BAUMOL'S COST DISEASE

Baumol's Cost Disease

The Arts and other Victims

Edited by

Ruth Towse

Lecturer in Economics, University of Exeter, UK

Edward Elgar

Cheltenham, UK • Northampton, MA, USA

Published by
Edward Elgar Publishing Limited
8 Lansdown Place
Cheltenham
Glos GL50 2HU
UK

Edward Elgar Publishing, Inc.
6 Market Street
Northampton
Massachusetts 01060
USA

A catalogue record for this book
is available from the British Library

Library of Congress Cataloguing-in-Publication Data
Baumol's cost disease : the arts and other victims / edited by Ruth
Towse.
Includes bibliographical references and index.
1. Performing arts—Finance. 2. Performing arts—Economic aspects. 3. Performing arts sponsorship. I. Baumol, William J. II. Towse, Ruth, 1943– .
PN1590.F55B38 1997
338.4'3791—dc21 97-24223
CIP

ISBN 1 85898 508 0

Printed and bound in Great Britain by
MPG Books Ltd, Bodmin, Cornwall

Contents

PART III THE COST DISEASE IN THE ARTS: EMPIRICAL EVIDENCE

PART IV POLICY IMPLICATIONS FOR THE ARTS

PART V THE DOCTOR PRESCRIBES!

Acknowledgements

The publishers wish to thank the following who have kindly given permission for the use of copyright material.

American Economic Association for articles: 'On the Performing Arts: The Anatomy of their Economic Problems', with W. G. Bowen, *American Economic Review*, 1965, **50**(2), May, 495–502; 'Macroeconomics of Unbalanced Growth: The Anatomy of Urban Crisis', *American Economic Review*, 1967, **57**(3), June, 415–26; Michael Keren, 'Macroeconomics of Unbalanced Growth: Comment', *American Economic Review*, 1972, **62**(1), March, 149; L. K. Lynch and E. L. Redman, 'Macroeconomics of Unbalanced Growth: Comment', *American Economic Review*, 1968, **58**(4), September, 884–6; 'Macroeconomics of Unbalanced Growth: Reply', *American Economic Review*, 1972, **62**(1), March, 150 and 'Unnatural Value: or Art Investment as Floating Crap Game', *American Economic Review*, 1986, **76**(2), May, 10–14.

Association for Cultural Economics for articles: 'The Mass Media and the Cost Disease', with Hilda Baumol, in William S. Hendon, Douglas V. Shaw and Nancy K. Grant (eds), *Economics of Cultural Industries*, 1984, 109–23 and 'The Future of the Theater and the Cost Disease of the Arts', with Hilda Baumol, in Mary Ann Hendon, James F. Richardson and William S. Hendon (eds), *Bach and the Box: The Implications of Television on the Performing Arts*, 1985, 1–18.

Blackwell Publishers for articles: 'On the Cost Disease and its True Policy Implications for the Arts', with Hilda Baumol, in David Greenaway and G. K. Shaw (eds), *Public Choice, Public Finance and Public Policy: Essays in Honour of Alan Peacock*, Basil Blackwell, 1985, 67–77 and references, and 'On the Economics of the Theater in Renaissance London', with Mary I. Oates, *Swedish Journal of Economics*, 1972, **74**(1), March, 136–60.

Cambridge University Press for article: 'On My Attitudes: Sociopolitical and Methodological', in Michael Szenberg (ed.), *Eminent Economists: Their Life Philosophies*, 1992, 51–9.

Columbia University Law School for article: 'Panel Discussion: Public Support for the Arts', *Columbia Journal of Art and the Law*, 1985, **9**(208), 214–28.

John Wiley & Sons for article: 'Electronics, the Cost Disease, and the Operation of Libraries', with Sue Anne Batey Blackman, *Journal of the American Society for Information Science*, 1983, **34**(3), 181–91.

Kluwer Academic Publishers for articles: 'On Finances of the Performing Arts during Stagflation: Some Recent Data', with Hilda Baumol, *Journal of Cultural Economics*, 1980, **4**(2), December, 1–11; 'Health Care, Education and the Cost Disease: A Looming Crisis for Public Choice', *Public Choice*, 1993, **77**, 17–28 and 'On the Economics of Musical Composition in Mozart's Vienna', with Hilda Baumol, *Journal of Cultural Economics*, 1994, **18**, 171–98.

Macmillan Press for articles: 'On the Career of a Microeconomist', in J. A. Kregel (ed.), *Recollections of Eminent Economists: Volume 2*, 1989, 209–34 and 'Performing Arts', in John Eatwell, Murray Milgate and Peter Newman (eds), *The New Palgrave: A Dictionary of Economics*, 1987, 841–3.

MIT Press for articles: 'On My Sculptures of Carved Wood', *Leonardo*, 1982, **15**(1), 40–42; 'Economics of Athenian Drama: Its Relevance for the Arts in a Small City Today', *Quarterly Journal of Economics*, 1971, **85**(3), August, 365–76 and 'Income and Substitution Effects in the Linder Theorem', *Quarterly Journal of Economics*, 1973, **87**(4), November, 629–33.

Peggy Heim for article: 'On Contracting with Publishers: or What Every Author Should Know', with Peggy Heim, *American Association of University Professors Bulletin*, 1967, **53**(1), March, 30–46.

Ruth Towse for articles: 'On the Economics of the Performing Arts in the USSR and the USA: A Preliminary Comparison of the Data', with Alexandre Rubinstein and Hilda Baumol, in Ruth Towse and Abdul Khakee (eds), *Cultural Economics*, Springer, 1992, 221–36.

Skandinaviska Enskilda Banken for article: 'The Cost Disease of the Personal Services and the Quality of Life', with W. E. Oates, *Skandinaviska Enskilda Banken Quarterly Review*, 1972, **2**, 44–54.

Springer-Verlag for article: David F. Bradford, 'Balance on Unbalanced Growth', *Zeitschrift für Nationalökonomie*, 1969, **29**, 291–304.

Theatre Development Fund for article: 'Last Minute Discounts on Unsold Tickets: A Study of TKTS', with Hilda Baumol, *Report 1, Last Minute Discounts on Unsold Tickets: A Study of TKTS*, 1974, 1–42.

The League of American Theatres and Producers for article: 'The Impact of the Broadway Theatre on the Economy of New York City', with Hilda Baumol, *The Impact of the Broadway Theatre on the Economy of New York City: A Study for the League of New York Theatres and Producers, Inc.*, Mathtech, 1977, 1–26.

The Wall Street Journal for article: 'A Growing Economy can Pay its Bills', *The Wall Street Journal*, 1992, 19 May, 1–3.

Twentieth Century Fund for articles: 'Trends in Over-all Cost of Performance', with William G. Bowen, *Performing Arts – The Economic Dilemma*, 1966, 181–207, 209–35; 'Trends in the Income Gap', with William G. Bowen, *Performing Arts – The Economic Dilemma*, 1966, 291–302 and 'On the Rationale of Public Support', with William G. Bowen, in *Performing Arts – The Economic Dilemma*, 1966, 369–86.

Every effort has been made to trace all the copyright holders but if any have been inadvertently overlooked the publishers will be pleased to make the necessary arrangements at the first opportunity.

Introduction

William Baumol is one of the world's most prolific, most cited and most respected economists. He is author, often co-author, of 30 books and some 400 articles in professional journals, as well as innumerable chapters in books, reports and articles for all kinds of publications. His first article appeared in 1946; 50 years later he continues to publish at a staggering rate. He has written on mathematical economics and operations research, micro- and macro-economic theory, welfare economics, industrial organization, environmental economics and a host of applied topics in economics. A citations count in 1990 showed him to be the fourth most cited economist, excluding Nobel Prize winners.[1] He was President of the American Economic Association in 1981 and was made a Distinguished Fellow of the Association a year later. He has received many other awards and honours. He has served on numerous professional bodies and has frequently been a consultant to business firms in the USA and other countries. He is also an artist, both practising and teaching art.

The Baumol and Bowen Book

In 1966 Baumol, with William Bowen, published *Performing Arts – The Economic Dilemma*. At a stroke the field of the economics of the arts (or cultural economics, as it has come to be called) was created. The book set the agenda for a stream of work on the live arts and (subsequently) on the media industries, on artists' labour markets, on non-profit organizations, and on private and public subsidies to the arts, all topics which still constitute the mainstream of work in this subject. Baumol, often working in partnership with his wife, Hilda, has contributed to cultural economics for over 30 years (at the time of writing). This book contains most of those contributions.

Baumol and Bowen's involvement in this major work turns out to have been serendipitous. Baumol describes it in his autobiographical essay (reprinted here as Chapter 1) as follows: 'Sheer misunderstanding led to my involvement in the economics of the performing arts'. The misunderstanding was a confusion over his dual role as an economist and artist which led to the assumption that he had worked on the economics of the arts. Luckily for cultural economics, it was a happy accident; other economists with a love of the arts, even with active administrative experience in the field of the arts, have not always retained the hard-headed objectivity that the discipline of economics requires when analysing the economics of the arts. Keynes is a classic example of an art-loving economist who failed to make any connection between the two; he never questioned the need for subsidy to the arts and, as the first Chairman of the Arts Council in England, set about seeking ever greater amounts of it. Lord Robbins, Baumol's friend and mentor (to whom *Performing Arts* is dedicated), was another great economist deeply involved in the arts in Britain. Unlike Keynes, he did write on the economics of the arts, but his heart occasionally overrode his head when he did so.[2]

In 1962 (or thereabouts), when Baumol was first approached by the Director of the Twentieth Century Fund to consider undertaking this unusual work, he was known as a formidable mathematical economist, having just published *Economic Theory and Operations Analysis* (1961). It was far from obvious that he would respond with such practical good sense as is evidenced in *Performing Arts* and subsequent empirical work of the 1980s (some of which is reprinted in Part III of this book). It would be rather like asking a modern game theorist to get her hands dirty with data-mining.

The person who literally did get her hands dirty collecting data was Hilda Baumol, Will's journalist wife and co-author of several major pieces of work in the economics of the arts. Arts organizations are not well known for their orderly book-keeping and Hilda often found herself in lofts and cellars poking about for evidence. Mary Ellen Bowen was also involved, being in charge of processing the many questionnaires. William Bowen (since then President of Princeton University and now of the Mellon Foundation) organized an army of student researchers, and so a huge empirical survey of the US performing arts (a phrase which, incidentally, Baumol disliked at the outset) was launched. There was, in addition, a British wing to this operation led by Muriel Nissel and Claus Moser.[3] Chapters 8 and 12 of *Performing Arts* are reproduced here as Chapters 13 and 14 to give a flavour of the detailed nature of the investigation. Even 30 years later, it cannot be faulted on the range and depth of the analysis. The big difference that the intervention of time has made is that the 'economic dilemma' of the arts has become a concern of many governments. Now it is a familiar problem. That was not so in the USA in the 1960s, and Baumol and Bowen's work must have struck many people, economists included, as extraordinary.

That two highly reputable academic economists should add their voices (or at least provide encouragement to) the clamour for increased state funding for the arts was perhaps a surprise. The way Baumol and Bowen put forward their case was no doubt greatly influenced by Baumol's early work in welfare economics.[4] This approach has now become so much part of the cultural economist's canon that it is hard to remember the first formulation of it (see below). That firmly set cultural economics on course as a branch of applied welfare economics, a course on which it has, in part, continued for the last 30 years.

Mathematica, Inc. and other empirical studies on the Arts

As Bowen's career took another direction, Hilda Baumol increasingly collaborated with Will on his work on cultural economics. She was a consultant to Mathematica, Inc., a research consultancy firm which Baumol helped to found, which undertook a series of commissions in the arts. The resulting publications on Broadway seat pricing and the economic impact of Broadway, long out of print, are reproduced here in full (Chapters 23 and 24). The empirical results are now of historical interest only, but their clarity of method and presentation make them relevant today.

Later studies took them from the realm of the live arts to testing the more optimistic hypothesis that, via the mass media, the arts could join the productive sector and so avoid the fate of the cost disease of the live arts. Two of these studies are reprinted here as Chapters 16 and 17. Hilda and William Baumol also played key roles in a conference on the specific effects of inflation on the live arts published as *Inflation and the Performing Arts* (Baumol and Baumol, 1984). Their earlier work on the arts during stagflation is reprinted in Chapter 15; also in Part III is their chapter in the book of essays in honour of Alan Peacock, an old friend and cultural economist (Chapter 18), and a paper resulting from their collaboration with the Russian, Alexandre Rubinstein (Chapter 19).

The cost disease and unbalanced growth

It is always interesting to discover the origin of great ideas. According to Baumol's own account (Chapter 1), the entire cost disease model came to him in the night, fully developed. This idea, which had its origin in the empirical study of the economics of live performance in the arts, has spread its influence into almost every area of life. It is predominantly a disease of certain service industries – the 'stagnant sector' – which includes libraries, education, health, restaurants, haircuts and garbage collection. Characterizing all economic activity as stagnant or progressive (with different shading levels in between), Baumol developed his model of unbalanced growth (the first analytical formulation of which is in his 1965 *American Economic Review* article, reprinted here as Chapter 4, which predicts the increasing relative cost of providing such services.

The same basic idea underpins a huge and diverse research programme in all the areas mentioned above, studies of which have been conducted by Baumol and a number of other economists. In this volume, Part VII contains some of Baumol's contributions (with various co-authors) on libraries, health and education. The idea has been honed over the years and has taken on board several strands of criticism. Comments by early critics, Bradford, Keren, and Lynch and Redman, as well as Baumol's response, are reprinted here (Part II). I find Baumol's final version of it in his entry on 'Performing Arts' in the *New Palgrave Dictionary of Economics* the most elegant statement, also reprinted in Part II.

Quite early on in its life, analysis of the cost disease was the inspiration for two historical studies on the performing arts by Baumol (with co-authors) on Athenian theatre and on Elizabethan drama at the time of Shakespeare. They were followed many years later by Hilda and Will Baumol's joint study of the economics of composing in Mozart's Vienna. Part VI consists of these papers. They testify to Baumol's love of history which undoubtedly has shaped his interest in economics. Part VI also includes another amazing piece of Baumoliana – his 1986 paper on art prices, an almost entirely new topic in the economics of the arts, which, again, has been the inspiration for a now burgeoning literature on that topic. Taking a long-run view, such as that embodied in the cost disease and the theory of unbalanced growth, is not frequently encountered in the modern economics. Baumol reminds us of the value of historical evidence as a basis for economic analysis. His award-winning book, with Blackman and Wolff (1989), on long-run productivity trends in the USA and other industrialized countries, amply demonstrates this point.

Baumol's style

It is clear from Baumol's two autobiographical essays (Chapters 1 and 2) that he believes in economics as an engine for social reform. That is part and parcel, I would say, of his New York Jewish upbringing, which at its best is enlightened, intellectual, cultured, hard-working, progressive and dedicated to active involvement in the search for improvement to society. We see that tradition echoed in the work of a number of other well-known economists with similar backgrounds in that generation. Economics fits comfortably with that tradition because it satisfies a taste for rigorous intellectual analysis as well as a desire for practical solutions to real world problems.

Baumol's lifetime of work in economics covers the whole gamut, as we can see, from mathematical economics to economic history. It is possible, however, to detect an underlying theme to the areas he has worked in, namely his belief that the capitalist system is one that can be made to work in the social interest with reasonable government intervention. Some of Baumol's most important recent work on the environment and regulation of utilities takes that position. Regulation, however, has costs which have to be balanced against its benefits. This is the view of a well-balanced welfarist (a term of approbation, not opprobrium, in Europe).

This *Weltanschauung* necessarily requires a view of what are desirable social values. Welfare economics, after all, is not value-free, any more than is society itself. I asked William Baumol how he had 'squared' his interest in the arts, which (as he was one of the first to demonstrate with firm evidence) are mostly the plaything of the better-off, not only in the USA but even in European countries with strong welfarist policies towards the arts. He replied that he believed society would be worse off without the arts and anyway there are social externalities; the need for equality of opportunity also must be satisfied; hence the case for subsidy. There is, therefore, complete consistency between his belief in the value of the arts and the analytical case for them which he has made via welfare economics.

Another aspect of the commitment to social reform that manifests itself in all Baumol's economics is how well he writes. It is his intention to convince people and you cannot do that if they cannot understand you. It must surely have struck other readers how vastly more legible and well motivated Baumol's writings are in (unfair, perhaps) comparison with those of most other economists! This has made his textbook in economics, co-authored with Alan Blinder and now (1996) in its seventh edition, one of the most popular of its kind in the USA. This is no accident, however. Baumol believes that thinking through how to explain an idea is as important as thinking the idea itself through. Poor writing is a sign of an inferiority complex. I daresay his activities as an artist have also contributed to his desire to communicate. Baumol's own observations on the different thought processes behind economics and sculpture are interesting (see Chapter 3). His advice on publishing is also worth taking note of (Chapter 22).

At the end of the day, however, what has mostly motivated Baumol's work is intellectual curiosity. The pre-eminent example of that is undoubtedly his work on the arts; the Twentieth Century Fund and the Rockefeller Brothers Fund apparently had a more modest study in mind when they first approached Baumol and Bowen. It was intellectual curiosity that propelled them to the thorough research that ended up as *Performing Arts – the Economic Dilemma*. Intellectual curiosity also led Baumol to his equally distinguished work in the history of economic thought (an interest he also shared with Lionel Robbins), among many other topics in economics. He has written on the history of monetary theory, on classical political economy and on Marxian economics; his collection of early writings in mathematical economics (Baumol and Goldfeld, 1968) involved him in translating from Italian, French, German (and even Latin); and his paper on 'Say's (at least) Eight Laws...' is a classic (see Baumol, 1986). In sum, Baumol is an economic polymath.

In addition he is a glutton for punishment! In 1989, he ended his essay, 'On the Career of a Microeconomist' by saying, 'as yet there is no conclusion to my story – all I can offer is a status report on a continuing stream of research...' since then he has produced half a dozen new books and over 50 chapters in books and refereed papers, besides writing numerous reviews, newspaper articles...

Notes

1. See Garfield (1990). Garfield believes that citation counts are reasonably good predictors of Nobel Prize awards in economics, hence the exclusion of past winners from the count.
2. The same might also be said of Martin Feldstein, whose acceptance of museum curators' view of deaccessioning certainly flies in the face of the opinion of other economists regarded as experts on museums, such as Frey and Montias. For a kinder view, however, see Baumol's review of Feldstein's book (Baumol, 1992).
3. At the time, Moser was the head of the Central Statistical Office, and Muriel Nissel, social statistician and wife of the Amadeus Quartet second violinist, Sigmund Nissel, held a senior appointment there too. (Sir Claus Moser subsequently became Chairman of the Board of the Royal Opera House, Covent Garden, succeeding Lord Robbins in this post – the interconnections are fascinating!) Audience members little knew that such eminent persons had left the questionnaire forms on their seats!
4. Welfare economics was the subject of his PhD thesis at the London School of Economics (supervised by Robbins). It was subsequently published in 1952 (see Baumol, 1952).

References

Baumol, William (1952), *Welfare Economics and the Theory of the State*, London: Longmans Green.

Baumol, William (1961), *Economic Theory and Operations Analysis*, Engelwood Cliffs, N.J.: Prentice Hall.

Baumol, William (1986), *Microtheory Applications and Origins*, Brighton: Wheatsheaf Books.

Baumol, William (1992), 'Review of *The Economics of Art Museums* by Martin Feldstein', *Journal of Economic Literature*, **30**, 942–3.

Baumol, Hilda and William Baumol (1984), *Inflation and the Performing Arts*, New York: New York University Press.

Baumol, William and Alan Blinder (1996), *Economics; Principles and Policy*, 7th Edition, Fort Worth: The Dryden Press, Harcourt Brace and Co.

Baumol, William and William Bowen (1966), *Performing Arts – The Economic Dilemma*, New York: The Twentieth Century Fund.

Baumol, William and Stephen Goldfeld (eds) (1968), *Precursors in Mathematical Economics: An Anthology*, London: London School of Economics.

Baumol, William, Sue Anne Blackman and Edward Wolff (1989), *Productivity and American Leadership: The Long View*, Cambridge, MA: MIT Press.

Garfield, Eugene (1990), 'Who Will Win the Nobel Prize in Economics? Here's a Forecast Based on Citation Indicators', *Current Contents*, **11**, 3–7.

PART I

AUTOBIOGRAPHICAL ESSAYS

[1]

On the Career of a Microeconomist

William J. Baumol

For as long as I can remember – certainly by my early teens – my desire to be an economist was never in doubt. In retrospect I can see that this was no accident. Both my parents were self-educated immigrants, but educated they were, as few undergraduates are today. Literature, older or current, language, politics and economics were constantly discussed in our house in a most fascinating manner, and I was expected from childhood to participate fully in the discussions. My father with his lower class background (his parents had run a tavern in a small town in Poland) was driven by passionate concern for humanity, and emotion ruled his talk. My mother, by contrast, coming from a line of Jewish Lithuanian intellectuals, epitomised logic and careful reasoning in pursuit of the same objectives. Both parents, particularly my father, were avid Marxists. The combination was irresistible. I was infected by their interests and their concerns. My reading provided a sampling of Marx's logical convolutions which, combined with tales of the adventure of the buccaneers of nineteenth-century business – Morgan, Vanderbilt, Gould, Rockefeller and others – sealed my fascination with the subject. Well before I entered college I had begun to read economic history, the works of the classical economists and the writings of Thorstein Veblen.

UNDERGRADUATE EDUCATION (1939–42)

I entered CCNY (the College of the City of New York) in 1939 as the great depression was drawing to an end and the threat of war hung over us. CCNY, then, was an extraordinary institution. There was no tuition charge and the students commuted from home every day by subway. The ambitious children of impecunious immigrants flocked to it as their ticket from poverty or grinding labour. Never did so many future Nobel Prize-winners congregate in one place. Passionate activity, discussion and debate flourished everywhere. The dining room was surrounded by alcoves each had been claimed by a permanent discussion group – there was the Trotskyist alcove, the Socialist alcove and one of every other variety. (There was even an alcove at which future comedians or rather, comic social commentators, some of them to become famous later, practiced their craft without let up.)

A number of economists of note emerged from there, Kenneth Arrow, Julius Margolis and Jules Joskow among them. But while CCNY at that time had many gifted teachers, the department of economics had very few. It was clear to us students that many of them were thoroughly behind the times, and could not teach us about the work of Keynes, Chamberlin and Joan Robinson which were then at the frontier. Besides, many of them just could not communicate very well. There seemed to us to be little choice, and so we organised our own classes, each specialising in a different field, devouring as much of the relevant literature as we could and then lecturing on it to the others. I was assigned the microeconomics, and suspect that I learned more economics there than ever before or since. This experience has always engendered uncertainty in my views on teaching. Can it be that, at least for some students, what is considered to be 'bad' teaching is really teaching in its most effective form, because it forces students to think and learn for themselves? I have long advocated some controlled experiments in which parallel classes are held, some taught in the conventional way by teachers of good reputation while in the others students are asked to fend for themselves, guided only by past examinations, perhaps by a reading list, and with no access to the faculty. It is my conjecture that the first group will perform better on the examination at the end of the semester, but that in an examination five or ten years later the self-taught group will far outdistance the other.

THE DEPARTMENT OF AGRICULTURE AND MILITARY SERVICE (1942–6)

Graduating in 1942, I spent a few months in Washington working (though it may seem odd) in the Department of Agriculture. The shadow of the receding depression led graduating students to accept with delight virtually any reasonable job offer, and I was considered very daring by the others in my class when I held out for – and received – a salary of $2000 a year. Happily the job was not undesirable. It was a sort of think tank for the Department, and many of the group, some of whom I still see, were exceedingly bright and creative persons. The head of the Department was Frederick Waugh, a bright and fatherly figure who then and later made a number of significant contributions to the economic literature. It was under his guidance and that of my young colleagues that I first learned how microtheory can be applied to concrete issues.

Just before leaving for Washington I had been married. We were both very young, but the US had just entered the war and many others were doing the same. I have had many occasions to congratulate myself on the wisdom (or luck) that guided that decision. We have ever since worked (and enjoyed life) together in many areas, most directly in our work on the economics of the performing arts. But I am getting ahead of the story.

My years in the US Army are pertinent only for the correspondence course in linear algebra I took, and, while stationed in Rouen, the mathematics books I was able to buy and devour. There, incidentally I made lifelong friends with a French family whose fabulous cellar, including samples of every great vintage of the century, introduced me to the delights of wine which I still collect. Just after the war in Europe had ended some German prisoners gave me my first lessons in wood sculpture which I now teach at Princeton University. (Before entering the army I had studied drawing and painting at the Art Student's League in New York City and my second main field of study at CCNY had been visual art – painting and lithography, particularly.)

After returning from the war there was another brief stint at the Department of Agriculture. But this time the task was very different: the allocation of the US grain resources among the countries of a hungry world. Two prime lessons emerged from this experience – the high costs of the negotiation process and the complexities of the calculations of fairness. The first lesson flowed from the fact that all of the senior and more experienced members of the division were almost fully employed in diplomatic negotiations involving international agencies and other governments. As a result, the actual decisions were, to our astonishment, left to another young man of equal inexperience and myself!

It was not a task to make for an easy conscience. The refrain we heard from virtually every country was the same; we are hungry. If we had one shipload to go either to country A or to country B, what were we to do if the evidence showed that we had already sent enough to A this month to provide each of its inhabitants more calories than before the war, but that B, whose per capita grain receipts were higher than A's, was nevertheless well below its pre-war consumption level? We did not, of course, enjoy the luxury of indecision that is available to pure research.

THE LONDON SCHOOL OF ECONOMICS (1946–9)

I had assumed that on my return to civilian life I would begin my postgraduate studies. My application to the London School of Economics was rejected, and I wrote again asking when it would be possible to apply for the following year. As later came out, compassion was still part of the admission process, and it was decided to accept me as a student for the masters degree only. As explained to me later, at LSE they had never heard of CCNY and, in any event, my undergraduate record was hardly outstanding. But CCNY soon made up for its handicap. The training in fierce debating – quarter neither asked nor given – soon got me (in my view, undeserved) attention in LSE's justly famous seminars. To my amazement, within weeks I had not only been transferred to the PhD programme, but was also offered a part-time teaching post which became full-time the following year. Lord Robbins afterwards told me that he went back to the records to see where they had made their mistake in rejecting me, and decided that, on the record, they had been right, after all.

LSE was an extraordinarily stimulating place to be. Besides Lionel Robbins I got to know Friedrich Hayek, Arthur Lewis, Nicholas Kaldor and, later, James Meade, among the economists, and Karl Popper and Harold Laski outside the department. Among the students there were Frank Hahn, undergraduate Ralph Turvey and an Australian, David Finch (now at the World Bank) who (in 1948!) was writing a thesis on the theory of stagflation. The weekly Robbins seminar and the stimulation in the common rooms where one met for avid and fruitful conversation were experiences I have never duplicated. The erudition and broad knowledge of Robbins and Laski revealed what humanistic learning can be. Popper, who had not yet reacquired any professional logician colleagues, was prepared to report his latest derivations frequently to a new assistant lecturer who had taken a course or two in formal logic at CCNY. Hahn, Turvey and other young people were sources of a continuing flow of new and fruitful ideas. Meade and Hayek were also full of ideas which they constantly tried out on the delighted newcomers.

Because few English faculty members had anything like a PhD and did not take the degree seriously, it was possible for me to write my dissertation at the same time that I held a full-time faculty position. I had already planned my dissertation during my military service, and Lionel Robbins agreed to be its supervisor. He never begrudged me time or advice, which was always very helpful. The thesis, later published as *Welfare Economics and the Theory of the State*, took off from the Marshall–Pigou theory of externalities, then a neglected subject widely considered to be of minor importance. It sought to generalise the idea to as diverse a set of subjects as the behaviour of competitors, the difficulty of cartel formation and the theory of inflation (all of which we were already characterising as a prisoners' dilemma problem in the new fangled theory of games).[1] More than that, I hoped to derive from the logic of externalities the rationale for all government intervention in the workings of the economy – notions later echoed in works of Buchanan and Tulloch and the writings of Mancur Olsen. In the hotbed of discussion that constituted LSE the dissertation's ideas were very much a group product. We had made an effort to revive the famous Cambridge, LSE, Oxford seminar of the 1930s, and these subjects were discussed at the joint sessions, bringing in ideas from outside the LSE. Jan de v. Graaff played a leading part, he and I spending large amounts of time discussing one another's work on welfare economics.

In the course of that seminar's travels, incidentally, I also met Dennis Robertson, Joan Robinson, R.F. Kahn, J.R. Hicks, Lionel McKenzie and others whose names already were or were about to become legendary.

At LSE I gave two courses. Lionel Robbins invited me to lecture on economic dynamics, and my lecture notes for that course formed the basis for what was to be my first book, *Economic Dynamics*, which still survives. But in return for that plum I had to give a set of lectures on the American economy, a subject on which, most regrettably, I was dismally ignorant and which, I am sure, were an embarrassment to everyone, even if most educational to me. Much of the dynamics course, like so much else, followed Paul Samuelson's pathbreaking explorations which I merely translated into forms more accessible to students. People have sometimes been kind enough to suggest that my writing on the subject is rather clear. I have responded that I tried to write the book so clearly that even I could understand it – and that was, in all seriousness, the truth of the matter.

In both my lectures and the dissertation there were substantial sections on the relevant *dogmengeschichte* on which Lionel Robbins was enormously helpful. The graphic translation of the dynamics of the Ricardian model seemed to me an obvious interpretation of a system universally understood within the profession and generally agreed upon. I was amazed to find it singled out for special commendation in John Williams's presidential address to the American Economic Association the year after publication, and to see it cited by writers on the history of thought many times thereafter. Since then it has become clearer that the substance of Ricardian economics is far from being agreed upon, as my former student Samuel Hollander has found in his debates with the neo-Keynesians of Cambridge and Italy and even with George Stigler and Paul Samuelson.

Our happy three years in London were drawing to an end. We had used the opportunity to travel about Europe a good deal. British exchange controls in that period of post-war austerity prevented us from using either my small earnings or my wife's comparable income, both in sterling, for the purpose. Fortunately, I also received support from the US Government in US currency, as an army veteran, and that permitted our first visit to Italy, which we have loved ever since. Of course, young graduate students did not expect many comforts while travelling or in their domestic arrangements so a small income served very adequately. There were severe shortages and strict rationing still continued. In London the foreign students and their spouses shared any packages received from abroad with their English friends. Often we would all pick up our six-week ration of one egg and one slice of bacon at the same time and get together to celebrate the feast. Heating was a great problem with tightly rationed coal of poor quality burnt in an open fireplace the main source of warmth in the home. One winter our water pipes froze for three months and produced a great indoor flood when they thawed and burst in the beautiful spring of 1947.

The dissertation was completed on schedule, and I had the most delightful oral examination on record over whiskey and sodas at the Reform Club with my examiners, Marcus Flemming and Lionel Robbins who still considered my pursuit of the PhD an American aberration. Professor Robbins knew we were determined to return to the United States, but he nevertheless made me a very generous offer at the LSE if I were prepared to remain. After I had refused with thanks most deeply felt, he recommended me with his characteristic kindness to Friedrich Lutz who was then visiting LSE from Princeton. Within weeks I had received and accepted an offer of an assistant professorship for the following academic year, and have remained at Princeton ever since.

Lifelong friends were acquired at the LSE – Lord and Lady Robbins and their children, Sir Arthur and Gladys Lewis to whom we had the pleasure of extending their first dinner invitation after they were married, Anne Bohm who brought sanity and order to the postgraduate programme, Frank and Dorothy Hahn, and others as well. We have since made still more close friends in London where our visits (or theirs to the US) have assumed the nature of reunions. In particular, Lord Robbins in his role as Chairman of the Royal Opera at Covent Garden and as Director of the National Gallery has over the years provided us with access to London's cultural activities such as few are privileged to enjoy.

PRINCETON UNIVERSITY (1949–)

At Princeton we were immediately welcomed into the community and the department. Richard Lester was chairman, and he quickly made us feel at home. Lionel Robbins had also written ahead about us to Jacob and Frances Viner with whom we remained on closest terms for the rest of their lives. I did not know Viner's terrifying reputation (which was belied completely by his natural but often deliberately concealed kindness). Consequently, I was foolish enough to disagree with him avidly and energetically whenever it seemed appropriate to the astonishment of many of our colleagues. Viner, who was obviously unused to such a response, was delighted. We spent many hours each week locked in debate. From time to time I needed information on economic history or on the history of ideas and was always very pleased when in response to literally any such question he would talk without interruption for at least an hour providing an amazing stream of illuminating material from his bottomless stock of knowledge. He would also regularly, but apparently casually, make some unsupported theoretical statement which I was sure was quite incorrect and which he would then challenge me to disprove. Each time, after a considerable struggle on my part, the mathematics showed unambiguously that he was right.

Years later a friend of his in another city recounted how Viner told him of a young friend on the faculty for whom he had set himself the task of presenting a new, paradoxical proposition in economic theory every week. What an education that was.

The following year Lester Chandler joined the Department, and from him I learned what little I understand about money and banking. Later we wrote a textbook together which, though it was unsuccessful, was an introduction to the pleasures of collaboration.

On arriving at Princeton we met two advanced graduate students, Martin Shubik and Harvey Leibenstein, with whom we have remained close friends. Within a year or two the department attracted an extraordinary group of undergraduate students including Richard Quandt, Otto Eckstein and Gary Becker with whom I wrote an article on Patinkin's dichotomy analysis and the pertinent materials in classical and neo-classical economics. We felt, and I still do, that Patinkin's discussions of the invalidity of the dichotomy between the real and monetary sectors of the economy, and of the problems caused by the assumption that supply and demand functions are homogeneous in prices alone, were brilliant pieces of work and constituted an extremely illuminating contribution. But at the same time some of the classical and neoclassical authors he accused of the resulting errors were, in my view, quite innocent of the charges. It should be added that the dispute was conducted just as such disputes should be, and that Professor Patinkin and I have become good friends and see one another both in Israel and the United States.

CONSULTING ACTIVITIES

In about 1953 Paul Lazarsfeld, the great sociologist then at Columbia University, asked me to work with him on one of his research projects. I quickly accepted the invitation, anxious to get to know more about his path-breaking work, and, of course, because of the additional income which greatly relieved the assistant professor's traditional poverty. A key premise in much of Lazarsfeld's analysis was that while human behaviour is stochastic, the relevant probabilities of the different options in tomorrow's behaviour depend on the state of affairs today. Thus the probability that some individual will vote socialist in the next election will depend on whether he voted as a socialist or a Christian democrat in the preceding election. This immediately leads to the employment of the theory of Markov chains which yields exactly that sort of relationship. It also translates itself at once into a simultaneous system of stochastic difference equations whose coefficients are the relevant probabilities. It was this translation which had attracted Lazarsfeld to my writings, and the work I did for him was subsequently used in a substantial expansion of *Economic Dynamics* in its second edition. Later I also joined Lazarsfeld in two seminars, each lasting several weeks, one held in Switzerland and the other in the beautiful mountains north of Turin. There our families got to know one another.

Just after my work on the Lazarsfeld project came to an end I spent the spring and summer as a visiting professor at Berkeley. We travelled from Princeton to Berkeley by car with our two small children, making the country seem even more enormous than it is. At Berkeley we met many delightful people, notably Aaron Gordon, Robert Dorfman, (and for the second time) Harvey Leibenstein and their wives. I also met Joe S. Bain from whose work the theory of contestable markets would later derive so much, and Howard Ellis who was then approaching retirement.

Soon after our return to Princeton, where I had been promoted to full professor, I was introduced to another remarkable person, Wroe Alderson, who was then serving on an advisory committee to the Princeton economics department. Alderson was Quaker and a devoted advocate of their social goals such as the promotion of peace and elimination of poverty. He was senior partner of Alderson and Sessions, a management consulting firm in Philadelphia. After one evening together at a meeting he invited me to come to his office to see whether a consulting arrangement would suit us both. That arrangement lasted for nearly a decade. I would travel to Philadelphia about once a week and work on one or more of the many projects on which the busy company was engaged. In those years I got some sense of the way big business in the US is conducted. I worked with large firms and small, among them major firms in chemicals, steel, food products and a variety of other lines. I studied their policies on pricing, advertising, product line, location and all of the other areas of interest to economic analysis. The work made use of demand theory, mathematical programming, inventory theory and many of the other tools of formal economic analysis. It was a very valuable experience, teaching me how theoretical instruments can be applied flexibly to the complex and messy problems of reality, and, above all, suggesting how firms actually behave in reality. It also led me to revise many of my theoretical ideas, and two of my books originated from my work at the consulting firm. *Economic Theory and Operations Analysis* (1961) started off as a compendium of the analytical tools that had proved useful in application to business activities, with illustrations derived from experience with firms. In its later editions the book has gradually evolved more into exposition of economic theory with particular emphasis on very recent developments. The relationship between business experience and theory was still more direct in the case of *Business Behavior, Value and Growth* and its sales-maximisation model. Several years of association with members of the managements of large firms finally forced me to recognise that there was a systematic difference between the way matters were viewed by them and by the standard economic models. Of the recommendations made to our clients, my impression was that about 60 per cent were accepted and adopted. It became clear, eventually, that those which were rejected were not chosen fortuitously, but, rather, constituted a fairly predictable pattern. It ultimately dawned on me that virtually any proposal that promised to increase profits but did so by sacrificing sales volume was almost certain to be spurned. I began to modify my recommendations accordingly and, as I remember it, the acceptance rate rose substantially.

The natural reaction of a microtheorist to such experiences was a re-examination of the standard profit-maximisation models which we had all been taught to employ. I found out, eventually, that other economists had, on the basis of interviews and other forms of observation, also reached the conclusion that in practice firms pursue objectives more diverse and complex than just maximisation of profits. But in one important respect the consulting experience had taken me beyond that observation alone, for it had shown that other goals such as maximisation of sales or growth of assets each had their own implications for business decisions and to each of these there seemed to correspond optimal values of the firm's decision variables. In other words, abandonment of the profit-maximisation premise did not leave one with no choice but chaos and indecision. Rather, it called for decisions which are different but equally determinate, and which can be analysed using all of the traditional tools and methods – marginal analysis, mathematical programming, etc.

Some months of working on the formal analysis provided the model of sales maximisation (later supplemented by a model of growth maximisation) which constituted the basis of the little book

Business Behavior, Value and Growth (1959). If this model does constitute a contribution I believe it consists not in the observation that management may have objectives other than profit, but in the demonstration that other objectives are perfectly consistent with fruitful theoretical analysis, as was later demonstrated so effectively by writers such as Oliver Williamson and Robin Marris.

Let me emphasise that I never maintained and do not believe that all firms (or even all oligopoly firms) seek to maximise sales, or that they all share any other common and simple objective. I merely asserted and still believe that many firms have some objectives other than profit alone, and that for some which I encountered sales maximisation is a reasonable approximation to their somewhat more complicated goals. Those goals are, in any event, rarely formulated expressly (except for purposes of public relations), they may change from time to time, and they are at most pursued only in a rough and ready manner. Moreover, I believe that in aggregative studies of industry behaviour the differences between the predictions of profit and sales maximisation are apt to be minor and unimportant. But for analysis of the behaviour of individual firms I believe the distinction is vital, as the reactions of business clients to our recommendations made under the two premises suggests strongly.

Partisans of the profit maximisation approach have suggested that the behavior patterns called for by the two models may be difficult to distinguish, and they have questioned the evidence presented in *Business Behavior, Value and Growth* which, admittedly, is all anecdotal. They have pointed out, rather cogently, that long-run profit maximisation may require resistance to elimination of unprofitable sales in the short run. I certainly cannot prove the contrary. I can only suggest that the change in the nature of our recommendations constituted what amounts to a (very poorly) controlled experiment of a sort rarely possible for economists. Moreover, the resulting observations were generally supported by careful discussion with businesspersons with whom I had established rather close relationships and who had little reason to slant their answers.

After the sale of Alderson Associates when Wroe Alderson retired my consulting work continued through the firms Mathematica, and Consultants in Industry Economics (CIE), which I helped to found. This work has usually proved fruitful and stimulating to me in more general research. Microeconomists are peculiarly fortunate in this respect, for while academic consultants drawn from other disciplines generally contribute by application of the learning they have acquired through research and teaching, for them benefits rarely seem to flow in the other direction.

THE PERFORMING ARTS

Sheer misunderstanding led to my involvement in the economics of the performing arts. In about 1960, the Twentieth Century Fund and John D. Rockefeller III had decided that the time was auspicious for a systematic study of that subject. On enquiry they were told of an economist at Princeton who was knowledgeable about the arts as well as economics. The person who had steered them to me had, of course, confused my activities in painting and sculpture with knowledge of the finances and organisation of opera, theatres, orchestras and dance companies. My father had instilled in me a great love of the performing arts, but little knowledge of the economic side of these activities accompanied my wife's and my frequent attendance.

I agreed to a meeting on the subject, having first discussed the matter with a young colleague, William G. Bowen, with whom I had worked earlier (and who has since become President of Princeton University). Talking with the potential sponsors of the study I emphasised my ignorance of the subject and then, on the basis of my consulting experience, proceeded to indicate how I believed it should be analysed dispassionately, as though one were dealing with the economics of the most banale of commodities rather than one which commands widespread expressions of adulation (if hardly universal attendance).

As it happened, Bowen and I were then both heavily committed to other projects. When it turned out that the potential sponsors had, for better or worse, decided that we were the right persons to conduct the study, we found ourselves resisting what was to prove one of the most exciting projects we had ever undertaken – so poor can foresight be!

The research turned out to be a major undertaking. It lasted somewhat more than three years, acquired and analysed data from several hundred organisations, distributed questionnaires to about 150,000 audience members at more than a hundred performances in dozens of cities. A small army of students and other investigators was trained and sent out to collect the materials using questionnaires which had been painstakingly designed and pre-tested. All of this was planned meticulously by Bowen and the work was organised and supervised by my wife, with whom all my subsequent work on the economics of the arts has been carried out in full partnership.

The overall design of the study and the planning of the empirical work is all to be credited to my co-author. His skill in dealing with messy data made it possible to determine many fundamental attributes of the activities in question. For example, he was able to show systematically that the composition of audiences in terms of education, income, age and sex varied only minusculely from one art form to another or one city to another. Audiences in London were, essentially, no different from those in Houston, Texas – all highly educated, and well-to-do relative to the population as a whole. Generally no more than 2 or 3 per cent of the audience was made up of blue collar workers; opera with 7 per cent of the audience derived from this economic group, constituting the only exception. Many fascinating observations peripheral to our central topic also emerged from Bowen's calculations. For example, he was able to show that the proportion of women among the performance in an orchestra at that time was almost perfectly inversely correlated with the income of the orchestra – a very tangible index of sex discrimination!

In the early 1960s collection of economic data on the performing arts in the US was no routine matter. It often took my wife to back offices, basements and lofts, where figures sometimes had to be pieced together from scraps of paper that constituted the only records that some group had kept. Since that time much more such information has been collected and some of it published on a regular basis. Indeed, we were asked to design and, for several years, collect some of the figures that now appear regularly in the official US government publications.

My own part in the study involved a role in the determination of the overall objectives and the general research design. I also wrote most of the final manuscript. However, my one contribution I consider to be significant is the cost disease model, which has since been used to help explain the behaviour of the cost of education, the budgetary problems of cities, etc. The basic point is that the *live* performing arts (in contradistinction to those employing the mass media such as film and television) are extraordinarily unadaptable to productivity-increasing technical change. A Boccherini string quartet written in the eighteenth century which takes half an hour to perform, required two-person hours of performance time then and requires exactly the same amount of time today. Meanwhile, in much of the remainder of the economy productivity has been increasing virtually without interruption in a manner that compounds and accumulates. If wages in the arts do not rise far more slowly than those in the remainder of the economy (and the evidence indicates that they do not) this means that cost per performance in the arts must rise steadily at a rate faster than costs in the remainder of the economy, roughly reflecting the difference in the productivity growth that characterises the two sectors. Over the years this can add up to an enormous differential. I estimate roughly that a typical manufactured good which cost about the same as attendance at a performance in 1800 now costs only about one twentieth as much! This means also that the funds supplied to the arts by government or private philanthropy must generally increase year in, year out, at a rate exceeding the economy's rate of inflation if artistic activity is not to be forced to retrench. Constancy of *real* contributions is simply not enough for the purpose. This, then, is what has since come to be called the cost disease of the arts (I am delighted that it is also sometimes called 'Baumol's disease'). If the hypothesis is correct (and there is a good deal of evidence consistent with it)[2] it helps to explain many economic phenomena outside the arts, such as the shift of the labour forces in a number of countries out of manufacturing and toward the services, the increasing use of disposable products to avoid repair, the rising relative cost of medical care and education, etc.

Because such incidents are sometimes considered noteworthy it may be worth reporting that the cost disease model entered my consciousness quite suddenly and unexpectedly, though it had no doubt lurked in my subconscious for some time before. One night I awoke from a deep sleep at about 3 a.m. with the entire model clearly in my mind. I left the bedroom, went to the next room, jotted down a few notes, and immediately went back to sleep. The next morning I was able to write the idea up systematically. Later I will recount another such incident which occurred about fifteen years afterwards.

Our study of the arts was sponsored by a private foundation, the Twentieth Century Fund, which generously paid the considerable costs of this project. Moreover, the Fund was careful to avoid interference of any sort with the nature of the research or the contents of the resulting book. Indeed, it withstood pressure from a representative of some of the larger performing organisations to suppress or weaken some of the materials showing the high incomes of the members of the audience, a piece of information which, it was feared, would make it more difficult to obtain financial support from the government and other sources. Happily, these fears proved to be unjustified.

As a matter of fact, it is now widely believed that the opposite occurred – that because of the accident of timing (or, perhaps it was no accident but a matter of good judgement of its sponsors) the book is now said to have played a role in launching substantial government support in the United States. It appeared at the same time as another report sponsored by the Rockefeller Brothers Fund (*The Performing Arts: Problems and Prospects*, 1965), in which Bowen and I had a peripheral part. The Rockefeller report was prepared by a committee composed to a considerable extent of businessmen whose strong statement of approval of funding for the arts contributed political respectability to the attempt to induce the United States to embark upon the sort of public sponsorship so traditional in Europe. The simultaneous appearance of our own book, which for the first time provided systematic data and some degree of analysis on the subject, apparently contributed ammunition to the campaign for public support of the arts.

The book was launched with a burst of publicity orchestrated by the Twentieth Century Fund. There were front page stories in the *New York Times* and the *Washington Post*. Newspapers throughout the world carried substantial reports. We were most amused by the story in Pravda which reported that two respectable economists from Princeton University had just published a book showing how capitalism destroys the arts!

PRINCETON AND NEW YORK UNIVERSITIES

The economics department at Princeton was an extraordinarily harmonious group, indeed. I believe virtually all of my colleagues had a deep affection for one another. We were sorry when Friedrich Lutz returned to Europe a few years after we arrived. In addition to members such as Viner, Oskar Morgenstern, Richard Lester, and Lester Chandler, the Department was fortunate to acquire W. Arthur Lewis and Fritz Machlup, both of whom were to become close friends. The Lewises had their home a few doors from ours, and our children grew up together. His lovely and charming wife also proved to be my most talented sculpture student, and has had several successful exhibitions of her own. Sir Arthur's general wisdom, his analytic intuition and his meticulous historical scholarship have always constituted standards difficult for the rest of us to emulate. Fritz Machlup, whose unexpected death earlier this year has left a major gap in our lives, was an incredible generator of ideas and research undertakings which he pursued with amazing determination and energy. At age 77 he undertook a research programme which was projected to yield a work in ten volumes. Three years later he had completed the first three of those books, and work on the others was well on its way.

He and Oskar Morgenstern reached retirement age virtually simultaneously. On attaining their emeritus status at Princeton they were immediately offered and accepted full-term appointments at New York University, where each of them continued to teach with energy and devotion for the remainder of his life.

At just about the time Machlup and Morgenstern left for NYU I had begun to think about my position. By then I had been at Princeton for nearly a quarter of a century. Our children had grown and left home. It seemed high time to make some change in our arrangements. Yet leaving Princeton altogether was virtually unthinkable. Half our lives had been spent there and it contained most of our close friends, both outside the department and within it.

The solution to our dilemma was an invitation to NYU, first, to come as a visitor for a year. Aside from visiting appointments at the Stockholm School of Economics and Berkeley this was our first protracted period away from Princeton since 1949, and it was a return to the city of our childhood. The department in New York proved most hospitable and a pleasant place in which to work. The students were far more heterogeneous than those at Princeton, both in ethnic background and in quality of their earlier training. The best of them were of outstanding quality, and they constituted a fascinating and enthusiastic group.

Consequently, when the next year I was offered a permanent appointment on a half-time basis, and received the consent of Princeton to the arrangement, I agreed readily. As it turned out, it was the beginning of what, in my own view, seems my most creative period.

It actually began with the completion of an exclusively Princeton enterprise; two volumes on environmental economics written jointly with my (then) Princeton colleague, Wallace Oates. One volume was almost entirely devoted to theory while the second sought to assemble the available empirical materials, adding some evidence acquired by ourselves.

Among the results provided by the theoretical volume two will be cited as illustrations. The first deals with the victims of externalities. It has, of course, been known, at least since the work of Pigou, that (with some restrictions) optimal expenditure on reduction of pollution emissions (or other detrimental externalities) requires a charge or tax upon the polluter equal to the marginal social damage of his emissions. This 'polluter pays' arrangement forces the polluter to bear the full social cost of his emissions, and therefore, to undertake any preventative measure whose (incremental) cost is less than the value of the damage thereby avoided. But what about the victims? It would seem that simple justice calls for some sort of compensation to those whose health or even whose cost of living is affected by pollution. Indeed, this intuitive judgement is readily confirmed formally with the aid of the mathematical theory of fairness provided in the work of Duncan Foley, David Schmeidler, Serge-Christophe Kolm and others. Yet it is proved in our theoretical volume that, unless it can be provided in a way whose incentive effects are zero (i.e. as a 'lump sum' payment), *any* compensation to the victims of externalities, however small, is incompatible with Pareto optimality in resource allocation in the economy. There is a simple theoretical explanation of this result. In the presence of detrimental externalities there is a Pareto optimal level of use of resources *by the victims* to protect themselves from their effects. For example, it may be appropriate to insulate or air condition homes and workplaces, or it may be desirable to move them away from the source of pollution thereby, perhaps, increasing transportation costs in the future. But if compensation is based on the amount of damage suffered by the victims, such compensation payments will induce them to spend less on self-protection against that damage. In effect, such compensation payments reduce the marginal net yield of outlays on self-protection. Here we then have a clear example of a conflict (or, rather, a trade-off) between Pareto optimality and fairness.

A second illustrative result of our theoretical analysis relates to the choice between a tax upon the generator of externalities and a subsidy to induce him to reduce his emissions. Common sense suggests that at appropriate tax and subsidy rates the effects of the two will be the same – the donkey can be moved either with the carrot or the stick. But while this conclusion (which had often been repeated in the environmental literature) has an element of truth, it turns out that subsidies have a second consequence which is more than likely to offset its pollution decreasing effect. It is true that in the short run either the tax or the subsidy will induce polluting firms to emit less. However, at least in the case of perfect competition, in the long run, the tax on emissions may *not* reduce the emissions of any one polluting *firm*, yet it will reduce the emissions of the *industry* by encouraging the exit of polluters. On the other hand, *the subsidy is likely to increase the industry's emissions* by encouraging the entry of polluters. These results are certainly true when there is a fixed proportion between output and quantity of emission. A fixed Pigouvian tax, t, per unit of emissions then contributes to the firm's total cost the amount tky, where y is output and k is the emissions-output ratio. The resulting addition to average cost is tky/y = tk = constant. Therefore, the Pigouvian tax simply causes a uniform upward shift in the firm's average cost curve, and so does not affect the location of its minimum point, i.e. its profit maximising output or emissions level. Yet we do know from a standard supply-demand diagram that with curves of the usual shape a tax must shift the supply curve upward and therefore must reduce industry output and, hence, its emissions, and the opposite must be true under a subsidy.

The investigation of the empirical data also produced a number of what, to us at least, were surprises. We had thought that the explosion in the world's population and in industrial activity would show that there was fairly universal growth in the rate of environmental damage, but the results were far more mixed. In some cases such as lead in the atmosphere and the generation of solid wastes our conjecture did indeed turn out to be true or, at least, to be supported by the evidence. But post-war emissions control efforts had substantial beneficial effects on air and water quality with, e.g. enormous decreases in the sulphur and particulate content of the atmosphere in major cities of the US and the United Kingdom. In other cases, e.g. the concentration of pollutants in Lake Superior in the United States and the oxygen content of the rivers surrounding Manhattan, matters had been improving long before that. In several cases such as the depletion of oxygen in the Baltic and the concentration of mercury in tuna it transpired that there was good reason to suspect that the causes were natural (e.g. a secular decline in rainfall in the sources of water for the Baltic). We were most surprised to find (after an extensive search that took us to the conservators' quarters at the Louvre, the Metropolitan Museum in New York and St Paul's

Cathedral in London) that there seems to be no conclusive evidence supporting the view that the deterioration of ancient sculpture and of stone buildings is accelerating or that it is attributable to increasing emissions of pollutants. We found many newspaper stories claiming categorically that this was so, but careful review of the scientific evidence simply forced us to accept the verdict 'not proven'.

Perhaps partly in consequence of this work I was elected to the presidency of the recently formed Association of Environmental and Resource Economists (AERE), an organisation which has since grown and expanded its activities.

THE THEORY OF CONTESTABLE MARKETS

Soon after the two books on the environment[3] made their appearance, I found myself embarked almost accidentally on what I consider to be the most fruitful piece of research in which I have ever participated. The word 'participated' is used advisedly, since the results stemmed from the work of at least a half dozen persons beside myself – my co-authors, John Panzar, then of Bell Laboratories and Robert Willig of Princeton University, Elizabeth Bailey, formerly Vice-Chairman of the Civil Aeronautics Board and now at Carnegie Mellon University, Dietrich Fischer, Thijs ten Raa, then at New York University, and Gerald Faulhaber at Bell Laboratories. Obviously there were three centres of activity: NYU, Princeton and Bell Laboratories.

My systematic work on the subject began with a project I had undertaken under the sponsorship of the Division of Information Science and Technology of the National Science Foundation in which an incidental part of the task was to provide a non-technical document discussing the rationale for and principles for the determination of the proper amount of government financial support for the dissemination of scientific and technical information in general and of scientific journals in particular. Assuming that a large part of the argument would rest on the sorts of market failure associated with public goods and scale economies, I set about what I expected to be the tedious task of redescribing a set of elementary and straightforward principles. The public goods portion of the discussion turned out just as expected – exactly as it is so well described in the literature. However, the theory of scale economies and the associated phenomenon of natural monopoly seemed to resist simple explanation. Each time I attempted a description of the logic of some obvious proposition it seemed to acquire complexity and turned out not to be quite correct. For example, in the case of a publisher who provided a half dozen journals rather than only one, scale economies did not seem to account for the firm's multiproduct character. Why was the enterprise a multiproduct firm, and what would society lose by breaking up the publishing firm into six separate publishers of single journals? It was considerations such as this which later led Panzar and Willig to formulate their concept of economies of scope – the savings which a firm may (or may not) enjoy from simultaneous provision of a multiplicity of products – and which had previously led me to formulate the more technical concept of trans-ray convexity,[4] a formal criterion of continuous complementarity in the production of different goods as output proportions change. At the same time it became clear that natural monopoly which is defined to mean that production of the industry's vector of outputs is cheaper when carried out by a single firm rather than by any multiplicity of firms, is not quite the same thing as scale economies. Indeed, it was proved eventually that scale economies throughout the relevant region of output space are neither necessary nor sufficient for natural monopoly.

Meanwhile, Gerald Faulhaber, who had been sent by Bell Laboratories to carry out his graduate work at Princeton, had quite independently, starting off from some earlier work of mine, begun research on the theory of natural monopoly. He found implications which had escaped me completely at the time the original work had been prepared. When Faulhaber showed me some of his work and asked me to supervise his PhD dissertation, I was astonished at the degree of overlap with my own work at NYU. Indeed, using a single-product game theoretic approach, his work was at that point in many ways ahead of mine.

The developments were sufficiently seductive to attract the attention of others, notably Panzar and Willig at Bell Laboratories, Dietrich Fischer at NYU, and Elizabeth Bailey who then held positions both at Bell Laboratories and NYU and who quickly took on the task of liaison in addition to the valuable contributions she directly provided herself.

Faulhaber had already proved for the single-product case that the concept underlying and, indeed, appropriately defining natural monopoly is a mathematical relationship called subadditivity of total cost. Specifically (for the multiproduct case) let y^I represent the vector of outputs of the industry and let y^i be any vector of outputs assigned to a hypothetical firm, i, in any partition of the industry's outputs, so that $\Sigma y^i = y^I$. If C(y) is the total cost function of a firm in the industry, then that cost function is strictly subadditive if $C(y^I) < \Sigma C(y^i)$ for each and every set of y^i summing to y^I. In other words, the cost function is subadditive at industry output vector y^I if it is cheaper for y^I to be produced by a monopoly than by any larger number of firms.

Faulhaber had also proved in the single product case, first, that economies of scale are sufficient to guarantee that the firm's average costs will decrease, second, that decreasing average costs are sufficient to guarantee subadditivity, and, third, that the converse is untrue – that subadditivity is no guarantee of decreasing average cost. In other words, in the single-product case he had shown that an industry could be a natural monopoly even if it did not exhibit scale economies and its average costs were not declining.

Soon Panzar and Willig produced several sets of necessary conditions for subadditivity in the multiproduct case, and I provided a set of conditions sufficient for multiproduct natural monopoly, conditions which have since been used rather widely in empirical studies of cost functions and their implications for the structure of an industry.

Panzar and Willig, working together, proposed a concept which Dr Bailey and I had also put forth on the same day – the concept of sustainability of prices. A vector of prices charged by a multiproduct monopolist is said to be *sustainable against entry* if a) it provides revenue to the monopoly at least sufficient to permit it to cover its costs, and b) there exists no other vector of outputs which an entrant can sell at those prices and which will permit the entrant to operate without loss. In other words, sustainable prices permit the incumbent to prevent entry without recourse to retaliatory measures or strategic responses. This concept was formulated as a first step toward transformation of the natural monopoly concept from one which was normative (when is natural monopoly the most efficient industry structure?) to something that was more or less behavioural (when will natural monopoly be immune from entry?).

Faulhaber was able to prove that where both economies and diseconomies of scale are present (at different ranges of outputs), even if a firm is a natural monopoly, no sustainable prices may exist for it. He did this with the aid of a remarkable numerical counterexample. Consider three communities for which electricity generating facilities of given capacity are to be built. Suppose any one of the communities' needs can be met at a cost of \$12 million, that any two of them can be served simultaneously for \$19 million while all three of them can be served by a single plant for \$30 million. Costs here are clearly subadditive since provision of the output by three separate plants costs 3 × \$12 million = \$36 million, while two-plant production costs \$12 + \$19 million = 31 million. Both other options are, therefore, more costly than the \$30 million outlay required for single-firm production. Yet, here, a single generating firm can find no prices which are sustainable. For if it were, for example, to propose to charge each community \$10 million in order just to cover its \$30 million cost, an entrant could offer to supply only two of the three communities at a cost of say \$9.7 million each, thus more than covering the \$19 million cost of the plant required for the purpose. Faulhaber's example thus showed that in some cases freedom of entry can prevent cost minimisation. But the bulk of our analysis was later to argue strongly for ease of entry.

A little later I provided a complementary theorem which rested on a result first derived by Frank Ramsey in 1927. As we know, where average costs are declining (and in a variety of related multiproduct cases), a firm which prices its products at their marginal costs must suffer losses. The question to which Ramsey addressed himself is if marginal cost prices are therefore precluded, what deviations of prices from marginal costs are required for the second-best allocation of resources, that is, for Pareto optimality under the constraint that supplying firms just cover their total costs? Ramsey was able to derive a formula for these second-best prices which was ignored by much of the economic literature for several decades but had by the 1970s received a great deal of attention. I was then able to prove (though the result took me completely by surprise) that a monopolist who decided to adopt Pareto optimal Ramsey prices would (under a set of rather reasonable assumptions) find those prices to be sustainable. In other words, such a commendable pricing decision would reward the monopolist by granting him immunity from entry.

I had arrived at this result in rather curious circumstances. My wife and I were attending a fund raising performance at one of New York's experimental theatres, and we were waiting in line to get in surrounded by persons in bizarre dress and make-up when, according to my wife, my face took on a rather distracted look. I told her that a theorem which hardly seemed plausible to me had come to me from nowhere, along with what seemed to me to be its entire proof.

Indeed, it transpired that the rigorous proof that emerged eventually did follow the outline that came to me suddenly in that theatre lobby, but it took weeks of hard labour by (a sceptical) Willig, Bailey (and myself) before it could be put into satisfactory form.

At about this time a small group of US economists was sent by the National Science Foundation to attend a conference in Leningrad, and Willig and I were among them. We sat up all night in the airplane discussing how our analysis of natural monopoly could be extended to other market forms and constitute the basis for a theory of the determination of industry structure. The vision had been mine, but Willig was to contribute the key step to its realisation. First, on our return, Fischer and I produced a paper showing how one can calculate the cost minimising structure of an industry, thereby determining whether it is or is not, say, a natural monopoly. For example, if it transpires that the industry's output vector can be produced most cheaply by say, four firms, one can say it is a 'natural oligopoly', and we showed under what circumstances this will be true. Similarly, we showed under what cost conditions the industry will be 'naturally perfectly competitive', etc.

Then Willig formulated the concept of what we were to call a perfectly contestable market – a market in which an entrant has access to all production techniques available to incumbents, in which the entrant is not prohibited from wooing the incumbent's customers, and in which entry decisions can be reversed without cost – that is, a market from which entrants can withdraw without loss of any of their investments. An example of an approximation to such a market is an airline route. If company A opens up for business on the route from New York to Los Angeles and business proves disappointing, he can simply withdraw and move them to another more promising route.

Where exit and entry are so easy and exit so costless incumbents are completely vulnerable to the threat posed by *potential* entry. It is possible to prove that, as a consequence, in a perfectly contestable market (a) no firm can earn any monopoly profit in the long run, (b) industry structure must always be efficient, i.e. the industry will tend to be composed of exactly the number of firms that can produce its output at minimum cost and (c) if two or more firms supply a given product to a market, in the long run the price of that product must equal its marginal cost.

Markets may be perfectly contestable even if they are characterised by scale economies in production and even if they contain only a small number of firms (even only a single firm). The theory thus generalises considerably the concept of perfect competition, showing how ease of entry and exit and the accompanying threat by potential entrants can elicit good performance even in industries with small numbers of firms.

It must be emphasised that our purpose was not apologetics. We do not believe that most industries are perfectly contestable or even nearly so. We do believe, however, that some industries with small numbers of firms *are* highly contestable, and that in those cases government interference with the market mechanism is difficult to justify. In other cases the contestability of the market can be increased by public policy and in those cases this will sometimes prove to be the most effective means to serve the public interest.

It should be added also that we are well aware of the heavy debt contestability analysis owes to earlier writing, and have tried to suggest some of its sources in our publications. But as Viner taught me long ago, one can never hope to achieve completeness in such an undertaking.

In my presidential address to the American Economic Association in December of 1981 I sought to provide a general introduction to the theory of contestable markets. This was followed several months later by the publication of our book with its lengthy analysis of multiproduct firms and industries and its examination of the market forces that determine the structure of an industry – whether it will emerge as an oligopoly, a monopoly or something else. As is to be expected, the analysis has generated controversy, raising legitimate questions many of which are still far from being settled. It has also led to a variety of research undertakings by others, both empirical and theoretical, and that has, of course, been most gratifying.

TOWARD FURTHER WORK

Happily, the area in which I work has experienced relatively rapid growth in the past few decades, and so my stock of teaching capital has undergone considerable obsolescence. Many of my former students and their contemporaries are now better equipped than I to teach the various courses in mathematical economics, virtually all of which I had inaugurated some thirty years earlier.

I flatter myself that this is not quite true in my research. In the two years since the appearance of the contestability book I have embarked on several other projects. I am working on applications of Duncan Foley's fairness concept to analyse the equitability of different rationing procedures, of peak-off peak pricing and of Pigouvian taxes on externalities. I am working on the theory of productivity growth and the feedback relationship between such growth and expenditures on research and development by private industry. I am also considering a study of the theory of nationalised industry – of the circumstances under which operation of a firm by the public sector may be superior in terms of the general welfare to operation by private enterprise, regulated or unregulated by government. Here it should be noted that analyses such as the theory of public goods are less pertinent than may at first appear to be the case since a public good can be produced by private firms if it is *financed* by government. If nationalised firms lack the incentives for efficiency provided by the market mechanism to private firms why, then, should government enterprise ever be preferred over private? I am working on a model which will, with a bit of luck, provide some answers and, perhaps, some additional insights.

In short, as yet there is no conclusion to my story – all I can offer is a status report on a continuing stream of research . . .

Notes

1. I am not certain the term 'prisoner's dilemma' had yet been invented; indeed, I seem to remember it was proposed by Professor A. Tucker at Princeton several years later. But the ideas of game theory had reached London and in discussions externalities were already being translated there into game theoretic terms.
2. The noteworthy exception seems always to have been a period of rapid inflation. Data for the period after the US Civil War, after the First World War and the inflation of the 1970s indicate that in such periods growth in cost per performance has not stayed ahead of the general price level. Presumably groups are not able to raise money quickly enough, and are therefore forced to retrench by reducing rehearsal time, simplifying costumes and scenery, etc. If this explanation is correct, it follows that the cost disease is not really in remission in such periods, but that its normal consequences are suppressed and emerge in a different form – that of reduction of standards and cutting of corners.
3. Baumol, William J. and Wallace, Oates, *The Theory of Environmental Policy*, Englewood Cliffs, N.J., Prentice Hall, 1975 and Oates, Baumol and Blackman, S.A., *Economics and the Quality of Life*, Englewood Cliffs, N.J., Prentice Hall, 1979.
4. For a formal definition see Baumol, W. Panzar and Willig, *Contestable Markets and the Theory of Industry Structure*, San Diego, Ca: Harcourt Brace Jovanovich, 1982, pp. 79–81.

Reference

The Rockefeller Report, *The Performing Arts: Problems and Prospects* (McGraw-Hill, New York, 1965).

[2]

WILLIAM J. BAUMOL

On My Attitudes: Sociopolitical and Methodological

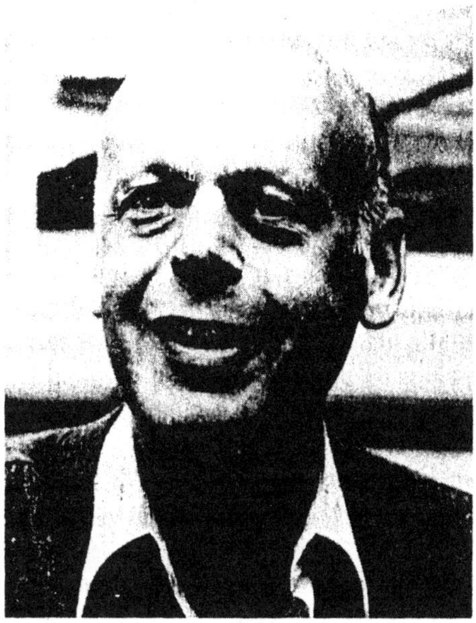

My goals for society have always derived from the left. However, they have nothing in common with the totalitarian persuasions of those who have hoodwinked society into believing that theirs are the only true antitheses of reactionary values.

I believe deeply, with Shaw, that there are few crimes more heinous than poverty. GBS, as usual, exaggerated when he told us that lack of money is the root of all evil. But he did not exaggerate by much. Perhaps barely second to the battle against poverty in my list of priorities is the struggle for human rights, the guarantee against arbitrary arrest, mutilation and murder either by officialdom or by terrorist groups, even those convinced that the nobility of their purposes exempts them from any constraints on their methods. To these objectives add the civil liberties which the late Senator McCarthy sought so hard to subvert and civil rights – freedom from discrimination on the basis of race, sex, nationality or beliefs.

It is quite fashionable to claim allegiance to these causes. Politicians who are prepared to cut expenditures on the poor before touching any other items in their budget show no shame in proclaiming their concern over hunger. Advocates of dangerous extensions of police powers and censorship trumpet their dedication to traditions of freedom. But such friends of these goals only underscore how difficult it is to achieve tangible progress toward their realization or even to prevent erosion of the progress that has already been achieved.

W. Arthur Lewis once remarked to me that throughout the world the veneer of civilization is very thin. It takes little to stimulate an outbreak of genocide; the Bill of Rights is an extremely recent phenomenon in human history – one which still encompasses a very limited portion of the globe, and even there it is often threatened.

My orientation toward the left (as I interpret the left) is come by honestly. My parents, Jewish immigrants from Eastern Europe, were part of the radical intellectual group engendered by the despotism of their homelands. My father was a devoted Marxist and remained pro-Soviet until the Hitler–Stalin Pact. My mother had had serious doubts much earlier and as a teenager I had already been revolted by the brutality of the Soviet government. But though divorcing myself from that totalitarian regime and its supporters I never lost faith in those ideals which had moved so many of the radicals who had populated my childhood world. I believe those are the objectives which I consider important still.

There is an opinion of a second sort which I also attribute to my Marxist upbringing. I feel a strong antipathy to acts whose only valuable consequence is likely to be the sense of virtue felt by those who undertake them. I have always interpreted Marx's quarrel with the "Utopian" socialists to have reflected similar concerns – the view that where an objective requires substantial and disquieting changes, few things are likely to be as damaging to the cause as an empty gesture. The opportunity cost is simply too great. That is why, for example, I have often opposed efforts to force *universities* to sell their stocks in firms which do business in South Africa. Such programs are unlikely to influence to any substantial degree the policies of the firms in question and cannot usually be expected to lead them to withdraw their investments. Moreover, even if some of them did withdraw, the effects on South African government policies would surely be minimal or may even drive them, in desperation, in an even more racist direction, with the bulk of the damage borne by the black population. True, those who worked hard for this cause must have felt more at peace with their consciences as a result. But the time and effort they spent on it might much better have been devoted to other approaches which might really have made a substantial contribution in the battle against discrimination. I know one case in particular in which a very promising opportunity to force increased hiring of blacks in a trade formerly largely barred to them was consciously neglected in order to throw all the available resources into the attempt to cleanse the universities' securities portfolios.

In sum, the causes I espouse face opposition from three sources: the forces of the right, the totalitarian left and what I term left-wing romantics.

What has all this to do with the discipline of economics? In my view, a great deal. There is a long tradition among economists of dedication to social causes. Frank Fetter's study of economists in Parliament in the nineteenth century suggests strongly on the basis of their attendance and voting records that they were responsible, dedicated and overwhelmingly supported what for their day were the radical causes – the secret ballot, enfranchisement of Catholics, extension of the suffrage. These causes were consistently supported by a far greater proportion of the economists than of the remaining members in Parliament. And they were supported by economists who stood to lose from the adoption of the measures at issue.

Yet economists have earned opprobrium by seeking to expose proposals for change which seemed to promise social benefits cheaply and easily but which they considered dangerous delusions. They have opposed rent control, believing that it is an incentive for neglect and abandonment and an obstacle to construction. For this they have been suspected of lacking sympathy for the ill-housed. Hoping to achieve substantial improvements in the environment they have advocated that polluters be required to pay for the damage they cause. For this they have been accused of espousing the sale of "licenses to pollute."

In short, given my orientation and my goals, I feel quite at home with those of a considerable number of my colleagues, particularly those who feel that a good deal must yet be done to provide work for the jobless, to raise the living standards of the homeless, to prevent the poisoning of our atmosphere and the degradation of our environment, who, in sum, are anxious to use our discipline to improve the circumstances in which people live.

ON POLITICAL POSITIONS BY PROFESSIONAL ORGANIZATIONS

While I am strongly predisposed toward colleagues who speak out on political and social issues and who are prepared to act on their convictions, I have always felt very differently about educational institutions and professional associations. I avidly opposed attempts to get the universities to take a stand on the Vietnam War or to induce the American Economic Association to take a public position on ratification of the Equal Rights Amendment, holding to this course even where I felt strongly that the cause for which endorsement was sought was just. There are two reasons for my opposition. First, any institution of the sort in question, precisely because it is not organized about any set of political opinions, is certain to encompass people whose views are diverse. If the organization then commits itself to some special political stand it must, consequently, misrepresent the views of at least some of its constituents – it must, by implication, distort such minority views, presenting to the world a spurious appearance of unanimity.

Second, the adoption of institutional positions imperils the organization and impedes pursuit of the purposes for which it was formed. If a professional organization which follows such a course drives away those members who differ from the "official" positions or, worse still, seeks to suppress their views, it loses its ability to promote the exercise of professional activities, the purpose for which it was founded. In an educational institution an official position is even more serious because it becomes a threat to academic freedom. True academic freedom is not merely a matter of willingness to listen to those with whom we disagree mildly. It requires the institution to offer a forum even to those whose opinions we vehemently detest. Official institutional positions are no encouragement to this principle, whose defense is apt at times to require considerable courage and tenacity.

It is sometimes suggested by those who advocate the adoption of organizational positions, particularly on critical public issues, that universities are repositories of wisdom, and that in times of crisis, it is a special responsibility of educational institutions to speak out. Fritz Machlup used to point out in reply that history does not support this conclusion – that with the onset of the Nazi regime the German universities *did* choose to speak out, but the position they adopted does them little credit.

In saying all this, I am not arguing against all political activities by universities and professional organizations. I have more than once urged the American Economic Association, or rather, the members of its executive committee, to do what they could for economists in other countries who had been imprisoned for the economic doctrines they held or advocated (I may add that the executive committee was in general quite willing to act in such cases). Similarly, I think it is quite appropriate for an educational institution to act on behalf of academic freedom whenever and wherever it is threatened. But that is because such a stand is entirely in line with its purposes, and constitutes no threat to its ability to function.

ON METHOD

My convictions on proper methodological approaches for economic analysis are relatively weak. Indeed, in the area of method I am not sure I have any deep convictions – I am quite happy to see a thousand flowers bloom. Mathematical economists, institutionalists, econometricians, economic historians, neoclassicists, followers of the Anglo-Italian path have each and all made valuable contributions. Yet none of them has found the philosopher's stone, and any of them that sees fit to denounce the others is apt to seem just a bit ridiculous. Economics *is* a difficult subject and we cannot afford to dispense with the services of anyone who has an approach that promises to provide any new light on the workings of the economy.

Having just trumpeted my unbounded forbearance on methodological issues, let me admit that there are some bounds to my tolerance. Indeed, I do have strong dislikes. I am particularly turned off by construction of models for their own sake or by painstaking attempts to complicate already available models, ostensibly for added realism.

A well-designed model is, after all, a judiciously chosen set of lies, or perhaps more accurately put, partial truths about reality, which have been chosen so as to permit us to reason more effectively about some issue than we otherwise could. The model *must* be an oversimplification if it is to be tractable analytically. Optimality in model construction must be based on the trade-off between these two desiderata – accuracy of representation of reality and usability in analysis.

Two conclusions follow from these observations. First, increased realism is not necessarily a virtue. Indeed, if it complicates the model to a degree that effectively precludes its use in analysis, it deserves to be treated as a mortal sin.

The second conclusion that follows is that a particular model can neither be judged good nor bad in the abstract. Only when related to the issue for whose analysis it is meant to be used can one judge its quality. A model which is admirably suited for the analysis of one such issue may be ill-adapted to another.

To make my point here let me give my favorite example. Models of the demand for cash can be said to be of at least three broad types. There are the macroeconomic models such as the liquidity preference or loanable funds constructs. The second type is the more microeconomic inventory theory model associated with Tobin's work and my own. The third type, generally unknown to economists, is based on the work of the psychologists. For example, there is one such construct in which the intensity of an individual's demand for money is related to his age at toilet training.

Whatever one may think of any of these models, it is clear that each of them is totally useless in dealing with some particular types of problem for which one of the others may be appropriate. For example, if one is asked to testify before the Joint Economic Committee of the U.S. Congress about the demand for money and the danger of increased inflation, the inventory theory model of the demand for cash will contribute little and the toilet training model probably even less. Here, only some one of the macro models offers any prospect of help.

Second, suppose an economist is hired as a consultant by the financial vice-president of a large corporation who seeks help in coping with the interest burden of the firm's cash reserves. Here, no macro model seems particularly promising, while the inventory theoretic model may conceivably be just what is needed.

Finally, imagine a distraught wife who seeks help because her wealthy but miserly husband is unable to part with cash and is keeping the family in penury. Here, what can be contributed by an analysis using either a macro model or one based on inventory theory?

The point is that each of the models is a highly specialized oversimplification – a set of partial truths which renders it fit only for use for the study of certain types of issues. What, then, can be the point of constructing a model for its own sake?

For these reasons, in building models I always prefer to work backwards, starting, if possible, with some hypothesis, some question I want to answer. Then I try to judge from this question and the range of possible answers what elements the model will have to contain and what features one can dispense with. That, to me, is the most effective way to try to make sure that the model is pertinent. It may seem as though this way of going about the process is likely to bias the result, predisposing it toward confirmation of the author's preconceptions. However, I have often found myself surprised at the results that emerged. Indeed, on a number of occasions the model's implications were completely opposite from my initial conjectures, and forced me to rethink the entire subject. I suspect that some of my most interesting articles emerged from surprises of this sort. The very fact that the result was unexpected meant that it was likely to suggest new ideas to some others beside myself. Moreover, it meant, at least sometimes, that the required analysis was more complex and subtle than I had anticipated.

ON SCIENCE AND ART

The fact that I spend a considerable amount of time working on painting and sculpture (I teach a course in wood sculpture at Princeton University) has forced me to think a bit about the relations between my two activities.

I put the matter that way because my preconceptions incline me to resist treating creative activity in the arts in a rigidly analytic manner. I like to approach the creative process in the arts as something that is best driven by feelings rather than systematic analysis. Art that emerges from a systematic intellectual process often seems to be threatened by sterility. Yet on a number of occasions I found myself forced to go beyond this purely negative statement.

The position I have arrived at over the years[1] is that ambiguity is perhaps the indispensable feature of a work of art, while it is at the same time the enemy of effective scientific work. There are at least two parts to the role of ambiguity in art. First, it seems to me that when a message can be transmitted rather unambiguously, any attempt to decorate it with an artistic superstructure is all too likely to degenerate into surface embellishment. I am not arguing that art should always have a message. When it has none, it is by definition all ambiguity. But where art *is* used to convey messages it seems appropriate to do so in cases where words fail the messenger – where it cannot be phrased in a manner that is direct and bears a unique interpretation. Allegory, poetry and other indirect communication media may then convey such imperfectly expressible messages more effectively than direct assertion.

There is a second reason why art must not avoid ambiguity. In a significant sense the artistic experience (whatever that term may connote) is produced by its audience as well as by its creator. Thus, the same work may evoke very different responses in individual A and individual B because the work and A together may involve a chemistry very different from the combination of that same work and person B. This is fortunate because otherwise a work of art could not long endure. A medieval altarpiece cannot possibly have had the same meaning for a fourteenth century monk that it does for a twentieth century observer from Japan. Without its ambiguity, its ability to be transmogrified as the members of its audience change, a work of art could not move different cultures or different ages. Without ambiguity, it can only attain the lifeless status of Soviet proletarian art or the art of the National Socialists.

Contrast this with appropriate standards for writing in our discipline. Anyone who has ever worked on the history of economic ideas is painfully aware of the extent to which ambiguity pervades our literature despite repeated attempts of economists to remove it from their writings. The persistence of discussions about what Ricardo or Marx really meant shows how imperfect is the economist's ability to preclude diversity of

[1] In arriving at this formulation of my views I have been helped enormously by the perceptive analysis of Louise M. Rosenblatt in her writings on literary criticism. See, for example, her *The Reader, the Text, the Poems*, Southern Illinois University Press, 1978.

interpretation of what they have written. Mathematical notation can, perhaps, help, but it is no panacea; witness, for example, the protracted and convoluted discussion of the meaning of the von Neumann–Morgenstern axioms on cardinal utility measurement which, while it has somewhat petered out, has still not come to an end.

Yet, while full success is out of the question, it is surely still part of the economist-writer's task to make the contents of his writings as clear and as unambiguous as possible. This is one of the reasons I have always stressed clarity of exposition and its importance as part of the student's training.

Though it is a disgression, I may add that it is by no means the only reason. I have often found that in the process of trying to rephrase a relatively difficult and obscure argument of my own, elements emerge of which I myself had previously been unaware, and sometimes the process even reveals errors or gaps in my analysis. Thus, exposition became not just an end in itself but a useful step in the creative process, one which is capable of generating ideas and of contributing even to more rigorous analysis.

ON APPLIED ECONOMICS

My rather strong views on social and political goals apply also to the work of economists. In line with many of my colleagues today, as well as their predecessors, I am particularly interested in what the discipline can contribute to improvement of the state of social welfare. To me the success of the discipline is to be measured primarily in the extent to which it can help to reduce unemployment and poverty and to improve the quality of life.

However, in arguing this I should not be taken to be questioning the value of "pure" economic research. I agree that additions to the state of knowledge are valuable in themselves. Veblen did have a point when he described the main motive for research as "idle curiosity." That, after all, is the primary business of the academic researcher – to achieve some reduction in the degree of our ignorance.

Moreover, at least occasionally, application is best approached by indirection. It is sometimes the purest of research which ultimately makes the greatest contribution to the social welfare. The only caveat I would address to those who are engaged in very abstract research is to urge the utmost caution before hastening to apply its results to the complex issues of reality. I suppose we are all prone to sin in that regard, ready to leap in with advice to the makers of public policy which is based on no more than an abstract analysis resting on obscure and unverified premises. That useful policy prescriptions may eventually derive from such work is true, but beside the point. Before completion of a careful process of testing and modifications to adapt it to the complications of reality, such a proposal might well be required to bear a label asserting, "This policy may prove dangerous to economic health."

William J. Baumol is Professor of Economics at Princeton and New York universities.

Leonardo, Vol. 15, No. 1, pp. 40–42, 1982
Printed in Great Britain

0024–094X/82/010040–03$03.00/0
Pergamon Press Ltd.

ON MY SCULPTURES OF CARVED WOOD

William Baumol*

1.

I write with feeling about the dichotomy between technical writing in the domain of political economy and the very different way sculpture must be described, because, even before I began my college education, I had acquired a passionate interest in these two fields, no doubt an unusual combination. Today, a half century later, I teach both subjects at Princeton University and at New York University.

I began my formal education in art in 1936 in the free classes made available by the Works Progress Administration (WPA) in the U.S.A. during its Great Depression when Franklin D. Roosevelt was President. The WPA, to relieve widespread unemployment, provided jobs whenever possible in fields in which people had been trained. It sponsored the painting of murals in public buildings, the organization of theatrical groups (notably Orson Welles' Mercury Theatre Productions) and excellent classes in the arts [1]. The economic depression affected both the themes that artists chose and the media used. A curious detail sticks in my memory—the advantage for lithography because it was then so inexpensive. Lithograph stones could be had for the trouble of carrying them home from a bank that had failed—for banks had once used lithograph stones to print certificates that would be hard to counterfeit.

In 1938 I ended my WPA classes. I then studied painting for three years at the Art Students League and, on entering the City College of New York (now part of New York City University), I concentrated on the two fields in which I still work.

My introduction to wood sculpture, in which, along with painting, I specialize today, was largely accidental. During World War II, I served in the U.S. Army, much of the time in France. My quartermaster unit spent one night in a ruined fortress near Cherbourg, recently recaptured from the Germans. In a pile of rubble I noticed a few tools that turned out to be those used in wood carving. Since no owner was to be found, I followed custom and simply took them with me. Months later, just after the war in Europe ended, I met a man among some prisoners working under my supervision, whom the Nazis must have drafted in desperation. An old socialist, little taller than a dwarf, he turned out to be a delightful person and a skilled wood-carver. He agreed to give me some lessons with the tools I had found.

*Sculptor, political economist and teacher in both subjects, Dept. of Economics, New York University, 8 Washington Place, Room 700, New York, NY 10003, U.S.A. (Received 20 May 1980)

2.

As sculptors of wood well know, the material has special properties and visual characteristics that can be utilized for artistic purposes. The grain of a log can be considered to be made up of a set of parallel cylinders, each composed of the strands that were added by a year's growth. Even if one cuts through a piece of wood carelessly, the grain is visible on the surface of the cut; not only is no skill required for the grain to be evident, it is an outcome that cannot be avoided.

But the carving of wood also presents certain difficulties—some are generic to the sculpting of any material, some are specific for wood. The direction of the strands of wood dictates the direction in which cuts should be made for physical reasons. If the wood is cut in the direction that forms an obtuse angle with the strands, they will be forced closer together, making a smooth surface. But if the cut is made in the opposite direction, they will be separated, sometimes even leading to the splintering of the wood. Often when a piece is carved, unsuspected knots and rot may be encountered that a carver may decide to allow to influence a preconceived sculpture. Of course, a painter and a sculptor of imagination learn through experience that a work while being made often takes on aspects that were not planned and that are accepted. In the case of a sculpture, it is practical to make only a few drawings from selected viewing points that one considers of prime importance. One can make clay models to guide one's carving of a wood sculpture, but the different properties of clay make this approach of limited help.

Sculpture of carved wood and stone is probably more difficult to plan than sculpture made of assembled components of various materials, as in constructivist works, both because wood and stone are not homogeneous and because carving involves special constraints not imposed by the assembly especially of prefabricated components, such as cracking and breaking. Several sculptors have discussed in past issues of *Leonardo* their experience of making carved sculpture and of making constructivist works.

3.

Until about 1965 my carved wood sculptures were based on figurative subjects, but now they are nonfigurative and my objective has been to make forms that lead viewers along paths that break out of two dimensions. In making these works I clearly owe some debt to Henry Moore in his figurative work and to Japanese sculptors whose goal seems to me to be the desire to present extreme simplicity in nonfigurative works. But I have not consciously sought to follow the lead of any particular sculptor or to produce any eclectic synthesis of the works of different sculptors.

I have focused primarily on selected silhouettes of a sculpture because I think that these first strike the eyes of viewers. The silhouette of a medieval European Christian sculpture of, say, the Virgin holding her Christ child typically has the form of a 3-dimensional *S*, with her head bent slightly and her hip thrust forward to support the child. I find this *S* form appealing, and I often introduce it in my nonfigurative sculptures.

In addition to this characteristic form, I seek to emphasize a spiral-like twist to accentuate the 3-dimensional aspect of sculpture. Without the spiral twist that leads the eye around the sculpture, a nonfigurative sculpture with flat surfaces, I find, can be visualized as a sculpture made up of several distinct 2-dimensional shapes.

4.

To bring out this point, I begin the discussion of my sculptures with a most recent piece, 'Wooden Form 258' (Fig. 1, left), which I regard as a deviation from my main artistic objective. Its form was cut on a band saw and then the edges were rounded by carving and sandpapering. I intended to imply a combination of motion and repose and to draw attention to the beautiful grain of the walnut. However, I find it is too pictorial in quality. The use of a band saw, unless one is very alert, tends to produce such '2-dimensional' sculptures because one usually chooses flat pieces of wood to cut and the saw lures one into making cuts having a fixed angle with the face of the sculpture.

Figure 2 (right) shows 'Wooden Form 134' and (left) 'Superimposed Figures'. The one on the right was first cut on a band saw, and I find it has a '2-dimensional' quality. The one on the left is a hand-carved piece in ebony. As one walks about it, one becomes aware of abrupt, even startling, configurations. To appreciate its complexity, one must walk around it in order to obtain a complete idea of its conception. If one does not, it is as though, in reading a story, one were to stop abruptly in the middle of its text. Another attribute of 'Superimposed Figures' that pleases me is that many viewers have considered the two related forms intertwined humans. I feel that the use of two or more related forms in a single sculpture enriches it, much as several voices in a fugue contribute to the appeal of such music.

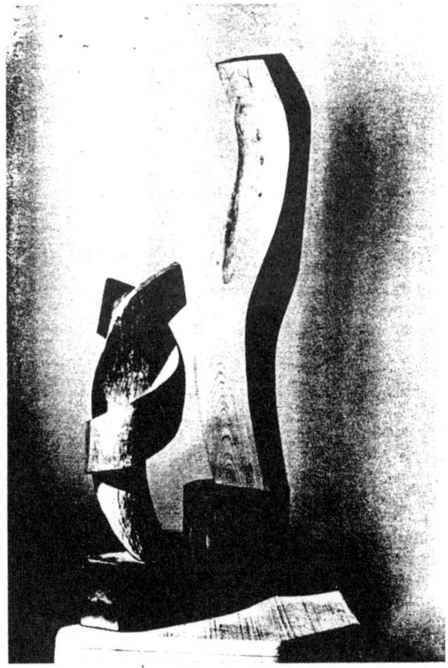

Fig. 2. (Left) ***'Superimposed Figures', ebony***, height 45 cm, max. dia. 12.5 cm, 1970; (right) ***'Wooden Form 134', elm***, height 81 cm, diam. at base 16 cm, 1974.

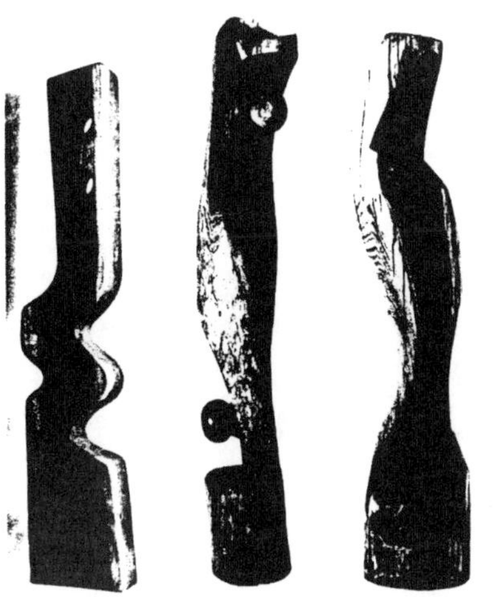

Fig. 1. (Left) ***'Wooden Form 258', walnut***, 71 × 14.5 × 6 cm, 1979; (center) ***'Twisted Figure', black cherry wood***, height 130 cm, dia. at base 20 cm, 1972; (right) ***'Woman', osage orange wood***, height 61 cm, dia. at base 12 cm, 1979.

Figure 3 (top) shows a sculpture consisting of two independent forms, and, for contrast, the one on the left was made of oak and the one on the right of birch. I intended the two forms to be complementary in the sense that both are based on the twisted shape of an *S*.

The pieces shown in Fig. 1 (center and right) were begun as nonfigurative pieces, however, as I carved them, they took on characteristics of human forms. The one at the center, entitled 'Twisted Figure' is 130 cm in height. A drawing based on a tracing of a photograph of one of the largest pieces I have carved is shown in Fig. 4. It was carved from a block of Guyanese saman wood taken from a log that weighed nearly two tons. The log was a gift sent to me from (formerly British) Guyana by a friend. I have provided the drawing instead of a photograph of the piece, as the beautiful grain of the wood draws one's attention from the special aspects that I shall mention. The piece consists of two abutting forms of clearly contrasting type. Only the column on the right has (on one side) the twist characteristic of my recent pieces.

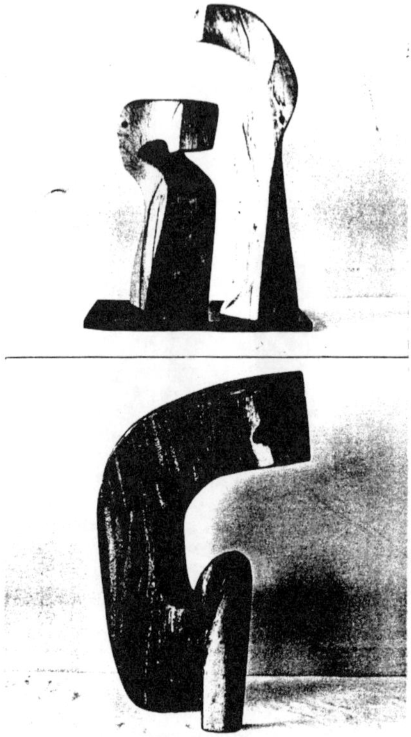

Fig. 3. (Top) *'Two Shapes', form on left of oak, form on right of birch*, 44 × 32 × 21 cm, 1978; (bottom) *'Seated Woman', Guyanese saman wood*, 50 × 30 × 20 cm, 1978.

The piece shown in Fig. 3 (bottom) was made from a block cut from the same log of saman wood as the block for the piece for which Fig. 4 has been provided. I have called the piece 'Seated Woman', because I sometimes imagine this twisted form resembles a woman seated on the ground with her knees drawn upward. The piece cannot be regarded as 2-dimensional from any viewing point. The rich qualities of the grain of saman wood are clearly visible in the photograph. The transition of the dark grain of the heartwood core to the lighter sapwood core is far more gradual for saman than for other kinds of tropical wood.

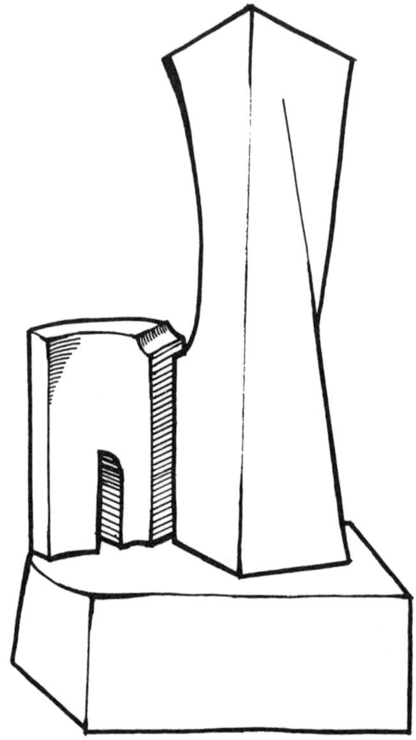

Fig. 4. Drawing based on a tracing of a photograph of a piece entitled 'H', Guyanese saman wood, height 150 cm, 1979.

5.

Sometimes, when looking at a piece I carved several years ago, I feel it was carved by another sculptor whose objectives were quite different from those I have now. Still, after a while, I recall what I had in mind when I carved it, and I realize that I am one of those sculptors who do not choose to make variation after variation of a single idea, but one who is interested in a wide variety of distinctive ideas that can challenge a wood-carver.

Reference

1. L. Rothschild, A Commentary on the Book *Art for the Millions, Leonardo* **10**, 141 (1977).

PART II

THE COST DISEASE DIAGNOSED

[4]

ON THE PERFORMING ARTS: THE ANATOMY OF THEIR ECONOMIC PROBLEMS*

By W. J. BAUMOL *and* W. G. BOWEN
Princeton University

I. *The Setting*

Romanticism long ago fixed in our minds the idea that there is something inevitable about the association between artistic achievement and poverty. The starving artist has become a stereotype among whose overtones is the notion that squalor and misery are noble and inspiring. It is one of the happier attributes of our time that we have generally been disabused of this type of absurdity. We readily recognize that poverty is demeaning rather than inspiring—that instead of stimulating the artist it deprives him of the energy, time, or even the equipment with which to create or perform.

While we have come to accept the idea that artists are often impecunious, even a cursory encounter with the facts of the matter usually proves surprising. One may or may not see something shocking in the fact that the median total income in 1959 of males classified by the census as actors was $5,640; that for musicians and music teachers the comparable figure was $4,757; and that for dancers and dancing teachers, $3,483.[1] But one must recognize that these figures include income from all sources, some of them (e.g., truck driving, lobster fishing, waiting on tables) rather unrelated to the performer's art.[2]

A detailed and specific investigation of economic conditions in the performing arts was conducted by Senate and House Committees in 1961 and 1962, and the volumes of *Hearings* which resulted are very

* This paper is based on a study being prepared by the authors for the Twentieth Century Fund, through the administrative channel of Mathematica. The study is still in progress, and this paper is nothing more than a brief introduction and a statement of certain theoretical ideas. The Fund has facilitated our work, not only by making generous financial provision for the extensive job of data collection and analysis which has been necessary, but also by helping to secure the cooperation of organizations and individuals and by allowing us full freedom to proceed as we wish. In the volume which will emerge from this study, we shall acknowledge our debt to the many people whose patient assistance has been essential to our work.

[1] U.S. Bureau of the Census, U.S. Census of Population: 1960, Subject Reports, *Occupational Characteristics*, Final Report PC(2)—7A, Table 25.

[2] As the Department of Labor's career guidance publication stresses: "Many performers . . . supplement their incomes by teaching, and thousands of others have to work much of the time in other occupations." (U.S. Dept. of Labor, Bureau of Labor Statistics, "Employment Outlook in the Performing Arts," Bulletin No. 1300-65, 1961, p. 214.) The BLS goes on to warn: ". . . the difficulty of earning a living as a performer is one of the facts young people should bear in mind in considering an artistic career" (*loc. cit.*).

revealing.[3] At that time the minimum weekly salary for Off-Broadway actors was $45 per week (it is currently $60); and what makes this figure significant is that most Off-Broadway actors are at the minimum. In such circumstances it is not difficult to see why Joseph Papp, producer of the New York Shakespeare Festival, was able to report that "banks and landlords consider him [the actor] a credit risk without visible means of support."[4]

Mrs. Helen Thompson, of the American Symphony Orchestra League, presented figures indicating that in 1961-62 the average salary paid to musicians in the twenty-six major orchestras in this country was $4,512; if the four highest-paying orchestras are excluded, the average for the remaining twenty-two major orchestras (again as of 1961-62) falls to $3,500.[5]

Dancers are in even worse financial circumstances, as illustrated by the case of a leading modern dance company whose members normally receive $25 after a trip which frequently includes four days of travel, a day of rehearsals, and a public performance.

In the main, performing artists are employed by organizations—by orchestras, opera and dance companies, producers and impresarios, resident theater companies—and the underlying economic pressures which manifest themselves in low performer salaries are transmitted through these organizations. Inadequate financial flows to these groups can threaten not only the welfare of individual performers but also the very existence of the institutions serving the entrepreneurial and managerial functions in the field of the performing arts. And, notwithstanding the publicity that has been given to the alleged "cultural boom" in America, we continue to hear frequently of theatrical groups which collapse, of opera houses whose seasons are in danger, and performing arts organizations of all kinds for whom financial emergency seems to have become a way of life. It is this situation and the threat that it poses for the cultural prospects of our society which constitutes the setting for the study we have undertaken.

The first objective of our study is to explain the strained economic circumstances which beset performing companies, to determine whether they are attributable mainly to fortuitous historical circumstances, to mismanagement or poor institutional arrangements, or whether there is something fundamental in the economic order which accounts

[3] U. S. House of Representatives, *Hearings Before the Select Subcommittee on Education of the Committee on Education and Labor,* "Economic Conditions in the Performing Arts," 87th Cong., 1st and 2nd Sess., 1962 (cited hereafter as "House Hearings"). U. S. Senate, *Hearings Before a Special Sub-Committee of the Committee on Labor and Public Welfare,* "Government and the Arts," 87th Cong., 2nd Sess., 1962.

[4] House *Hearings,* p. 111.

[5] House *Hearings,* p. 47.

for these difficulties. On the basis of our analysis we hope to produce some conditional forecasts of the financial future of the performing arts, the prospective costs, the operating revenues likely to be associated with various levels of activity, and the proportion of the resultant financial gaps which one can expect to be met from current sources of contributed income.

This session is intended to deal with theoretical matters and, while much of our work has been empirical, we welcome this opportunity to try to describe the basic economic relationships which seem to us to underlie the financial problems of the performing arts.

II. *Basic Economic Characteristics of Nonprofit Organizations*

Before we turn to the special economic properties of the performing arts, it is useful to devote some discussion to the economics of nonprofit-making organizations in general, for only in this way can the difficulties which beset the performing arts be seen in perspective.

Nonprofit organizations as a group share at least two characteristics: (1) they earn no pecuniary return on invested capital and (2) they claim to fulfill some social purpose. These two features are not wholly independent. Any group which sought to fulfill no social purpose and earned no financial return would presumably disappear from the landscape. Moreover, its goals themselves often help explain why no money is earned by such an organization. While an automobile producer may take pride in the quality of his cars, he is much less likely to regard product quality per se as an ultimate objective of the enterprise than is the head of a nonprofit organization. Nor is the auto producer likely to be nearly as concerned about the social composition of his clientele.

The significant point is that the objectives of the typical nonprofit organization are by their very nature designed to keep it constantly on the brink of financial catastrophe, for to such a group the quality of the services which it provides becomes an end in itself. Better research, more adequate hospital facilities, more generous rehearsal time, better training for those engaged in these activities—all these are not merely incidental desiderata. They are fundamental goals in themselves, and with objectives such as these, the likelihood of surplus funds is slim indeed. These goals constitute bottomless receptacles into which limitless funds can be poured. As soon as more money becomes available to a nonprofit organization, corresponding new uses can easily be found, and still other uses for which no financing has been provided will inevitably arise to take their place. Any lively nonprofit organization always has a group of projects which it cannot afford to undertake and for whose realization it looks hopefully to the future. Once this fundamental fact is grasped, it is hardly surprising that such groups feel themselves constantly strapped. It becomes clear that they are simply built that way.[6]

Nor is it just through its quality aspirations that the social goals of the nonprofit enterprise contribute to its financial difficulties. The concern of the typical nonprofit organization for the size and composition of its clientele often causes operating revenue to be lower than would be the case if services were priced to satisfy a simple profit-maximization goal. Since such a group normally considers itself to be a supplier of virtue, it is natural that it should seek to distribute its bounty as widely and as equitably as possible. The group is usually determined to prevent income and wealth alone from deciding who is to have priority in the consumption of its services. It wishes to offer its products to the needy and the deserving—to students, to the impecunious, to those initially not interested in consuming them, and to a variety of others to whom high prices would serve as an effective deterrent to consumption. In short, a low price for the product of a nonprofit group is normally an inevitable consequence of its objectives, and indeed sometimes becomes an article of faith. The ancient doctrine of "just price" is imbedded in the operations of these groups and carries with it all the difficulties which inevitably accompany an attempt to put it into practice.

The desire to provide a product of as high a quality as possible and to distribute the product in a manner other than that which maximizes revenue combine to produce a situation which is unusual in yet another respect. For such an enterprise a substantial increase in the demand for its product may well worsen the organization's financial health! Marginal costs may well exceed marginal revenues over the relevant interval. An increased number of student applications, an increased number of hospital patients, an increased number of orchestral performances may well increase the size of the contributions required for solvency. More generally, it follows that, contrary to widespread impressions, the much publicized cultural and educational "booms," whatever their composition, may in many cases prove a very mixed financial blessing.

Yet even in such circumstances the organizations cannot simply refuse to expand their activities in response to an increase in demand. By such a refusal the organization would renege on its fundamental

[6] The fact that any nonprofit organization can always find uses for a temporary excess of funds—and indeed may be embarrassed to report to its contributors that it has some money left at the end of the year—makes it very difficult to determine its cost functions. If an auto producer finds that a sudden increase in demand has swollen his receipts, he is only too happy to report higher profits; a nonprofit enterprise, however, may well use the extra revenue in a way which, in effect, deliberately raises it costs.

objectives, and, incidentally, it might even produce a loss in private and community support.

III. *The Performing Arts in Particular*

It is apparent that all of the standard problems of nonprofit organizations which have just been discussed beset the performing arts. It is not surprising, therefore, that the survival of the great majority of its organizations requires a constant flow of contributions. We can then easily understand why the arts find themselves in their present unhappy financial circumstances. But, up to this point, our discussion has offered no portents for the future. Here we don the inherited mantle of the dismal scientist and argue that one can read the prospects of the arts tomorrow in the economic structure which characterizes them today. The evidence will suggest that the prospects offer no grounds for complacency—that there are fundamental reasons to expect the financial strains which beset the performing arts organizations to increase, chronically, with the passage of time.

To understand the prospective developments on the cost side, it is necessary to digress briefly and consider in general terms the implications of differential rates of growth in productivity within the economy for the relative costs of its various outputs.[7] Let us think of an economy divided into two sectors: one in which productivity is rising and another where productivity is stable. As an illustration, let us suppose that where technological improvements are possible they lead to an increase in output per man-hour of 4 percent per annum, but that output per man-hour remains absolutely constant in the stable productivity sector. If these sectors are assigned equal weights in the construction of an economy-wide productivity index, the aggregate rate of increase in output per man-hour will be 2 percent per annum. For the moment let us assume that there is only one grade of labor, that labor is free to move back and forth between sectors, and that the real wage rate rises *pari passu* with the aggregate rate of change of productivity, at 2 percent per annum. Finally, let us suppose that the money supply and the level of aggregate demand are controlled in such a way that the price level is kept stable. Assuming that there are no changes in the shares of capital and labor, this means that money wages will also increase at the rate of 2 percent a year.

The implications of this simple model for costs in the two sectors are straightforward. In the rising productivity sector, output per man-

[7] There is, of course, nothing new in the following observations on the effects of differential rates of productivity change on costs and prices. See, e.g., Tibor and Ann Scitovsky, "What Price Economic Progress?" *Yale Rev.*, Autumn, 1959. Only its application to the state of the arts is novel.

hour increases more rapidly than the money wage rate and labor costs per unit must therefore decline. However, in the sector where productivity is stable, there is no offsetting improvement in output per man-hour, and so every increase in money wages is translated automatically into an equivalent increase in unit labor costs—2 percent per annum in our example. It should be noted that the extent of the increase in costs in the stable productivity sector varies directly with the economy-wide rate of increase in output per man-hour. The faster the general pace of technological advance, the greater will be the increase in the overall wage level and the greater the upward pressure on costs in those industries which do not enjoy increased productivity. Faster technological progress is no blessing for the laggards, at least as far as their costs are concerned.

It is apparent that the live performing arts belong to the stable productivity sector of our economy. The legitimate theater, the symphony orchestra, the chamber group, the opera, the dance—all can serve as textbook illustrations of activities offering little opportunity for major technological change. The output per man-hour of the violinist playing a Schubert quartet in a standard concert hall is relatively fixed, and it is fairly difficult to reduce the number of actors necessary for a performance of *Henry IV*, Part II.

Moreover, from the standpoint of long-term developments, the essence of the matter is not absolute or relative levels of productivity at a given date but the rates of change in productivity over time. This means that even if the arts could somehow manage to effect technological economies, they would not solve their long-term cost problem if such savings were once-and-for-all in nature. In order to join the ranks of the rising productivity industries, the arts would somehow have to learn not only to increase output per man-hour but to continue to do so into the indefinite future. Otherwise, they must at some juncture fall behind the technologically progressive industries and experience increases in costs which stem not from their own decisions but from the inexorable march of technological change in other parts of the economy.

True, some inefficiencies of operation are to be found in the field, and their elimination can help matters somewhat. Moreover, performing arts organizations can reduce the rate of increase in their unit costs by permitting some deterioration in the quality of their product—by fewer rehearsals, the use of more poorly trained performers, shoddy costumes and scenery. But such a course is never popular with organizations dedicated to quality, and, furthermore, it may lead to loss of audience and community support. Nevertheless, it is not an uncommon "temporary" expedient, imposed by the realization that the cutting of corners may be the only alternative to abandonment of the enterprise.

There is one other important avenue for cost saving open to the performing arts which has so far not been considered. We refer to wages paid performers. In the simple model sketched above, we postulated a situation in which a single, market-clearing wage was paid to all persons regardless of the industry in which they were employed. In actual fact, the live performing arts constitute a rather special labor market—a market in which the need for great native ability and extensive training limits the supply, but in which the psychic returns to those who meet these tests often offers a very substantial inducement to remain in the field. For these reasons, the performing arts are relatively insensitive to general wage trends, especially in the short run. It is largely for this reason that performing arts organizations in financial difficulty have often managed to shift part of their financial burden back to the performers—and to the managements, who also are generally very poorly paid by commercial standards. The level of the incomes in this general field must be considered remarkably low by any standards, and particularly so in light of the heavy investment that has often been made by the artists in their education, training, and equipment. And it is surely explained at least in part by the willingness of those who work in these fields to sacrifice money income for the less material pleasures of their participation in the arts.

However, there are limits to the financial sacrifices society can extract from the performers in exchange for psychic returns. One may reasonably expect that rising incomes in other sectors will ultimately produce untoward effects on the supply of talent. At what point this will occur depends partly on the income elasticity of the demand for psychic income. As the general level of real income rises, it may well be possible to persuade performers to accept a lower relative position in the income hierarchy. However, there are symptoms which suggest that, in some specialized areas, effects involving both quantity and quality are already being felt, though, overall, excess supply continues to be one of the market's most notable characteristics.

In sum, the cost structure of the performing arts organizations promises them no easier future. One might anticipate, therefore, that this structural problem would produce discernible effects on pricing policy. Certainly, in most of the industries in which productivity is stable, we would expect the price of the product or service to rise relative to the general price level. And there is a widespread impression that the arts have indeed behaved in accord with this anticipation—that ticket prices have been soaring. Yet our preliminary evidence suggests strongly that this view is incorrect and is largely a product of money illusion. Indeed, our preliminary data indicate that the rate of increase of ticket prices has barely managed to keep up with the price level and has lagged substantially behind increases in costs.

One might undertake to account for the surprisingly modest rate of increase in ticket prices in terms of a revenue maximization model—on the hypothesis that arts organizations believe the demand for their product to be highly elastic. We suspect, however, that a more valid explanation is the role of a doctrine of just price in the objectives of these organizations.

The tendency for increases in prices to lag behind increases in costs means simply that arts organizations have had to raise larger and larger sums from their contributors—and our analysis leads us to expect this trend to continue. Thus our analysis has offered us not only an explanation for the current state of affairs; it has also provided us with a basis for speculation about the future. What it has shown will not, we are afraid, be reassuring to those to whom ready availability of the arts constitutes an important objective of society. If our model is valid, and if, as may be suspected, there are limits to the amounts that can be obtained from private contributors, increased support from other sources will have to be found if the performing arts are to continue their present role in the cultural life of this country and especially if it is intended that they will expand their role and flourish.

[5]

MACROECONOMICS OF UNBALANCED GROWTH: THE ANATOMY OF URBAN CRISIS*

By William J. Baumol

There are some economic forces so powerful that they constantly break through all barriers erected for their suppression. Such, for example, are the forces of supply and demand which have resisted alike medieval efforts to abolish usury and contemporary attempts to control prices. In this paper I discuss what I believe to be another such mechanism which has colored the past and seems likely to stamp its character on the future. It helps us to understand the prospective roles of a wide variety of economic services: municipal government, education, the performing arts, restaurants, and leisure time activity. I will argue that inherent in the technological structure of each of these activities are forces working almost unavoidably for progressive and cumulative increases in the real costs incurred in supplying them. As a consequence, efforts to offset these cost increases, while they may succeed temporarily, in the long run are merely palliatives which can have no significant effect on the underlying trends.

The justification of a macroeconomic model should reside primarily in its ability to provide insights into the workings of observed phenomena. Its aggregation of diverse variables usually deny it the elegance and the rigor that are provided by microeconomic analysis at its best. Yet macro models have succeeded in explaining the structure of practical problems and in offering guidance for policy to a degree that has so far eluded the more painstaking modes of economic analysis. This article hopes to follow in the tradition—the structure of its basic model is rudimentary. Yet it can perhaps shed some light on a variety of economic problems of our generation.

1. *Premises*

Our model will proceed on several assumptions, only one of which is really essential. This basic premise asserts that economic activities can, not entirely arbitrarily, be grouped into two types: technologically progressive activities in which innovations, capital accumulation, and economies of large scale all make for a cumulative rise in output per

* The author is professor of economics, Princeton University. He wishes to thank the Ford Foundation and the National Science Foundation whose grants greatly facilitated completion of this paper. The basic hypothesis was originally developed jointly with William G. Bowen in the study of the performing arts conducted for the Twentieth Century Fund. In this paper there is no attempt to document the illustrative empirical observations though in every case the data have been examined and appear to support the assertions.

man hour and activities which, by their very nature, permit only sporadic increases in productivity.

Of course, one would expect that productivity would not grow at a uniform rate throughout the economy so it is hardly surprising that, given any arbitrarily chosen dividing line, one can fit all goods and services into one or the other of two such categories in whatever way the dividing line is drawn. I am, however, making a much stronger assertion: that the place of any particular activity in this classification is not primarily a fortuitous matter determined by the particulars of its history, but rather that it is a manifestation of the activity's technological structure, which determines quite definitely whether the productivity of its labor inputs will grow slowly or rapidly.

The basic source of differentiation resides in the role played by labor in the activity. In some cases labor is primarily an instrument—an incidental requisite for the attainment of the final product, while in other fields of endeavor, for all practical purposes the labor is itself the end product. Manufacturing encompasses the most obvious examples of the former type of activity. When someone purchases an air conditioner he neither knows nor cares how much labor went into it. He is not concerned one way or the other with an innovation that reduces the manpower requirements for the production of his purchase by 10 per cent if the price and the quality of the product are unaffected. Thus it has been possible, as it were, behind the scenes, to effect successive and cumulative decreases in the labor input coefficient for most manufactured goods, often along with some degree of improvement in the quality of the product.

On the other hand there are a number of services in which the labor is an end in itself, in which quality is judged directly in terms of amount of labor. Teaching is a clear-cut example, where class size (number of teaching hours expended per student) is often taken as a critical index of quality. Here, despite the invention of teaching machines and the use of closed circuit television and a variety of other innovations, there still seem to be fairly firm limits to class size. We are deeply concerned when elementary school classes grow to 50 pupils and are disquieted by the idea of college lectures attended by 2000 underclassmen. Without a complete revolution in our approach to teaching there is no prospect that we can ever go beyond these levels (or even up to them) with any degree of equanimity. An even more extreme example is one I have offered in another context: live performance. A half hour horn quintet calls for the expenditure of $2\frac{1}{2}$ man hours in its performance, and any attempt to increase productivity here is likely to be viewed with concern by critics and audience alike.

The difference between the two types of activity in the flexibility of their productivity levels should not be exaggerated. It is a matter of degree rather than an absolute dichotomy. The jet airplane has increased the productivity per man hour of a faculty member who is going from New York to California to give a lecture. Certainly the mass media have created what may be considered a new set of products that are close substitutes for live performance and by which productivity was increased spectacularly. In addition, there are, as the reader will recognize, all sorts of intermediate activities which fall between the two more extreme varieties. Yet, the distinction between the relatively constant productivity industries and those in which productivity can and does rise is a very real one, and one which, we shall see, is of considerable practical importance.

In addition to the separability of activities into our two basic categories I shall utilize three other assumptions, two of them primarily for ease of exposition. The reader will recognize, as we proceed, that neither is essential to the argument. The first of the incidental premises consists simply in the assertion that all outlays other than labor costs can be ignored. This assertion is patently unrealistic but it simplifies greatly our mathematical model. A second, far more important, and more realistic assumption is that wages in the two sectors of the economy go up and down together. In the long run there is some degree of mobility in all labor markets and consequently, while wages in one activity can lag behind those in another, unless the former is in process of disappearing altogether we cannot expect the disparity to continue indefinitely. For simplicity I will in the next section take hourly wages to be precisely the same in both sectors, but the model is easily complicated to allow for some diversity in wage levels and their movements.

A final inessential assumption which is, however, not altogether unrealistic, asserts that money wages will rise as rapidly as output per man hour in the sector where productivity is increasing. Since organized labor is not slow to learn of increases in its productivity it is likely to adjust its wage demands accordingly. This assumption affects only the magnitude of the absolute price level in our model, and does not influence the relative costs and prices that are the critical elements in the analysis.

2. *A Model of Unbalanced Expansion*

Assume that the economy is divided into two sectors, sector one, in which the productivity of labor is constant, while in sector two output per man hour grows cumulatively at a constant compounded rate, r. Thus we have for the respective values of outputs Y_{1t} and Y_{2t} in the two sectors at time t:

$$Y_{1t} = aL_{1t} \tag{1}$$

$$Y_{2t} = bL_{2t}e^{rt} \tag{2}$$

where L_{1t} and L_{2t} are the quantities of labor employed in the two sectors and a and b are constants.

We suppose wages are equal in the two sectors and are fixed at W_t dollars per unit of labor, where W_t itself grows in accord with the productivity of sector 2, our "progressive" sector, so that

$$W_t = We^{rt}. \qquad (W = \text{some constant}) \tag{3}$$

We may now derive several properties of such a system. First and most fundamental is *Proposition 1:* The cost per unit of output of sector 1, C_1, will rise without limit while C_2, the unit cost of sector 2, will remain constant.

proof:

$$C_1 = W_t L_{1t}/Y_{1t} = We^{rt}L_{1t}/aL_{1t} = We^{rt}/a$$

$$C_2 = W_t L_{2t}/Y_{2t} = We^{rt}L_{2t}/bL_{2t}e^{rt} = W/b.$$

Note that the *relative* costs will behave in this manner whether or not wages increase in accord with (3) for we have

$$C_1/C_2 = (L_{1t}/Y_{1t})/(L_{2t}/Y_{2t}) = be^{rt}/a.$$

In practice, we would expect in these circumstances that market demand for the output of sector 1 would decline. Suppose, for example, the elasticity of demand for the two outputs were unity in terms of prices which were proportionate to costs. Then relative outlays on the two commodities would remain constant, i.e., we would have

$$\frac{C_1 Y_1}{C_2 Y_2} = \frac{We^{rt}L_{1t}}{We^{rt}L_{2t}} = \frac{L_{1t}}{L_{2t}} = A(\text{constant}).$$

Hence the output ratio of the two sectors would be given by

$$Y_1/Y_2 = aL_{1t}/bL_{2t}e^{rt} = aA/be^{rt}$$

which declines toward zero with the passage of time. Thus we have *Proposition 2:* In the model of unbalanced productivity there is a tendency for the outputs of the "nonprogressive" sector whose demands are not highly inelastic to decline and perhaps, ultimately, to vanish.

We may inquire, however, what would happen if despite the change in their relative costs and prices the magnitude of the relative outputs of the two sectors were maintained, perhaps with the aid of government subsidy, or if demand for the product in question were sufficiently price inelastic or income elastic. Then we would have

$$(b/a)\,Y_1/Y_2 = L_1/L_2e^{rt} = K.$$

Let $L = L_1 + L_2$ be the total labor supply. It follows that

$$L_1 = (L - L_1)Ke^{rt} \quad \text{or} \quad L_1 = LKe^{rt}/(1 + Ke^{rt}) \tag{4}$$

and

(5) $$L_2 = L - L_1 = L/(1 + Ke^{rt}).$$

Hence, as t approaches infinity, L_1 will approach L and L_2 will approach zero. Thus we have *Proposition 3:* In the unbalanced productivity model, if the ratio of the outputs of the two sectors is held constant, more and more of the total labor force must be transferred to the nonprogressive sector and the amount of labor in the other sector will tend to approach zero.

Finally, we may note what happens to the overall rate of growth of output in the economy if the output ratio for the two sectors is not permitted to change. We may take as an index of output a weighted average of the outputs of the two sectors:

$$I = B_1Y_1 + B_2Y_2 = B_1aL_1 + B_2bL_2e^{rt}$$

so that by (4) and (5)

$$I = L(KB_1a + B_2b)e^{rt}/(1 + Ke^{rt}) = Re^{rt}/(1 + Ke^{rt})$$

where

$$R = L(KB_1a + B_2b).$$

Therefore

$$\begin{aligned} dI/dt &= R[re^{rt}(1 + Ke^{rt}) - Kre^{2rt}]/(1 + Ke^{rt})^2 \\ &= rRe^{rt}/(1 + Ke^{rt})^2. \end{aligned}$$

As a result, the percentage rate of growth of output will be

$$(dI/dt)/I = r/(1 + Ke^{rt})$$

which declines asymptotically toward zero as t increases. We have, then, arrived at *Proposition 4:* An attempt to achieve balanced growth in a world of unbalanced productivity must lead to a declining rate of growth relative to the rate of growth of the labor force. In particular, if productivity in one sector and the total labor force remain constant the growth rate of the economy will asymptotically approach zero.

3. *Discussion of the Propositions*

The logic of the entire analysis can be restated rather simply in intuitive terms. If productivity per man hour rises cumulatively in one sector relative to its rate of growth elsewhere in the economy, while wages rise commensurately in all areas, then relative costs in the nonprogressive sectors must inevitably rise, ***and these costs will rise cumulatively and without limit.*** For while in the progressive sector productivity increases will serve as an offset to rising wages, this offset must be smaller in the nonprogressive sectors. For example (ignoring nonwage costs) if wages and productivity in the progressive sector both go up 2 per cent per year, costs there will not rise at all. On the other hand, if in the nonprogressive sector productivity is constant, every rise in wages must yield a corresponding addition to costs—a two per cent cumulative rise in wages means that, year in year out, costs must be two per cent above those of the preceding year. Thus, the very progress of the technologically progressive sectors inevitably adds to the costs of the technologically unchanging sectors of the economy, unless somehow the labor markets in these areas can be sealed off and wages held absolutely constant, a most unlikely possiblity.

We see then that costs in many sectors of the economy will rise relentlessly, and will do so for reasons that are for all practical purposes beyond the control of those involved. The consequence is that the outputs of these sectors may in some cases tend to be driven from the market. If their relative outputs are maintained, an ever increasing proportion of the labor force must be channeled into these activities and the rate of growth of the economy must be slowed correspondingly.

4. *Some Applications*[1]

These observations can be used at once to explain a number of observed phenomena. For example, there is evidence that an ever increasing portion of the nation's labor force has been going into retailing and that a rising portion of the cost of commodities is accounted for by outlays on marketing. Now there have been several pronounced changes in the technology of marketing in recent decades: self service, the supermarket, and prewrapping have all increased the productivity per man hour of the retailing personnel. But ultimately, the activity involved is in the nature of a service and it does not allow for constant and cumulative increases in productivity through capital accumulation, innovation, or economies of large-scale operation. Hence it is neither mismanagement nor lack of ingenuity that accounts for the relatively constant productivity of this sector. Since some sort of marketing effort is an inescapable element in economic activity, demand for this service is quite income elastic. Our model tells us what to expect in this case—cumulatively increasing costs relative to those of other economic activities, and the absorption of an ever growing proportion of society's resources by this sector—precisely what seems to have been observed.

Higher education is another activity the demand for whose product seems to be relatively income elastic and price inelastic. Higher tuition charges undoubtedly impose serious hardships on lower-income stu-

[1] Some of the ideas in this section arose out of discussions with Eugene Beem of Sperry and Hutchinson.

dents. But, because a college degree seems increasingly to be a necessary condition for employment in a variety of attractive occupations, most families have apparently been prepared to pay the ever larger fees instituted in recent years. As a result higher education has been absorbing a constantly increasing proportion of per capita income. And the relatively constant productivity of college teaching leads our model to predict that rising educational costs are no temporary phenomenon—that they are not a resultant of wartime inflation which will vanish once faculty salaries are restored to their prewar levels. Rather, it suggests that, as productivity in the remainder of the economy continues to increase, costs of running the educational organizations will mount correspondingly, so that whatever the magnitude of the funds they need today, we can be reasonably certain that they will require more tomorrow, and even more on the day after that.

But not all services in the relatively constant productivity sector of the economy face inelastic demands. Many of them are more readily dispensable than retailing and education as far as individual consumers are concerned. As their costs increase, their utilization tends therefore to decrease and they retreat into the category of luxury goods with very limited markets or disappear almost completely. Fine pottery and glassware produced by the careful labor of skilled craftsmen sell at astronomical prices, though I am told the firms that produce them earn relatively little profit from these product lines which they turn out primarily for prestige and publicity, obtaining the bulk of their earnings from their mass production activities. Fine restaurants and theaters are forced to keep raising their prices, and at least in the case of the latter we know that volume is dwindling while it becomes ever more difficult for suppliers (the producers) to make ends meet.

An extreme example of an activity that has virtually disappeared is the construction (and, indeed, the utilization) of the large and stately houses whose operation even more than their construction allows for little in the way of enhanced productivity, and whose rising costs of operation have apparently decreased their salability even to the wealthy.

These observations suggest something about the likely shape of our economy in the future. Our model tells us that manufactures are likely to continue to decline in relative cost and, unless the income elasticity of demand for manufactured goods is very large, they may absorb an ever smaller proportion of the labor force, which, if it transpires, may make it more difficult for our economy to maintain its overall rate of output growth.

The analysis also suggests that real cost in the "nonprogressive" sectors of the economy may be expected to go on increasing. Some of the services involved—those whose demands are inelastic—may continue viable on the free market. Some, like the theater, may be forced to leave this market and may have to depend on voluntary public support for their survival. Our hospitals, our institutions of private education and a variety of other nonprofit organizations have already long survived on this basis, and can continue to do so if the magnitude of contributions keeps up with costs. Some activities will either disappear or retreat to a small scale of operation catering primarily to a luxury trade. This fate may be in store for restaurants offering true *haute cuisine* and it is already the case for fine hand-worked furniture and for clothes made to measure. Some activities, perhaps many of the preceding among them, will fall increasingly into the hands of the amateurs who already play a considerable role in theatrical and orchestral performances, in gastronomy, in crafts such as woodworking and pottery. Finally, there is a considerable segment of nonprogressive activity that is dependent on tax support. Some of the problems that go with this position will be considered in the remainder of this paper.

In all the observations of this section there is one implicit underlying danger that should not escape the reader: the inherent threat to quality. Amateur activity has its virtues, as an educational device, as a good use for leisure time and so forth. But in a variety of fields it offers a highly imperfect substitute for the highly polished product that can be supplied by the professional. Unbalanced productivity growth, then, threatens to destroy many of the activities that do so much to enrich our existence, and to give others over into the hands of the amateurs. These are dangers which many of us may feel should not be ignored or taken lightly.

5. *On the Financial Problem of the Cities*

One of the major economic problems of our times is the crisis of the larger cities. Together with their suburban periphery the cities are attracting ever greater segments of our population. Yet at least the core of the metropolis is plagued by a variety of ills including spreading blight as entire neighborhoods deteriorate, increasing pollution of its atmosphere, worsening traffic, critical educational problems, and, above all, mounting fiscal pressures. The financial troubles are perhaps central to the entire issue because without adequate funds one cannot hope to mount an effective attack on the other difficulties. More than one reform mayor has taken office determined to undertake a radical program to deal with the city's difficulties and found himself baffled and stymied by the monstrous deficit which he discovered to be hanging over him, a deficit whose source appeared to have no reasonable explanation. There seems in these cases to be no way to account for the growth in the city's financial needs—for the fact that a municipal budget far above that which was roughly adequate a decade earlier threatens to disrupt seriously the city's most vital services today. Where the political process is involved it is easy to blame growing costs on inefficiency and corruption but when they take office, reform administrations seem consistently puzzled by their inability to wring out the funds they require through the elimination of these abuses.

A critical element in the explanation becomes clear when we recognize how large a proportion of the services provided by the city are activities falling in the relatively nonprogressive sector of the economy. The bulk of our municipal expenditures is devoted to education which, as we have already seen, offers very limited scope for cumulative increases in productivity. The same is true of police, of hospitals, of social services, and of a variety of inspection services. Despite the use of the computer in medicine and in traffic planning, despite the use of closed circuit television and a variety of other devices, there is no substitute for the personal attention of a physician or the presence of a police patrol in a crime-ridden neighborhood. The bulk of municipal services is, in fact, of this general stamp and our model tells us clearly what can be expected as a result. Since there is no reason to anticipate a cessation of capital accumulation or innovation in the progressive sectors of the economy, the upward trend in the real costs of municipal services cannot be expected to halt; inexorably and cumulatively, whether or not there is inflation, administrative mismanagement or malfeasance, municipal budgets will almost certainly continue to mount in the future, just as they have been doing in the past. This is a trend for which no man and no group should be blamed, for there is nothing that can be done to stop it.

6. *The Role of Static Externalities*

Though these may be troubles enough for the municipal administrator, there are other compelling forces that plague him simultaneously. Among them are the general class of externality problems which have so long been the welfare economist's stock in trade.

Since the appearance of Marshall's and Pigou's basic writing in the area a most significant development has been the growing impact of external costs on urban living. No longer are road crowding and smoke nuisance only quaint cases serving primarily as textbook illustrations. Rather, they have become pressing issues of public concern—matters discussed heatedly in the daily press and accorded serious attention by practical politicians. Newspapers devote headlines to an engineer's prediction that the human race is more likely to succumb to its own pollutants than through a nuclear holocaust, and report with glee the quip that Los Angeles is the city in which one is wakened by the sound of birds coughing.

Now there are undoubtedly many reasons for the explosion in external costs but there is a pertinent observation about the relationship between population size in a given area and the cost of externalities that seems not to be obvious. It is easy to assume that these costs will rise roughly in proportion with population but I shall argue now that a much more natural premise is that they will rise more rapidly—perhaps roughly as the square of the number of inhabitants. For example, consider the amount of dirt that falls into the house of a typical urban resident as a result of air pollution, and suppose that this is equal to kn where n is the number of residents in the area. Since the number of homes in the area, an, is also roughly proportionate to population size, total domestic soot-fall will be equal to soot per home times number of homes $= kn \cdot an = akn^2$. Similarly, if delays on a crowded road are roughly proportionate to n, the number of vehicles traversing it, the total number of man hours lost thereby will increase roughly as n^2, since the number of passengers also grows roughly as the number of cars. The logic of the argument is simple and perhaps rather general: if each inhabitant in an area imposes external costs on every other, and if the magnitude of the costs borne by each individual is roughly proportionate to population size (density) then since these costs are borne by each of the n persons involved, the total external costs will vary not in proportion with n but with n^2. Of course I do not maintain that such a relationship is universal or even that it is ever satisfied more than approximately. Rather I am suggesting that, typically, increases in population size may plausibly be expected to produce disproportionate increases in external costs—thus pressures on the municipality to do something about these costs may then grow correspondingly.

7. *Cumulative Decay and Dynamic Pareto Optimality*

Economic theory indicates yet another source of mounting urban problems. These are the processes of cumulative urban decay which once set in motion induce matters to go from bad to worse. Since I have discussed these elsewhere I can illustrate the central proposition rather briefly. Public transportation is an important example. In many urban areas with declining utilization, frequency of service has been sharply reduced and fares have been increased. But these price rises have only served to produce a further decline in traffic, leading in turn to yet another deterioration in schedules and another fare increase and so on, apparently *ad infinitum*. More important, perhaps, is the logic of the continued flight to the suburbs in which many persons who apparently would otherwise wish to remain in the city are driven out by growing urban deterioration—rising crime rates, a growing number of blighted neighborhoods, etc. Once again, the individuals' remedy intensifies the community's problems and each feeds upon the other. Those who leave the city are usually the very persons who care and can afford to care—the ones who maintain their houses, who do not commit crimes, and who are most capable of providing the taxes needed to arrest the process of urban decay. Their exodus therefore leads to further deterioration in urban conditions and so induces yet another wave of emigration, and so on.[2]

It is clear that these cumulative processes can greatly increase the financial pressures besetting a municipality and can do so in a variety of ways: they can increase directly municipal costs by adding to the real quantities of inputs required for the upkeep of buildings, to maintain levels of urban sanitation, to preserve the level of education attained by an average resident, etc.; they can reduce the tax base—the exodus of more affluent urban inhabitants cause a decline in the financial resources available to the city; and with the passage of time the magnitude of the resources necessary to arrest and reverse the cumulative processes itself is likely to grow so that the city may find it increasingly difficult to go beyond programs that slow the processes slightly.[3]

[2] As is to be expected, such dynamic processes may be monotonic or oscillatory, stable or unstable. As examples we might expect the public transportation scheduling problem to grow monotonically while automotive road crowding may be inherently oscillatory. More specifically, let f represent frequency of public bus departure and p be the number of bus passengers. We would expect the relevant relationships to be something such as

$$p_t = a + bf_t \quad \text{(demand for public transport) and}$$
$$f_{t+1} = w + vp_t \quad \text{(lagged public transport supply response)}$$

so that

$$f_{t+1} = w + av + vbf_t$$

in which the coefficient vb is presumably positive. On the other hand, if D represents average delay on some road and A is the volume of automotive traffic, the corresponding relationships would be

$$D_t = a' + b'A_t \quad \text{(delay grows with traffic volume) and}$$
$$A_{t+1} = w' - v'D_t \quad \text{(delays today lead to lower traffic tomorrow)}$$

so that we have a negative coefficient $-b'v'$ in the difference equation

$$A_{t+1} = w' - a'v' - b'v'A_t.$$

Since monotonic and oscillatory time paths correspond respectively to positive and negative variable coefficients in a first-order difference equation, our result follows. An intuitive explanation is fairly simple in each case: increased automotive traffic today causes delays and so may reduce traffic tomorrow. But a decline in number of passengers which causes a deterioration in service leads to still another fall in volume.

As stated, the time path in each case may be stable. But in the latter case, even though the declines will not be unbounded, the limit toward which they tend may be very low and totally unacceptable as a matter of public policy.

[3] I have argued that the cumulative processes involve what may be considered dynamic externalities. Each passenger who uses public transportation less frequently imposes the increased likelihood of poorer schedules not only on himself but on others as well. As a result these processes will yield results that do not maximize social welfare. For the private and social marginal rates of transformation between present and future will then differ from one another. The individual will tend to cut down on his use of public transportation by an amount greater

8. *Conclusion—The Financial Problems of the Large City*

The story is perhaps completed if we add to the preceding observations the fact that each city is in competition with others and with its own surrounding areas for industry and for people with the wherewithal to pay taxes. No city government acting alone can afford to raise its tax rates indefinitely. Even if they were politically feasible, mounting tax rates must eventually produce diminishing and perhaps even negative returns as they depress the tax base further.

We can now quickly pull the pieces of our story together. We have just seen that our municipalities are perhaps unavoidably subject to a variety of growing financial pressures: the limited sources of tax funds, the pressures imposed by several processes of cumulative decay, the costs of externalities which seem to have a built-in tendency to rise more rapidly than the population. These phenomena imply that the activities of the municipality will have to be expanded if standards of city life are to be maintained. But the funds available for the purpose are extremely limited. And over all this hangs the shadow cast by our model of unbalanced growth which has shown that the costs of even a constant level of activity on the part of a municipal government can be expected to grow constantly higher.

The picture that has been painted is bleak. It suggests strongly that self-help offers no way out for our cities. All of this would then appear to offer stronger theoretical support for the Heller-Pechman proposal that the federal government can provide the resources necessary to prevent the serious crisis that threatens our larger urban communities and whose effects on the quality of life in our society may become one of the nation's most serious economic problems.

References

1. W. J. Baumol and W. G. Bowen, *Performing Arts: The Economic Dilemma.* New York 1966.
2. Jean Fourastié, *The Causes of Wealth.* Glencoe, Ill., 1960.
3. Tibor and Anne Scitovsky, "What Price Economic Progress?" *Yale Review,* Autumn 1959, *49,* 95–110.

---

than that which is optimal because he himself does not bear all of the costs of his action. There is a marginal rate of transformation between the utility derived from public transportation today and that obtainable from transportation tomorrow. If relative prices do not equal that marginal rate of transformation a misallocation of resources is likely to result. The consequences may even be what might be called Pareto-nonoptimal. That is, everyone may be harmed. For example, when automobile traffic becomes sufficiently bad it may become clear that everyone will be better off if passenger cars are banned completely from the downtown area in order to make possible a faster, more efficient public transportation system.

[6]

Macroeconomics of Unbalanced Growth: Comment

By Michael Keren*

An unfortunate error of misinterpretation mars some of the conclusions of William Baumol's illuminating paper on the "Macroeconomics of Unbalanced Growth."

The paper develops a model of a two-sector economy: a "progressive" sector where labor-saving technical change takes place, and a nonprogressive sector where there is no technical change. His production functions are[1]

$$(1) \qquad Y_{1t} = aL_{1t}$$

$$(2) \qquad Y_{2t} = bL_{2t}e^{rt}$$

where Y_{jt} and L_{jt} stand, respectively, for output and labor input at time t, and the subscript $j=1, 2$ refers to the unprogressive and progressive sectors respectively. With labor the only input, (given perfect competition), the price ratios of the outputs always equals the labor cost ratio. Letting W_t represent the wage rate,

$$(3) \qquad \frac{P_{1t}}{P_{2t}} = \frac{W_tL_{1t}/Y_{1t}}{W_tL_{2t}/Y_{2t}} = \frac{L_{1t}}{L_{2t}}\cdot\frac{Y_{2t}}{Y_{1t}}$$

If we suppose that the elasticity of demand for the outputs were unitary, the ratio of outlays on both outputs would remain constant:

$$(4) \qquad \frac{P_{1t}Y_{1t}}{P_{2t}Y_{2t}} = \frac{W_tL_{1t}}{W_tL_{2t}} = \frac{L_{1t}}{L_{2t}} = A(\text{constant})$$

The output ratio will then be

$$(5) \qquad Y_{1t}/Y_{2t} = (aL_{1t})/(bL_{2t}e^{rt}) = (aA/be^{rt})$$

which declines toward zero as t grows.

This result is interpreted in *Proposition 2:* ". . . There is a tendency for the outputs of the 'nonprogressive' sector . . . to decline and perhaps, ultimately, to vanish" (Baumol, p. 418).

It is this *proposition* which is false. The output of the nonprogressive sector 1, per capita of the working population, is *constant*, rather than declining. The output ratio of (5) falls because the denominator is rising, not because the numerator is falling. This becomes obvious by reference to equation (4). Assume that the total input of labor remains constant: the number of workers employed in each sector would also stay constant, and a constant input of labor produces, by equation (1), a constant output in the "nonprogressive" sector.

Several of Baumol's conclusions depend on the false Proposition 2. Thus, if the provision of higher education belongs to sector 1, and if the wage level is geared to the rising productivity in sector 2, it is true that the cost of higher education will rise (see p. 421). It does not follow that the relative outlays on higher education should rise, unless relatively more or better education is being provided. The same is true for municipal services. Let R be municipal revenues and L_1 labor inputs into municipal services. Then the proportion of municipal deficits to municipal spending is

$$(6) \qquad \begin{aligned} \frac{W_tL_{1t} - R_t}{W_tL_{1t}} &= 1 - \frac{L_t}{L_{1t}}\cdot\frac{R_t}{W_tL_t} \\ &= 1 - \frac{A+1}{A}\cdot\frac{R_t}{W_tL_t} \end{aligned}$$

This proportion will rise only if the share of municipal revenues in total income (R/WL) falls over time. In other words, only if the income elasticity of municipal taxes is below unity will the financial problems of cities grow, provided the level of services remains unchanged. This could happen if the municipal tax base does not grow as fast as labor income.

REFERENCE

W. J. Baumol, "Macroeconomics of Unbalanced Growth," *Amer. Econ. Rev.*, June 1967, *57*, 415–26.

* Lecturer in economics, Hebrew University, Jerusalem.

[1] The equations, and their numbering, are not identical with those of Baumol.

[7]

Macroeconomics of Unbalanced Growth: Comment

W. J. Baumol, in a very interesting paper published in the June 1967 issue of this *Review*, sought to examine the consequences of what he called a powerful economic force operating in our economy: that in certain important service activities—municipal government, education, the arts, restaurants—the impossibility of significant technological improvement tends to increase their costs without limit.

A two-sector model was developed, in which the labor force was held constant, and productivity increased at a continuously compounded rate in one (the "progressive") sector and remained constant in the other (the "nonprogressive") sector. Under the assumptions that costs other than labor are zero, and that money wages in the nonprogressive sector rise with money wages in the progressive sector, the model was used to demonstrate first that costs in the nonprogressive sector rise without limit, and second that an attempt to maintain balanced growth would lead to a transfer of resources from the progressive to the nonprogressive sector, and a declining rate of economic growth. Two conclusions were drawn from the first result which do not necessarily follow.

Assuming that price equals cost, Baumol concluded first that rising costs create a tendency for the outputs of the nonprogressive sectors whose demands are not highly inelastic to vanish. But Baumol overlooked the fact that *real income,* as well as the prices of nonprogressive goods, is rising and therefore that price elasticity is not a sufficient condition for the demands for certain nonprogressive goods to vanish. Only those nonprogressive goods for which the absolute value of the elasticity of demand with respect to price is less than the absolute value of income elasticity, or those for which the income effect is negative, will tend to vanish.

The particular nonprogressive sectors which Baumol asserts are threatened with extinction because of rising costs (the performing arts, handcrafted goods, gourmet restaurants, and stately homes) would appear to be sectors for which income elasticity of demand is high—luxuries for which the market consists chiefly of the wealthy. If the outputs of these sectors have declined, absolutely or relative to population, it may be the result of a change in the relative *distribution* of income—proportionately fewer of the extremely wealthy who can afford luxury items—and/or it may be the result of a shift in demand, brought about by our changing value system with its emphasis on mass culture and conformity. In any case, the decline cannot be attributed to relative price changes without presenting supporting empirical evidence.

The Urban Crisis

Municipal services fall in the "nonprogressive" category, and therefore their costs tend to rise without limit. Baumol's second conclusion was that this tendency, intensified by externalities—tax base erosion and increasing per capita demands for municipal services as a city's population increases—is responsible for urban financial problems.

Here again though, Baumol overlooked the effects of real income increases. We contend that externalities are the basic force creating urban financial problems and that technological inertia in municipal services simply magnifies them. In fact, if we assume no externalities, no productivity changes in municipal services, and positive productivity changes in some other industries, then sufficient revenues to pay for the increasing costs of municipal services could easily be generated out of rising real income with no increase in urban tax rates.

This would be possible because as cities grew, the real per capita outputs of municipal services, measured in terms of levels of protection, would not have to rise. The per capita outputs of the progressive industries would increase because productivity is increasing. Thus in real terms, the ratio of municipal services output to total output would decline. In monetary terms, if Baumol's wage equality assumption holds, the ratio would remain constant. Given that output equals income, both real and money incomes would rise, and the percentage of total money income allocated to municipal services would remain constant. To the extent that municipal services are financed by income taxes (such as city payroll taxes) revenues would rise in proportion to income without rate changes. Where property is the major tax base, its value would rise (generating additional revenue) to the extent that property as a factor of production shared in the increasing money income. Sales tax revenues would also increase without rate changes. Thus, with no externalities, additional revenues to partially offset the increasing costs of urban services would be generated under present urban tax structures, and the remainder could be obtained through changes in the tax *structure* without alteration of tax *rates*.

This argument does not eliminate the political aspect of the problem discussed by Baumol. The costs per unit of urban services will, no doubt, continue to rise without any explanation apparent to the layman, whether or not externalities are present. Thus, the unprogressive technological nature of urban services is sufficient to cause embarrassment to urban politicians who have promised to reduce budgets. But without externalities, an urban fiscal arrangement dependent entirely upon a proportional income tax would automatically provide sufficient incremental revenues to maintain the quantity and quality of urban services.

In summary, we have argued that Baumol failed to consider increases in real income in his analysis of the rising relative costs in the service or nonprogressive industries and consequently may have been misled in concluding that declines in the outputs of certain nonprogressive sectors are due to relative price changes; and in attributing the major financial problems of cities to factors inherent in the technological structures of the municipal services industries.

L. K. Lynch*
E. L. Redman*

* The authors are, respectively, senior economist and sociologist at Spindletop Research, Inc. They are indebted to Professor W. J. Baumol for his comments and suggestions on an earlier draft.

Zeitschrift für Nationalökonomie 29 (1969), 291—304

Balance on Unbalanced Growth

By

David F. Bradford*, Princeton, New Jersey, USA

With 6 Figures

(Received January 22, 1969)

In a recent article William J. Baumol presented and analyzed a simple unbalanced growth model [1]. Baumol's model economy consists of two outputs produced by a single factor, labor. In the "lagging" sector 1 (the archetypal service sector and the urban public service sector in particular), Y_1 is produced with constant labor productivity. In the "progressive" sector 2 (the ideal manufacturing sector), as a result of continuing technological progress[1], labor produces Y_2 with productivity growing continually at constant rate r.

Contemplating this model world, Baumol draws some rather gloomy sounding conclusions. He recognizes, of course, that through time the economy's ability to produce the one commodity is continually increasing, without any diminution in its ability to produce the other. Of relevance for his discussion, however, are the negative conclusions which follow from an interest in the time path of the price of Y_1 in terms of Y_2 (continually up), the likely response of the demand for Y_1 (continually down), and from an interest in the implications of pursuing a policy of balanced expansion (i. e., holding Y_1 and Y_2 in constant proportion) for the allocation of resources (ultimately all concentrated in sector 1) and for the growth rate of a real output index (ultimately zero).

The simple model which Baumol advances provides considerable insight into the economic events with which he wishes to deal. Certainly the rising opportunity cost of labor to direct services, deriving from technological progress in other sectors, has had, and will continue to have, extremely important effects. These effects will include shrinking

---

* The author is assistant professor of economics at Princeton University. He wishes to thank the Brookings Institution and the Ford Foundation for financial support which facilitated the writing of this paper, and to acknowledge helpful discussions with colleagues William J. Baumol, Richard R. Cornwall and Dennis E. Smallwood.

[1] Capital deepening and returns to scale are also cited by Baumol as sources of differential labor productivity growth between progressive and lagging sectors of the economy, although the model actually analyzed does not explicitly incorporate these features.

demands for the services in question, when income elasticities are relatively low, and lagging provision of resources to the public sector, where the "backward" good is supplied by the government. The process of adjustment to such unbalanced technical change is certain to be costly to some individuals and institutions (although the predictability of the backward sectors asserted by Baumol will tend to reduce the costs in the form of mistaken investment and career decisions), and Baumol's analysis illuminates the plight of a variety of institutions, from theaters to city governments. However, although there is good cause to view with alarm the current situation of the theater and urban governments in the United States, and of other institutions struggling against "Baumol's disease", the conclusions which Baumol draws from his model seem to me to leave a too pessimistic impression of unbalanced growth. In particular, I contend that in his article he attaches too great an importance to the rate of exchange between the two commodities, to a rather unlikely expansion path, and to a growth rate of doubtful welfare significance.

Whether or not this is the case, I propose in this paper, utilizing the graphical tools of elementary economics, to look on the sunny side, to balance the treatment of unbalanced growth by concentrating on the production possibilities available to the model society through time. As Baumol presents his results in the form of four propositions ([1], pp. 418 to 419), in keeping with the theme of balance I present my principle findings in four more-or-less opposing propositions. A section below is devoted to each of the four pairs; Baumol's propositions are, in part, in my paraphrasing. A fifth section contains a demonstration that the single-factor assumption adopted by Baumol for simplicity is not altogether innocuous.

I. Propositions 1 and 1'

Proposition 1 (Baumol): Through time the cost per unit of output of the lagging sector 1, relative to that of the progressive sector 2, will rise without limit.

Proposition 1' (Bradford): Through time the cost per unit of output of sector 2, relative to that of sector 1, will fall to zero in the limit, while the set of feasible output combinations will continually expand.

These propositions, as well as the rather less trivial ones below, are easily derived graphically because the model economy has at each moment of time a linear production possibility frontier. The production functions for the two outputs, Y_1 and Y_2, at time t are

$$Y_{1t} = a L_{1t} \quad (1)$$

$$Y_{2t} = b L_{2t} e^{rt} \quad (2)$$

where L_{1t} and L_{2t} are the quantities of labor emlpoyed in the two sectors, and a and b are positive constants. The production possibility frontier of this simple economy at time t is thus a straight line [PP (t) in Fig. 1] with slope $-a/b\,e^{rt}$, Y_1 intercept $a L_t$, and Y_2 intercept $b L_t\, e^{rt}$, where L_t is the total labor force available.

With a fixed total labor force, the "motion" of the production possibility frontier through time under the effect of the continued productivity advance in sector 2 is obvious. It simply pivots on the Y_1 intercept, P, with slope decreasing in absolute value: the total amount of Y_1 produceable remains constant at aL, while the maximum potential output of Y_2, bLe^{rt}, rises steadily. In Fig. 1, a second production possibility frontier,

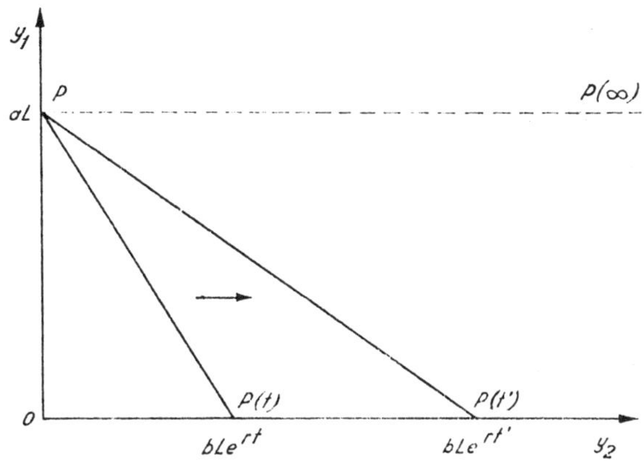

Fig. 1

$PP(t')$, is shown, for a time t' later than t. The horizontal frontier, $PP(\infty)$, is approached asymptotically with the passage of time, enclosing an ever-expanding set of output combinations. Correspondingly, the opportunity cost of a unit of Y_2, the amount of Y_1 which must be foregone to obtain an additional unit of Y_2, which is measured by the negative of the frontier's slope, steadily falls toward zero. This establishes Propositions 1 and 1'. With a growing labor force the behavior of the slope of the production possibility frontier is unchanged, though its Y_1 intercept moves away from the origin at the labor force growth rate.

It should perhaps be observed explicitly that, assuming both goods are always desired by someone, in this situation society's utility possibility frontier is shifting continually outward (though possibly approaching a limit; see footnote 7 below), regardless of what happens to the price ratio. However, the process may well be accompanied in the real world by utility losses for some. Furthermore, there may be political factors making the demand for the increasingly expensive public services (when that is the technologically lagging sector) "unduly" price elastic, so that society fails to reach its utility possibility frontier by ever increasing margins[2]. This would appear to be the only ground for being concerned with the time path of the exchange rate between Y_1 and Y_2 per se — that in some sense the degree to which an optimal provision of a public service is approached

[2] On welfare comparisons on the basis of utility possibility frontiers see Samuelson [4] or Graaff [2]. Graaff, in particular, makes use of a distinction between utility possibility and utility feasibility frontiers. Of course, the meaning to be attached to distance or "nearness" in utility space is not obvious.

is sensitive to the prevailing relative prices. Baumol cites the loss of confidence of the electrorate in their governments as a result of rising budgets without a corresponding rise in service quantity as a source of such a phenomenon ([1], pp. 422—423).

On the other hand, in the case of private goods, such as the wares of fine restaurants and theaters, or the services of stately mansions, it is by no means clear why one should be worried, as Baumol is ([1], p. 422), about rising prices. Within the constraints usually placed upon normative reasoning in welfare economics, such a concern would have to be based on a worsening of the situation of someone or some group. In the model world, unless the distribution of current income changes, everyone becomes continually better off in the unambiguous sense that everyone's consumption opportunity set continually expands, with no feasible combinations of Y_1 and Y_2 lost and new combinations steadily becoming available. The mechanism for this continual improvement in individual positions is, of course, the steadily increasing wage in Y_2 units, which is also a constant wage in Y_1 units. People can purchase as many *haute cuisine* repasts and theater tickets as before, and at the same time buy ever more and better air conditioning. That people choose to buy somewhat less *haute cuisine,* if they do, and even more air conditioning or, worse, TV dinners, is generally taken to indicate that they feel better off as a result.

We do not live in a single-factor world, so that income distribution is affected by technical change (cf. Section V below), and by other forces and public policies as well. In this case the very process of change, signalled in part by changing relative prices, may systematically worsen the position of some groups in the economy, either through falling money income shares or through rising relative prices of commodities normally consuming a relatively large share of the budgets cf the damaged groups. The fact of changing relative prices by itself tells us nothing about such processes, however.

One may, to be sure, deplore popular tastes and regret a decline in consumption of particular goods. Certainly the extreme individualistic model of welfare economics, with tastes taken as autonomously given, is too simple. Judgments about tastes, and especially about the dynamic process of taste formation, have valid content and cannot be ruled out. As yet, however, we have no carefully worked-out normative theory of the "external economics" of tastes and their formation; and most conclusions on the subject stand as obiter dicta, unsupported by ethical presumptions of such apparent acceptability as those of conventional welfare economics. As one who enjoys *haute cuisine* and theater performances, I should be happy to see such activities subsidized. I might not be so happy with a shift in popular tastes in this direction, however, since, in a many-factor world with a bowed-out production possibility frontier, this would tend to raise the prices of these goods, though returns to scale here — through maintenance of a large pool of trained chefs and actors interacting to improve quality, for example — could change matters.

In any case, the outlook for a growing demand for the output of the lagging sector, or at least maintenance of a fixed level, may not be quite so grim as Baumol's Proposition 2, to which we now turn, suggests.

II. Propositions 2 and 2'

Proposition 2 (Baumol): Unless demand for it is highly inelastic, output in the lagging sector will decline and perhaps vanish.

Proposition 2' (Bradford): By maintaining a constant proportion between expenditures on the two goods (at current prices), individuals can purchase a constant amount of Y_1 and an ever growing amount of Y_2. Alternatively, a constant proportional money income tax will suffice to finance the provision of a constant (per capita) amount of Y_1 allowing taxpayers a continually growing consumption of Y_2.

In fact, the analysis underlying these two propositions is the same; Baumol misinterpreted it in deriving Proposition 2. If we equate, as Baumol does, "unit elasticity of demand for both outputs"[3], with constant relative outlays at opportunity cost prices, the corresponding expan-

[3] The ordinary partial equilibrium concept of price elasticity measures the effect on the amount demanded of a change in a commodity's price, all other prices and money income (i. e. purchaseable combinations of all other commodities) held constant. Since in this case only the amount of Y_1 "purchaseable" is held constant, it is, strictly speaking, only possible to discuss the price elasticity of demand for Y_2, and this only with a fixed labor force. Generalizing from the fact that where demand elasticity, with respect to either price or income, is greater than, less than, or equal to unity, the fraction of the budget devoted to the commodity in question increases, decreases, or is constant under a fall in price or increase in income *as appropriate to the definition* involved, Baumol has implicitly defined a hybrid elasticity. Attention is drawn to this in the text by putting quotation marks around "elasticity" when used in his sense.

The possibility of defining "elasticity" depends upon the assumption that the fraction of the budget devoted to a commodity depends only upon the set of relative prices. In the two-commodity case, let $f_1(p)$ denote the fraction of the budget devoted to purchase of Y_1 when the price of a unit of Y_1 in terms of Y_2 is p. Then demand for Y_1 will be said to be "elastic", "unit elastic", or "inelastic" according as $f_1'(p)$ is less than, equal to, or greater than zero. If $f_2(p)$ is the budget fraction devoted to Y_2 we shall call its demand "elastic" if this fraction *increases* with an increase in p, etc., since p is the inverse of the price of Y_2 in terms of Y_1. Of course, $f_1'(p) + f_2'(p) = 0$, so demands for both goods are of the same "elasticity".

Though the assumption that the fraction of the budget devoted to the various commodities depends only upon relative prices is a rather strong one, it does not appear to affect the analysis and does simplify the exposition. It does imply, and is implied by, unit income elasticity at all income levels and at all sets of relative prices. This in turn places restriction on price elasticity as usually defined, and on "elasticity" as well, for a consumer obeying the axioms of revealed preference (e. g. rules out expansion paths, in Fig. 2, with a slope at any point greater than that of a ray from the origin to that point). However, there is no necessity for society to behave according to the axioms of revealed preference.

sion path of chosen combinations of Y_1 and Y_2 traces points lying at the same fractional distance from the endpoints of the production possibility frontiers, society's successive budget constraints. In the constant-total-labor force case, elementary geometry tells us that in our diagram such paths are horizontal lines, such as XX' in Fig. 2, where A and B label the

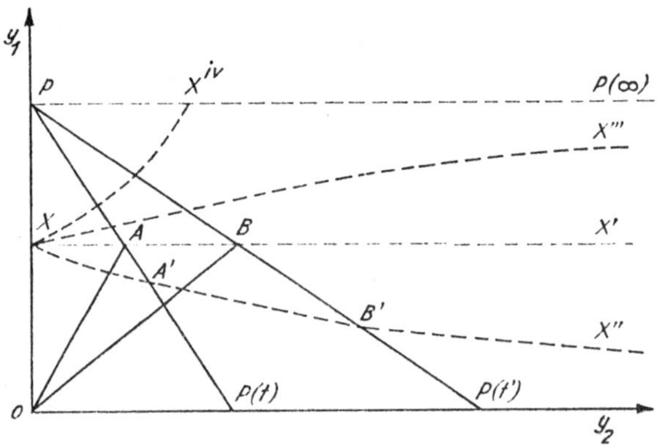

Fig. 2

combinations chosen at times t and t' respectively. Along XX' the fraction of the "budget" spent on Y_1 is given by the distance ratio $AP(t)/PP(t) = BP(t')/PP(t')$, etc.; that on Y_2 by $PA/PP(t) = PB/PP(t')$, etc. The ratio, Y_1/Y_2, of the chosen outputs of the two sectors at point A is given by the slope of the line from A through the origin, OA. At a later date, at point B, the ratio is given by the slope of line OB, etc. As time marches on, the chosen combination of outputs moves infinitely far out on the line XX', and correspondingly the ratio of the chosen output of Y_1 to the chosen output of Y_2 tends toward zero. If the total labor force is growing, the analysis is unaffected. In this case the production possibility frontier at, say, time t', would be parallel to $PP(t')$ in Fig. 2, but farther away from the origin. The output combination chosen under the "unitary elasticity" assumption would lie along the same ray, OB, extended to intersect the new frontier.

Baumol's Proposition 2 is incorrect in its interpretation of the vanishing of the chosen ratio Y_1/Y_2, attributing it to the decline to zero of the amount of Y_1 demanded. For notice that a constant relative outlay on the two goods (in the case where sector 1 is public output, a government budget which is a constant percentage of national income in current dollars, e. g. financed by a constant proportional money income tax) buys a constant amount of Y_1, the output of the nonprogressive sector[4]. This is our Proposition 2'. With "unitary elasticity" of demand, the tendency to zero of Y_1/Y_2 is caused entirely by the tendency toward infinity of the

[4] With a growing labor force, the absolute level of output of Y_1 chosen would actually increase through time.

denominator, the chosen output of Y_2. Of course, if the demand for Y_1 were to be and remain "elastic", in the sense that the fraction of the resource budget devoted to it declined with an increase in its relative price, the expansion path would look like XX'' in Fig. 2, with combination A' chosen at time t, B' at time t'. With labor force fixed, ultimately Y_1 would vanish absolutely as well as relatively[5]. With a growing labor force, even this won't assure the vanishing of Y_1.

It should be pointed out that a path of "inelastic" demand for Y_1, perhaps more illuminatingly described as a path of high income elasticity, cannot be ruled out a priori. When television sets are priced at $ 1 each I may gladly give up a couple of dozen for a handmade pottery ash tray. In such a case, moving along an expansion path like XX''', or XX^{iv} in Fig. 2, the desired Y_1/Y_2 ratio can do anything[6].

For example, the demand for leisure, the production of an hour's worth of which always requires an hour of labor time, is apparently "inelastic" relative to other goods. If it weren't, we would see the fraction of time spent in production of goods increasing (path XX'' in Fig. 2) instead of decreasing. The approach of an infinite price for the lagging sector's output need not signal the approach to zero of the demand for that output. If there indeed exist free goods (the usual example: air), anything we are now consuming with positive money price can be thought of as having an infinite price relative to the free good.

III. Propositions 3 and 3'

Proposition 3 (Baumol): In order to maintain balanced expansion (i. e., a constant ratio between the outputs of the two sectors), the fraction of the labor force allocated to the lagging sector must approach unity.

Proposition 3' (Bradford): It seems unlikely that individuals (or society collectively) will choose a balanced expansion path in a world of unbalanced productivity change.

Since labor productivity is constant in the output of Y_1, the fraction L_1/L of the labor force allocated to sector 1 is equal to the ratio of the output of Y_1 actually chosen, aL_1, to the maximum produceable amount, aL. For example, in the "unit elastic" demand case, discussed above and illustrated in Fig. 2 by expansion path XX', the fraction of the available labor force devoted to Y_1 is given by OX/OP. Disregarding the question of why we should be interested in the allocation of resources per se, it is easy to see that maintaining fixed proportions between the two outputs means following an expansion path which is a ray through the origin,

[5] Strictly speaking, to assure this the "elasticity" of demand for Y_1 must be bounded away from unity as long as any fraction of the labor force is still allocated to sector 1. Otherwise XX'' could have everywhere negative slope but be bounded away from the Y_2 axis.

[6] We might rule out an indefinite rise in the Y_1/Y_2 ratio, which would mean tending toward the point labelled P in Fig. 2. If point P represented bliss it might be argued that the curve would have to start as well as end there. But on this point see the final remark of footnote 3.

such as OZ in Fig. 3, and that this will require ultimately allocating the entire labor force to sector 1 (Baumol's Proposition 3). In the diagram, combinations C and D represent those which must be chosen at times t and t', and OC'/OP, OD'/OP the corresponding fractions of the labor force which must be devoted to the production of Y_1, to maintain the desired output ratio. It is evident that with the passage of time, as the production possibility frontier swings around toward PP (∞), to keep the desired ratio of output the fraction of the labor force allocated to sector 1 must tend toward 1. Again, this proposition is independent of the growth rate of the labor force.

It is less easy to imagine why an individual (or a society) should ever choose such an expansion path. While no path can be ruled out a priori, and satiation with a free good must be recognized as a possibility, sector 2 was designed to represent the manufacturing sector, where

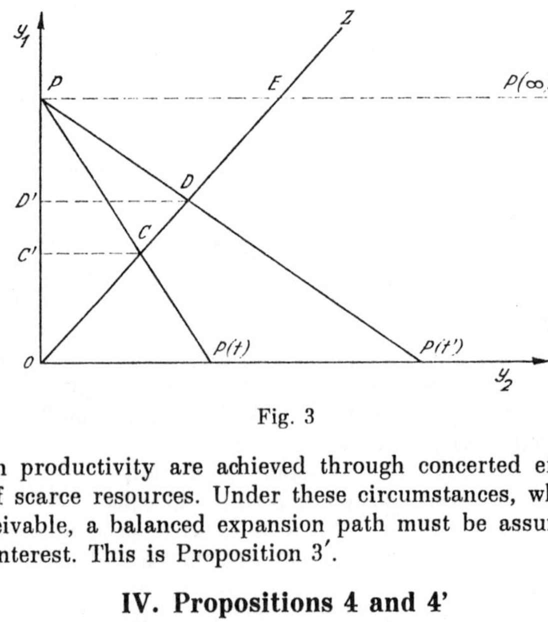

Fig. 3

advances in productivity are achieved through concerted effort and investment of scarce resources. Under these circumstances, while certainly not inconceivable, a balanced expansion path must be assumed to be of little real interest. This is Proposition 3'.

IV. Propositions 4 and 4'

Proposition 4 (Baumol): An attempt to maintain balanced expansion must lead ultimately to a zero rate of growth of real output per man.

Proposition 4' (Bradford): As long as any ceiling, however close to 1 (but less than 1), is placed on the fraction of the labor force allocated to the lagging sector, the average rate of growth of real output per man over the long run will equal the maximum sustainable level, which is the rate of growth of productivity in sector 2.

It is useful to begin this section by demonstrating Baumol's Proposition 4 geometrically, using the fact that level lines of a weighted average of the two outputs (i. e., of any fixed-weight measure of real output) consist of parallel straight lines. In Fig. 4 level lines for values k_1 and k_2 of the weighted average $w_1 Y_1 + w_2 Y_2$ have been drawn through output combinations C and D. The ratio of real income at D to that at C, k_2/k_1, is equal to the distance ratio OD''/OC'', or, equivalently, OD/OC.

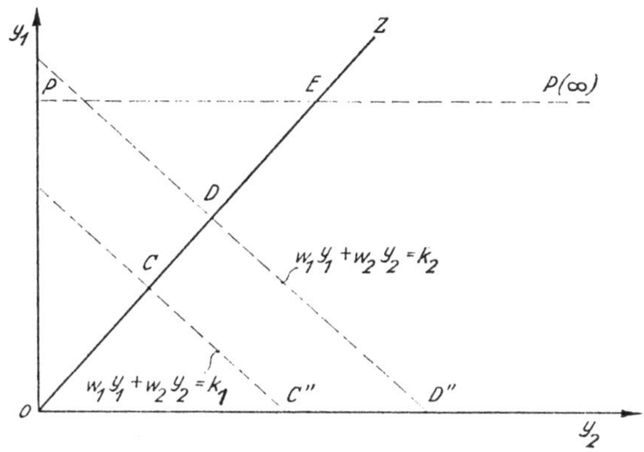

Fig. 4

In fact the ratio of *any* fixed- (positive) weighted average of two output combinations lying along a ray through the origin is equal to the ratio of their distances from the origin. Since, in the model world, the point E puts a ceiling on the attainable output combinations in a Y_1/Y_2 ratio given by the slope of OZ, it is evident that the growth rate of any real output measure must eventually approach zero. It should also be evident that if, instead of a constant labor force, we have a growing one, then the point E will move away from the origin at a rate equal to the growth rate of the labor force, and ultimately the growth of real output, with sector output combinations constrained to lie along OZ, must approach this rate. This is Baumol's Proposition 4.

There may be a lesson to be drawn from this proposition relevant to the politics of growth. It is clear that the maximum rate of growth of any index of real output in the short run is to be attained by concentrating all production in the progressive sector and in the long run (cf. Proposition 4′) by keeping some minimum quantity of resources in that sector. If, through the marketplace or otherwise, society should choose to stay on a path such as OE, is it behaving irrationally in thus choosing, ultimately, zero growth? (We have just argued that it would be behaving rather peculiarly, though not irrationally.)

We can put this another way. Imagine the model society to be made up of individuals with independent utility functions each of whom, confronted with the successive price ratios of the two goods and the income provided him by socially optimal lump sum distributions, chooses to consume the same constant ratio of the two goods. The economy of this society would then trace out through time an expansion path like OE of Figs. 3 and 4. Evidently, any program designed to increase the rate of growth of any real income measure by shifting resources into the "progressive" sector, such as by forced industrialization, will actually reduce the welfare of the citizens[7]. This is a commentary on the risks of focusing attention on an index of real output; it does not, of course, address the more difficult issue of determining the "correct" social discount rate for investment decisions.

However, if the model society is worried about its entry in the international real growth score-book it can take comfort from our Proposition 4′. This proposition can be developed intuitively from the geometry in the constant labor force case when it is noted that the expansion path corresponding to the *slowest* rate of growth of real output which can be realized, under the specified restriction on the amount of labor allocated to sector 1, is one like XX' in Fig. 2, although X might be located much closer to P than it is in this example. Along such a path the real output index consists of a constant term, corresponding to the constant output of Y_1, plus a term growing at the constant rate r, corresponding to the output of Y_2. In the long run the second term completely dominates the first, and the rate of growth of the index tends toward r. Along an arbitrary expansion path lying in the "strip" between the Y_2 axis and the slowest-growth path (like XX' in Fig. 2) real output may not approach any particular growth rate in the limit [the path may "wiggle back and forth" along pieces of successive frontiers like $AP(t)$ and $BP(t')$ in Fig. 2, and thus may repeatedly have short periods of negative growth]. However, the long run average rate of growth (barring failure to stay on the production possibility frontier) cannot be lower than that along XX', which we have seen tends toward r.

This result, and the corresponding result per man with a growing labor force, stated as our Proposition 4′, may be more rigorously, but still very simply, demonstrated analytically. Let $m(t)$ be real output per man at time t. By average growth rate from time 0 to time t we mean that constant rate s at which m would have to grow to reach $m(t)$ in a period of time of length t, i. e., the solution to

$$m(0)\,e^{st} = m(t). \tag{3}$$

Taking logarithms and solving for s, this becomes

$$s = \frac{\log m(t)}{t} - \frac{\log m(0)}{t}. \tag{4}$$

[7] If we think of real output as having welfare significance, the best that our model society is able to achieve may indeed ultimately be a zero rate of real output growth. That is, the individuals become satiated with the output of the progressive sector while the absolute limit on the output of the nonprogressive sector prevents further welfare advance. That such absolute limits exist on (a) the supply of direct personal services and (b) the supply of certain objects, such as masterworks of art, was the basis for Harrod's argument against the possibility of economic satiety [3]. I wish to thank Dr. S. G. Long of the University of Iowa for this reference. Long pointed it out to Baumol who pointed it out to me.

As t approaches infinity the second term vanishes, so that it is only necessary to show that, under our assumptions,

$$\lim_{t \to \infty} \frac{\log m(t)}{t} = r. \tag{5}$$

Let $n_2(t)$ denote the fraction of the labor force allocated to the progressive sector, and let ε be the specified allowable minimum for this fraction, so that

$$1 > n_2(t) \geqq \varepsilon > 0. \tag{6}$$

By definition,

$$m(t) = w_1 a [1 - n_2(t)] + w_2 b e^{rt} n_2(t). \tag{7}$$

Since, by (6), the first term on the right cannot exceed $w_1 a (1 - \varepsilon)$, for t sufficiently large, again in view of (6),

$$w_1 a (1 - \varepsilon) + w_2 b e^{rt} \varepsilon \leqq m(t) \leqq w_2 b e^{rt}, \tag{8}$$

from which we see,

$$w_2 b e^{rt} \varepsilon \leqq m(t) \leqq w_2 b e^{rt}, \tag{9}$$

and, taking logarithms,

$$\log w_2 b \varepsilon + rt \leqq \log m(t) \leqq \log w_2 b + rt. \tag{10}$$

Dividing through by t and "taking the limit", we obtain the desired result:

$$r \leqq \lim_{t \to \infty} \frac{\log m(t)}{t} \leqq r. \tag{11}$$

V. The Single-Factor Assumption

It remains to provide the promised demonstration that Baumol's single-factor assumption is not as innocent as it might appear. The implication of the single-factor assumption (coupled with a constant-returns-to-scale assumption and separability of the two production processes) is that the production possibility frontier of the model economy is a straight line, or, equivalently, that the marginal rate of transformation between Y_1 and Y_2 is independent of the proportions in which they are produced at any moment in time. Baumol's Propositions 1 and 2 depend upon this fact.

When more than one factor of production is incorporated to the model, a curved production possibility frontier is to be expected (constant returns to scale in the [separable] production processes assures that the frontier will be concave to the origin). We can no longer speak of the (marginal) cost of one commodity in terms of another without specifying precisely where on the frontier of the moment such a quantity is to be calculated. Fig. 5 illustrates a case in which technological progress results in a continually rising price of a marginal unit of the progressive sector output, Y_2, in terms of the lagging sector output, Y_1, when the latter output is kept constant through time at OX. The economy's capacity to produce Y_1 is not changing, while its capacity to produce Y_2 is continually expanding, yielding successive production possibility frontiers *PP* (*t*), *PP* (*t'*), *PP* (*t''*), etc. But the slope of successive frontiers when Y_1 output

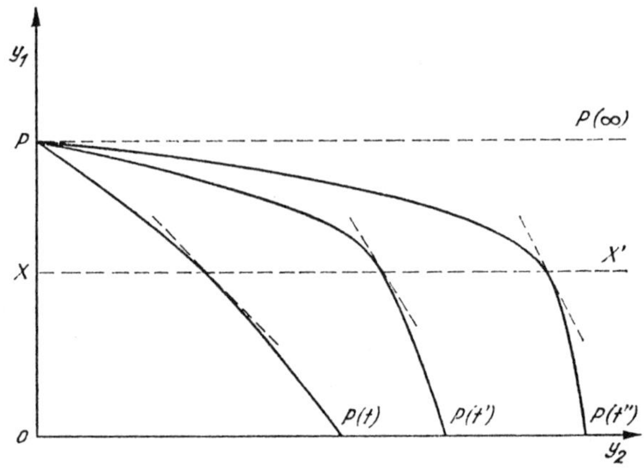

Fig. 5

is held constant at *OX* continually increases. There appears no obvious reason for ruling out this sort of technical change a priori.

For example, suppose that Y_1 is produced with unskilled labor (*Lu*) alone, with constant productivity, so that

$$Y_1 = a' \, L u_1 , \tag{12}$$

while in sector 2, unskilled labor, skilled labor (*Ls*), and capital (*K*) are combined according to the constant returns to scale production function

$$Y_2 = b' \, (L u_2 + c \, e^{rt} \, L s)^{\alpha} \, K^{1-\alpha} \tag{13}$$
$$0 < \alpha < 1.$$

According to (13), the effect of technical progress is to make skilled workers increasingly productive in sector 2. Assuming factor supplies fixed, and holding Y_1 at some prescribed level by holding Lu_1 (and hence Lu_2) constant, the marginal product of unskilled labor in sector 2 at any time is given by

$$\frac{\partial Y_2}{\partial L u_2} = b' \, \alpha \, (L u_2 + c \, e^{rt} \, L s)^{\alpha - 1} \, K^{1-\alpha}. \tag{14}$$

Since $\alpha - 1 < 0$, as time passes this marginal product, and hence the Y_2 price of Y_1 at the margin, continually falls.

This is the situation depicted graphically in Fig. 6. The points labelled *A* (*t*) and *A* (*t'*) represent the output combinations produceable at those times if *all* unskilled labor is allocated to sector 1. As time goes on, the production possibility frontiers become more and more like *PB* (*t*) *P* (*t*) and *PB* (*t'*) *P* (*t'*) (i. e., the increment in Y_2 obtainable by shifting the entire unskilled labor force from sector 1 to sector 2 approaches zero).

Ultimately the production possibility space approaches, as in the previous model, the "strip" bounded by the axes and the line *PP* (∞).

It may be pointed out that Baumol's Propositions 3 and 4 continue to hold in this world (substituting "unskilled labor" for "labor" in Proposition 3), but the balanced expansion path would clearly never be

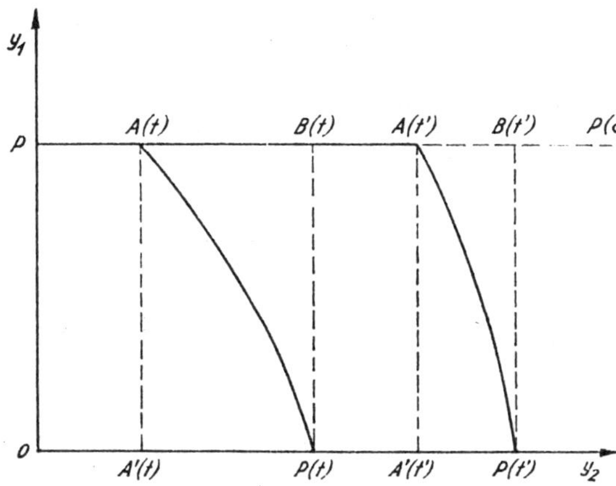

Fig. 6

chosen here, since along such a path Y_2 becomes literally free at the margin after a finite length of time. If it is assumed that all factor supplies grow at the same rate (or all remain constant) it is not difficult to show that full employment of all factors (in fact, full employment of capital and skilled labor alone) assures that average real output per man over the long run will grow at the maximum possible rate, which is αr.[8]

[8] Let n_u be the unskilled fraction of the labor force, n_s the skilled fraction and k the ratio of the capital stock to the total labor force. If all factor supplies grow at the same rate, n_u, n_s, and k are constant through time. The "per man economy", under the constant returns to scale assumption, looks like a scale model of Fig. 6. Full employment of at least capital and skilled labor assure an output combination lying somewhere in successive triangles like $A(t)\ A'(t)\ P(t)$. The actual real output per man will lie between the real output values of points like $A'(t)$ and points like $B(t)$, where at $A'(t)$ all unskilled labor is "thrown away", and at $B(t)$ all unskilled labor is treated as employed simultaneously in both sectors. If $m(t)$ is real output per man and w_1 and w_2 the weights applied to Y_1 and Y_2, this means that

$$w_2 b' [c e^{rt} n_s]^{\alpha} k^{1-\alpha} \leq m(t) \leq w_1 a' n_u + w_2 b' [n_u + c e^{rt} n_s]^{\alpha} k^{1-\alpha}. \qquad (15)$$

Recalling the proof of Proposition 4′, take logarithms and divide by t to obtain

$$\frac{\log (w_2 b' c^{\alpha} n_s^{\alpha} k^{1-\alpha})}{t} + \qquad (16)$$

$$+ \alpha r \leq \frac{\log m(t)}{t} \leq \frac{\log (w_1 a' n_u + w_2 b' [n_u + c e^{rt} n_s]^{\alpha} k^{1-\alpha})}{t}.$$

VI. Conclusions

In his paper Baumol raised a number of important issues. Included are several knotty problems of an empirical nature: Can measures of outputs which we normally classify as services be reasonably divorced from measurement of the inputs of labor involved in their provision? Can commodities be satisfactorily divided into two classes: those for which the technology of production is inherently stagnant, and those for which technological progress is possible? It should be clear that in this paper no attempt has been made to address these or any other factual questions.

What has been attempted is a demonstration that, on their own grounds, Baumol's rather pessimistic propositions about the behavior of an economy undergoing unbalanced productivity change can be balanced by rather more positive ones. Furthermore, those grounds have themselves been questioned: It has been argued that few normative implications can be drawn from the movement of relative prices, especially in the one-factor world used illustratively by Baumol, that a balanced expansion path is unlikely to be desired in such a world, and that little significance can be attached to changes in a real output index in this context. Finally, it has been shown that assuming a one-factor world results in hiding some of the important possibilities (for relative commodity and factor price behavior) under unbalanced growth. In particular, with not very unlikely sorts of factor complementarity, two of Baumol's propositions no longer hold.

References

1. W. J. Baumol: Macroeconomics of Unbalanced Growth: The Anatomy of Urban Crisis, The American Economic Review *LVII* (1967), pp. 415–426.
2. J. de V. Graaff: Theoretical Welfare Economics, Cambridge 1957.
3. R. F. Harrod: The Possibility of Economic Satiety, in: Problems of U. S. Economic Development, Vol. I, Committee for Economic Development, New York 1958.
4. P. A. Samuelson: Evaluation of Real National Income, Oxford Economic Papers, N. S., *II* (1950), pp. 1–29.

Address of author: Prof. Dr. David F. Bradford, Princeton University, Department of Economics, Princeton, New Jersey 08540, U. S. A.

As t approaches infinity the left hand side evidently approaches ar. That this is the upper as well as the lower bound to the long-run average rate of growth can be shown by using L'Hospital's rule to prove that the right hand side approaches the same limit.

[9]

Macroeconomics of Unbalanced Growth: Reply

By William J. Baumol*

There is no doubt that Michael Keren is right and that the point is important.[1] In the initial discussion of my model, I simply misinterpreted the rising relative cost of the urban public services to mean that it will become harder for society to provide them. As Keren shows, the rising productivity elsewhere in the economy that is the source of the increasing opportunity cost of the services, also automatically means that the community will be able more easily, if it wishes, to pay for these services, despite their rising cost.

The implications of Keren's point are worth spelling out. The basic argument of the original analysis still remains valid: the financial problem of the cities increases (in part) because the costs of the services rise more rapidly than the general price level. This may well lead to cumulative deterioration in the quality and quantity of the services, even though it is not forced on the economy by lack of resources.

Because of their rising relative costs, the community may in fact *want* less of some or even most of these services. But the danger is that the nature of the political process and the tax system will also force it to accept a decline in even those services which the public would in fact prefer to expand, an expansion which, as Keren shows, society will well be able to afford. The problem is to find means by which the rising resources of the community can be channelled into *those* public services at a rate that grows more rapidly than their costs.

* Princeton University.

[1] My error has also been pointed out by several others, though sometimes not so clearly as in Keren's note. See, e.g., illuminating papers by David Bradford and by L. K. Lynch and E. L. Redman.

REFERENCES

D. Bradford, "Balance on Unbalanced Growth," *Zeitschrift fur Nationalokonomie*, 1969, *29*, 291–304.

I. K. Lynch and E. L. Redman, "Macroeconomics of Unbalanced Growth: Comment," *Amer. Econ. Rev.*, Sept. 1968, *58*, 152–55.

[10]

W. J. Baumol and W. E. Oates:
The Cost Disease of the Personal Services and the Quality of Life

There are a number of economic activities which are widely thought to be fundamental to a high and improving quality of life. It is a diverse group encompassing such services as education and medicine, theatrical and musical performances, protection from crime, the operation of libraries and, perhaps, of fine restaurants. These activities also have another characteristic in common, one whose implications many will consider very unfortunate: they have all, at least in recent years, been exhibiting phenomenal rates of increases in their costs.

For example, in the United States during the period 1947—1967, the cost of elementary education **per pupil** has risen about 6 1/2 per cent per year compounded.[1] Similarly, for university libraries the cost **per volume** held has gone up over six per cent per year compounded.[2] The figures for the other activities in the list all suggest similar patterns of increasing costs, and this has occurred during a period when costs in the remainder of the economy, as indicated by the standard price indices, have risen on the average less than 1 1/2 per cent per year.

In the United States such rapidly increasing costs have in many cases led to significant decreases in the quality or the quantity of these outputs supplied. The streets grow increasingly dirty; libraries have curtailed the hours during which they are open; and hospitals become increasingly overcrowded. Many even believe that the quality of the elementary schools has been affected significantly. Any recent visitor to the United States must be all too aware of the dismal list.

[1] D. F. Bradford, R. A. Malt, and W. E. Oates. "The Rising Cost of Local Public Services: Some Evidence and Reflections," **National Tax Journal** (June, 1969), p. 190.
[2] Association of Research Libraries.

W. J. Baumol and W. E. Oates are economists at Princeton University, New Jersey, USA. Professor Baumol was visiting professor at the Stockholm School of Economics during the first half of 1971.

Nor are other countries immune to these problems. Those capitals of Europe which are most noted for their cleanliness grow increasingly dirty, and visibly so. The costs of their theaters run ahead of their subsidies, and so on.

Yet this is so despite the fact that public expenditures on these services have not remained stationary. On the contrary, in the United States, expenditures of state and local governments, which are in considerable part devoted to such services, have risen from a total of $11 billion in 1946 to some $121 billion by 1969, a more than ten-fold increase in less than 25 years, during a period in which GNP increased at less than half as rapid a rate. Surely, budgetary increases of this magnitude should have permitted not only the maintenance of the quantity and quality of these services, but significant increases in both. Their failure to do so certainly requires explanation.

We typically find these problems attributed to three basic causes: governmental inefficiency, growth in population served, and inflation. But on closer inspection, those do not appear to be the real villains. In the United States, for example, many universities, and much of medical and theatrical activity is not run by the government. Yet the costs of these activities go up just as rapidly as the others. Indeed, the cost of medicine has increased most quickly of all.

Nor can the explanation be the growth in the size of the population served. True, the postwar baby boom did increase the number of children to be educated and that, in turn, obviously added to the educational budget. However, the educational figures given before referred to cost **per pupil;** i.e. it had already been deflated to eliminate the effects of population growth. It was after elimination of these effects that we were able to report that cost of education (i.e., cost per pupil) had increased at 6 1/2 per cent per annum. Obviously, the growth in student population does not explain this sensational rate of increase, except perhaps to the extent that the increased demand for teachers bids up their salaries somewhat more rapidly than they would have risen otherwise.

Finally, we cannot ascribe the problem to inflation. If inflation were the explanation, in an economy where prices rose at 1 1/2 per cent per year we would expect cost per pupil also to rise at about 1 1/2 per cent—not 6 1/2 per cent—per year. Obviously, even after we take account of the effects of increasing price levels, we still have some 5 of the 6 1/2 per cent growth in cost per pupil left over to be explained.

There is, of course, no single explanation for the paradox of the rapidly rising public budgets required to supply public services that seem to grow increasingly inadequate. Rural-urban-suburban migration patterns, the rising student population, the rather inflexible tax base in most cities, and a host of other problems have contributed to the financial plight of the public sector. Some of these may be problems peculiar to recent decades which may or may not persist in the future. However, we will argue that, in addition to these sources of rising costs, there exists a chronic cost disease that infects not only the public services but also a wide variety of services provided by private industry and by private nonprofit institutions. This cost disease threatens to price out of the market many of those services which we usually consider to be important contributors to the quality of life. Among the afflicted services, we find elementary and higher education, medical services, the handicrafts, the live performance of music, drama, and dance, libraries, and cuisine; in short, many of the things which we associate with a vital and attractive civilization.

We will contend that a substantial portion of the cost problems that beset these services must be ascribed to the nature of their technology, rather than to any of the villains that are usually conjured up—inflation or inefficiency, corruption (where the item in question is supplied by government) or greed and profiteering (where it is supplied by private industry). This cost problem has, in fact, beset the services for a long time and is likely to continue to do so for the foreseeable future.

It appears, moreover, that there is no painless cure for this disease. We can predict with confidence that the costs of these services will rise continually at a rate more rapid than costs for the economy as a whole. There is, however, one encouraging aspect of the problem. As we will show, the very process which causes these compounding increases in the costs of services also generates the additional resources needed to meet those costs. The problem thus becomes that of society deciding which and in what quantity and quality particular services should be supplied. The real danger is that, unless the nature of the process is made clear, public misunderstanding or neglect may lead to the deterioriation (or even the extinction) of certain services, some of which it may well be in our interest to perpetuate.

1. Lagging technological progress in the production of services

A calculation based on several centuries of rather remarkable data suggests that the purchasing power of a day's wages (or what economists call **real** wages) are some twenty times as high in the United States today as they were in Elizabethan England.[3] This rise in the value of a day's work reflects primarily the increased productivity of labor: with modern techniques of production, a

[3] See E. H. Phelps Brown and Sheila Hopkins, "Seven Centuries of the Prices of Consumables," **Economica**, N. S. 23, Nov., 1956, pp. 296—314.

man can produce many more goods and services per hour than he could three centuries ago. Continual improvements in methods of production have over time thus increased the productive capability of labor and thereby raised the **real** earnings of the typical worker.

It is not surprising to find that increasing output per man has been much more dramatic in some forms of productive activity than in others. However, these differences in rates of productivity increase have not assumed a random pattern with one set of activities experiencing rising output per man over one period, while another set realizes rapid increases in productivity at another time. Rather, there is a broad class of activities, which we will call (admittedly with some oversimplification) the **personal services,** that have shown themselves over the centuries to be relatively resistant to productivity-increasing innovation.

The personal services typically possess one or both of two closely related characteristics which make increases in output per man relatively difficult to come by. The first is that some of their outputs are inherently unstandardized so that techniques for their mass production are difficult to develop. Certain types of medical care are a good example. While, in some cases, standard patterns and treatment are available for particular ills, we know of too many cases of faulty diagnosis even in the finest medical laboratories to place great faith in routinized diagnostic procedures. Even where two patients are known to share a common ailment, the treatment appropriate for one may produce dangerously allergic reactions in the other. Consequently, most of us are extremely reluctant to forego the personal attention of the examining physician. It is not difficult to think of other activities for which standardization is virtually impossible, including such disparate services as painting, the teaching of children with special problems, and the repairing of watches.

The second obstacle to rapid and continued increases in productivity is the frequently intimate connection between the quantity of labor and the quality of the end product. It is not easy, for example, to imagine how we can mechanize the teacher's reading and criticism of students' papers, which appears so important for the development of writing skills. An increase in gross instructor productivity, in the sense of an increase in the number of students per teacher, would seem to have serious consequences for the quality of the "product." Once again, we can readily find further examples in widely different fields. The need for study and interpretation of certain legal problems requires the input of trained lawyers. On quite a different matter, the personal service and attention accompanying the serving of a good meal is frequently regarded as an integral part of the experience of dining out. In all these instances, reduced reliance on the use of labor is likely to have adverse effects on the quality of the service provided.

In some cases, product specifications seem effective to prevent any reductions in manpower below some point (which often has already been reached). The single bus driver who collects the fares, as well as driving the vehicle, in most American or Swedish cities represents the minimum number of persons possible for the job. In the New York subways in the 1920's there were six employees per train. This number was reduced one by one over the next two decades until, by the postwar period, there remained only the motorman and the conductor who operated the doors.

In the live performing arts, the obstacles limiting increases in productivity are perhaps the most clear-cut of all. A Schubert trio scored for a half-hour performance simply requires one and a half man-hours of labor in its public presentation, and that is all there is to the matter. As Alan Peacock has put it, "Removing Judge Bouck from the cast of **Hedda Gabler** would certainly reduce labor input to Ibsen's masterpiece, but it would also destroy the product. Nor could one increase the productivity of the cost by performing the play at twice the speed. Anyone who doubts this proposition should try playing modern long-playing disks at 28 revolutions per minute."[4]

We do not mean to say that in most of these activities increases in productivity are impossible. On the contrary, from time to time one can expect significant labor-saving innovations in their production. The use of programmed teaching materials has no doubt raised the teacher's productivity to some extent. The jet airliner has done the same for the live performing arts by permitting performers to travel from city to city much more quickly. If one is willing to accept modifications in the product, still greater reductions in the number of man hours per unit of output become possible. The mass media, for example, have certainly yielded spectacular increases in the productivity of the actor and the musician.

Yet, while sporadic increases in labor output are possible and do occur in the personal services, it is nevertheless much more difficult to achieve regular and frequent increases in productivity than elsewhere in the economy. The techniques used today, for example, by the policeman in "pounding his beat," or those of the violinist or the master chef hardly differ from those employed by their counterparts a century ago. In how many lines of manufacturing can the same be said?

[4] Alan Peacock "Welfare Economics and Public Subsidies to the Arts," **The Manchester School of Economic and Social Studies,** (December, 1969).

2. Slow growth in productivity and the costs of services

Where real wages are low, the personal services are usually comparatively cheap. Anyone who travels to a less affluent country is impressed by the particularly low cost of servants and haircuts. Indeed, it has been suggested that the cost of a haircut relative to that of manufactured goods is a good rough and ready index of the state of development of an area. Similarly, the low cost of theater tickets in the unsubsidized theater in London relative to that in New York is no accident; it reflects, at least in part, the relative real wages in the two cities.

However, as productivity in the economy rises with the passage of time, the personal services find themselves at a growing cost disadvantage. The relationship is exhibited most clearly where wages follow the growth of productivity in manufacturing. In practice, where productivity in a firm or industry engaged in wage negotiations has been rising five per cent per year, it is hard to imagine a wage proposal by the union calling for less than a five per cent rate of increase. Moreover, as far as that industry is concerned, the cost effect of such a wage rise is exactly counterbalanced by the productivity gains. The hourly wage may rise five per cent, but so does the number of units of product per man, so that the labor cost per unit of output neither rises nor falls.

But for the economy as a whole that is not the end of the matter. The labor markets for the personal services and in manufacturing are not isolated from one another. If wages of policemen, teachers, or street cleaners fall significantly behind those in manufacturing, in a prosperous economy labor will simply move out of the former occupation and look for jobs in the latter. Scarcity of labor supply will force wages in the personal service upward, close behind those in the remainder of the economy. The evidence suggests that over longer periods wages in the personal services keep up with those paid elsewhere much more frequently than is sometimes believed.

Suppose then, to get back to our example, that because wages (and productivity) in manufacturing have been rising at an annual rate of 5 %, wages in the services are forced to increase at, say, 4 % per year. As was just observed, the wage rise in manufacturing will then not increase its labor costs. By contrast, if productivity in the services goes up, say, only 1 %, the more modest wage rise of 4 % will necessarily cause the costs of the services to increase some 3 per cent annually. Only one percentage point of the wage rise will have been absorbed by productivity increases. **More generally, we see that, in a sector of the economy such as the personal services, where productivity does not grow as rapidly as wages rise, the cost per unit of output must rise persistently and cumulatively over time.**

Of course, a 2 or 3 per cent differential in a given year does not amount to much. However, since the differential is continuing and cumulative, over a longer period it can become very substantial. In fact, with the passage of time, the arithmetic of compounding can produce spectacular results. It may prove helpful at this point if we follow through a hypothetical case to illustrate this whole process. Consider the history of two products: a personal service, say a haircut, and the other a manufactured good, say a fountain pen. Let us assume for simplicity that each is produced solely with labor and that in the initial year, it takes one man-hour to produce a haircut and one man-hour to produce a pen; so that a haircut and a pen have the same initial cost. If a man-hour of labor costs $1 in this first year, then the unit cost of each item will be $1. Let us suppose, however, that technical progress generates increases in the output of pens per man-hour at a rate of 3 % annually, while the annual rate of increase in haircuts per man-hour is only 1 %.[5] Finally, we postulate as earlier, that wages rise at the same rate as productivity in the production of pens, namely at 3 % per annum. Since unit cost is simply equal to the hourly wage divided by output per man-hour, we find that the cost per pen remains unchanged over time at $1: rising wages are at each step precisely offset by increased output per worker. In contrast, productivity increases in the provision of haircuts are insufficient to keep pace with the rising wages; as a result, the cost of a haircut increases steadily at 2 % annually (the difference between the rate of increase in wages and that of output per man-hour). While the cost of a pen remains at $1, the cost per haircut increases to $1.02 in year 2, to $1.22 by year 10, to $2.67 in year 20, and finally, **after the passage of a century, a haircut will cost more than seven times as much as a pen.**

The evidence in fact shows that such differentials between the rate of change of costs for many personal services and those in manufacturing have been with us for over a century, and that in recent decades they have in several important instances (such as the costs of education) been substantially larger than the differential in our preceding example. And this, we are convinced, has been a powerful force contributing to the growing fiscal distress of state and local governments throughout the United States and in other industrialized countries as well.

[5] These rates of increase in productivity are, incidentally, fairly realistic. A study of the barbering industry found that, over the period 1939 to 1963, output per man had increased at an average annual rate of 0.6 per cent. In contrast, from 1947 to 1965, output per man in manufacturing rose on average at 3.0 per cent annually. See Victor Fuchs, **The Service Economy,** New York: Columbia University Press, 1968, pp. 109, 51.

48

We should emphasize that while our illustration has assumed (fairly realistically) that wages constantly rise, increasing money wages really are not the source of the problem. So long as wages in the two sectors of the economy maintain approximate parity, whether they rise or fall, the **relative** cost of the personal services must increase in the manner described. Suppose money wages were to remain absolutely fixed over time. In that case in our example, the dollar cost of a haircut would actually decrease 1 per cent per year. But the cost of a pen would then fall 3 per cent per year, so that the annual 2 per cent differential rise in relative costs would remain.

In summary, **in an economy in which one sector of the economy persistently lags behind the rest in terms of rate of productivity growth, the products of that sector must invariably rise in cost relative to cost levels in the rest of the economy, and that rise will be persistent and cumulative.** This must be true so long as **relative** wages in the various sectors of the economy remain the same, and whether or not the overall level of wages is rising, falling or constant.

Thus, a slowing down of the rate of increase in money wages does not cure the cost problem of the personal services. Their difficulty, rather, is that with increasing productivity an hour of labor becomes more valuable in terms of the manufactured goods that it can turn out. In these circumstances it becomes more and more expensive in terms of the potential output of its labor elsewhere (what economists call its "opportunity cost") to continue to supply the service. The service, in short, is the victim of technological progress in other sectors of the economy, and its problems grow worse with the increased efficiency achieved elsewhere by innovation. Faster technological progress is no blessing for the laggards!

3. Rising costs and the supply of the personal services

With costs that are likely to rise cumulatively over the foreseeable future, continued supply of the personal services will obviously run into a variety of difficulties. However, the market mechanism and governmental decision-making processes are most unlikely to treat all services similarly. Depending upon political pressure and consumer responses to rising prices and incomes, some services will fare better than others. Already we can see examples of at least four different developments. First, some services have virtually disappeared from the market, or at least their volume has fallen drastically. Handmade furniture, butlers and full-time maids are growing increasingly unusual. The doctor's house calls are also largely gone. No doubt certain other personal services will follow this pattern.

Second, some services will not disappear, but as an offset to their rising costs, their quality will be allowed to deteriorate progressively. Dirtier streets, subways with increasing accident rates, larger classes in some schools, and shorter rehearsal periods for plays are all examples of this phenomenon. The reader will have little difficulty in supplying others.

Third, certain other services will be transformed, in whole or in part, into unpaid amateur activities. Handmade pottery and furniture are now mostly produced as hobbies. Shaving is an interesting example of a successful takeover by the nonprofessional.[6] In this case the change has inspired innovations which permit the amateur barber to provide a reasonably satisfactory substitute for the work of the professional.

[6] This example was pointed out by Professor Carolyn Bell. See her "Macroeconomics of Unbalanced Growth: Comment," **American Economic Review,** (September 1968), pp. 877—84.

Finally, there are the services, notably medicine, and perhaps education, for which the public has at least so far generally resisted a curtailment in supply or in quality. For this we have had to pay the price: expenditures have simply had to keep pace with the cumulatively rising costs. Everyone who has recently purchased either of these services in the United States knows all too well how painful these rising costs can be.

4. Employment in the service industries

In fact, as incomes have risen people have demanded more education and better medical treatment. Obviously this has led to even greater outlays on these services than their rising costs alone can explain. This expansion in demand, along with the innovation-resistant technology of the personal services, has led to another important phenomenon: a significant shift in the allocation of the economy's labor resources. With the disappearance of personal servants and other types of service activities and the growth of amateurism in others, one might perhaps expect a decline of the proportion of the labor force employed in the services. The facts indicate that precisely the opposite has occurred. Since World War II the labor force in the United States has risen by almost 30 per cent from 61 million in 1947 to over 84 million by 1969. Yet the number of persons employed in manufacturing and agriculture is little larger today than it was in 1947. The great bulk of the increase in employment has occurred in the services. This phenomenon has led Victor Fuchs to describe the United States as the world's first "Service Economy," the first country in which more than one-half of the labor force is employed in the provision of services. Where the service sector accounted for 40 % of employment in 1929, this had risen by 1967 to 55 %.

The analysis of this paper can help to explain this striking pattern of development. Suppose that, as the economy's real income rises, the public desires to maintain constant the proportion of the personal services in the market basket of goods and services that it consumes: that is, when the consumption of manufactured goods goes up 20 % it wishes to increase its educational training by 20 % as well. Then, with the quantity of labor required per unit of manufactured goods declining at a rate significantly more rapid than that in the services, there must be continuous reallocation of the labour force from manufacturing to the services. As it takes comparatively less and less time to produce the manufactures, to prevent a change in the relative outputs of the two types of products, more and more of the economy's labor force must go into the services. This appears to represent a reasonably accurate description of what has occurred in the United States in recent decades. After adjusting for the effects of price changes, Fuchs found that the share of total output in the economy originating in the service sector was about the same in 1965 as it was in 1929. But in spite of its relatively stable share of output, the service sector has, as noted earlier, absorbed a continually larger share of the labor force. "The major explanation for the shift of employment," Fuchs concludes, "is that output per man grew much more slowly in the service sector than in the other sectors."[7]

[7] Fuchs, p. 4. Fuchs suggests that, in addition to a slower rate of technological progress in the service sector, the more rapidly increase of output per man in industry is also attributable to a more rapid growth in physical capital per worker in industry than in the services, to a relative decline in the length of the working day in the service industries, and to a relatively growing reliance on more highly skilled workers in the industry sector. The differential in technological progress, according to Fuchs's estimates, accounts for about one-half of the difference in the rate of growth of output per man between the two sectors.

In particular, Fuchs's own estimates of the average annual increase in output per man by sector over the period 1929—1965 are:

Agriculture	3.4 %
Industry	2.2 %
Service	1.1 %

This pattern of development in which the service sector accounts for a growing share of employment over the time seems to characterize the experience of most other countries as well. Fuchs has found a similar expansion in service-sector employment over time among the western European countries; and, in a statistical study covering several countries at various points in time, discovered a strong positive correlation between the level of per capita income and the percentage of employment in the service sector. Similarly, Simon Kuznets, in a study of thirteen countries, finds for most a substantial increase over time in the share of the labor force employed in the production of services.[8] Thus, the phenomenon we are considering by no means appears to be confined to the United States. Rather, it seems to be a typical characteristic of economic growth.

One word of caution is in order here. The service sector, as defined for accounting purposes, includes a highly diverse group of public and private activities, including everything from education and health services to laundries, insurance companies, and auto-repair shops. This "promiscuous ensemble of the service industries," as Georg Stigler has called it, makes generalization rather precarious.[9] As one might expect, the experience among some service industries in terms of rates of productivity increase and changing levels of employment has been quite different from that of others. Nevertheless a number of studies of individual service industries do indicate quite clearly that many of the services normally associated closely with the quality of life do fit well the general description we have provided.

[8] **Modern Economic Growth,** New Haven: Yale University Press, 1966, Chapter 3.
[9] George Stigler, **Trends in Employment in the Service Industries,** Princeton University Press, 1956, p. 166.

5. Changes in the quality of services

It is sometimes objected that the preceding analysis misses an essential element: the improvement in quality of many of the services that has occurred over the years. Productivity changes in the services, it is suggested, have taken the form of better output rather than increased quantity per unit of labor input. Although the direction of change in the quality of education or in the adequacy of repair services is sometimes questioned, there seems little reason to doubt, for example, that an appendectomy today is a much better product than the corresponding operation in 1900. While today's patient may pay more (directly or via taxes) for a piece of surgery, he certainly gets more for his money.

There is little question about the validity of this argument and the significance of such improvements in quality for the welfare of the community. But it is equally important to recognize that they are largely irrelevant for the central point of our present discussion—the rising quantity of money required to procure the service. The fact is that neither a 1900 appendectomy nor a 1900 education is available today no matter which of them the consumer prefers. He must be prepared to lay out today's higher prices if he is to obtain the service at all.

It may be comforting to the harassed mayor of a city to be assured that his constituents' children are getting a better education for the rapidly rising quantity of money he must budget for public schools. But this does not necessarily help him to raise the requisite funds. The basic point is that the **relevant magnitude in the calculation of cost is the crude gross productivity figure, the number of persons served per hour of labor.** Improved quality, with all of the difficulties involved in its estimation, need not affect the growth rate in the unit cost of the service, the issue with which we are primarily concerned here.[10]

Yet, the point should not be overstated. Changes in product quality do affect the analysis in at least two ways. First, we noted before that rising costs tend to induce decreases in the quality of some services as a means to offset or conceal the effects on their prices. Obviously for those services for which improved techniques have managed to yield higher quality, the danger of quality deterioration is correspondingly smaller. Second, where quality rises sufficiently, society may actually be willing to reduce the quantity of a particular service that it acquires. If students were now able to learn in five years everything that they formerly absorbed in eight, then one might wish to consider a corresponding reduction in the number of years of schooling financed by the public sector. Yet such reductions in output have been proposed for few, if any, of those public services whose quality has patently been improved. As a result, their demands upon the public budget have continued to increase as rapidly as those of the public services whose product specifications seem not to have changed with the passage of time.

[10] It is, incidentally, by no means clear that difficulties in measuring the quantity or quality of output in the service sector have led to underestimates of rates of productivity increase for the services. Fuchs concludes that, "Although there are serious questions concerning the measurement of real output, it does not appear that the differential in (the rate of growth of) output per man is attributable to biases in the measure of output," **op. cit.**, p. 4.

6. Society's ability to finance the rising costs of services

Our analysis seems to suggest that there is no real cure for the cost disease of the services; one can hope for palliatives, for means to ease the pain, but not for any permanent remedy. That is true, but the conclusion is not as gloomy as it may sound. If the preceding analysis is correct, the disease, by its very nature, provides the means with which it can be treated.

The analysis in essence shows that the rising relative cost of the personal services is part of the price of economic progress, for it results from the cumulative **increases** in productivity in manufacturing (and agriculture). Underlying the problem is the fact that manufactures are becoming progressively **cheaper** to produce (in terms of labor), while productivity in the personal services remains unchanged or rises relatively slowly. Since in this process productivity does not decline in any sector of the economy, it follows as a truism that society's command over goods and services must be increasing. It can afford some more of everything because its productive powers are rising generally.

The very process that generates the rising costs of the services automatically provides income sufficient to permit society to continue to purchase them. Should it so choose, the community can obtain ever increasing quantities of the personal services despite the continuing increases in their prices. To do so, it only needs to shift each year some fraction of the labor force engaged in the manufacturing sector into the services. Taking an extreme example, suppose that output per man in manufacturing rises at 3 % per year while there is absolutely zero increase in productivity in the services. In this case, if 1 or 2 per cent of the manufacturing labor force were transferred annually to the production of services, then an ever increasing supply of both manufactured goods and services would be the result. The output of services would rise, because more labor is continually being devoted to their production; at the same time, manufactures would also increase since the decline in workers in this sector would be more than offset by the continuing rise in output per man. As we noted earlier, a process of this general type seems in fact to have characterized the historical experience of the advanced, industrialized countries. Society therefore possesses the means to maintain or even increase the output of personal services over time should it desire to do so.

7. The future of the personal services

We are certainly **not** entitled to conclude from all this that society should necessarily choose to increase the supply of each and everyone of the personal services. After all, we will undoubtedly assign different degrees of importance to different services. Some may be judged essential despite their increasing price, while others may not be considered worth their higher opportunity cost (i.e., the increased quantity of manufacturing goods that one must give up for the service). We do not want to suggest that the maintenance of the quantity and quality of any particular service is a matter of public virtue or social obligation. That is a matter that the public must decide for itself.

We are concerned, however, that some services will deteriorate and disappear, not because it has been decided that their price is more than they are worth, but simply through negligence and lack of foresight. When a service runs into financial problems, it is rarely threatened by a cataclysmic collapse. Rather, it undergoes gradual reductions in quality which are disguised as artfully as its suppliers can manage; the supply itself dries up bit by bit, each loss often passing by unnoticed, until it is realized too late that the product has disappeared. Three years ago there were two professional chamber orchestras in the United States; today there are none. Many attended their concerts, but few were present at the funeral rites. Perhaps they did not justify their cost and so their demise may have been appropriate, but it is quite clear that their fate was determined more by happenstance than by deliberation. For many years, there was an annual decline in the number of new plays produced by the Broadway theaters, but hardly anyone may have been aware of the change from year to year.

Professor Kahn has described such a process as "the tyranny of the small decision."[11] Each of the groups whose decisions afffect the final outcome is concerned only with its immediate problems— the current tax rate or the rising price of theater tickets. In selecting its course of action, the individual or single group is in no position to give substantial weight to the consequences for the community as a whole. Yet the fate of a service that is important to the community can be determined inadvertently as the more or less haphazard consequence of a myriad of small, myopic decisions.

The character of the budgetary process contributes substantially to the problem. The services with their constantly rising costs are particularly vulnerable to unconsidered budgetary restrictions made without understanding of the cost behavior that their technology forces upon them. It is only natural, when the cost of some activity doubles or trebles in a decade when the quality of its product seems to be declining and other prices are relatively stable, to feel that somehow waste and inefficiency must be at the root of the problem. This is particularly true in the public sector where the connection between services received and taxes paid is often only vaguely understood

[11] Alfred E. Kahn, "The Tyranny of Small Decisions," **Kyklos** (1966), pp. 23—46.

by the individual citizen. He naturally abhors the significant increases from year to year in his tax bill; since these tax monies support a wide variety of public services, it is often difficult to establish the link between his tax liability and the quantity and quality of particular public services. Thus, we often find the same individual or group resisting forcefully proposed increases in taxation, while at the next moment, bemoaning the lack of adequate public service. Unfortunately, this pattern of behavior, while perfectly understandable, is likely to produce a cumulative deterioration in the level and quality of many of the personal services.

A difficult educational process will be required to convince both those who construct the public budgets and the taxpayer that the rising cost of the public services is not necessarily a manifestation of mismanagement. Once we understand the nature of their cost structure, we can begin to calculate how much money will be required to maintain a particular service over the long run, and only then can we decide rationally whether it is worth the price. If, all things considered, it is determined that the service in question should not be permitted to deteriorate, then the necessary resources must be provided. Whatever its form, the supply of the requisite resources will entail a long-term budgetary commitment which implicitly takes cognizance of the fact that, because of the nature of its technology, the amount that is sufficient to finance a personal service today will be inadequate tomorrow, and the amount that is adequate tomorrow will not be enough the day after that.

Failure to understand and to provide for these rising costs must condemn the service to decay and perhaps even to extinction. As we have seen, we can expect the wealth of our society to grow rapidly enough to permit it to meet these cost increases. There is, therefore, no excuse for the failure to provide sufficient financing for those of the services which rational deliberation determines to be worth their cost.

[11]

INCOME AND SUBSTITUTION EFFECTS IN THE LINDER THEOREM *

WILLIAM J. BAUMOL

In his illuminating book Linder dispels some common illusions about leisure and, in particular, the prediction that its growth will constitute an increasing social problem. His observations lead to quite a different view — that for substantial groups leisure is becoming scarcer.

In an appendix he goes beyond this, showing formally that a rise in real wages ("productivity") will lead to a reallocation of time to the disadvantage of cultural and other time-consuming pursuits. His model is overly restrictive, and the argument requires curious assumptions such as linear homogeneity of the utility function. However, a modified formulation indicates clearly the range of applicability of Linder's hypothesis and ties the analysis more closely to standard choice theory. The results support Linder's conclusions and offer little comfort to the conventional view. They show that the substitution effect of a rise in real wages will decrease consumption of some good or service if the time needed to consume one dollar's worth of the item is greater than the average time used to consume a dollar's worth of all other commodities (in the proportions he consumes them). Thus, the substitution effect always works in the direction Linder predicts — rising "productivity" does decrease the demand for commodities whose consumption is expensive in time or inexpensive in money. As we become richer, we have less time for leisurely consumption and must become more efficient in getting rid of our money, buying more of those items that dispose of more cash per unit of time.

Later we will consider the income effect whose sign, as usual, is ambiguous. But first we offer a simple analysis of the substitution term.

* The author is most grateful to the National Science Foundation under whose grant the writing of this paper was supported.

1. THE MODIFIED LINDER THEOREM

Let x_1 = quantity of good 1 purchased
x_2 = the quantity purchased of a composite of all other goods
x_3 = quantity of labor time expended
p_1, p_2 = prices of goods 1, 2
w = wage rate
t_1, t_2 = time necessary to consume a unit of goods 1, 2.

Then we may take the individual's objective to be the maximization of his utility,

(1) $U = U(x_1, x_2, x_3)$,

subject to his money and his time budget constraints,[1]

(2) $p_1x_1 + p_2x_2 = M + wx_3$

(3) $t_1x_1 + t_2x_2 + x_3 = t^*$,

where M is nonlabor income and t^* is the total time available to him. Substituting (3) into (1), then multiplying (3) by w and adding it to (2), we are left to maximize

(1′) $U(x_1,x_2,x_3) = U(x_1,x_2,t^* - t_1x_1 - t_2x_2) = V(x_1, x_2)$,

subject to

(2′) $(p_1 + wt_1)x_1 + (p_2 + wt_2)x_2 = M + wt^*$.

This is now the Slutsky model, only with what, following Becker, we may call "time prices," $p_i + wt_i$, substituted for the money prices p_i. By the Slutsky theorem, after elimination of the income effect, $\partial x_1/\partial w$ will depend on the effect of w on relative time prices. That is, considering only the substitution effect, $\partial x_1/\partial w > 0$ if and only if an increase in w will *decrease* the time-price ratio,

$$\frac{p_1 + wt_1}{p_2 + wt_2} = \frac{p_1}{p_2}\,\frac{1 + wt_1/p_1}{1 + wt_2/p_2}.$$

Since a rise in w will decrease the last fraction if and only if $t_1/p_1 < t_2/p_2$, our result follows.[2]

This result is surely one of the most noteworthy products of the comparative statics technique. Despite its minimal assumptions about the consumer's predilections, the argument produces a result whose implications are profound. We have become used to compar-

1. The argument assumes that the p_i and t_i are fixed. However, it does not preclude the use of more or less close substitutes that differ from the commodity under discussion in price and required consumption time. That is, it leaves open the possibility that the individual will turn to less time-consuming substitutes as w rises.

2. Note that as w rises the consumer will *not* increase absolutely his consumption of a more expensive or less time-utilizing substitute, i, unless t_i/p_i is less than the average for his overall consumption.

ative statics arguments whose results are remarkable for their banality — a rise in excise taxes will tend to increase prices, or a rise in the price of a product is likely to reduce its demand. But the Linder Theorem, assuming only that consumption takes time as well as money [3] and that the consumer maximizes some vaguely defined utility function, yields a result that is perhaps contrary to conventional wisdom and is certainly far from obvious beforehand.

The fly in the ointment is the income effect that, as usual, precludes us from drawing a clear-cut conclusion. But as is also usually the case, there is good reason for the ambiguity.

2. The Role of the Income Effect

In the modified Linder model the reason that the income effect may offset the substitution effect is obvious enough. If time-consuming activities are not inferior goods, consumers will want more of them as their incomes rise. They can afford to expend more *money* on time-consuming activities even if rising pay scales increase their dollar opportunity costs.

This effect may seem to be more damaging than helpful to the Linder position. After all, the income effect of a rise in wages is likely to be substantial, unlike that of a change in the price of some minor item in the consumer's budget. With income effects substantial and leisure not likely to be an inferior good, it would appear that the demand for leisurely activities can be expected to grow. We are apparently not all that far away from the standard position.

There are, however, two important reservations. The first is a formal matter. In the Linder model there are two constraints. The one that really bites is the *time* constraint, not the money budget. If our individual had additional time, he could make more money, but that is prevented by the twenty-four-hour limit to his day. To paraphrase a more ancient discussion, in this model money income is really congealed time *and not vice versa.* Additional time will purchase more income, but additional income does not purchase more time.[4] The wage increase does ease the budget constraint, but does not loosen the constraint that really binds.

3. It also assumes away the possibility that the individual's employment offers him no option on hours of work or that consumption time is sometimes taken from periods that would otherwise be spent in boredom rather than genuine leisure.

4. Again this is an oversimplification. By spending money, one can save time. I can purchase in expensive shops instead of taking the time to go bargain hunting or hire someone to keep records for me that I would otherwise keep myself. But there are obvious limits to this sort of time saving unless

Whether for this reason or because the money-income effect is weak or because leisure activities really are inferior goods, observation suggests that for a large class of people the demand for leisurely activities does not rise with real income.[5] This is notably the case for persons with "responsible" positions. We academics need only look about us at our harried and harassed colleagues. It may be hard to explain to those outside the university that a six-hour teaching load really means something closer to a sixty-hour week, but the important point is that many of those sixty hours are spent *by choice*, particularly by those who do not need them to improve their academic positions. Among top executives, weekends are also likely to be the periods when one does the work that is prevented by everyday activities.

That these are the classes to which Linder's analysis applies most strongly is itself of significance. For it is these groups — the educated, the well-to-do, the professionals and management — from which the "culture consumers" are normally drawn. Theaters, orchestras, and museums derive the bulk of their audiences from here not only in the United States but, apparently in every other country in which the matter has been studied.[6]

3. Concluding Comment

We see then that the ambiguity of the sign of the income effect increases the richness of the Linder theorem. It can encompass those cases that fit the more usual hypothesis about ever-increasing amounts of uncommitted time and a corresponding rise in demands for leisurely activities.

But it indicates also that the activities that are often said to make for a gracious and rich existence — music, the theater, the dance, and fine cuisine — are under simultaneous attack from two directions. Earlier, W. G. Bowen and I had shown why the cost of such activities can be expected to grow cumulatively and persistently. Linder has now shown that for a rather independent reason

we can take all our pleasures vicariously by hiring others to carry out every one of our time-using consumption processes.

5. Note that I am relying here on no more than casual observation — the model itself seems to carry us no further. It is true that it can be used to show that both the income *and* substitution responses to a given rise in wage rate d_w fall with the level of w. However, it can be shown that the response to a fixed *percentage* rise in wage rate $d_w/_w$ need not tend to fall.

6. This includes a number of European countries in which the arts are heavily subsidized. For the case of Sweden, in which per capita subsidies of many of the arts are about as high as they are anywhere, see Swedish Ministry of Education and Cultural Affairs, 1970, pp. 24–25.

the demand for them may decline persistently, as it becomes more difficult for their traditional consumers to find the time in which to consume them. It is not for me to say whether the decimation of the fleets of transatlantic luxury liners is a net loss to society; however, their demise is easily explained. And other prospective victims of these forces are not difficult to identify.

PRINCETON AND NEW YORK UNIVERSITIES

[12]

performing arts. In the past two decades a substantial international literature on the economics of the arts has accumulated. Aside from the importance of the cultural contribution made by the arts, interest in the subject among economists has been elicited by some special attributes of the economics of the arts which have proved interesting analytically and whose analysis has had significant applications outside the field. Notable is the 'cost disease of the performing arts' which has been proposed as an explanation for the fact that, except in periods of rapid inflation, the costs of artistic activities almost universally rise (cumulatively) faster than any index of the general price level. Another major theoretical issue with which the literature has concerned itself is the grounds on which public sector funding of the arts can be justified.

ORGANIZATION AND FUNDING. The structure of the performance industry is similar in many of the industrialized countries. The largest enterprise in terms of budget and personnel is the opera, followed, in rank order, by the orchestra, theatre and dance. The theatres are the only group that contains a substantial profit seeking sector. All of the others, and many of the theatres as well, receive a substantial share of their incomes from government support and private philanthropy. The US, with its policy of tax exemptions, is probably the only country in which the share of private philanthropy is large, and there it exceeds the amount of government funding by a large margin. In many countries the bulk of such financing is provided by only a single agency, while in the US an arts organization whose application has been rejected by one funding source can usually turn to others for reconsideration.

The available statistical evidence suggests that demand for attendance is fairly income elastic but quite price inelastic, at least in the long run. This suggests that the widely espoused goal of diversity in audiences prevents ticket prices from rising more than they have, although fear that such rises will cause temporary but substantial declines in revenues and will reduce philanthropic or government support no doubt also plays a part.

In every country in which systematic audience studies have been carried out, the audience has been shown to be drawn from a very narrow range. It is far better educated than the average of the population, it has a far higher average income, it is somewhat older, and it includes a remarkably small proportion of blue-collar workers. Even free or highly subsidized performances affect this only marginally.

While total expenditures on ticket purchases have, of course, risen over the years, the pattern is modified substantially when corrected for changes in population, the price level and real incomes. Thus, in the US, the share of per capita disposable income devoted to admissions to artistic performances declined from about $0.15 out of every $100 in 1929 to about $0.05 in 1982. The latter figure has been virtually unchanged throughout the period since World War II.

THE COST DISEASE OF THE PERFORMING ARTS. One of the special features of the economics of the performing arts that seems to colour their cost structure is their 'cost disease'. This condemns the cost of live performance to rise at a rate persistently faster than that of a typical manufactured good. An illustration comparing the costs of watchmaking and of musical performance over the centuries shows the reason. There has been vast and continuing technical progress in watchmaking, but live performance benefits from no labour-saving innovations – it is still done the old-fashioned way. Toward the end of the 17th century a Swiss craftsman could produce about 12 watches per year. Three centuries later that same amount of labour produces over 1200 (non-quartz) watches. But a piece of music written three centuries ago by Purcell or Scarlatti takes exactly as many person hours to perform today as it did in 1685 and uses as much equipment.

These figures mean that while one has to work just about as many hours to pay for a ticket to an opera today as one would have in similar jobs 300 years ago, the cost of a watch or of any other manufactured good has plummeted, in terms of the labour time we must pay for it. In other words, because manufactured goods have benefited from technological advance year after year while live performances have not, almost every year theatre and concert tickets have become more and more expensive in comparison with the price of watches. This phenomenon has been called 'the cost disease of live performance'.

To facilitate comparison with the discussion of the cost structure of the mass media that follows, it is helpful to describe the cost disease formally. Let

y_{it} = output of product i in period t
x_{kit} = quantity of input k used in producing i
AC_{it} = average cost of i in period t
w_{kt} = (real) price of k in period t
$\pi_{it} = y_{it}/\Sigma w_{kt}x_{kit}$ = total factor productivity in output i
$*$ = rate of growth, i.e. for any function, $f(t)$
$f^* = \dot{f}/f$.

Then we have:

Proposition 1. Let y_{1t} and y_{2t} be two outputs produced by single product firms. Then, if $\pi^*_{1t} \leqslant r_1 < r_2 \leqslant \pi^*_{2t}$, so that output 1 may be called relatively 'stagnant' (and output 2 is relatively 'progressive'), the ratio of the average cost of output 1 to that of output 2, AC_{1t}/AC_{2t} will rise without limit.

Proof: By definition

$$AC_{1t}/AC_{2t} = \pi_{2t}/\pi_{1t}$$

so that

$$(AC_{1t}/AC_{2t})^* = \pi^*_{2t} - \pi^*_{1t} \geqslant r_2 - r_1. \qquad \text{Q.E.D.}$$

Here, of course, y_1 may be interpreted as the output of live performance and y_2 as the output of manufactured goods. It follows that the prices of manufactured goods can be expected to rise less quickly than those of concerts, dance or theatrical performances. Ticket prices must therefore rise faster than the economy's overall rate of inflation, since the latter is an average of the increases in the prices of all the economy's goods.

It is sometimes suggested that the mass media – film, radio, television and recording – can provide the cure for the cost disease, but recent analysis suggests that despite their sophisticated technology many of the mass media are in the long run vulnerable to essentially the same problem. As a matter of fact, the data indicate that the cost of cinema tickets and the cost per prime-time television hour have been rising at least as fast as the price of tickets to the commercial theatre. The explanation apparently lies in the structure of mass media production, which is made up of two basic components that are very different technologically. The first comprises preparation of material and the actual performance in front of the cameras, while the second is the transmission or filming.

Television broadcasting of new material requires these two elements in relatively fixed physical proportions – one hour of programming (with some flexibility in rehearsal time) must be accompanied by one hour of transmission for every one hour broadcast. However, since the first component of television is virtually identical with live performance on a theatre stage, there is just as little scope for technical change in the one as in the other, while the second component, on the other hand, is electronic and 'high tech' in character and constantly benefits from innovation.

Industries with this cost structure have been referred to as 'asymptotically stagnant'. The evolution of such an industry over time is characterized by an initial period of decline in total cost (in constant dollars) which *must* be followed by a period in which its costs begin to behave in a manner more and more similar to the live performing arts. The reason is that the cost of the highly technological component (transmission cost) will decline, or at least not rise as fast as the economy's inflation rate. At the same time, the cost of programming increases at a rate surpassing the rate of inflation.

If each year transmission costs decrease and programming expenses increase because of the cost disease that besets all live performance, eventually programming cost must begin to dominate the overall budget. Thereafter, total cost and programming cost must move closer and closer together until virtually the entire budget becomes a victim of the disease, with the stable technological costs too small a fragment of the whole to make a discernible difference.

These results are encompassed in the following propositions: *Proposition 2.* Suppose an activity, A, uses stagnant input x_1 and progressive input x_2 in fixed proportion v, so that $x_{2t} = vx_{1t}$. If w_{1t}, the unit price of x_{1t}, increases at a nonnegative rate no less than r_1 and w_{2t} increases at a rate no greater than r_2, where $r_2 < r_1$, then the share of total expenditure by A that is devoted to x_{1t} will approach the limit unity. Moreover, for any g such that $0 < g < 1$, there exists T such that for all $t > T$

$$1 \geqslant w_{1t}x_{1t}/(w_{1t}x_{1t} + w_{2t}x_{2t}) \geqslant 1 - g.$$

Proof: We are given

$$w_{1t} \geqslant a_1 e^{r_1 t}$$
$$w_{2t} \leqslant a_2 e^{r_2 t}, \qquad x_{2t} = vx_{1t}.$$

Then,

$$1 \leqslant \frac{w_{1t}x_{1t} + w_{2t}x_{2t}}{w_{1t}x_{1t}} = 1 + \frac{vw_{2t}}{w_{1t}} \leqslant 1 + (a_2/a_1)v\, e^{(r_2 - r_1)t}.$$

Q.E.D.

Along similar lines one can prove:
Proposition 3. Let A in Proposition 2 be supplied under conditions of perfect competition, and let its output, y_t satisfy $y_1 = ux_{1t}$ (u constant) and let its price be p_t. The p^* will approach that of the price of its stagnant input.
Corollary. The smaller the value of w_{2t}, i.e. the more progressive is the progressive input of A, the more rapidly will the behaviour of A's price approximate to that of its stagnant input.

GROUNDS FOR PUBLIC SUPPORT. Several economists have explored the grounds, if any, on which public support for the performing arts can be justified. They have examined all the usual criteria and found most of them weak. For example, income distribution concerns surely do not explain public financing of activities consumed largely by persons with incomes above the average. The beneficial externalities of attendance of the arts are not only difficult to document but are even hard to describe in the abstract. The same is true of the public good properties of performance. The best that has been done is to argue (1) that they have an 'option value' – even those who do not care to attend, themselves, may want to keep the arts alive for their grandchildren; and (2) that they constitute a partially public good through their part in the educational process and the (national) pride they engender even in those who do not attend themselves (or the embarrassment they avoid among those who do not want to belong to a nation of philistines). In the last analysis, it is simply argued that the arts deserve support because they are 'merit goods' (to use Musgrave's term). But that amounts to substitution of nomenclature for analysis. What the discussion comes down to is that the evidence suggests strongly that the public considers the arts worth supporting, and that in a democracy the public has the right to support what it wants to. Welfare theory has little to contribute here.

The cost disease analysis has been used by administrators throughout the world as justification for support but, of course, the fact that an activity is under financial pressure is, by itself, no valid reason for public subvention, as economic theory shows so clearly. However, if support is decided upon on other grounds, the cost disease analysis does legitimately help to give guidance on the amounts it will be appropriate to provide. It also warns us of the dangers of underfinancing as a result of what W.E. Oates has called 'fiscal illusion'. The cost disease implies that the cost of performance will rise faster than the general price level. If so, when government support for the arts increases only marginally faster than the general price level, politicians are likely to conclude that, though they have increased the real level of support, the quantity and quality of activity the public is getting for its money is declining. Mismanagement and waste are then likely to be blamed and budgets may be trimmed, on those grounds, below the level that is called for by the public's actual preferences.

WILLIAM J. BAUMOL

BIBLIOGRAPHY
Baumol, H. and Baumol, W.J. (eds) 1984. *Inflation and the Performing Arts.* New York: New York University Press.
Baumol, W.J. and Bowen, W.G. 1966. *Performing Arts: The Economic Dilemma.* New York: Twentieth Century Fund.
Blaug, M. (ed.) 1976. *The Economics of the Arts.* London: Martin Robertson.
Feld, A.L., O'Hare, M. and Schuster, J.M.D. 1983. *Patrons Despite Themselves: Taxpayers and Arts Policy.* New York: New York University Press.
Netzer, D. 1978. *The Subsidized Muse.* New York: Cambridge University Press.
Throsby, C.D. and Withers, G.A. 1979. *The Economics of the Performing Arts.* New York: St Martin's Press.

PART III

THE COST DISEASE IN THE ARTS: EMPIRICAL EVIDENCE

[13]

Trends in Over-all Cost of Performance

IN THIS chapter we discuss trends for the first time. Here we are primarily concerned with rates of change in the costs of a performance and their relationship to trends in the general price level. The behavior of these variables constitutes a direct test of our central analytic hypothesis, for, if it is valid, we would expect costs per performance to rise more rapidly than the over-all price level.

A tremendous data problem besets this sort of inquiry. If the data do not span a very considerable number of years, we run the risk of being misled by temporary aberrations that have little or no relation to the underlying trends. But statistical series which are continuous over a considerable time interval are difficult to find. Few organizations have long, continuous histories, and fewer still have preserved their early records. Fortunately, however, we have been able to obtain some remarkable sets of records spanning very long periods. These case histories enable us to form a clear picture of long-term trends and cyclical patterns in costs and prices for two major orchestras. The data are sufficient to enable us to report on a wide range of art forms.

Our investigation of costs has also permitted us to undertake a somewhat more ambitious analysis. We have sufficient information on the major orchestras to investigate how costs per unit (costs per concert) vary with the scale of activity. Knowledge of this relationship enables us to determine the extent to which performing organizations have available to them the economies of large-scale production: whether it is true for them, as it is for many industries, that an increase in output can yield a reduction in cost per unit of output.

This chapter shows very clearly that costs per performance have risen more rapidly than costs of other activities in the economy as a whole. This finding is documented in terms of several long-period case histories, in terms of the different stages of the business cycle, and for all organizations for which we have been able to assemble postwar data. The detailed discussion in the chapter will be of interest primarily to those readers who are especially concerned with historical relationships and wish to know precisely what the record shows.

Some Evidence on Cost in the British Theater

There is still extant a set of 21 account books for the Drury Lane and Covent Garden Theatres in London which span the period 1740–1775.[1] These are the earliest usable data found, and they permit a crude comparison between costs for that period and current costs on the London stage. In interpreting our results it should be recognized that such comparisons involve two difficulties. First, the scale of activity has changed: length of season today is not the same as it was in the 1700's. This source of error can be corrected, at least to some extent, by dealing with cost per performance instead of cost per year or season. Second, there have probably been changes in the elaborateness and quality of production which also influence costs. Unfortunately, as we have no way to measure these changes, we can do little to allow for them. Historical records may shed some light on qualitative changes, but this is a problem which will plague us throughout the chapter.

To determine cost trends for the London theater, we calculated the average cost per performance in the Drury Lane over the five year period 1771–72 through 1775–76 and the 1963–64 cost per performance of the present Royal Shakespeare Theatre. The earlier figure came to £157 and the more recent figure was £2,139.[2] Comparing them, we conclude that costs per performance have risen

[1] These records are tabulated in Stone, pp. ccxxxiv–ccxxxv.

[2] Calculated by taking 1/8 of the total weekly expenditure at the Royal Shakespeare, there being 8 performances per week.

some 13.6 times over this period, which is the same as saying that there has been an average annual rate of increase of 1.4 per cent compounded.

The key issue, of course, is whether this rate of increase in costs is greater or less than the rate of increase of prices in general. Thanks to the efforts of two British economists, there is available a price index which can be used to answer this question.[3] Over the period 1773–1964 we find that the price level rose to about 6.2 times its initial level; that is, prices grew at a compound rate of about 0.9 per cent per year. Thus, the average annual rate of increase in costs per performance was nearly 60 per cent greater than that in prices, and the cost per performance over the period as a whole went up more than twice as much as the price level.

One may ask whether qualitative changes in the theater between the two periods can account for this difference — whether theatrical costs might have risen much more slowly if the two companies had been more similar in their operations. An examination of the facts suggests the contrary. During the earlier period, although contemporary dress was frequently worn, costumes and scenery were quite expensive and elaborate.[4] More telling is the fact that at the Drury Lane Theatre at that time some 51 different full-length plays and 25 different "afterpieces" seem to have been performed each season, and many of these were new productions.[5] It is hard to believe that any contemporary theater could operate on this scale without a substantial rise in its costs.

[3] For our price index we use the index of a "composite unit of consumables" constructed by E. H. Phelps Brown and Sheila V. Hopkins for the years 1260 to 1954. (See their "Seven Centuries of the Prices of Consumables, Compared with Builders' Wage-Rates," in *Essays in Economic History*, Vol. II, edited by E. M. Carus-Wilson, Edward Arnold Ltd., London, 1962, pp. 179–96.) Their index is based on 1451–1475 = 100, and for the years between 1771 and 1776 its median value is 835. In the last year of their index, 1954, the value is 3,825. We projected this value forward to 1964 by assuming that it increased at the same rate over this recent period as the official retail price index, which rose from 125 in 1954 (1950 = 100) to 169 in 1964. (See United Kingdom, Ministry of Labor, *Statistics on Incomes, Prices, Employment, and Production*, No. 13, June 1965.) This gives us a projected value for the Phelps Brown–Hopkins index of 5,174 for 1964.

[4] Stone, p. clx ff.

[5] Stone, p. clxii ff.

Continuous Histories:
The New York Philharmonic and Cincinnati Orchestras

So far we have compared costs at two distinct points in time and for two different organizations whose similarity is not entirely clear. Analysis of year-to-year changes in a single organization's costs over a long period of time is a much more satisfactory procedure, and, through the cooperation of the managements of the New York Philharmonic and Cincinnati Symphony Orchestras, this is possible.

The New York Philharmonic was founded in 1842 and is the oldest orchestra in this country. From its extraordinary collection of historical materials we were able to compile financial data for 100 of the 122 years of its existence. The gaps in our data correspond to the periods 1876–1883, 1909–1914 and 1920–1927, at least two of which were somewhat troubled periods in the history of the orchestra.

Our other long series describes the Cincinnati Orchestra from 1920 through 1964. Though the Cincinnati data do not go back as far as those for the New York Philharmonic, they are continuous over the period of the 1920's when there is a serious gap in the Philharmonic records. The existence of this second, very detailed case history lessens the danger of our being misled by some quirk in the history of the New York Philharmonic.

The expenditures of the New York Philharmonic amounted to less than $3,000 in 1850 as compared with its total outlay of roughly $3 million in 1965–66. It was then composed of 64 musicians — about three fifths of its current membership — and was organized as a cooperative.[6] Figure VIII–1 summarizes graphically the total expenditures of the orchestra over the entire period, and shows that its growth was very steady despite some relatively brief but violent fluctuations.[7] This graph, like most in this chapter, is drawn on a semi-logarithmic scale. It will be recalled from the discussion of this device in the preceding chapter that

[6] Some of the flavor of the early operations of the orchestra is conveyed by the financial statement for the year 1850, reprinted in Appendix Table VIII–A.

[7] There are a number of accounts of the history of the New York Philharmonic: Krehbiel, Erskine, and Mueller (pp. 37–69). On the history of the Cincinnati Orchestra see Mueller, pp. 113–22.

FIGURE VIII–1

NEW YORK PHILHARMONIC: TOTAL EXPENDITURES, 1843–1964

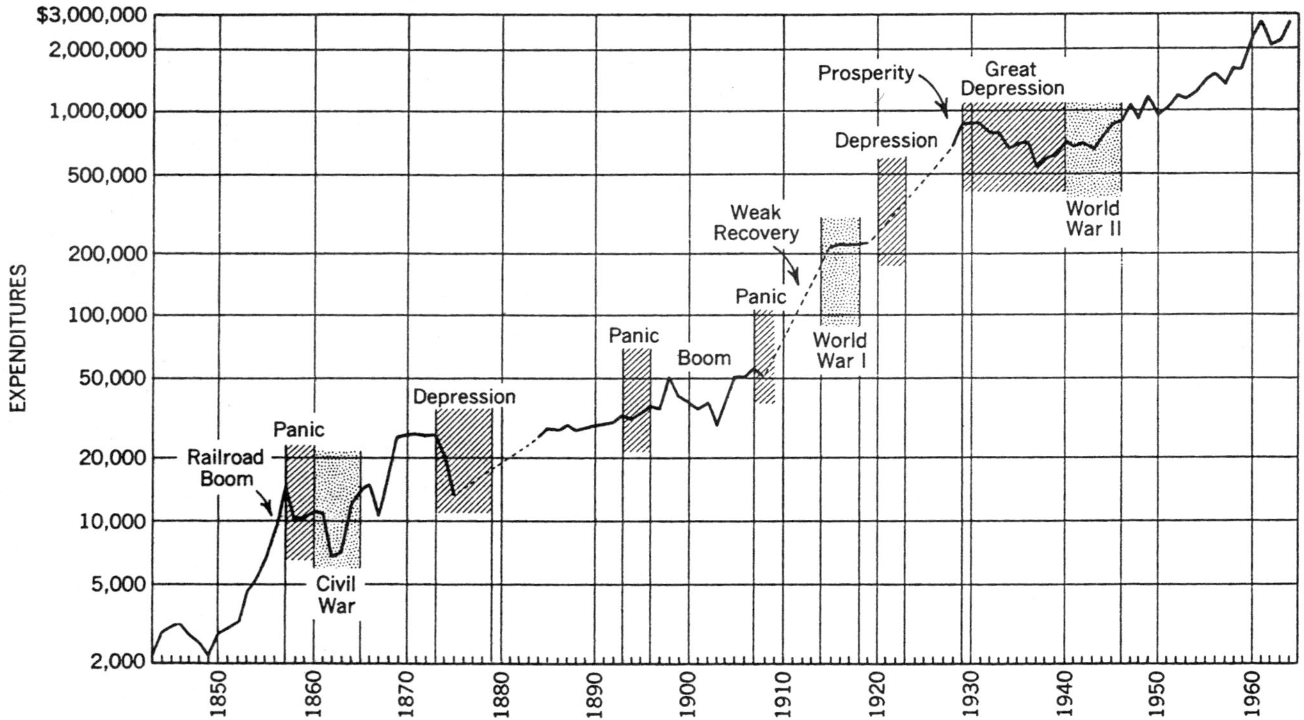

In this and the following graphs the years shown represent the end years of seasons; 1954, for example, refers to the season 1953–54.

on a scale of this kind a *constant* compound rate of growth will yield a graph which is a straight line. Thus, the fact that the graph in Figure VIII–1 is a fairly good approximation of a straight line (short-period variations aside) attests to the steadiness of the long-term growth in expenditures of the Philharmonic.

Specifically, between the terminal years 1843 and 1964 expenditures rose at a compound annual rate of 6.1 per cent. Part of this very rapid growth in outlay is a result of the increase in the number of concerts per year (from 4 performances in 1843 to 183 in 1964), and we must, therefore, turn once again to expenditure per performance to obtain a series capable of indicating the rise in cost of a given amount of activity.

Figure VIII–2 depicts the history of expenditures per concert and the course of the wholesale price index.[8] (Cincinnati Orchestra expenditures per concert are also shown on this graph, but they will be ignored for the moment.)

It will be noted that while the two graphs start out at about the same level, the cost per concert graph slopes upward much more sharply than the wholesale price line. In interpreting the magnitude of this differential rate of increase, it must constantly be remembered that a semi-logarithmic scale compresses absolute differences as we move to points higher up on the graph. Had the diagram been drawn on an ordinary graph scale, the widening gap between the cost per concert and the wholesale price index would have shown up much more sharply. The extent of this differential in rates of increase can be brought out most clearly by calculating numerical growth rates.

Considering first the longest period for which data are available (1843–1964), we find that costs per concert for the New York Philharmonic grew at an annual rate of 2.5 per cent per year over the entire period, while the price index went up only 1.0 per cent per year. (These growth rates, and others discussed in the next two sections, are summarized in Table VIII–1.) This difference is sig-

[8] For our purpose the wholesale price index seemed more appropriate than the consumer price index. The reasons for this, the consequences if we had used a consumer price index in our calculations and some possible sources of bias in our calculations are discussed in Appendix VIII–1.

nificant. Over 121 years, the length of our period, an amount increasing at 2.5 per cent is multiplied twentyfold by compounding, whereas an amount increasing at a 1 per cent growth rate merely quadruples. In other words, over our 121 year period the cost of a New York Philharmonic concert rose five times as much as the wholesale price index.

Between 1890 and 1964 cost per concert grew at a remarkably steady rate of 2.5 per cent per year, while the wholesale price index, after a long period of decline (1865–1887) rose at a rate of 1.6 per cent.

If we start our long-term comparison from 1920 we are also able to include the Cincinnati figures.[9] Again the disparity between the rate of increase of orchestral costs and wholesale prices is clear and considerable. The annual growth rate for the Philharmonic was 3.9 per cent; for Cincinnati, 2.2 per cent; and for wholesale prices, only 0.4 per cent.

In appraising these growth rates it would be misleading to ignore changes in the quality of the New York Philharmonic, to which some of the rapid rise in its cost per concert must undoubtedly be ascribed. Probably throughout its early history and certainly at the turn of the century, because of its continued adherence to what Mueller describes as "the obsolete system of cooperative organization,"[10] it was a thoroughly second-rate enterprise. Some of the performers were poorly qualified, and all were inadequately disciplined and rehearsed. As late as World War I, "The Philharmonic could not escape odious comparison with its sister orchestras."[11] It must have been expensive to turn a mediocre orchestra into the outstanding organization it subsequently became. As a result, for our purposes, we must discount some of the high rate of increase in cost per concert shown in our graphs, treating it not as a manifestation of the technology of performing organizations in

[9] We use 1920 only because that is when our Cincinnati figures began. It is not a good base year, since it came just at the end of a period of sharp wartime inflation, which affected wholesale prices more than orchestral costs.

[10] It is noteworthy that the four London orchestras are all currently operating as cooperatives.

[11] Mueller, p. 54. On problems of quality in the Philharmonic at the turn of the century see Mueller, pp. 46–51.

FIGURE VIII–2

NEW YORK PHILHARMONIC AND CINCINNATI ORCHESTRAS: EXPENDITURES PER CONCERT AND THE WHOLESALE PRICE INDEX, 1843–1964

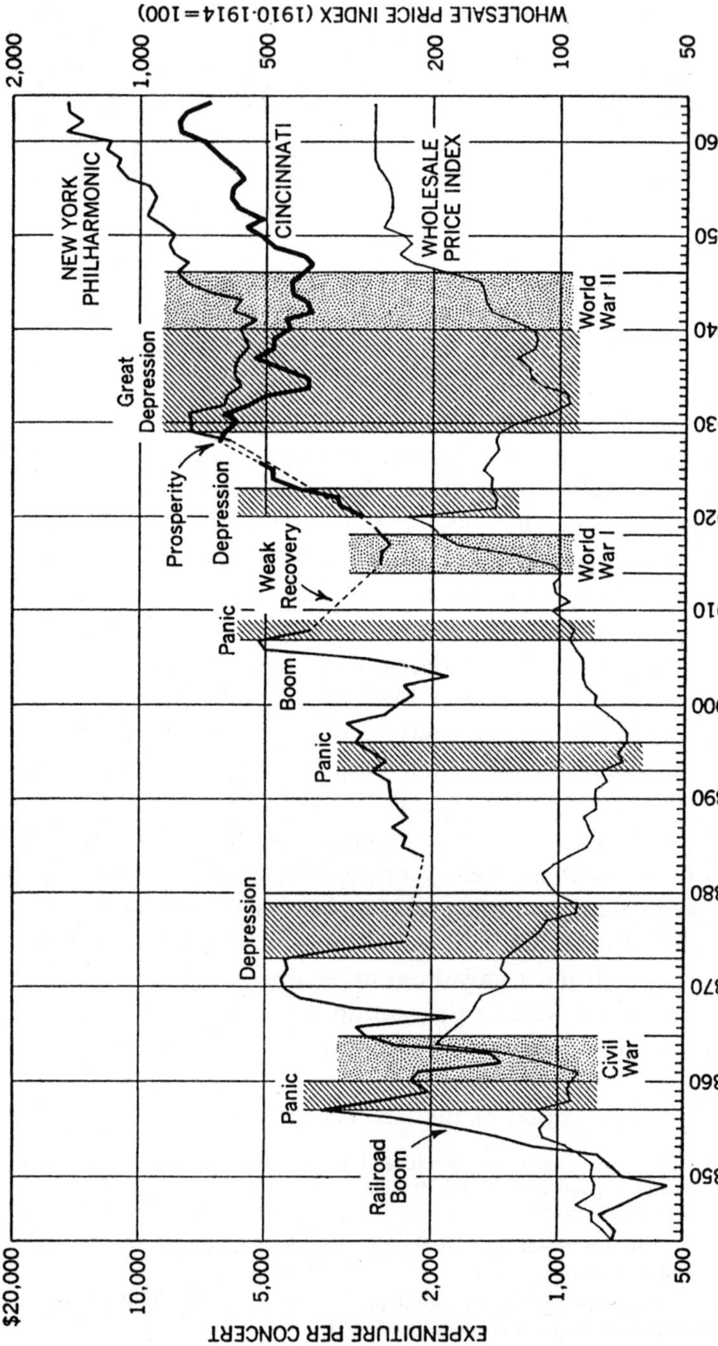

188

(Notes on opposite page)

general, but as a result, in part, of the peculiar history of this particular group.[12]

Prosperity, Depression and Wartime Inflation

Long-period trends, by definition, are mute with regard to the relation between fluctuations in economic activity and variations in orchestral costs. Yet to understand the economics of the performing arts it is important to see how the fortunes of an arts organization are affected by prosperity and depression, by war and inflation. Furthermore, only by relating the history of orchestral costs to contemporary economic circumstances can we tell whether the observed long-period differences in the growth of costs and general prices are an accident of the years chosen for comparison or whether they really reflect underlying economic phenomena. The length of the time series at our disposal makes this kind of cyclical analysis possible.

Our historic period encompasses the Civil War and the two World Wars. During each of the corresponding periods of wartime inflation the data go in the opposite direction from that predicted by our hypothesis — in each case the price level rose more rapidly

[12] It should be noted that changes in the nature of an orchestra's operations can bias our cost per concert growth rate downward as well as upward, depending on the direction of change and the base year used. For example, the "true" rate of increase in the costs of a given concert of the Cincinnati Orchestra between 1931 and 1964 is surely understated by comparing costs in 1931, the year in which Fritz Reiner left, and 1964. During most of the 1920's Reiner was conductor of the orchestra, and he apparently insisted on such exacting standards that the costs of the Cincinnati Orchestra almost equaled those of the New York Philharmonic. And this was at the time that Toscanini, with his reportedly astronomic salary and demanding rehearsal requirements, had pushed New York's costs to an extraordinary level!

Notes to Figure VIII–2

Between 1884 and 1905 it was customary for the Philharmonic to put on an equal number of regular concerts and public rehearsals (e.g., 6 of each in 1884 and 9 of each in 1905). Apparently, fees were collected for attendance at the latter. For this reason, and because it is difficult to separate these performances and their associated costs from the regular performances of the group, we have counted these rehearsals as part of the total number of concerts. Since public rehearsals are not mentioned after 1906, there is some question as to the validity of the segment of the graph corresponding to the period when the practice changed. Data for this graph were obtained from records of the two organizations; on the derivation of the wholesale price index see the notes to Table VIII–1.

TABLE VIII–1

Trends in Expenditures Per Concert (two major orchestras) and in the Wholesale Price Index, Selected Periods, 1843–1964

Time Period	Average Annual Percentage Increase (compound rate)[a] — Expenditures per Concert: New York Philharmonic	Expenditures per Concert: Cincinnati Symphony Orchestra	Wholesale Price Index
Long-Period Comparisons:			
1843–1964	2.5		1.0
1890–1964	2.5		1.6
1920–1964[b]	3.9	2.2	0.4
Wartime Inflations:			
Civil War: 1861–1864[c]	27.0		30.0
World War I: 1915–1919	0.8		18.8
World War II: 1940–1948	4.5	–0.9	9.7
Depressions:			
1857–1860	–15.2		–5.7
1893–1897	1.1		–3.4
1920–1921	n.a.	11.0	–37.0
1929–1932 (1931–1934)[d]	–9.1	–14.7	–32.0
1929–1940	–2.3	–3.4	–17.4
"Good Times":			
1843–1857	12.1		2.8
1897–1905[e]	–0.4		3.5
1922–1928	n.a.	10.9	0.0
1948–1964	3.8	4.0	1.5

SOURCE: Orchestra expenditures per concert were calculated from data generously made available by the respective orchestras. The source of our wholesale price index for the years 1843–1951 is U. S. Bureau of the Census, *Historical Statistics of the United States, Colonial Times to 1957*, Washington, D. C., 1960, Chapter E, esp. pp. 102–3, 115–17. We use the "all commodities" series. The original source of the figures for 1843 to 1890 is George F. Warren and Frank A. Pearson, *Prices* (John Wiley and Sons, New York, 1933). The Warren-Pearson index is ideal for our purposes because it was intended to correspond with the Bureau of Labor Statistics (BLS) index, which is the primary source of data for years 1890 on. Also, the Warren-Pearson index is based mainly on New York City prices, which is fortunate since we wish to compare this series with costs and prices for the New York Philharmonic. The BLS series from 1890 to 1951 (*op. cit.*, pp. 116–17) uses

than cost per concert. Only during the Civil War did orchestral costs come close to keeping up with prices. During World War I the wholesale price index rose 18.8 per cent per year, almost doubling between 1915 and 1919, while orchestral costs hardly increased at all. During World War II and its inflationary aftermath, wholesale prices went up almost 10 per cent per year, while costs per concert of the Philharmonic rose at a rate of 4.5 per cent. There was an absolute decline in the cost per concert of the Cincinnati Orchestra, much of which can be ascribed to the fact that it increased the number of its performances sharply during this period and so reaped substantial economies of larger-scale operation.

Thus, the prediction of our basic analysis is wrong — consistently wrong — for periods of wartime inflation. There are several

Notes to Table VIII–1 continued

1926 = 100 as its base, and in order to have one continuous series we recalculated these numbers using the Warren-Pearson base period of 1910–1914 = 100. (For 1890 the Warren–Pearson index is 82 while the BLS index, with 1926 = 100, is 56.2; hence, the BLS index can be put on the Warren–Pearson base of 1910–1914 = 100 by multiplying each number by 82/56.2.) The original source of the BLS figures for years 1952–1964 is the *Economic Report of the President*, January 1965. Since this current series uses a base of 1957–1959 = 100, it was necessary to put it on the 1910–1914 = 100 base in a manner analogous to that used to transform the 1890–1951 series.

[a] Calculated on the basis of terminal years only, except that the 1964 figure for Cincinnati is the mean of the figures for 1962, 1963 and 1964; the atypical nature of the 1964 Cincinnati observation would have distorted growth rates calculated by the terminal year method.

[b] The New York Philharmonic rate applies to the period 1919–1964 because no figure was available for 1920.

[c] The New York Philharmonic growth rate is for the period 1862–1865 rather than 1861–1864. We have a choice here, because the 1862 orchestra figure is actually for the season 1861–62; and, as Figure VIII–2 shows, it is the 1862–65 period which corresponds most closely to the behavior of the wholesale price index between 1861 and 1864.

[d] Whereas the decline in the wholesale price index can be dated from 1929, the decline in costs per concert for both of our orchestras did not start until 1931. We have, therefore, calculated our "sharp" rate of decline for the orchestras from 1931 to 1934, this being the period analogous to 1929–1932 for the wholesale price index.

[e] We end this period in 1905 because, beginning in 1906, the method of counting New York Philharmonic concerts may have changed. (See the note to Figure VIII–2.)

possible explanations for this pattern. First, patrons may be less inclined to support their orchestras during wartime, and expenditures may be held down correspondingly; it might seem unpatriotic to increase orchestral expenditures markedly during a time of national crisis. Second, earnings in most salaried occupations are notoriously slow to respond to inflationary or deflationary conditions — they are "sticky" — and it may well be that the behavior of musicians' salaries during sharp inflations conforms to this pattern. This possibility will be examined in some detail in the next chapter when we analyze trends in the salaries of performers. Still a third possibility is that in wartime there tend to be shortages of many of the commodities represented in the wholesale price index, and the pressure of excess demand produces sharp increases in the prices of these commodities. Whatever the reasons, the plain fact is that during wartime inflations orchestral costs have lagged behind the wholesale price index, and the consistency of the pattern suggests that our observations do not represent mere historical accident.

Looking next at depressions, there are four periods of "hard times" covered by our data — 1857–1860, 1893–1897, 1920–1921 and 1929–1940 — and with one exception they tell a consistent story which certainly *is* in line with our hypothesis. The exceptional period is the first, the pre-Civil War Panic of 1857–1860, when the wholesale price index fell at a rate of nearly 6 per cent per year but cost per concert fell almost three times as rapidly.[13]

[13] Here we must rely on an *ad hoc* explanation. The 1856–57 season was extraordinarily successful, with receipts more than 50 per cent higher than in any previous year and much higher than in any year for nearly a decade to come. That season was the culmination of nearly ten years of sharply rising orchestral income. In 1857–58 receipts fell slightly below the amount which had prevailed in 1855–56, and there they remained for several years. As a result, payments to musicians, which were determined residually under the cooperative system, also declined. (An important general point to be noted here is that our cost figures are highly dependent on demand conditions, because musicians' incomes were determined by what was left over from orchestral receipts after payment of other expenses. But all other cost data for the performing arts share this characteristic to a degree. For example, any arts organization tends to trim its costs when its income falls. In this respect, then, all of our cost data may be considered impure, and any test of our hypotheses in which we use these figures is correspondingly imperfect.) If we look at the change in costs between 1856–57 and 1857–58 alone, what may

However, this pattern was reversed during our next major depression, the Panic of 1893 (and the longer depression period of 1888–1897).[14] Cost per concert continued to rise despite a substantial rate of decline in the wholesale price index. We come next to the brief period of depression following World War I. There is a gap here in the Philharmonic data, but we do have Cincinnati figures. Between 1920 and 1921, while the wholesale price index fell 37 per cent, the Cincinnati's cost per concert went up about 11 per cent. The great depression of the 1930's is the one slump for which we have very good orchestral data. These show a clear pattern. Costs per concert declined for both orchestras, whether we include in our calculation only the initial period of the greatest depression or take into account the entire decade of the 1930's. But for neither orchestra in neither period was the decline anywhere near so precipitous as the fall in wholesale prices.

Thus, with the exception of the very special case of the 1850's, every depression seems to have shown a pattern consistent with our analysis. Cost per concert either rose despite a falling whole-

from a longer viewpoint be regarded merely as a leveling off, looks like a precipitous drop. In addition, in 1858–59 the Philharmonic began an eight year period in which it performed five concerts per season, having offered only four concerts during each of the preceding fifteen years. Since there was no corresponding increase in orchestral outlays, this additional concert automatically caused a 20 per cent drop in expenditure *per concert*. Finally, in 1858–59 the Philharmonic moved back from the large and apparently expensive Academy of Music to Niblo's Garden. Together, these three facts explain the extraordinary drop in expenditure during the depression period of 1857–60 — a fall more rapid than that in the price level. (See Krehbiel, pp. 115–17.)

[14] It is unfortunate that our series spans only the first three years of the 1873–1879 slump. While during these years expenditure per concert dropped precipitously, this was the result of a very special set of adverse circumstances in the history of the Philharmonic.

In 1867 R. Ogden Doremus, Professor of Chemistry at New York University, accepted the presidency of the Philharmonic on the condition that membership in the orchestra be increased to 100 performers and that it hire prominent soloists (Mueller, p. 43). This caused a near doubling in cost per concert, at which level the orchestra continued to operate through 1873. At this point, however, the Philharmonic seems to have run into deep trouble, partly because of energetic competition from various sources.

Our data, consequently, show a precipitous drop in cost per concert during the next two years, and then the figures disappear altogether. It is hardly surprising that the two years for which figures exist exhibit a decrease in orchestral costs greater than the fall in wholesale prices.

sale price level, or declined less rapidly than the level of prices. In other words, *cost per concert rose relative to wholesale prices* during each of these periods.

Finally, we look at the prosperous peacetime periods in our history. Here again there is one exceptional case — the period 1897–1905 when cost per concert for the New York Philharmonic fell even though the price level was rising.[15] But during every other period of peacetime prosperity for which we have figures, cost per concert rose substantially more than the price level. This is true of the "railroad boom" of the 1850's when the annual rate of increase in orchestral costs was more than four times as high as that in wholesale prices. And it is true of the 1920's. At Cincinnati costs per concert rose nearly 11 per cent per year compounded, while wholesale prices remained virtually constant.[16]

The final prosperous period covered by our orchestral series is the interval from the end of World War II to the present. The evidence from this period is, of course, most directly applicable to the current financial circumstances of performing arts organizations, and we shall presently analyze the available data. Here it will suffice to note that once again cost per concert for both orchestras increased far more rapidly than the wholesale price index.[17]

[15] This is easily explained, since this period marked the final collapse of the old cooperative orchestra just before its reorganization under Gustav Mahler in 1909. Moreover, the data for this period are rather questionable, for it is somewhere in this interval that the paid public rehearsal, which we find so difficult to classify, seems to have been abandoned.

[16] This sharp rate of increase in orchestral costs may be ascribable in part to Fritz Reiner's exacting standards. Unfortunately, we lack annual observations for the New York Philharmonic during this period. However, if we calculate the growth rate of the Philharmonic's costs per concert between 1919 and 1928 — years for which we have figures — we obtain a rate of 10.2 per cent per year, a rate of increase almost exactly as high as that for the Cincinnati Orchestra. This is probably a consequence, in part, of the demanding requirements of Toscanini, who took over the baton toward the end of the decade. Note also another curious coincidence — the fact that in both orchestras expenditures per concert reached a peak in 1929, fell in 1930, and rose again to a higher peak in 1931 before embarking on a protracted decline. (See Figure VIII–2.)

[17] Cost per concert rose 3.8 per cent per year for the New York Philharmonic and 4.0 per cent for the Cincinnati Orchestra between 1948 and 1964, while the wholesale price index rose 1.5 per cent per year. If we calculate the or-

Trends in Costs on Broadway

Unfortunately, we have no continuous data series for the Broadway theater because of the absence of permanent theatrical companies. Hence we must do what we can with isolated figures assembled from a variety of sources.

The pattern, however, is unmistakable. Costs rose much more rapidly than the wholesale price index in every period for which we have figures. The single exception is the decade encompassing World War II: between 1940 and 1950 the price index went up 7.3 per cent per year, while Broadway's weekly running costs increased only 1.4 per cent per year and its production costs rose by 6.7 per cent per year. It is noteworthy that this period of wartime inflation is the same exception that we found in the orchestral data, and the explanations offered there may also apply to the Broadway theater.

Table VIII–2, which summarizes our Broadway figures, shows another curious phenomenon — production costs seem consistently to have gone up more rapidly than nightly running costs. This interesting fact, which was first noticed by Moore, will be discussed in the next chapter when we consider the components of the general cost increases in the performing arts.

The Postwar Evidence in More Detail

The period since World War II is, of course, of greatest current interest, and for this interval we have far more extensive data. These are summarized in Figures VIII–3 and VIII–4 and Table VIII–3.

Our most reliable figures are once again orchestral data. For this period we need no longer rely on two isolated case studies; thanks to the managers of the major orchestras, we have at our disposal time series for 23 of the majors. For reasons explained in Appendix

chestra growth rates by fitting a trend line to the annual observations rather than just using terminal years, we obtain slightly higher growth rates — 4.0 per cent and 4.2 per cent, respectively. Moreover, the rate of growth per concert was very steady, as shown by the R^2 of .98 for the Philharmonic and .90 for Cincinnati, where an R^2 of 1.00 means absolutely steady growth.

TABLE VIII–2

Growth in Broadway Costs and in the Wholesale Price Index, Selected Periods, 1913–1961

Time Period	Average Annual Percentage Increase (compound rate): Broadway Costs	Average Annual Percentage Increase (compound rate): Wholesale Price Index
1913–1928:		
"Misleading Lady" — production costs	5.3	2.2
Over-all estimate — production and running costs	5.1–8.2	
1934–1952:		
"Children's Hour" — production costs	12.9	4.7
1928–1940:		
Production costs	4.1	1.8
Weekly running costs	1.3	
1940–1950:		
Production costs	6.7	7.3
Weekly running costs	1.4	
1950–1961:		
Production costs	6.3	1.4
Weekly running costs	5.5	

SOURCE: For wholesale price index, see Table VIII–1. The growth rates for Broadway costs were calculated from several sources, in the manner explained in that table. The 1913–1928 "Misleading Lady" production costs were originally calculated by Bernheim (p. 204), and were also used by Poggi. Bernheim compared the actual costs of the 1913 production with a detailed estimate of what the production costs would have been in the 1928–29 season had the standards of the 1913 production been duplicated. Poggi made the over-all estimate that production and operating costs "more than doubled but less than tripled" between 1914 and 1928. Our average annual growth rates are equivalent to this estimate of the over-all percentage change.

The 1934–1952 estimate for "Children's Hour" comes from a paper prepared by Norris Houghton for the Rockefeller Brothers Fund study. Houghton reported that when Herman Shulman presented the "Children's Hour" in 1934 it cost $6,000 to open; when Kermit Bloomgarten revived the play eighteen years later with the same physical requirements and a cast of the same size it cost $60,000.

The estimates for the remaining periods, 1928–1940, 1940–1950, 1950–1961, come from Moore (text Table 5 and Appendix Table A–9). Moore presents only "deflated" figures; we multiplied these by the appropriate price index values in order to restore them to current dollar values. Moore's original sources are explained in detail in his manuscript; it suffices here to note that he relied heavily on Bernheim and on information collected by the League of New York Theatres.

III–2, most of our calculations are conducted in terms of a subgroup which we call our "basic eleven." For this set of eleven orchestras, costs per performance rose at an average rate of 3.2 per cent per year from 1947 to 1964.[18]

We also have detailed information about the finances of the Metropolitan Opera, obtained with the generous assistance of its management. The Metropolitan's expenditure per performance, plotted in Figure VIII–3, increased at an average annual rate of 4.4 per cent. This rate of increase was somewhat greater than that for the orchestras, and was extremely steady ($R^2 = .96$), though an acceleration can be observed between 1961 and 1963. It should be recognized that 4.4 per cent is a very rapid rate of compound growth. It means a doubling every 16 years, so that costs per performance at the Metropolitan at the end of 1964 were more than twice what they were right after the war.

Theater data on which to base trend calculations are much more difficult to obtain. We have few continuous series, and in some cases for which we do, the structure of the enterprise has changed so substantially that a direct comparison of costs over the period would be misleading. We managed to obtain two time series which may be taken to represent reasonably homogeneous activities — the American Shakespeare Festival at Stratford, Conn. and the Bucks County Playhouse, a summer theater in New Hope, Pa., both of which have been in operation for a number of years. Both experienced increases in cost per performance well beyond the growth in the price level, though a little slower than the growth rates for the orchestras.

For a number of other organizations we obtained what might be described as "spot data" — figures for several isolated years, not all of which are directly comparable. These provide the basis for

[18] The steadiness of this growth is evident from the orchestra curve in Figure VIII–3, which shows a slight dip in 1955–1957 and a steady rise thereafter until 1961. Since 1961, the *rate* of increase has been mounting. Indeed, it is noteworthy that during the four years 1961–1964 costs per performance rose faster than the average rate of increase for the entire postwar period.

The results are also highly consistent from orchestra to orchestra. While there has been some variation, and the financial difficulties of an occasional organization have forced a decrease in costs, ten of our basic eleven orchestras experienced increases in costs per performance more rapid than the rise in the price level.

FIGURE VIII–3

EXPENDITURES PER PERFORMANCE AND THE WHOLESALE PRICE INDEX, 1947–1964

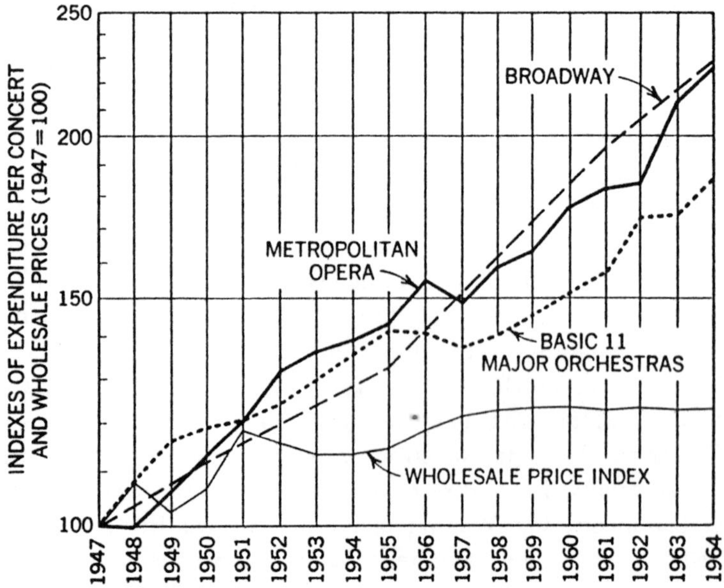

The basic data for this graph appear in Tables VIII–1 and VIII–3.

the growth rates in Table VIII–3 which are not italicized. Each of these rates also fits the general pattern described so many times in this chapter. The pattern holds even for the City Center Opera and the New York City Ballet, whose costs per performance rose more slowly than those of any other organization for which we have data.

The over-all results, then, are sufficiently clear and dramatic. They confirm the impression that costs in the performing arts do indeed rise, and that they outstrip prices in the rest of the economy. Whatever else one may conclude, it is clear that the cost problems besetting the performing groups are no mere reflection of the rate of inflation characteristic of the economy as a whole.

TABLE VIII–3

Growth in Expenditure Per Performance and in the Wholesale Price Index During the Postwar Period

Organization	Time Period	Average Annual Percentage Increase (compound rate)[a] Expenditure Per Performance	Wholesale Price Index
Major Orchestras:			
"Basic 11"	1947–1964	*3.2*[b]	1.3
All 23	1947–1964	*3.1*[b]	1.3
"Basic 11"	1961–1964	*4.9*[b]	0.1
All 23	1961–1964	*3.9*[b]	0.1
Opera Companies:			
Metropolitan Opera	1951–1964	*4.4*	0.3
Opera Company A	1958–1963	5.0	0
City Center Opera	1958–1963	2.0	0
Dance Companies:			
New York City Ballet	1958–1963	2.3	0
Theaters:			
Broadway Sample	1950–1961	*6.0*	1.4
Regional Theater A	1958–1963	*11.2*	0
Regional Theater B	1958–1963	*6.0*	0
Regional Theater C	1955–1963	2.5	0.9
Summer Theater	1954–1963	*3.6*	0

SOURCE: The growth rates for the major orchestras were calculated from the compiled reports of the American Symphony Orchestra League. For definitions of the "basic 11" and "all 23," see Appendix III–2. Broadway data were obtained from Moore (see Table VIII–2 for the exact source). All other growth rates were calculated from expenditure and performance information acquired directly from the individual organizations.

[a] The italicized growth rates were obtained by fitting a trend line to the logarithm of annual observations over the period indicated. Rates not in italics were obtained simply by assuming a constant (compound) rate of growth between the terminal years, the only years for which data were available in the case of these organizations. The italicized rates are, of course, more reliable.

[b] This is a weighted average of the growth rates for all eleven orchestras, the weights being mean (arithmetic average) expenditures over the period as a whole. This gives us an over-all industry figure. We also calculated an unweighted average which tells us about a typical orchestra without regard to size. This unweighted average comes to 2.9 per cent per year. The fact

And Great Britain Once More

Having just conducted the reader through a labyrinth of American statistics, we had hoped merely to reassure him that things were similar in the United Kingdom and perhaps to report this in a footnote. On examining the British figures, however, we found a rather interesting relationship which merits some attention.

Little can be done with British data by way of long-period comparisons because most of the older records seem to have been lost during World War II. Where figures exist, some crucial piece of information, such as number of performances, is usually missing. However, we do have data for the Royal Shakespeare Theatre for the period 1949–1964. Expenditures per week (and so, we presume, per performance) grew at a rate of 9.6 per cent per year, as compared with a growth rate of 3.4 per cent in the retail price index. At the regional orchestra for which we have figures, total costs increased at a rate of 7.3 per cent per year over this period; and, since the number of concerts per year rose by only a negligible amount between 1955 and 1964, a 6 to 7 per cent growth rate in expenditure per concert seems a very conservative estimate.

At Covent Garden it is difficult to calculate a meaningful cost per performance figure since so many types of performance are given. Not only does Covent Garden offer both ballet and opera, but it also provides what are referred to as "special" and "ordinary" performances. However, since the total number of house performances actually decreased between 1951 and 1964 (from 326 to 282), the 7 per cent annual increase in total expenditures clearly understates somewhat the growth in cost per performance. Furthermore, if we exclude years with big tours, the growth rate figure for total expenditures increases to 9.3 per cent per year.

These, however, are not the most interesting observations to be made on the British figures. If we compare the rate of increase in costs with the rate of increase in the price index, we notice that at

Notes to Table VIII–3 continued

that it is slightly lower than the weighted figure suggests that expenditure per concert has grown more rapidly for the larger orchestras. Note also that the growth rate for the entire group of majoı orchestras has been slightly lower than that of the basic eleven alone. The difference is negligible, and in any event the rise is still far more rapid than the rate of growth of the price level.

Covent Garden, at the regional orchestra and at the Royal Shakespeare Theatre, costs have risen at an annual rate about twice as great as the rate of rise in the price index. Cost per performance rose at a rate of 7 to 10 per cent while prices went up at about a 4 per cent rate. If we now turn back to the figures for the United States, we find that *the ratio between cost and price increases was very similar*. Costs rose during the postwar period at an annual rate close to 4 per cent, while prices went up somewhere between 1 and 2 per cent, depending on which index one employs.

One cannot place too much of a burden on this very rough relationship, but it should not wholly surprise us. What it says is that after we correct for changes in the purchasing power of the dollar and the pound, real cost per performance seems to have been rising at about the same rate in both countries. If much of the rise is attributed to a structural problem in the technology of the arts that knows no national boundaries, one might have expected to find just such a result.

Economies of Large-Scale Operation[19]

Changes in the cost of most enterprises reflect not only movements in the prices of the factors of production they employ, but also changes in the scale of their operations. Experience with a number of manufacturing enterprises has taught us that in some types of activity an increase in output can reduce per unit cost. Where items can be standardized and mass produced, each unit can be provided more and more cheaply as the market expands. One may well ask whether this pattern fits the performing organizations — whether they too can benefit from economies of scale when they increase the availability of performance to the public.

Figure VIII–4 shows the relationship between cost per concert (vertical axis) and number of concerts given (horizontal scale) for one of the nation's major orchestras. For example, the dot marked 1950 indicates that in 1950, when 80 concerts were performed during the season, the cost per concert was 70 "units of real cost" (expenditure adjusted for changes in the purchasing

[19] Appendix VIII–2 contains a more technical discussion of the analysis underlying this section.

FIGURE VIII–4

REAL EXPENDITURE PER CONCERT AND NUMBER OF CONCERTS, FOR A MAJOR ORCHESTRA, 1936–1964

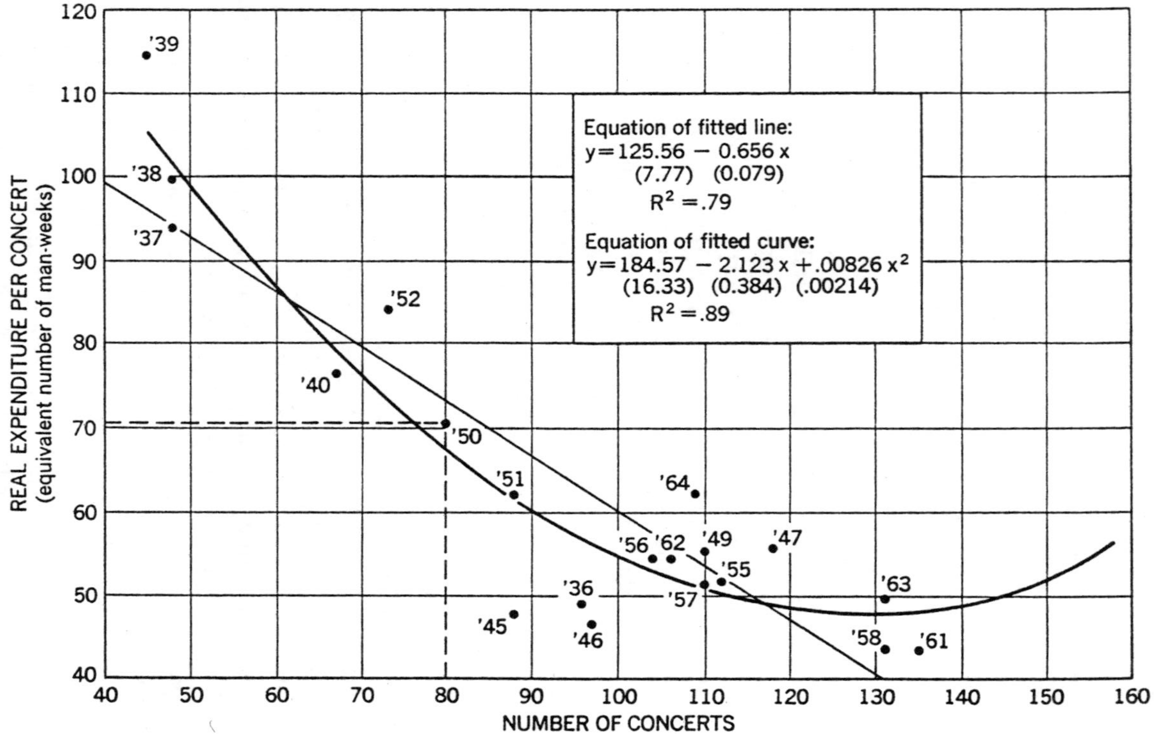

For the derivation of this graph see Appendix VIII–2.

power of the dollar to our orchestras).[20] Notice how closely the curve fits the dots representing the actual data for the years indicated. Moreover, the curve very clearly slopes downward from left to right — there are very marked and clear-cut economies of scale, though they level off (the curve flattens out noticeably after the scale of operations becomes fairly large).

This sort of analysis was undertaken for each of our basic eleven orchestras. The data for six of the eleven fell into similar patterns, though the curves were by no means identical — they were not equally steep, nor did they begin to level off at about the same number of concerts per year. Some orchestras reached what appeared to be a minimum cost level after as few as 90 concerts per year, while others still went on enjoying economies of scale until they had played nearly 150 concerts per year.[21]

What do these results mean, and how do we account for them? They suggest that up to a point the orchestras enjoy economies of large-scale operation, but that beyond this point further lengthening of the concert season will produce no further reductions in cost per concert.

Administration is one activity which offers obvious scope for such economies. A 10 per cent increase in the number of concerts performed may not require a corresponding increase in managerial personnel. If so, an increase in the number of concerts will reduce the administrative cost *per concert.*

A more important opportunity to economize is presented by the possibility of making rehearsal time cover more performances. Suppose an orchestra has been running three series of identical programs per season and decides to run four. This will not add to the number of different pieces of music performed. Each item will

[20] Our criterion of purchasing power was the salary of the musician, which constitutes the bulk of the orchestra's expenditures. We measured expenditures in terms of the number of musicians the orchestra could hire for one year at the relevant minimum rate if it devoted all of its expenditures to this purpose. In other words, had dollar expenditures quadrupled over a given period while the musicians' minimum annual wage had doubled, we would conclude from our calculation that the orchestra's *real* expenditures had merely doubled because they would be equivalent to only twice as many musician-years as before.

[21] See Appendix VIII–2 for a detailed presentation of all of our cost curve regressions.

now be repeated before four different audiences instead of three, and little, if any, increase in rehearsal time will be required. If rehearsal costs were $120,000 for the season, with three series the rehearsal cost per series would be $40,000, and with four series it would fall to $30,000. Here, then, is an opportunity to achieve very substantial economies.

This also suggests why the lowest cost per concert occurs at different levels of activity for different orchestras. One would surmise that the lowest unit cost corresponds to the largest number of parallel series for which the orchestra can find audiences. If one orchestra operates in a large city with many music lovers, it may, perhaps, be able to give six such concert series and thereby achieve economies up to that level of operation. But an orchestra located in a smaller, less musical metropolis may find that beyond four concert series any further expansion requires the presentation of different programs in order to attract the same subscribers back. In that case rehearsal cost per concert will rise when the number of concerts expands any further. If, in addition, these added concerts require noted guest conductors or soloists to attract audiences, it is easy to see why unit costs might cease falling. This explanation is, of course, only a hypothesis, which may or may not be valid.[22]

Similar reasoning can be applied to the stage. We know that there are some economies of scale to be obtained in the theater when the length of run of a play is increased. The production cost of a play, which encompasses the cost of rehearsals, scenery, costumes, etc., usually constitutes a very substantial proportion of the total cost for the run of that play. Consequently, as the length of run increases, the proportion of the fixed production cost that is ascribed to each week of operation declines. If a show costs $100,000 to produce, the production costs for a ten week run would be

[22] After the preceding comments had been written we undertook a simple test of our hypothesis. For the six orchestras whose data showed a strong statistical relationship, we compared size of population in the home city with the cost-minimizing number of concerts per season. For five of the six, the ordering by population size was exactly the same as the ordering by length of season — the more populous a city, the longer the season for which its orchestra could operate without running into diminishing returns. Even the one exceptional orchestra was not far out of line with what one might have expected from our hypothesis.

$10,000 per week. By the time the show has run 20 weeks the production costs will have fallen to $5,000 a week. Thus, the longer the run, the smaller the production cost per week — which is what we mean by economies of scale.

We do not know whether the weekly running costs of a play also decline with length of run. In part this is because the requisite data are not available. The practice of classifying certain cost items sometimes as production costs and sometimes as running costs does not help matters. Things are confused even more when some of the personnel involved accept cuts in pay in order to keep a relatively unsuccessful play running, for these cuts might seem from the records to represent a decline in running cost resulting from length of run. Our data for the Bucks County Playhouse did enable us to compare the costs of the second week of a two week run with those of the first week (at that theater plays are usually given for two weeks). There the figures show that on the average the second week's operations cost 11 per cent less than the first.

Our economies of scale analysis has an implication which affects our interpretation of the cost trends described earlier in this chapter. It was stated in a previous section that for a few of our orchestras, costs failed to rise more quickly than the price level. We can now suggest a possible explanation for those exceptional cases: during the period for which our cost trends were calculated those orchestras may well have been increasing the number of concerts they gave per year, and as a result they may have achieved economies of scale sufficient to offset any real cost-increasing trends.

This is illustrated in Figure VIII–5, which reports the expenditures per concert for one of our orchestras over the period 1937–1964 (bottom curve). This curve shows that expenditures per concert rose during that period, but for the orchestra under scrutiny they rose a little less rapidly than the wholesale price index (middle curve). The top curve, however, shows how much costs would have risen had the orchestra enjoyed no economies of increased scale.[23] This curve shows clearly that had the orchestra not in-

[23] This upper curve was calculated with the aid of an average cost curve for that orchestra like the one shown in Figure VIII–5. For each year, in effect, we undid the economies that resulted from any increase in the number of concerts above the 1937 level. For this purpose we utilized the following expression: corrected expenditure per concert in year t = $(Y_{x37} / Y_{xt}) \times$ (actual ex-

FIGURE VIII–5

EXPENDITURE PER CONCERT WITHOUT ECONOMIES OF SCALE, FOR A MAJOR ORCHESTRA, 1937–1964

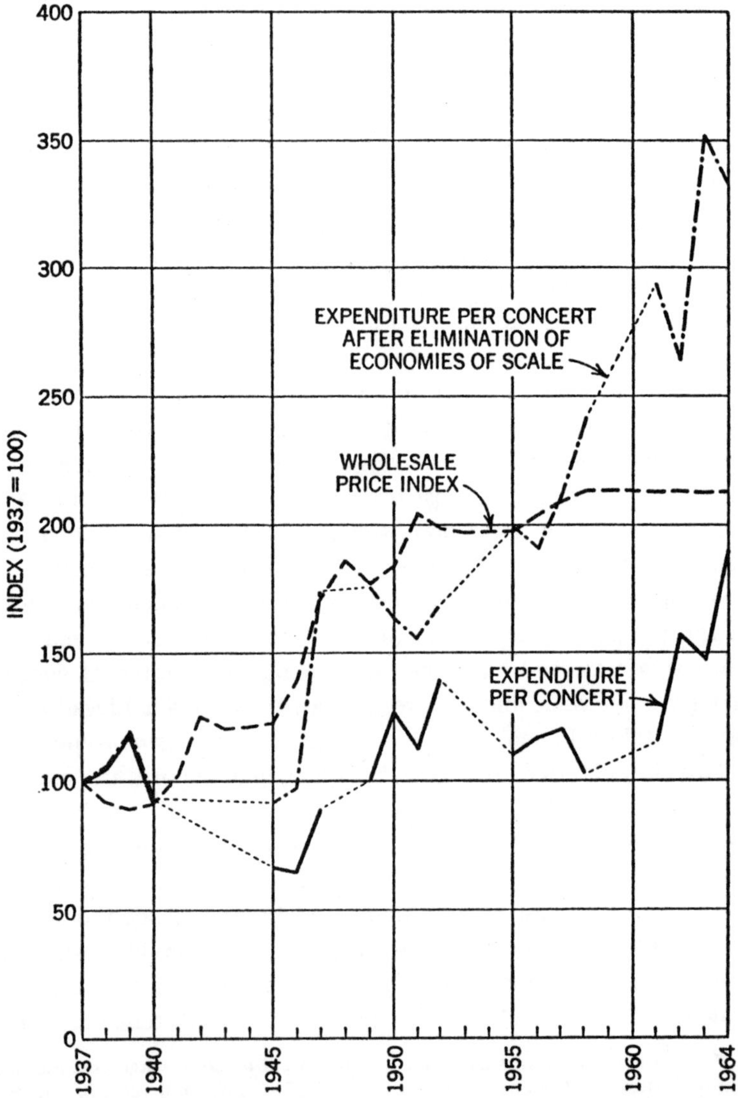

creased its scale of operations, its costs would undoubtedly have risen far more rapidly than the price level. This finding implies that in many other cases the rate of increase in cost per concert shown in our previous calculations also significantly understates the rate at which the entire cost curve has been shifting upward.

The major thrust of this chapter is summed up very simply. As our analysis in the previous chapter suggested, the real costs of performance almost always rise. These can sometimes be offset by economies of scale, and periods of war seem to constitute a consistent exception, but otherwise one can find few cases in which price rises in the economy fail to be exceeded by the state of increase in the costs of performance. This tells us clearly that inflation alone is not the villain of our story. It also indicates once more that the financial pressures upon the performing arts cannot be expected to ease with the passage of time.

penditure in year t) where $Y_{xt} = f(X_t)$ is the equation of the average cost curve for that orchestra (see boxed equation and heavy line in Figure VIII–4) so that X_t and X_{87} are, respectively, the number of concerts in the two years and Y_{x87} and Y_{xt} are the corresponding unit costs as given by the cost curve regression equation.

Trends in Performer Salaries and Other Components of Cost

LET US now examine the components of the rise in over-all costs of performance. Such an inquiry will help us to understand the source of these cost pressures and will make it easier to forecast the pattern of the future.

We begin the chapter by considering the broad components of total costs; in particular, outlays on artistic personnel as compared with all other expenditures. We then study trends in the cost of auxiliary services and equipment — scenery, stagehands' salaries, advertising, etc. Finally we re-examine performer salaries in greater detail, relating their growth to that of other incomes in the economy and considering the effects of salary changes on the supply of performers and the demand for them. In general, we shall see that performer incomes have been rising at a rate faster than that of the price level, but still have not kept up with incomes elsewhere in the economy, and that salary payments have constituted a declining portion of over-all costs of performance in recent years.

Expenditures on Artistic Personnel as a Percentage of Total Costs

Given the nature of the available data, the most consistent way to break down the costs incurred by performing organizations is to classify them into expenditures on artistic personnel and "all other expenditures." Payments to artistic personnel are the largest item in the operating budgets of performing organizations, and merit

FIGURE IX–1

EXPENDITURES ON ARTISTIC PERSONNEL AS PER CENT OF TOTAL EXPENDITURES, ELEVEN MAJOR ORCHESTRAS, 1937–1964

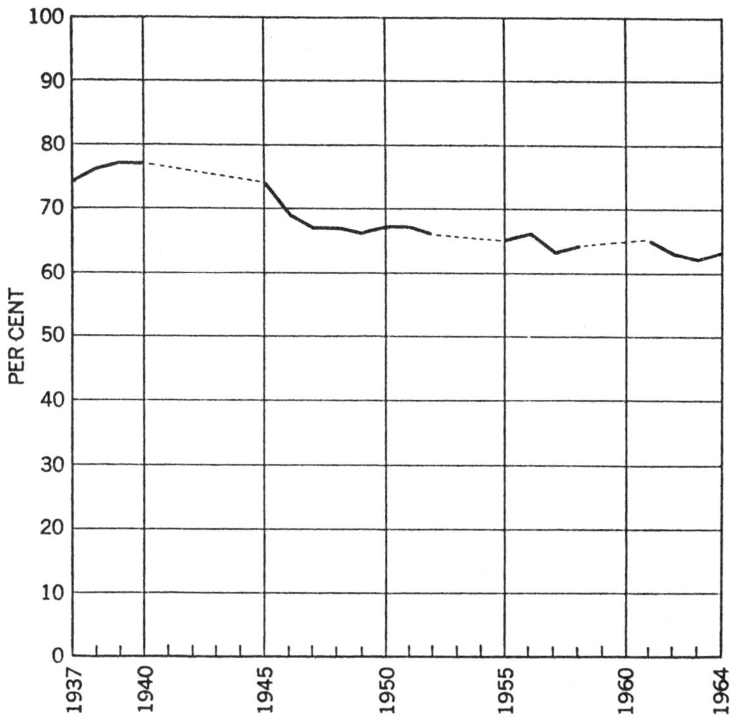

Based on major orchestra compiled reports. Data used here are averages for the basic set of eleven major orchestras.

special attention also because performer compensations are critical for the welfare of the arts.

Costs in both of these broad categories have risen substantially, but not always at an equal rate. The figures for one major orchestra over the whole period for which we have data — 1929–1964 — indicate that there has been considerable variability but no obvious long-term trends (Figure IX–2), although outlays on artistic personnel in 1964 were a slightly smaller proportion of total costs (about 55 per cent) than they were in the 1940's (60–65 per

FIGURE IX–2

EXPENDITURES ON ARTISTIC PERSONNEL AS PER CENT OF TOTAL EXPENDITURES, FOR A MAJOR ORCHESTRA, 1929–1964

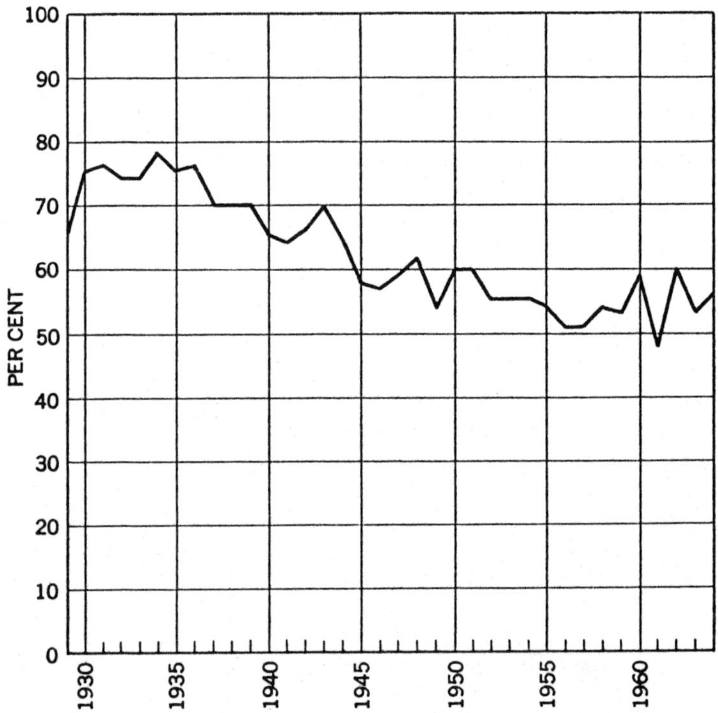

cent). Nor is there any clear-cut relation to the business cycle. For example, relative to total costs, expenditures on performers rose after 1929, but fell after the panic of 1893. Figures for another major orchestra show the same inconclusive patterns. Relative to total costs, personnel costs were high for both orchestras during the great depression.

For the postwar period, our most comprehensive and reliable figures are again those for the major orchestras. The data for our basic eleven major orchestras are shown in Figure IX–1, and Figure IX–2 shows similar data for one particular orchestra extending over a slightly longer period. Both graphs reveal a small but fairly persistent downward trend in the salaries of artistic personnel as a proportion of total expenditures. This has been offset in part by substantial improvements in fringe benefits in recent years — pensions, Blue Cross, major medical insurance and sick leave. Nevertheless, it is clear that the increase in over-all costs of performance among major orchestras cannot be ascribed to a particularly rapid rate of increase in the costs of artistic personnel. But because payments to performers constitute so large a proportion of total costs, they account for the bulk of the *absolute* increase in orchestral expenditures. For a typical major orchestra, total costs have gone up about $560,000 between 1942 and 1964, and some 60 per cent ($336,000) has consisted of increases in salary payments to performers.[1]

The declining proportion of the performer wage bill relative to total costs during the postwar period has not been confined to the major orchestras. It appears to hold for most other performing organizations, including the Metropolitan Opera, Broadway, Covent Garden and a major symphony orchestra in London. Later in the chapter we shall present the most pertinent of these data and consider the reasons for this phenomenon.

Trends in Other Types of Expenditure

What are the items other than artistic personnel whose costs have been rising? For once, the major orchestra data are of little help. It was not possible to obtain a detailed cost breakdown which could be applied consistently to all the orchestras. At best we were able to divide orchestra expenditures into three broad categories: artistic personnel costs; production expenses (including stage expenses, hall rental or operating costs, etc.); and "all other." Each of the last two classes of expenditure has increased somewhat more rapidly than personnel costs over the postwar period.

A more detailed classification of personnel costs for the Metropolitan Opera, in Table IX–1, shows that outlays on salaries of wardrobe and scenic personnel have risen much more slowly than other expenditures. There was great similarity in the rates of growth of all the other cost components, though artistic person-

[1] Calculated from compiled reports of the major orchestras.

TABLE IX–1

Trends in Components of Costs, Metropolitan Opera, 1948–1964

Expenditure Category	Average Annual Growth Rate[a]	R^2 *
Salaries:		
Artistic Personnel	5.38%	(.97)
Stage Department	6.16	(.97)
Building Operating	5.83	(.89)
Executive and Clerical	6.41	(.88)
Wardrobe and Scenic	2.96	(.11)
Total Salaries	5.62	(.98)
All Expenses	5.73	(.99)

SOURCE: Calculated from data supplied by the Metropolitan Opera Association.

[a] Calculated by fitting a trend line to the logarithms of the annual observations.

* This measure of closeness of relationship is explained in the note on semi-logarithmic graphs at the end of Chapter VII.

nel costs constituted the second most slowly rising item. It is possible that the rate of increase in fringe benefits received by performers might have been sufficient to put them higher on this scale.

In the theatrical field, fairly detailed accounts are available both because of the transitory nature of the organizations and the degree of subcontracting. When a production disbands, each expenditure must be accounted for to the investors. Cost statements of this type, provided by Moore, enabled us to calculate the percentage distribution of expenditures for several Broadway productions during four different periods of time (Table IX–2).

The cast salary component of *production costs* on Broadway rose between 1928 and 1961, mainly because rehearsal pay did not become general until after the late 1920's. In spite of the trend, however, cast salaries are still a small proportion of the total initial production outlay. The largest single item in production costs — scenery — has undergone a major relative decline, as have directors' fees and outlays on crew and stagehands; on the other hand, advertising has risen most rapidly. This refers only to pre-opening advertising expenditures, which have undoubtedly risen because of

TABLE IX–2

Components of Broadway Costs, 1928–1961

	Percentage Distribution			
	1927–28 and 1928–29	1949–50 and 1950–51	1954–55 and 1955–56	1960–61
PRODUCTION COSTS				
Director's Fee	8.9	7.0	6.0	4.4
Cast Salaries	4.4	5.9	6.2	6.0
Crew and Stagehands	8.6	4.5	6.4	5.3
Scenery Designer	5.0	5.2	4.4	3.5
Scenery	30.5	28.1	23.4	22.3
Costumes	9.7	11.3	7.9	9.2
Advertising	7.0	5.5	7.0	12.0
	74.1	67.5	61.3	62.7
Remainder	25.9	32.5	38.6	37.4
Total	100.0	100.0	100.0	100.0
WEEKLY OPERATING COSTS				
Cast Salaries	51.3	41.3	36.9	37.1
Crew and Stagehands	4.5	8.0	7.3	6.4
Author's Royalties	13.5	15.4	14.8	11.9
Director and Designer	—	3.4	3.2	3.5
Stage and Company Managers	3.5	5.4	5.6	4.9
Publicity and Advertising	18.5	12.3	11.2	16.8
	91.3	85.9	78.9	80.6
Remainder	8.7	14.1	21.1	19.4
Total	100.0	100.0	100.0	100.0

SOURCE: Calculated from data collected by Moore, Ch. III.

the increased risk to which Broadway productions are subject. To minimize that risk, producers advertise more before the opening of a play in order to have as large an advance sale as possible. The miscellaneous category of production costs has also risen sharply since 1928. At that time it was made up entirely of props and electrical and sound equipment, but more recently managerial expenses, press agent salaries and legal and auditing fees have also become items to be reckoned with.

Weekly running costs on Broadway exhibit patterns not entirely similar to those found among production outlays. The share of actors' salaries has declined, and while proportional outlays on crew and stagehands rose between 1928 and 1950, they have subsequently fallen. The proportion spent on publicity and advertising, while down relative to 1928, has gone up in recent years, as has "the remainder."

Our data, in general, support the contention that the incomes of stagehands have been going up relative to the incomes of most other persons in the theater. As Appendix Table IX–A shows, the weekly minimum pay scale of stagehands increased more rapidly than the minimum scales of other Broadway theater employees between 1960 and 1965, and stagehands ranked third in rate of increase of minimum salary among the thirteen occupations for which we have data for the interval 1953–1965 (only assistant managers at musicals and wardrobe attendants experienced more rapid increases in minimum weekly pay). These comparisons do not take account of overtime payments and fringe benefits, which together constitute a significant proportion of stagehands' earnings. But neither do they include the wage rates of the "grips" — the lowest paid but most numerous category of stagehand.

Over the period 1953–1965 the rate of increase in Broadway actors' pay has placed them at about the middle of the list. They are outranked in this respect not only by assistant managers, wardrobe attendants and stagehands, but also by ticket takers, ushers and treasurers. However, the minimum scales of actors went up more rapidly than those of stage managers, department heads (stagehand and wardrobe), cleaners, porters and musicians. It is noteworthy that contract musicians performing at musical comedies are at the very bottom of the list — their pay rates rose more slowly than those of anyone else in the theater.

Since advertising outlay has risen so sharply, we investigated it in some detail. The results of a study of the amount of theater advertising lineage in the *New York Times* and the *Times'* advertising rates are presented in Appendix Table IX–B. Over the period 1957–1962 price per agate line increased about 3 per cent on the average for Broadway productions, a rate slightly higher than the rate of growth of the consumer price index (2 per cent per year)

FIGURE IX–3

TRENDS IN SALARIES OF ORCHESTRAL MUSICIANS, BROADWAY ACTORS, TEACHERS, WORKERS IN MANUFACTURING, AND IN THE CONSUMER PRICE INDEX, 1929–1964

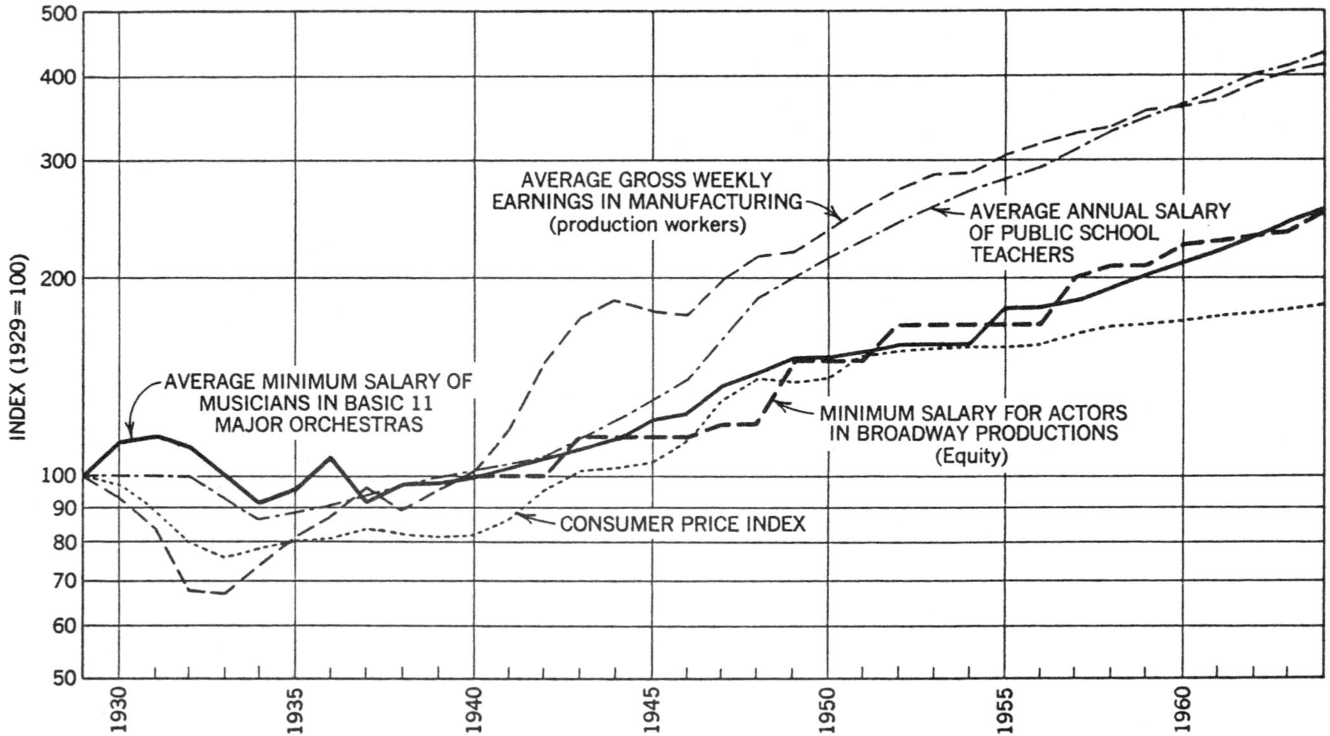

For the derivation of this graph see the notes to Table IX–3.

and about twice as large as that of the wholesale price index (1.3 per cent per year). In this period the volume of advertising went up 4.3 per cent per year on Broadway and 14.8 per cent per year off-Broadway. These last figures, however, reflect changes in the number of productions as well as variations in advertising lineage per performance. The latter increased 3.7 per cent per year on Broadway, but declined 1.4 per cent per year for the off-Broadway theater. Thus, the increased cost of advertising space, together with a growth in advertising lineage per performance, produced a rise of about 11 per cent annually in advertising costs on Broadway.

The general conclusion to which the foregoing evidence leads is that rising costs of performance can certainly not be laid to increases in performers' wage levels alone. Cost increases have been pervasive and have affected almost all categories of expenditure.

Trends in Performers' Salaries: General Comparisons

Since expenditures on performers' salaries have been rising, we are naturally led to ask how much this has helped the performer himself. Has his salary kept up with the price level and with compensation in other occupations?

Figure IX–3, our key graph, plots the course of three types of earnings: (minimum) performer salaries, earnings in manufacturing and teachers' salaries. These are expressed in index form, using 1929 as a base year, so that relative changes can be seen clearly. The consumer price index is also plotted on the diagram, as a means of showing how the various groups have fared in terms of purchasing power.[2] Table IX–3 summarizes the trends that are illustrated in Figure IX–3, and also includes data for college teachers.

There are several clear-cut conclusions to be drawn from the data:

(1) For the period 1929–1964, salaries of both Broadway actors and major orchestra musicians rose, on the average, 2.7 per cent annually. Since the annual increase in the consumer price

[2] Since the consumer price index is designed to measure cost of living, it, and not the wholesale price index, is the relevant measure in this instance.

TABLE IX–3

Trends in Actors' and Musicians' Salaries, in Teachers' Salaries and in Earnings in Manufacturing, 1929–1964

	Average Annual Percentage Change[a]									
	1929–1939	1940–1948	1948–1961	1961–1964	1929–1948		1948–1964		1929-1964	
Performers:										
Broadway Actors[b]	0.0	2.3	5.0	3.6	1.0	(120)[c]	4.7	(208)[c]	2.7	(250)[c]
Major Orchestra Musicians[d]	–0.2	4.7	3.3	5.1	1.9	(143)	3.6	(177)	2.7	(254)
Others:										
Production Workers in Manufacturing[e]	–0.5	9.9	4.4	3.9	4.1	(215)	4.2	(195)	4.2	(418)
Public School Teachers[f]	–0.1	7.8	5.7	4.5	3.3	(186)	5.5	(235)	4.3	(437)
College Teachers[g]	–0.5	4.2	4.7	5.3	1.6	(135)	4.8	(212)	3.0	(286)
Consumer Price Index	–2.1	7.0	1.7	1.2	1.8	(140)	1.6	(129)	1.7	(181)

[a] Compounded between terminal years.

[b] Equity minimums for Broadway. Compiled from files of agreements and back records made available by Actors' Equity.

[c] Figures in parentheses are index numbers (1929 = 100).

[d] Between 1929 and 1937 these figures are based on an index of average remuneration paid to New York Philharmonic musicians, exclusive of recording income and other "extras." Between 1937 and 1964 the figures represent an adjusted average of the weekly minimums paid by our basic eleven orchestras. Because some orchestras failed to report every year, the raw averages could not be used; they would have seemed to decline in years when an orchestra paying relatively high salaries did not report and to increase sharply in years when a lower paying orchestra did not report. We estimated the missing salary figures by averaging the preceding and following values.

[e] Average gross weekly earnings. Data from *Economic Report of the President*, January 1965.

[f] Average school-year salaries. Data for years prior to 1957 are from U. S. Bureau of the Census, *Historical Statistics of the United States, Colonial Times to 1957;* data from 1957 on were supplied by the U. S. Office of Education. The 1962 and 1963 values are National Education Association estimates.

[g] Average academic year salaries. Data for 1929–1952 are from *Historical Statistics of the United States*. (The original source of this series is George Stigler, *Trends in Employment in the Service Industries*, Princeton University Press, Princeton, N. J., 1956.) The estimates for 1960 and 1965 are from the *Bulletin of the American Association of University Professors*, Summer 1965, p. 249. The AAUP figures are for a specially selected sample of 36 relatively high paying institutions, but this fact does not necessarily imply a similar bias in the rates of change; studies made by the AAUP suggest that, if anything, salaries at these 36 institutions have risen somewhat less rapidly than academic salaries in general in recent years.

index was only 1.7 per cent, the performers' real income went up at an average rate of about 1 per cent per year.

(2) However, the performers' minimum salary fell behind the wages of production workers in manufacturing, public school teachers and college teachers, whose respective average rates of increase were 4.2, 4.3 and 3.0 per cent per year. Looked at another way, between 1929 and 1964 performers' salaries rose to about 2.5 times their initial level; but manufacturing workers' wages rose about 4.2 times, and school teachers' pay about 4.4 times during the same period. Thus, in a relative sense, performers grew poorer over the period as a whole.

(3) We see that performers do not constitute a completely insulated group. Their pay rates are affected by general economic conditions; for example, as in most other occupations, the money wages of performers were reduced during the great depression. However, the connection between the behavior of the general economy and performers' salaries is a very loose one, involving substantial lags and variations in pattern.

(4) More specifically, performers' pay rates did not fall as much as manufacturing wages during the depression. Performers really lost out, relatively speaking, during World War II. Manufacturing earnings rose nearly 10 per cent per year during the war, as compared with 2.3 and 4.7 per cent rises for Broadway actors and major orchestra musicians. Over the postwar period the rates of increase in all the job categories on which we have reported have been fairly similar except for the musicians, who have only recently begun to catch up.[3] There is a very close parallel between the

[3] An interesting specific case is the off-Broadway theater, where wages are still extremely low by any absolute standards, but have been creeping up on those paid on Broadway (Appendix Table IX–C). Sixty-five dollars per week (the 1965–1967 off-Broadway minimum) is still far from affluence, but minimums have risen from 35 per cent of the Broadway levels in 1954 to about 50 per cent of the Broadway figure today. And rehearsal pay has gone up from 9 per cent ($5 per week) to roughly 60 per cent ($65 per week) of the 1965 Broadway figure ($107.50). These figures help to explain why off-Broadway earning levels have managed simultaneously to keep actors poor and yet to impose very difficult financial burdens on the producer. The decline in the off-Broadway theater in 1964–65 has been ascribed to these increases in pay rates. (See the article by Lewis Calta, *New York Times*, Oct. 17, 1964, p. 18.) But surely this argument is primarily a commentary on the shaky finances of the off-Broadway theater, and not meant to suggest that off-Broadway performer incomes have reached immodest heights.

course of performers' salaries and those of college teachers. Both ended the 1930's with about the same money wages they had at the start. Both lost out relatively during World War II, did better between 1948 and 1961 and best between 1961 and 1964. Over the period as a whole both lost out relative to manufacturing workers and to elementary and secondary school teachers.

(5) Finally, we may observe that our figures support one of the postulates employed in developing the basic analytic argument of Chapter VII. The difference between the rate of growth of manufacturing wages (4.2 per cent) and that of the consumer price index (1.7 per cent) is an annual average net increase of 2.5 per cent. This is the average annual rise in real earnings (earnings measured in dollars of constant purchasing power). It is also the approximate annual rate of increase in productivity per man-hour, so that over the entire period 1929–1964 real wages in manufacturing increased at roughly the same pace as productivity.[4]

We offer one further general comparison of trends in wages of performers with those in other occupations. The Census data which we used in Chapter V to report on incomes in professional occupations in 1959 are, in general, available for 1949, so that it is possible to determine the rate of growth of earnings in each of these occupations over the ten year period.

Musicians and actors are right in the middle of a list in which professions are ranked in the order of rate of growth in income — they are, respectively, numbers 23 and 24 out of 48 (Table IX–4).[5] The implication is that over the decade they have just about kept their place relative to other professions. It may well be argued that

[4] The comparison is not wholly valid because the work week has been shortened since 1929; *hourly* pay in manufacturing must, therefore, have risen somewhat more quickly than 4.2 per cent per year.

[5] The table refers only to males. We have a similar table for women, but since the data are less complete and show very similar results, it is not reproduced.

There is some danger of misinterpretation of these figures. The period encompassed excludes the years since 1959 when, for example, musicians' incomes, at least in a number of major orchestras, have gone up markedly. The occupational categories in the Census lists are not as cleanly defined as one might have wished; for example, the "Musicians" category is distorted not only by the inclusion of music teachers but also by the presence of players of popular music. Nevertheless, the information provided by the Census data, in its broad outlines, is most illuminating.

TABLE IX–4

Income of Men in 48 Professional Occupations, 1949 and 1959

Rank (based on percentage rise in income)	Occupational Group	Median Income 1949	Median Income 1959	Percentage Rise in Income, 1949 to 1959	Percentage Change in Number, 1950 to 1960
1	Athletes	$2,336	$5,394	131	–64
2	Veterinarians	4,220	9,178	117	15
3	Optometrists	4,343	8,772	102	11
4*	Airplane pilots and navigators	5,263	10,514	100	92
4*	Librarians	2,294	4,592	100	91
6	Photographers	2,941	5,692	94	3
7	Dentists	6,448	12,392	92	11
8	Aeronautical engineers	4,828	9,127	89	195
9*	Funeral directors and embalmers	3,179	5,967	88	–6
9*	Natural Scientists (n.e.c.)	4,245	7,965[a]	88	60
11	Electrical engineers	4,657	8,710	87	73
12*	Chiropractors	3,471	6,463	86	16
12*	Metallurgical engineers	4,657	8,639	86	51
12*	Therapists and healers (n. e. c.)	3,011	5,591	86	35
15	Mechanical engineers	4,594	8,494	85	40
16	Physicians and surgeons	8,302	15,013	81	18
17*	Chemical engineers	5,005	8,948	79	26

/Continued overleaf

17*	**Lawyers and judges**	**6,284**	**11,261**	**79**	**17**
19	Artists and art teachers	3,552	6,333	78	35
20*	Chemists	4,091	7,245	77	13
20*	Pharmacists	4,170	7,385	77	5
20*	Social scientists	4,446	7,868	77	76
23	MUSICIANS AND MUSIC TEACHERS	2,700	4,757	76	5
24	ACTORS	3,260	5,640	73	–28
25*	Clergymen	2,410	4,151	72	22
25*	College presidents, professors, and instructors	4,366	7,510	72	44
25*	Industrial engineers	4,519	7,790	72	137
25*	Miscellaneous engineers (except mining)	4,965	8,522[a]	72	116
29	Social and welfare workers (except group)	3,196	5,481	71	54
30	Accountants and auditors	3,977	6,758	70	21
31	Civil engineers	4,590	7,773	69	26
32*	Authors	4,033	6,745	67	115
32*	Draftsmen	3,470	5,794	67	62
34*	Entertainers	2,217	3,674	66	–19
34*	Nurses, professional	2,645	4,400	66	50
34*	Sports instructors and officials	3,300	5,519	66	53
37	Teachers (elementary and high school)	3,465	5,709[a]	65	65
38	Foresters and conservationists	2,997	4,873	63	25

TABLE IX–4 (continued)

Rank (based on Percentage rise in income)	Occupational Group	Median Income 1949	Median Income 1959	Percentage Rise in Income, 1949 to 1959	Percentage Change in Number, 1950 to 1960
39	Surveyors	2,773	4,486	62	73
40*	Architects	5,509	8,868	61	29
40*	Personnel and labor relations workers	4,754	7,669	61	81
42*	Osteopaths	6,458	10,279	59	–21
42*	Technicians: medical and dental	2,908	4,614	59	55
44	Farm and home management advisers	4,059	6,159	52	14
45	Radio operators	4,016	5,975	49	68
46	DANCERS AND DANCING TEACHERS	2,385	3,483	46	0
47	Religious workers	2,316	3,241	40	66
48	Recreation and group workers	3,155	4,395	39	123
	All men in professional occupations	3,949	6,778	72	50

SOURCE: Compiled by Professor T. A. Finegan from *U. S. Census of Population, 1960: Subject Reports*, Final Report PC(2)–7A, Table 25.

[a] A weighted average of medians for component subgroups.

* Indicates tie ranking. n.e.c.: not elsewhere classified.

just keeping up is not good enough for a group that had fallen behind the rest of the community over a considerable earlier period, as this merely preserves their low relative position in 1949. Some figures we gave a little earlier suggest that there has been some catching up since 1961, though we cannot be sure that this is so since we do not have comparable data for all of the other professions.

In the Census data dancers, as usual, are at the bottom of the list — only in two other professional occupations have incomes increased more slowly than in theirs.

The pattern of salaries of British performers has been similar to ours (Appendix Table IX–D). Weekly pay rates lagged behind the average weekly earnings of "operatives" (manual workers) over the 1946–1963 period (a 4.2 per cent annual increase for the former as against 6.1 per cent for the latter). The lag decreased between 1950 and 1963, and performers have improved their relative position slightly during the most recent interval for which data are available (1957–1963).

The British data, in conjunction with our American figures, bring out a fundamental point relevant to our basic analysis. They show that in Great Britain, where prices and industrial wages have been rising more rapidly than here, performers' salaries have also increased more quickly. This confirms that performing arts organizations confront a labor market which is heavily influenced by developments in the rest of the economy.[6]

Wages, Supply and Demand

The prevalence of low wages that have, at times, fallen even further behind those of the rest of the community might reasonably be expected to reduce the supply of skilled performers. It would be highly desirable to test this hypothesis by analyzing the effects of changing wage levels on the supply of and the demand for performers. Unfortunately, empirical answers are extremely difficult to

[6] In *real* terms, both earnings of operatives and salaries of performers have risen less quickly in Great Britain than they have here. This is noteworthy in light of the fact that productivity has increased somewhat more slowly in Great Britain than in the United States.

come by in this area. Since the real world is a hodgepodge of simultaneous occurrences, one cannot be sure whether a variation in the supply of performers subsequent to a change in wages can legitimately be ascribed to the wage change or whether it resulted from any one of the many other events which are certain to have occurred at the same time. Consequently, the materials we offer now cannot pretend to do more than hint at the nature of the underlying relationships.

We begin with some Census figures which show that between 1950 and 1960 there was a decline of 28 per cent in the number of actors (Table IX–4).[7] The number of dancers and dance teachers has remained about the same, and there has been a small increase in the number of musicians and music teachers. While these figures seem to suggest that the over-all supply of performers has been diminishing, it is hard to know what they imply about the nature of supply responsiveness. A reduction in supply may be a consequence of inadequate demand, of low earnings levels or of any number of fortuitous circumstances, and these influences cannot be disentangled from the available data.

Some evidence on supply in relation to demand is provided by a series of interviews we conducted with producers and managers. These 56 interviews involved the full range of art forms — theaters, orchestras, chamber groups, dance companies and operas. Only 4 respondents indicated that they experienced difficulty in hiring performers of satisfactory quality, 18 reported moderate difficulty and 25 reported no problem at all. All indicated that they ended up with performers who were either usually or always satisfactory. When asked whether hiring had become harder or easier over the past five years, 7 respondents indicated that it had grown more difficult, 17 that it was about the same and 13 stated that it was now easier.

It is true that one cannot always take such statements at face value. Our own response categories were at best vaguely defined. The quality of performers is difficult to evaluate, especially in com-

[7] In his dissertation Watts (pp. 8–9) reports that according to the Census the number of self-designated actors and actresses has been falling since 1930. This number doubled during the first decade of the century, was stable in the next decade and grew about 30 per cent during the 1920's. In the 1930's the number fell about 50 per cent; it has since been declining more slowly.

parisons extending over a period of time, and a manager is not likely to admit to having hired unsatisfactory performers. Still, there is nothing in these interviews to suggest a general shortage of performers.

Though perhaps the most important issue involved in supply is the quality of performers, the sheer number available is also of interest. On this point impressive evidence is provided by the Census counts of the number who are unemployed. These figures may be interpreted as a measure of net oversupply — the number of performers supplied minus the number demanded — with some qualifications. In two respects the Census figures probably understate the true level of unemployment in the performing arts: they do not count as unemployed those who are without professional work at the time of the Census but *are* working as waiters or in some other unrelated job; and they do not count those who have become sufficiently discouraged to leave the labor force altogether. On the other hand, many persons list themselves as actors, dancers or musicians though neither their training nor their seriousness of purpose gives much justification for their doing so, and the number of unemployed performers is enlarged in consequence. One may well question whether all would-be performers — actresses, for example — can realistically be regarded as part of the reservoir of talent available to performing organizations.

According to the 1950 Census, the unemployment rate was 18 per cent among actors and 7.4 per cent among (male) musicians and music teachers.[8] The larger proportion of unemployment among actors is ascribable in part to the scarcity of permanent companies. Since actors must change jobs often, it is only natural that many are "between jobs" at any given time. Despite this fact, an unemployment rate of 18 per cent is extremely high in comparison with the rate of roughly 5 per cent for the labor force as a whole in 1950. It represents a degree of economic hardship for the actor which is hard to duplicate elsewhere in the economy.

A comparison with the figures a decade later is even more revealing. The 1960 data, reported in Chapter V, show that during the preceding decade there was a drop in unemployment among

[8] *U. S. Census of Population, 1950: Occupational Characteristics.*

musicians and music teachers to a rate of 4.7 per cent. But by 1960 the average unemployment rate for actors had risen to an enormous 29 per cent. Here is strong evidence that the supply is still well ahead of the demand, despite a considerable decline in the number of actors reported by the Census.

Special Areas of Performer Shortage

There are reports of shortages of particular types of performer. For example, we were told that good character actors, many of whom find jobs in television and the films, are fairly hard to locate. There also seems to be general agreement that good orchestral players of string instruments are scarce.[9] Curiously, the same shortage has been reported in British and continental orchestras.[10] It is interesting that players of exactly the same instruments should be scarce in several countries simultaneously. Perhaps the universality of the shortage may be ascribed in part to the international mobility of skilled performers; they can be enticed into deficit areas from any country in which they are more abundant. Mobility has also affected the employment patterns of young American singers, who are apparently oversupplied in the United States but frequently find jobs in European opera houses.[11] Specialized performers of other types also appear to be in short supply; for example, few actors are flexible enough, by training, to work effectively in repertory.

The evidence that there is a shortage of at least some types of orchestral musician suggested to us a test which, as it turned out, revealed rather strikingly one way in which the market goes about meeting such a situation. We surmised that the shortage has helped to open the orchestral field to women, but that for a variety of reasons — perhaps prejudice, but also scheduling difficulties caused by women's family obligations — orchestras prefer to hire men. We then conjectured that the less affluent orchestras are forced to hire more women because, as a general rule, orchestras

[9] See, for example, *New York Times*, Aug. 20, 1963, p. 36.

[10] Report of the Committee on the London Orchestras, Arts Council of Great Britain, p. 9.

[11] See, for example, testimony of Anthony A. Bliss, House Hearings, II, p. 78.

employ women only when they cannot obtain men of comparable ability at their prevailing wage scales. The following table provides spectacular confirmation of this hypothesis, for it shows with what perfect regularity the proportion of women employed varies inversely with the budget of the orchestra.[12]

Size of Orchestra's Annual Budget (millions)	Number of Orchestras in Category	Women as Per Cent of Total Performers
$1.5 and over	5	3.6
$0.8–$1.49	6	11.3
$0.6–$0.79	5	19.2
$0.4–$0.59	6	27.3
Under $0.4	3	36.3

The "stars" constitute another special group in short supply. In part, this means only that the very best people in any profession are always eagerly sought after. Though this is an especially sensitive area, and though we have no hard evidence,[13] we were told by many sources that fees for stars have been going up at an exceedingly rapid rate.

One of the important factors at work here is the demand of the mass media. A star who captures the affection of the public holds very considerable economic power as a consequence of the extremely large audience to which the mass media cater.[14] If he agrees to appear in a film rather than a live play, he may increase the number of viewers (and box office receipts) by several million, and his earnings may be expected to reflect this fact. If the live performing arts wish to compete for the services of such stars, they must expect to pay dearly.

[12] These figures were calculated from information contained in the American Symphony Orchestra League report for the major orchestras, 1963–64.

[13] Even those organizations which were most willing to open their books to us balked when we broached the subject of salaries of star performers, and it is easy to see why they felt this way.

[14] The difference between the size of audiences for the living arts and for the electronic media is even greater than is sometimes recognized. It has been estimated, for example, that the few network productions of Shakespeare's plays, although they were far from successful by ordinary television standards, were seen by more persons than have seen a live performance of these plays from the day they were written. Here indeed is a revolution in output per man-hour!

Yet, on the whole, the mass media have probably caused a reduction in the demand for performers below the topmost echelon, since a single film or a record often replaces thousands of live performances. While there may be some offsetting factors, such as the increased market for the services of dancers that accompanied the advent of television, it is doubtful that the net effect of the mass media has been to increase performer incomes or professional employment.

If wages and employment in live performance decrease sufficiently, the over-all supply of skilled persons will probably also eventually fall. There must be limits to the dedication even of musicians, dancers and actors (although we have come across cases where these limits are hard to imagine). The number of actors has already been declining, and a decrease in the number of well-trained performers of other types available for the living arts is certainly conceivable.

Such a decline may ultimately produce a serious problem for the mass media as well, for the living arts serve as an important training ground for the performers needed to produce recordings, films and television programs. Perhaps the mass media will yet have to learn to contribute more directly to the financial health of live performing groups. Motion pictures and television cannot afford much experimentation and failure, as the penalty for not attracting the public is as extreme as the reward for pleasing it. Yet first-rate talent can be developed only if there are opportunities to experiment and freedom to fail. Since the live performing arts do perform these essential functions for the mass media, it may not be far-fetched to suggest that the mass media may some day undertake to compensate them.

Remarks on Union Activity

The performing arts are one of the most highly unionized sectors of the economy, the spectrum of membership including such diverse personnel as stagehands, ticket takers, press agents, musicians, actors and business managers. While in many fields, such as the automobile industry, a single union represents the great majority of the unionized employees, workers in the performing arts are organized into a large number of independent craft unions. The main unions in this field include Actors' Equity, the American Federation of Musicians, the American Guild of Musical Artists (AGMA), the American Guild of Variety Artists (AGVA), the Theatrical Protective Union and the Directors and Choreographers Guild.

The craft union structure of its labor organizations means that managements must deal with several sets of union negotiators, and that some performers may belong to several unions at the same time.[15]

Perhaps a more important consequence of craft unionism is that rather rigid lines are drawn between different kinds of work, and the exclusive right to each of its job functions is carefully protected by each craft. Irritation is often caused when an actor or a director is not permitted to move a chair on a set, this being the exclusive province of the stagehand.

The long history of unionism in the performing arts[16] is attributable to several causes. The relatively chaotic and impermanent nature of the operation of many organizations in the industry has meant that unions such as Actors' Equity have served to introduce a degree of stability to the industry. Thus, they have played a role similar to that of the unions in the needle trades. Economic hardship and poor working conditions have, no doubt, also served to spur unionism, as has the concern with social problems which has long been characteristic of artists.[17]

Today, the unions in the performing arts, like most other labor organizations, concern themselves mainly with improvements in

[15] We were told, for example, that during a brief visit one foreign performer who worked in opera, appeared briefly off-Broadway and made a few television appearances, had to be a member of AGMA (for his work in opera), Equity (for his stage appearances), the American Federation of Television and Radio Artists (for his television appearances), and that, had he made a movie, he would also have had to join the Screen Actors Guild.

[16] The American Federation of Musicians was founded in 1896 and Actors' Equity in 1913. (See Leiter.)

[17] Actors' Equity was a pioneer in the struggle against discrimination. As long ago as 1947, because of some highly publicized incidents in the nation's capital, it added a clause to its rule book specifying that "the actor shall not be required to perform in any theater in Washington, D.C. where discrimination is practiced against any actor or patron of the theater by reason of his race, color or creed."

the wages, employment opportunities and working conditions of their members. They pursue these objectives not only through collective bargaining, but also by working to stimulate greater public interest in the arts and more governmental support.

The unions have sought to publicize the inadequacy of performers' earnings levels, a judgment generally shared by performer and management alike. Though standards of fairness are not easily defined, few persons in the performing arts feel that compensation levels are adequate, and hardly anyone seems to argue that the issue ought to be left exclusively to the market forces of supply and demand.[18] Managements usually argue only that they cannot afford to pay better. Ultimately, the level of wages is heavily influenced by the general financial state of the performing organization. The dilemma posed by what are considered to be the requisites of justice and the limitations imposed by financial constraints was nicely summed up by one prominent Broadway producer when, in commenting on the outcome of negotiations with Actors' Equity, he remarked, "My colleagues and I feel that this was a very fair settlement. We can't afford it, but it is a fair settlement."[19]

In some cases unions have attempted to help both performing and non-performing personnel by imposing work rules that are often denounced as "featherbedding." Unfortunately, the subject is more elusive than might be thought, and our rather intensive efforts at documentation brought meager results. In our discussion of this subject we must, therefore, rely on the views of persons more closely acquainted with the field.

It is easy enough to provide illustrations of the sort of practice that is alleged to occur.[20] A particularly forceful statement appeared in a newspaper article written by a Broadway producer. There he suggested that

> . . . to bring back to its doors the men and women who love and should go to the theater . . . [one should answer] some pertinent questions, such as, why does it cost as much to move a one set

[18] For an exception see the statement by Sigmund Spaeth, House Hearings, II, p. 169.

[19] *New York Times*, June 7, 1964, p. 31, quoting David Merrick.

[20] Featherbedding is not a new problem for the theater. Poggi, (Chapter 10, p. 17) gives examples going back nearly fifty years.

> show four city blocks as to ship an entire householder's goods from New York to far away Tibet; why a play with two people requires 22 stagehands; why a performance starring two entertainers, one a pianist and the other a monologist, who appear in dinner jackets, requires a wardrobe mistress; why an actor signed for a run-of-the-play contract, but who on the second day of rehearsal is relieved of the role, must necessarily be paid $1,700 a week for the entire run, while this artist is doing work in television and in films; why it costs as much to build and paint on canvas a one set interior, as it does to build a seven-room house; why a straight play's producer must employ four standby musicians who are paid *not* to play.[21]

If nothing else, this statement illustrates what a tremendous irritant "featherbedding" practices have been to theatrical management and helps to account for the disproportionate amount of time that is sometimes spent in dealing with union representatives on such matters.

But perhaps the most illuminating evaluation of the subject was written by A. H. Raskin of the *New York Times*. In a background paper written for the Rockefeller Brothers Panel, he first reminds the reader of the example

> . . . provided in the 1961 season by "An Evening with Mike Nichols and Elaine May" at the Golden Theater. With only two performers, the show had fifteen stagehands. This automatically stirred memories of the parade of eleven carpenters, electricians, property men, and grips Victor Borge used to call up for a bow at the final curtain of his one-man show of comedy and piano improvisations in the period from 1953 to 1956. The procession of unionists battening off Mr. Borge's talents never failed to send the audience home chuckling, but also vaguely disquieted.
>
> However, Alexander H. Cohen, producer of the Nichols and May show, saw nothing either funny or excessive about his fifteen-man stage crew. He considered every man necessary from the standpoint of the artistic integrity of the production, even though he was aware that eight men could readily have been dropped if the settings were laid out differently. . . .
>
> What the producers find especially galling about . . . payments for work not done is that . . . [some of the unions have] no unemployment problem. Since the advent of television, . . . [one of them] has had more jobs than members, and employers assert that "moonlighting" — the practice of holding two or three jobs at the same time — is widespread. The union not only maintains a tight rein on the admission of new members, but it cracks down on any producer who seeks to have a stagehand perform work in more than

[21] Joel Schenker, *New York Times*, June 21, 1964, Section 2, p. 3.

one department classification. This means that a man whose sole task is to push a light switch once an evening cannot be used to move a chair offstage in another scene a half hour later. If he has anything to do with lights, he is an electrician and cannot also serve as a prop man. . . .

Despite the vast amount of grumbling among producers about the multiplicity of extra costs for stagehands, many admit privately that the shows that get hurt most in this regard are usually those in which the employer has been insufficiently vigilant in protecting his own interests. If he determines his needs carefully and makes it plain to the union that he will resist any overcharges, he can often temper the overexuberance of a business agent eager to saddle him with more men than the rules require. . . .

He concludes:

I can think of nothing less useful than a repetition . . . of the sterile, and largely baseless, complaint that high union wages and restrictive union rules represent a principal obstacle to the financial health of professional groups in the performing arts. It is undoubtedly true that the standards built up to protect those with jobs would cheerfully be waived by younger artists of talent who would like an opportunity to demonstrate their ability. It is also true that experimental groups often find manpower and other requirements imposed by unions representing stage hands, electricians, etc., an obstacle. But if the groups are determined enough they usually can obtain waivers. Similarly, in the professional theater, music, and opera, where producers stand up with sufficient vigor for their rights, abuse is much less frequent than where submission comes without even the appearance of a fight.

Unions in the arts — in common with those in social agencies, hospitals, and other nonprofit organizations — reject the notion that their members should be expected to make what is, in effect, a charitable contribution to keep worthy organizations afloat. Nevertheless, when they are convinced of the genuineness of the financial emergency, modifications of rules and even of union scales are made with the agreement of unions and their members.[22]

In trying to account for movements in wages one would normally look to three types of influence: the general economic situation, which pulls wages in most fields along with the remainder of the economy; the nature and extent of union activity; and special circumstances affecting the particular field of endeavor, in this case the presence of the mass media and shortages of particular skills. In this chapter we have commented briefly on each of these

[22] Raskin, "Labor as Performer and Practitioner in the Arts."

types of influence. In looking at performer earnings from these various angles, however, one runs some risk of losing sight of the two main conclusions to which this chapter points:

(1) Artists' earnings are not the only component of cost of performance that has been rising. Indeed, other costs have grown more rapidly. In recent years, at any rate, expenditures on artistic personnel have been a declining portion of the total expenditures of the typical performing organization.

(2) While the money wages of performers have risen and have increased more rapidly than the price level, for long periods they have lagged well behind those in other occupations. Thus, in relative terms, performers have grown poorer over the rather long period examined. Only in the last few years do they seem to have stopped falling further behind.

[14]

Trends in the Income Gap

THIS CHAPTER, though the briefest in the book, is one of the most important. It reports the most significant conclusions which we have derived from our financial data, and in the process seeks to develop a unified pattern from the many pieces of information which have been presented. It undertakes to answer the basic factual question: Have the income gaps of the performing organizations grown larger, and, if so, at what rate?

Trends in Earned Income, Expenditures and the Financial Gap

The data used in this chapter pertain to five organizations or groups of organizations: the New York Philharmonic (from 1895), the Cincinnati Orchestra (since 1920), the Metropolitan Opera (since 1951) and the basic set of eleven major orchestras (since 1937). Unfortunately, we have no theatrical data. The regional theaters are almost all too new to provide significant trend information, while annual "gap" figures have no obvious meaning for Broadway and off-Broadway.[1]

The data are described in six graphs and an appendix table, which we can discuss simultaneously. Figure XII–1 shows the available data on earned income and total expenditures for the New York Philharmonic since 1895. The Philharmonic data for the nineteenth century and the first decade of the twentieth are, unfortunately, largely useless for our present purposes. During this

[1] It would have been highly desirable to have figures from which one could judge profit trends on Broadway. The League of New York Theatres is making efforts to provide better data, and has begun to collect some figures for recent years.

period, when the orchestra operated as a cooperative and all earnings in excess of expenditures were shared out among the musicians, orchestral earnings *had* to be identical with *net* operating income (except for occasional unimportant additions to or withdrawals from reserves kept in a savings account). This correspondence is seen very clearly in the pre-1910 portion of the graph. What the experience of the New York Philharmonic during this early period does show is that there was a time when an important orchestra was able to operate in the main on a profit-making basis.[2]

Even where the cooperative system was not employed (Figure XII–1 after 1910 and Figures XII–2, XII–3, XII–4 and XII–5), there is a clear parallelism between movements in earned income and expenditure.[3] Again, this undoubtedly represents a combination of interactions. When public demand for tickets caused an increase in the funds available to organizations, performer salary levels were increased; and when pressure from the performers forced a rise in remuneration levels, ticket prices were usually increased or extra performances were put on to raise the necessary funds.

The bottom sections of Figures XII–1 to XII–5 show how earned income has varied over time as a percentage of expenditure. The last three of these graphs seem to show a declining ratio of income to expenditure. Yet there is a great deal of fluctuation, and the trend is not always clear-cut, particularly for the Metropolitan Opera and our basic set of major orchestras in the early postwar period. This need not mean that there has been no clear trend in the income gap. On the contrary, in every organization for which we have data, *the income gap has been growing, and it has been doing*

[2] We say "in the main" because there is evidence that, even during this early period, some musicians in the Philharmonic and their friends were contributing services. Moreover, at least a small part of the fees and dues collected from the "subscribers" and "associate members" should, no doubt, be regarded as a contribution to the Society, and not just as the purchase of the right to attend concerts and public rehearsals.

[3] The use of a semi-logarithmic scale produces a seriously misleading impression in Figure XII–1. It looks as though the Philharmonic's income gap has been growing constantly smaller and has all but vanished in recent years. However, this illusion is only a result of the fact that semi-logarithmic scales compress the higher values on a graph. See Chapter VII, pp. 176–179.

FIGURE XII–1

TOTAL EXPENDITURE, EARNED INCOME, AND INCOME AS PER CENT OF EXPENDITURE, NEW YORK PHILHARMONIC, 1895–1964

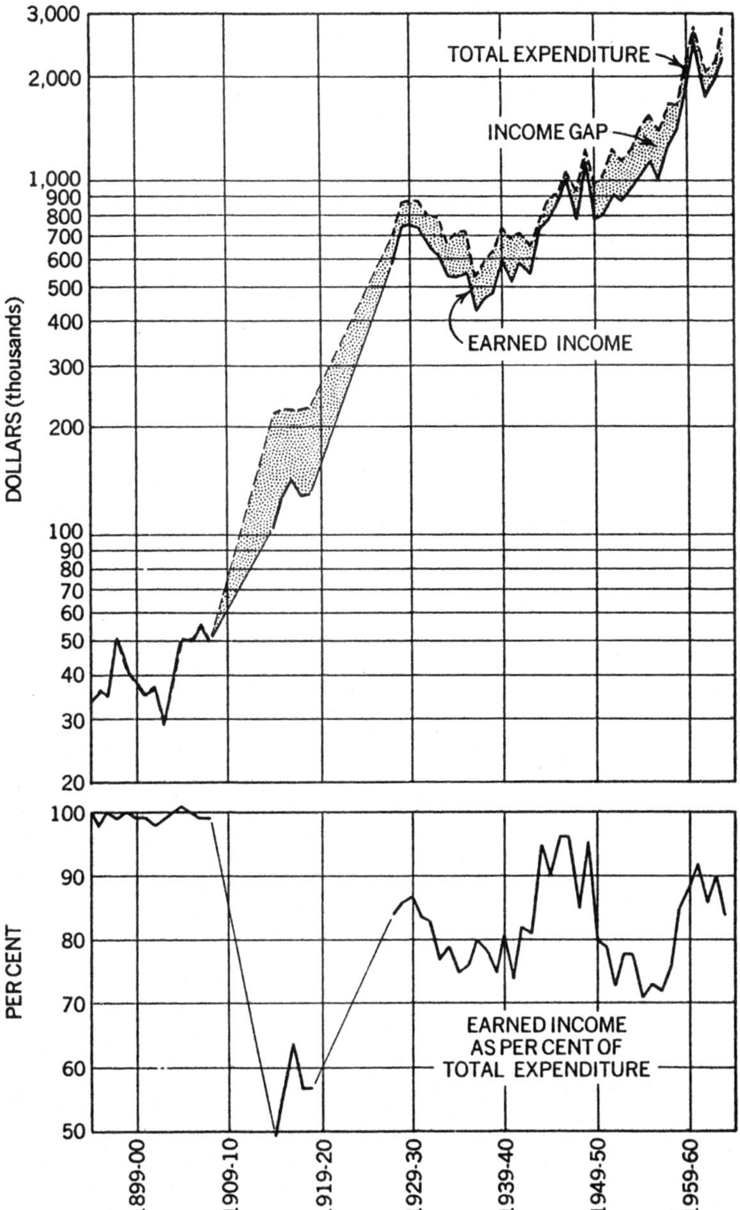

Basic data for this graph were supplied by the New York Philharmonic Orchestra.

FIGURE XII–2

TOTAL EXPENDITURE, EARNED INCOME, AND INCOME AS PER CENT OF EXPENDITURE, CINCINNATI ORCHESTRA, 1920–1964

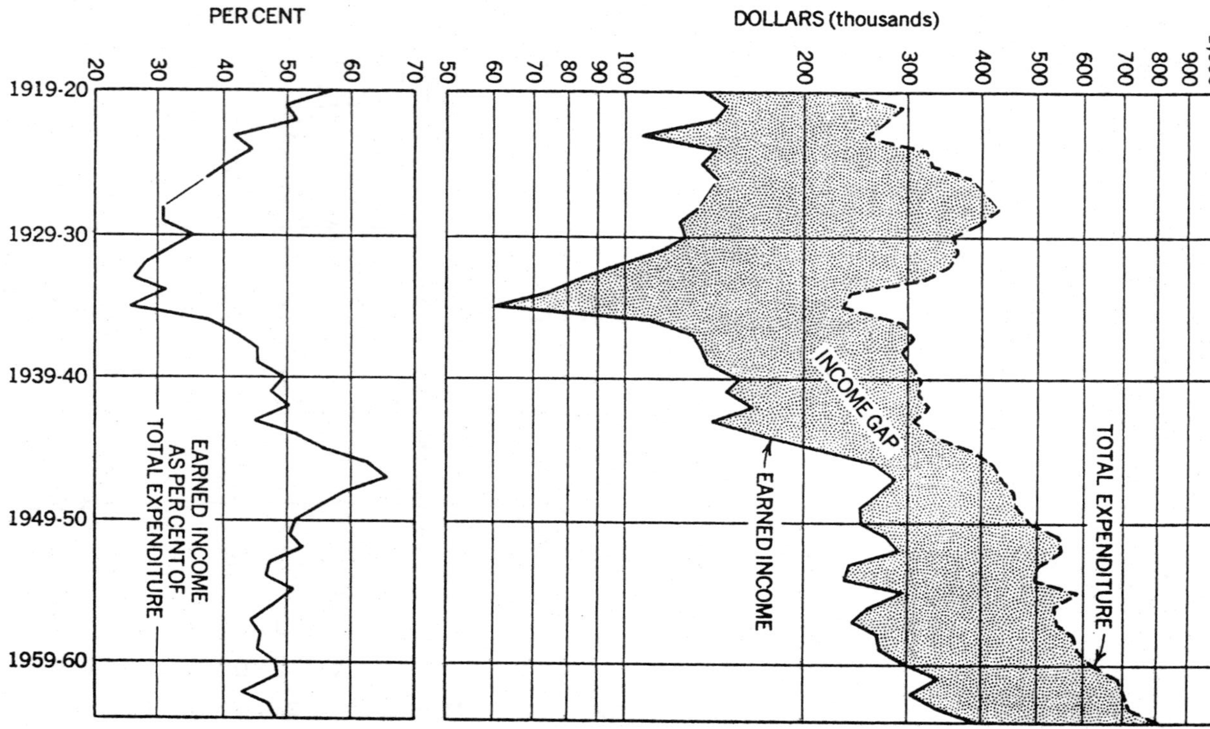

Basic data for this graph were supplied by the Cincinnati Symphony Orchestra.

FIGURE XII–3

TOTAL EXPENDITURE, EARNED INCOME, AND INCOME AS PER CENT OF EXPENDITURE, AVERAGE OF BASIC ELEVEN MAJOR ORCHESTRAS, 1937–1964

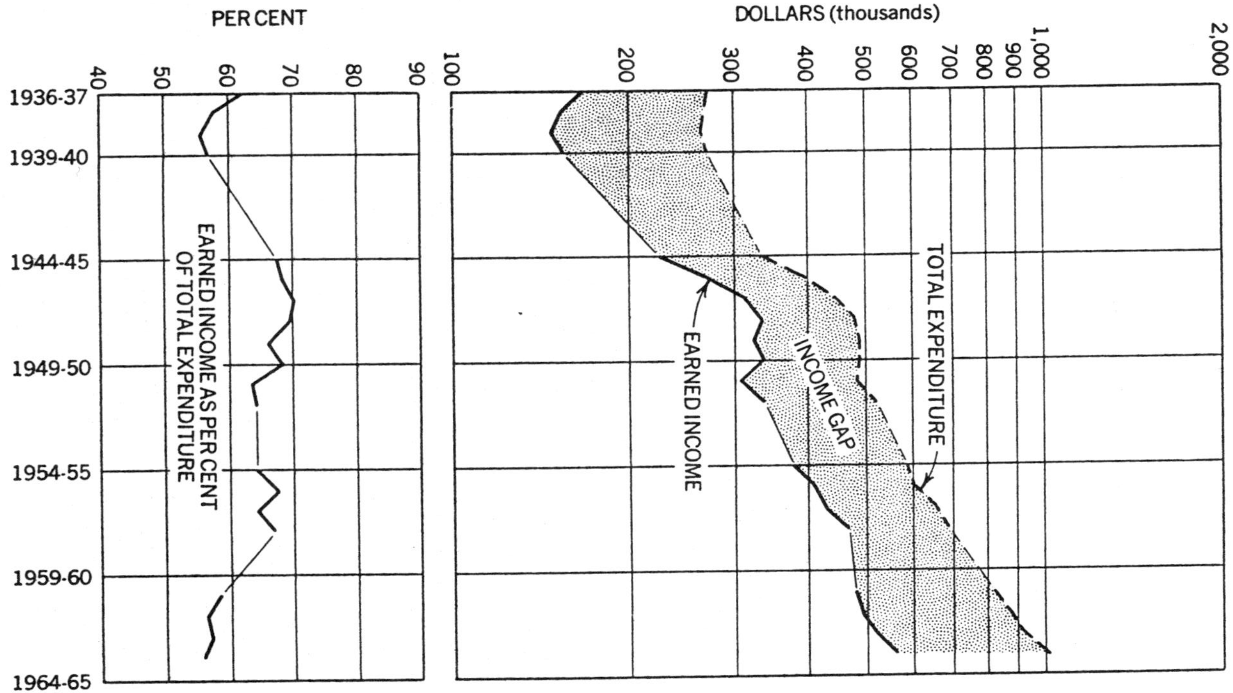

Data for this graph were obtained from compiled reports of major orchestras.

FIGURE XII–4

TOTAL EXPENDITURE, EARNED INCOME, AND INCOME AS PER CENT OF EXPENDITURE, METROPOLITAN OPERA, 1951–1964

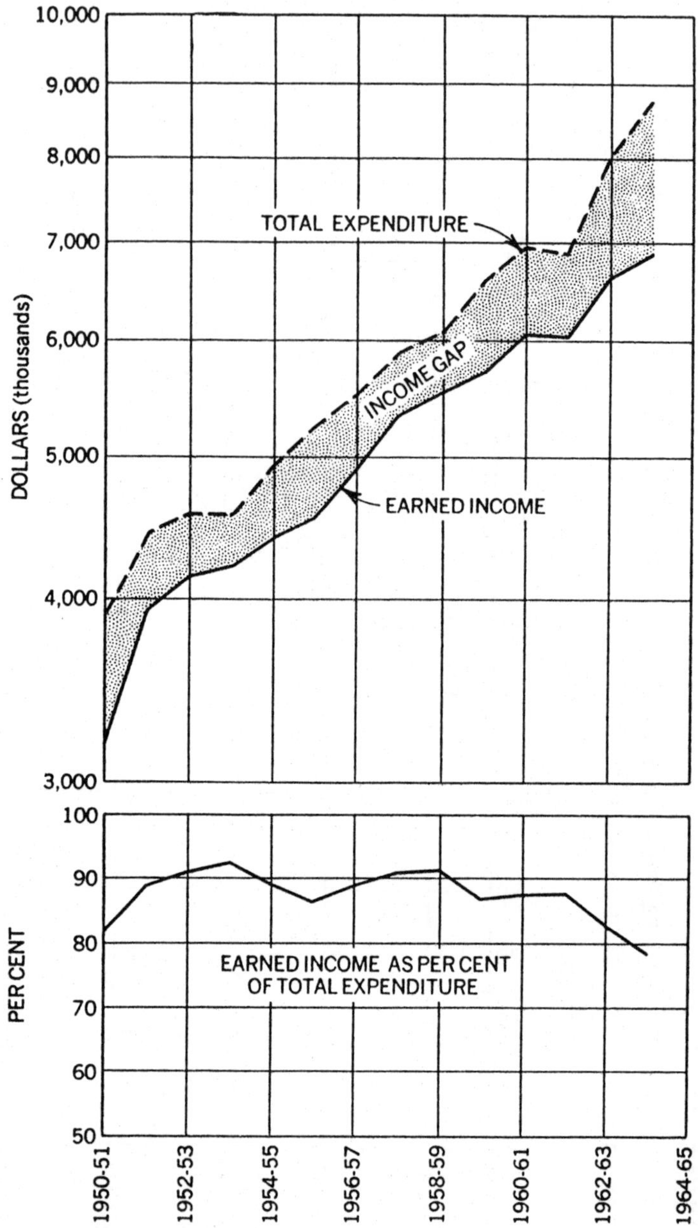

This graph is based on data supplied by the Metropolitan Opera.

FIGURE XII–5

TOTAL EXPENDITURE, EARNED INCOME, AND INCOME AS PER CENT OF EXPENDITURE, COVENT GARDEN, 1951–1964

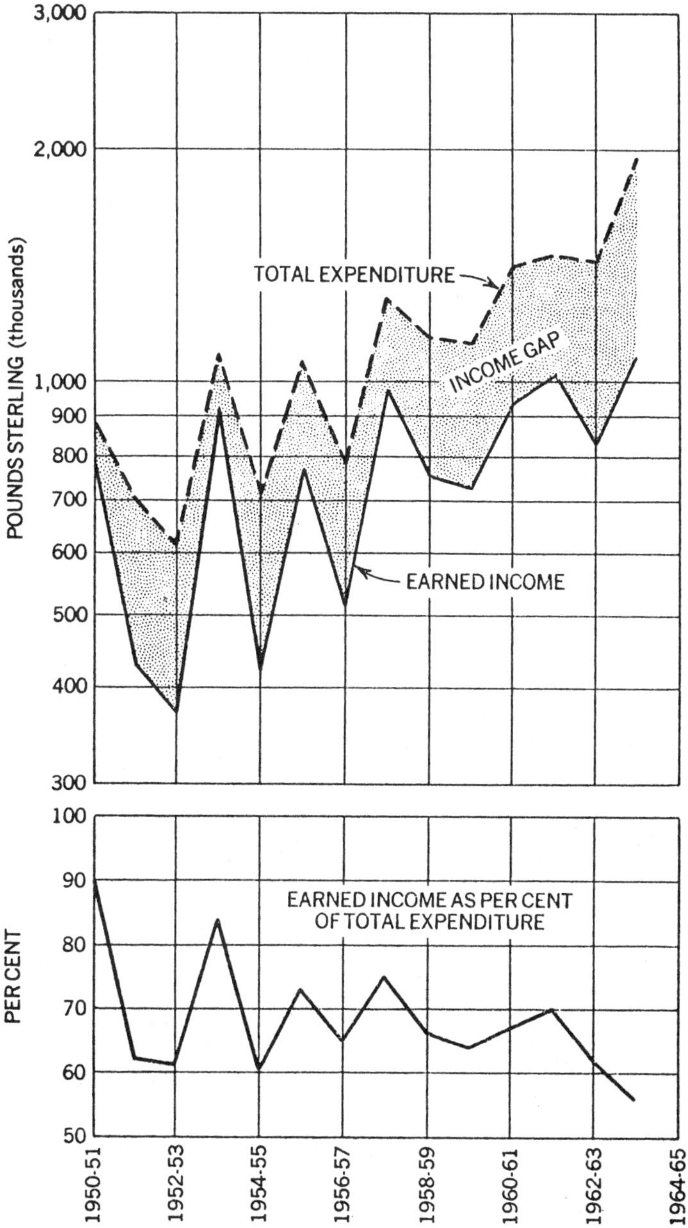

This graph is based on data supplied by Covent Garden.

so quite steadily. This is shown in Figure XII–6. Despite some ups and downs in the graph (in part the consequences of intermittent tours), the tendency for the income gap to grow is quite obvious in this last graph.

Even when earned income does not decline as a proportion of expenditure, if both rise at the same compound rate, so does the gap. If income is 60 per cent of expenditure, and both income and expenditure double, the gap will still be 40 per cent of expenditure, but in dollar terms it will be twice as large as before. For example, in 1951 the Metropolitan Opera's earned income was 82 per cent of its expenditure, and in 1963 the figure was virtually the same — 83 per cent. Yet during that time its gap nearly doubled, growing at an average annual rate of 5.8 per cent. Since, in fact, earned income has constituted a declining proportion of expenditure for many organizations over the postwar period, we would expect that over that interval gaps have risen quite substantially. To test this assertion we fitted trend lines to our postwar gap statistics and found the annual growth rates for the income gaps to be 5.2 *per cent per year for the New York Philharmonic, 4.7 per cent for the Cincinnati Orchestra, 6.9 per cent for the basic eleven major orchestras, 8.2 per cent for the Metropolitan Opera and 9.2 per cent for Covent Garden.*[4]

Gaps have also increased in countries other than the United States and Great Britain. For example, we have financial records for three of the leading Swedish performing organizations going back to 1947–48. In each case attendance has been virtually stationary, and while the Swedish price level has been rising during the postwar period at 3.9 per cent per year, the income gap of the Royal Opera in Stockholm has been growing at a rate of 10.5 per cent per year, and the gaps of the Royal Dramatic Theater in Stock-

[4] See Appendix Table XII–A for details of the calculations, including the tables involved.

The *real* rate of growth of Covent Garden's gap is actually lower than that of the Metropolitan Opera's because the price level in Great Britain was growing about twice as quickly as ours over this period. In constant dollars the annual growth rates in the gaps are very roughly: New York Philharmonic, 4.5 per cent; Cincinnati, 3 per cent; basic eleven orchestras, 5 per cent; Metropolitan Opera, 7 per cent; and Covent Garden, 6 per cent.

FIGURE XII–6

THE INCOME GAP: BASIC ELEVEN MAJOR ORCHESTRAS, METROPOLITAN OPERA AND COVENT GARDEN, 1948–1964

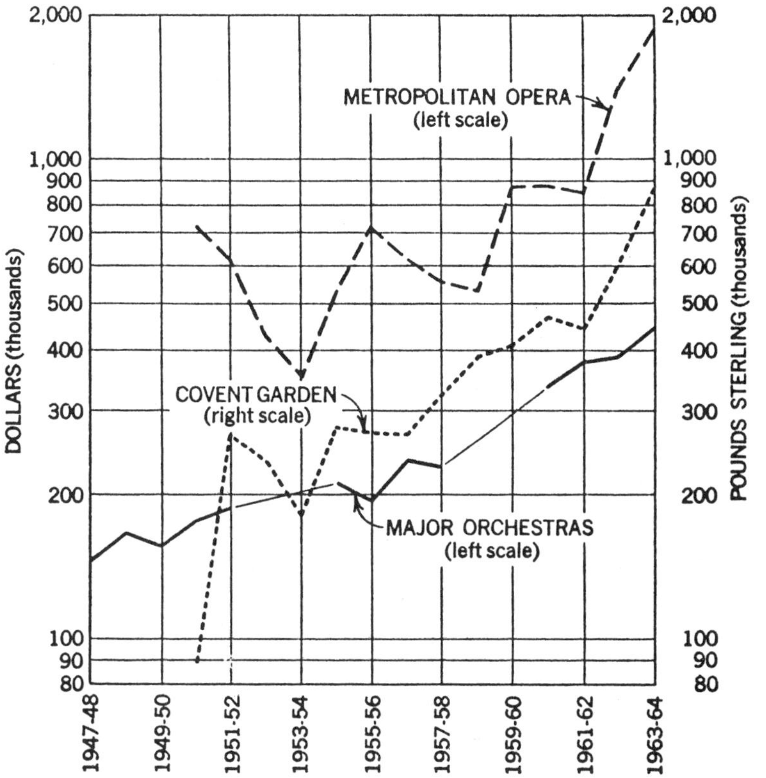

For the data used, see Appendix Table XII–A.

holm and the municipal theater in Malmö have increased at annual rates of 19.5 and 12.5 per cent respectively.[5]

The reader will recall that up to this point a 4 per cent annual

[5] The data on performing groups in Sweden were supplied by the Swedish Centre of the International Theater Institute. The data for the Royal Opera are for 1947–48 to 1963–64. Figures for the Royal Theater span 1947–48 to 1962–63 and those for the Malmö municipal theater are for 1947–48 to 1964–65. The index of prices used is the Consumer Price Index (Cost of Living Index) for 1947–1964, from United Nations, *Monthly Bulletin of Statistics*.

growth rate seemed rather sizable. In fact, not one of our calculated gaps has been growing as slowly as this. It should be noted that an amount growing at 5 per cent per year doubles every 14 years, while one growing at 8 per cent doubles every 9 years. Thus the figures suggest that the typical performing organization's gap is compounding at a very rapid rate. These figures, then, quantify the rate of growth of the financial pressures impinging on some of our leading performing organizations.

Some Indications of a Growing Gap

Calculation of the growth rates of the income gaps is an essential step in the projection of the size of future gaps — a task which we shall undertake in the last chapter of this book. Growth rates by themselves, however, convey only a stark and skeletal image of the underlying realities which they reflect. A few illustrations may suggest somewhat more concretely the nature of the problems which arise out of a growing gap, and indicate their universality.

Perhaps the most sensational illustration of the fact that the financial pressures which beset the arts are not exclusively an American phenomenon is provided by a 1965 news story headlined "Operas in Italy May Face Closing,"[6] in which Robert C. Doty reported:

> The Rome Opera and many of the other major Italian companies may have to face the threat of a close-down early in August unless the Government can raise the equivalent of $5.6 million to meet July payrolls.
>
> Massimo Bogianchino, artistic director of the Rome Opera, now holding its summer season in the ruins of the Baths of Caracalla, said the salaries of more than 400 orchestral and choral musicians, dancers, technicians and office workers — nearly $200,000 — could not be paid this month without state help. . . .
>
> Almost all of the 13 major operatic and symphonic companies in Italy were in similar straits, Mr. Bogianchino said. . . .
>
> Opera-going is a deeply ingrained Italian tradition, and interruption of the supply of Puccini, Verdi, Mozart and Donizetti would be almost as great a public disaster as a utility strike.
>
> Yet the opera patrons here are no more able to foot the entire bill for their favorite entertainment than are their fellow enthu-

[6] *New York Times*, July 26, 1965.

siasts in New York and the current crisis is a symptom of a chronic disease — deficit.

In New York and many other American cities, the deficit is filled by rich, individual contributors. In Italy, the state is the patron, appropriating annually more than $18 million for subsidies to music. But, with lavish Italian production standards and rising wages and other costs, the 13 major state-subsidized organizations have built up debts of more than $22 million.

Similar problems have arisen in Great Britain. In its 1952–53 annual statement, the Arts Council of Great Britain reported:

> The year which ended last March was an anxious one for many of the bodies with which the Arts Council is associated. The cost of producing the arts continues to mount, and several wages awards had to be met by the Symphony Orchestras and the Grand Opera and Ballet Companies. . . . The losing battle in which some of the Repertory Theatres are engaged called for emergency action. *It must be emphasized that most of these anxieties were not provoked by a falling-off in audiences, but rather by the inexorable increase in the costs of presentation.* In such circumstances the providing bodies, and especially the major ones, are confronted with a dilemma. If they decide to economize by, let us say, reducing the number of new productions in opera, ballet and drama they run the risk of a decline at the box-office. There is a limited audience for any given opera or ballet or classical play; and the programme must be frequently changed if attendances are to be maintained. Morton's Fork is a familiar phenomenon in administering the arts.
>
> With the aid of a supplementary vote from Parliament, and the use of its 1951 Festival reserve fund, the Arts Council was able to stave off disaster. For the present year its grant has been substantially increased by Parliament and, at least, breathing-space has been secured.[7]

Since Great Britain is now behind the United States in man-hour output in manufacturing, and hence in manufacturing wages, one might surmise that the cost pressures on British arts organizations are correspondingly lower; and the relatively narrow financial gaps exhibited by a number of organizations whose data we have examined would appear to bear this out. But with productivity rising progressively in the British economy it is only a matter of time before the financial problems of British performing organizations become as serious as ours. Travelers have often commented in the

[7] Arts Council of Great Britain, *The Public and the Arts*, Annual Report for 1952–53, pp. 14–15. Italics ours.

past on the relative aura of prosperity which surrounds the British commercial theater. The large number of new productions offered and the relatively low ticket prices have been cited as evidence. But if our analysis is valid, the unsubsidized West End should not remain immune for very long from the problems which have beset Broadway for some time, and which recently undermined the off-Broadway theater. As wages rise in the British economy, costs of theatrical production will be forced upward, and the increased risk and profit squeeze will be on. Indeed, oral reports indicate that such pressures are already beginning to be felt, and that the British commercial theater will, regrettably, soon join the international brotherhood of arts in perpetual crisis.[8]

What is being done to meet the challenge which a rapidly growing income gap poses for the economic viability of the arts will be considered in the next few chapters, in which we examine sources of contributed income.

[8] Since this was written we found an article which reported that "As far as the rank and file West End theaters were concerned this (1963–64) was one of the most disastrous seasons since before the war. Of twenty-three straight plays only five achieved lengthy runs." (*Theater World Annual*, No. 15, p. 19.) Further investigation confirmed that in London, though there was a sharp increase in 1963–64 in the number of plays performed, the total number of performances and the number of performances per production have declined fairly steadily over the past five years. The number of performances fell from a high of nearly 17,000 in 1954–55 to to a little over 11,000 in 1961–62 and a little over 9,000 in 1962–63 (see Appendix Table XII–B).

Incidentally, if off-Broadway plays are included, the sheer volume of theatrical activity is considerably greater in New York than in London. In 1962–63, for example, 83 different plays were running in London, while in New York 71 were running on Broadway and 131 off-Broadway.

[15]

On finances of the performing arts during stagflation: some recent data

with Hilda Baumol

The cost disease, which seems to contribute so heavily to the financial problems of live performance, is perhaps the most widely cited conclusion of the 14 year old Twentieth Century Fund report on the economics of the arts with which both authors of this article were concerned (Baumol and Bowen (1966). See Notes to Figure 2 for full reference.) The argument is that live performance is at an inherent disadvantage relative to manufacturing in terms of the scope for productivity-increasing innovations. Since the beginning of the 19th century the productivity of labor in manufacturing has probably risen something like 2000%, but the number of person hours directly required to perform a Mozart quintet has not changed. As a result, cost per unit of output in the arts will rise persistently and cumulatively faster than those in the economy as a whole. What has not been widely noted is that our historical data seemed generally to confirm this cost pattern for all states of the economy *with the notable exception of periods of inflation*. For example, financial data for the New York Philharmonic, going back to 1842, indicate that costs failed to keep ahead of the general price level only during the inflationary periods associated with the Civil War and World Wars I and II (Baumol and Bowen, p. 190). We conjectured that this lag in outlays during periods of inflation was to be attributed to erosion of philanthropic support, measured in real terms, and to money illusion which inhibited rises in nominal ticket prices, particularly during a time of national emergency.

Since we are now undergoing the most protracted and substantial inflation in recent American history, it may therefore be interesting to see whether these phenomena are recurring. Here we offer a preliminary report based on some spotty evidence. We will see that in at least one sector, orchestral performance, real cost per performance has actually been holding its own. Real financial support, at least by the public sector, has risen substantially. All this has been accompanied by some increase in attendance and in a widening of the geographic distribution of the audience. Our overall conclusion is that the arts have fared better in terms of support and earned income than might have been feared during such a period of stagflation.[1]

1 On orchestral finances

The extraordinary heterogeneity of arts organizations in their structure and in their financial records is one of the major handicaps besetting systematic analysis of their financial statistics. Orchestras, obviously, hardly can be considered replicas of one another. Nevertheless, their activities and their structures have a basic similarity. Perhaps equally important for our purposes is the standardization in the data which they provide to the American Symphony Orchestra League (ASOL). For this reason the orchestras were a mainstay of the statistical analysis in Baumol–Bowen, and we are fortunate now to have been given recent ASOL data. The larger orchestras are classed as Major Orchestras (those with income over $2 million), Regional Orchestras (budgets of £500,000–$1,999,999), and Metropolitan Orchestras (budgets between $100,000–$499,999). We have figures for a fixed sample of some 160 orchestras for the six years 1973–74 through 1978–79 (Table 1), giving attendance, number of performances, total expenditures and revenues, and grants from different sources. For the moment we are concerned only with the behavior of costs. In nominal terms, over the period total costs rose from $114.7 million to $221 million, an increase of 93%. Using the GNP implicit price deflator (base year 1972) this is transformed into a real rise from $98.8 million to $133.5 million, a rise of 35%. While somewhat more modest, this is, of course, by no means negligible. However, this increase in outlays was accompanied by a rise in attendance and in number of performances. It transpires that, in 1972 dollars, costs per attendee[2] actually rose only slightly from $5.40 to $5.96, while cost per performance actually declined, from $7,100 to $6,000. (Table 2)

This suggests that recent behavior of unit cost is consistent with the historical record. During inflationary periods real performance outlays (like real faculty salaries at colleges and universities) fail to keep ahead of the general price level, even though, because of the relatively slow growth in productivity in the arts and education, their costs rise more rapidly than the general price level at almost all other periods.

Thus, a superficial glance at the data may suggest that increased efficiency of operation has permitted the orchestras to counteract the effects of their inherently lagging productivity. We are, however, rather skeptical about such a sanguine view. At least some of the organizations have offered an alternative view – that the reduced real expenditures are at least partly the result of painful belt-tightening forced upon the orchestras. Cuts in real salaries, in rehearsal time and other such 'economies' may provide a good part of the explanation. Some plausibility is supplied for this view by analogy, such as the well-documented fact that in higher education decreases in real wages have occurred in every inflationary post-war period, including this one.

However, there is a second, equally unhappy phenomenon which may also help to account for the failure of cost per performance to rise. It will be recalled that the cost disease arises from the technology of the live performing arts which inhibits their sharing in the productivity growth enjoyed in the manufacturing sector of the economy. But, as we all know, in the last decade productivity growth in manufacturing has been slowed drastically, and in the last year it has actually been negative. This means that it is no longer so difficult for the arts to keep up in the race. For the moment the tortoise may even be outpacing the hare, and for this reason relative costs in the arts may actually decline.

While for the moment this may represent a welcome pause in the progress of the cost disease, a continued diminution in the general rate of productivity growth in the economy will, in the long run, probably prove a mixed blessing for the arts. Growth in output per labor hour provides rising incomes which make increased

Table 1 Financial and Operational Statistics – Major, Regional and Metropolitan US Orchestras – 1973/74–1978/79

(dollars and numbers, in thousands)

	1973–74	*1974–75*	*1975–76*	*1976–77*	*1977–78*	*1978–79*
Earned income (ticket sales and fees)	48,265.7	57,046.0	64,862.6	74,180.0	86,370.3	103,458.4
Tax-supported grants	16,195.1	18,757.1	20,023.7	20,814.2	25,074.6	32,036.6
Private sector support	33,755.1	34,843.0	38,675.7	44,314.8	50,504.0	62,196.8
Endowment and interest	13,151.0	13,892.9	13,420.4	14,759.4	16,111.4	19,051.1
Gross income	111,366.9	124,539.0	136,982.4	154,068.4	178,060.3	216,741.9
Artistic personnel expense	69,877.8	77,623.5	84,875.8	96,055.2	105,931.4	121,331.5
Production expense	29,031.3	33,728.4	36,403.2	41,380.2	49,947.0	64,399.3
Administrative expense	15,751.1	18,151.1	20,257.7	23,475.4	27,203.4	35,243.7
Gross expense	114,660.2	129,503.0	141,536.7	160,910.8	183,081.8	220,974.4
(Deficit)	(3,293.3)	(4,964.0)	(4,554.3)	(6,842.4)	(5,021.5)	(4,232.5)
Total Attendance	18,336.2	18,326.6	20,058.3	21,032.1	21,383.3	22,405.1
Total Performances	13.9	14.2	14.8	17.4	18.0	22.1
Total Musicians Employed	9.7	8.8	7.5	8.8	9.5	10.7

Source: American Symphony Orchestra League.

Table 2 *Real Income and Expenses (dollars and numbers in 000's) – Major, Regional and Metropolitan US Orchestras – 1973/74–1978/79*

(Using GNP Implicit Price Deflator, 1972 = 100)

	1973–74	*1974–75*	*1975–76*	*1976–77*	*1977–78*	*1978–79*
Earned income (ticket sales and fees)	41,601.1	44,865.1	48,491.7	52,383.3	56,788.9	62,512.6
Tax-supported grants	13,958.9	14,751.9	14,969.8	14,698.2	16,486.6	19,357.5
Private sector support	29,094.2	27,403.0	28,914.2	31,293.5	33,206.6	37,581.1
Endowment and interest	11,335.1	10,926.3	10,033.1	10,422.5	10,593.3	11,510.6
Gross income	95,989.3	97,946.5	102,409.0	108,797.6	117,075.6	130,961.9
Artistic personnel expense	60,229.0	61,048.7	63,453.7	67,830.8	69,650.4	73,312.1
Production expense	25,022.6	26,526.4	27,215.3	29,221.2	32,840.4	38,912.0
Administrative expense	13,576.1	14,275.3	15,144.8	16,577.5	17,886.3	21,295.3
Gross expense	98,827.9	101,850.5	105,813.9	113,629.5	120,377.2	133,519.3
(Deficit)	(2,838.5)	(3,904.0)	(3,404.8)	(4,831.8)	(3,301.6)	(2,557.4)

Source: See Table 1.

attendance and increased philanthropic support possible. Obviously, a growing economy can be more generous in its support of the arts than one which is stagnant.

2 Ticket prices

We are easily shocked by the prices of tickets. A $50 admission fee to the opera and a $20 charge for theatre attendance offend our sense of proportion. But the question is whether this reaction is largely a matter of money illusion or whether these prices have actually risen spectacularly in real terms. Here we turn to another sector, the Broadway theatre, for our information, for here we have access to data spanning more than half a century. Of course, these figures may or may not represent what has happened in other art forms.

There is no fully satisfactory way to calculate the behavior of ticket prices over so long a period. Some theatres have closed and been replaced by new ones. Most have been re-equipped with larger numbers of seats more closely packed to one another. The relative prices of say, orchestra and balcony seats, have changed, and the number of seats included in the higher cost categories, has also risen over the years. Yet, as a rough indicator of price trends it seems reasonably suggestive to use the top ticket price for a musical and a 'straight play'. The data, converted into real terms, are shown in Figure 1. They indicate virtually no trend in real ticket prices since World War II, and, despite the boom in attendance of the past several years, real prices have actually declined substantially in comparison with the prewar period!

3 Audiences

In Baumol–Bowen, 14 years ago, we went to great lengths to puncture inflated contentions then current alleging that the nation was undergoing a great cultural boom. Matters have changed since then in an important way. There is no question that audiences have grown, particularly for some arts activities. The growth is heartening, though not so sensational as to justify the claim that the long awaited 'cultural boom' has finally arrived. What does seem to have arrived is a greatly increased geographical dispersion of arts activity and audiences, so that 'cultural wastelands' have demonstrably and significantly been reduced. Between 1969 and 1977 the number of states offering summer theatre with some degree of professionalism has risen 32%. A recent study of 95 members of the Theatre Communications Group showed that 76% of them were founded since 1962. Dinner theatres, which rose to popularity in the 1970s, are estimated to have provided 32,000 performances in 1977, serving an audience of over 11 million people in every region of the country. Interestingly, the heaviest concentration of dinner theatres is found not in the northeast but in the east, north, central, and south Atlantic states, which formerly showed relatively little interest in performance. The 'road', the presentation of Broadway theatre productions outside of New York, which a decade ago was considered dead, now grosses more than Broadway itself.[3]

We have further evidence that total theatrical activity is increasing from Actors' Equity, which reports total employment of Equity members in terms of work weeks. Employment of actors fell in the late 60s, dipping to 165,000 total playing

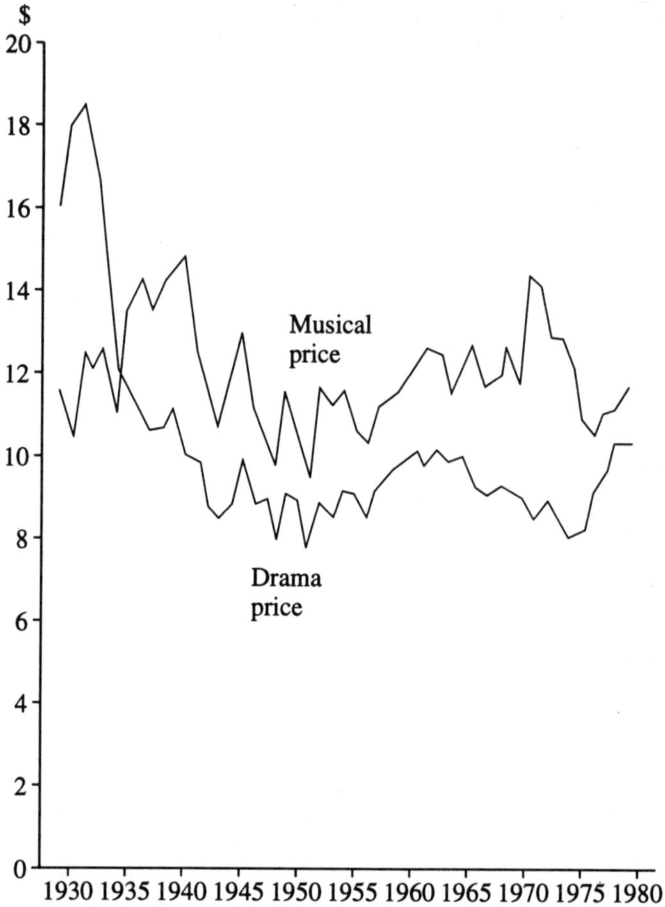

Source: League of New York Theaters and Producers, Inc.

Figure 1 Real Broadway Ticket Prices 1928/29–1978/79 (Top Prices, Musicals and Dramas, Adjusted by GNP Implicit Price Deflator, 1972 = 100)

weeks in 1967–8 and a low of 147,000 in 1970–71. Employment rose after that, slowly at first, and then more rapidly, reaching 204,000 in 1978–9, a 39% rise from its low point eight years earlier.[4]

We have dealt with theatre in such detail because the most recent comprehensive study deals with this art form, but similar trends are manifested elsewhere. The American Symphony Orchestra League reports that in the five years since 1973–4 the audience for major, regional and metropolitan orchestras has risen from 18.3 million to 22.4 million, an increase of 22%.

Thus, interest in the performing arts has grown during the last decade and has spread throughout the country. It is not possible to say whether or not this proliferation is only the beginning, or whether we can expect further growth in the future. It may, however, increase the attractiveness to politicians of government support for the arts, as interest is no longer confined primarily to the inhabitants of the east and west coasts.

Audiences are not only larger but seem to bring in larger revenues. For example, in six years, after correction for changes in the price level, earned income for the ASOL sample of orchestras rose some 50% from $41.6 million to $62.5 million. The earnings of Broadway theatres rose even faster. Between 1972–3 and 1978–9, even in terms of 1972 dollars, total grosses rose from $42.8 million to $82.5 million, that is, by 93%, even though, as we have seen, real ticket prices have not changed substantially. There is evidence that other sectors of the arts are moving in the same direction.

Yet, as already suggested, we should not leap to the conclusion that the great cultural boom has at last arrived. On the contrary, the evidence indicates that there has been no increase in the share of the outlays of consumers going to the arts. Figure 2, a diagram from Baumol–Bowen which we have just brought up to date, dramatizes the story.

This graph gives, for the 33 year period 1946–79, an index of total expenditures on admissions to artistic performances (1929 = 100) as reported in the Survey of Current Business. This is shown by the uppermost curve in the graph, and it indicates that the absolute rise (expressed in nominal dollars) has been very extensive.

But the lower curves show, successively, the behavior of real expenditure, real expenditure *per capita* and, finally, expenditures on admissions as a share of disposable personal income. It is, of course, the last two curves that are of prime significance as a measure of the behavior of public interest in the performing arts. While total expenditure in nominal dollars has increased more than tenfold since 1929 (= 100), in real terms it has just (a bit more than) doubled. More important, *per capita* real expenditure has risen only 12% in half a century, and as a percentage of disposable personal income it has actually fallen 40%! Obviously, attendance of live performances remains far from top priority to the public.[5]

4 Problems for government and private contributions

Before we turn to the evidence which will show that funding for the arts has held up to a surprising degree, it is appropriate to consider why those who advocate such funding might well have been apprehensive (and why, as a matter of fact, many of them continue to be).

There are a number of grounds for concern about the behavior of philanthropic support of the arts during the 1970s and its prospects for the immediate future. As was suggested before, inflation in the past seems generally to have brought harder times for the arts, and that is perhaps in part attributable to money illusion on the part of donors who may not have been prepared to adjust their contributions proportionately to the rise in price level. The inflation rates we are now experiencing are, historically speaking, most extraordinary, and recent bouts of double digit inflation have given us a new sense of proportion about what constitutes normalacy in the behavior of the price level. We now consider a 6% inflation rate a most difficult target and 4% perhaps an unattainable ideal. Yet a historical comparison shows how sharply and quickly such standards can change. The great Tudor infla-

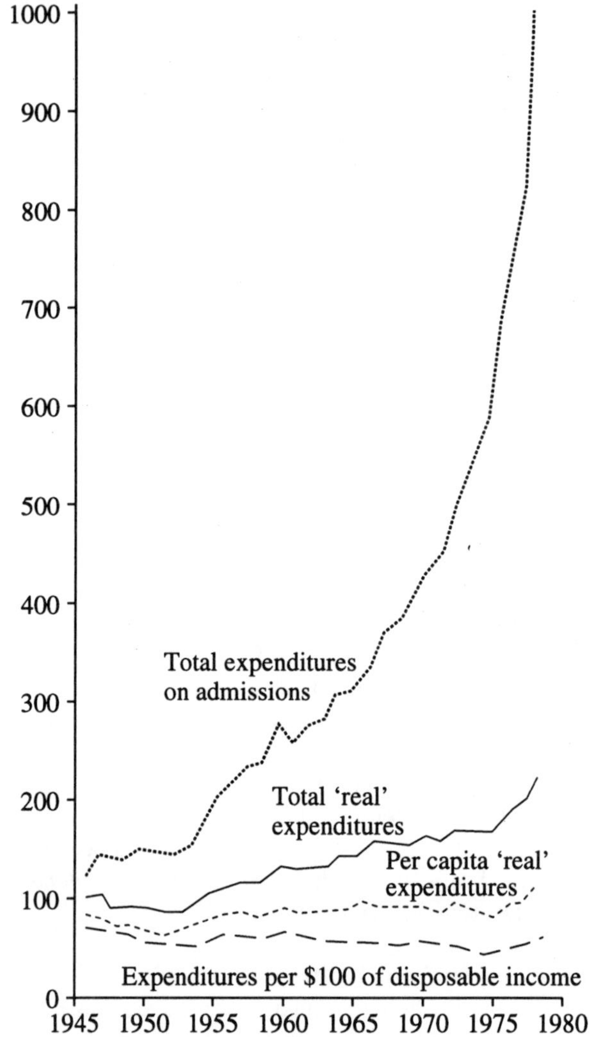

Notes: For data sources and methods of calculation, see Baumol and Bowen, *Performing Arts: The Economic Dilemma* (New York: 20th Century Fund, 1966), p. 430. The main data source is the Survey of Current Business, Personal Consumption Expenditures: Admissions to Legitimate Theaters and Operas and entertainments of nonprofit institutions (except athletic).

Figure 2 Indexes of Expenditures on Admissions 1946–78

tion was the worst in English history. From 1510, one year after Henry VIII's accession, to 1650, the year the Commonwealth was established, prices rose eightfold. Persons living at that time were appalled. Yet a straightforward calculation shows that the rise in prices amounted to no more than 1.3% per year compounded!

Today's economy impedes private contribution in another way. In the past, inflation was rarely accompanied by recession, and the present recession has created financial difficulties for the individuals and the foundations providing funds for the arts. Few people realize how serious the fall in the real value of stock prices has been. Alan Blinder, in an unpublished calculation, has shown that in one year, between January 1973 and December 1974, the fall in purchasing power of an average stock was almost exactly as great as during the worst years of the Great Depression, 1929 to 1933. Thus both the endowments and real incomes of many traditional sources of support for the arts have been severely eroded.

The financial problems affecting support by private individuals and foundations are at least matched by those facing state and local governments. One long-term source of this difficulty lies in the fact that the public services provided by state and local governments also suffer from the cost disease. Education, welfare, and police and fire protection traditionally account for the bulk of their budgets, but none of them are amenable to labor-saving or technological change. It is not surprising, therefore, as evidence confirms, that over longer periods state and local government costs have kept step with costs of the performing arts, and have steadily exceeded the rate of growth of the general price level. Add to this the special problems of the cities in recent years and the success of Proposition 13 and its counterparts elsewhere, and the difficulties threatening state and local support of community cultural centers and arts organizations in general become very clear.

5 On the behavior of real contributions

Despite all of the problems discussed in the preceding section which might have been expected to inhibit giving to the arts, the data we have been able to assemble suggest that real financial support has not declined, and that real support from some sources has actually risen dramatically.

Because there are serious gaps in the data on giving to the arts we can offer only a partial report on their recent behavior. The most comprehensive information available is, once more, that for the orchestras. According to the ASOL figures, in the six year period 1973–4 through 1978–9 real government contributions rose 39%, from $14.0 to $19.4 million (in 1972 dollars). Real private support rose as well, increasing some 30%, from $29.0 million to $37.6 million. As a result, the orchestras have managed to hold their *real* deficit virtually constant.

The experience of the orchestras is reflected in patterns of giving by the major sources of support for the arts. The overall trend of contributions made to the arts by individuals is not quite clear because of the lack of consistent figures. We saw that in the case of the orchestras private contributions actually rose faster than public funding, but, unfortunately, we can find no other reliable time series.

We do know, however, that the annual total of foundation grants to the humanities, which includes grants to the arts, has shown extremely wide fluctuations for the past 6 years.[6] In 1972 dollars, the annual subvention has gone as high as $67.2 million to a low of $46.6 million. The most recent available figure, $57.2 million in 1978, is a little higher than the first one of $53.9 million reported in 1973. Taken as a whole, there seems to have been a very slight declining trend in financing of the arts and humanities by private foundations.

However, government support shows a very different picture (Figure 3). The American Council for the Arts has reported the appropriations of all State Arts

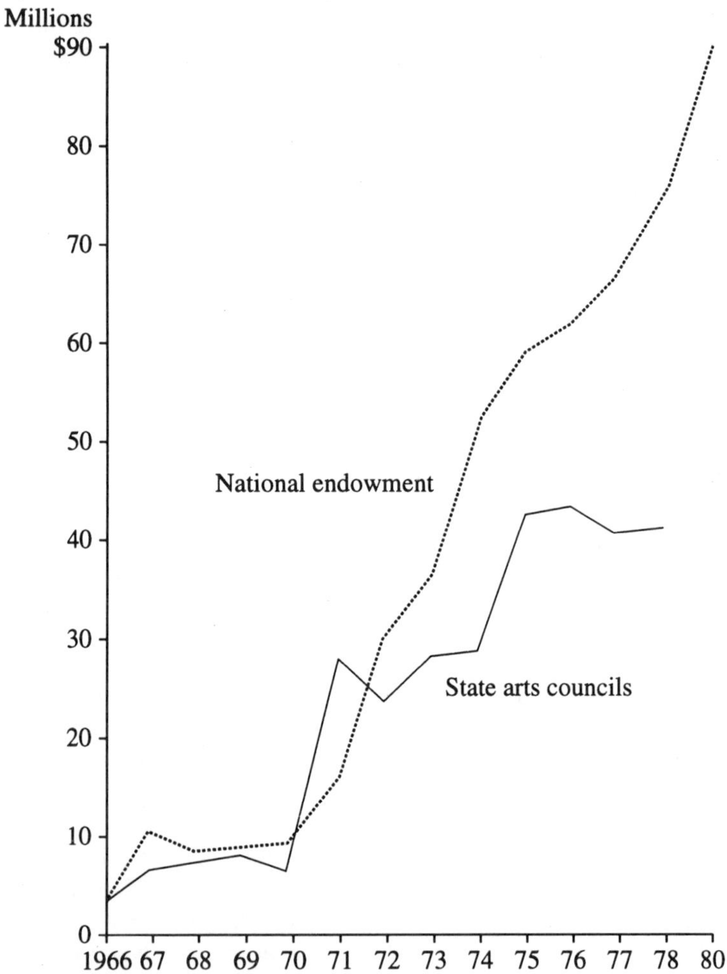

Sources: National Endowment for the Arts, *Annual Reports*; American Council for the Arts, Annual Survey of States Arts Agency legislative appropriations.

Figure 3 *Real Public Support for the Arts, National Endowment and State Arts Councils, 1966–1979 (Adjusted by GNP Implicit Price Deflator, 1972 = 100)*

Councils since 1966. As we might expect, state support showed very modest beginnings ($3.5 million in 1972 dollars for the entire United States in 1966), with an enormous rise at the outset (to $28 million constant dollars in 1971). But our main concern is the behavior of this important source of funding in recent years. Our graph shows a slight fall off *in terms of purchasing power*, but this is still negligible. For all practical purposes the state subventions have managed to rise rapidly and then to keep up with inflation ($40.8 million 1972 dollars in 1978). It is noteworthy, however, that there have been significant exceptions, disturbingly enough including the two capitals of the arts world, California and New York. This is hardly surprising given the well known financial problems of New York and of New York State and the effect of Proposition 13 in California.

The situation remains bright in the case of the National Endowment. Again in 1972 dollars, the history of federal giving shows the same pattern as the State Councils in the earlier years. From a meager $3.3 million in 1966 the total subvention rose to $10.1 million the next year, and then levelled off until 1971. Since then it has risen and re-risen, doubling and redoubling, until in 1979 it reached $90 million. Thus, year after year, the National Endowment's budget has risen significantly faster than the price level!

Concluding comment

The basic conclusion from the facts we have presented is that the stagflationary period thus far has not had the disastrous effect upon the arts that some had feared. Moreover, there is reason to believe the pattern may continue. Past evidence suggests that even in the most difficult periods the arts have managed, by and large, to find financial resources. In the United States, with greater and more widespread interest in the arts being manifested than ever before, the political base for public support for public contributions should grow increasingly firm. This does not imply that the arts organization will have an easy time of it, on the contrary, for them crisis is likely to remain a way of life. But crisis is not the equivalent of disaster.

Mathematica, Inc. Princeton and New York Universities

Notes

1. We are very grateful to Lisa Gonzalez of the American Symphony Orchestra League, George Wachtel of the League of New York Theatres and Producers, Mary Mateja and Thijs ten Raa for their generous assistance. A grant from the Sloan Foundation greatly facilitated completion of this paper. An earlier version was given as a talk at the annual conference of the Association of College University and Community Arts Administrators, Inc. (ACUCAA).
2. While the number of performances rose some 58%, total attendance went up by about 22% during the five year period. Normally we would have preferred cost per performance rather than cost per attendee as our measure of production cost behavior. However, the disparity in the behavior of the two is explainable, at least to a considerable degree, by the growing frequency of chamber music performances by only a small portion of an orchestra's personnel. This seems to have increased substantially in recent years, and therefore reduces considerably the comparability of the figures on number of performances at different dates. In any event, it is clear that real cost per attendee did rise slightly over the period, while cost per performance actually declined significantly.
3. National Endowment for the Arts, Research Bureau Report No. 11, *Conditions and Needs of the Professional American Theatre*, Washington, D.C., April 1980.
4. Actors' Equity Association, Hewitt Report, various years.
5. In saying this we are *not* proposing any value judgement about the merits or demerits of this pattern of consumer expenditures. We cite the figures merely as a comment on the view in recent years that there has been an explosion in US demand for professional arts activities.
6. The Foundation Grants Index, The Foundation Center, New York, 1976–79.

[16]

THE MASS MEDIA AND THE COST DISEASE

Hilda Baumol and William J. Baumol

Ever since the appearance of the Baumol-Bowen volume on the economics of the performing arts, its central hypothesis, the cost disease of live performance, has regularly elicited the comment that the mass media surely provide the cure for the disease. The resistance of live performance to growth in productivity such as the manufacturing sector has been able to achieve means that the costs and prices of manufactured goods must admittedly fall continuously and cumulatively relative to those of performance (meaning that live performance must grow continuously more expensive relative to manufactures and to the price level generally). However, this surely (so the argument goes) is not true of the mass media with their heavy reliance on sophisticated electronics, whose design and productivity contributions improve constantly. Thus, on this view, the costs of the mass media per performance or per member of the audience served(1) should not be expected to rise relative to the general price level, and they should surely be expected to fall relative to the comparable costs of live performance.

In this paper we show both empirically and with the aid of a theoretical analysis that this expectation has in fact been disappointed, and that this is to have been expected, at least in the cases of broadcasting (either TV or radio) and movies (though not necessarily in phonograph records and tapes). First, a matter of terminology: We use the term "progressive" to refer to activities (such as computer hardware and telecommunications) with relatively rapid productivity growth, and the term "stagnant" to connote those (like education and live performance) in which growth is characteristically slow. We will show that, for example, broadcasting, by the very nature of its technology, falls into a hybrid group which we describe as "initially-progressive", meaning that after an initial spurt of cost behavior very similar to that of a progressive industry, its cost is condemned to behave more and more like that of a stagnant activity.

Movie and Broadcasting Production Costs: Some Illustrative Data

The expectation that prices and costs in the mass media will fall relative to those of live performance is easily dispelled by the data. There is a widespread impression that the rate of rise in the prices of Broadway theater tickets has been extraordinary and extreme, at least in recent years, which is what the cost disease analysis (which we are about to summarize briefly) should lead us to expect. We may, therefore, appropriately use these prices as a conservative standard against which to measure the price performance of the mass media.

Table 1 and Figure 1 show the behavior of movie and theater admission prices for a number of years over the postwar period for which we were able to acquire the required data. It is obvious at a glance that over the bulk of the postwar period the price of admission to movie performances has been going up more rapidly than that to straight plays (which, in turn, rose somewhat more quickly than musicals).(2) In the past

Table 1

Ticket Prices, Movies and Commercial Theater, 1948-1983

Year	Film	Drama	Musicals	Indexes (1948=100) Movies	Indexes (1948=100) Drama	Indexes (1948=100) Musicals
1948	$0.36	$ 4.71	$ 6.18	100.00	100.00	100.00
1954	$0.49	$ 5.61	$ 6.52	136.11	119.11	105.50
1958	$0.68	$ 6.68	$ 8.07	188.89	141.83	130.58
1963	$0.86	$ 7.30	$ 8.94	238.89	154.99	144.66
1971	$1.65	$ 9.09	$12.95	458.33	192.99	209.55
1974	$1.89	$10.65	$13.64	525.00	226.11	220.71
1978	$2.34	$17.94	$21.23	650.00	380.89	343.53
1983	$3.30	$37.00	$41.00	916.67	785.56	663.43

SOURCES: Film: The Encyclopedia of Exhibition, National Association of Theater Owners, New York City, 1983. The figures are averages from reports of Association members throughout the U.S.

Theater: League of New York Theaters and Producers, Inc. Based on top ticket price data from Variety.

Figure 1. Ticket Price Indices
Movies and Commercial Theater 1948-83

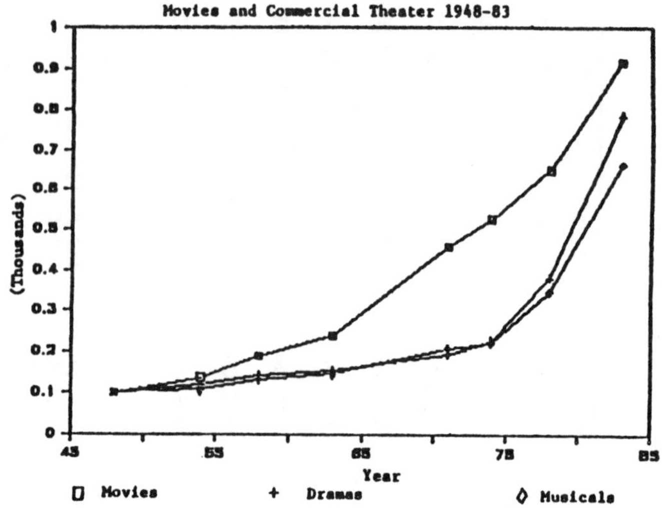

Source: See Table 1

few years the commercial theater has narrowed the gap somewhat, but it has by no means been eliminated.

Table 2 and Figure 2 provide a comparison between cost per hour of prime-time television (averaged for the three networks) and ticket prices for straight plays on Broadway, for 1964/65 to 1976/77, the years for which we have data. For a number of obvious reasons, notably that price is a charge per audience member while the broadcasting data deal with cost per performance, this comparison can at best be suggestive. Yet suggestive it is. Over the 13 year period in question the broadcasting costs rose 63 percent more quickly than Broadway ticket prices.(3)

So much, then, for the hypothesis that the mass media are immune from the cost disease and that their costs and prices will not rise anywhere near as quickly as those of live performance. We will explain soon the logical flaw in this conjecture and the reason the observed behavior we have just reported could have been expected a priori. First, however, we provide a brief review of the old cost disease model as a foundation for the remainder of our discussion. We urge all those who have heard this song before to skip the next section and go on to our new material.

Recapitulation: The Cost Disease Analysis

The model which led to the conclusion that the performing arts are predestined to be victims of a cost disease which condemns their cost (say, per performance) to rise persistently faster than the economy's rate of inflation rests on the basic premise that the technique of live performance is inherently stagnant. Both their labor productivity and total factor productivity is inherently resistant to change. A string quartet written in 1800 for a half-hour performance requires almost exactly as much capital (four instruments) and as much labor (two person-hours) today as it did in the year it was written.(4) Meanwhile, productivity in the manufacturing sector of the economy, having risen at an estimated average rate between 1 and 1.5 percent per annum, compounded over the entire period has gone up something like an astonishing twenty-fold in the interval. As an example, there was a hundred-fold estimated increase in labor productivity in the manufacture of (non-electronic) watches over the 300 year interval since the last decades of the 17th century (on this, see David Landis' marvelous volume (1983), pp. 254 and 351). If the wages of watchmakers and musicians have remained about the same over this period it means that the ratio of the cost of a performance of music to the cost of a watch must have risen about one hundred-fold. That is, the opportunity cost of admission to a theater in terms of number of watches it would have bought would have gone up about 100 times. The relative rise in admissions prices can be expected to persist year in - year out, compounding and adding up as in fact it has.(5)

This, then, in summary is the cost disease analysis which we have offered as an explanation of the behavior of the costs and prices of live performance and which, as we will see, underlies our analysis of the cost behavior of broadcasting and movies.

On The Cost Structure of Initially-Progressive Activities

Broadcasting is a prime example of an activity which we call

Table 2

Cost Per TV Program Hour and Broadway Drama Ticket Prices
1964/65 - 1976/77

Season	Cost Per Program-Hour	Program Index	Drama Price	Drama Index
1964	126	100.0	7.27	100.0
1965	136	107.9	7.06	97.1
1966	156	123.8	7.24	99.6
1967	176	139.7	7.73	106.3
1968	181	143.7	7.83	107.7
1969	188	149.2	8.16	112.2
1970	195	154.8	8.27	113.8
1971	200	158.7	9.09	125.0
1972	208	165.1	8.93	122.8
1973	204	161.9	9.42	129.6
1974	213	169.0	10.65	146.5
1975	252	200.0	12.37	170.2
1976	306	242.9	13.65	187.8

SOURCES: Television: Charles River Associates. Based on data in *Television and Broadcasting* magazines. The data are average costs for the three networks per program hour, all evening entertainment series, and exclude movies, sports and news programs.

Theater: Same as Table 1.

Fig. 2. TV Costs vs Drama Ticket Prices
Indices 1964-76 (1964=100

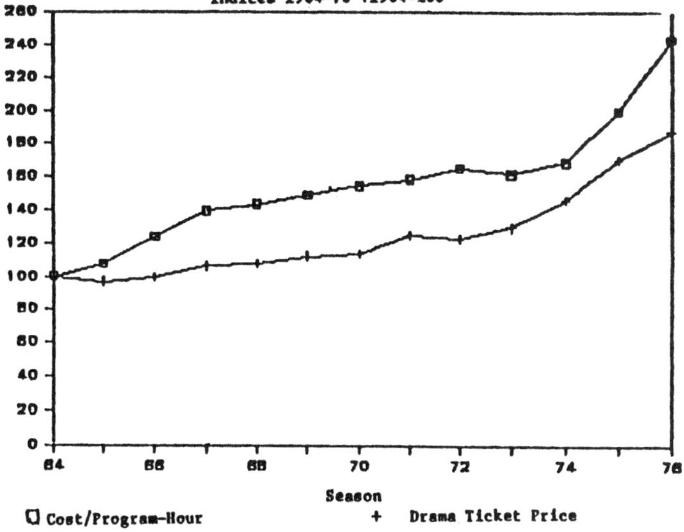

Source: See Table 2

initially-progressive. It has two basic components: (1) programming, that is, the writing, set design and construction, and performance (acting, playing the music, etc.) of the actual programs, and (2) transmission, the delivery of the programs to their distant audiences. The first is extremely stagnant in its productivity growth; it is, indeed, virtually identical with live performance on a theater stage. The second, electronic and high tech in character, is highly progressive. These are the defining attributes of an initially-progressive activity—the progressivity of one of the two dominating inputs and the stagnancy of the other, and the relatively fixed physical proportions of the two inputs—one hour of performance (with some flexibility in rehearsal time) and one hour of transmission per one-hour broadcast. There are other examples of such activities; electronic computation, with its reliance on progressive hardware and stagnant software, is our favorite example.(6)

What predetermined fate awaits such an initially-progressive activity? Its destiny is dictated irremediably by the underlying relationships just described, unless there is a fundamental technological change which leads to the elimination of one or more of the defining attributes. Otherwise, as we will show now, such an activity may be expected to be characterized by an initial period of declining real cost (hence the term "initially-progressive") followed by a period in which its costs begin to behave in a manner more and more similar to those of a purely stagnant activity. Thereafter, the cost behavior of the two (say, broadcasting and live performance) need never again diverge to any significant degree.

The reason for this sort of time path of costs is straightforward. Because one input is progressive its cost will tend to decline or at least not to rise in real terms, thus exerting a reducing influence on the overall price of the initially-progressive activity. At the same time, the stagnant component will rise in unit cost at a rate faster than the general price level. These two facts, the relative lag in the price of the progressive component and the relative rise in the price of the stagnant component, together with the fixed proportion in which they are employed, means that the progressive input must constitute an ever-declining share of the overall budget of the enterprise, while the stagnant input must for the same reason constitute an ever-increasing share of that budget. Ultimately, the outlay on the stagnant component will necessarily have to constitute almost the entire budget of the supplier of the activity. In sum, the very progressivity of the more high tech input automatically causes its ultimate demise as a significant component of the total cost of the enterprise.

Figure 3 is a hypothetical history of the costs of such an initially-progressive activity. To dramatize the time pattern the growth rates chosen are those appropriate for computation rather than those for broadcasting where matters proceed far more gradually, as we will see. But in the long run the qualitative properties of the time paths of costs in the activities must be the same. That is an inescapable logical consequence of the premises implicit in the defining attributes of an initially-progressive activity.

In the figure we show transmission cost initially constituting 80 percent of total costs. Those costs are here assumed to fall 25 percent per

Figure 3. Initially-Progressive Behavior: A Cost Simulation

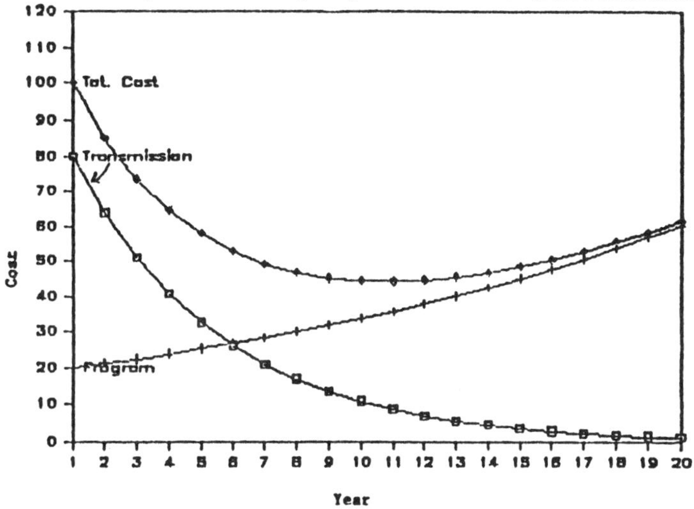

year in real terms (about the right figure for computer hardware, starting in about 1970). Programming, the remaining 20 percent of costs in year 1, are taken to rise 6 percent a year (a reasonable estimate for software costs in reality). We see that for the first ten years or so, because transmission costs are falling and start out as so high a proportion of the whole, the total cost at first falls almost as rapidly as transmission costs, and continues falling, but at an ever-declining rate. By the 10th year, transmission costs are reduced to about 10 percent of the total and the upward time path of programming cost will begin to dominate the overall budget. Thereafter, total cost and programming cost must move closer and closer together, until they become virtually indistinguishable.

This is the prototype life cycle of any initially-progressive activity. Note, however, that if the progressive component is relatively small to begin with, the period of declining cost of the overall activity may be fairly brief or may not occur at all. However, the rising cost portion of the life cycle and its increasing similarity to the behavior of the cost of the stagnant component, is an inescapable consequence of the defining attributes of such an activity.

This model, then, is sufficient to account for the cost and price behavior of broadcasting and the movies that was reported earlier. The analysis tells us that in the long run broadcasting and moviemaking cannot promise an escape from the cost disease that besets live performance. On the contrary, the model shows that the cost disease can be contagious and that at least some of the mass media may already be in an advanced stage of the illness.

On Further Evidence

The preceding theoretical analysis is easily rephrased in rigorous mathematical terms which readily confirm the conclusions that have been drawn from it. However, as usual, empirical evidence requires more work.

The sequence of events in the research reported here already provides some supporting evidence. Had we first observed the behavior of movie ticket prices and of broadcasting costs and then sought to explain it by means of the model, then, as we know, the data would constitute no confirmation of the formal analysis. But the fact is that we proceeded in just the opposite way. First, we hit upon the formal analysis and only turned later to the figures to check their consistency with the model's predictions. That, of course, does constitute evidence which at least does not "disconfirm" the basic analytical structure.

A second prediction of the model can be used as a further check. The model tells us that with the passage of time the <u>share</u> of the overall budget constituted by the stagnant input will rise <u>relative</u> to the progressive input. Figure 4, revised from Baumol, Blackman and Wolff (1984) and based on U.S. Federal Communications Commission data, shows that this was indeed the case. While matters moved far more slowly than in computation, technical expenses fell from 28 percent of the total of the two in 1960 to only 19.7 percent of that total in 1980.(Table 3)

In constant dollars, calculated using the GNP deflator, technical expenses actually rose, but at the rate of 0.8 percent per year. Real programming costs, however, rose at an annual rate of 3.1 percent, while

Figure 4. Technical and Program Expense
Average U.S. TV Station, 1960-1980

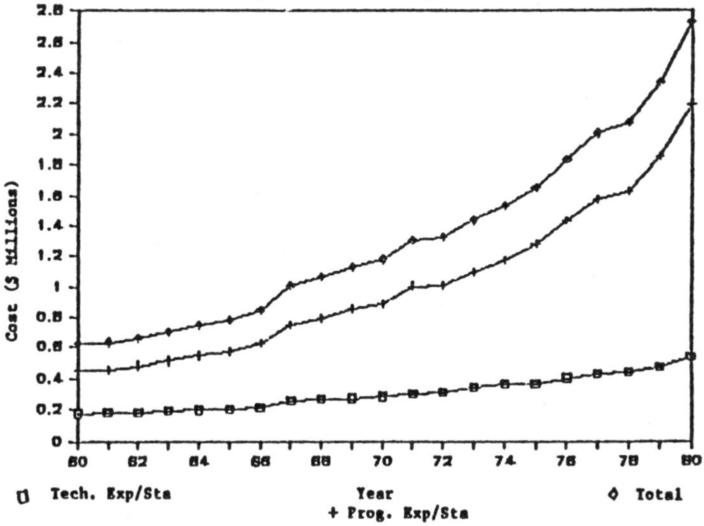

Table 3

Technical and Program Expenses Average U.S. TV Station 1960–1980, in Millions of Dollars

Year	Technical Expenses	Program Expenses	Technical and Program Expenses	% of Expenses in Programs
1960	92.9	239.1	332.0	72.02
1961	96.2	245.2	341.4	71.82
1962	101.3	265.4	366.7	72.38
1963	106.3	290.5	396.8	73.21
1964	113.8	315.1	428.9	73.47
1965	120.2	338.8	459.0	73.81
1966	131.1	380.1	511.2	74.35
1967	141.4	409.2	550.6	74.32
1968	151.5	449.1	600.6	74.78
1969	161.4	504.9	666.3	75.78
1970	170.6	534.7	705.3	75.81
1971	179.6	599.2	778.8	76.94
1972	196.5	628.6	825.1	76.18
1973	210.5	677.9	888.4	76.31
1974	228.3	733.7	962.0	76.27
1975	229.6	805.3	1034.9	77.81
1976	256.7	912.3	1169.0	78.04
1977	270.3	995.1	1265.4	78.64
1978	318.4	1162.5	1480.9	78.50
1979	346.3	1343.6	1689.9	79.51
1980	390.0	1588.3	1978.3	80.29

SOURCE: U.S. Federal Communications Commission, Annual Report, various years. Excludes the three major networks but includes network-owned and operated stations.

total real cost rose at a rather similar rate, 2.9 percent per year.

While we were not able to get actual cost figures from the television networks, one major network very kindly made inquiries among their knowledgeable personnel for us. The consensus was that 10 years ago above-the-line costs for a TV series (actor, producer, director, music, etc.) constituted 35 to 40 percent of the budget and below-the-line costs (roughly, production costs) were 60 to 65 percent. Now, they are roughly equal.

The declining spread between the two types of costs are doubtless attributable in good part to the various economizing innovations that have been introduced in the technological area, among them, increased automation, the use of tape instead of film wherever possible, the editing of film after first putting it on tape, etc.

While other influences undoubtedly have played a role in the cost developments described in this section, they clearly are consistent with our hypothesis that TV broadcasting is an initially-progressive activity with an inherent tendency to fall victim to the cost disease.

Concluding Comments

The preceding discussion may perhaps be helpful to groups presenting live performance, to broadcasters and to movie producers alike. For example, theater owners and producers can now assert that while the rate of increase in their ticket prices is disturbing, it is certainly not out of line with and perhaps even somewhat more modest than the cost and price rises in those mass media whose products are most directly comparable with their own. Broadcasters and moviemakers can now provide evidence strongly indicating that the very rapid increases in their costs are not manifestations of waste and extravagancies, but, rather, reflect the technological imperatives of the production of their outputs and the inherent requirement that their activities' stagnant segments occupy an ever-rising share of their overall budgets.

As we have noted, the analysis also shows that the mass media are by no means immune to the cost disease. The evidence is that film and broadcasting may in fact both be suffering from a well-advanced case of the illness.

It should be noted, however, that there is a possible offset for the mass media. This is clearest for phonographic tape and recording, but a similar possibility arises for the other mass media which may conceivably become relatively immune from the consequences of the disease, at least if calculated in terms of cost per person served. The fact that a tape or a record can be replayed as many times as one desires for as many additional persons who care to listen or watch, without any addition in performance inputs, may be able to offset the consequences of the cost disease of the original recording if the audience size per recording rises cumulatively at a sufficiently rapid rate. The same may be true of any of the mass media. If the audience per broadcast or per movie should rise at a rate faster than the cost of performance increases, then their real unit prices may actually fall. In fact, however, the number of households watching television on the major networks has been decreasing for the last decade, and movie audiences have been declining sharply for a period that is even longer.

Finally, we may note that the fact that the cost disease seems to pervade the mass media as well as live performance is a ground for concern but not for despair. For there is little reason to expect the disease to be terminal (except, perhaps, for some financially marginal enterprises) — but it certainly can be debilitating.

Industry Economics Princeton and New York University

FOOTNOTES

1. Production cost per performance and cost per audience member do not, of course, necessarily behave in the same manner. Strictly speaking, the cost disease phenomenon we will be discussing implies only that the cost per TV broadcast or the cost per movie produced will ultimately tend to rise like cost-per-performance in live theater. If the size of the audience per TV broadcast or per film rises quickly enough it is still possible for real cost per audience member to decline.

   The distinction between cost per performance and cost per audience member is a problem for our empirical discussion. The nature of the available data leads us to compare price per ticket to a Broadway performance (where audiences have fluctuated but shown little trend over the postwar years) with price per movie ticket, where audiences have fallen significantly. It also leads us to compare cost per ticket to a Broadway play (a rough indicator of cost per audience member) with cost per hour of prime-time television, an indicator of cost per performance. The comparisons, thus, are highly imperfect. Yet the robustness of the observed behavior does lend support to our conclusions.

2. The result is, of course, attributable in part to the rather sizable fall in movie audiences, as well as the technological cost-disease influences with which we are concerned. We have made a rough estimate of what the rise in movie tickets might have been had the audience size not declined. Using data provided by Fritz Machlup and Michael Rubin on total expenditures on movie admissions in the U.S. in 1958 and 1980 and the ticket price data in Table 1, we estimated total audience sizes in those two years. Then, extrapolating linearly to 1948 and 1983 we corrected the ticket price figures for the two years on the assumption that the same total costs would have been covered, despite the change in audience size. This reduced the value of the movie price index for 1983 from 916 to 521, making the rise in movie prices somewhat less than that in theater tickets, though still leaving them similar in magnitude. It is clear that the 521 value of the index is a considerable underestimate since, if attendance in 1983 had risen some 75 percent to its 1948 figure, that would have created demand pressures toward higher ticket prices even if it reduced cost per attendee.

3. According to Levin (1980), who used data for different years, between 1960 and 1970 the cost of a half-hour of prime-time television rose 3.5 percent per annum in constant dollars. From 1952 to 1974 in real terms the cost of a half-hour film rose 7.4 percent per year (!) and total network program expenditures even went up a bit faster.

4. There are some savings. For example, performers do spend much less time today traveling between engagements.

5. For supporting data, see Baumol and Bowen (1966), Chapter VIII. A noteworthy exception occurs in periods of sharp inflation when costs per performance have, almost without exception, not risen faster than the general price level (see Baumol and Bowen, pp. 189-191, and for more recent data, Baumol and Baumol (1984, forthcoming)). We believe that what goes on during inflationary periods is suppression, not remission, of the cost disease. That is, the difficulty of raising sufficient funds either through ticket sales or contributions gives rise to cutting of corners (reduced rehearsal time, reduced number of sets, smaller casts, etc.) rather than to any significant increase in efficiency (productivity). But that is the subject of another article which we are now writing.

6. For data on computation and a formal analysis of the behavior of costs in such an initially-progressive industry, see Baumol, Blackman and Wolff (1984). There, instead of "initially-progressive" we use the barbaric term, "asymptotically stagnant."

REFERENCES

Baumol, Hilda and William J. Baumol. "On Inflation and the Performing Arts: A Summing Up," Inflation and the Performing Arts, New York: New York University Press, 1984 (forthcoming).

Baumol, William J., Sue Anne Batey Blackman, and Edward N. Wolff. "Unbalanced Growth Revisited: Asymptotic Stagnancy and New Evidence." C.V. Starr Center, New York University, Economic Research Reports, January 1984.

Baumol, William J. and William G. Bowen. Performing Arts: The Economic Dilemma. New York: Twentieth Century Fund, 1966.

Landis, David. Revolution in Time. Cambridge, Mass.: Bellnop Press (Harvard University Press), 1983.

Levin, H. J. Fact and Fancy in Television Regulation. New York: Russell Sage Foundation, 1980.

The future of the theater and the cost disease of the arts

with Hilda Baumol

The only conviction we have on the future of the theater is that it will survive. The question is only the degree of hardship creative activity will face, and the degree of economic, and thus artistic, risk producers will allow themselves. This is as true of the commercial theater as the not-for-profit. No one can foresee the economic conditions of the distant future, but we may be able to learn something from today's pertinent trends, which are the subject of this paper.

The unusual aspect of this paper is that a ten year set of data for small- and medium-sized nonprofit theaters has become available, which lends itself to comparison with orchestral data. Up to now the American Symphony Orchestra League had been the only source of annual, comparable statistical data. We will analyze these two sets of data which permit a fairly systematic ten year comparison of costs and revenues and some of their components for theaters and orchestras. These and some other related data will be examined for their implications for the future of the theater in terms of the cost disease model with which we have been associated. This model predicts that, because of the nature of their technology, the costs of the performing arts have an inherent tendency to rise persistently and cumulatively faster than the economy's overall rate of inflation. Finally, we will discuss whether mass media such as films and television offer a respite from the cost disease of live performance.

First we will show that during the past decade the cost disease has continued to plague both theaters and orchestras in the US, suggesting that their economic future is unlikely to grow easier in the foreseeable future. Second, we will provide evidence that the cost disease has been partly camouflaged by 'economies' which actually threaten the quality of the performing arts. Finally we will indicate that the mass media offer no way out of the problem in the long run because they, too, have fallen victim to the cost disease for reasons that will be explained.

Since the cost disease is central to the analysis of this paper, it is necessary to review the nature of this malaise of live performance. Eighteen years ago one of the authors of this article and William G. Bowen, now President of Princeton University, showed that the performing arts are predestined to be the victims of a cost disease which condemns the cost per live performance, be it *Hamlet*, *The Barber of Seville*, or a rock concert, to rise at a rate persistently faster than that of a typical manufactured good.

The cost disease and inflation

Since the cost disease was described in 1964, arts administrators throughout the world have been using the model to back up their requests for increases in government support for the arts. It has repeatedly been argued that since performance budgets must inevitably rise faster than the general price level, increases in support which merely match the economy's price level must condemn the arts to decline and deterioration. So long as the data continued to show that *real* costs per performance or per attendee were indeed continuing to rise as predicted all seemed well in the continuing relationships between the funding agencies and the recipients of their support. However, when recent data revealed some cases in which such costs were falling behind the inflation rate, more than one such group underwent feelings of panic and betrayal. The reliable old cost disease law had failed them. What had gone wrong? Or, rather, had something unexpectedly gone *right* for costs in the arts?

As a matter of fact, nothing has gone wrong with the cost disease model's predictions. Neither is there any reason to believe that matters have improved in any way for the costs of performance. There are two reasons a slowdown, and perhaps even a decline, in real per unit costs should have been and were, in fact, expected.

First, as we have seen, the cost disease is a manifestation of the *relative* lag in productivity growth in performance. Performance suffers because manufacturing productivity habitually rises so rapidly and pulls wages up with it. But in the 1970s, for reasons that are in some dispute, productivity growth in manufacturing in almost every industrialized economy slowed down to a crawl. Thus, the engine that triggers the cost disease virtually ran out of fuel during that decade.

Second, even the earliest study of the cost disease of the arts (Baumol and Bowen, 1965) indicated that while for well over a century orchestral cost per performance had *almost* always risen faster than the general price level, there was one persistent exception – periods of inflation. During each of the brief postwar inflations that the United States experienced before World War II, the rise in cost per performance consistently fell behind the general price level. Though we have no clear cut evidence, our hypothesis is that in such periods the public resists increases in outlays on the arts which exceed the growth in the price level to the degree typical of uninflationary periods. Since in the performing arts expenditures must, in the long run, adjust themselves to receipts, cost per performance then lags as a matter of economic necessity.

Whether this explanation is or is not valid, the fact remains. In inflationary periods experience should have made it clear that cost per performance does not necessarily rise faster than the general price level when an economy is undergoing an inflationary period such as that of the 1970s. Thus, both the record of the past and the logic of the cost disease analysis should have warned us (and did) that the symptoms of the cost disease may become more moderate or may even (temporarily) disappear altogether during an era such as that we are now experiencing. Also, this inflation differs from previous ones in the US. No earlier inflation has ever lasted as long as that of the 1970s, and never before has so much direct support been provided to the arts by the federal, state, and local governments and by private foundations. The question then remains, what did happen to real per unit costs? We now have some facts which can help us to answer the question.

The ASOL and TCG data

Until a few years ago virtually the only available US data that permitted systematic intertemporal comparisons of costs pertained to orchestras. Each theatrical production was typically organized as an individual enterprise with its own records and its own financial arrangements, and this, added to the heterogeneity of the plays themselves, impeded the accumulation of comparable records over time for costs of drama and musical comedies. However, in the last few decades the United States has experienced the growth of a national network of theaters, each having a permanent organization and each offering a number of different productions every season. Their organization, the Theater Communications Group (TCG), has, among its many valuable activities, collected data on income, expenditures and activity of the sort previously available only for the orchestras from the venerable and respectable American Symphony Orchestra League (ASOL). The figures for both these groups are compiled annually by the respective organizations. Tables 1 and 2 provide the data in question in terms of 1972 dollars. We need only offer a few remarks about the sample. The ASOL figures are more or less a universal sample of the organization's membership, which includes all professional and most semi-professional orchestras in the US. The sample therefore varies somewhat from year to year as new orchestras are founded, others die, and some of the smaller ones fail to provide data. Yet the variability is not as great as that may suggest. The figures are dominated by the relatively large budgets of the so called Major Orchestras (defined as those whose budgets exceed $3.4 million per year), whose population does not change from year to year and who never fail to provide their reports to ASOL.

The TCG sample consists of a homogeneous group of 22 theaters for nine of the ten years. In the most recent year a change in the sample was required as one of the theaters in the previous sample ceased operations. Fortunately, TCG provided several years of overlap of data for the two sample groups, so that it was quite easy to adjust the 1983 data for the new sample to make them comparable with the figures for the earlier nine years.[1]

Summary of conclusions from the data

Our first conclusion is that the data tell us unambiguously that the cost disease is still very much with us. In the ten year period for which we have data (Tables 3 and 4), cost per performance rose relative to the general price level at a compound rate of 1 percent a year for the theaters and 0.9 percent a year for orchestras. Similarly, *real* cost per attendee increased 2.2 percent a year for theaters and 2.4 percent a year for orchestras. That may not seem like much, but because of compounding it was sufficient over the decade to raise cost per attendee by 25 percent relative to the average price of commodities in the economy as a whole. Over a 35 year period, such a rate of increase is sufficient to double the cost of attendance measured in dollars of constant purchasing power.

However, there is more to the story. We note that cost per performance rose considerably more slowly than cost per attendee. This means that both theaters and orchestras were increasing the number of their performances significantly faster than audiences were growing. Indeed, this led to a remarkable phenomenon. Between 1974 and 1979 the number of orchestral performances was growing so

Table 1 *Income, Expenses and Activity: 22 Regional Theaters 1974–1983 (millions of current dollars except as noted)*

	1974	1975	1976	1977	1978	1979	1980	1981	1982	1983	Growth rate (%)
Income earned	13.8	15.8	17.4	20.0	23.0	29.1	27.7	34.7	37.2	42.5	11.9
Contributions											
federal	1.4	1.9	1.8	1.9	2.6	3.3	2.4	3.0	2.7	2.9	7.6
state and local	0.6	1.0	1.0	1.9	1.3	1.5	2.0	2.0	2.1	2.4	14.9
individual and other	2.9	3.7	3.3	3.7	4.6	5.5	6.7	7.7	8.3	9.2	12.2
foundations	2.3	1.9	2.2	1.9	1.6	1.9	2.1	2.2	2.3	3.1	3.0
corporations	0.4	0.5	0.5	0.6	0.9	1.0	1.1	1.3	1.5	2.9	21.9
Total income	21.4	24.7	26.2	29.1	33.9	42.3	42.0	50.9	54.2	61.3	11.1
Expenses											
artistic salaries	5.9	6.6	7.7	8.7	9.9	10.7	10.6	12.0	13.6	15.1	9.9
administrative salaries	3.0	4.0	4.2	4.6	5.4	6.4	7.3	8.1	10.0	11.6	14.5
technical salaries	2.5	3.5	3.7	4.2	4.6	6.3	6.0	7.9	8.7	9.1	13.8
non-salary expenses	10.5	10.4	11.1	12.3	14.5	18.3	17.8	22.6	22.5	25.7	9.4
Total expenses	21.9	24.4	26.7	29.8	34.3	41.7	41.7	50.6	54.8	61.5	10.9
Surplus	–0.5	0.3	–0.5	–0.7	–0.4	0.7	0.3	0.4	–0.6	0.2	
Performances (000)	7.3	7.7	8.0	9.0	8.9	9.0	8.5	8.9	8.7	9.2	2.3
Attendance (mil)	3.5	3.6	3.8	3.8	4.0	4.3	4.2	4.2	3.8	3.9	1.1

Source: Theater Communications Group, *Theater Facts*, various years. The sample changed in 1983, and our figures for 1983 are adjusted accordingly. Attendance and Performance figures for 1974 and 1983 are also estimates.

Table 2 Income and Expenses: 22 Regional Theaters 1974–1983 (millions of 1972 dollars)

	1974	1975	1976	1977	1978	1979	1980	1981	1982	1983	Growth rate (%)
GNP deflator	147.7	161.2	170.5	181.5	195.4	217.4	246.8	272.4	289.1	298.4	
Income earned	9.34	9.80	10.21	11.02	11.77	13.39	11.22	12.74	12.87	14.24	4.3
Contributions											
federal	0.95	1.18	1.06	1.05	1.33	1.52	0.97	1.10	0.93	0.97	0.3
state and local	0.41	0.62	0.59	1.05	0.67	0.69	0.81	0.73	0.73	0.80	7.1
individual and other	1.96	2.30	1.94	2.04	2.35	2.53	2.71	2.83	2.87	3.08	4.6
foundations	1.56	1.18	1.29	1.05	0.82	0.87	0.85	0.81	0.80	1.04	–4.0
corporations	0.27	0.31	0.29	0.33	0.46	0.46	0.45	0.48	0.52	0.97	13.6
Total income	14.49	15.32	15.37	16.03	17.35	19.46	17.02	18.69	18.75	20.54	3.6
Expenses											
artistic salaries	3.99	4.09	4.52	4.79	5.07	4.92	4.29	4.41	4.70	5.06	2.4
administrative salaries	2.03	2.48	2.46	2.53	2.76	2.94	2.96	2.97	3.46	3.89	6.7
technical salaries	1.69	2.17	2.17	2.31	2.35	2.90	2.43	2.90	3.01	3.05	6.1
non-salary expenses	7.11	6.45	6.51	6.78	7.42	8.42	7.21	8.30	7.78	8.61	1.9
Total expenses	14.83	15.14	15.66	16.42	17.55	19.18	16.90	18.58	18.96	20.61	3.3
Surplus	–0.34	0.19	–0.29	–0.39	–0.20	0.32	0.12	0.15	–0.21	0.07	

For source and notes: see Table 1.

Table 3 Real Cost Per Performance and Per Attendee: 22 Regional Theatres 1974–1983 (thousands of dollars)

	Cost per performance	Cost per attendee
1974	2.0	4.2
1975	2.0	4.2
1976	2.0	4.1
1977	1.8	4.3
1978	2.0	4.4
1979	2.1	4.5
1980	2.0	4.0
1981	2.1	4.4
1982	2.2	5.0
1983	2.2	5.3
Growth rate (%)	1.0	2.2

For source and notes: see Table 1.

rapidly that the real cost per performance actually fell fairly steadily from $5,600 to $4,600. (See Table 4.)

What was going on? As we understand it, in this period, many of the major orchestras, having signed contracts agreeing to provide full year employment to their musicians, sought income producing ways of keeping them busy. Chamber concerts by small groups of musicians drawn from an orchestra was one widely used means to do so. Such concerts added considerably to the *number* of performances, but with the typically small attendance of chamber concerts they did not increase audiences nearly commensurately.

The important implication of this observation is that the cost disease forces performing groups to find ways to sublimate the problem – to trade off increasing costs for money saving changes in the way they conduct their activities. Table 5 provides a convincing illustration of this phenomenon. One obvious way to suppress the cost disease is to cut down the number of artists the performing organization has on its payroll. In the theater, the obvious way to do so is to produce plays which call for small casts. Table 5 shows what has happened to the cast size of all plays (except musicals) produced by the Broadway theater for roughly five year intervals since 1946. The almost perfectly steady decline was sufficient to cut the average cast size *in half* from the 16 person figure with which the postwar period began.

We are convinced that this is but one dramatic example of a very pervasive phenomenon. Major orchestras and opera houses have surely reduced the frequency with which they make use of outside soloists and star guest performers. Smaller budget orchestras and theaters have probably cut expenditures on rehearsal time. In theaters and opera houses it is our impression that there has been a rise in frequency of use of single sets which eliminate the need for scene shifting stagehands.

Table 4 Theater Income, Expenses, Activity (Indices: 22 Regional Theaters)

	1974	1975	1976	1977	1978	1979	1980	1981	1982	1983
Income earned	100.0	114.5	126.1	144.9	166.7	210.9	200.7	251.4	269.6	308.0
Contributions										
federal	100.0	135.7	128.6	135.7	185.7	235.7	171.4	241.3	192.9	207.1
state and local	100.0	166.7	166.7	316.7	216.7	250.0	333.3	333.3	350.0	400.0
individual and other	100.0	127.6	113.8	127.6	158.6	189.7	231.0	265.5	286.2	317.2
foundations	100.0	82.6	95.7	82.6	69.6	82.6	91.3	95.7	100.0	134.8
corporations	100.0	125.0	125.0	150.0	255.0	250.0	275.0	325.0	375.0	725.0
Total income	100.0	115.4	122.4	136.0	158.4	197.7	196.3	237.9	253.3	286.4
Expenses										
artistic salaries	100.0	111.9	130.5	147.5	167.8	181.4	179.7	203.4	230.5	255.9
administrative salaries	100.0	133.3	140.0	153.3	180.0	213.3	243.3	270.0	333.3	386.7
technical salaries	100.0	140.0	148.0	168.0	184.0	252.0	240.0	316.0	348.0	364.0
non-salary expenses	100.0	99.0	105.7	117.1	138.1	174.3	169.5	215.2	214.3	244.8
Total expenses	100.0	111.4	121.9	136.1	156.6	190.4	190.4	231.1	250.2	280.8
Activity										
Performance (000)	100.0	105.5	109.6	123.3	121.9	123.3	116.4	121.9	119.2	126.0
Attendance (mil)	100.0	102.9	106.6	108.6	114.3	122.9	120.0	120.0	108.6	111.4

For source and notes: see Table 1.

Table 5 Percent Distribution. Theater Income, Expenses

	1974	1975	1976	1977	1978	1979	1980	1981	1982	1983
Income earned	64.5	64.0	66.4	68.7	67.8	68.8	66.0	68.2	68.6	69.3
Contributions										
federal	6.5	7.7	6.9	6.5	7.7	7.8	5.7	5.9	5.0	4.7
state and local	2.8	4.0	3.8	6.5	3.8	3.5	4.8	3.9	3.9	3.9
individual and other	13.6	15.0	12.6	12.7	13.6	13.0	16.0	15.1	15.3	15.0
foundations	10.7	7.7	8.4	6.5	4.7	4.5	5.0	4.3	4.2	5.1
corporations	1.9	2.0	1.9	2.1	2.7	2.4	2.6	2.6	2.8	4.7
Total income	100.0	100.0	100.0	100.0	100.0	100.0	100.0	100.0	100.0	100.0
Expenses										
artistic salaries	26.9	27.0	28.8	29.2	28.9	25.7	25.4	23.7	24.8	24.6
administration salaries	13.7	16.4	15.7	15.4	15.7	15.3	17.5	16.0	18.2	18.9
technical salaries	11.4	14.3	13.9	14.1	13.4	15.1	14.6	15.4	15.9	14.8
non-salary expenses	47.9	42.6	41.6	41.3	42.3	43.9	42.7	44.7	41.1	41.8
Total expenses	100.0	100.0	100.0	100.0	100.0	100.0	100.0	100.0	100.0	100.0

For source and notes: See Table 1.

Surely the gradual replacement of the three act/six scene play by plays with a far smaller number of changes of locale is an indicator of this phenomenon.

All of this boils down to the obvious choices relating to the cost disease. There are two different ways to live with inflation – either raise the price or debase the product. In the performing arts, coping can take the form of escalating real costs per attendee and rising real ticket prices. Or, instead, these obvious responses to the disease can be suppressed, and its virulence channeled into other consequences which many will consider still more serious – cuts in rehearsals, restrictions on the sorts of plays that can be produced (large cast Elizabethan plays becoming economically unsustainable), less expensive performers, larger theaters, safer programming, and other reductions in the economically feasible range of artistic options. It is thus responsible for the phenomenon which has been referred to as the artistic deficit.

Clearly, a disease whose symptoms are camouflaged in this way is not a disease that has been cured. In sum even if real cost per attendee or real cost per performance rises more slowly than expected, or, even for a while, fails to rise at all, that is no justification for withdrawal of support by the agencies that help to fund the arts or for a relaxation of fund raising efforts.

Let us turn to some other conclusions that can be drawn from our data. First, we may note that there is absolutely no trend in deficits when measured in current dollars – they have had their year to year ups and downs; but in 1982 the combined deficit of the 22 theaters in the sample was almost exactly the same as it was in 1974 (about half a million dollars) and in 1983 the combined deficit of the orchestras was about the same as in 1974 (a bit under $3.5 million). This means that in real terms those deficits must have been falling. This is confirmed by the excess of the growth rate of real incomes (3.6 percent per year for theaters and 4.5 percent per year for orchestras) over the annual percentage growth rates of their real expenditures (theater: 3.3, orchestras: 4.3).

Within the income and expense categories there have also been some noteworthy changes. The classifications provided in the theatrical and orchestral data for the ten year period are different so there are limits in the degree to which they can be compared here. Nevertheless, the scenarios they report are at least roughly similar.

First, as far as incomes are concerned we note that earned incomes (box office and other payments for services) have risen relative to other sources of funding. In the case of the theaters, over the decade they increased from 65 to 69 percent of the total and for the orchestras they went up from 43 to 49 percent of overall income (percentages calculated from Table 2). Thus they are not only rising but also constitute the largest single source of funds for the organizations studied.

These data also indicate that individual private contributions are the second largest single source of funds and that these too have been rising. The fastest growing component of income is the corporation grant, whose contributions to the theaters expanded at an average annual rate of 22 percent over the ten year period, or 14 percent faster than the average rate of growth of the economy's price level. Nevertheless these business contributions still constitute less than 5 percent of the total income of the theaters ($.97 million as a percent of $20.54 million).

Foundation giving to the theater has declined at about 4 percent a year in dollars of constant purchasing power. Federal support grew rapidly until 1979, and then fell, and later levelled off in terms of current dollars. Over the ten years as a whole real income from this source for the theaters rose at an annual rate of about 0.3 of 1 percent compounded. It should be said, moreover, that many government outlays are matching grants and have generated additional private support.

The poor performance of the stock market also held down the income of the orchestras' endowments, which rose 2 percent annually in real terms, and fell from 12 to 9 percent of their total income over the ten year period.

The components of expenses, too, exhibited some noteworthy patterns. First, as is hardly a surprise, every reported category of expense rose faster than the general price level, at rates ranging from 2 to 7 percent per year compounded (Tables 6 and 7).

Second, the total expenditures devoted to administrative salaries and technical salaries rose far faster than the average. With total real expenses of the theaters going up 3.3 percent per year, outlays on administrative and technical salaries rose, respectively, 6.7 and 6.1 (Table 6). In the case of the orchestras this was manifested as a rise in the relative share of production costs (Table 7). The theater data, which report a wider range of component costs, suggest that this is ascribable to the expansion of their salary component, rather than to non-salary expenses which increases only 1.9 percent per year in constant dollars.

A component of cost whose rise was below average was expenditure on artistic salaries, which lagged significantly behind total expenses in both the theaters and the orchestras (Tables 6 and 7). This does not necessarily mean the actors' and musicians' wages lagged behind the prices of other inputs, but it may be ascribable entirely or partly to economies such as the declining size of casts (which we have already noted) and decreased use of high priced guest artists on the part of the orchestras. This is an issue that clearly calls for further study.

One expected difference between the theaters and the orchestras is the large share of non-salary outlays in the total budgets of the former. Set construction, costumes and lighting constitute the most significant share of the cost of operation of the theater and, despite the relative lag of these costs, their share of the total has only fallen from 48 to 42 percent over the ten year period. For orchestras' artistic salaries, the largest component of costs, declined from 61 to 53 percent of total outlays, while in the case of the theater (where they constitute the second largest cost component) they fell from 27 to 25 percent of overall expenses.

Administrative salaries increased from 14 to 19 percent of the total outlays of the theaters and from 14 to 16 percent of the total for the orchestras. It is our hypothesis that much of this significant increase is ascribable to the rise in the amount of effort that is devoted to fund raising to compensate for the fall in federal government foundations' support.

Attendance is the last set of figures on which we will comment. In both the orchestras and the theaters attendance rose moderately between 1974 and 1979 or 1980, and then levelled off or fell, though ending off at a level slightly above that at the beginning of the ten year period (Figure 1). Over the period as a whole attendance rose 1.1 percent a year for the theaters and 1.9 percent a year for the orchestras – a significant rate, but hardly a cultural boom (Tables 6 and 7).

Table 6 Income, Expenses and Activity: ASOL Orchestras 1974–1983 (millions of current dollars except as noted)

	1974	1975	1976	1977	1978	1979	1980	1981	1982	1983	Growth %
Income earned	48.3	57.0	64.9	74.2	86.4	102.7	118.3	135.1	155.3	168.8	13.3
Contributions											
government	16.2	18.8	20.0	20.8	25.1	31.6	33.4	36.1	37.4	36.3	8.4
private	33.8	34.8	38.7	44.3	50.5	62.0	71.7	89.5	100.5	110.4	12.6
endowment	13.2	13.9	13.4	14.8	16.1	19.1	23.0	28.1	32.4	32.8	9.5
Total income	111.4	124.5	137.0	154.1	178.1	215.4	246.4	288.8	325.6	348.3	12.1
Expenses											
artistic salaries	69.9	77.6	84.9	96.1	105.9	120.2	135.8	155.3	172.6	186.5	10.3
production expenses	29.0	33.7	36.4	41.4	49.9	64.0	79.8	89.6	104.2	110.0	14.3
administration expenses	15.8	18.2	20.3	23.5	27.2	35.1	36.5	44.4	50.8	55.2	13.3
Total expenses	114.7	129.5	141.5	160.9	183.1	219.3	232.1	289.3	327.6	351.7	11.9
Deficit	–3.3	–5.0	–4.6	–6.8	–5.0	–3.9	–5.7	–0.5	–2.0	–3.4	
Attendance (mil)	18.3	18.3	20.1	21.0	21.4	22.4	22.6	22.8	21.9	22.0	1.9
Performance (thou)	13.9	14.2	14.8	17.4	18.0	22.1	22.2	19.3	19.2	19.2	3.3

Source: American Symphony Orchestra League, annual reports, various years. Sample size varies from year to year.

Table 7 *Real Budgets: ASOL Orchestras 1974–1983 (millions of 1972 dollars)*

	1974	1975	1976	1977	1978	1979	1980	1981	1982	1983	Growth rate (%)
GNP deflator	147.7	161.2	170.5	181.5	195.4	217.4	246.8	272.4	289.1	298.4	
Income earned	32.7	35.4	38.1	40.9	44.2	47.2	47.9	49.6	53.7	54.6	5.6
Contributions											
government	11.0	11.7	11.7	11.5	12.8	14.5	13.5	13.3	12.9	12.2	1.0
private	22.9	21.6	22.7	24.4	25.8	28.5	29.1	32.9	34.8	37.0	4.9
endowment and interest	8.9	8.6	7.9	8.2	8.2	8.8	9.3	10.3	11.2	11.0	2.1
Total income	75.4	77.2	80.4	84.9	91.1	99.1	99.8	106.0	112.6	116.7	4.5
Expenses											
artistic salaries	47.3	48.1	49.0	52.9	54.2	55.3	55.0	57.0	59.7	62.5	2.8
production expenses	19.6	20.9	21.3	22.8	25.5	29.4	32.3	32.9	36.0	36.9	6.5
administration expenses	10.7	11.3	11.9	12.9	13.9	16.1	14.8	16.3	17.6	18.5	5.6
Total expenses	77.7	80.3	83.0	88.7	93.7	100.9	102.1	106.2	113.3	117.9	4.3
Deficit	–2.2	–3.1	–2.7	–3.7	–2.6	–1.8	–2.3	–0.2	–0.7	–1.1	

For source and notes: See Table 6.

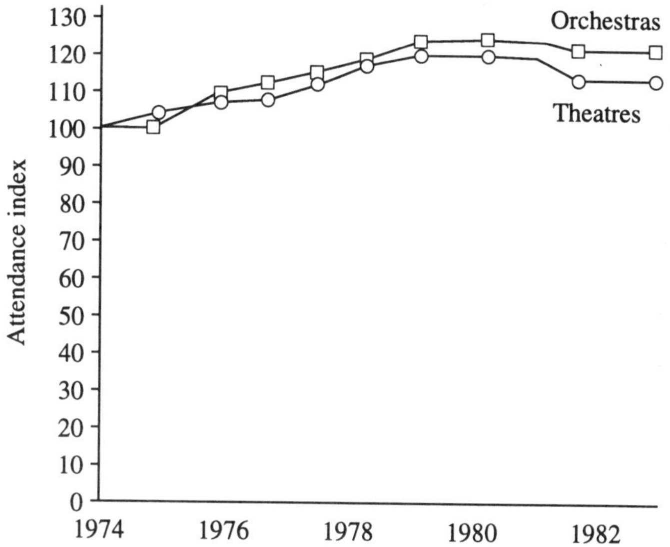

Notes:
1. Members of the Theater Communications Group, T.C.G.
2. Members of the ASOL, American Symphony Orchestra League.

Source: T.C.G. and ASOL.

Figure 1 Attendance Indices: Theaters (1) and Orchestras (2)

The mass media and the cost disease

Some people, seeing live performance become ever more vulnerable to remorselessly rising costs and continuing to need ever more government and philanthropic aid, have expected the mass media to provide an escape from the cost disease. They have argued that performance need not take place in hallowed halls to provide entertainment, pleasure, enrichment, or whatever other values are transmitted. Any possible diminution in the quality of the performance when it is purveyed by electronic transmission is offset by the vast size of the audience served, many of whom would otherwise have no access to professional performance of any kind.

It seemed obvious that the costs of delivering performance via the mass media would be contained by their ability to use the most modern technology and the stream of innovations from which it benefits year after year. Optimism about the cost containing capability of the mass media is also bolstered by their ability to serve vast and ever growing audiences. Even a hit play on Broadway never reaches an audience greater than two or three thousand persons each time it is performed, while one performance brought into the home by the electronic miracle of television can reach 50 or 60 million. Prints of a movie are sent in cans to every city and hamlet of the world and viewed by scores of millions of paying customers. A phonograph record of a 30 minute Haydn string quartet, while still requiring two person hours to perform, can be sold to a vast public with no further effort than the mechanical reproduction of disks.

Unfortunately, there is more to the story. For example, anyone who thinks, as a result, that the price of theater tickets must have been rising faster than the price of movies and the costs of television production is actually quite wrong.

Between 1948 and 1983, the price of admission to a Broadway musical rose about six and one half times and to a straight play nearly eight times. Meanwhile, the average price of admission to a movie house has increased over nine times! In the 12 years between 1964 and 1976, the price of a ticket to a Broadway play rose nearly 90 percent, but the cost of providing an hour of prime time television went up over 200 percent.

If the cost disease analysis is right, it would seem to make the figures on the rapid rise of movie tickets and broadcast costs even harder to believe. After all, broadcasting is a high tech electronic industry with plenty of room for innovation, and the technology of film making has not exactly been stagnant. The cost problem that besets these mass media is a bit more complex and more subtle than the cost disease of live performance.

Television broadcasting is typical of a number of fields (among them the computer industry) in that it has two basic components which are very different technologically. The first includes the actual performance in front of the television cameras – what television companies call 'over the line' costs. These cover the labor intensive activity of preparing and presenting programs, complete with writers, performers, musicians, directors, and whatever else is required to put a show on the air. In the computer business, the comparable labor-using activity is the preparation of software. The second basic component of broadcasting is the actual transmission; the high tech delivery of the programs to their distant audiences, which incurs what are called 'under the line' costs. In the computer field, the corresponding high tech component is the hardware. The first component of TV is virtually identical with live performance on a theater stage, and there is, therefore, just as little scope for technical change in the one as in the other. The second component, broadcasting transmission, is electronic and high tech in character, and constantly benefits from innovation. Television broadcasting requires these two elements in relatively fixed physical proportions – one hour of programming (with some flexibility in rehearsal time) must be accompanied by one hour of transmission in each and every one hour broadcast.

A predetermined fate awaits an industry with such a pattern of components, one of which is highly amenable to technical change while the other is not. Such an industry will be characterized by an initial period of decline in total cost (in constant dollars) followed by a period in which its costs begin to behave in a manner more and more similar to the live performing arts. The reason is that the cost of the highly technological component (transmission cost) will decline, or at least not rise as fast as the economy's inflation rate. At the same time, the cost of programming increases at a rate surpassing the rate of inflation.

If each year transmission costs decrease and over the line or programming expenses increase as a manifestation of the cost disease that besets all live performance, eventually programming cost will begin to dominate the overall budget. Thereafter, total cost and programming cost must move closer and closer together until virtually the entire budget becomes a victim of the disease, with the stable technological costs too small a fragment of the whole to make a discernible difference.

This entire story is really no more than a bit of arithmetic. If a budget is composed of two items, one of which gets smaller and smaller while the other gets larger and larger, sooner or later the budget will be dominated by its rising cost component. In actual fact, one of the major networks reported to us that while over the line costs composed 30 percent to 35 percent of a dramatic presentation ten years ago, they now constitute 50 percent of the budget, and have only been kept down to that proportion by stringent economies.

The evidence for the mass media

Moving to more detailed evidence, Figure 2 gives us the trend of the average price of movie admission throughout the US over much of the period since World War II. This is compared to the trend in the price of tickets to Broadway shows during that period. In 1948 it cost on the average $.36 to get into the movies, $4.71 was top price for a Broadway play and $6.18 paid for the best seat in the house for a Broadway musical. Inflation took its toll, and by 1983 we were paying an average of $3.30 for a movie, $34.00 (average top) for a drama and $41.00 for a musical. In percentage terms, musicals rose the least (only!) 563 percent. Drama admissions came next, rising 622 percent, and the price of movies rose 817 percent. During the last five years, there has been a leap in theater ticket price which narrowed the gap somewhat, but it certainly has not reversed the trend.

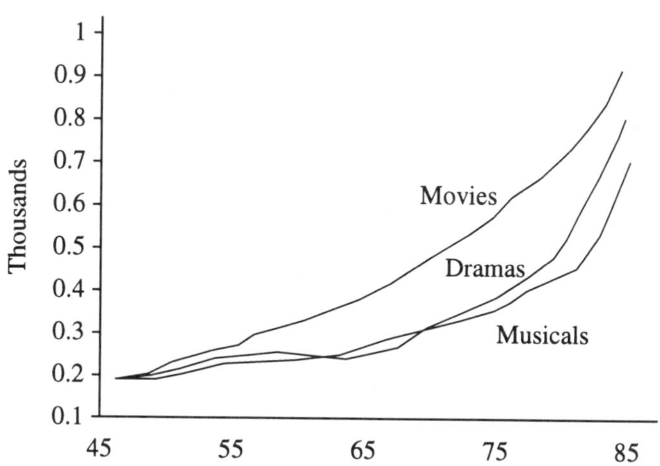

Sources: Movies: *The Encyclopedia of Exhibition*. National Association of Theater Owners, New-York City, 1983. The figures are average from reports of Association members throughout the United States.

Theater: League of New-York Theaters and Producers, Inc. Based on top ticket price data from *Variety*.

Figure 2 Ticket Price Indices, Movies and Commercial Theater 1948–1983

We can also compare cost per hour of prime time TV entertainment series (averaged for the three networks) and ticket prices for straight plays on Broadway for 1964 to 1976, the years for which we have data. The trends are shown in Figure 3. For a number of obvious reasons, notably that price is a charge per audience member while the broadcasting data deal with cost per performance, this comparison can at best be suggestive. Yet suggestive it is. Over the 13 year period in question broadcasting costs rose 55 percentage points more quickly than Broadway ticket prices.

So much, then, for the belief that the mass media are the means to escape the rising costs of live theater, opera, music, and dance. The analysis tells us that in the long run television and movie making cannot provide an escape from the cost disease of live performance. On the contrary, it shows that the cost disease can be contagious, and that at least some of the mass media may already be in an advanced stage of the illness.

It is interesting that electronic computation has suffered from exactly the same problems. The cost of computer hardware has been falling some 25 percent a year for decades. Meanwhile, software costs, which are analogous to programming costs in television in that they are highly labor intensive, have gone up about 6 percent a year. As a result, the cost of software has now become a major component of a computation budget, and is estimated to be about 70 percent of the total cost of

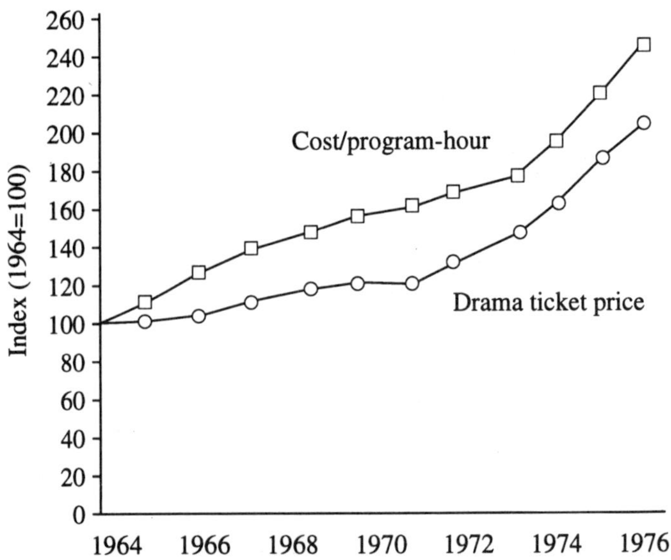

Source: Television: Charles River Associates; Based on data in Television & Broadcasting Magazines. The data are average costs for the three networks per program hour, all evening entertainment series, and exclude movies, sports, and news programs.

Theater: League of New-York Theaters and Producers, Inc. Based on top ticket price data from *Variety*.

Figure 3 TV Costs and Drama Ticket Prices

using a computer. Total computation costs are now widely reported to be on the rise despite all the wonders innovation contributes to this field every year.

Falling mass media audiences

The fact that movie tickets and television costs have actually risen faster than live theater prices is more extreme than we would expect on the basis of our analysis. We should expect mass media prices and costs to rise almost as fast as theater tickets but not faster, because the falling relative costs of the high tech parts of the mass media operations do still offer some advantage to movie and television production. We suspect there are two main reasons the price of movie tickets and television program costs have actually increased faster. First, the movie audience has shrunk drastically over the postwar period (the TV network audience has also declined recently), and the price increase in part represents an attempt to cover costs in the face of falling ticket sales. Second, poverty is not yet a way of life in the mass media as it has long been in live performance. For many years, theater producers, managers of symphony orchestras, and others concerned with the finances of live performance have been forced to learn how to keep costs down. This is often done by underpaying the performer, a strategy that is not possible in the media.

We must set aside as a pipe dream the expectation that performance cost will rise at a modest rate in the media. Moreover, no one need be culprit. To explain the rising costs we do not have to conjure up pictures of free spending movie moguls, wasteful television executives, greedy Broadway producers, or featherbedding unions. Some villains, of course, exist, but the real story needs no such scapegoats. The underlying problem, it turns out, is just a dull matter of economics and technology.

Concluding comment

The implications of our data for the future of the theater and the other performing arts seem clear. There is absolutely no evidence of any threat to their survival. Just as in the past they have survived wars, persecutions, and other catastrophes; they are surviving inflation and withdrawal of government funding. Overall deficits measured in real terms (as they should be) are, if anything, falling. Contributions and earned incomes are both rising significantly faster than the price level. There is no reason to believe that the existence of artistic performance is threatened.

However, they do face another threat which must be considered very serious, and which is rather more insidious. That is what has been called the artistic deficit, which serves to camouflage the cost disease but which may actually well be one of its most serious manifestations. It restricts the opportunities to experiment, limiting the character of plays and the content of musical programs to those which offer the promise of being viable financially. It involves cutting of corners in terms of quality of performers (when their high salaries threaten budgets), in terms of rehearsal time, and in terms of freedom of artistic choice. The evidence here is still highly incomplete, but such evidence as there is indicates dramatically that the threat is very real.

Those who provide support for the arts must surely not ignore this threat and must take its financial demands into account in planning their funding targets. For otherwise there is danger that they will find themselves underwriting a body of activities the quality of whose product ever decreasingly deserves the attention of the community and even the inadequate resources they are absorbing.

The moral is clear. In periods when real cost per attendee is rising, increasing funding of the arts may be required to sustain their health. But when cost per attendee falls, increased funding may be more urgent still!

Industry Economics
Princeton and New York University

Note:

1. The estimates for 1983 were calculated simply by adjusting them by factors of proportionality obtained for the four years in which we had figures for both samples. There was sufficient stability in ratios year to year in the period of overlap to elicit some confidence in the defensibility of the 1983 estimates.

[18]

On the Cost Disease and its True Policy Implications for the Arts

HILDA BAUMOL AND W. J. BAUMOL

5.1 INTRODUCTION

The cost disease of the performing arts seems to have become a mainstay in the arguments of those seeking public support in a surprisingly broad range of geographical arenas. Its logic has been mastered thoroughly by those who rely on it to help their cause. Yet, at least two misunderstandings seem widespread, and both of these weaken the case for public support of the arts. In this paper we seek to clear up these misunderstandings.

Specifically, the first of these is the judgement that the cost disease analysis must necessarily presage a grim future for the live performing arts and perhaps for quality of life generally – in short, just what is to be expected from a discipline justly dubbed 'the dismal science'. We will show, on the contrary, that the cost disease phenomenon inevitably means that society can expect to be able to support arts ever more generously and effectively while simultaneously increasing its consumption of material things – if only society chooses to do so.

The second of the misunderstandings with which this paper concerns itself is the view that when, as has often happened during periods of inflation, cost per performance or cost per attendee rises more slowly than the general price level, the cost disease is (apparently) cured, or is at least in remission, so that deceleration of public support may become appropriate. On the contrary, we will show that there is good reason to believe that in such periods the disease is not in remission but is, rather, suppressed, and that its suppressed variant threatens even more serious harm to the arts than its overt form. In short, when the disease assumes its suppressed form, that is no signal for friends of the arts to relax their efforts. Instead, it becomes appropriate for them to work even harder to provide adequate resources for the artistic activities they desire.

5.2 THE COST DISEASE: BRIEF SUMMARY OF THE ANALYSIS[1]

Since the cost disease is central to the analysis of this paper, it is necessary to review the nature of this malaise of live performance. Eighteen years ago, one of the authors of this paper and William G. Bowen, now president of Princeton University, showed that the performing arts are predestined to be the victims of a cost disease which condemns the cost per live performance, be it *Hamlet, The Barber of Seville* or a rock concert, to rise at a rate persistently faster than that of a typical manufactured good. An illustration will help clarify the reason. Compare what has happened to the cost of producing a watch with the cost of a musical performance over the centuries. There has been vast, labour-saving technical progress in watchmaking, which is still continuing, But live violin playing benefits from no labour (or capital) -saving innovations – it is still done the old-fashioned way, as we want it to be.

Towards the end of the seventeenth century a Swiss craftsman could produce about 12 watches per year. Three centuries later that same amount of labour produces over 1,200 (non-quartz) watches. But a piece of music written three centuries ago by Purcell or Scarlatti takes exactly as many person-hours to perform live today as it did in 1684.

What do these figures mean? They mean that, while one has to work just about as many hours to pay for a ticket to an opera today as one would have in similar jobs 300 years ago, the cost of a watch or any other manufactured good has plummeted in terms of the labour time we must pay for it. In other words, because manufactured goods have benefited from technological advance year after year while live performances have not, almost every year theatre and concert tickets have grown more and more expensive in comparison with the price of watches. This phenomenon has been called 'the cost disease of live performance'.

The message is simple. Prices of manufactured goods do not rise as quickly as those of concerts, dance or theatrical performances because manufacturers benefit from labour-saving innovation while the performing arts do not (to any large extent). This is another way of saying that cost per attendee or per performance must rise faster than the average price of other things; arts budgets therefore must rise faster than the economy's rate of inflation, which is simply the average increase in the prices of all the economy's outputs.

5.3 THAT BENEFICENT COST DISEASE[2]

It is almost impossible to tell the cost disease story without giving it the aura of a tragedy. What a dismal failure it seems to foretell, one in which every major ingredient of the quality of life is gradually priced out of the market by its irresistibly, remorselessly growing costliness. It suggests a barren society where the arts have been reduced to uncompensated amateur activities – without museums or libraries, with little education, vestigial garbage removal and even vanishing police protection. Indeed, there is a danger that society, misled by appearances, will resign itself to such a future, and that by its resignation it may bring about just these dismal circumstances that it could so easily avoid. This may well be a course on which we are already embarked, as a glance at deteriorating municipal services surely suggests.

Yet its inevitability is all a matter of misunderstanding. To those who understand the logic of the cost disease analysis this bleak future is presaged by the exponentially rising budgetary resources that will be required to prevent it. To others, the grim prospect seems to be approaching because of a mysterious acceleration of the budgetary demands of the services, which seem every year to require more money, in real terms, even as their quality deteriorates visibly.

Where in this unhappy prospect are there any rays of hope? We will show now that there is more than a mere ray. Properly interpreted, the moral of the cost disease analysis is sanguinity embodied. It tells us that humanity can have even more of everything – more manufactured goods, more municipal services, more arts activity – if only it chooses to apportion its resources in a manner consistent with this goal of growing abundance in every field.

A moment's thought confirms that, in a world characterized by the cost disease, this must be true. The disease originates from the fact that, even though there is *some* productivity growth in the stagnant services, it is significantly slower than productivity growth in the remainder of the economy. But a society whose productivity is growing everywhere, albeit in some areas more slowly than in others, obviously will be able to afford to consume constantly more, and certainly will not be forced to consume less and less. It has the means to enjoy more of all outputs, or it may instead choose to devote all of its increased productive capacity to a selected smaller group of items; but that is a decision to be made by society as a whole. The cost disease had created the illusion that society can no longer afford many things it used to be able to obtain. But the opposite is in fact true. A society beset by the cost disease can each year afford at least a bit more of each item it obtained the year before. It *can afford* more and slightly better endowed artistic activity each successive year, despite the rising real cost, and more manufactured goods as well.

A simple example brings out the sort of range of options to society that must inevitably go along with the cost disease.[3] Table 5.1 describes the output bundles from which a hypothetical economy can choose at a future date after unbalanced productivity growth of the sort that

Table 5.1 *Hypothetical arts and services scenarios, 1984 and 2008**

(Prices: 1984 = 100)

	(1) Nominal GNP	*(2) Real sevices cost*	*(3) Nominal services cost (trillions)*	*(4) Real arts activity*	*(5) Nominal arts activity*	*(6) Mfg*	*(7) %increase in Mfg over 1984*
1984	1	0.25	0.25	0.0025	0.0025	0.75	—
2008							
Constant services and arts output	2	0.25	0.50	0.0025	0.0050	1.50	100
Constant shares of total output	2	0.40	0.80	0.004	0.008	120	60
Doubled services and arts output	2	0.50	1.0	0.005	0.01	100	33.3

* Assumes constant 3 per cent per year rate of growth of productivity in manufacturing, zero growth in productivity in stagnant services, constant input quantities, wages and prices increasing at a rate of growth of manufacturing productivity.

engenders the cost disease has had a substantial period in which to manifest itself. For the sake of simplicity, we shall begin our hypothetical history with a GNP of £1 trillion, 24 per cent of which consists of stagnant services whose productivity is not growing at all. The remainder consists of manufactures whose productivity is growing at a steady 3 per cent per year compounded, so that with a given bundle of input flow output will double approximately every 24 years. Arts expenditure is assumed throughout to be 1 per cent of the outlays on the stagnant services. Wages and other primary resource prices are assumed to reflect productivity and hence to rise 3 per cent per year. Produced items are taken to be supplied competitively so that their prices correspond to their costs as determined by the prices and productivity of their inputs.

The first row in the table, the one labelled '1984', shows the assumed initial state of affairs. The interesting phenomena manifest themselves in the three rows labelled '2008', corresponding to three of the options open to society under the circumstances posited: (1) constant services output, which assumes that society will devote the same absolute volume of inputs to the arts and the other stagnant services that they did in 1984, so that with zero productivity growth their activity levels will remain absolutely fixed; (2) proportionate output growth, which assumes that society will choose to expand these activities strictly in proportion to manufacturing output; (3) doubled services output, which assumes that society will provide enough resources to the arts and the other stagnant services to double their 1984 activity levels.

The first thing to be noted is that, even in the most modest constant services output scenario, in nominal terms the required budget for the arts and other services in 2008 will have doubled from its 1984 value (columns (3) and (5)). Instead of £0.25 trillion, the services' budget will have risen to £0.5 trillion, and the arts budget will have gone up from £0.0025 to £0.005. This is because input prices will double in 24 years, and with no increase in productivity and constant outputs these budgets must, consequently, double.

Under this scenario, manufacturing output must also take a great leap, increasing from £0.75 trillion to £1.5 trillion. Thus, the doubling of outlays on the services can hardly be taken to constitute much of a real burden upon society.

Case 2 represents a less conservative goal for the arts and other services. Now the economy transfers to them a quantity of resources sufficient to permit them to expand their real outputs in strict proportion to manufactures. Nominal outlays on the services generally and the arts in particular must rise to £0.8 and £0.008 trillion, respectively.

Nevertheless, the transfer of resources to the services causes only some moderation in the outpouring of manufactures, which now rise only 60 per cent above their 1984 levels (columns (6) and (7)).

Society can afford even more ambitious service (and arts) outputs. For example, it can double them both from their 1984 output levels (last row of the table), thereby necessarily quadrupling their required

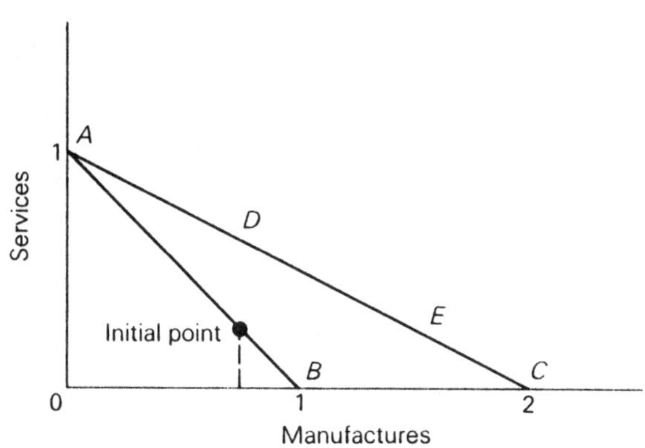

Figure 5.1 *GNP. Growth and expansion of the service and manufacturing sectors*

budgets while still enjoying a quadrupling of the output of manufactured goods.[4]

The same example can be used to demonstrate the sort of fiscal illusion that the cost disease analysis is intended to expose. Suppose that by the year 2008 society increases the outlays devoted to services, including the arts, by 60 per cent, from £0.25 to £0.4 trillion. Since on our assumptions the prices of the services must have doubled, this means the real resources devoted to them will have fallen (in 1984 prices) from £0.25 trillion to £0.20 trillion. Yet the overall price level will have risen only 11 per cent, since the prices of manufactures will be constant, and with the resources devoted to manufacturing having gone up from £75 to £80 trillion in 1984 prices and productivity having doubled, manufacturing output must rise to 160. Hence, the 2008 price level must be

$$\frac{2(20) + 1(160)}{20 + 160} = 111$$

Thus nominal outlays on the services will have risen 60 per cent i.e. *by more than five times the rise in the general price level*,[5] and yet the quantity of services supplied will have fallen by 20 per cent from its initial level of £0.25 trillion in 1984 prices. No wonder the public will be driven to fear that it cannot afford to keep the supply of the services at their initial level, much less undertake any expansion in the resources devoted to them.

But, as we have seen, this conclusion is quite wrong. Here let us choose our words with care. We are saying that an implication of the circumstances that produce the cost disease is that it will actually be possible to expand significantly the resources devoted to the arts and the other services. The public *will be able to afford* to do so, and to experience substantial increase in the creature comforts they enjoy at the same time. But to say that they can afford it is not the same as saying they ought to do so. That is a judgement no economic analysis can entitle us either to make or to deny. All that we can say in good conscience is that society should be kept from making a negative decision, that is a decision to cut back on the arts and the other services contributing to the quality of life, solely by the misapprehension that it cannot afford to do otherwise.

Put in another way, fund-raisers who have used the cost disease as one of their arguments for ever increasing support may well profit by studying what has just been said here; for it permits them in good conscience to carry a banner inscribed with the motto, 'Yes, you can afford it!'

5.4 THE COST DISEASE AND INFLATION

Since the cost disease was described in 1964, arts administrators throughout the world have argued that, because performance budgets must inevitably rise faster than the general price level, increases in support that merely match the economy's price level must condemn the arts to decline and deterioration. So long as the data continued to show that *real* costs per performance or per attendee were indeed continuing to rise as predicted, all seemed well in the continuing relationships between the funding agencies and the recipients of their support. However, when recent data revealed some cases in which such costs were falling behind the inflation rate, more than one such group underwent feelings of panic and betrayal. The reliable old cost disease law had failed them. What had gone wrong? Or, rather, had something unexpectedly gone *right* for costs in the arts?

As a matter of fact, nothing has gone wrong with the cost disease model's predictions. Neither is there any reason to believe that matters have improved in any way for the costs of performance. There are two reasons why a slowdown, and perhaps even a decline, in real per-unit costs should have been, and were in fact, expected.

First, as we have seen, the cost disease is a manifestation of the *relative* lag in productivity growth in performance. Performance suffers because manufacturing productivity habitually rises so rapidly and pulls wages up with it. But in the 1970s, for reasons that are in some dispute, productivity growth in manufacturing slowed down to a crawl in almost every industrialized economy. Thus, the engine that triggers the cost disease virtually ran out of fuel during that decade.

Second, even the earliest study of the cost disease of the arts (Baumol and Bowen, 1965) indicated that, while for well over a century orchestral cost performance had *almost* always risen faster than the general price level, there was one persistent exception: periods of inflation. During each of the brief postwar inflations that the United States experienced before the Second World War, the rise in cost per performance consistently fell behind the general price level. Though we have no clear-cut evidence, our hypothesis is that in such periods the public resists increases in outlays on the arts which exceed the growth in the price level to the degree typical of uninflationary periods. Since in the performing arts expenditures must, in the long run, adjust themselves to receipts, cost per performance then lags as a matter of economic necessity. Whether this explanation is or is not valid, the fact remains. Experience has shown that in inflationary periods cost per performance does not necessarily rise faster than the general price level.

Thus, both the record of the past and the logic of the cost disease analysis should have warned us (and did) that the symptoms of the cost disease may become more moderate or may even (temporarily) disappear altogether during an era like the present.

5.5 ON THE SUPPRESSED FORM OF THE COST DISEASE

The important implication of the preceding explanatory hypothesis about the lag of real costs in inflationary periods is that the cost disease forces performing groups to find ways to sublimate the problem – to trade off increasing costs for money-saving changes in the way they conduct their activities. We shall now provide a convincing illustration of this phenomenon. One obvious way to suppress the cost disease is to cut down on the number of artists the performing organization has on its payroll. In the theatre, the obvious way to do this is to produce plays that call for smaller casts. Figures 5.2, 5.3 and 5.4 show what has happened to the proportions of plays and musical comedies, and to the cast size of all plays (except musicals), produced by the Broadway theatre for roughly five-year intervals since 1946. The almost perfectly steady decline was sufficient to cut the average cast size *in half*, from the 16-person figure with which the postwar period began.

We are convinced that this is but one dramatic example of a very pervasive phenomenon which is unfortunately very difficult, if not impossible, to document quantitatively. Major orchestras and opera houses have surely reduced the frequency with which they make use of outside soloists and star guest performers. Smaller budget orchestras

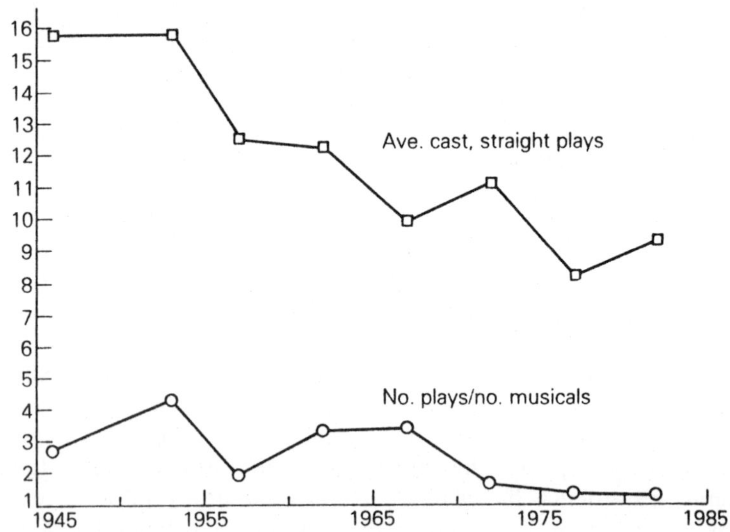

Figure 5.2 *Cast sizes, and ratios of straight plays to musicals, Broadway theatre, 1945–83*

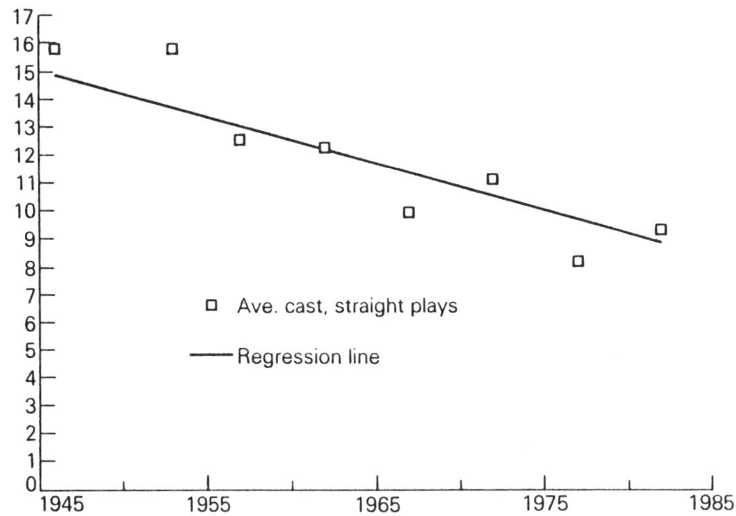

Figure 5.3 *Average cast sizes in straight plays, Broadway theatre, 1945–83*

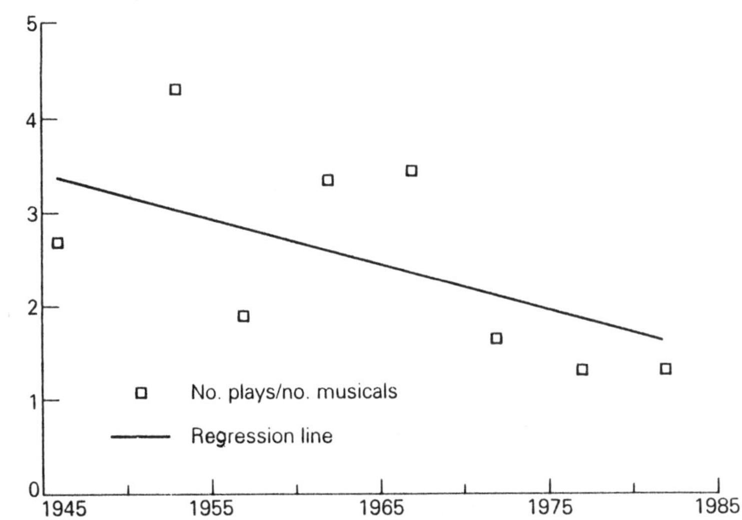

Figure 5.4 *Ratios of straight plays to musicals, Broadway theatre, 1945–83*

and theatres have probably cut expenditures on rehearsal time. In theatres and opera houses it is our impression that there has been a rise in the frequency of use of single sets, which eliminates the need for scene-shifting stagehands. Surely the gradual replacement of the three act–six scene play by those requiring a far smaller number of scene changes is an indicator of this phenomenon.

All of this boils down to the obvious choices relating to the cost disease. There are two different ways to live with inflation: either raise the price, or debase the product. In the performing arts, 'coping' can take the form of escalating real costs per attendee and raising real ticket prices. Or, instead, these obvious responses to the disease can be surpressed, and its virulence channelled into other consequences which many will consider still more serious – restrictions on the sorts of plays that can be produced (large-cast classics becoming economically unsustainable), cuts in the number of rehearsals, less expensive performers, larger theatres, safer programming and other reductions in the economically feasible range of artistic options. It is thus responsible for the phenomenon that has been referred to as the artistic deficit.

Clearly a disease whose symptoms are camouflaged in this way is not a disease that has been cured. In sum, even if real cost per attendee or real cost per performance rises more slowly than expected, or even (for a while) fails to rise at all, that is no justification for a withdrawal of support by the agencies that help to fund the arts, or for a relaxation of fund-raising efforts.

5.6 CONCLUDING COMMENT

We see, then, that two basic misunderstandings about the nature of the cost disease have impeded its utility to those responsible for funding the arts. The first of these is the illusion that the analysis implies a growing inability of society to maintain the funding that is required if the quantity and quality of performance activity are not to be eroded. What has been shown here, on the contrary, is the firm implication of the cost disease that the sources that are responsible for its occurrence also automatically provide the resources that can serve as its antidote or even its cure. Inability to pay the rising costs of the arts is simply not a valid excuse for starving the arts in a society destined to grow increasingly affluent because of rising productivity.

The second misunderstanding of the cost disease corresponds to a rather insidious threat to the viability of the arts which has been called the 'artistic deficit'. This has served to camouflage the cost disease, but may actually be one of its most serious manifestations. It restricts the opportunities to experiment, limiting the character of plays and the content of musical programmes to those that offer the promise of being viable financially. It involves the cutting of corners in terms of quality of performers (when their high salaries threaten budgets), in terms of rehearsal time, and in terms of freedom to utilize more costly options when appropriate, such as large casts or multi-set plays. The evidence here is still highly incomplete, but such evidence as there is indicates dramatically that the threat is very real.

Those who provide support for the arts must surely not ignore this threat and must take its financial demands into account in planning their funding targets; otherwise there is danger that they will find themselves underwriting a body of activities the quality of whose product ever decreasingly deserves the attention of the community and even the inadequate resources they are absorbing.

The moral is clear. In periods when real cost per attendee is rising, increasing funding of the arts may be required to sustain their health. But when cost per attendee falls, increased funding may be more urgent still!

NOTES

The authors are grateful to the Starr Centre for Applied Economics, New York University, for its assistance in the preparation of this paper.

1 Readers who have heard the cost disease story repeated ad nauseum are avidly urged to omit this section.

2 The substance of this section draws heavily on Bradford (1969).

3 The reader will recognize that the logic of the argument is perfectly general and in no way depends upon the particular numbers that happen to have been chosen for our illustration.

4 It is easy to show that, under the circumstances postulated, society could increase the resources devoted to the services to 250 per cent of their 1984 levels without suffering any diminution in manufacturing output. The general situation can be depicted diagramatically (figure 5.1). We have implicitly assumed away any diminishing marginal rate of transformation between the services and manufacturing and have selected output units so that the initial $MRT = 1$. Thus the initial production frontier is that labelled AB. The initial point is that labelled on AB. With a doubling of productivity in manufacturing, the frontier shifts outward to AC. It is clear that any point on the new frontier that falls on line segment DE, above and to the right of the initial point, constitutes a feasible increase in both manufactures and services.

5 In general, if the share, k, of the stagnant services remains constant and wages keep abreast with the constant growth rate of productivity in the remainder of the economy, then the price level at time t will be

$$p_t = ke^{rt} + (1 - k)$$

where r is the difference between the growth rate of productivity elsewhere and that in the stagnant services. Then, with a constant level of service activity, the growth in its cost relative to the growth in the price level over its value in period 0 must be

$$\frac{(e^{rt} - 1)}{p_t - 1} = \frac{(e^{rt} - 1)}{k(e^{rt} - 1)} = \frac{1}{k} > 1.$$

References

BAUMOL, W. J. AND BOWEN, W. G. (1965) 'On the Performing Arts: The Anatomy of their Economic Problems'. *American Economic Review*, vol. 55.

BRADFORD, DAVID (1969) 'Balance on Unbalanced Growth'. *Zeitschrift fur National-ökonomice*, December.

[19]

On the Economics of the Performing Arts in the USSR and the USA: A Preliminary Comparison of the Data

Alexandre Rubinstein — American Soviet Theater Initiative

William Baumol — Princeton University

Hilda Baumol[1]

INTRODUCTION

The possibility that we might gather a set of roughly compatible statistics for the costs and incomes of performing arts organizations in the USSR and the USA constituted an irresistible opportunity for a comparative study. While we did not achieve the degree of comparability we would have liked, we believe we still have something of interest to present. The materials readily obtainable pertain only to three years spanning a single decade. We found that the determination of what is included in a specific art form and the aggregation of performing entities that are grouped for statistical purposes in the two countries differed substantially. It seemed to us, however, that there remained a basis from which inferences could be drawn if treated with sufficient caution and labelled with suitable warnings. This paper provides a summary of the data, offers some rudimentary analysis, and ends up with some conclusions suggested by the figures. These conclusions appear to be of some interest in themselves, but their main value may prove to be the guidance and stimulus they offer for future cooperative work in the area.

We may note at the outset that the analysis did bring a number of surprises. First, the western reader may find it astonishing that, unlike its American counterpart, musical performance in the USSR does not seem to suffer from serious problems of financial deficits, and seems to obtain only small government contributions. After all, in the West it had always been understood that the Soviet government is relatively generous toward the arts. What seems to be the case, however, is that in the USSR only a comparatively small proportion of musical performances needs to be subsidized, because earned income, largely box office receipts, cover a far higher proportion of musical expenses in the USSR. Theatrical performance is, however, subsidized substantially. Second, the fact that administrative costs constitute a far-higher proportion of US expenses both in music and theater requires some explanation. Third, while in both countries the statistics indicate that the performing arts suffer from the problems associated with "Baumol's disease" - the propensity for cost per audience member or per performance to rise faster than the economy's overall price level because productivity in the live performing arts necessarily grows more slowly than it does in the economy generally - the manifestations of the problem seem to be considerably milder in the USSR than they are in the USA. Later in this article, these and other observations will be documented and some explanatory hypotheses will be offered.

To western readers, however, the most informative part of the article may well be the description of the evolving forms of financial organization and support of the performing arts in the USSR. We find that the 1980s have brought to the Soviet Union a surprising variety of additions to its traditional means of funding which now includes tax deductions for voluntary support by individuals or firms, profit-seeking theatrical activity, emergence of a spate of small theater groups and tax exemption even for quasi commercial theaters. Details on these remarkable developments are reported in the sections that follow.

OVERALL VIEW OF PERFORMING ARTS ACTIVITY IN THE USSR

At the end of the 80's there were over 2,000 performing arts organizations in the USSR: about 1,000 repertory theaters and studio-theaters and almost an equal number of philharmonic orchestras and variety-show groups. These figures include about 400 drama theaters, 200 children's theaters and 100 music theaters (opera, ballet, operetta), over 50 symphony and 100 chamber orchestras, about 60 choruses and almost 600 groups (pop, rock, jazz, folk, etc.) and orchestras. Together, these various performing arts organizations gave about 1 million performances annually, attended by almost 4 billion people. The total annual income generated by these organizations exceeds half a billion rubles.

Most theater performances and concerts in the USSR are arranged by state-owned theaters, concert agencies (philharmonic societies) and individual performing groups. Their activities rely on a mix of financing by state subsidies (All-Union, Republic, and local) and by box office receipts. Because of the nature of their activities they can reasonably be compared with "not-for-profit" organizations. Like those in the United States their objectives are purely artistic and not profit oriented. As in some other countries in the west, these organizations are exempt from most taxes and other payments to state budgets.

In recent years public opinion in the country has recognized the necessity of attracting additional financial resources to the arts, and has led the government to consider further tax exemptions. Thus, in April of 1990 the Supreme Soviet of the USSR adopted (in a first reading) a law under which theaters and concert organizations will be able to receive contributions from corporations and private persons, enabling the latter to reduce their payments to the state in the form of taxed incomes.

THEATER IN THE USSR

The non-commercial nature of the activities of theaters and philharmonic organizations is traditional for the performing arts organizations in the USSR. Since the time of Stanislavsky the vision of the Moscow Arts Theater has guided the development of staging in the country. Permanent companies in repertory theaters and permanent orchestras form the basis of such development, and state subsidies covering about 50 percent of the expenses of these organizations constitute their main source of financial support.

"Non-commercial" theaters include about 600 permanent companies working in different Republics, regions and cities. These theaters can be divided into four groups: All-Union, Republican, regional and city. They have corresponding managing bodies: the Ministry of Culture of the USSR, the Ministries of Culture of Union Republics, Regional and City Councils, all of which provide state subsidies to the theaters. These theaters serve large audiences in their respective regions and also participate in a relatively extensive and ongoing tour exchange. About half of all the performances are given by theaters not on their own stages but while touring other cities. Such broad tour exchange helps to extend the market for theater services and adds to the interest of the audiences.

Apart from the state management bodies there is another powerful public organization which also represents the interests of Soviet theaters. The Theater Workers Union of the USSR is comprised of over 50,000 actors, directors, set designers, playwrights, managers and representatives of other theater professions. TWU owns a large number of factories, and with this means of financial self support in hand it conducts a rather effective independent policy which has a significant influence on the theatrical process The end of the 80's marked a new period in the development of Soviet theater. This new period is characterized by an extremely active amateur movement - the emergence of a whole group of varied theater companies, the so-called "cellar" theaters, and studios, which are trying to find their own ecological niche and work within a broader economic and organizational framework than the traditional state-owned repertory companies. This process has resulted in the emergence of a large group of studio theaters which have become a part of the professional theater world. There are now over 300 totally independent theater companies. The powerful artistic and political messages as well as organizational innovations of these small studio theaters have become a serious challenge to the traditional theater.

The most important feature of the studio theaters is that they are financially self sustaining. And although in most cases they are trying to begin to extract some commercial profit, they have managed to stay financially independent of the state. This is built into the very aesthetics of the studio theaters which are typically impecunious theaters with small companies. All the actors have contracts and also perform various duties at the theater such as those of a technical crew. Dispersed around the country, these theaters also enjoy tax-exempt status, and any profits they make remain in the theater and are used to satisfy artistic needs and to remunerate members of the studio.

Without any subsidies from the state, studio theaters nevertheless play an important role in the theater process. They have become an alternative theater force and, unlike the state theaters, they are very flexible. Some of their organizational innovations which encourage economic freedom and independence as well as the contractual system attract more and more attention from the managers of traditional theaters. Their interests are now represented by a young, but nevertheless quite powerful, public organization -- an All-Union Studio Theaters Association.

In order to provide a full picture it is also necessary to mention the amateur theaters which are found throughout the country and subsidized directly by various clubs, higher educational institutions and other organizations out of their own resources. Very often it is these amateur theaters that feed the studio theater movement and the traditional theater.

In contrast with the US, where box-office income is relatively higher, the direct funding of theaters out of the state budget accounts for about one half of their expenses. The previously-mentioned tax exemptions and contributions from corporations and private persons are at the moment negligible, and are not made on a regular basis. Thus, it is clear that contributed support of performing art is derived preponderantly from allocations from the state budget. Such single-source funding has led to the dependence of theaters on the decisions of fiscal bodies, the politicizing influence of state subsidies and, what is most important, to the absolute power of the administrative system because of its ability to provide or deny financial support. To make the situation even worse, the members of the creative community were cut off from the process of decision making in these matters. In practice, the financial welfare of a theater was actually determined by civil servants.

By the end of the 80's the situation had changed. The government, under pressure from the theater community, instituted changes in the prevailing system of financing. The new model, which is to be introduced in 1990, envisages the establishment of local arts development foundations funded by state budgets according to a fixed norm (calculated per capita). Decisions on the distribution of financial resources by such foundations among the theaters will involve active participation by the creative community.

Thus, the reorientation of the system of financing of the performing arts in the USSR is characterized by two developments which are quite similar in nature and orientation to the processes currently found in the United States and Western Europe. First of all, the shift towards the use of inducements (the "inspirer")[2] entailing the traditional (for the United States) use of tax incentives and numerous independent sources of financing the arts. And, second, there is the shift towards the "patron"[3] which involves transition to the British pattern of arms length management and the creation of regional foundations for arts development. Most probably the 90's will witness continuation of the process of ever-growing similarity between the approaches to financing of non-commercial theater in the USSR and the United States.

MUSIC IN THE USSR

All philharmonic concert activities in the USSR are sponsored by the state concert organizations which do not pursue commercial objectives. There are about 200 concert agencies, including 150 philharmonic societies. They are found in every Union Republic, and every more-or-less important region. The majority of professional music groups (orchestras, ensembles, choruses) operate within these organizations and are fully dependent on their support. There are only 70 philharmonic music collectives which have an independent status and are funded directly from the state budget (All-Union, Republic or local). In addition, concert agencies and philharmonic societies schedule the work of solo musicians who are either on their permanent payroll or have a temporary contract with these organizations.

By analogy with the theaters, concert agencies can be divided into four major groups: All-Union, Republican, regional and city. The corresponding management bodies (the Ministry of Culture of the USSR, Ministries of Culture of the Union Republics, Regional and Local Councils) provide state subsidies for concert agencies (philharmonic societies) and independent music collectives. Like theaters, the concert organizations serve large audiences in their regions and also participate in the touring process. The scale of touring activity in this field is even greater than that of the theaters. The requirements of musical activity force them to maintain a very intense touring schedule.

Apart from the state management bodies, the interests of musicians are also represented by the All-Union Music Society. However, this public organization is less influential than the Theater Workers Union of the USSR. In April of 1990 a new association was formed to complement its activities - the All-Russian Union of Concert Performers. Members of the music community place their hopes in these two professional associations. Today there is a very good prospect that they will be able to develop an independent policy of efficient support of concert activities in the country.

The pattern of funding of philharmonic activities is identical with that of the non-commercial theater, and all the changes that occurred in the late 80's also applied to philharmonic activities, including enhanced tax privileges and creation of independent regional foundations for arts development.

Variety shows constitute a large component of concert activities. For the most part they are organized by the same state concert organizations, philharmonics, and independent collectives. Within the concert organizations one can find about 500 variety-show groups, and only 20 of these enjoy independent status.

Variety show business is entirely profitable, and although it would not be fair to say that the objective of the state concert organizations in the field of variety shows is to extract profit, this type of activity cannot be described as non-commercial. Up to 1980 the presence of these two occupants (commercial and non-commercial) under a single roof permitted the management of the concert organizations to use profits from the one to finance the other. Since 1980 the traditional pattern has changed, and all profits from variety show activities are returned to the state budget in the form of taxes and other payments, which are then used to fund philharmonic activities. For example, in 1985, of the 44.4 million rubles of philharmonic subsidy, 30 million rubles came from the state budget and 14.4 million from the profits of variety show activities. In the late 80's this practice also changed: profits from variety show activities were retained by the concert organizations while the funding of philharmonic concerts by the state budget remained intact. Thus, the variety show activities of the state concert organizations were given a type of non-commercial status which make them tax exempt.

All these changes in the late 80's were accompanied by another important new phenomenon in the organization of variety show activities - the emergence and rapid growth of cooperative (in certain ways, private) concert agencies independent of the state. Popular groups prefer to work with these agencies, selling their services via contracts with the organizers of such concerts. Acting on the basis of the Law on Cooperatives, these music agencies exclusively pursue profit-making objectives. Profits remaining after payment of taxes can be used at their own discretion. Indirect protection of the interests of such agencies is provided by yet another new organization -- The Union of Cooperative Workers of the USSR.

OVERALL VIEW OF PERFORMING ARTS ACTIVITY IN THE US

Some musical and dramatic performances in the United States are presented for individual profit by private investors while others are funded by a mixture of box office receipts, grants from the federal government, the individual states, individuals, private foundations and business firms. The latter are known as "not-for-profit" organizations.

The amount of direct government funding in the United States seems (and no doubt is) surprisingly low. It should be mentioned that the amount of direct funding by government sources is only part of the total picture. As already noted, not-for-profit cultural organizations are operated as tax-exempt institutions, and can receive gifts from private sources on which the tax is forgiven. Private foundations operate with funds that have already been given tax exemption and have been dedicated irrevocably to approved public causes. The amount of tax foregone by government in these ways is large, and should be considered a form of subsidy.

The National Endowment for the Arts, an agency of the Federal Government, makes grants to small and large organizations on the basis of their professional quality and contribution to the life of people throughout the country. Grants are allocated by professional panels whose constituency changes regularly. Efforts to politicize giving to the arts are fought off, often successfully, by the artistic community.

Each state and territory has an independent Arts Council. About 20 to 25 percent of federal grant money is redistributed by them to local arts organizations, and is augmented by grants from the individual state governments and other sources. This system encourages arts activities throughout the country rather than only in certain urban centers.

Touring productions range from commercial travelling shows to long- term programs by regional theaters and other not-for-profit artists, and special funds to cover the extra cost are available from the National Endowment for the Arts and most of the state Arts Councils.

It is considered by many an important advantage of the system in the United States that there is a multiplicity of sources of support, because it means that some funding is available for each of the various styles and philosophies of performance, and for a variety of ideologies.

The interests of the individual artists are protected by labor unions whose principal function is to negotiate contracts covering salary, working conditions and, in most cases, provisions for health insurance and retirement pensions. The most important are the powerful Actors Equity and American Federation of Musicians, both of which have called very effective strikes to enforce their demands. There are other specialized unions for television and radio artists, playwrights, scenic designers etc.

THEATER IN THE US

The not-for-profit theater may be the most fertile source of innovation both in material and production techniques at the present time, often providing material to the profit-seeking sector. These theaters have tax-exempt status, which means that they may receive contributions for which the donors are permitted to reduce their federal tax payment proportionately. The theaters pay taxes and pay salaries to their workers, but may not operate for the profit of any individual. They bring business to their areas by attracting visitors from distant areas who use the local restaurants, hotels and other facilities.

The nonprofit theaters include an elite group of 67 "regional" theaters located throughout the country. Each theater must obtain considerable local financial support from individuals, local governments and others in order to survive. They serve large regional audiences in their home theaters and by touring, and many are distinguished artistically.

The many smaller professional theaters scattered throughout the country also depend on a mix of box office, federal and state grants and private and business contributions. Together with the regionals some belong to the Theater Communication Group which provides many services, keeps statistics and disseminates information through its publications and other efforts.

It is estimated that there are about 600 additional small, professionally-oriented theaters, often offering an artistic or a political message. They are not always funded directly by government, but are eligible for tax exempt status.

In theater, there are also many productions presented by private capitalists with the hope of financial gain. There is a good profit to be made from staging plays of wide popular interest, and the Broadway stage has a proud history of artistic achievement financed in this way.

By far the largest supplier of drama and musical comedy in the United States is the private, profit-seeking sector which radiates from Broadway. This sector is a clear net contributor to the economy; it receives no subsidy and provides a demand for services such as set construction, costume production and transportation, restaurants and tourist services. Successful plays are organized into "road companies" which travel to the larger cities bringing the latest shows which are still running on Broadway to the rest of the country and abroad. Smaller communities must wait a while longer and be satisfied with less opulent productions, because they are served, in the private sector, by smaller travelling groups that spend only a few days in any one locality, or even specialize in one night stands. They typically pay a fee for the use of copywrited plays.

Another large part of the private sector is the dinner theater where a play and a meal are sold to the public at rather low prices. This is not, however, an innovative branch of theater artistically, and typically provides minimal productions of proven favorites.

ORCHESTRAL MUSIC IN THE US

All orchestral music in the United States is provided by not-for-profit orchestras. Their funding pattern is approximately the same as for non-profit theater. One of the main jobs of the orchestra manager is to seek funding, and he or she works to ensure that the organization remains a valued part of the community.

Orchestras are represented by the American Symphony Orchestra league (ASOL), which provides various services to its members and keeps an elaborate statistical analysis from year to year for their use and guidance. The ASOL separates its members into seven categories determined by size of annual budget. There are 41 elite orchestras, distributed throughout the country, with budgets of over $3.4 million. The 53 orchestras with budgets between that sum and $1 million are also fully professional and usually of excellent quality. Below that, with budgets between $240,000 and $1 million are 87 smaller orchestras which can include non-professional musicians. Estimates show that there are about 1000 low budget orchestras in various locations. All of these orchestras are fully independent entities with their own managements who make all their own artistic and business decisions.

Choruses and large chamber groups, similarly, are typically organized as not-for-profit entities. Individual performers, however, and many small groups, still find it advantageous to operate as profit-seeking entities, and contract their services directly to individual concert organizers.

DESCRIPTION OF THE TABLES

Tables 1-6 report the data and the ancillary calculations for the incomes and expenses of musical-performance groups in the USSR and the U.S.A., and Tables 7-12 provide the corresponding information for theaters in the two countries. Tables 1 and 7 give the raw data in current rubles or dollars (as appropriate); that is, there is no attempt to correct the figures for inflation in either country. The tables also give figures on attendances and number of performances in the reported sample, as well as price indices for the USSR and the U.S. There are two USSR indices, Index I, provided by the Soviet co-author of this paper and Index II, provided by the U.N. For the U.S. there are also two indices reported, the GNP deflator and the CPI. Throughout, the analysis uses USSR Price Index I and the U.S. GNP deflator. All data are for the three years 1975, 1980 and 1985 for which the information was readily available.

Tables 2 and 8 translate the current dollar and ruble figures into real data, by adjusting for inflation, so that the rubles and dollars shown remain constant in purchasing power over the decade under discussion.

Tables 3 and 9 make a rough correction for the differences in the USSR and U.S. samples by calculating revenues and costs on a *per-attendee* basis, thus to some degree making up for the far larger number of USSR performances reported.

Tables 4 and 10 translate all the figures into a single currency unit - rubles of 1975 purchasing power, as calculated by an international group of specialists. This is the first table in which the USSR and the US figures can be compared directly. The dollar-ruble exchange rate used is the Purchasing Power Parity (PPP) exchange rate taken from Marer (1985, p. 85).

Tables 5 and 11 translate the preceding tables into indices, with 1975 (arbitrarily) set equal to 100, so that we see how rapidly comparative costs in the two countries have risen. For ease of comparison both countries are started out equal in 1975 (1975 = 100).

Tables 6 and 12 show the percentage breakdowns of costs and revenues in the two countries, where possible, reporting the percent of total cost constituted by compensation of artistic personnel, the percent of total income made up of box office receipts, etc.

Table 1 Musical (Orchestral) Income, Expenses, etc. USSR, US (Current rubles, dollars, in millions)

	1975 USSR	1975 US	1980 USSR	1980 US	1985 USSR	1985 US
1 Total income	220.9	137.0	281.7	288.8	309.9	480.5
2 Earned	213.6	64.9	259.7	163.2	280.2	282.4
3 Govt Contrib	7.3	20.0	22.0	36.1	29.7	49.7
4 Priv Contrib	0.0	38.7	0.0	89.5	0.0	148.4
5 Endowment		13.4				
6 Total expenses	220.9	141.5	281.7	244.5	309.9	467.1
7 Salaries	80.6	105.2	108.5	189.5	115.7	307.2
8 Artistic	41.2	84.9	59.0	155.3	62.0	252.3
9 Admin	4.2	20.3	6.1	34.2	6.7	54.9
10 Other	35.2	0.0	43.4	0.0	47.0	0.0
11 Other exp	140.3	36.4	173.2	55.0	194.2	159.9
12 Gap (surplus)	0.0	4.6	0.0	0.5	0.0	10.7
13 Attendance	133.9	20.0	147.5	22.8	141.5	25.4
14 USSR pr index I	100		106.0		121.0	
15 USSR index 2 (UN)	100		103.2		107.9	
16 US GNP deflator		100		144.5		187.5
17 US CPI		100		153.1		199.9

Table 2 Real Musical (Orchestral) Income, Expenses, etc. USSR, US (Using USSR price index 1 and US GNP deflator)

	1975 USSR	1975 US	1980 USSR	1980 US	1985 USSR	1985 US
1 Total income	220.9	137.0	265.8	199.9	256.1	256.3
2 Earned	213.6	64.9	245.0	112.9	231.6	150.6
3 Govt Contrib	7.3	20.0	20.8	25.0	24.5	26.5
4 Priv Contrib	0.0	38.7	0.0	61.9	0.0	79.1
5 Endowment	0.0	13.4	0.0	0.0	0.0	0.0
6 Total expenses	220.9	141.5	265.8	169.2	256.1	249.1
7 Salaries	80.6	105.2	102.4	131.1	95.6	163.8
8 Artistic	41.2	84.9	55.7	107.5	51.2	134.6
9 Admin	4.2	20.3	5.8	23.7	5.5	29.3
10 Other	35.2	0.0	40.9	0.0	38.8	0.0
11 Other exp	140.3	36.4	163.4	38.1	160.5	85.3
12 Gap (surplus)	0.0	4.6	0.0	0.3	0.0	5.7

Table 3 Real Musical (Orchestral) Income, Expenses. Per Attendee.

	1975 USSR	1975 US	1980 USSR	1980 US	1985 USSR	1985 US
1 Total income	1.6	6.9	1.8	8.8	1.8	10.1
2 Earned	1.6	3.2	1.7	5.0	1.6	5.9
3 Govt Contrib	0.1	1.0	0.1	1.1	0.2	1.0
4 Priv Contrib	0.0	1.9	0.0	2.7	0.0	3.1
5 Endowment	0.0	0.7	0.0	0.0	0.0	0.0
6 Total expenses	1.6	7.1	1.8	7.4	1.8	9.8
7 Salaries	0.6	5.3	0.7	5.8	0.7	6.5
8 Artistic	0.3	4.2	0.4	4.7	0.4	5.3
9 Admin	0.0	1.0	0.0	1.0	0.0	1.2
10 Other	0.3	0.0	0.3	0.0	0.3	0.0
11 Other exp	1.0	1.8	1.1	1.7	1.1	3.4
12 Gap (surplus)	0.0	0.2	0.0	0.0	0.0	0.2

Table 4 Real Ruble Musical (Orchestral) Income, Expenses. Per Attendee at 1980. (Purchasing power parity rate: 2.5 dollars = 1 Ruble)

	1975 USSR	1975 US	1980 USSR	1980 US	1985 USSR	1985 US
1 Total income	1.6	2.7	1.8	3.5	1.8	4.0
2 Earned	1.6	1.3	1.7	2.0	1.6	2.4
3 Govt Contrib	0.1	0.4	0.1	0.4	0.2	0.4
4 Priv Contrib	0.0	0.8	0.0	1.1	0.0	1.2
5 Endowment	0.0	0.3	0.0	0.0	0.0	0.0
6 Total expenses	1.6	2.8	1.8	3.0	1.8	3.9
7 Salaries	0.6	2.1	0.7	2.3	0.7	2.6
8 Artistic	0.3	1.7	0.4	1.9	0.4	2.1
9 Admin	0.0	0.4	0.0	0.4	0.0	0.5
10 Other	0.3	0.0	0.3	0.0	0.3	0.0
11 Other exp	1.0	0.7	1.1	0.7	1.1	1.3
12 Gap (surplus)	0.0	0.1	0.0	0.0	0.0	0.1

Table 5 Real Ruble Musical (Orchestral) Income, Expenses. Per Attendee 1975-1985. Indexes: 1975 = 100

	1975		1980		1985	
	USSR	US	USSR	US	USSR	US
1 Total income	100.0	100.0	109.2	128.0	109.7	147.3
2 Earned	100.0	100.0	104.1	152.7	102.6	182.7
3 Govt Contrib	100.0	100.0	258.1	109.6	318.2	104.4
4 Priv Contrib		100.0		140.4		161.0
5 Endowment		100.0		0.0		0.0
6 Total expenses	100.0	100.0	109.2	104.9	109.7	138.6
7 Salaries	100.0	100.0	115.3	109.4	112.3	122.6
8 Artistic	100.0	100.0	122.6	111.0	117.7	124.8
9 Admin	100.0	100.0	124.4	102.3	124.8	113.6
10 Other	100.0		105.6		104.4	
11 Other exp	100.0	100.0	105.7	91.7	108.3	184.5
12 Gap (surplus)		100.0		6.6		97.7

Table 6 Musical (Orchestral) Income, Expenses, etc. USSR, US. Percentage Breakdowns.

	1975		1980		1985	
	USSR	US	USSR	US	USSR	US
1 Total income	100.0	100.0	100.0	100.0	100.0	100.0
2 Earned	96.7	47.4	92.2	56.5	90.4	58.8
3 Govt Contrib	3.3	14.6	7.8	12.5	9.6	10.3
4 Priv Contrib	0.0	28.2	0.0	31.0	0.0	30.9
5 Endowment	0.0	9.8	0.0	0.0	0.0	0.0
6 Total expenses	100.0	100.0	100.0	100.0	100.0	100.0
7 Salaries	36.5	74.3	38.5	77.5	37.3	65.8
8 Artistic	18.7	60.0	20.9	63.5	20.0	54.0
9 Admin	1.9	14.3	2.2	14.0	2.2	11.8
10 Other	15.9	0.0	15.4	0.0	15.2	0.0
11 Other exp	63.5	25.7	61.5	22.5	62.7	34.2
12 Gap (surplus)	0.0	4.6	0.0	0.2	0.0	10.7

Table 7 Theater Income, Expenses, etc. USSR, US (Current rubles or dollars) (millions)

	1975 USSR	1975 US	1980 USSR	1980 US	1985 USSR	1985 US
1 Total income	197.6	24.7	255.0	42.0	293.8	67.5
2 Earned	126.6	15.8	135.8	27.7	145.1	46.6
3 Govt Contrib	71.0	2.9	119.2	4.4	148.7	6.14
4 Priv Contrib	0.0	6.1	0.0	9.9	0.0	15.3
5 Total expenses	197.6	24.4	255.0	41.7	293.8	67.6
6 Salaries	113.2	13.9	152.5	23.9	167.1	39.1
7 Artistic	60.6	6.6	82.3	10.6	89.6	16.3
8 Admin	9.2	4.0	13.3	7.3	15.1	12.3
9 Other	43.4	3.3	56.9	6.0	62.4	10.5
10 Other exp	84.4	10.4	102.5	17.8	126.7	28.2
11 Gap (surplus)	0.0	0.3	0.0	0.3	0.0	-0.1
12 Attendance	115.7	3.6	119.2	4.2	123.9	3.8
13 USSR price index	100.0		106.0		121.0	
14 US GNP deflator		100.0		144.5		187.5

Table 8 Real Theatrical Income, Expenses (Using USSR price index 1, US GNP deflator)

	1975 USSR	1975 US	1980 USSR	1980 US	1985 USSR	1985 US
1 Total income	197.6	24.7	240.6	29.1	242.8	36.0
2 Earned	126.6	15.8	128.1	19.2	119.9	24.9
3 Govt Contrib	71.0	2.9	112.5	3.0	122.9	3.3
4 Priv Contrib	0.0	6.1	0.0	6.9	0.0	8.2
5 Total expenses	197.6	24.4	240.6	28.9	242.8	36.1
6 Salaries	113.2	13.9	143.9	16.5	138.1	20.9
7 Artistic	60.6	6.6	77.6	7.3	74.0	8.7
8 Admin	9.2	4.0	12.5	5.1	12.5	6.6
9 Other	43.4	3.3	53.7	4.2	51.6	5.6
10 Other exp	84.4	10.4	96.7	12.3	104.7	15.0
11 Gap (surplus)	0.0	0.3	0.0	0.2	0.0	-0.1

Table 9 Real Theatrical Income, Expenses. Per Attendee.

	1975 USSR	1975 US	1980 USSR	1980 US	1985 USSR	1985 US
1 Total income	1.7	6.9	2.1	10.0	2.4	17.8
2 Earned	1.1	4.4	1.1	6.6	1.2	12.3
3 Govt Contrib	0.6	0.8	1.0	1.0	1.2	1.6
4 Priv Contrib	0.0	1.7	0.0	2.4	0.0	4.0
5 Total expenses	1.7	6.8	2.1	9.9	2.4	17.8
6 Salaries	1.0	3.9	1.3	5.7	1.3	10.3
7 Artistic	0.5	1.8	0.7	2.5	0.7	4.3
8 Admin	0.1	1.1	0.1	1.7	0.1	3.2
9 Other	0.4	0.9	0.5	1.4	0.5	2.8
10 Other exp	0.7	2.9	0.9	4.2	1.0	7.4
11 Gap (surplus)	0.0	0.1	0.0	0.1	0.0	0.0

Table 10 Real Ruble Theatrical Income, Expenses. Per Attendee.
(At 1980 PPP exchange rate: 2.5 dollars = 1 Ruble)

	1975 USSR	1975 US	1980 USSR	1980 US	1985 USSR	1985 US
1 Total income	1.7	2.7	2.1	4.0	2.4	7.1
2 Earned	1.1	1.8	1.1	2.6	1.2	4.9
3 GovtContrib	0.6	0.3	1.0	0.4	1.2	0.6
4 PrivContrib	0.0	0.7	0.0	0.9	0.0	1.6
5 Total expenses	1.7	2.7	2.1	4.0	2.4	7.1
6 Salaries	1.0	1.5	1.3	2.3	1.3	4.1
7 Artistic	0.5	0.7	0.7	1.0	0.7	1.7
8 Admin	0.1	0.4	0.1	0.7	0.1	1.3
9 Other	0.4	0.4	0.5	0.6	0.5	1.1
10 Other exp	0.7	1.2	0.9	1.7	1.0	3.0
11 Gap (surplus)	0.0	0.0	0.0	0.0	0.0	0.0

Table 11 Real Ruble Theatrical Income, Expenses, per Attendee.
Indexes: 1975 = 100

	1975		1980		1985	
	USSR	US	USSR	US	USSR	US
1 Total income	100.0	100.0	125.3	145.7	138.8	258.9
2 Earned	100.0	100.0	104.1	150.3	107.0	279.4
3 Govt Contrib	100.0	100.0	163.0	130.0	195.6	200.6
4 Priv Contrib		100.0		139.1		237.6
5 Total expenses	100.0	100.0	125.3	146.5	138.8	262.5
6 Salaries	100.0	100.0	130.8	147.4	137.8	266.5
7 Artistic	100.0	100.0	131.8	137.7	138.1	234.0
8 Admin	100.0	100.0	140.3	156.4	153.3	291.3
9 Other	100.0	100.0	127.3	155.8	134.3	301.4
10 Other exp	100.0	100.0	117.9	146.7	140.2	256.9
11 Gap (surplus)		100.0		85.7		-31.6

Table 12 USSR, US Theatrical Income, Expenses.
(Percentage breakdowns)

	1975		1980		1985	
	USSR	US	USSR	US	USSR	US
1 Total income	100.0	100.0	100.0	100.0	100.0	100.0
2 Earned	64.1	64.0	53.3	66.0	49.4	69.0
3 Govt Contrib	35.9	11.7	46.7	10.5	50.6	9.1
4 Priv Contrib	0.0	24.7	0.0	23.6	0.0	22.7
5 Total expenses	100.0	100.0	100.0	100.0	100.0	100.0
6 Salaries	57.3	57.0	59.8	57.3	56.9	57.8
7 Artistic	30.7	27.0	32.3	25.4	30.5	24.1
8 Admin	4.7	16.4	5.2	17.5	5.1	18.2
9 Other	22.0	13.5	22.3	14.4	21.2	15.5
10 Other exp	42.7	42.6	40.2	42.7	43.1	41.7

NOTES ON THE DATA

Unfortunately, as we expected, the data are not as consistent as one might, ideally, have hoped. Not only are the American classifications far from consistent with those of the USSR, but the US orchestral breakdown is very different from those for US theaters.

Statistical data on the Soviet performing arts organisations are more representative and detailed. The data relate to the activities of practically all professional theatres (note that the number of studio-theatres until 1986 was negligible), orchestras, ensembles, choruses, other concert groups and individual performers for 1975-1985. These data reflect not only the "end" parameters of the performing art (attendances, performances, incomes, expenses, etc.) but also which is at least as important gives an idea of the "interim" parameters. Such detailed statistics representing a large volume of information on the individual expense and income items in the budgets of the performing art organisations appeared as the result of long efforts and intense work with accounting books, including the search in the archives of the Ministry of Culture of the USSR. This was accomplished by a group of research workers from the All-Union Scientific and Research Institute of Arts Studies under the guidance of one of the authors of this paper. The first publication of the above mentioned information will occur in the near future.[4]

The data for American musical performance pertain only to orchestras while, as noted, the Soviet figures refer to an amalgam of performing groups ranging from chamber music to rock performers. The figures were provided by the American Symphony Orchestra League, which maintains very extensive and very careful records provided to it by its member orchestras. Our sample includes only orchestras in the top groups in terms of total expenditures, in accord with the ASOL's classification. The size of the sample varies from year to year in accord with the numbers of orchestras that fell into those two groups in any particular year, and the number that chose to submit reports in that year.

The theater data were provided by the Theatre Communications Group, and relate to their membership of more-successful regional theaters. Though these theaters are located throughout the country, the figures cannot pretend to be representative of American theaters, since they exclude, among others, the commercial theaters at one economic extreme, and a considerable majority of smaller organizations at the other. However, the theater figures have the great virtue of relating to an unchanging group of 22 theaters, with 10 years of consistent data available for the members of this group. Unfortunately, the data are not available for just those 22 theaters in 1985, so that regression calculations had to be employed to extrapolate the figures for that year. Other data, extending from 1981 through 1985, were analyzed to make sure that 1985 was not an outlier in its financial behavior. With each of the trend regressions having R squared values of 0.9 or higher, the extrapolated financial figures are offered with some degree of confidence. Regrettably, the same cannot be said of the vital attendance figure for that year, since the attendance data are considerably more volatile.

IMPLICATIONS OF THE DATA

Both the similarities and differences that show up for the two countries are striking.

First, as is seen from Table 6, artistic salaries represent a far smaller share of the total cost of *musical performance* in the USSR than in the U.S., though the share in the U.S. has been declining. This may represent either the higher level of wages in the U.S., or the inclusion of some types of capital costs in the USSR other expense figures that are excluded from the U.S. data but, more likely, is an artifact of the differences in the types of performing groups included in the data for the two countries.

Table 6 shows a difference that is even more remarkable - the far-higher share of total of musical performance expenses that are covered in the USSR out of earned income (largely box office receipts) rather than out of government (or private) subvention. This certainly dispels the western illusion that the arts in the USSR are far more liberally supported by subsidy.

Still, it is noteworthy that the more-directly-comparable figures for *theater* in the USSR and the US are much more similar than those for musical performance. In both countries the share of contributions in total income expenses were relatively close in 1975, though that proportion in the USSR has since grown considerably (Table 12). On the side of expenses (Tables 6 and 12), the USSR share of artistic salaries is consistently higher for USSR theaters than for those in the US. This is the direct reverse of the relationship observed in music finances. Still more striking is the far-higher share in US budgets of administrative salaries. In the theater the percent of administrative salaries in the US budget was consistently more than three times as high as that in the Soviet Union, and in music that disparity was considerably greater.

Also noteworthy is the fact that in every category cost per attendee in the US is far higher than that in the USSR. This is not put in doubt by questions about the trustworthiness of our PPP ruble-dollar exchange rate on which this comparison depends. For it seems clear that if anything the 2.5 to 1 exchange rate we have used, if anything, underestimates the relative purchasing power of the dollar, so that any correction is virtually certain to increase the disparity between the per attendee costs in the two countries.

Finally, Tables 5 and 11 show the relative time trends in rubles of constant purchasing power. They show that in both countries performance costs have increased substantially faster than the rate of inflation, but that the cost disease has grown acute at a far more rapid rate in the U.S.

TWO FORMS OF "BAUMOL'S DISEASE"

The relatively slow growth of real cost per attendee in the performing arts in the USSR should probably be ascribed to the policy of rigid price control on the part of the state. This suppresses inflation but leads to shortages of goods and services. Performing arts organizations have experienced increasing difficulties in acquiring materials, sound and light equipment. The result is a non-price form of "Baumol's Disease" peculiar to centrally-planned economies with rigid state price control. Any movement towards a market economy would release suppressed inflation which would then be expressed in monetary terms and "Baumol's Disease" would take its familiar form.

Comparing the data for the USA and USSR we suggest that there are two forms of the same "Baumol's Disease". In the US it takes the form of rising real costs; in the USSR it takes the form of increasing shortages of goods and services needed for the operation of performing arts organizations.

HYPOTHESES TO ACCOUNT FOR THE OBSERVED PATTERNS

The fact that, until recently, a high share of total music performance cost was covered by box-office income in the USSR, can be explained by the structure of arts delivery to the public, which was, in effect, entrusted to large conglomerates consisting of every level of musical activity from solo performances and one man shows to symphony orchestras. Some of these activities, usually those of individuals or small groups, are typically profitable. In the U.S. they receive no subsidy, while in the Soviet Union, during the period to which our data pertain, they received a form of cross subsidy, with more popular types of musical performance covering the deficits of those that are less popular.

A second explanatory influence may be the fact that the overall level of productivity in the US is still the highest in the world, which means that the cost disease is in a relatively advanced stage in that country, making the cost of performances relatively high and hence making it considerably more difficult to cover those costs by the sale of tickets alone.

The fact that government subsidies to theater in the USSR are far higher than those for music confirms that the theater was not the recipient of cross subsidies from more-popular types of performance, and so its deficits had to be covered by the state.

However, the relatively high costs per attendee of the American performances and the greater rapidity of the rate of increase in those real costs do lend support to the hypothesis that the cost disease in the US is in a considerably more advanced stage than that in the USSR.

Finally, the very high proportion of administrative cost in the American budgets is almost certainly attributable largely to the high cost of fund raising. With contributions never a foregone conclusion, and with the most if not all organizations having to raise more than a third of their income from a substantial multiplicity of contributors, it should not be surprising that the outlays required for the purpose are so substantial.

CONCLUDING COMMENT

This paper is intended only as a preliminary comparative exploration of the economics of the arts in our two countries. We began with the data that were readily available and took their analysis as far as the sparse information permitted. Yet it has offered some tentative conclusions and provided some insights. Above all, we hope that careful examination of the assembled materials will provide a useful agenda for the future.

But in this case it is the descriptive materials that surely emerge as the focus of the reader's interest. The revolutionary changes in the financial organization of the performing arts in the USSR during the last decade are remarkable and largely unrecognized in the west. We will all have a good deal to learn by watching them as they evolve in the next few years and are firmly incorporated into the institutional fabric.

FOOTNOTES

[1]The authors are extremely grateful to Gregory Nersesyan for his very useful comments, for his indispensible role in translation, and, above all, for his friendship. We must also thank the American Symphony Orchestra League and the Theatre Communications Group for their generous cooperation in the process of data gathering and interpretation.

[2]See Chartrand (1987).

[3]See preceding footnote.

[4]See Rubinstein (1990)

REFERENCES

Chartrand, H.H. (1987) "Cultural Economics of Arts Funding: Five Variations on a Theme" in *Paying for the Arts*, Association for Cultural Economics, pp. 3-16.

Marer, P. (1985) *Dollar GNPs of the USSR and Eastern Europe*, Johns Hopkins, Baltimore.

Rubinstein, A. (1990) *Introduction to the Economics of the Performing Arts*, Supplement I-IV, Moscow.

PART IV

POLICY IMPLICATIONS FOR THE ARTS

[20]

On the Rationale of Public Support

EVIDENCE of growing financial gaps in the budgets of performing arts organizations and recurrent crises in their operations inevitably gives rise to the suggestion that more support should be provided to the arts by government. For some people, evidence that the typical income gap is likely to continue to grow is enough to settle the issue. Convinced that the performing arts make a contribution to our culture and are valuable as an end in themselves, they feel that the responsibility of society, as represented by its government, is perfectly clear. The argument is simple: if through no fault of their own the arts cannot survive without public support, the necessary support must be provided.

However, the conviction that government should do more for the arts is by no means universal. Even among members of symphony boards the case for government aid has hardly been considered obvious. As recently as 1953 a survey by the American Symphony Orchestra League showed that 99 per cent of the members of orchestra governing boards were strongly opposed to federal aid. Even though by 1962 a much larger proportion of this group took at least a middle ground and by 1965 "in a dramatic reversal of position . . . presidents and managers of nearly forty symphony orchestras endorsed federal support,"[1] doubts about the desirability of government support continue to be raised even by friends of the arts.

[1] American Symphony Orchestra League, *Newsletter*, March–April–May 1965, p. 1.

In this chapter we shall, therefore, examine some of the fundamental pros and cons of government support, paying particular attention to those issues which are amenable to economic analysis.[2]

Some Arguments for Government Support

"We are the only major nation on earth whose government still does so little about the nation's cultural treasure in the performing and visual arts, and it is high time that we caught up."[3] With these words a noted Senator stated clearly one of the most common arguments for government support — the argument by example. It is done elsewhere, why not here? The argument by precedent also takes another form: "Our government came to this conclusion [that federal assistance is warranted] about United States shipping in 1950, about agriculture in 1862, about education even before this."[4]

Though these analogies may be effective in forcing us to think about the issue, they suffer from two serious shortcomings. It does not necessarily follow that because support is appropriate for some social and economic activities it is equally desirable for others. Even more important, the argument by analogy provides no evidence that government assistance to the other activities cited was justified in the first place. To remedy this deficiency a variety of beneficial side effects reputed to flow from the arts are frequently brought to our attention, consequences ranging from those which serve the noblest purposes to those which cater to the most material ends, from the enrichment of the nation's expanding leisure time to the provision of employment opportunities.

Most often, however, the advocacy of public support is made to rest ultimately on what might be considered higher grounds, the "intrinsic value" of artistic activity. Lord Bridges put the matter most forcefully in his Romanes Lecture in 1958 when he stated, "The heart of this matter is surely that the arts can give to all of

[2] For a concise discussion of some of the subject matter of this chapter, see Robbins, Section II.

[3] Senator Jacob K. Javits, quoted in Stoddard.

[4] Stoddard, p. 3.

us, including those who lack expert knowledge of any of them, much of what is best in human life and enjoyment; and that a nation which does not put this at the disposal of those who have the liking and the capacity for it, is failing in a most important duty."[5]

Arguments Against Government Support

The one argument which most of us today would regard as an antediluvian manifestation is that poverty is good for the arts and stimulates creativity. "We want to develop a hungry theater," said one witness at the House Hearings on economic conditions in the performing arts, who went on to assert that only a hungry man feels compelled to say "what's in him."[6]

A more thoughtful objection to the use of government funds for the arts asserts that there are higher priorities, that poverty, disease, crime and ignorance have a stronger claim on government funds. Thus, Lord Bridges notes in his address a case where an expenditure related to the arts was attacked in the press on the basis that the money could have been used "to build six bungalows for old people" in the area. While this alternative use of funds may be appealing, it must be recognized that, as a practical matter, the money in question, if not used for the arts, may well not be employed to construct "six bungalows" or for any other similar purpose. In any event, even if one believes that more money should be spent on the poor, it does not follow that less should be spent on the arts. Perhaps economies should be effected instead in some other part of the government budget, or perhaps total outlays by the public sector should simply be increased. It is capricious and arbitrary to attack expenditures on the arts just because one believes some other projects have a higher priority. Such an argument is valid only if one can think of *no* better source of the requisite funds, and if one can be reasonably sure that the monies denied the arts would, in fact, be devoted to the six bungalows, or to whatever else is deemed worthier.

[5] 1958 Romanes Lecture, pp. 12–13.

[6] House Hearings, II, testimony of John D. Wentworth, managing director of the Washington Theater Club, Washington, D.C., p. 533.

An argument of a very different sort is that government support of the arts would serve mainly to displace private funds, which in turn implies that a great deal of government money would have to be spent to bring about a small increase in the total resources available to performing arts organizations.

Unfortunately, there is little evidence on the basic factual issue — the effect of government grants on private contributions.[7] We do know, at least on an impressionistic basis, that in Western European countries there is little private giving to the arts; and, as was noted in the last chapter, governments do provide considerable direct support in these countries. One possible inference is that government grants have discouraged private giving, but it is at least equally plausible that causation has flowed in the opposite direction — that it is because of a lack of private support that continental governments have felt obliged to spend considerable sums on the arts. To the best of our knowledge no strong tradition of private giving to the arts exists in any European country, and it may well be that private contributions would be small even in the absence of government grants.

Our audience survey shed some interesting sidelights on this question. If we compare by income class the proportion of persons who contribute to the performing arts regularly in Great Britain and the United States, we find that in the lower income brackets the proportion giving regularly is about the same in the two countries, but in the upper brackets there is a much lower rate of contribution in the United Kingdom. This distinction may be one result of the greater tax incentives provided in the United States, or it may mean that the wealthy are the first to reduce their contributions when the government begins to finance artistic activity. Of course, other explanations are also possible — for example, the effect of the higher over-all level of per capita income in the United States has to be considered — and it would be fatuous to pretend that the implications of these results are unambiguous.[8]

[7] Great Britain would seem to be an excellent locale for such a study, since a comparison of current patterns of giving with patterns before World War II and the inauguration of the Arts Council might be very enlightening, but no such investigation seems to have been conducted.

[8] The results of this comparison are summarized graphically in Appendix Figure XVI–A.

On the whole, we were somewhat surprised at the high proportion of contributions reported in our English audience surveys, as our examination of the financial records of leading performing organizations indicated that they obtained relatively little money from private contributions. We, therefore, studied the organizations to which English respondents said they contributed. Comparing a London orchestral audience with an orchestral audience in the United States, we found that in the American case two thirds of the organizations to which respondents reported donating were major professional groups, whereas in the London sample semiprofessional or amateur groups made up nearly half of the total. This finding suggests that where the state takes a major share of responsibility for the support of professional organizations, a higher proportion of private contributions will go to amateur activity.

An historical study of English philanthropy has emphasized that time and again private donors have directed attention to a need, and then, when society at large assumed responsibility for ministering to that need, moved on to new fields.[9] This does not mean that government grants to the performing arts would necessarily drive away private donors in the United States. Developments in the field of education provide evidence to the contrary. Here the government has been doing more and more, and yet private contributions have also been rising at a very substantial rate indeed.[10] It is also reassuring that the institution of private philanthropy seems so well established in the United States. For this reason, and perhaps because of our greater wealth, total charitable contributions are higher in this country than abroad. Moreover, no one has proposed government grants of a magnitude which would make private support redundant.

Another argument against public support is the danger of public control. Senator Barry Goldwater voiced the fears of many peo-

[9] See David Owen, *English Philanthropy, 1660–1960*, Belknap Press, Cambridge, Mass., 1964. Welfare activities and hospitals are obvious examples.

[10] See Council for Financial Aid to Education, *Guide Lines to Voluntary Support of America's Colleges and Universities*, Report on surveys conducted in 1954–55, 1956–57, 1958–59 and 1960–61, which shows that 728 institutions reported receiving somewhat less than $290 million in private support in 1954–55, while only eight years later, in 1962–63, 1,036 institutions reported receiving $911 million from private sources.

ple when he said that "the Federal Government eventually will do more harm in this field than good by overregulating it, by overcontrolling it."[11] Americans are still haunted by the memory of the atmosphere of thought control which surrounded the demise of the Federal Theatre Project, and it is not easy to forget the moment when counsel for the House Unamerican Activities Committee asked Hallie Flannigan: "You are quoting from this Marlowe. Is he a Communist?"

This objection, that public support implies public control, though one of the most persuasive, has turned out to be one of the least valid in practice. There is ample evidence that government support in Western Europe has not meant public control. John E. Booth, reporting on the European experience, writes:

> The performing arts, under government support, are manifestly free from political pressure or interference. Broadly speaking, and exceptions exist, government does not impose its view. . . . Within the bounds of public acceptance, all are free to be exposed, experimentation is encouraged.
>
> The extent of the freedom is evidenced in the testimony of all concerned — government officials, producers, playwrights, and critics. . . . the freedom is implicit in the range of works produced year in and year out.[12]

And in our own country a review of experience suggests strongly that we must regard as unfortunate aberrations the WPA history and the more recent outburst of two Congressmen of considerable repute against "eroticism" in the dances of Martha Graham. In our researches we encountered no case of interference by state or local governments, even where the amount of assistance provided has been relatively large.[13] An official concerned with the Library of Congress concert series, one of the oldest government supervised arts programs in the country, told us that he could recall no instance where his decisions had been questioned or

[11] Senate Hearings, p. 180.

[12] Booth, p. vi.

[13] In an article in the *Newsletter* of the American Symphony Orchestra League (November–December 1963, pp. 13–14), the manager of the Milwaukee Symphony reported that his organization had been receiving funds from the city for four years and that not one city official had tried to interfere in any way. He suggested that his experience was applicable elsewhere.

where any attempt was made to influence his program, aside perhaps from an occasional call by a Congressman suggesting hesitantly that he would appreciate a hearing for a performer from his constituency.

Indeed, one can make a strong case to the effect that interference by private patrons is far more frequent and poses a far more imminent threat than does government control. It has been charged more than once that some performing organizations share the tribulations of the group "controlled by a handful of people who consider the operation as their own private domain. They dictate not only administrative policy, labor policy, fund raising policy, but public standards of taste . . ."[14] We know of at least one case where a leading patron of an orchestral group has virtually banned contemporary music; and where, in addition, the occasional performance of a pre-nineteenth century piece is suffered only as an obvious exercise in forbearance. Even the foundations have not escaped charges of undue influence — the Harkness Foundation's rift with the Joffrey Ballet is a notable case in point.[15] In such circumstances government support, instead of reducing the freedom of the arts, can serve to increase it. We conclude, then, that there is little factual basis for the fear that control would be an inevitable concomitant of government assistance.

There is, however, an associated danger which has much more substance. While government assistance may not circumscribe the freedom of the arts in any direct sense, it can effectively dampen their vitality. If support is channeled exclusively to old, established organizations, it can discourage experimentation and make for general stagnation. We have seen in the preceding chapter that this charge has been leveled against the Arts Council of Great Britain. However, the indictment is more telling in connection with arts programs in several other countries, where some of the famous old theaters and opera companies, recipients of heavy government support, are apparently suffering from an advanced

[14] House Hearings, II, statement of Mrs. Diane Fivey, San Francisco Executive Secretary of the American Guild of Musical Artists, p. 350. See also the letter by a member of the San Francisco Arts Commission, *New York Times*, Nov. 29, 1964, p. 49.

[15] *New York Times*, March 18, 1964, p. 48.

case of ossification. If, on the other hand, government support is spread thinly over a variety of enterprises of widely varying quality, in order to avoid the charge of "favoritism," the inevitable result is a diffusion of mediocrity. This is not an imagined danger. The state of stagnation of several European systems of higher education can be attributed at least in part to a misplaced egalitarianism in the distribution of government funds. When fifth-rate institutions and research projects are supported on a scale not far below the support given those of the highest quality, insufficient financing at the top level can lead to a "brains drain" if there is somewhere else to go.

But these perils, while potentially very serious, seem unlikely to apply in the case of the United States, at least in the imminent future. No one is suggesting support on a scale which would make government the exclusive source of funds for any activity, and a pluralistic arrangement in which private and public support both play a role automatically acquires checks and balances. Such a mixed system has been highly successful in maintaining the vitality of our system of higher education, and there is no obvious reason why it should not work just as well in the arts.[16]

The Market Test

There remains the fundamental objection to public support which arises out of the application of the market test to the performing arts. The Philistine is surely entitled to ask: If the arts do provide so much to their audiences, why are the audiences not willing to bear their cost? The most basic objection to government support of the performing arts is simply that those who want to see them ought to pay the price. "The small percentage of people who enjoy opera does not qualify it for public financial support," wrote one commentator, who went on to say: "If opera cannot pay for itself, the fault is with opera, . . . It has never been a principle

[16] There is, however, some danger that individual giving will follow patterns set by government grants. The psychological "seal of approval" conferred by government aid may supplement the effects of matching-funds requirements in diverting the flow of private funds toward the pattern adopted by public agencies. Apparently this has been the experience in Canada. (See Hendry, p. 64.)

of our society that the people as a whole should be forced to pay for the entertainment of a few — and it must not be so now."[17]

Though some may find it distasteful, this objection is not without merit. Insolvency *per se* does not constitute adequate grounds for public assistance. No doubt when the automobile first came into general use financial catastrophe threatened manufacturers of buggies, yet we hardly feel that public funds should have been poured into that industry. The reason is clear: if consumers did not value buggies sufficiently to purchase them in quantities and at prices high enough to permit their continued production, the manufacturers no longer had any reason for survival. They had failed the stern test of the market which says that goods and services should be produced only if they are worth their keep to the consumer. But then, one may ask, does not the same test apply just as harshly to the performing arts? If audiences do not want them sufficiently to cover their costs through admission charges, why should this fact be construed as a *prima facie* case for public support? Might it not argue the contrary — that live performance is an obsolete vestige of a handicraft economy which deserves no public assistance precisely because effective demand for it is inadequate?

This is a particularly telling argument in a discussion of government assistance, for government funds, unlike private gifts and contributions, are supplied *involuntarily* by many individual members of the public. If the arts are to receive help from government sources, it becomes important to explain why the performing arts should be among those privileged activities which are granted exemption from the market test.

The proper response, it may be felt, cannot be given on a materialistic level. Rather, it must be phrased in terms of finer and less tangible concepts: the inherent value of beauty and the ineffable contribution of aesthetic activity. To the man in the street, however, this may not be an acceptable answer. Indeed, it is likely to smack of things he rightly considers dangerous: paternalism, dictation of tastes and violation of consumer sovereignty. He may

[17] Letter from Mr. William Eugene Hudson of New York City, printed in the *New York Times Magazine*, November 12, 1961, and quoted in House Hearings, II, p. 236.

well ask whether we are to base the allocation of the nation's resources on the aesthetic standards of some group of individuals who consider the true standards of beauty to have been revealed only to them. If public funds are to be spent to provide "good performance" which the public does not seem to want, then might not the next step be the proscription of other types of performance which the public does desire — perhaps the prohibition of immoral drama, or the discouragement of jazz, or of modern art or of anything else which does not appeal to those who dictate the aesthetic standards. If we accept the sovereignty of the public — the fundamental principle that in a democracy choices are to be made by the citizens of the community — an appeal for the sanctity of the arts simply will not suffice.

But if, as we have shown, audiences are drawn from so limited a segment of the community, can one ever expect to demonstrate that government support of the arts accords with the desires of the public? The answer is to be sought in the nature of activities which, by general consent, are exempted from the market test. One does not expect the defense establishment to show a profit, the courts to pay for themselves or the elementary schools to cover their costs out of their revenues. There are good grounds for these exemptions — grounds fixed firmly in economic analysis and involving no departure from democratic ideals. Much of the remainder of this chapter will be devoted to a discussion of these grounds and an examination of their applicability to the performing arts.

It should be emphasized that our analysis is not intended to pre-judge the amount of government support that is desirable, or even, for that matter, to argue that government funds should necessarily be devoted to such purposes. Rather, it is our intention to describe the logic on which such a decision, one way or the other, should be based if it is to satisfy the criterion of rationality.

The Egalitarian Grounds

The economist recognizes three basic grounds which can legitimately be used to defend government subsidy of unprofitable activities. The first ground for government intervention in the economy is inequality of opportunity. We generally take it as an article of faith that it is undesirable for anyone to be kept from achieving as much as he can through the abilities with which he is endowed. It is, therefore, widely agreed that no market test need support the flow of public funds devoted to the opening of opportunities to the impecunious. This exemption is neither capricious nor merely a matter of tradition. The market test has been described as an election in which the consumer decides what commodities shall be produced and in what quantities. He decides this, not by casting votes, but by the way in which he spends his dollars. But it is very important to remember that under this system not all men have the same number of votes. The affluent consumer has a far greater influence on the course of events than does a purchaser whose finances are quite limited. Therefore, government funds intended to promote equality of opportunity directly or indirectly may be viewed as a means for improving the way in which the market election is conducted.

Now, one may well argue that the extremely narrow audience for the arts is a consequence, not of limited interest, but of the fact that a very large segment of the community has been denied the opportunity to learn to appreciate them. In part this may be so because many persons cannot easily afford the admission charges. However, the lack of facilities in many of the nation's communities also constitutes a denial of opportunity. How can people learn to enjoy the living arts if no plays, no concert performers and no dancers are available to them? People can be deprived of opportunities by phenomena other than poverty and ignorance, and if the government wishes to improve the situation as far as the arts are concerned, it may have to help in the provision of opportunities for attendance in many parts of the country where professional performance is now totally unavailable.

The Education of Minors

A second legitimate reason for government support can be dealt with briefly. It is maintained that while in a democracy most individuals can be left to decide for themselves how their incomes should be spent, some classes of people are not competent to make their own decisions. In particular this argument is applied to minors, with the result that the latter are not permitted to purchase alcoholic beverages, drive automobiles, or decide for themselves whether funds shall be devoted to their schooling. The application to the arts is immediate, and is not unrelated to our accepted policies on education. It is felt that if children and adolescents are not exposed to artistic performance during their minority, by the time they become adults it will be too late. The arts must be made available early, while tastes are still being formed and behavior patterns developed.

It should be made clear that while the logic of this argument is acceptable enough, it rests also on an allegation of fact which has yet to be tested: the hypothesis that taste for the arts is instilled by early experiences. No one seems to have any overpowering evidence that this is so. No one has tracked down the children who attended the New York Philharmonic's young people's concerts which were given continuously from 1898 (by the New York Symphony Society before it merged with the New York Philharmonic) until 1939, or the WPA performances, to see whether they subsequently showed greater interest in the arts than persons coming from otherwise similar backgrounds.

Public Goods and the Market Test

The third ground which can be used to justify government expenditures involves the class of commodities and services which the economist calls "public goods." Public goods are items which, when provided to one person, automatically and unavoidably become available to other members of the community as well. For example, if current efforts succeed in reducing air pollution in Los Angeles, pure air will have been supplied not just to one Angeleno and his family but to all the inhabitants of the city.

The provision of public goods cannot be entrusted to market forces alone. The profit motive and free enterprise, which work so effectively in bringing private goods to consumers when and as they want them, are subject to a fatal limitation as regulators of the supply of public goods. The reason is that commodities of the latter type lack the basic requisite of the market — saleability.

This is seen most easily in the case of an item such as national defense. To pose the relevant question — can the operation of our military forces be left in the hands of private enterprise? — is to answer it. The proposition is ridiculous on its face. Defense benefits everyone, but if an individual were sold "a piece" of it, just what would he have purchased? National security, which is vital to all citizens, cannot be sold to any one of them. When someone desires a good such as a shirt or a pound of potatoes he must pay its price or the seller will refuse to hand the item over to him. But if an individual cannot be excluded from the enjoyment of the benefits of a good, there is no way a private seller can enforce the payment of a fee which would cover his costs. One cannot hope to sell rights to unpolluted air in the city streets, and for this reason the idea of an air cleaning firm has never attracted private investors.

While public goods cannot pass the market test, it does not follow that such items are unwanted by the general public. Even though consumers cannot be made to pay for them, they may regard them as well worth their cost. In such a case it is the normal commercial mechanism and not consumer demand which has failed to function. A government's decision to supply a public good is, therefore, not necessarily a decision to flaunt the wishes of the consumer. On the contrary, government financing may be the only way in which the wishes of the body of consumers can be put into effect.

The Case of "Mixed Commodities"

The situation is slightly more complicated in the case of mixed commodities — goods and services whose characteristics are partly private, partly public. Education is a prime example. When a student attends a school or a university his own welfare (including his future earning ability) is thereby increased. In this sense education is a *private* good — it can be sold to an individual purchaser because it yields benefits specifically to him. But at the same time education is also a *public* service because it enriches society as a whole — it not only increases the productivity of the individual, it makes for a better life for everyone in the community. Without general education the democratic process as we know it could not function effectively.

Unlike pure public goods, mixed commodities can be expected to cover part of their cost by sale to the public. One can charge a price for the direct benefits which flow from the provision of facilities for higher education, for inoculations against contagious diseases, slum clearance projects, etc. This is possible because the consumer can be excluded from the enjoyment of direct benefits if he does not pay the fee. A student who refuses to pay tuition may not be permitted to attend the university, and a tenant who chooses not to pay his rent can be evicted.

The consumer cannot, however, be excluded from the indirect benefits associated with mixed commodities, since these are unavoidably made available to all members of the community. Therefore, the price tag which can be put on quasi-public goods may be insufficient to cover their cost of production. But, in this case, failure to pass the market test does not necessarily mean that the goods in question are unwanted; it merely reflects the fact that they are not amenable to ordinary commercial standards of valuation. In these conditions public support may be entirely justified as the only available means to make demand effective.

The Performing Arts as "Mixed" Services

The reader can readily see where all of this is leading. If the performing arts are mixed commodities which confer direct benefits on those who attend a performance but which also offer benefits to the community as a whole, government support of the arts might well be completely consistent with the desires of the entire community. To determine whether the arts do or do not fall into this category it is necessary to look closely at the advantages they offer to the public at large.

There are at least four types of general benefit which may flow from the arts. The first of these may perhaps be considered unworthy, but it is, nevertheless, very real — it is the prestige conferred on a nation by its performing arts. Many persons who themselves have no desire to attend an opera or a program of contemporary dance take pride in the international recognition conferred on our singers and the creativity of our choreographers. To them the availability of a number of fine orchestras is a measure of the achievement of America, and is therefore a prime source of satisfaction. They would be most unhappy if the United States became known abroad as a cultural wasteland, a nation in which mammon had put beauty and art to rout.

Lest this phenomenon — the prestige conferred by cultural activity — be considered insufficient justification for any substantial support, it need only be recalled that concern with our image is the prime justification behind many of the billions currently being expended on the space race. If the national feeling of achievement which would attend getting to the moon at an early date is worth the outlay of tens of billions on the propulsion of astronauts into space, then the expenditure of a small fraction of this amount to obtain the prestige offered by a viable performing arts establishment may also be justified. It is in this connection that the potential role of the arts in U.S. foreign policy has been stressed. George London testified before a House committee that "the arts were being used as a potent propaganda weapon of the cold war." He suggested that in many parts of the world the United States is considered "a purely materialistic country devoted to profits and consumers' goods, and bereft of spiritual or cultural values. This is a theme which particularly the Soviets pound upon and make political capital of."[18] The use of State Department funds to finance international tours of American companies can be regarded as a small first countermove.

A second equally materialistic set of indirect benefits which flows from the arts is the advantage that the availability of cultural activity confers on business in its vicinity — the fact that it brings customers to shops, hotels, restaurants and bars. On a national level, distinguished performing arts organizations may serve, analogously, as a significant tourist attraction.[19] A particularly good illustration was provided in an editorial in the *New York Times*

[18] House Hearings, II, p. 21.

[19] Booth (p. iii) points out that the encouragement of tourism is an important motivation behind some of the support provided in Western Europe.

Support whose form seems to recognize the relationship between performance and some types of business activity has been provided in San Francisco, where a tax is levied on hotel rooms and the proceeds are divided between convention bureaus and the arts.

which commented on competition among 117 communities in 46 states, each seeking to become the site of a $280 million facility for experimentation in nuclear physics. The editor reported:

> In setting up its criteria for a choice, the [Atomic Energy Commission] noted that the location should have adequate cultural and educational facilities for those who will work at the facility. The result has been much soul-searching in communities that would like to have the accelerator and realize that past neglect of local educational and cultural institutions casts a blight over their chances.
>
> Many local readers over the country are now becoming aware that a strong research-oriented university, a thriving symphony orchestra and a lively theater no longer can be ranked as frills. They are essentials for a community's economic expansion in an age when science and scientists play an unprecedentedly important role.[20]

A third and far more appealing type of social contribution credited to the performing arts involves future generations. One may well feel that ability to appreciate the arts cannot always be achieved without a suitable period of training and acquaintance.[21] We have all met people who admit they have never themselves learned to enjoy a particular art form, but feel it important that such an opportunity be available to other members of their families. This same phenomenon has a significant extension to the posterity of the community as a whole. We support programs for the conservation of natural resources and for improvement of architecture in part because few of us are willing to take the responsibility of passing on to future generations a country whose beauty has been destroyed.

But provision for the future requires support for the arts in the present. Though it is demonstrably false that the arts "when once destroyed can never be supplied," it is true that their rehabilitation is not likely to be quick or easy. There is the old saw about the

[20] *New York Times*, Aug. 15, 1965, p. 85. Note that all of the indirect benefits in such a case are usually derived locally, and so this is an argument which can serve as justification primarily for local support.

[21] We have already had occasion to note another type of indiscriminate benefit associated with training children to appreciate the arts. This is the fact that because of the great mobility of the American population, an organization providing children's concerts in one city is likely to be building future audiences for other cities. This clearly argues for federal rather than local support.

man who asked the secret of the lush lawns at Versailles and was told that the answer was simple: they need only be watered daily for three hundred years. The development of mature cultural activities, of exacting standards of performance, and of an understanding audience cannot be achieved overnight. Funds must be provided today if the arts are to be kept alive for tomorrow. A program to preserve the arts for the nation's posterity is a case of indiscriminate benefits *par excellence*. No one can say whose descendants will profit one hundred years hence from resources now devoted to that purpose. Neither can these benefits be priced and their cost covered by an admission charge. Though most Americans may be happy that future generations will have the arts available to them and are content to have funds spent for the purpose, there is no way in which the free market, unaided by public funds, can enable these desires to be realized.

Still another type of indirect benefit provided by the arts is their educational contribution.[22] If, as is generally conceded, a liberal education confers indirect and non-priceable benefits upon the community, the same must be true of the arts. If the teaching of the humanities makes for a finer civilization, for a richer community, for a better life for everyone, this is necessarily so with the arts as well; for without the arts a vital element is taken from the humanities. How can drama be taught if there is no drama available for the student to experience? What can the teaching of music mean if no one can hear performances of professional quality? If the arts are reduced to an atrophied relic of ancient history, a critical component of our educational system must concurrently be lost.

One main conclusion can be drawn from the analysis central to this chapter. If one agrees that the performing arts confer general benefits on the community as a whole, in the manner described above or in other ways, he must conclude that in part, and perhaps in large part, the arts are public goods whose benefits demonstra-

[22] The items mentioned are not the only indirect and indiscriminate benefits provided to the community by the performing arts. There are others; for example, the fact that the live performing arts serve as training grounds for the mass media.

bly exceed the receipts one can hope to collect at the box office. It is a long-standing tenet of economics that if the wishes and interests of the public are to be followed in the allocation of the nation's resources, this is the ultimate ground on which governmental expenditures must find their justification. Government must provide funds only where the market has no way to charge for all the benefits offered by an activity. When such a case arises, failure of the government to provide funds may constitute a very false economy — a misallocation of the community's resources, and a failure to implement the desires of the public. In such circumstances, government outlays are no manifestation of boondoggling bureaucracy, no evidence of creeping socialism, but a response to one of the needs of the society at large.

IV. PANEL DISCUSSION: PUBLIC SUPPORT FOR THE ARTS

Virginia Smith, Moderator*

Professor William J. Baumol**

There seems to be an impression that to justify public support for the arts it is sufficient and, perhaps, necessary to provide evidence documenting the benefits they yield. To any economist this statement is misleading on two separate scores. First, the fact that they yield *some* benefits is evident almost on its face. Second, this fact alone is not sufficient ground for public subsidy. After all, the obvious fact that shoes and books are beneficial is not a convincing excuse for subsidies either to shoe manufacturers or to commercial publishers. Economists have produced a considerable body of literature examining what grounds *do* constitute a tenable justification for public sector funding of some activity. As an economist it is to be expected that I will make my stand on the principles that emerge from that literature, which I do believe provide the one defensible set of criteria for the purpose.

In this paper I will review those criteria, showing what burden of proof they impose on defenders of public subsidy of the arts. I will also consider which of those criteria may be expected to be easy to satisfy or, at least, for which it may be relatively easy to provide the requisite evidence, and for which the task may be difficult or even hopeless. I will also distinguish the standards which are defensible logically from those which promise to be "saleable" politically, arousing in sufficient degree the emotions and enthusiasm needed to spur politicians on. Perhaps it is fortunate that evidence for the former, the standards that would appeal to a disinterested, unemotional and understanding observer, is apt to be far more difficult to come by

---

* President, Board and Society for Values in Higher Education.
** Professor of Economics, Princeton and New York Universities.

than the evidence that offers some reasonable prospect of moving public opinion, and thereby galvanizing the lawmakers into action.

Finally, I will discuss the sorts of studies that are usually conducted in practice to provide quantitative evidence of the benefits generated by artistic activity. I will show that these generally relate only to very peripheral and, perhaps, inherently less worthy benefits of the arts—their ability to attract business to a particular area, to support tourism or to generate taxes. While these are neither irrelevant nor unconvincing, it must be conceded that they are entirely irrelevant to the fundamental contributions of the arts—those that all of us consider to constitute their true virtues, and the reason they merit the dedicated effort so many are prepared to devote to them.

1. *Total Benefits, Unmarketable Benefits and Public Support*

Any commodity which does no one any harm demonstrates its benefits the moment it finds a buyer. The very fact that a consumer is willing to devote part of his hard-earned income to the item means that to justify the expenditure, he feels himself sufficiently better off as a result of possession of the item than he would be without it. Indeed, the benefit must *exceed* the value of the money the individual lays out for it or else the consumer would not take the trouble to make the exchange. Economists call this net benefit the item's "consumer's surplus." Thus, unless we are prepared to take the paternalistic view that we know better than the consumer what is beneficial to him or, worse yet, that he does not know at all what is good for him, it follows indisputably from the logic of the matter that the most commonplace and pedestrian commodities generate net benefits, attested by the fact that they find voluntary purchasers.

Yet few of us are ready to conclude from this fact that a program of subsidies should be adopted to encourage the manufacture of shirts, electronic games and cosmetics. I bring all this up because it shows that the task of erecting a logically defensible argument for subvention of the arts is far more formidable than a mere showing that they have beneficial consequences.

There is another way of looking at the matter which is, perhaps, somewhat more direct. The fact is that the arts do attract paying audiences. People do pay for admission to museums and concerts and they purchase paintings and pieces of sculpture, just as people buy skirts, neckties and tickets to professional football games. Why is it that expenditures on items of the latter variety are expected to cover their costs and perhaps a bit more, while we consider it proper that audience expenditures on the arts should fall far short of covering their costs?[1] If the attendees at a performance of a string quartet are those who benefit from it, why should they not cover its costs? Or put another way, if an evening of theater costs $40,000 to present and the audience is unwilling to pay more than $25,000 for it, do they not thereby demonstrate that the costs incurred by the performance exceed its benefits, as indicated by the amount at which the audience values it?

It is not enough at this juncture to seek to bludgeon the economist into silence by reminding him of Oscar Wilde's quip that his training teaches him to recognize the price of everything and the value of nothing. For that evades the fundamental issue. Just why do you and I, when we visit a museum or attend a performance of modern dance, deserve to have our enjoyment subsidized? Do we really have such special merits that we deserve to be fed at the public trough when others who consume only more worldly goods deserve to be turned away?

The truth is that such an argument will not wash, and most of us would no doubt be embarrassed to offer it. A valid reason for subsidy, at least as writings in economics view the matter, must take a very different direction. Valid grounds must somehow assert that the benefits of that dance performance go beyond the enjoyment of the immediate audience. That is, even if the attendees do pay for what they themselves get from the performance, so that their expenditure is a reasonable indicator of its private benefits to those actually present, there must be some reason suggesting that the performance actually generates some *un*remarkable benefits which cannot reasonably be expected to be borne by those who derive them.

It is evidence of the existence of such a *surplus* of total social benefits over the immediate private benefits obtained by the actual attendees that economists who study the arts seek in order to justify a program of subvention of the arts.

2. *Externalities, Public Goods and Redistribution as Grounds for Public Support*

It should be emphasized that in raising these issues economists are not seeking to deny the possibility of legitimate grounds for public support for the arts, for education, for research or for a variety of

1. It is not enough to argue that the costs in question are high and that left to the marketplace alone many arts activities would fail financially. The argument is an equally good (or, rather, an equally poor) justification for subsidies designed to save every failing industry.

other deserving activities. On the contrary, our literature has provided a considerable body of materials deriving what we accept as defensible grounds for such support. In particular, we have derived three primary grounds on which subsidies can legitimately be justified, which may be referred to respectively as the *redistribution*, the *public goods* and the *externalities* foundations for public subsidy. Each of these grounds, if it can be shown to be present and substantial enough in magnitude, is sufficient by itself to provide the justification we desire. That is, it is not necessary for all three of the corresponding criteria to be satisfied in order for public support to be judged defensible.

Let us then examine the three grounds in turn and consider their pertinence to the arts.

(i) *Redistribution*: The most straightforward of the three grounds relates to redistribution—to the desire for increased equality of income, equality of wealth or equality of opportunity. For example, it is frequently held that unless funding is provided by government for the support of elementary schools, the poor will be denied equality of opportunity. Economists recognize that this is one of the legitimate social goals the market mechanism may not be able to help achieve. The free market does not tend to reduce the gap between rich and poor. On the contrary, its celebrated productive efficiency and abundance of output is attributable to the generous rewards it provides to those who are successful in increasing efficiency and in producing what buyers are willing to pay for, as well as to its remorselessness in penalizing failure. The free enterprise system is, indeed, an arrangement to make the rich grow richer and, even if some of its benefits also reach the poor eventually, it is hardly to be considered a great levelling force.

Thus, if society adopts some degree of equalization as one of its goals, it must turn to government to do something about it, because the free market will not be of much help on this matter. Aid to education, medical assistance to the poor, welfare programs and the progressive income tax are all means widely adopted for the purpose, although they may not be equally effective and efficient in carrying out the task.

To some extent one can employ the redistributive goal as a justification for support of the arts. If the poor cannot afford to go to the theater or they are denied a suitable arts education, there may be little hope that they will develop an interest in the arts. That, of course, is denial of equality of opportunity.

Yet the redistributive argument is a dangerous one for supporters of the arts. Audience surveys are virtually unanimous[2] in their conclusion that those who attend the theater, musical or dance performances are characterized by education, income levels and status in the hierarchy of occupations well above the average for their community. The differences are large and virtually universal. In short, subvention of admission to artistic performances must be admitted to amount to support of the relatively overprivileged. It constitutes what has been described as a reverse Robin Hood redistribution.

(ii) *Public Goods*: In economics a "public good" is a very technical term, not meaning merely that the item in question provides benefits to the public. Rather, a public good, whose antonym is a "private good" is one which, while it is beneficial, simply will not (and should not) be supplied by a free enterprise arrangement left to itself. That is, if such a good is to be provided it must and should be supplied by the *public* sector because the *private* sector will not do so by itself, at least not on terms considered acceptable on economic principles. Two characteristics that account for the market's inability to supply such items are usually associated with the public goods and are, indeed, used to define it. These two attributes are called *unexcludability* and *undepletability*.

A commodity is called "unexcludable" if, once the item is supplied to any one individual, it is either impractical or impossible to preclude anyone else from enjoying its benefits. Shoes are an example of an excludable public good. Any individual who is unwilling to pay their going price simply can be denied access to a pair of shoes by the shopkeeper. In contrast, once a lighthouse shines its beacon to warn those ships that have paid for its upkeep that they are approaching dangerous shoals, it also warns all other ships with equal effectiveness, whether or not they have paid toward a share of its upkeep. Thus, ships making use of the services of a lighthouse cannot be excluded from its benefits. The same is true of individuals who breathe the air which has been purified by a costly program to control the emission of particulates, and of citizens who are protected from foreign invasion by their nation's defense establishment. Air purity, national defense and lighthouse protection, then, are all unexcludable goods.

The relevance of the unexcludability attribute is straightforward. A product for which it may not be possible to force customers to pay

2. For a fascinating exception see, G. Rahav, S. Weitz & G. Zeltzer, The Emergence of a New Theatre Audience in Israel, Tel Aviv University (Nov. 1981) (available in Tel Aviv University Department of Theatre).

their share (or to pay anything at all) is not the sort of item whose production is apt to recommend itself to a profit-seeking business firm. Such enterprises do not operate for eleemosynary purposes and they are hardly likely to incorporate into their product line commodities which are apt to attract few paying customers, even if they bring in many satisfied users. Only government can afford to finance the supply of nonexcludable goods and services and that is why the financing of lighthouses, cleansing of polluted waterways and national defense are all usually left to the public sector.

The second defining property of public goods is what I have called nondepletability. Like the widow's curse, their usefulness does not decline with the appearance of additional users of their products. Again, examples will bring out the point. Fuel is a private good because it is depletable. The more I use up by driving my car the less there will be left for other people to enjoy. However, a public good is not like that. The fact that a lighthouse provides a warning to ten ships does not reduce its ability to provide the same information to an eleventh, which derives the same message by seeing its light. Similarly, if I enjoy the cleaner air that an anti-pollution program has brought to my city it does not reduce its ability to please my neighbor, reduce his laundry bills and decrease the likelihood that he will suffer a respiratory disease. So improved air quality is also a (relatively) undepletable good.

The undepletability feature of a public good militates against its supply by the private sector in a way that is different from the unexcludability attribute. The latter makes private financing impractical or even impossible, as we have seen. The former renders it undesirable, even if it were feasible. Before discussing why this is so, we may note that a product may satisfy the excludability criterion even if it is undepletable. A broadcast television signal can be scrambled so that it cannot be received by anyone who fails to pay the price. Yet it is undepletable in the sense that additional viewers do not reduce the supply available to anyone else, and need not add to the broadcaster's costs.

The catch besetting private supply of undepletable items is that because an additional user of an undepletable good harms no one and if it does generally benefit the user, anything that discourages additional users is socially undesirable. Put another way, any such discouraging influence is economically inefficient because it wastes an opportunity to benefit someone at no cost to society. But price is the prime means that the economy uses to discourage consumption. Whenever a price is charged for some item marginal users are dissuaded from acquiring it. Thus, any price that is charged for consumption of an undepletable good is economically wasteful, for it prevents consumption of the item by persons who would otherwise derive some benefit thereby, and it does not provide any offsetting cut in use of input resources.

In sum, nonexcludability makes it impossible to charge a nonzero price for a public good, while nondepletability makes it undesirable to do so. Either of these, then, rules out private supply as a good way to provide public goods. In other words, either of these *can be* a valid justification for public support.

How do the arts make out on these criteria? Here they do indeed get some mileage, though, as we will see is true of virtually all of the demonstrable grounds for support of the arts, the items at stake here are somewhat tangential to what most of us would consider the basic purposes and achievements of the arts (intangible though those may be).

Specifically, there are at least three social benefits of the arts which fall into the category of public goods as economists define the term. The first is referred to as their "option value." The second may perhaps be called "national pride" and the third, "pleasure from support of virtue." All of these are psychic benefits and while they may, at least to some degree, strike one as far-fetched, there is strong evidence that a considerable proportion of the public is prepared to lay out considerable amounts of money in support of the arts on these grounds.[3]

Option value is the term used to denote the value that an individual places on the ability to use some service at some future date (or for their descendants to do so) even though at the moment that person has neither the desire nor the intention of taking advantage of this option. For example, apparently many persons who have not plans to visit Bryce Canyon were incensed at ex-Secretary Watt's proposal to permit strip mining nearby, on the ground that once the vistas were destroyed they could never be restored, and so the option of enjoying them would be precluded to themselves and to all future

3. For a straightforward interview study that comes to this conclusion see the survey carried out by the Harris Poll, Associate Council of the Arts, Americans and the Arts, New York National Research Center of the Arts, Inc. (1975). A highly sophisticated investigation providing safeguards against respondent misrepresentation and bias, deliberate or unintentional, has recently been carried out by C. David Throsby and Glenn A. Withers in Australia, and they reach very similar conclusions. See their Strategic Bias and Public Good Valuation: Survey Evidence on Free-Riding, The Australian National University, Faculty of Economics, Canberra, (Dec. 1982) (working paper 080).

generations. Similar feelings are obviously possible about the arts. There are those to whom, for example, the prospect of being taken to the opera is a terrifying threat and who nevertheless feel that cessation of operatic activity would constitute loss of a vital national resource and a deprivation to our posterity. (I once was acquainted with a well-known and generous donor to the arts who seemed to me to cringe when a visit to the opera was suggested to him.)[4]

The national pride ground for support is more straightforward. We do not like to think of ourselves as a nation of philistines and barbarians, and neither do the citizens of other lands. Whether or not we derive much pleasure from attending a museum or a theater ourselves, we might well be pleased if we were to find that the support provided to the arts by the public sector in the U.S. was not notably inferior to that in other countries.

The third public goods type of benefit of support for the arts is perhaps the least tangible of the three. It is the pleasure one feels when one's political system produces results which we consider virtuous. It makes us feel good about ourselves and about our government.

As I have indicated, all three of these benefits are psychic, but have little relation to aesthetics—to the direct products that artistic activities engender. Yet they are sufficiently substantial to account, probably, for a nonnegligible part of the political climate that has made it difficult to cut budgets of public support to nearly the extent some politicians have proposed.

What is to the point here is that each of the three psychic benefits to the public that I have just discussed possesses both of the defining attributes of a public good in the economists' sense. First, they are unexcludable—once public funding is provided, how can I be deprived of any of those benefits even if I make no direct contribution to their funding? Of course, the tax collector can always extract a payment from me, but not just by threatening to deny me access to the benefits in question. Second, the benefits are undepletable—my psychic pleasure is not reduced by the fact that you are pleased to have the arts preserved for this generation or for posterity. If I consume this benefit it does not reduce the potential benefit available to you from the same source.

The public goods argument, then, does offer a defensible ground

---

4. "Although responsible for The San Carlo in Naples, the finest opera house in Europe, Don Carlos (Carlos III, King of Spain) had purposely placed his box where he would be least disturbed by the music." R. Kirkpatrick, Domenico Scarlatti 132 (1953).

for public sector support of the arts. The argument satisfies the abstract logical requirements of validity so far as economists are concerned, and its grounds probably are rather more satisfying emotionally to the general public.

3. The Externalities Argument

The third possible rationale for support of the arts that has some standing among economists is what is called the production of external benefits. In some ultimate sense, this is probably where one can hope to find the most fundamental reasons for public subvention of the arts. But these reasons are elusive and empirical evidence is sometimes hard to find.

An externality is defined as an incidental benefit or burden which is imposed on third parties by some activity or transaction. For example, my purchase of electricity increases the amount of coal that the supplier of electricity must burn and that in turn, contributes to pollution, laundry bills, mortality or morbidity and to loss of quality of life. The electricity producer and I have, between us, imposed that burden on others, and we may neither know nor care about it. The pollution emission, in this case, is a detrimental externality generated by the increased consumption and production of electricity. Similarly, an activity can generate beneficial externalities in a variety of ways. Firm A's research may invent new investigative techniques that incidentally facilitate research and development by firm B in a totally unrelated industry. The opening of a business enterprise in a less developed country may provide infrastructure that incidentally makes it easier for native firms to operate effectively.

Beneficial externalities are recognized by all economists as a justification for public support. The reason is quite simple. Private enterprise produces only that quantity of a good or a service whose benefits elicit a payment by the recipient. But the incidental third party benefits that make an externality what it is clearly yield no revenues to the supplier of the commodity. As a result, the market will generally provide less of an external benefit-generating activity than it would be in the public interest to produce. For example, the market will elicit less research than the social interest requires; hence the public funding of research activities. The market will provide less infrastructure than economic efficiency calls for. Hence, infrastructure is financed by the public sector.

Now, in this connection it is sometimes suggested that the problem of evidence of the presence of beneficial externalities is solved by the assertion that the arts are educational. Unfortunately, that does not end the matter because educational support faces similar difficulties in the provision of evidence. As the literature on the economics of education confirms, while it is generally believed that education offers such incidental benefits, not only is it difficult to provide tangible evidence—it is not even easy to identify just what those benefits are.

It is, for example, suggested that schooling creates better citizens, that persons who have been educated are less likely, as a result, to commit crimes, and that there are therefore incidental third party benefits to the persons who might otherwise have been victims of criminal behavior. This is all very plausible, though difficult to document. More important, it is clearly peripheral to what education is all about. The essence of education is knowledge, and the spread and generation of ideas and not primarily crime prevention.

The issue for the arts is not dissimilar. No one denies their ability to generate external benefits, but the list generally cited seems curiously distant from the heart of the target. What are those identifiable benefits? They do, of course, include those attributed to general education, notably the making of better citizens. In addition, a number of economic external benefits are commonly cited, most of them with a narrowly local geographic reference. For example, it is noted that when a firm which needs engineers and physicists for successful operation opens for business in some area, the presence of cultural activity will facilitate the hiring of the educated personnel they require. Similarly, it is often noted that theaters and museums attract visitors and thereby offer business to hotels, restaurants and taxicabs, among other lines of activity. Finally, it is often noted that the arts create income and employment. But this last assertion must be handled with care since the same can probably be said of a subsidy to virtually any industry if that subsidy leads the industry to expand. The issue here is what is special about the arts as sources of income and employment that makes them deserve support when other activities do not receive it. Even more to the point, where does the basic aesthetic contribution of the arts, that is their central purpose, enter this list of externalities? Has it somehow eluded us, or is it hidden somewhere in the list of public goods and externalities? No doubt the answer, to some extent, is the latter. The last of our public goods arguments, the pleasure the public derives from the support of activities it considers virtuous, certainly encompasses, to a degree, the essence of artistic activity. Similarly, the ability of the arts to attract skilled personnel or tourists must in the last analysis, rest on aesthetics. Yet, it seems to me that there remains something here of a performance of Hamlet without the prince of Denmark. Something fundamental still seems to be missing.

Perhaps the best approach we can manage involves, simply, a cutting of the Gordian knot. One can *appear* to solve the problem by just giving it a name. Economists have provided such a term—"merit goods." The argument is that the public has a right to support anything it considers meritorious, whatever the grounds—even sheer gut feeling will do. Is this a good argument for public support? I confess that I am not happy with it, but then I don't know a better one to which to direct anyone.

If we concede that the preceding list of defensible grounds for support of the arts is incomplete, we may note again that the list also includes items which seem to lie very far from the spirit of the arts—perhaps a rather poor exchange. The ability of the arts to help one city compete with another for hotel or taxi business seems an external benefit which has little to do with artistry and can indeed be considered rather on the vulgar side. That is not to say that we should reject such arguments when they are available to help the arts in their desperate need for funds. Still, it is not inappropriate to recognize them for what they are. We shall presently have occasion to return to the role of such "vulgar" benefits.

4. Is All This Discussion Necessary?

One may understandably grow impatient at much of the preceding discussion. It may seem rather academic and to have only a tangential relation to what the general public and politicians are probably really after. To that subject, too, I will return and conclude this paper with a few pertinent comments.

First, however it is well to reconsider why I have gone through the exercise and why, in my view, it cannot legitimately be avoided.

The problem is that without such arguments, we who are inclined to defend funding for the arts are left in a logically tenuous position. The issue is that the arts do have a body of consumers, who are, incidentally, relatively well-to-do, in general. If they are the only ones who benefit, why should they not be expected to pay all the costs incurred in providing their benefits? Why should citizens who do not attend, who derive no pleasure from the arts, and many of whom are less affluent than the attendees, be forced by the tax collector to contribute to support of arts activity?

The only defensible answer must be that persons who are not in the audience *somehow* benefit as well. But if that is our answer and it is to be backed up by more than hand waving, we must be able at least to identify those benefits that do not derive only from attendance. It is to that unavoidable task that this paper has addressed itself up to this point.

5. Documentation of Public Benefits in Practice

Fundraisers for the arts have not been oblivious to the need to show that they generate benefits to persons other than the actual members of the audience. In facing up to this need they have commissioned studies by market researchers and others to provide the required evidence. Hilda Baumol and I have, indeed, carried out such a study ourselves.[5] A few words on the character of such studies and what may be achieved with their aid seems a fitting way to conclude my discussion.

It should be emphasized that such studies do seems to work. Whatever their shortcomings, they do seem to provide helpful ammunition when, for example, a financing bill is before a state legislature or some form of help from a municipality is up for review. Perhaps it is because friendly politicians simply need ammunition to bolster their case and are prepared to welcome such help. Whatever the reason, such a study is often worth its effort and cost. There also exist short cut methods by means of which a public benefits report can be provided with rather little outlay or exertion.[6] But, of course, such a quick-and-dirty study is likely to yield a report that is less impressive than that of a full scale investigation.

Most studies of the social benefits of the arts concentrate on their more tangible returns—those that one can hope to quantify more or less directly. As a result, they tend to confine themselves to what I have described as vulgar benefits—the business activities the arts stimulate, the taxes they yield, at least indirectly through the incentives they provide for taxable business activities, and the jobs they provide.

Most of the studies go at the collection of such information in a very straightforward manner. They do so with the aid of audience questionnaires asking members of the audience whether they ate at a restaurant before coming to the theater, how much they spent at the restaurant, whether they stayed at a hotel, etc. Experience suggests

---

5. H. Baumol and W. J. Baumol, The Impact of the Broadway Theatre and the Economy of New York, The League of New York Theatres and Producers (1977).

6. For a set of instruction for such short-cut studies see id. at 43-46.

that the estimates of this sort provided by a questionnaire are reasonably accurate.

But the rule is that this information by itself is insufficient for the purpose. The fact that two people stayed overnight at a hotel *and* went to the theater is not enough to justify the conclusion that they did so *in order to* attend the theater. That is, the real issue is whether, had the theatrical performance not been available, those persons would have occupied the hotel room anyhow. If so, it is clearly not the performance that can be assigned responsibility for this bit of economic activity.

One can deal with this problem, too, with the aid of the audience questionnaire. For one can ask the respondents the hypothetical question how their outlays would have changed had they not attended a performance that evening. But here reliability is by no means certain. Long experience indicates that interview responses to hypothetical questions are not terribly dependable. Respondents often tend to give answers which they believe to suggest that their own behavior has been commendable, and they also tend to provide responses they believe will please the interviewer. Even if such biases do not turn out to be substantial, the fact is that few people are used to thinking in such hypothetical terms and the replies are therefore apt to be somewhat confused and imperfectly related to the facts (which are unknown even to the respondent). There are other difficulties. Even if respondents had not gone to the theater the night the interview occurred, they might nevertheless have done so had tickets for a performance been available the night before or the night after. If so, the availability of the artistic activity should still be credited with the contribution to the economy, but the hypothetical question suggested before to deal with the problem would clearly miss out in dealing with such cases. There are, obviously, other complications besetting the interview or questionnaire approaches to evaluation of the financial contribution of the arts. However, this is not the appropriate place for such detailed considerations. For here it is germane only to illustrate the available approaches and the attendant problems in very general terms.

One can sometimes get around the difficulties just discussed when an opportunity arises for an approximation to an experiment. For example, some years ago a strike closed down a considerable proportion of the commercial theaters in New York. It then became possible for us to evaluate the resulting damage to the economy directly by determining from restaurants, taxi and hotel associations and others likely to be affected their weekly volume of sales during a period before and after the strike and comparing those figures with the weekly volume during the strike period. This method, too, is far from foolproof. Many restaurant owners are secretive and refuse to divulge the information, fearing it will go to competitors. In any event, it is not easy to track down all the restaurants and parking lots that might have been affected. Some small business firms turned out to have very poor and unsuitable weekly records.

This is only a sample of the problems that typically beset such a study and they would be very serious if a high degree of accuracy were very important. Fortunately, in this arena, literally nothing depends on the quantitative precision of the results. What matters is the order of magnitude of the economic stimulus the arts provide. For example, if a municipality is considering the adoption of a new tax whose proceeds are to be dedicated to the arts, the wisdom of the proposal interpreted purely as a financial investment for the city is unlikely to be affected one way or the other by a ten or even a twenty percent adjustment in the available estimates of the contribution of the arts to the city's economy.

Given the broad tolerance limits appropriate for such studies, they can be carried out with reasonable success. That is, experience indicates that their results can be relied upon as sufficiently acceptable approximations to the pertinent facts. And as such they can, indeed, serve the purpose for which they are carried out.

It must be reemphasized that such studies can only hope to get at a portion (and, very likely, just a small portion) of the benefits of the arts that fall to others than their immediate audience. The rather long list of such benefits that is provided in this paper, but which such a survey cannot usually encompass directly, indicates that this is so.[7]

It is, consequently, important in writing out the results of such a study to point out most emphatically that it only represents a lower bound upon an acceptable estimate of the pertinent benefits. Because so many types of relevant benefit are inevitably omitted altogether from such a study the true magnitude of the arts' contribution can be taken with a considerable degree of confidence actually to be larger, and perhaps substantially larger, than its numbers show. By describing some of the omitted benefits qualitatively, one can impart further

7. But note that the approaches used by the Harris Poll and in the Throsby/Withers study, supra note 3, can get at *some* of those other benefits, thus supplementing the sort of study discussed in this section.

credibility to this observation and strengthen the effectiveness of the study overall.

6. Concluding Comment

True to the traditions of the dismal science, this paper has devoted itself heavily to the doubts and difficulties which must beset the evaluation or even the identification of the sorts of benefits that can justify the provision of public support for the arts. It is true that the task is not easy and that it nevertheless cannot be avoided by anyone undertaking a responsible evaluation of arts support policy.

Yet, I must protest that the basic conclusions of the paper are sanguine. It shows that it is certainly possible to deduce what sorts of benefits are relevant and that one can go far in spelling many of them out in detail. One can hope to provide reasonable estimates of the magnitudes of at least some of them. Above all, in pursuing this avenue of experience indicates that the arts can contribute effectively to efforts of the policy makers who seek to help them.

The problems I have raised here have not been brought up to carp at those who are working in the area to encourage anticipatory surrender. Rather, my objective has been to erect signposts which can be helpful in avoiding some of the pitfalls and to provide a bit of guidance to those who are engaged in the quest for analysis and evidence that can assist in the funding of the arts.

The discussion also leaves us with at least one immediate issue. As I have emphasized, both the nature of the available data, and what seems to constitute political prudence, has led to emphasis on the more mundane benefits such as increased tourism, increased local incomes and the like. I do not wish to denigrate such studies, but I do raise one question about them. Has not the repeated failure to focus discussions of the benefits of the arts on their aesthetic and cultural contribution bought us short run gains at the expense of long run difficulties? If so, what, if anything, can be done about it? This, perhaps, is the crucial item on the agenda for which we do not know even how to begin an attack.

PART V

THE DOCTOR PRESCRIBES!

Reprinted from AAUP Bulletin, Spring, 1967.

On Contracting with Publishers: or What Every Author Should Know

By WILLIAM J. BAUMOL and PEGGY HEIM[1]

Though, notoriously, publication is one of the more pressing immediate objectives of a large segment of our profession, the academic author has available to him curiously little information about the terms on which publication can be arranged. Data on the range of terms provided in publishers' contracts are not readily available. When the professor embarks on negotiations with the representative of a press, he has little basis on which to judge, even in comparative terms, the contractual provisions which are being offered to him.[2] Few authors seem to be aware of the fundamental fact that—particularly where a contract is signed before the manuscript has been completed—usually, and almost unavoidably, the publisher is not committed to bring out the book in question, though the author is committed to offer his manuscript to the publisher with whom the contract is signed; that the contract binds the author without really committing the publisher.

This article undertakes to supply some of the pertinent information in a more or less systematic manner. We have attempted no exhaustive analysis of all the formalities of the contract, nor have we pursued in depth the legal status of copyrights or any similar matters.[3] Rather we have sought to collect information which most faculty members are likely to find useful in arriving at an arrangement with their publishers. We describe the range of those financial terms that seem to be of most widespread interest—royalties, including the rather confusing and not readily comparable variety of bases on which they are calculated, advances, cost of corrections, discounts on copies of the book purchased by the author, etc. In the appendix to this article many other contractual provisions are also described. This information was obtained by examination in detail of a substantial number of contracts representing a variety of publishers, academic institutions, and disciplines.

Next we present the results of a survey in which over 350 faculty members were polled to determine the types of books they had published, the royalty rates they had received, the payments made to them for reviewing or editing of manuscripts, the general relationships between themselves and the publisher. The results of this survey, while not necessarily representative, do give a somewhat clearer picture of the circumstances of the author.

It transpires that the academic rather is generally well satisfied with what the publisher has done for him—to an extent perhaps even surprising in a profession not noted for the reticence of its criticism. Nevertheless, as was to be expected, a number of unfortunate cases, some of them involving rather questionable practices, did turn up. Several such cases are described in one of the later sections of this article. They are not to be interpreted as an oblique attack on the performance

[1] The authors are highly indebted to Professor Leo J. Raskind of the College of Law of the Ohio State University, Mr. Herbert Bailey, Jr., of the Princeton University Press, Mr. A. W. Goodyear of Prentice-Hall Inc., and Mr. Frederick Seiler of St. Martin's Press, Inc., for their extremely helpful comments. Without the contributions of Mrs. Maryse Eymonerie, who assisted in the processing of the questionnaire forms and statistical analyses, Mrs. Deborah Trzyna, who helped edit the manuscript, the diligent and conscientious campus representatives who distributed the questionnaire forms and secured the cooperation of their colleagues, and the respondents who completed the regrettably somewhat tedious forms, this study would not have been possible. To all of them we are deeply grateful.

[2] cf, however, J. C. Hogan and S. Cohen, *An Author's Guide to Scholarly Publishing and the Law*, Prentice-Hall, Englewood Cliffs, N. J., 1965, especially Chapter 4; and O. Cargill, W. Charvat, and D. D. Walsh, "The Publication of Academic Writing," *Publications of The Modern Language Association of America*, Vol. LXXXI, Sept. 1966, pp. 39-45. The second of these references is primarily a brief compendium of items of good advice to the young author. For a legal treatise on copyright, see Melville B. Nimmer, *Nimmer on Copyrights*, Matthew, Bender Co., Inc., 1966.

WILLIAM J. BAUMOL is Professor of Economics at Princeton University and Chairman of the Association's Committee Z on the Economic Status of the Profession. PEGGY HEIM is Associate Secretary and Economist in the Association's Washington Office.

[3] If there are questions on these matters, as with any legal document, the advice of counsel before execution of the contract can prove very valuable.

of publishers in general, but as a warning pointing out explicitly the types of problems that occasionally arise. At least some of them arise because insufficient care is exercised in the consideration of the contractual terms or in the discussions preceding the signing of the contract.

This article presents two proposals to publishers which we believe can contribute substantially to better relations between them and their authors. In addition to standardization of the base in terms of which royalties are calculated, we suggest the adoption of a standardized information form (Figure 1) which will report to the author data that are highly important to him but which are not now supplied to him as a matter of course. We believe such a form will impose no serious burden, will help to avoid needless misunderstandings, and enable both publishers and authors to perform their work more effectively.

Unfortunately there are some problems of publication that cannot simply be handled in terms of contractual provisions. Neither an information form nor a contract can guarantee that copy editing will be of satisfactory quality or that promotion will be vigorous or that the printer's work will be good. Publishers vary enormously in the effort they devote to the quality of the volume and to its sale, and an author may often find it preferable to select a house whose record on these matters is very good, even if its royalty rates are lower than those offered elsewhere. On all these issues there seems to be no substitute for checking past performance. Before signing with any publisher an author is therefore well advised to speak, if he can, with one or more people who have had books published by the firm in question and to examine other more or less similar volumes that the publisher has put out, as well as some of the company's relevant advertising and other promotion material. There is probably no more reliable way than this to obtain information on the quality of a publisher's service in its many aspects—concerns of great significance for the author which are difficult, if not impossible, to cover explicitly by contractual provisions.

Types of Financial Arrangement

Standard financial arrangements take four main forms: (1) royalty agreements; (2) sale-of-rights agreements; (3) stock-option agreements; and (4) subsidy publishing agreements.

The Royalty Agreement

Basically, the royalty agreement, which is the most common arrangement in use today, provides for the payment of some specified percentage of list price, gross proceeds, or net proceeds on the number of copies sold. Generally, terms are not the same for domestic and foreign sales, and the contract spells out the degree to which the author shares in the proceeds from the sale of subsidiary rights. Under most circumstances, the author will probably find the royalty agreement more advantageous than any of the other three forms of compensation agreement described here. (There are exceptions, however; for example, a book with wide appeal which is marketed effectively under a private publication arrangement.)

The Sale-of-Rights Agreement

Under a sale-of-rights agreement the author receives a fixed sum for which he assigns to the publisher the copyright and all other rights and interests in the book. In effect, the author receives a flat fee for his writing service and the use of his name. Disposition of the product is then in the hands of the publisher. The sale-of-rights contract generally offers the author very little protection. Unless the contract provides specifically a procedure for revised editions, the publisher can appoint a second party to revise the book (generally a text, an industrial manual, etc.) and the original author, without resorting to potentially costly litigation, and perhaps not even then, has no more control over the revisions than the publisher is willing to grant him. Indeed, the problems to which a sale-of-rights contract may lead can be so troublesome that the author is well advised to consult legal counsel before signing any such agreement.

Stock-Option Agreements

These are usually used only by small or new publishing houses. The agreements are essentially profit-sharing arrangements in which the author receives compensation in the form of stock shares. Their value, of course, depends upon the success of the company and upon the existence of a market for the stock. The author may also receive stock options for the purchase of additional shares. In some cases, royalty agreements are combined with some form of stock arrangement.

Publishing Subsidy Agreements

Many contracts call for direct payments to the publisher by the author before the book is brought out. In our survey, some ten per cent of the contracts required some subsidy payment ranging from $200 to $8350, with an average of $2090 for hard cover books.

These subsidies are designed to permit publication of manuscripts which might otherwise not be financially feasible for the publisher to undertake, or, if the author expects very large sales, to insure the bulk of the profits for the author, or to make the book available at a price lower than the one at which it would otherwise have been sold. While often such subsidy agreements are entered into with standard publishing houses, particularly with university presses, they are most frequently employed by what is known in the trade as the "vanity press," which handles purely private publication which authors arrange entirely on their own behalf.[4]

While some of our respondents have stated that they have been pleased with the results of private publica-

[4] If a manuscript is not of interest to a commercial publisher or a university press but the scholar nevertheless wants to arrange for its publication, he may find it useful to consult *Literary Market Place, The Business Directory of American Book Publishing*, which provides a list of commercial printers who perform this service and the names of independent agents who, at author's expense, give technical advice (e.g., on book design, pricing policy, etc.), and who handle promotion and advertising.

FIGURE 1

PROPOSED INFORMATION FORM FOR AUTHORS

from Period____________ to ____________

Name of Book: ____________

Name of Author: ____________

Name of Publisher: ____________

1.

Sales	Number of Copies (1)	List Price (2)	Publishers' Proceeds* (3)	Royalty Terms (as ___% of which col.) (4)	Royalty (5)
Domestic:					
Trade					
Text					
Foreign					
Other types					
Total sales					

Cumulative total sales from date of publication:

Of current edition	
Of earlier editions	

2. Other types of proceeds to publisher

Other types of proceeds to publisher (1)	Payment to Author (2)
(1) Rental of plates, sales of sheets, etc.	
(2) Translations or other editions (including paperbacks) already contracted for	
(3) Proceeds from licenses, fees, etc. not covered above	
Total of "other proceeds"	

3. Translations or other editions contracted for:

	Language or Other Specification (1)	Publisher (2)	Payment to Author (3)
(1)			
(2)			
(3)			
(4)			

4. Number of books in stock____________ as of (date)____________ **

* to be supplied only where royalties are based on proceeds

** The author will be notified if it has been decided to let the book go out of stock, and will also be notified when it is decided to reprint so that he can submit lists of any errors for correction.

tion (one said that he would publish no other way), others have reported unsatisfactory experiences. The most common complaint is that the net cost to the author was underestimated, generally because sales, and therefore royalty income, were overestimated, despite relatively high royalty rates designed to make the contract look attractive. In another instance, the agreement obligated the author to pay the costs without stipulating a maximum payment by the author, and the cost of publication exceeded the estimate by a significant amount.

In publication by standard presses, direct prepublication payments to publishers are sometimes requested to permit the book to be sold at a price lower than would otherwise prevail. However, a number of authors who provided prepayments on these grounds indicated that their lower price expectations were, in fact, not realized. Clearly this may represent a misunderstanding and failure of communication on the part of both parties. However, if lower selling price is the object, it would appear to be desirable to have some specific price agreement *in writing* from the publisher rather than to rely upon some general reference to "keeping the price low," which may mean different things to author and publisher.

On occasion, the special research funds available to scholars in some of the more progressive and higher-paying liberal arts colleges and private universities are also used to help subsidize publication, particularly where the institution does not have its own press. Sometimes, when the subsidy is paid by an organization or institution, a special provision may be included in the contract stipulating that payment of royalties to the scholar will not begin until the subsidy provided by the institution or by a foundation has been repaid.

Royalty Rates

Bases Used in Calculating Basic Royalty Payments

Royalty payments are usually calculated as a percentage of one of three alternative bases—list or retail price, gross proceeds (sometimes called net price), and net proceeds. The term "gross proceeds" generally refers to list price less discounts to booksellers.[5] While the difference between gross proceeds and net proceeds is not clearly defined, net proceeds, as used by some publishers, means gross proceeds less other discounts, returns, and allowances—items of significant magnitude in some instances. Apparently, other publishers consider the two terms synonymous.

Of the three bases, list price is apparently the one most frequently used. From our sample of some 80 contracts (see footnote 10, below, on the nature of our sample), we reviewed standard contract forms—some single, some multiple samples—for seventeen relatively well-known commercial publishers and (by sheer coincidence) for seventeen university presses, though the number of contracts with university presses was much smaller than that for commercial presses. About 60 per cent of the publishers used list price as the royalty base for hardcover books, another six per cent used two different bases, one of which was list price, and the remaining 34 per cent used gross or net proceeds. The percentage breakdown by type of publisher is shown here:

Royalty Base Used by Publisher	*Type of Press*		
	Commercial	*University*	*Combined*
List price	53%	67%	60%
Gross or net proceeds	35	33	34
Both list price and gross or net proceeds	12	0	6

It is probable that a larger sample of contracts from each press would show that a higher percentage of publishers used a combination of both list price and gross or net proceeds, depending upon the particular book.

Royalty Bases and Rate Structures—Textbooks

Because publishers use different systems of discounts and pricing, depending upon whether a book is sold as a trade edition or as a text—there are other variations too which we shall not attempt to explain here—there is no easy and accurate way to describe royalty rate structures for purposes of comparison. The system places the author at a great disadvantage in his effort to evaluate the royalty terms proposed in his contract.[6] Thus the apparently simple conversion of list-price-based royalties on a college text to the equivalent royalty rates on gross sales normally runs into a major complication. In addition to sale as an adopted text, the book (usually with a different cover and jacket) is often sold in a trade edition at a higher list price—about one-third more than the text—and at a higher discount to the bookstore. This discount to the bookstore commonly runs about 20 per cent of the textbook's list price for the educational edition and about 40 per cent of trade list for the trade edition.[7] Yet the two editions are commonly priced to yield approximately the same gross proceeds to the publisher. As a result, an author whose royalties are based on gross receipts will do equally well from either type of sale, but an author paid a fixed percentage of list price will earn more from the sale of a trade edition copy than from a copy of the text version if the royalty rates on both editions are the same. Of course, if, as publishers suggest, sales of textbooks in

[5] Where books are sold by the publisher directly to the final purchaser at list price (as when books are sold by mail), the corresponding portion of gross proceeds is identical with list price. Often a substantial proportion of the sales of a volume is of this variety.

[6] The author can obtain some useful information by asking the publisher with whom he is negotiating for sample information on royalty rates and total royalty payments on a volume similar to his own.

[7] A further complication is introduced by the "agency plan" which is apparently becoming more important for academic authors. A bookseller who undertakes such an arrangement is given a 33⅓ per cent discount on books that would otherwise be sold to him at a "short," say 20 per cent, discount, but in return he commits himself to handle some minimum number of copies of every book the publisher produces in the given subject area.

trade editions are often relatively small and hence unprofitable, the author may well find it desirable to accept a lower royalty rate on the trade volume in order to induce the publisher to provide such an edition.

Royalties on Specialized, Technical, and General Books

Scholarly volumes which are not textbooks are priced for sale to the trade (i.e., for sale by regular retailers). Hardcover volumes frequently, but not always, are sold to retailers at a price equal to 66 2/3 per cent of list price (a discount to the bookstore of about 33 1/3 per cent). The discount is usually less than 40 per cent, and sometimes goes as low as 20 to 25 per cent on single copy sales.

A conversion table may help the scholar compare royalty rates based upon list price with those quoted on another base, such as gross proceeds, when the latter is a more or less fixed proportion of list price (e.g., where gross proceeds are 80 per cent of retail). Of course, because of the complex system of pricing and discounts any such calculation must be an over-simplification which does not take into account retail price differences between books sold to the trade primarily as technical, specialized, or general works and those sold as college texts.

Illustrative Conversion Table
For Gross (or Net) Proceeds: Royalty Rate Equivalents

Average Gross Proceeds as Per Cent of List Price	Average Gross Proceeds Equivalents for List-Price Royalty Rates		
	10% of List	12% of List	15% of List
80 Per Cent	12.5% of Gross	15.0% of Gross	18.8% of Gross
75 Per Cent	13.3% of Gross	16.0% of Gross	20.0% of Gross
70 Per Cent•	14.3% of Gross	17.2% of Gross	21.5% of Gross
60 Per Cent	16.7% of Gross	20.0% of Gross	25.1% of Gross

This table indicates, for example (figure with •), that if gross proceeds are 70 per cent of retail price, the author would need royalties of 21.5 per cent of gross proceeds in order to be as well off as he is with rates calculated at 15 per cent of list price.[8]

Fixed or Graduated Rates

The basic rate may be stated as a fixed percentage on all copies sold, or the rate may be graduated upwards as sales increase, e.g., it may be set at 10 per cent of the first 5000 copies, 12.5 per cent of the next 5000, and 15 per cent on the remainder. There are various reasons for the use of graduated rates. If the book is going to be published anyway, the procedure may serve to reduce the financial risk to the publisher; if publication is uncertain, the arrangement may help a specialized book with limited sales-appeal see the light of day. On the other hand, one can look at the provision through publishers' eyes and say that it gives the author an opportunity to participate in the profits derived from a larger volume of sales.

The graduated rates usually employ no more than three steps, but the number of thousands of copies involved varies significantly among publishers and even among contracts with the same publisher. Most commonly, royalties begin with the first copy sold, but a wide variety of alternative arrangements exist. Royalties may be omitted on the first one to three thousand copies sold, or, on occasion, this number may be extended to five or even seven thousand. Some contracts go a step further and provide that no royalty will be paid until the publisher recovers the cost of producing the book. Under the latter provision, the scholar relies on the good faith of the publisher, generally a university press.

Another variation of the graduated rates uses a less favorable royalty base, as well as a lower rate, on the first several thousand copies sold. Simply by changing an adjective the effective basic rate can be lowered significantly without its being very apparent to the author. The following illustration shows the real effect of the arrangement:

		List Price Equivalent
First 3000 copies	10% of net price (defined as 70% of list)	7% rate
Second 3000 copies	10% of list price	10% rate
Above 6000 copies	15% of list price	15% rate

This technique is, of course, used to merchandise the royalty package. By changing the descriptive term rather than the figure, the rate structure can be made to look more attractive than it really is. Apparently, this practice is relatively new and uncommon.

It may be noted here that the direct financial return from the publication of a volume is generally not the most important consideration to the scholar, and this may help to account for the fact that many of the respondents in our survey did not indicate what royalty base is used in the calculation of their royalties. In the opinion of some authorities, publication of a first book may provide returns in the form of higher academic salary far greater than any royalty payment. It has been surmised that having a widely distributed book to his credit may well be worth over $20,000 to the young faculty member in terms of increased lifetime earning power aside from any royalty payments.

In any event, the preceding discussion suggests very clearly that a high confusion cost is incurred by the use of three different bases for the calculation of royalties—in terms of retail price, gross, and publisher's net. Whether the result is deliberate or unintentional, it is obviously unfortunate and constitutes a major obstacle to the author's deliberations.

It is recommended to publishers, therefore, that they abandon this system and that, in the future, all royalties be expressed in terms of actual retail price paid, a mag-

[8] Some contracts utilizing gross proceeds as the base state that the term shall be construed to mean some specific proportion, such as 75 per cent of list price.

nitude whose meaning is readily understood. Thus differences in returns to publishers between trade and text editions could be reflected, without misunderstanding, by a difference in royalty rates on the two types of editions. Any publisher unwilling to convert to the standardized system advocated here could instead base royalties on receipts by the publisher, and any of its subsidiaries,[9] *simultaneously informing the author in detail about the structure of the firm's discounts so he can compare the royalties he is likely to receive with those offered by a competing publisher who uses a retail price base for his royalty calculations.* At a minimum, the author should be supplied with information on the average relationship of retail price to gross and to net so that he can perform a translation from one to the other for himself. Surely an author will have some justification for the suspicion that any publisher who refuses to do so must have something to hide.

Royalty Rates in Practice

We can get a better idea of the range of royalty rates paid out in practice from the results of our survey. Unfortunately, many of our respondents did not indicate the nature of the royalty base (list price, gross proceeds, or net proceeds) and their rate information could, in most instances, not be used for the subsequent analyses. The resulting sample is therefore reduced in size. Partly for this reason some categories of books, such as fiction or nonfiction for the general public, include too few respondents to make the figures statistically significant. The data are summarized in Table 1, which shows how royalty rates varied by type of book, number of copies sold, and the base on which royalties were calculated.[10]

As might be expected, the average royalty rate for undergraduate texts (13-14 per cent) is higher than that for technical or specialized books (12.6-13.6 per cent) when royalties are based on *list* price. But it is interesting that this is not true when gross proceeds are used as the base, although even in this case the textbook *median* remains higher than that for technical or specialized books. Apparently because the list price of texts often includes only a very small mark-up for the retailer, competition forces the publisher to give a particularly high royalty rate on list price to many textbook authors to make up for this relatively smaller component in the base on which their total royalties are calculated.

Another interesting conclusion to be drawn from the figures arises out of a comparison of the royalty rates based on list price with those calculated from gross proceeds. Since list price is always at least as high as gross proceeds one would expect royalty rates to vary in the opposite direction to make up for the difference—the higher list price should offer a lower royalty rate and vice-versa. But for undergraduate and graduate texts the pattern is curiously reversed—the rates based on gross proceeds are generally no higher than those on list price, and indeed the former are typically somewhat lower! This suggests strongly that a gross proceeds base is often used by a publisher as a device to conceal low real royalty rates. The author might therefore be justified in regarding the use of a gross proceeds base in the royalty provisions of his contract as evidence that the publisher's royalty rates are low![11]

Finally, a particularly significant conclusion can be drawn from the table on royalty rates paid to editors of reprint volumes—the persons who put together books of "Readings" consisting of selections of articles or portions of books by other authors. It is noteworthy that *while the authors of the reprinted pieces often receive little or nothing for the republication of their works, the editor of the reprint volume is paid at almost the same rate as that offered the author of a technical or specialized volume.* We will have more to say on this point presently.

Until now, our discussion has dealt with the basic royalty rate structure. In addition, most contracts call for different terms on various special types of sales. The categories most commonly covered include foreign sales, special editions, and disposal of overstock. The contract may also include clauses relating to other special circumstances, such as sales through radio or coupon advertising and reduced royalties when rates of sale drop below a specified point.

Foreign Sales

Most contracts make special provisions for foreign sales. In some cases, the financial arrangements on Canadian sales are the same as those on domestic sales; sometimes Canadian sales are treated simply as foreign sales and sometimes somewhere between the two.

In most cases, foreign rates are lower than the domestic rates. The rough rule-of-thumb seems to be that the royalty rate on sales abroad is either a flat five per cent of the amount received by the publisher or, alternatively, about half that provided on domestic sales, except that net proceeds, or some similar figures, are used as the royalty base, even if domestic rates are based on list price. The use of net proceeds can probably be attributed in part to ease of calculation, for foreign sales may take the form of books, sheets, or

[9] An exception should be made where the publisher owns and operates his own bookstores, in which case the usual retailers' discounts would be excluded in determining the royalty base.

[10] Royalty rates will also vary substantially by discipline. In the humanities, where sales of scholarly books are frequently very limited, royalty rates are often much lower than those on a technical book in engineering, where sales volume is typically much larger.

[11] It is also possible that the statistical result reflects the better terms which can be commanded by the authors of potential best sellers among texts—that they can demand and get both higher royalty rates and the more favorable list price royalty base. Such a switch in bases only adds, of course, to the confusion inherent in the multiple base system. Would not the publisher who uses a gross receipts base contribute to clearer understanding of all concerned by offering his star author eighteen or twenty per cent on gross instead of switching suddenly, say, to fifteen per cent of list?

Table 1

Royalty Rates on Hard Cover Books Based upon List Price, Gross Proceeds, and Net Proceeds When Number of Copies Sold Reach Stated Numbers, by Type of Book[1]

(Rates Based upon Books Published Since 1953)

Type of Book and Statistical Measure	Rate on List Price		Rate on Gross Proceeds		Rate on Net Proceeds	
	5,000 Copies	10,000 Copies	5,000 Copies	10,000 Copies	5,000 Copies	10,000 Copies
Undergraduate Text						
Mean	13.1%	13.9%	12.7%	13.7%	14.0%	14.5%
Median	15.0	15.0	12.5	15.0	15.0	15.0
Upper Decile	15.0	15.0	15.0	15.0	18.7	18.7
Maximum	19.0	19.0	20.0	20.0	20.0	20.0
(No. in Sample)	(84) •	(84) •	(51) •	(51) •	(16) •	(16) •
Graduate Text						
Mean	12.6	13.6	12.8	14.4	15.2	15.2
Median	15.0	15.0	12.5	15.0	15.0	16.0
Upper Decile	15.0	15.0	15.0	15.0	18.7	18.7
Maximum	20.0	20.0	20.0	20.0	18.7	18.7
(No. in Sample)	(51) •	(51) •	(30) •	(30) •	(8) •	(8) •
Technical or Specialized Book						
Mean	10.9	11.8	12.6	13.1	12.8	12.8
Median	10.0	12.0	10.0	10.0	12.5	12.5
Upper Decile	15.0	15.0	15.0	15.0	15.0	15.0
Maximum	20.0	20.0	45.0	45.0	15.0	15.0
(No. in Sample)	(65) •	(65) •	(27) •	(27) •	(16) •	(16) •
Book of Readings						
Mean	10.3	10.5	12.9	13.4	10.0	10.0
Median	10.0	10.0	12.5	15.0	10.0	10.0
Upper Decile	15.0	15.0	16.0	16.0	10.0	10.0
Maximum	20.0	20.0	16.0	16.0	10.0	10.0
(No. in Sample)	(16) •	(16) •	(10) •	(10) •	(2) •	(2) •

[1] Royalty data obtained from a questionnaire completed by 158 faculty members chosen by random means of selection in over 50 colleges and universities and covering 294 hard cover books, many of which served multiple purposes, e.g., an undergraduate text and a specialized book for sale to the trade.

•Number of books in the category, including those serving other purposes as well.

plates, each having its own financial arrangements. Where the domestic rate is graduated, the foreign rate is usually half of the lowest domestic rate. If the author is successful in negotiating a higher domestic rate than the one provided in the publisher's standard contract, the foreign rate, when given as a standard fixed percentage, does not generally appear to be adjusted upwards. In a very few contracts, authors have reserved for themselves the right of arranging for foreign sales or for sales in certain countries, such as those belonging to the British Commonwealth.

Copies Sold through Special Marketing Channels

Special channels may include radio, television, mail order, or coupon advertising direct to the consumer. Some publishers who base their domestic rates on gross proceeds cut their royalty rate in half on sales of this kind, while some standard contract forms apply to them a royalty rate of five per cent. These low rates reflect the unusually large costs of selling, shipping, and collecting on these special types of sale.

Special Editions, Including Paperbacks

The most common type of special edition is the paperback, for which there are so many variations in terms of compensation that we shall describe only a few more prevalent types. The royalty rate on paperbacks is lower than the basic domestic rate on the hardcover edition. Sometimes this lower rate is achieved by basing the special edition rate on net proceeds, while the basic domestic rate is set on list price. In other cases, the percentage figure is simply reduced, e.g., by one half. A few use a double-barrelled approach: they cut the rate and shift the base downward. In still other cases, the royalty is set at a fixed amount, say 5 cents if the price is $1.50 or less; more, if the price is higher. An author is not likely to become rich from paperback sales, except perhaps by editing a collection of readings, which may sell in large volume.

Disposal of Overstock

Many publishers make special royalty provisions for disposal of overstock. If the book is sold at a price below publisher's cost, or manufacturing costs plus royalties, royalties will not be paid at all. Sometimes there is a flat provision, without reference to cost, that royalties will not be paid on copies disposed of as overstock.

In the more generous provisions, the author receives the usual domestic rate, but the base is shifted from list price to net proceeds. It is apparent that, under these circumstances, the author must rely upon the integrity of the publisher, and it is noteworthy that our survey turned up few complaints on payments on overstock.

Reduced Sales

In order to make it possible to keep books in print for longer periods of time, special rates may go into effect when sales fall below specified limits for any given period of time. For example, if sales during a six-month period fall below a specified number, say 150 or 250 copies, the royalty rate may be cut in half. This type of arrangement is relatively uncommon.

Payment for Subsidiary Rights

There is a considerable degree of similarity in the various provisions made for the division of proceeds from the sale of subsidiary rights such as translation, condensation, serial rights, book-club editions, reprint editions, dramatic, motion picture, radio, and television rights, recordings, microfilms, and programmed learning editions.

Proceeds are generally divided on a 50-50 basis, but, particularly where performing rights are involved, a few publishers are more generous, offering the author 75 or 85 per cent of the net amount received. At the other extreme, under some contracts the author may receive nothing at all. This generally applies when the contract contains a blanket assignment to the publisher of all subsidiary rights and makes no general provision for the sharing of proceeds derived from sale of licensing of these rights. In some rare cases, the right to license a subsidiary right remains the property of the author.

The author should certainly beware of any blanket provision assigning subsidiary rights to the publisher which includes *no* general formula for the sharing of proceeds. At the very least, the author may want the protection of a general clause, e.g., the author will be paid 50 per cent of the net amount actually received by the publisher, except as otherwise provided.

Some Other Contractual Provisions

In addition to the terms of the contract determining the author's earnings there are a number of other provisions of widespread interest and particular importance. This section describes some of these provisions. Certain other contract terms are discussed in the appendix.

Advances

Many contracts provide that the publisher will pay to the author a fixed amount of money at one or several specified dates, before royalties have been received and often before the manuscript has even been delivered. These payments are subsequently returned to the publisher, who retains future royalties until (if ever) all advances have been repaid. Such advances on royalty payments are an important benefit to the author. They shift part of the risk of the publication from the author to the publisher—if royalty payments never add up to the amount of the advance, the difference is simply borne by the publisher. Moreover, the author, by receiving his money earlier, if he wishes, can bank it sooner and earn additional interest. It is noteworthy that if a publisher decides, on grounds of quality, not to publish a book for which he has signed a contract before he had seen the complete manuscript, he often does not ask for a return of his advance payments.

In our survey, we found that 27 per cent of the contracts for hard cover books involved advance payments ranging from $50 to $6000, with the median advance payment (for books on which any advance was offered) amounting to $580.

Right to Quote, Abridge, and Reproduce

Where the publisher controls the right to permit others to quote from the work (frequently done on the ground that it helps promote sales) and to extract, digest, condense, abridge, and reprint, the publisher is under no contractual obligation to consult with the author on questions relating to this use of the work. While some publishers will routinely refer these questions to the author, others do so only intermittently or not at all. It should be pointed out that consultation with the author is a chore; sometimes the author cannot readily be located and, in any case, consultation imposes additional correspondence on the staff of the publishing firm and thereby increases its cost of doing business. In the event that the author is uncooperative in granting permission, consultation may also serve to reduce the book's visibility which, in turn, affects sales and possibly also the net proceeds that could be derived from the licensing of subsidiary rights. In any event, excessively rigid consultation requirements may constitute an undesirable obstacle to the diffusion of knowledge. On the other hand, the author may find that, if his writings are reprinted in whole or in part without his permission, they are taken out of context and used to promote causes which he opposes or to defend positions with which he does not concur. Quotation of the work of a writer may tend to associate him indirectly, if not overtly, with the views held by the person who quotes him. Still another problem may arise where, in the process of abridgement or condensation, passages of critical importance in the author's eyes are omitted or emasculated. The scholar also may want his writings brought up-to-date before they are reprinted. Unless the work is reissued principally as a matter of historical interest, he may feel a moral obligation to call attention, through footnotes at least, to important new developments or new research which may affect his previous conclusions. In all of these matters he has a professional reputation to protect.

Specific contract provisions requiring the publisher to consult with and receive the approval of the author (in effect granting the author veto power) might impose an unreasonable burden on the publisher. But an alternative and less rigid approach to the problem has much to be said for it. The author may well find it useful to protect his interests by asking for the insertion in his contract of a somewhat flexible clause on the subject. Such a clause would require that when the author's work is to be quoted *at length*, abstracted, condensed, digested, abridged, or reprinted the publisher will make reasonable efforts to consult the author before granting permission.

Number of Free Copies and Price of Additional Copies

Most contracts provide that the author will receive a number of copies of his book when it appears. The number of free copies usually ranges from six to ten, with these two extreme figures occurring most frequently.

The author is usually also entitled to purchase at a discount as many additional copies of the book as he desires for his own use. The discount on these purchases varies quite widely, usually ranging from 20 to 40 per cent of the list price. Though it is not specified explicitly, presumably the author also receives royalty payments on the copies he purchases at a discount, since the discount would appear to consist largely of retailer's margin which is avoided by the elimination of the middleman.

Pricing

The contract normally leaves the pricing decision entirely in the hands of the publisher who need neither explain nor even inform the author of his decision. Since most contracts are signed well before the final manuscript is delivered, it is of course not possible for the publisher to commit himself to a selling price for the book at that time. However, it might be desirable for the publisher to explain the nature of his pricing calculations to the author, particularly since this might induce the author to take more careful account of printing costs as he works. In any event, *the author should be informed of the pricing decision as soon as it is made.* Many publishers provide to the author soon after publication information on price, and number of copies printed, promotion plans, review copies sent, etc. This can help cement relations between author and publisher, and frequently the author is able to make useful suggestions on the basis of this information. And where the author is induced to accept unusually low royalties or to provide a publishing subvention as a means to keep down the retail price of the volume, the publisher should be required to indicate *in writing* exactly how the retail price will be affected. In this way much unpleasantness and some abuses can be prevented.

Cost of Corrections

Contracts usually include a clause protecting the publisher from the cost of excessive corrections in proof. On rare occasions, the author is required to bear the cost of any corrections other than those occurring as a result of the printer's errors. In some cases, the author is asked to pay half the cost of corrections, with the publisher's liability limited to some fixed amount, ordinarily one or two hundred dollars. More commonly, the author is permitted to supply corrections in proof at no cost to himself so long as they do not exceed five or ten per cent of the entire cost of setting the volume into type. In a few contracts, this percentage may be raised to fifteen or even twenty per cent. Since corrections may cost as much as 75 cents a line, they can well constitute a major expense for the publisher, and, therefore, for the author.

Options on Subsequent Writings

A contract often commits the author to submit his next book (or sometimes his next two books) to the same publisher, who has the option of undertaking publication on terms that are "mutually agreeable" after "negotiation in good faith." It is not clear what choices are open to the author if some other publisher offers him rates on a subsequent manuscript higher than those proposed to him under the option contract.

Most option clauses require the publisher to indicate that he will exercise his option, i.e., that he will let the author know whether he is willing to publish the book within 60 or sometimes 90 days after the manuscript has been received. If the author has not heard from the publisher by that time he is free to submit his manuscript elsewhere. The absence of such a time limit in the option clause can sometimes constitute a real disadvantage to the author because it can result in a very substantial delay in publication of his book. The author is therefore well advised to check for the presence of such a time limit in any option provision.

Some clauses specify that he may not publish the book elsewhere at substantially the same or at lower rates. This practice may lock in the scholar who has been dissatisfied with the past performance of the publisher and his distribution efforts.

Another serious danger in the option clause is the fact that it is usually signed *before* the author has had his book produced by the publisher. As a result, he may find himself committed to turn over his next work to the same publisher even if he has been extremely dissatisfied with the publisher's performance in the production and distribution of his previous book. Apparently, publishers have recently been placing much less weight on such clauses and rarely make any attempt to enforce them. Where an option clause is included in the contract, the author may find it desirable to bargain for a provision under which he could, within 120 days of the publication of the work, give notice to the publisher (by registered mail) of dissatisfaction with the manufacturing or marketing of his work, with such notice serving to terminate his obligation to submit future manuscripts to this publisher under the terms of the option clause.

Singular Provisions

The appendix to this article undertakes a more comprehensive survey of the major provisions of publishers' contracts, attempting to indicate the variety of arrangements that may be included. However, having discussed in the text the contractual stipulations selected because of their wider interest, we now pause to list a few of the less conventional clauses that appear in the contracts we have examined.

Contractual terms designed to limit the amount of royalties actually paid to an author in a given tax year are now generally of lesser importance. Since 1963 the Internal Revenue Code permits income averaging over several years. Contractual provisions designed to improve further on the treatment of the Revenue Code are most likely to be strongly resisted by the Internal Revenue Service.

Somewhat more unusual is the contract provision stipulating that "if the Author . . . leaves . . . the profession of teaching before the work has been set in type, the Publisher shall have the right to cancel this agreement."

Another contract with a major publisher made publication of the book conditional on the results of "a formal marketing test," and one contract permitted the publisher to "license publication of the work in braille or photographing and/or microfilming for sale to the physically handicapped without payment of fees and without compensation to the author." Clearly virtue itself does not go unprotected in the contractual arrangements!

On Author-Publisher Relations in Practice

So far we have discussed contract provisions *per se.* But there is much in the relationship between authors and publishers which does not appear in contracts. Our survey offers us some information which goes beyond the terms of contractual arrangements.[12]

The most noteworthy result was the almost uniform satisfaction reported by authors with the quality of service provided by publishers. Authors were asked their opinions of the help provided by publishers with editing and promotion, the speed of publication, assistance in obtaining criticism by other readers, indexing, design and quality of printing, help in correction of errors, arranging for translations, etc. On each of these various items the proportion of authors expressing dissatisfaction rarely exceeded ten per cent and more usually ran to about five or six per cent of the respondents. The highest proportions of dissatisfaction involved editing, where nine per cent were displeased; indexing, nine per cent; delays in publication, eleven per cent; and promotion, seventeen per cent.

Where differences in author attitudes were significant, dissatisfaction with the university presses was generally somewhat more frequent than complaints about commercial publishers. For example, eight per cent of the authors publishing with commercial presses complained about indexing, whereas the corresponding university press figure was fifteen per cent. Those who were unhappy with promotion came respectively to 16 and 22 per cent of the totals for commercial and university presses. On the other hand, four per cent of the authors publishing commercially complained about lateness in royalty payments while there were no such criticisms of university presses.

There was remarkably little dissatisfaction about provision of information by the publisher (four per cent), printing and design (four per cent), adequacy of time for proofreading (five per cent), promptness of royalty payments (two per cent), and arranging of translations or multiple editions (four per cent). Overall, the median figure on proportion of authors expressing dissatisfaction came to five per cent, surely a very small figure by any standards.

Payment for Editorial Services

Our survey produced many other pieces of information reported in various portions of the article. Only one further result will be described here because of its inherent interest. Of the 364 scholars authoring at least one book, 12 per cent indicated they served as consultants to publishers, as regular editors, as occasional readers of manuscripts or under various intermediate arrangements. Excluding one exceptional individual who received $9000 per year for consulting and other services, 24 scholars gave data for both the total compensation received and the number of days spent reading manuscripts and performing other tasks for publishers. They worked on the average 21 days during the year for which they received a compensation of $670, or about $30 for each day worked—hardly a munificent wage. The exceptional individual described above fared much better, for he averaged about $120 for each day worked.

Some Cases of Abuse

In any relationship such as the one between author and publisher there are bound to arise occasional cases of inadvertent mishandling and even isolated cases of deliberate abuse. The examples which are described in this section, some of them rather hair-raising, are, with the exceptions subsequently noted, well documented. But they are, obviously, *not* typical. Most of them were sent in response to an explicit appeal for documented examples of mishandling (*AAUP Bulletin,* Summer, 1965, p. 269), and, as such, it should be apparent, they represent a deliberately biased sample. But our purpose is not to cast aspersions on the publishers' integrity. Rather, it is to alert authors to the nature of such sporadic problems so that they can guard more effectively against being caught up in them and to point out the difficulties to publishers, many of whom will doubtless want to do something about these issues. In reading this section the reader should recognize that publishers

[12] Since this section is based entirely on the results of our survey, this seems an appropriate point to indicate something about the nature of the survey itself. An effort was made to select the sample randomly, drawing faculty members according to a prescribed formula from alphabetical lists in over 70 colleges and universities, chosen to form a representative institutional sample. Apparently it was not always practicable to follow directions completely. Altogether more than 360 authors responded, giving varying amounts of information on about 660 books published since 1950. About 75 per cent of the books gave royalty data in sufficient detail for analysis. Authors were also asked to submit photocopies of their contracts and in this way we obtained 80 executed contract forms involving seventeen different commercial publishers and seventeen different university presses. The work of collection and analysis of these data was enormous despite the limited size of the sample. The survey was conducted in 1965.

can certainly just as easily come up with examples of questionable behavior on the part of authors.[13]

Delays in Editing and Publication

One of the most common sources of friction occurs when the publisher falls behind the schedule he has promised or at least suggested to the author. Of course, in preparing a production schedule it is always tempting to make rather optimistic estimates which leave little room for normal mischance. One should perhaps learn to regard the editor's time estimate as a distant kin of the home builder's cost estimate—as something of a lower bound. But while one soon learns to live with some delays, a few are stretched to inexcusable lengths, and, as will be seen below, on occasion insult is added to injury.

Normally, a book appears less than a year after completion and acceptance of the manuscript. The results of our survey indicate that it can take as little as two months or as much as 49 months to publish a volume after delivery of the final manuscript. While most books took seven months to a full year to appear, large percentages ranging from 37 to 40 per cent in the various categories came out in half a year or less, except in the case of texts published by university presses. Only about three per cent of the books in our sample took two or more years to appear in print.

Cases of extreme delay can be very unpleasant. We have in our files a documented case involving a well-known commercial publisher who was sent most of an accepted manuscript of a textbook in political science in May of 1963, and the remaining chapters by July. The authors had been promised some copy-edited chapters by May or June of 1964. Over a year later (August of 1965), the authors had received only two edited chapters. Nor was there apparently any question of quality, since the publisher absolutely refused the authors' offer to withdraw the manuscript.

Even more extreme is the history of a manuscript submitted to a well-known university press in September, 1962. Not having heard from the publisher, the author wrote prodding letters on the following January 7, May 31, October 28, and January 8, 1964 (!) (asking politely for the return of the manuscript by the end of February if no decision had yet been reached). On March 28, the author sent a somewhat less patient reminder, and wrote a demand for its return on May 13. On May 14, the author received what was almost certainly, in part, a form letter totalling eight lines in length. It said only of the nearly two-year lapse since the manuscript had been submitted "please accept my most profound apologies for the long delay in the consideration of your manuscript. I am chagrined, especially since the Committee has finally acted against it. . . . You may be sure that your manuscript has had adequate and careful consideration. . . . The manuscript is going forward to you with my thanks and good wishes. Sincerely yours."

Problems of Good Faith

As a transition, we turn to a case involving not only inexcusable delays but also conduct that raises serious questions of the publisher's ethics. We have the file of letters between an assistant professor of mathematics and the president (no less) of a well-known publishing house specializing in reprints and translations. On March 22, 1964, the professor wrote to the publisher proposing to translate several works and to undertake some other writings if they appealed to the publisher. The president of the publishing house wrote back on April 10 that he "had not yet had an opportunity to consider your suggestions. . . . I will write to you in about a month or so. . . ." Apparently unbidden, the author sent in a sample chapter of one of the proposed translations on January 27, 1965. On February 1, the company president acknowledged the manuscript, stating, "as soon as we have had a chance to review the book and translation I will let you know whether we'd like to see your completed manuscript." On April 2, the author asked for the return of the manuscript "even if you have not reached a decision. . . ." On April 7, the publisher wrote in reply that " . . . your manuscript [is] in the hands of our consultant . . . we are very interested and I hope we will be able to get together. I will have a decision in a week and I will write to you then." On April 14, the president wrote again (this is virtually the complete letter). "Dear Professor———: About a year ago we entered into an agreement with Mrs.——— to do a translation of [the same book]. When your translation came in we had to check to see whether her work was satisfactory. Mrs.——— is about finished with her translation and it does seem competent. I must, therefore, regretfully decline your offer."

Poor Information and Communication

Publishing houses differ in the amount of information they supply to authors. Some often go to considerable lengths to make certain their authors are well informed, while others seem to interpose a curtain between themselves and those who have written for them.

One example is provided by the case of an associate professor of philosophy and religion at a Southern college who was invited by a European publisher to submit his doctoral dissertation to them. He sent a copy, and several months later (early in 1964) received a contract. The author was somewhat annoyed to find that the contract called for a subsidy to the publisher amounting roughly to one quarter the estimated cost of publication, the cause of the annoyance not being the request for a subvention but the fact that ***the publisher had not previously mentioned the basis on which it would consider publication of the book.*** "Particularly vexing was the fact that in October, right after I had agreed to give [the publisher] permission to consider my manuscript, I received a letter from the editor of [a university] press asking similar permission. Since I believe multiple

[13] Indeed, we have proposed to several publishers that they prepare some such materials, not in a spirit of recrimination, but in an attempt to show authors some of the things they can do to improve their relations with their publishers, to facilitate the process of publication, and to improve the quality of the published product.

submissions of the same manuscript to be unethical,[14] I did not send a copy to [the second] press." The author's college was willing to pay the subsidy requested by the foreign press, so he decided to go ahead rather than wait for other presses to read over his manuscript. After signing his contract, in April of 1965, the author sent in his manuscript. The publisher never acknowledged receipt of the manuscript, nor did he reply to three subsequent letters asking whether the manuscript had been received, what production schedule was planned. etc. Three months later, when the author wrote to us, he had still received no communication from the press.

More important than the occasional breakdown of communications is the fact that most publishers do not, as a matter of course, supply certain types of information. Illustrative are the experiences of one of the authors of this article with a well-known publisher. First, the publishing house failed to inform him when a second printing of his book was to appear; in fact, he only learned of this accidentally by coming across a copy marked "third printing." As a result, both reprintings still contained all the errors which had been discovered since the book first made its appearance. Second, this same publisher permitted the book to be out of print for well over a year without notifying the author, who found out about it by deduction, from the sharp dip in his royalties. Finally, the publisher did not notify him about inquiries for translations and foreign editions or even about agreements that had been reached on the subject. On several occasions (also with other publishers) he has found out about a translation only when a package arrived in the mail containing several copies of the translated book.

It is not only foreign editions that sometimes go unreported. One author, a professor at an outstanding New England liberal arts college, wrote that his book, which had been published by a major university press, was subsequently reprinted in a paperback edition by another university press without his permission or knowledge and without any remuneration. He found out about it only when his daughter came across an advertisement of the paperback edition.

On one occasion, a foreign publishing house wrote to a scholarly author because it had received no answer to an inquiry sent to his American publisher. When the author asked his publisher about the situation, the editor first denied that any such inquiry had ever been received and, only after confrontation with the letter received by the author, did he finally admit, apparently after some checking in his files, that the communication was in his hands.

We doubt whether this is ordinarily intentional. Most publishers do not want to keep their authors in the dark. It just seems to be too much trouble or there is perhaps no standardized procedure designed for the purpose. We suggest that much could be gained if publishers were to adopt a standardized information form of the sort shown in Figure 1, which could be sent to the author along with his statement of royalties. Such a form should help improve author-publisher relations, reduce errors, and perhaps even make it easier to keep up sales.

Misunderstanding of the Terms of the Contract

The publisher can hardly be blamed when his contract is misinterpreted because it has not been read carefully, and it is inevitable that some misunderstandings will arise in this way. However, there are some provisions the consequences of which are such that the publisher could avoid much unpleasantness later by pointing out their implications to the author. There are also at least a few cases where the publisher may have abused the terms of the contract by stretching his interpretation in a manner that seems questionable at best.[15]

A relatively mild example is that sent in by a professor of nursing at an urban university whose contract did *not* call for the cost of index preparation to be borne by the (commercial) publisher (a company which has already appeared twice in the cases described in this section). However, what was not made clear was the open-endedness of the sum involved. The subject editor had assured the author that $350 was enough to cover the cost, and she apparently signed a separate indexing contract on this basis (we have not actually seen the contract in question). She writes: "At the time the contract was signed the book had already reached the stage of page proofs. Therefore the size of the manuscript should have been no surprise to anyone. However, I received another bill for $475 with the statement that the index was much longer than expected." There is a lesson in the fact that, when she protested against the added cost (prompted by her view that the index was of very poor quality), the company agreed to assume the additional financial burden.

A case raising very real issues of propriety involved a relatively unknown publishing company which contracted for a junior high school text, paying the senior author " . . . at the rate of $0.05 a word" which, according to the contract, constituted "full cash payment." Several years after the appearance of the book, he received a letter from his former co-author, an employee of the publishing company, stating that the firm was planning to publish an enlarged edition of the book, and enclosing a copy of the long introductory section asking him to check for anything to which he might "violently object." Later, he was sent some alternative sets of statistical figures and was asked to recommend those which seemed most appropriate. For this he received an honorarium of $25.00. The revised volume appeared subsequently with the names of both the original authors. It contained substantial changes which had never been shown the senior author of the original

[14] One editor remarked that he saw nothing unethical about multiple submissions provided that all the publishing houses were informed. He commented that this might redound to the disadvantage of the author of a marginal manuscript but, where the manuscript was very promising, it might well improve the terms offered to the author.

[15] On such matters the author will sometimes find it advisable to seek the help of counsel.

edition, and, aside from the $25.00 honorarium and six free copies of the revised edition, no suggestion of any payment for the revised edition was ever mentioned. Aside from the issue of compensation, however, the author was most concerned with the company's use of his name without his authorization and without his having had an opportunity to see the materials that were being ascribed to him in print. It is not clear from the wording of the contract that, upon payment to the author of the fixed fee for the original materials, the materials became the property of the publisher to do with as he wished. We are not prepared to say how the courts might regard the issue if it were brought to them. But if the publisher regarded this as the appropriate interpretation of the contract, it was surely incumbent on him to make this clear to the author from the very beginning, even if it increased the risk that the latter might never have agreed to the arrangement.

We have an undocumented letter from a well-known mathematician at an ivy-league university which provides another example of abuse of contract provisions. The issue arose out of a large sale of one of his books to an organization. The author writes: "The publisher, according to their statement, was paid a flat fee in addition to their expenses; half of the small fee was turned over to the author. I reminded the publishers that according to the contract I should be entitled to a percentage stipulated for all sales even for those at a much reduced rate. But this argument was refused by the publisher under reference to a contract quotation. The statement, however, did not occur in my contract. When so informed the publisher referred to the original contract with the statement that the case was covered by an 'etc.' in the clause concerning radio rights. No settlement was ever made."

The Contract Not an Obligation to Publish

Though it rarely causes much difficulty in practice, because publishers are anxious to publish their authors' works, one of the most prevalent misunderstandings relating to contracts is the widespread failure to recognize that a publisher's contract often does not even constitute a commitment to publish. This is particularly true where the contract is signed before the manuscript has been completed. Taken at face value, such a contract is a one-sided affair which commits the author to deliver the manuscript to no other publisher, but does not bind the publisher to bring out the author's materials. We have documented illustrative cases involving a number of relatively well-known publishers. One example concerns a contract signed in 1960, under the terms of which a manuscript was submitted in 1962. For three years, there was no progress toward publication. Finally, the editor who was working on the book informed the author that he would receive proofs in February of 1965. However, in November of 1964, the editor left the company, and apparently about the same time there was a change in the ownership of the publishing house. Shortly thereafter, the author received a letter from the publisher informing him that "in the past two weeks our copyeditor has encountered so many difficulties with the text of ——— that we have been forced to reappraise the whole project. I am sorry to say that we have now decided not to publish the book. . . . Although I know it will be little consolation to you, I am sure you will understand that our decision represents as great a loss to us as it does to you, in view of the $1200 advance that we must forfeit and in view of the considerable expense already incurred in terms of editorial time. . . . You have received the full amount of the advance and, needless to say, this will be found money, if, as I honestly hope, you are able to sign a new contract with another publisher."

Options on Subsequent Works

A number of authors wrote to us emphasizing the unpleasantness which arose out of the clauses sometimes included in contracts which give the publisher an option on some of the author's subsequent work. The difficulty often occurs because such a contract is normally signed before the author has had a chance to judge the quality of the publisher's work. In one case, a professor of chemistry reported that publication of his first book underwent numerous delays and appeared more than a year after the galleys were returned. After publication, the publisher failed to answer letters from individuals who wanted to consider adopting the book, two of whom ultimately wrote to the author. The book apparently contained many errors, a substantial proportion of them introduced after the proofs had been returned. The author also considered the advertising to be misleading, and there was no answer to his request for a list of adoptions. As a result of these experiences, the author understandably sought a release from the option to his second book. After some correspondence in which the request was first ignored, then tentatively agreed to and finally rejected, an attorney was finally brought in by the author and the release was obtained.

Most option clauses limit the time which the publisher can take in making up his mind on a manuscript submitted under its terms, and usually the option is limited to one subsequent book. But we have come across exceptions—a case where a young author granted the publisher an option on his next three works (not documented), and cases where publication of a manuscript was unduly delayed when the publisher sat on it far too long before either accepting or rejecting it. The letters we received thus substantiate the dangers in the option clause and suggest that authors should try to have them eliminated altogether, or at least be sure that they are adequately circumscribed. After all, good service is the most effective way for a publisher to keep a writer "in his stable of authors," (the justification provided by an editor of one major publisher to an author who considered the option clauses in his successive contracts to constitute "indentured servitude").

Volumes of Reprints

We come, finally, to an issue that has assumed increasing importance in recent years, though, strictly speaking, it does not fall within the limits of the subject of this article since it involves abuse of the authors of journal articles rather than of writers of books. The problem arises out of the compilation of "books of readings" composed of articles or even sections of books and articles cut and pasted together to form a volume.

Normally, the author of the reprinted piece receives no compensation or is given a token payment in the form of a flat fee, usually no more than $100. More important, *the author is often not asked his permission for the reprinting,* and he may even come across the reprinted piece only by accident. Some publishers or journals which hold the copyright grant permission to reprint routinely on receipt of some standard fee which is frequently not shared with the author. Some relatively impecunious journals keep the entire fee for themselves, a practice which is not necessarily objectionable if authors have been informed about this policy before they agreed to have their articles published by the journal. In any event, it should be noted that the author frequently receives little or nothing for the reprinting of his paper. Meanwhile, as has already been reported, the editor of the volume, who has not incurred work nearly comparable with the writing of a book, is, according to the results of our survey, paid royalties whose rates are just about as high as those given the writer of an original volume. No doubt this is a very good thing for the editor and, perhaps, for the publisher, but those who have actually made the substantive contributions to such a volume, the authors of the pieces that are included, can be pardoned for questioning the equity of an arrangement which sometimes does not even provide them with free copies of the book.

But probably even more serious is the fact that the writer has no control over the nature of the volume in which his piece appears or the quality of the other writings with which it is associated. One noted sociologist recounted "an outrageous experience in which I found myself reprinted three times in a melange which purported to be an introduction to the social sciences. This was done without my knowledge, consent, or, of course, any compensation. In fact the publisher resented my asking for three free copies of the book, and, after an exchange of a number of letters, ended up grudgingly by sending me one, and that one a paperback."

In another recent case, a pair of economists found reprinted a section of their textbook in which they discussed the things that can be accomplished by the pricing system. The reprint volume was a right-wing publication whose apparent purpose was to demonstrate the virtues of an unregulated business economy and the dangers of public intervention in the economy. Thus, by reprinting in such a book, the passage on the price system was converted from a purely descriptive piece into one which might be interpreted to imply that, if only the government would keep its hands off, all would be for the best in this best of all possible economies.

Concluding Comment

We believe this article has shown that, by and large, relations between authors and publishers are usually straightforward and satisfactory. The neophyte author need not feel that when he undertakes to arrange for publication he is entering a jungle in which the publisher will take every possible advantage of him.

Nevertheless, there are dangers. There are a number of special difficulties that occasionally beset relationships between author and publisher, among them delays in publication, failure to supply adequate information to the author, and abuses of option clauses. Above all, there is the danger that the author will be inadequately informed about the range of terms that is currently being offered and the meaning of the provisions of the contract. This article has sought to supply at least a substantial proportion of the requisite information on many of these items so that the author can be better prepared when he negotiates a contract. If it succeeds also in persuading publishers to supply on a regular basis some of the information which our study shows to be provided unsystematically, if at all, despite its importance to authors, and if it can lead to greater standardization of the terms in which royalties are expressed, we shall feel it will have accomplished a very great deal.

Appendix: Other Contractual Provisions

The following materials describe a number of provisions made in publishers' contracts and the range of terms which they generally offer. While these have not been discussed in the text of the article, some of them are likely to prove important to the author.

Warranty and Indemnity

This provision requires the author to guarantee that he is the sole owner of the work and has full power and authority to copyright it and make this agreement; that the work does not infringe any copyright, violate any proprietary rights, contain any scandalous, libelous, or unlawful matter, or constitute an invasion of privacy. Most contracts provide further that the author will defend, indemnify, and hold harmless the publisher against all claims, suits, costs, damages, and expenses that the publisher may sustain or incur by reason of any scandalous, libelous, or unlawful matter contained or alleged to be contained in the work, or any infringement or violation by the work of any copyright or property right.

Most commonly, the contract is worded in such a way that the publisher can hold the author liable in full for legal expenses that may be incurred, as well as damage awards or settlements, but a few limit the author's indemnity in the case of libelous or unlawful matter (but not suits for copyright violation or infringement) to some fixed share, e.g., half. The scholar is cautioned that he does not avoid liability if the contract omits the term *indemnify* and uses only the phrase "hold the publisher harmless"; *indemnify* merely adds another nail to a provision that is already tightly fastened. Some, but not all, contracts go one step further to protect the fiduciary interests of the publisher; they specify that sums due the author may be withheld as security for his obligations.

The Copyright

Contracts specifically provide for the securing of the copyright. Generally, the actual act of obtaining it is performed by the publisher, sometimes in the name of the author himself, at other times in the name of the publisher (upon proper authorization). Except in the case of private publication, the cost is usually borne by the publisher.

This appears to be an appropriate place to mention another matter of importance, the copyrighting of journal articles, which is significant because the entire article or portions of it may later be incorporated into a larger work or into collections of readings. While journals may copyright the entire contents of each issue published, the author can protect his own interests by copyrighting his own article independently as well. Apparently, the author obtains some degree of protection simply by attaching a footnote to the title of his article, reading "Copyright 19— by [name of author]." This gives the author some degree of control over subsequent use of his article, though the primary purpose is to notify the editors of the journal that he wants to be consulted before permission to reprint his article is granted to anyone.

Infringement of Copyright

To protect the publisher's interest, most contracts provide that the publisher shall have the right to bring action if he believes the copyright of the work has been infringed, but the financial arrangements vary among publishers. The more generous ones, in effect, bear the cost if the legal action is unsuccessful and share equally with the author any net balance (over and above expenses) from any settlement or damage award. Other contracts provide that litigation may be undertaken jointly, in which case both expenses and net proceeds are shared jointly; in the event one party declines action, the other—or at least the publisher—has the right to proceed on his own, bearing all expenses and retaining any net proceeds which may result.

Fees and Permissions to Use Copyrighted Materials

Understandably, the publishing house is most explicit in imposing a contractual requirement upon the author to obtain and furnish to the publisher written permission to use any and all copyrighted material quoted or reproduced in the work. In the vast majority of contracts reviewed for purposes of this study, permission fees, if any, are borne by the author. The subject is open to bargaining, however, and so there are some exceptions, usually in the form of a specified maximum amount, e.g., $500, to be paid by the publisher. This rather uncommon arrangment must be distinguished from the somewhat more frequent provision stating that permission fees will be paid by the publisher but that such sums are merely advances which are to be deducted from the author's earnings. From the standpoint of the author himself, it seems preferable to have the publisher pay the fees, even though they are treated as an offset against future royalties—he does not have to advance the money and, in the rare cases where the publisher fails to bring out the book, these costs at least have been shifted from the writer's shoulders.

Form of the Manuscript

Besides the usual title page, preface (if any), table of contents, and bibliography, most but not all contracts require that the author supply final copy for submission to the printer, complete with illustrations, charts, and diagrams properly prepared, and that the author shall have the option of revising it to the publisher's satisfaction or of commissioning the publisher to have it properly prepared at the author's expense. He is usually called upon to provide an index or, sometimes without any choice on his part, to pay for its preparation. There is often a time limit and an escape clause for the publisher to arrange for preparation of the index at author's expense if the commitment is not met. The author may also be called upon to supply a teacher's manual and a student workbook, and he frequently receives no royalty on the former, which is usually given away, and is typically paid a reduced royalty on the latter. The financial terms relating to illustrations, charts, index, manuals, and workbooks are, on occasion, bargainable issues. It is unusual but not unknown for the publisher to pay the cost of having the index and, less frequently, manuals and workbooks prepared by someone other than the author.

Editing by Publisher

Contracts commonly reserve to the publisher the right to edit the work for the original printing and any subsequent reprintings, providing such editing or alteration does not materially change the meaning or otherwise materially alter the text. While most presses customarily seek the author's approval of editing changes—and it is really only the author who can determine whether a proposed modification is suitable—some presses accept this obligation less conscientiously. In a few cases, unpleasant conflicts arise over differences of opinion on style and contents or as a result of failure by the publisher to get the author's approval of editorial changes. A few contracts protect the author explicitly with a proviso to the effect that the author shall be given the opportunity to approve or disapprove any changes.

Grounds for Not Publishing

Contracts often provide the publisher with one or more grounds on which he may decide not to publish the volume. The two most important of these relate to the specified date of submission and the quality of the manuscript. If the manuscript is not already completed when the contract is drawn, the date for submission is usually specified. If the manuscript is not submitted on time, the publisher generally has the privilege of cancelling the contract. In addition, the contract often specifies, if the manuscript is not already in hand when the contract is signed, that the author be required to submit "a complete and satisfactory manuscript" where the term "satisfactory" is not defined.

Since the agreement seems to be designed to work primarily in the publisher's favor, effectively imposing an obligation on the author but not on the publisher, the scholar may well question the advantage of signing a contract before completion of his manuscript. If a work is expected to have a limited market, the author who postpones the negotiation of an agreement until completion of his manuscript may discover that the presses which he most prefers may consider themselves to be overcommitted on such "prestige books." More important is the effect of the publisher's moral obligation to print the work if at all feasible. It is really quite rare for a publisher to back out of a contract, perhaps in part because he is leary of any adverse publicity that might follow.

Other Decisions Left to the Publisher

Typically, contracts reserve to the publisher decisions as to price, paper, printing, binding, timing of publication, advertising, and selling. The pricing decision is, of course, of particular importance to the author, but traditionally the publisher has come to treat this as his exclusive concern and the author is rarely consulted or even informed of the pricing decision. This sometimes leads to unpleasantness, particularly where the author believes strongly that the book should be inexpensive in order to encourage wider use. Some publishers also reserve the privilege of changing the title, though in practice this is usually not done without consultation with the author. In some cases, timing of publication may be a major issue between the press on the one hand and the scholar on the other. The latter has a professional interest in its early release, for earlier publication may affect decisions on promotion, salary, and offers of appointment at other institutions. The press has to gear publication to its production schedule and, especially in the case of texts, to seasonal marketing factors. If a book appears too late in the season to be available for adoption as a textbook, it may be preferable from a sales standpoint to bring it out at a later date, particularly if doing so will change the copyright date to make the book appear more recent and up-to-date.

Reprintings and Revised Editions

While the typical contract does not include any special section giving the author the right to correct errors or make minor changes when a reprinting occurs, presses commonly give the author this privilege. Unfortunately, however, the author is often not informed of planned reprintings, so that he is effectively deprived of the opportunity even to correct typographical errors that have come to light since the previous printing. One way to avoid such situations is for the author to inform his publisher automatically of any errors as soon as they come to light, whether or not he knows of any planned reprinting.

With respect to revisions, the publisher typically reserves the right to decide whether the work shall be revised. There is some tendency for publishers to ask for more frequent revisions of popular texts than the author desires, in order to increase the volume's marketability. Publishers are often understandably reluctant to undertake the expense required to bring a technical work up to date. On each of these issues the author has at his command only his powers of persuasion, which in author-publisher relationships are not always negligible. The publisher's property interests are usually protected by a clause stating that, should the author fail to make the revision within a reasonable time after the request is made or should the author be deceased, the publisher may have the revision prepared and charge the cost against the author's royalties. Unless the contract so specifies, an author who does not personally revise his work has only such influence on the selection of the individual to make the revision or in approving and disapproving textual changes as the publisher is willing to permit. To protect himself, the author of a textbook (since the problem is only likely to arise in the case of a text) may seek to have inserted in the contract a provision to the effect that the publisher may select, subject to mutual consent, some other person(s) to make the necessary revisions on terms satisfactory to all contracting parties *or* that it is understood that such revision, if prepared by outside authority during the author's lifetime, shall be subject to review by the author. The reviser, on his part, should also have a clear understanding not only of the financial arrangements, but on textual differences in the event the contracting parties cannot agree.

Decision to Discontinue Publication

The decision to take a book out of print usually rests solely with the publisher. Occasionally the contract specifies a minimum number of copies which must be sold per year if the company is to continue selling copies out of stock. More usually there is a sales figure (higher than the preceeding) which constitutes a prerequisite for reprinting of the volume. Some contracts provide that, when sales drop below the minimum considered acceptable by the publisher, the press may discontinue manufacture and destroy the plates, sheets, and books without liability to the author. Other contracts provide in detail for their disposal, and provisions vary widely in the terms under which the author may take title to sheets, copies, and plates. For example, the purchase price of plates seems to range anywhere from their value as old metal to 100 per cent of full manufacturing cost, and that of bound copies from 50 to 100 per cent of full cost, or sometimes it is set at some specified proportion of list price.

Some contracts do not provide specifically, when the publisher allows the work to go "out of print," that all rights under the contract revert to the author, and even fewer provide time limits for the publisher to make and carry out a decision to reprint a work and make it available for sale. While such a provision is usually little more than a formality, since the author will probably find no market elsewhere for a book which his own publisher does not want to reprint, there are many exceptions. Moreover, there have been cases where publishers have delayed for a considerable period the decision between reprinting and release of the work to the author. Often the author has not even been told the book was out of print. An author should therefore try to arrange for a contract clause requiring the publisher to notify him when the book is no longer in stock, and setting a limit on the time during which he can delay the decision on republication.

[23]

Last minute discounts on unsold tickets: a study of TKTS

with Hilda Baumol

Introduction

On June 25, 1973, Theatre Development Fund launched an experimental program for the theatre to attract additional audiences, to contribute to the relief of their financial problems, to increase the accessibility of their performances for less affluent individuals, and to revive last-minute impulse buying that can contribute so much to the excitement of the theatre.

To carry out this experiment, a special box office was opened in the theatre district on 47th Street where Broadway and Seventh Avenue meet. This box office was named the Times Square Theatre Centre (TKTS). It offers tickets to a wide variety of productions that are theatrical in nature – to Broadway, off-Broadway, Lincoln Center, the Brooklyn Academy of Music, City Center, and others. These are sold only on the day of performance at half price plus a 50¢ service charge for tickets with face value under $10, and a $1 service charge for more expensive tickets. The service charge is retained by TKTS for expenses, and the ticket income is returned to the production. The TKTS booth is open seven days a week: from 3–8 p.m. Monday through Saturday, from 12 noon–2 p.m. on matinee days, and from 12 noon–7 p.m. on Sunday.

TKTS offers no luxuries to its patrons. They sometimes wait in long queues in all sorts of weather. Heaters have been installed above each of the box office windows, but very little shelter is provided. Opposite the box office windows is a listing of all productions for which tickets are available, but no information on availability is given by telephone. At its outset the booth sold about 7,000 tickets weekly, and it is now, in the summer of 1974, selling as many as 14,000 tickets per week.

TKTS has undoubtedly served its users not only with tickets at reduced prices but by acting as a central box office,[1] a marketing innovation that has been discussed for many decades but never put into operation. The TKTS booth has also made it possible for anyone to decide on the day of performance that an evening at the theatre is a good idea, for it has reduced the risk of getting to a theatre and being left high and dry. Finally, it is possible that a person casually passing by will be attracted by available tickets and will attend on impulse.

Despite its attractions, the opening of TKTS met with some reservations. A few ticket brokers expressed fears of competition, arguing that their existence was already precarious. Some theatre owners and producers feared that instead of bringing in new audiences it would merely encourage theatregoers to purchase at half price what they would otherwise have bought at face value. They were also afraid that potential ticket purchasers would postpone their buying decisions, thereby increasing the risk borne by the theatres and their vulnerability to adverse weather and other unforeseen events. Indeed, about half a dozen productions refused to participate in the program at all, and a few others have used it sparingly (one popular musical used it exactly one day).

The reasons for non-participation differ widely. The producer of *Pippin* did not believe in the concept of the TKTS booth; a highly effective television campaign helped maintain large audiences for the show. Sellouts, such as *A Moon for the Misbegotten* or *Uncle Vanya*, find the booth superfluous. Shows that have very high running costs, particularly if they are in smallish theatres, cannot afford to run with discounted tickets and will simply close when audiences dwindle. Other productions that do substantial business send a few tickets to TKTS, partly to sell unpopular locations and partly to avoid publicizing the inevitable moment when participation in TKTS may make the difference between closing and a longer run.

Soon after the inception of the program, a survey of the users of the TKTS box office was designed and carried out to analyze and document the experiment and to assess whether or not there were grounds for the reservations described.[2] More than 800 persons, randomly selected, were asked to fill out questionnaires – some 400 while waiting to purchase tickets and another 400 after they had made their purchases.

The results of that study were reassuring. They indicated that the box office was contributing additional audience, not simply luring audiences away from traditional ticket-selling channels. Moreover, it seemed to be bringing in an audience younger and less affluent than that which usually attends performances at the participating theatres. However, since this initial survey was carried out before the operations of the new box office had been given a chance to assume longer term patterns, and because it had unavoidably left a number of significant questions unanswered, a second investigation, the one whose results are described in this report, was undertaken later on.

Objectives of the study

The first objective of this study is to provide an evaluation of TKTS to help determine whether it should be continued or even expanded. This evaluation should also enable performing groups outside New York City to judge whether or not a similar undertaking might be useful to them. The second objective is to investigate whether or not the workings of the box office can be improved, and if so, how this can be done.

Specifically, the study provides the material that will be helpful in answering the following questions:

- Does TKTS attract a net addition to audiences?
- Does TKTS add to the net revenues of the theatres, and, if so, how much?
- What are the characteristics of the audiences it attracts and how do they differ from the usual audiences at similar theatres?
- Does TKTS lead to a significant amount of impulse buying or buying with little advance planning?
- Do TKTS sales compete with sales by theatre box offices or ticket brokers?

- How costly and complex are TKTS administrative arrangements?
- What might be the consequences of innovations such as acceptance of phone or credit card orders, variations in discount by time of performance (i.e., higher discounts for performances on Tuesday, Wednesday, and Thursday evenings), or the opening of additional box offices?

Some of these questions are answered here rather conclusively; for others a strong presumption is provided. However, only broad inferences have been drawn on the potential effect of these innovations and a more definitive evaluation must be left to future investigation.

TKTS' operations

Administration, ticket revenue and volume

The Theatre Centre is administered by Theatre Development Fund (TDF), a nonprofit corporation created in 1967 to assist all aspects of the theatre.

To establish the booth, individuals and foundations granted TDF over $60,000 for one time only, in the expectation that the TKTS booth would quickly become self-sustaining or nearly so. The largest contribution was $35,000 from the Ford Foundation; other contributions were made by the Rockefeller Brothers Fund, Edward John Noble Foundation, Fanton Foundation, New York Times Foundation, Cultural Council Foundation, The Shubert Foundation, Inc. Irving Berlin Charitable Trust, Mrs Russel Crouse, and Messrs Harold Prince and Neil Simon.

The total cost of establishing the booth, excluding the first week of operation, was $27,542.26. Over half of the initial grants were used for one-time expenses and as a contingency fund, and the remainder for a public information program.

Other gifts were the TKTS facility (whose design was coordinated by the Office of Midtown Planning and which was installed by the City at a cost of approximately $27,000), rent-free space on Duffy Square that is maintained by the Department of Parks, and the installation of power lines that the New York City Department of Commerce and Industry donated at a cost of $2,188.

Space for posting TKTS publicity was donated as a public service by Metro Transit Advertising, New York Subways Advertising, and Transportation Displays, Inc. This brought the message to buses, subways, train stations, and airports. Time was also contributed as a public service on virtually every metropolitan radio station and on WNEW-TV. A public relations firm was retained to prepare the material. There was also extensive coverage in newspapers and on radio and television news programs.

Disregarding the first week of operation, which fell into a prior fiscal year, the 52-week total revenue for the sale of 450,715 tickets was:

Total cash received:	$2,339,617.94
Total paid to theatres:[3]	2,051,897.94
Total retained by TDF:	287,720.00

The staff of the TKTS Centre was:

A general manager
Five treasurers
A cleaner/porter (part-time)
Three messengers/maintenance (routine maintenance only)
Temporary employees to cover vacations, etc.
TDF administrative personnel.

The administrative and operating costs of the Centre now amount to a little less than $6,000 per week, and it is planned to continue at that level in the absence of any change in scale of operation of severe inflationary pressure. Of this amount, about two-thirds consists of salaries, 4 percent public information expenses, and the remainder maintenance, telephone and utilities, security, professional fees, etc. For fiscal year 1973–74, TKTS ran at a modest deficit of about $14,000 supplied by restricted grants to TDF. A smaller deficit is projected for 1974–75.

Weekly ticket sales have ranged from a low of 5,778 in November 1973 up to 14,003 in June 1974, and even more during the subsequent summer. The average weekly sale for the 1973–74 fiscal year was 8,668 tickets. Figure 1 shows week by week, since its inception, the sales at the TKTS box office. After a brief downward trend, sales have climbed steadily and today are about twice as high as they were at its inception. The relatively small volume of off-Broadway and Lincoln Center tickets sold has held fairly steady apart from the first month of operation.

Publicity and other sources of information

As already indicated, almost half the opening budget, more than $12,000, was spent informing the public of the existence and function of TKTS. In addition to the opening publicity mentioned, there has been subsequent publicity including the main story on the front page of *The New York Times*' Arts and Leisure Section in December 1973, and a brief coast-to-coast television report at the time of the celebration of TKTS, first anniversary.

Table I lists the sources from which TKTS users report having first heard of the booth. It is noteworthy that despite all of the publicity received, approximately 40 percent of TKTS patrons learned about the booth from friends, while about 9 percent simply noticed it while passing by.

Participation of Broadway productions

As reported, not all eligible producers and productions have actually made use of the TKTS facilities. Some have had reservations about the entire procedure. Others have chosen not to participate so long as their production was highly successful, preferring to leave the impression that they had sold out all seats even when a small number were still available. As one of them is reported to have said: 'I'd rather not advertise the fact that I don't have a sellout.'

Different theatres have different strategies for using the TKTS booth: some box office managers have routinely sent in the same number of tickets every day; strong shows tend to send tickets to locations that are hard to fill, such as balcony seats; weaker shows send in a selection of seats that, if sold, will 'dress' the house (give

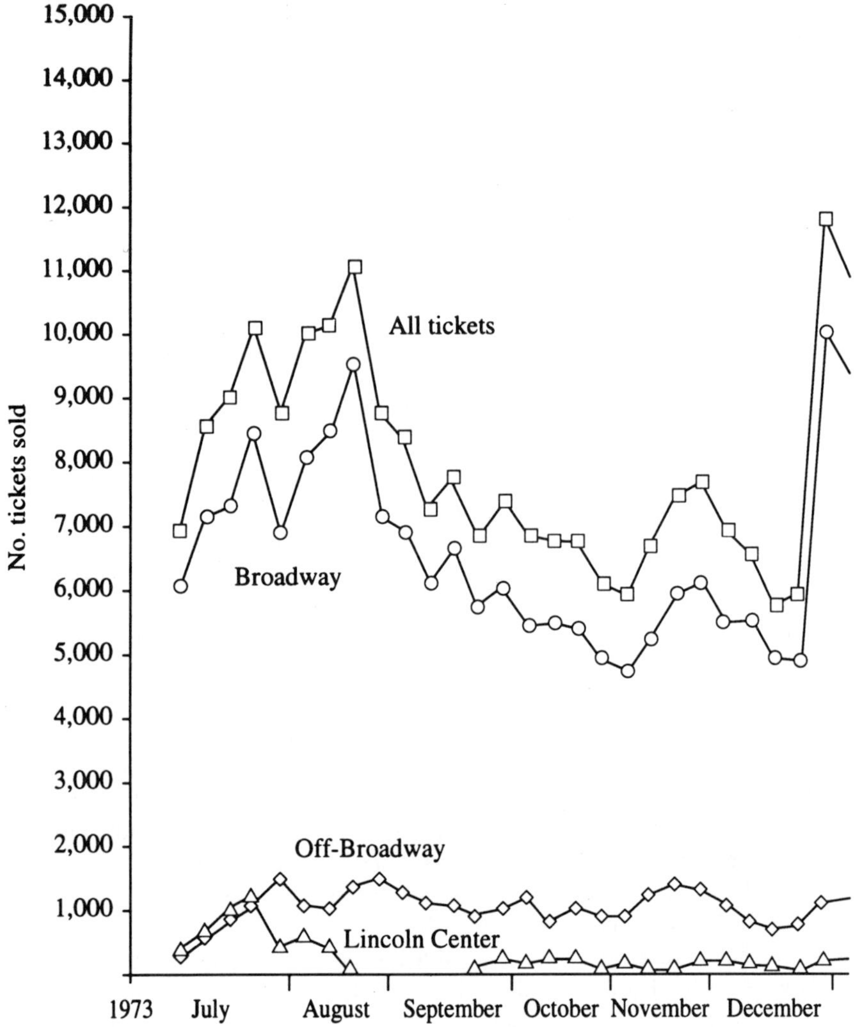
15,000
14,000
13,000
12,000
11,000
10,000
9,000
8,000
7,000
6,000
5,000
4,000
3,000
2,000
1,000
No. tickets sold
All tickets
Broadway
Off-Broadway
Lincoln Center
1973
July
August
September
October
November
December

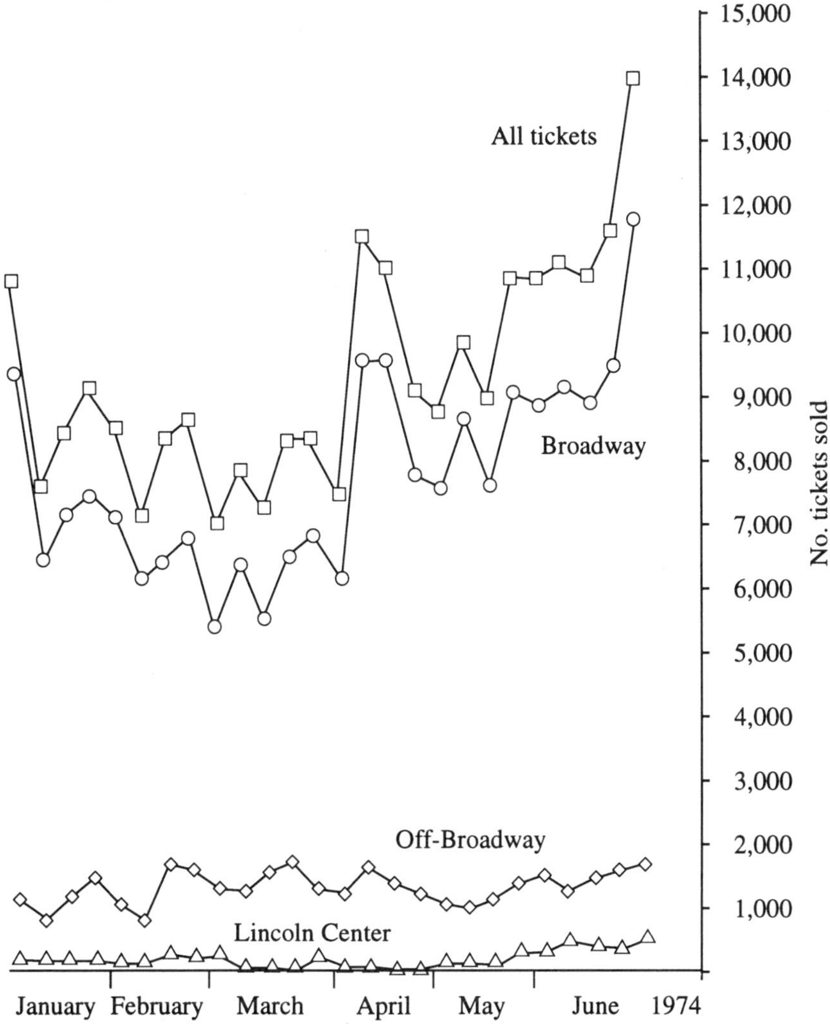

Source: Theatre Development Fund. 7/1/73–6/30/74, 53 weeks.

Figure 1 TKTS: TKTS Weekly Sales Volume

Table I TKTS: How Patrons Heard of TKTS

	August	February	May	Average for the Three Surveys
	Number of Responses*			
	512	173	199	
	%	%	%	%
Newspapers	25.69	36.42	30.15	30.75
Radio	5.69	2.31	.50	2.83
Television	8.43	2.89	2.01	4.44
Subway billboard	8.04	3.47	2.01	4.51
Bus poster	2.55	–	.50	1.02
Railroad poster	1.57	.58	–	.72
Friend	33.72	41.04	44.22	39.66
Teacher	.59	2.31	–	.97
Noticed booth	7.25	6.36	14.57	9.39
Other	6.47	4.32	6.03	5.71

Note: * Respondents could check more than one category.

Source: August 1973, February and May 1974 surveys at TKTS.

the appearance of a well-filled theatre). Most seats allocated to TKTS are for the orchestra, if only because there are more of those than for other locations.

There is frequent communication between the TKTS personnel and the individual box offices on direct lines that connect the booth to the theatres. If the initial allocation runs low at the booth, one of the treasurers calls the theatre. The theatre manager decides whether or not he can sell what he has by the end of the day or whether he should send another allocation to TKTS. In this way, new allocations may be sent to the booth until curtain time.

Table II indicates for three different weeks the number of Broadway theatres in operation, and the number for which tickets were available to the TKTS booth at least once during that week. It indicates that during the season roughly half to two-thirds of the available productions made use of the TKTS facility.

It is, of course, too early to judge trends in participation. However, as early fears about the effects of the Theatre Centre prove unfounded, the great majority of productions now use its facilities. This may depend on the number of productions that are 'hits'. Figure 2 shows the number of Broadway shows running, the number that were 'sellouts',[4] and the number whose tickets were available at TKTS. It indicates that the number of shows using TKTS has remained roughly constant. However, as the number of productions grew during the second half of the season, the non-participating group grew commensurately. As is to be expected, non-participation tended to be higher in periods when attendance at the theatres was relatively high.

Table II TKTS: Participation in TKTS (Broadway Theatres)

Week	Number of Theatres in Operation	Number with Tickets at TKTS	Participants as Percent of Total
7/30–8/5/73	12	8	66.7
10/29–11/4/73	15	9	60.0
2/25–3/3/74	15	7	46.7

Source: *Variety* and TDF records.

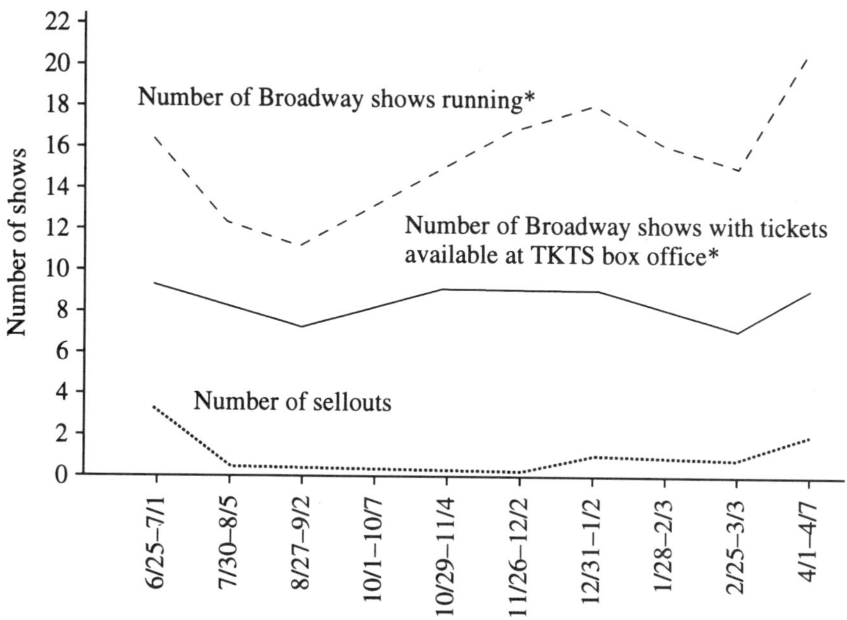

Note: * Including Beaumont Theatre.

Source: *Variety* and TDF records. Selected ten weeks: the first week of every month, from July 1973 (inception of program) to April 1974.

Figure 2 TKTS: Number of Broadway Shows Running, Tickets Sold by TKTS, and Number of Sellouts

Availability of tickets by time of performance

Obviously the availability of tickets at TKTS will vary inversely with demand through normal distribution channels, and that varies in turn by day of performance. It is well known, for example, that on Broadway the demand for tickets on Tuesday, Wednesday, and Thursday evenings is much lower than for weekends and

Wednesday matinees. We have examined the availability of tickets at TKTS by night of week to see whether it follows a corresponding pattern. This is important for two reasons: first, it can be helpful to patrons of the Centre, indicating to them the times when they will probably find the widest choice of tickets; second, it can help in the design of pricing policy, suggesting which performances seem to be over- or under-priced in relation to market demand. It may be worth considering a simple variation in both box office and TKTS prices by time of performance as steps toward a more effective policy for the marketing of theatre tickets.

Table III shows, by day of performance, both average number of tickets available and percentage of Broadway shows for which tickets are available at TKTS.[5] Several interesting behavior patterns may be observed from the table. First, there is a sharp drop in the percentage of Broadway shows that use the box office on Saturday matinees and evenings. While on Wednesdays, Thursdays, and Fridays, about half of the shows running offer tickets at TKTS, on Saturdays only about one-third participate. This is not surprising because Saturday is traditionally a day of heavy attendance and consequently many shows might be expected to sell well at their own box offices. Indeed, what is surprising is the wide selection of tickets that has typically been available on Friday nights, also a night on which audiences tend to be large.[6]

This attendance pattern contrasts curiously with the distribution by day and time of performance of number of seats sold by TKTS. In Table III we see that TKTS actually sold more tickets on Friday and Saturday evenings than at any other performance time – about 900 tickets per day. On Tuesdays through Thursdays, including Wednesday matinees, sales through TKTS amounted to about 700 tickets. This means that on non-weekend performances, theatres have more tickets left unsold and yet sell fewer through TKTS than they do on weekends. This perverse

Table III TKTS: Ticket Availability by Time of Performance (Selected Ten Weeks)*

	Mon	Tues	Wed		Thur	Fri	Sat		Sun
	E	E	M	E	E	E	M	E	M
Average number of tickets sold by TKTS	488.5	639.4	765.6	799.6	707.4	895.1	684.0	917.1	482.6
Average percent of shows running available at TKTS	44.7	47.0	45.8	52.5	51.0	50.0	35.8	34.8	47.8
Decile on percent of shows available									
– Lower decile	12.5	23.5	31.3	38.9	38.9	37.5	20.0	20.0	0
– Upper decile	72.7	66.7	63.6	66.7	66.7	66.7	50.0	50.0	100.0

Note: * The first week of every month, from July 1973 (inception of TKTS program) to April 1974.

Source: TDF records, *New York Times*, *Cue Magazine*, and *Variety*.

pattern is what might be expected, since TKTS offers no significant price bonus for purchases of tickets to midweek performances.

TKTS audience

Composition of TKTS patrons and comparison with general Broadway audience
To determine the differences in characteristics of TKTS patrons with those of the theatre box offices, 375 patrons of the TKTS booth were interviewed, roughly half in February and half in May 1974. These interviews supplemented those conducted in August 1973 after the opening of TKTS. (Details of the questionnaires, sampling methods, and other pertinent materials are given in Appendix A and individual results of the three surveys appear in Appendix B, 1–4.)

The results of all these interviews were remarkably consistent, so that larger interview samples are quite pointless. This is confirmed by Table IV, which shows absolutely no change from the samples in median age, income, or education, although there are some changes in their distribution.[7] Table V indicates TKTS users' residences.

Table IV TKTS: Seasonal Variation, TKTS Box Office Patrons

	August 1973	February 1974	May 1974
Median age	30	30	30
Median income	$16,397	$15,500	$15,500
Median education	4 years college	4 years college	4 years college

Source: August 1973, February and May 1974 surveys at TKTS.

Table V TKTS: Residence of TKTS Patrons

	August 1973	February 1974	May 1974
	%	%	%
Manhattan	19.95	31.21	27.14
Other boroughs	17.52	15.03	20.10
Long Island	9.98	11.56	9.55
New York State (other)	5.11	8.67	6.53
New Jersey	12.17	15.03	11.56
Other states	29.93	17.34	21.61
Abroad	5.34	1.16	3.52

Source: August 1973, February and May 1974 surveys at TKTS.

For this report, what is important are the similarities and differences of TKTS patrons and the Broadway theatrical audience as a whole. In order to carry out the comparisons, the characteristics of the Broadway audience had to be inferred from several sources. The source of the most recent information available is a Metromedia, Inc. survey of theatre audiences for *Playbill* in 1973. We could not always use their figures because of differences in the categories employed by the two surveys. There were other discrepancies arising from their procedure of obtaining information at the respondents' homes, rather than at the theatre. To fill the gaps, we supplemented their data with figures taken from an earlier survey for the Twentieth Century Fund in 1966.[8]

The results of the comparisons, reported in Figures 3–6, can be summarized as follows:[9]

Occupation (Figure 3): TKTS users include both a higher proportion of professionals and a higher share of blue collar workers than the overall Broadway audience.

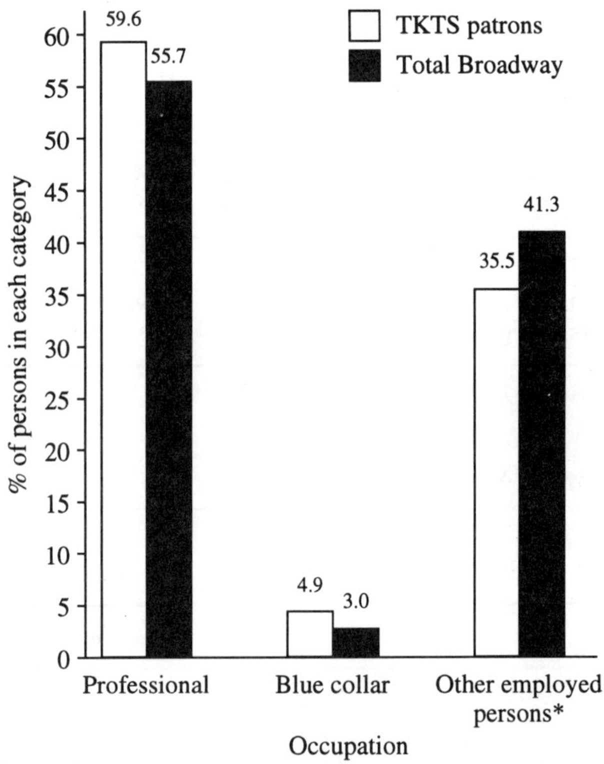

Note: * Includes managerial, clerical, sales, and general white collar.

Source: TKTS surveys, average of August 1973 and February and May 1974; Baumol and Bowen survey (Twentieth Century Fund, 1966), p. 458.

Figure 3 TKTS: Occupation: TKTS Users vs. General Broadway Audience

Age (Figure 4): TKTS patrons are considerably younger. Their median age is nearly 10 years less than that of the typical attendee at a Broadway theatre.

Education (Figure 5): TKTS users are far better educated than Broadway audiences overall, with a far smaller proportion of the former having completed no more than high school and a far higher percentage having attended graduate school.

Income (Figure 6): TKTS patrons had a $1,300 lower median income than that of the overall Broadway audience, with a higher representation in the $5,000–$15,000 range, and smaller numbers in the very low and very high income groups. Median income of TKTS users was $15,799; median income for the total Broadway audience was $17,127.

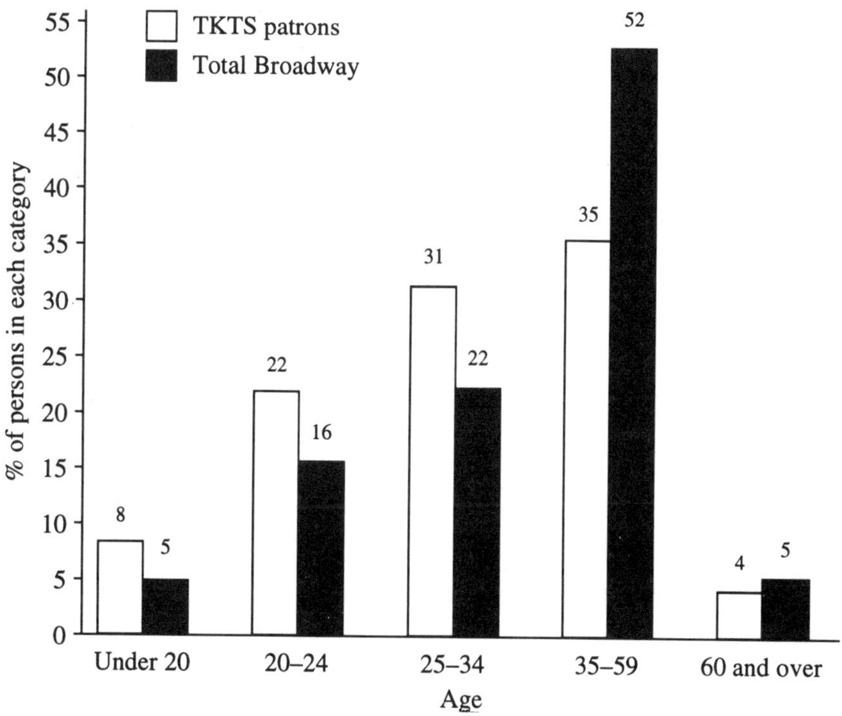

Source: The percent distribution of the total Broadway audience is a composite of *Playbill* and Twentieth Century Fund figures. The percentages for under 20 and over 60 are taken from the Twentieth Century Fund; the 25–34 figure was taken from *Playbill* and multiplied by 16/100 to account for the approximately 4 percent of audience in the under 18 category; the 20–24 figure was taken from *Playbill* and again adjusted to account for 4 percent of the population under 18. The 35–59 figure equals 100 minus the sum of other percentages. (*Playbill* survey, Metromedia, Inc., 1973; Baumol and Bowen, Twentieth Century Fund, 1966, p. 458.) The TKTS audience figures are from the TKTS surveys, average of August 1973 and February and May 1974.

Figure 4 TKTS: Age: TKTS Users vs. General Broadway Audience

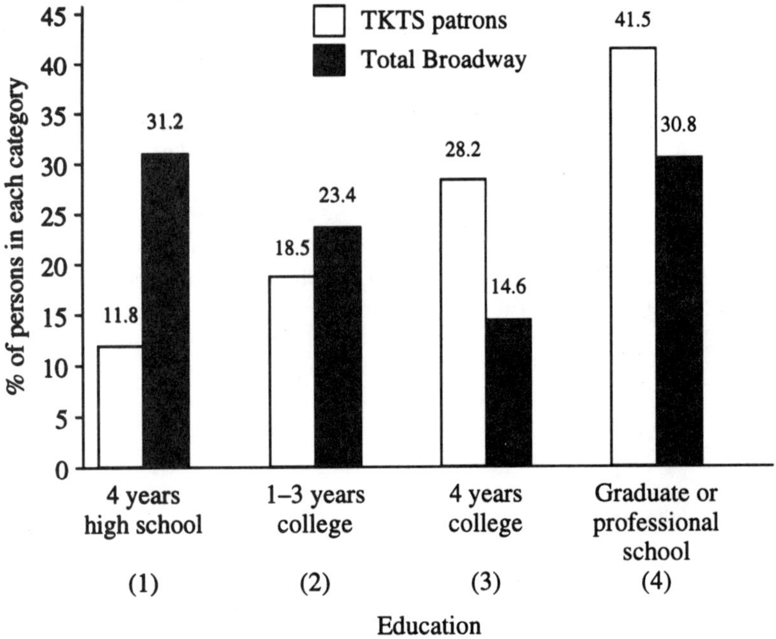

Source: TKTS surveys, average of August 1973 and February and May 1974; Baumol and Bowen (Twentieth Century Fund, 1966), p. 458; *Playbill* survey, Metromedia, Inc., 1973 (Note that the *Playbill* survey does not include a graduate or professional school category. The total Broadway percentage in this category was calculated by splitting the figure given in *Playbill* for four years of college between categories (3) and (4) according to the same ratio as that in the Baumol and Bowen survey).

Figure 5 TKTS: Education: TKTS Users vs. General Broadway Audience

It seems clear that there are differences between the groups of persons who use the TKTS box office and those who do not. The information suggests that TKTS is bringing in new patrons and new revenues, but it is, of course, by no means conclusive. This matter must be investigated directly in terms of the earnings of the theatres themselves, an issue we discuss presently. First, however, we deal with one additional and very important characteristic of the TKTS patron – the issue of impulse buying.

Impulse buying

Besides differing in age, economic, and educational characteristics, one may surmise that the TKTS and non-TKTS users differ in the amount of advance planning they devote to the decision to attend the theatre. While we have no data for non-TKTS users, our impression is that they do very little last-minute purchasing. As many as 60 percent of the TKTS users, however, decide to attend on the day of performance or one day earlier. Well over 80 percent of the TKTS users made their attendance decision no more than a week in advance (Figure 7).

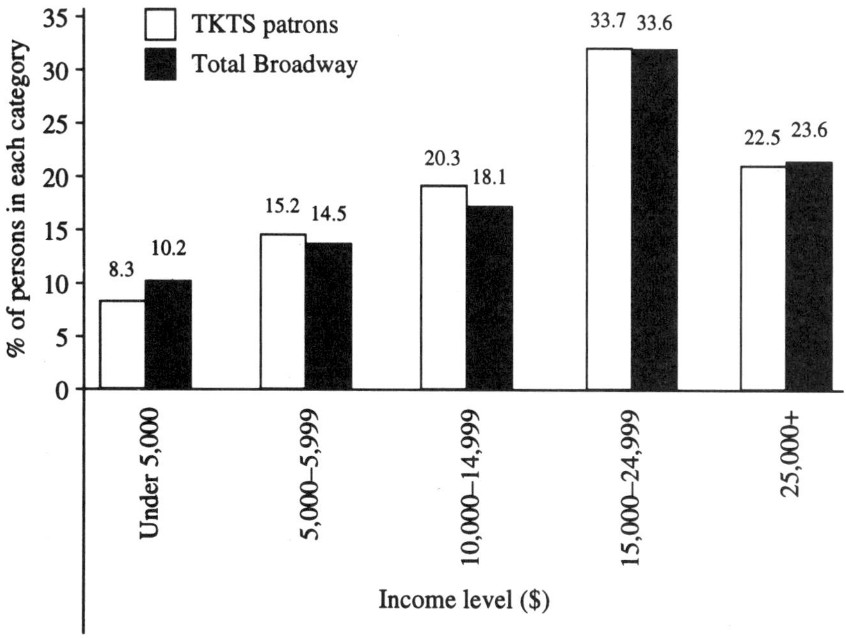

Source: TKTS survey, August 1973 (The percent distribution for TKTS users here is derived from August data only, rather than an average of the three months in which surveys were taken, because it was the only month in which income intervals comparable to those of the *Playbill* survey were used); *Playbill* survey, Metromedia, Inc., 1973.

Figure 6 TKTS: Income: TKTS Users vs. General Broadway Audience

There was a slightly higher percentage of impulse buying in February than in May. We could hypothesize that since the weather was on the mild side (for February), the weather was a factor in the sudden decision to attend. But still, 58 percent of the May sample planned no more than two days in advance, and the figure might well have been even higher had the weather not been wet and unpleasant (for May).

On the other hand, ticket purchases at the TKTS booth, apparently unlike those at the theatre box offices, do not seem to dip to any marked degree in foul weather. It seems to take a convulsion of nature to keep the impulse buyers away. This observation is confirmed by the graph on weekly sales of TKTS (Figure 1) that shows clearly that the Christmas–New Year period was one of very heavy sales and that business continued very good during the winter months of January and February despite the lack of protection from the elements provided to persons waiting to purchase tickets. Any relationship between weather and impulse buying is further weakened by the know-how acquired by the very visible group of TKTS clientele that attends the theatre every week, or which 'goes to see everything now.' People in these categories were at a loss to state when they had made the decision to attend, since ticket buying at the booth had become part of their weekly routine. They take pot luck on what show they see, make their purchases at non-peak times

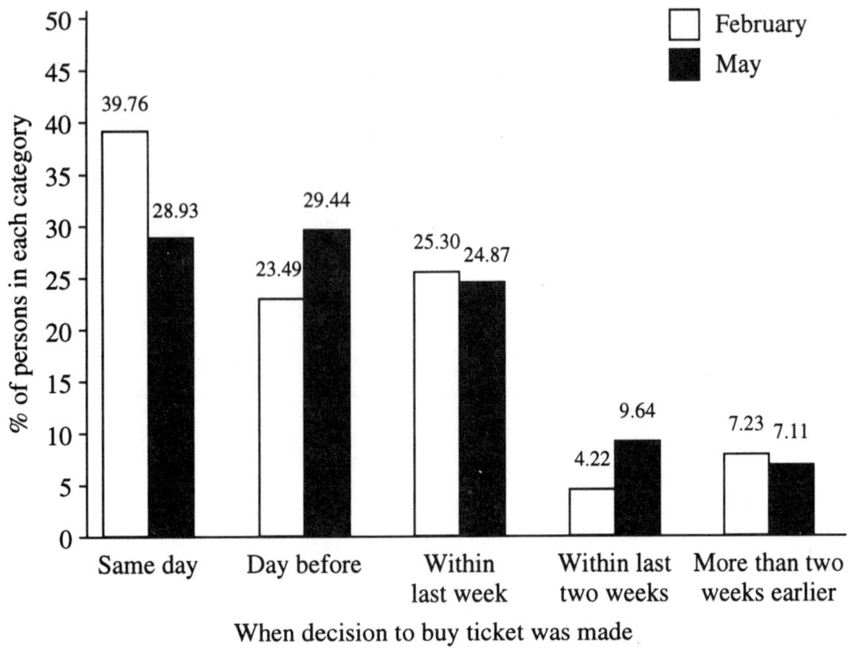

Source: TKTS surveys, February and May 1974.

Figure 7 TKTS: Advance Planning of Ticket Purchases by TKTS Users

(4–5 p.m. and after 7:30 p.m.), knowing that allocations of tickets continue to arrive throughout the afternoon.

The new audience

It seems quite clear from the preceding results that TKTS is contributing to audience size. In order to get a sample of what kind of person was being attracted, we selected all the responses to the TKTS survey where the respondent had indicated that zero months had elapsed since his first use of the TKTS booth, and also replied that he had attended Broadway and off-Broadway performances zero times within the last twelve months. Nine percent of the sample fell into this category.[10]

Table VI gives the profile of these newcomers and, for contrast, of all TKTS users. It is noteworthy that the new attendees exhibit a completely different spread in education, occupation, and income distribution, all in the direction of the middle categories. Fewer of them are high school graduates only, fewer went to graduate or professional school, and significantly fewer are professionals.

*Table VI TKTS: Profile of Newcomers to TKTS**

		All Newcomers to Theatre and TKTS		All TKTS Users (February and May)	
Sex	Male	54.3%		51.4%	
	Female	45.7%		48.7%	
Age	Under 20	2.8		7.0	
	20–24	22.2		19.7	
	25–34	33.3		31.9	
	35–44	19.4		17.6	
	45–59	13.9		18.9	
	60 and over	8.3		4.9	
	Median age		36		30
Marital status	Married	57.6		46.1	
	Single	42.4		53.9	
Children	Median number		1		1
Residence	New York City	2.9		46.8	
	Long Island	8.6		10.5	
	New York State	20.0		7.5	
	New Jersey	14.3		13.2	
	Other states & abroad	54.4		22.0	
Education	Finished high school	14.7		13.1	
	1–3 years college	20.6		16.9	
	4 years college	26.5		29.4	
	Graduate or professional school	38.2		40.7	
	Median category		4 years college		4 years college
Occupation	Professional	20.7		38.3	
	White collar	34.5		30.8	
	Blue collar	6.9		3.3	
	Not employed	37.9		27.6	
Income	Under $7,000	17.7		12.6	
	$7,000–$14,999	41.2		35.0	
	$15,000–$24,999	32.4		27.5	
	$25,000 and over	8.8		24.9	
	Median income		$14,265		$15,500

Note: * Newcomers are defined as those patrons who had not attended Broadway or off-Broadway within the last twelve months.

Source: February and May 1974 surveys at TKTS.

TKTS contributions to theatre

Contributions to audience size and theatre grosses

One of the most critical issues for an evaluation of TKTS is its contribution to audience and to theatrical finances. This obviously cannot be judged directly from the number of tickets sold by the box office or by subsequent payments to the theatres, since there remains the difficult problem of determining what proportion of TKTS patrons would have purchased full-price tickets if the TKTS box office had not been available. While we cannot say definitely whether or not a given patron of TKTS represents a net contribution to audience size, there are various ways in which we can draw convincing inferences.

The first source of evidence is our audience survey at TKTS. We determined that the relevant characteristics of the users of TKTS are very different from those of other theatre patrons, supporting the hypothesis that TKTS is bringing in new categories of theatre patrons as its customers. We reported, for example, that TKTS patrons tend much more than the remainder of the Broadway audience toward the median categories of education, income, etc., and have a substantially lower representation in the extreme end categories.

We were also able to use statistical methods to obtain two direct numerical estimates of TKTS' net effects on the size of total audience and of theatrical earnings during the first year of its operations. These two estimates were calculated by diverse methods on the basis of different data obtained from separate sources. The fact that the two calculations yielded extremely similar results should increase confidence in their reliability.

The first of these estimates utilized data on grosses of individual theatres obtained from *Variety* for ten weeks immediately before and ten weeks immediately after the opening of TKTS. By comparing trends in sales before and after, both for productions using TKTS and those which were not, we were able to infer that a very substantial proportion of TKTS sales represented a *net* contribution to theatre revenues.

The second of our statistical approaches utilized the interview data on the relative frequency of previous attendance by newcomers to TKTS and by those who had used TKTS for some time before their interviews. It was possible to infer from these figures how much TKTS was adding to net frequency of attendance of its users and, hence, to deduce its net revenue contribution. As already noted, the two calculations yielded completely consistent results.

Before describing these two calculations and their results in detail, it is important to indicate why it is so difficult to determine how much TKTS contributed on balance, and why, therefore, such relatively complicated estimation methods had to be employed.

The major complication besetting the use of statistical data on box office grosses is that the availability of TKTS is far from the only influence affecting the revenues of a particular production. Aside from seasonal and other influences that affect the sales of all theatres simultaneously, the gross of a particular theatre is influenced by all sorts of special circumstances – the length of its run up to the date in question, the loss of a popular star, etc. To minimize the effects of special circumstances of individual productions we utilized figures for as many theatres as possible. To allow for seasonal and other common influences we compared trends in grosses of the theatres that made use of TKTS not only with their own past sales trends, but also with those of theatres not using TKTS. An example will illustrate the logic of this procedure. Suppose that in the ten weeks after TKTS opened theatres using TKTS had experienced a 7 percent increase in grosses, but that grosses at other theatres had risen by 5 percent over the same period. Then we would have attributed to TKTS only the 2 percent 'edge' that grosses in TKTS-using theatres had over those in theatres not using TKTS. That is, we would not have ascribed to TKTS anything like the entire 7 percent rise.

The basic difficulty in the use of interview data to estimate TKTS net contribution to audiences and grosses is that hypothetical questions – such as 'Would you have gone to the theatre tonight *if* there were no TKTS box office?' – do not yield reliable information. Interviewees rarely know the answers to such questions themselves and there is a well-known bias in the direction of an answer which the respondent believes will increase his status in the eyes of the interviewer.

Instead, we confined our questions to behavior and actions that had already transpired and on which there was a good chance of getting reasonably accurate reports. For example, those interviewed were asked the number of times they had attended Broadway performances in the preceding year, whether they had usually bought the tickets at theatre box offices, from brokers, etc., and if they ordinarily sat in the orchestra, mezzanine, or balcony.

Box office data and TKTS contributions to revenues

So far we have drawn only the broad inference that TKTS has increased audiences for participating theatres, mostly from the evidence that the composition of the TKTS audience is quite different from that of the Broadway audience generally. This section describes how we arrived at quantitative estimates of this effect and discusses how TKTS data permitted us to estimate net revenue contributed to the theatres. In the following section, interview data will be utilized to determine the amount of audience and revenue TKTS has contributed overall.

The most direct way to test the effect of the TKTS booth on box office and attendance would be to get complete data on receipts and attendance for productions that ran for a reasonable time before participation in the TKTS program and similar data for the period after their entry into the program. This proved unfeasible, however, partly because participation of individual productions is often erratic, and also because the beginning of any run usually involves pre-booked theatre parties whose returns are not normal box office receipts.

Instead, we identified nine productions that entered the program at the very beginning which already had substantial runs before the opening of the TKTS booth. Two were rejected for erratic participation, but detailed records on grosses and TKTS receipts were accumulated for the remaining seven productions for a period of ten weeks prior to the opening of the TKTS booth and ten weeks afterward. Corresponding data were obtained for four productions that did *not* make use of TKTS during this period.

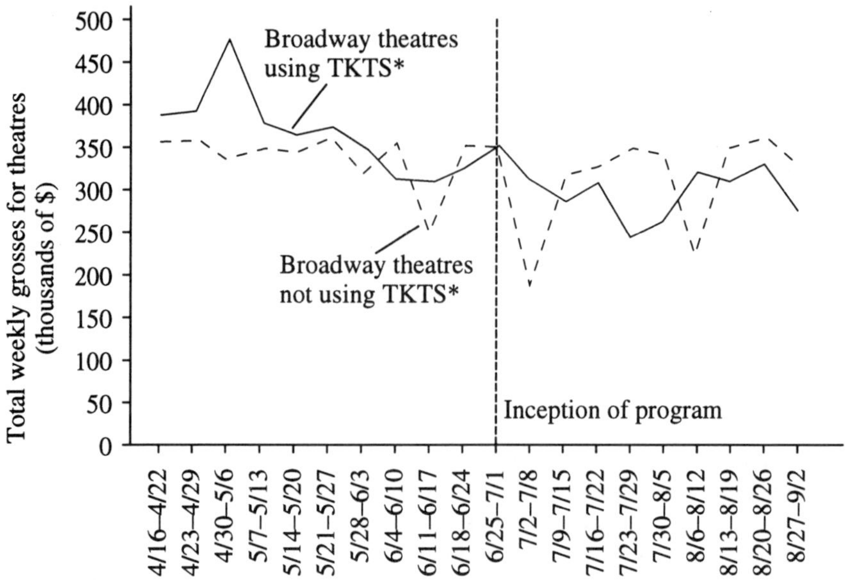

Notes:

* The seven theatres are the Booth, Shubert, Music Box, Broadhurst, Uris, Edison, and O'Neill. (The Edison was closed the week of 6/4–6/10 – *Cope* was in Cleveland. The Uris was closed 7/23–7/29 – *Seesaw* was in St. Louis.)

** The four theatres are the Royale, Atkinson, Imperial, and the Minskoff. (The Minskoff was closed 7/2–7/8 – vacation for *Irene*, and 8/6–8/12 when *Irene* played St. Louis.)

Source: *Variety*.

Figure 8 TKTS: Pre and Post Program Inception Weekly Grosses for Broadway Theatres Using and Not Using TKTS

Figure 8 shows the total actual aggregated gross earnings of all seven participating theatres for ten weeks preceding and ten weeks succeeding the opening of TKTS, and shows the same for the four theatres that had not participated in the TKTS program at its inception.

It is very difficult for the naked eye to draw any conclusion from the graph itself. There are at least three basic problems in disentangling the effect of TKTS on ticket sales:

1. The summer is traditionally a slack time for theatre sales (though not for sales through TKTS – see Figure 1).
2. The trend in grosses prior to and after TKTS is difficult to quantify.
3. The stronger shows tend not to use the booth, so that the data will show high TKTS use in a period of declining sales.

The three problems taken together make it rather difficult to determine what would have happened to the basic box office data had TKTS never opened. But the real issue is not how much the grosses dropped, but whether they dropped by a smaller amount after the availability of TKTS than would have been expected from the seasonal experience of previous years.

A brief summary of the available information will make this clearer. There are eleven shows for which relatively clean data are available, and the data are summarized in Table VII. For of these – shows 8 to 11 in the table – made essentially no use of TKTS. The remaining seven made varying use of the booth. The ratio of the pre-TKTS average weekly gross to the post-TKTS gross was .96 for the non-TKTS shows and .87 for the shows using TKTS – in other words, a much greater decline in the summer for the shows using TKTS. Furthermore, comparison[11] indicates that the individual shows that made extensive use of the booth were by far the weaker shows.

TKTS, of course, is hardly responsible for this weakness, since many of these productions were already in various stages of decline. This can be quantified in a crude way by looking at various sub-periods *prior* to the introduction of TKTS,[12] which show the TKTS-using productions were already in a downtrend *even before* TKTS started since they suffered much more of a decline in the period just before

Table VII TKTS: Data on Broadway Grosses Just Before and Just After Inauguration of TKTS

Play #	A*	B*	C*	D*	E*	F*	G*	H*
1	34,414	29,900	.87	.97	.94	2,763.7	.092	.79
2	106,563	101,657	.95	1.01	1.01	3,363.1	.033	.92
3	22,312	21,161	.95	.83	.71	3,088.5	.146	.81
4	48,600	32,850	.68	.83	.79	3,662.9	.112	.60
5	83,465	66,660	.80	.88	.90	14,047.5	.211	.63
6	23,211	22,609	.97	1.06	1.03	910.7	.040	.93
7	28,075	24,888	.89	.74	.72	3,946.1	.159	.75
8	62,293	64,616	1.04	1.01	1.00			
9	32,510	29,347	.90	.93	.93			
10	106,620	102,104	.96	.97	.96			
11	139,553	132,702	.95	.97	.96			

Note:
*Headings:
A. Average weekly gross (in dollars) 10 weeks before TKTS started.
B. Average weekly gross (in dollars) 10 weeks after TKTS started.
C. Ratio of B to A (B/A).
D. Ratio of average gross in second 5-week period to first 5-week period.
E. Ratio of average gross prior to July 1 in last 4 weeks to first 9 weeks.
F. Average TKTS receipts.
G. Ratio of F over B (F/B).
H. Ratio of B minus F over A (B–F) /A.

Source: The Shubert Organization and Theatre Development Fund.

July 1st than did the non-TKTS shows. The problem is to decide how to extrapolate this decline into the post-July 1st period. What we want to know is if TKTS sales simply substituted for box office sales or were a full net addition to the box office, or, what is most likely, something in between.

There are a variety of ways one can arrive at a rough estimate of this. The actual pattern of relative revenues that was observed is the following:

	Before July 1		After July 1
	1st 5 weeks	2nd 5 weeks	10 weeks of TKTS
TKTS Shows	$1	90¢	83¢
Non-TKTS Shows	$1	97¢	95¢

In other words, for every $1 for TKTS shows in the first 5-week period, 90¢ was grossed in the second 5-week period, and 83¢ in the last 10 weeks. (For non-TKTS shows, the results are much flatter.)

Of the 83¢, roughly 9¢ comes from TKTS and 74¢ from other box office sales. *If* one is willing to make the assumption that the trend observed prior to TKTS would otherwise have continued after July 1, then box office receipts in the last 10 weeks (if TKTS did not exist) would have been 77¢.[13] If one adds to this the slight seasonal decline evident for the non-TKTS shows, this can be reduced to 75¢. In other words, under this assumption, of the 9¢ attributable to TKTS, only between 1¢ and 3¢ would have shown up at the box office anyway. Put another way, *between 67 and 89 percent of TKTS revenues were apparently above and beyond what these shows could have expected.*

As a check on this conclusion we can employ an alternative breakdown using the data for slightly different periods than before (i.e., by using figures corresponding to column E of Table VII):

	Before July 1		After July 1
	9 weeks	4 weeks	10 weeks
TKTS Shows	$1	87¢	84¢
Non-TKTS Shows	$1	96¢	95¢

If, once again, one uses the assumption that the trend observed prior to the opening of TKTS would otherwise have continued after July 1, the estimate of the revenues provided by TKTS becomes higher than before.

Even on the very conservative assumption that the trend evident in the five weeks before July 1 would have slowed down by 50 percent in the subsequent period, then the first estimate implies that somewhere between 30 and 50 percent of TKTS revenues constitutes a net addition to earned income for participating theatres, while the second estimate implies that about 80 percent of the revenues represents such a net addition.

Taking all of these figures into account, one seems justified in estimating that, of the $2 million paid by TKTS to the theatres during its first year of operation, something roughly between $1 million and $1.6 million represented a *net* addition to their grosses. Presently, we will describe a second and independent method that was employed to estimate this amount, using totally different data. The results of this second process, as we will see, turned out to be consistent with the preceding estimates.

The interviews and contribution to audience

First calculation The basic interview data from which we carried out our second estimate of the amount TKTS added to audiences and to grosses were figures on frequency of past attendance and on the length of time they had been using the discount box office. To elicit these data, we asked respondents how many months previously they had first used TKTS, how often they had attended the theatre during the past twelve months, and how often they attended the theatre since their first visit to TKTS. We wanted to compare the rate of ticket purchase by TKTS users since they began using the box office to their purchase rate of the preceding year.

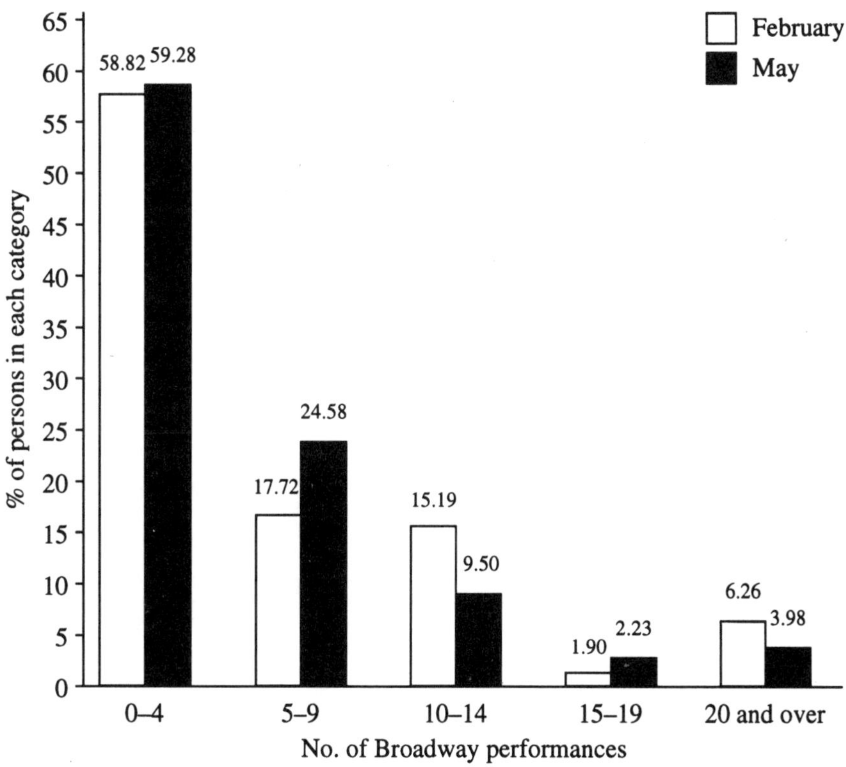

Source: TKTS surveys, February and May 1974.

Figure 9 *TKTS: TKTS Users Who Have Attended Broadway Performances Within the Past Year*

Figure 9 shows the distribution of number of tickets purchased in the preceding year by current TKTS purchasers. It indicates immediately that TKTS must have brought some patrons to the theatre, since almost 60 percent of the TKTS patrons sampled bought no more than 0–4 tickets in the preceding year.

In the August survey, which followed almost immediately the opening of the TKTS booth (in June 1973), 34 percent had not attended any performances on Broadway in the preceding six months, and 84.87 percent were in the 0–4 category.[14] Fewer of the patrons seem to be newcomers to the theatre in the later surveys, but more people seem to be going more frequently, and while about 20 percent in the later surveys attended 5–9 times per year, less than 10 percent had that many attendances in the August survey.[15]

These figures seem to indicate that the booth is getting fewer newcomers, perhaps as many begin to use it more regularly. This interpretation is supported in the data in Figure 10 which selects newcomers to TKTS (defined as having replied that zero months had elapsed since their introduction to the TKTS booth), and shows

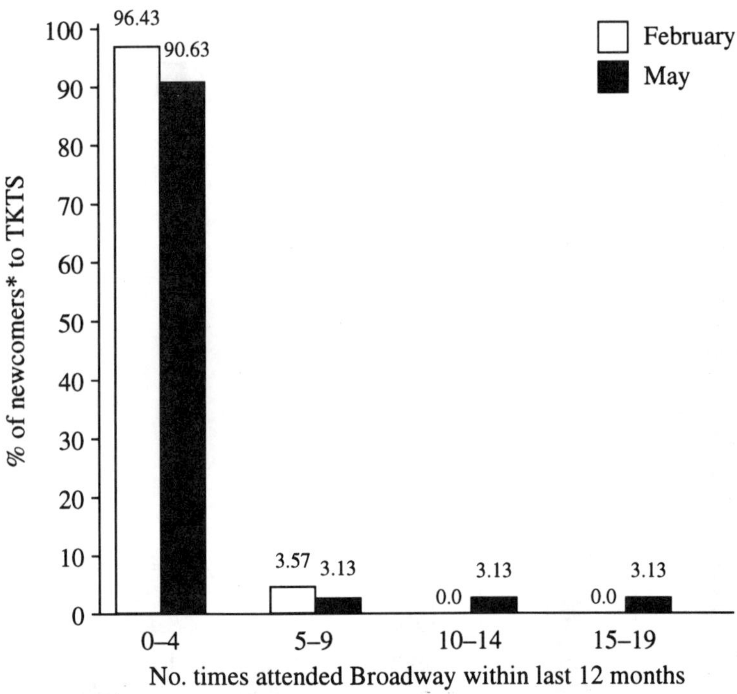

Note: * Newcomers are defined as those TKTS users who answered zero as the number of months that had elapsed since they first used TKTS.

Source: TKTS surveys, February and May 1974.

Figure 10 TKTS: Broadway Attendance Within the Last Twelve Months by Newcomers to TKTS

the frequency of their Broadway attendances. Not more than 10 percent of this group fall outside the 0–4 attendances category![16] Table VIII shows the distribution of TKTS respondents by number of months they had been using the booth. It indicates that nearly 40 percent of the respondents had first used TKTS during the month of the interview, many of them, it may be surmised, on the day they were interviewed. Apparently, at least at that date, TKTS was still selling a very substantial proportion of its tickets to newcomers to the booth.

Table VIII TKTS: Months Elapsed Since TKTS Patrons First Used TKTS

Number Months Elapsed	Percent of Patrons	Number Months Elapsed	Percent of Patrons
0	37.09	6	10.60
1	12.58	7	2.65
2	5.96	8	3.31
3	5.30	9	2.65
4	5.30	10	5.96
5	2.65	11	5.96

Source: TKTS survey, May 1974.

Second calculation We will now estimate the contribution of TKTS to overall ticket sales by comparing seasonal patterns and trends in ticket sales before and after the inauguration of TKTS and will attempt to quantify this contribution.

We can easily proceed from the data in Figures 9 and 10 to an estimate of TKTS overall contribution to audience size. TKTS has been selling tickets at a weekly rate ranging from 6,000 to 14,000 tickets. The actual average weekly sale was 8,668 tickets, and the average during the last six months (after the initial introductory period) was 9,290. This then corresponds to an annual rate of sale of about 483,000 tickets, the figure which would have been realized if that sales rate had held throughout the year. But not all of these represent a net addition to sales.

From the data in Figure 9, we estimate that in May 1974, each TKTS user had attended Broadway performances an average of about 5.4 times during the preceding year.[17] However, from Figure 10, we see that for newcomers to the box office, previous attendance was only 2.9. The current group of users consisted of 37 percent newcomers, while 12.6 percent of them had been introduced to the box office only one month earlier (See Table VIII). Assuming that a rate of 2.9 purchases in the previous year is characteristic of persons when they first get to use the booth, this means that to bring the overall average figure of new entrants and old users to the overall figure of 5.4, there must be a very large increase in attendance once people begin to patronize TKTS. Indeed, that overall figure must be about 11.9 visits to the theatre per year.[18] (This figure becomes plausible after one has met as many persons as we have who report that since they were introduced to TKTS, they have begun to attend the theatre almost weekly.)

From these data we summarize that the advent of TKTS increased the attendance of its patrons in a ratio something on the order of 11.9 to 2.9 – about four to one. In other words, of total TKTS sales only approximately 25 percent represent attendance that would have occurred even in the absence of the TKTS booth. In sum, it can be estimated that the 450,000 tickets sold by TKTS represent a net increase in attendance of approximately 340,000 attendees.

An alternative estimate of net revenue contribution

From the net audience contribution figure, we can move on to attempt a second and independent estimate of the TKTS box office net contribution of revenue to the theatre. For this purpose we need to know the prices of the tickets sold by TKTS and the prices of tickets that might otherwise have been sold to TKTS users from other channels. These figures are essential and must be handled with care if serious pitfalls are to be avoided. For example, the replacement of a ticket sale through other channels by a sale through TKTS does not necessarily produce a 50 percent reduction in revenues to the theatre. Indeed, if the buyer would otherwise have bought a balcony seat at $5.00 and now buys an orchestra ticket whose face value is $12.00, there will have been a dollar increase in revenues to the theatre as a result of the switch to the discount box office.

The typical prices of tickets sold by the discount box office is easily obtained from TKTS records: tickets sold by TKTS had an average face value of $9.08 per ticket. Thus at a 50 percent reduction in price, the average value of a ticket was $4.54. To derive an estimate of the price the individuals in our sample might have

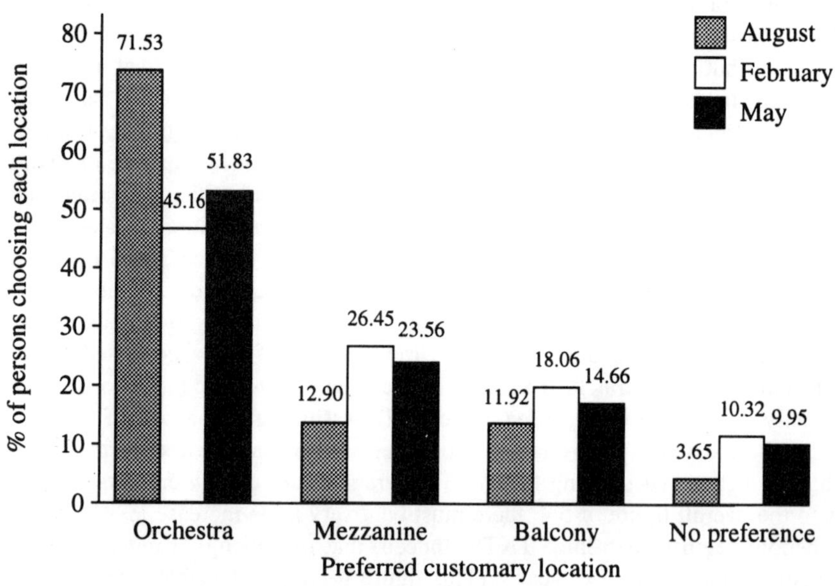

Source: TKTS surveys, August 1973, February and May 1974.

Figure 11 TKTS: Usual Non-TKTS Seat Locations of TKTS Patrons

paid had they not used TKTS, they were asked where they had normally sat in the previous season. The results are reported in Figure 11.

Using these data and the actual ticket prices for the productions that utilized TKTS, it was estimated[19] that the average ticket price that would have been paid by patrons of TKTS if they had bought full-price tickets would have been $7.00. In other words, TKTS users, on the average, buy better seats at TKTS than they would have bought otherwise, but this type of upgrading alone would only partially offset the 50 percent discount.

We can now quickly complete our second calculation of TKTS net contribution to theatre revenues by drawing together the price and attendance calculations. We have estimated that use of TKTS turns a theatregoer who typically attends the theatre 2.9 times a year at an average price of $7.00 per ticket into one who attends 11.9 times a year at an average ticket price of $4.50 for the theatre.[20]

This means that for every $53.55 (= $4.50 × 11.9) in revenue contributed by TKTS, a total of $20.30 (= $7.00 × 2.9) in revenue is lost to the theatre in potential purchases through other channels. In sum, every dollar in gross contribution to the theatre by TKTS represents a net contribution of

$$\frac{(\$4.50 \times 11.9) - (\$7.00 \times 2.9)}{\$4.50 \times 11.9} = \$0.62.$$

This leads us to the estimate that of the $2 million in gross box office contribution of TKTS in its first year of operation, a total of some $1.24 million represents a net addition to theatre revenues. It should be noted how closely this figure corresponds to our earlier and independently derived statistical estimate of this same figure.[21]

Competition with other marketing agencies

Inevitably, TKTS must compete at least to a minor degree with other sources of ticket supply, for we have seen that TKTS did produce some net reduction in sales by other channels. One can then ask where they would otherwise have taken place. Table IX indicates where respondents' last three sets of tickets bought from other agencies than TKTS were purchased. It will be noted that the bulk of competition (73 percent) was with theatre box offices (including mail orders), while less than 3 percent of the responses indicated that users had previously patronized ticket brokers and 10 percent reported previous use of Ticketron. Obviously, the typical user of TKTS is not prone to use relatively expensive ticket sources.

Purchase of tickets that were not customer's first choice

One way in which TKTS contributes to theatrical revenues is by inducing customers to purchase tickets to a substitute production if there are no tickets available to the one they might most have wanted to see. Many patrons commented that they had no first choice, but at most a list of acceptable shows. Out-of-towners, in particular, often asked the interviewers which of the shows they would recommend, and bought what was available.

In the written responses in our questionnaires, close to three out of four people indicated that they had substituted another show when their first choice was not

Table IX TKTS: Ticket Agencies Previously Used by TKTS Patrons

	August	February	May	Total	
	Number of Responses*				
	431	153	185	#	%
Box office	227	97	115	439	65.2
Ticketron	50	11	8	69	10.2
Mail order	28	12	14	54	8.0
Student discount	12	7	n.a.	19	2.8
Department store	4	3	–	7	1.0
Ticket broker	14	4	1	19	2.8
Two-fer	18	9	4	31	4.6
Other	16	10	9	35	5.2
				673	100.0

Note: * Respondents could check more than one category.

Source: August 1973, February and May 1974 surveys at TKTS.

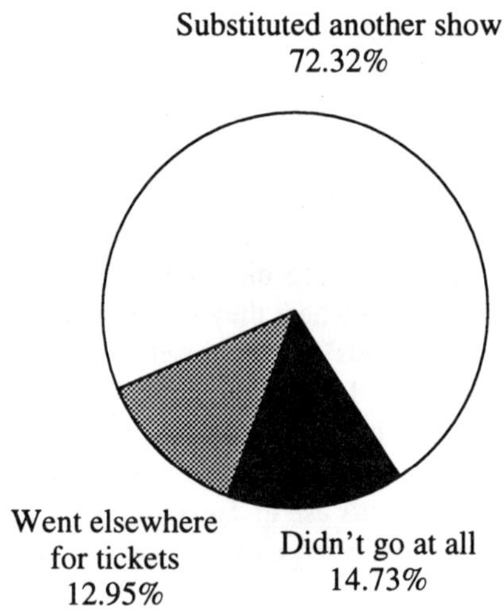

Source: TKTS surveys, average of August 1973, February and May 1974.

Figure 12 TKTS: Actions of TKTS Patrons for Whom First Choice Was Not Available

available. (See Figure 12.) This suggests another way in which TKTS has contributed to ticket sales – by making it easier for prospective theatregoers to get a second-choice ticket when no tickets are available to their first-choice performance.

Proposals for modifications of TKTS

Obviously, no experimental and innovative undertaking can be expected to emerge full blown in its ideal state, although, from the comments we have had, it would seem that TKTS came closer than most. Some modifications in its operation were suggested by experience, and others are changes worth considering but which require analysis and experimentation before their merits can be evaluated.

Modifications undertaken

A year after the opening of TKTS, it strikes one as naive that those who planned it seem to have had in mind the unhurried ambience of a sparsely patronized Broadway ticket booth. They made no arrangements for the crowding that accompanies the sale of 1,500 tickets in two hours or the queues that reach from one end of Duffy Square to the other in all kinds of weather. While some steps have been taken to improve organization, the problem has not been solved. About an hour before the booth opens, two lines leading to the end windows form. If business is heavy, three or four windows will be opened, and there is a disorganized rush to the new stations that is unfair to those who have waited their turns.

One of their first modifications dictated by experience was the discontinuation of the telephone information service that reported on ticket availability. Aside from the staff time it took, the information provided was extremely unreliable as tickets are often received and sold out at any hour of the afternoon. In addition, this amenity seemed to offer direct competition with the regular box offices. For all these reasons, TKTS decided instead to provide a taped telephone message, recorded by Broadway personalities, that states the ground rules of the box office and provides detailed information on its services.

Second, performances for which tickets were available had been posted on one board just a few feet above ground level where wooden signs could easily be attached and removed as tickets became available or sold out. This caused confusion as people crowded around the one board, and those at the front of the line could not see it to make their final decisions before arriving at the window. There are now two boards, one on either side of the booth, and mounted much higher so that people entering the window area from queues on either side file by and have a good view of all available productions.

The booth also found it expedient to print a small brochure with a map of the Broadway area that patrons can consult and take away.

Improved amenities for ticket purchasers

We invited and received some comments from respondents to our questionnaire, though only about 9 percent of them chose to volunteer their opinions. Almost half were unqualified praises. Many of the others suggested a better organization of the queueing process, more amenities (such as extended hours, a wider selection of seats, and a 'number' system for those in the queue), and a better supply of tickets. TKTS, of course, has no control over the number of tickets consigned to the booth or which shows choose to participate.

The merits of instituting any change that increases the ease of ticket purchases by reducing the waiting time for buyers, by increasing their comfort, and by bringing box office outlets closer to where they live, are not as clearcut as they may appear at first. Any such suggestion must be considered with two reservations: first, such an 'improvement' may not be worth the cost involved, and second, TKTS may then begin to compete with standard distribution outlets and cut seriously into sales of theatre tickets at full price.

It should be remembered that it is not the purpose of TKTS to produce an overall decrease in ticket prices. Indeed, the fact that ticket prices over the years have kept up neither with theatrical costs nor with the per capita income of the general public suggests that such an *overall* reduction may be inappropriate. Rather the purpose of TKTS is to bring to the theatre an audience that it may once have had, one composed of people who are willing to buy at the last minute, who are interested in productions other than the 'smash hits', and who are willing to exchange some waiting time and some lack of amenities for a bargain in attendance.

It has been suggested that TKTS might stimulate sales by taking orders by telephone, particularly on the basis of credit cards or by keeping special accounts in which customers could deposit small amounts against which telephone purchases would be debited. There is undoubtedly virtue in such a proposal, but one may well question whether it is appropriate for a facility that specializes in discounted tickets for last-minute sale. Probably it would be better for the theatrical community to organize such an enterprise as a second and independent entity, one whose prime attractive feature is customer convenience rather than low prices.

Attitudes toward TKTS[22]

Users of TKTS generally seemed enthusiastic in their attitude toward the institution even though a few of them felt that some details of its operation might be improved. Some theatre owners, producers, and box office treasurers are, however, quite unhappy about the establishment of the discount box office. They feel that the booth is attracting business away from the individual box offices. They are particularly disturbed at the number of inquiries received at their box offices asking whether tickets to the production at their theatres are available at TKTS. While in the past they have received similar questions about their participation in other discount programs such as the student rush and two-fers, it was their impression that the number of such inquiries had risen since the establishment of TKTS.

They feel also that while the individual producer nominally has freedom of choice in deciding whether or not to use the booth, the producer of a marginal show in fact does not have that luxury if his competitors sell tickets at TKTS, for potential patrons of productions with many unsold seats naturally favor a production whose tickets are more economical. Most troublesome to those who hold this viewpoint is the possibility that more and more regular patrons of the theatre box offices will learn that they can get to see almost any show at half price merely by waiting a few weeks until it is carried by TKTS. At that point they feel the half-price sale will become the normal transaction, with purchases at full price the rare exception, a situation from which only the smash hit will be able to protect itself.

On the other side, it has to be pointed out that the evidence so far strongly suggests that TKTS has contributed many more customers to the theatre than the number it has attracted away from full-price channels, and that the difference has been sufficiently large to bring in a substantial net contribution to the revenues of the theatre. The presence of TKTS has not prevented the summer of 1974 on Broadway from being relatively prosperous despite the unfortunate state of the nation's economy. It has not deterred an unusually high number of bookings of new productions for the 1974–75 season which are reported to exceed those in any of the preceding five years.

For the longer run, one must question whether an increasing number of full-price ticket buyers will be willing to queue in the unprotected lines before the TKTS booth or whether they will be willing to leave the determination of the play they will see until the actual day of the performance when they discover whether their first choice is available at the booth. As we have seen, users of the booth have included virtually no users of ticket broker services.

It seems that those who want prime locations, quick service, credit privileges, and certainty in their plans are not promising converts to TKTS. Perhaps the best way for the industry to retain its purchasers of full-price tickets is to improve services to these patrons still further, extending the use of credit cards, telephone orders, and a central switchboard for the purpose.[23] Such innovations should preserve most of the theatre's full-price ticket customers and perhaps even attract some others.

Certainly, with theatre seats often going more than 40 percent unsold and with the number of unsold tickets still exceeding manyfold those that are purchased through TKTS, the suppression of an institution specializing in the sale of tickets that would otherwise go unsold is a highly questionable proposal.

Publicity

The same theatre people with whom we discussed TKTS were uniformly critical on only one attribute of the operations: its advertising practices. They all objected strongly to billboards at airports and railroad stations which were in their view almost certain to attract to the booth the out-of-town visitors who are natural patrons of the ticket brokers and theatre box offices. They were particularly appalled at radio spots that reportedly invited ticket buyers to 'beat the system' by buying tickets at half price at TKTS, although no advertising copy to this effect has been issued by TDF. The discontent on this issue, whether or not it is justified, is sufficiently vocal to warrant a re-examination of this portion of the public information program.

A small number of these critics of TKTS has also argued that the booth should be relocated to take it out of the theatrical district where the purchasers can conveniently stroll from TKTS to the theatre. This suggestion is obviously intended primarily to undermine the operations of TKTS altogether and its discussion is therefore implicit in our comments on the criticism of the institution *per se* by a segment of the theatre industry.

The opening of additional TKTS booths

As already indicated, the patrons of TKTS come from a wide variety of areas (see Table V). This, the high volume, and long queues at the 47th Street ticket booth suggest that it might be desirable for TKTS to open some branch offices. However, even if this proves desirable in terms of prospective costs and benefits, thought must be given to the strategy of location of new box offices. A TKTS office in Brooklyn or the Bronx, or on a university campus, might clearly be desirable in terms of TKTS' objectives if there is potential volume to justify the undertaking. However, it may be more realistic financially to open one or more branches in areas where a larger number of customers can be found. If this area is somewhat further from the theatres' box offices than the present ticket booth, it might well minimize any incremental competition with other ticket distribution channels.

Variations in ticket discounts

TKTS sells all tickets at a 50 percent discount from face value, whether demand for the production is moderately high or low, whether the date of performance is at the height of the season or in one of its traditional doldrums, or whether the time of performance is Saturday evening when demand is at its maximum or Tuesday, Wednesday, or Thursday evenings when customers are at their scarcest. It is consequently to be expected that there will be sharp oscillations in TKTS volume, at least within the week, and great differences in its sales from production to production.

Table X recapitulates some material that has been discussed earlier, reporting how TKTS volume varied by time of performance. It shows average sales for the months of July 1973 through April 1974 by time of performance, contrasted with an independent sample of patterns of number of unsold seats by time of performance. In the Broadway theatre overall, according to this sample, the number of unsold seats on Tuesday, Wednesday, and Thursday evenings exceeds by a factor of

Table X TKTS: Broadway Ticket Volume by Performance Time and Patterns of Unsold Seats

Time of Performance	Average Number of Tickets Sold by TKTS[a]	Relative Number of Unsold Tickets to Number Unsold on Friday[b]
Monday evening	488.5	3.8
Tuesday evening	639.4	4.0
Wednesday matinee	765.6	2.2
Wednesday evening	799.6	4.1
Thursday evening	707.4	4.1
Friday evening	895.1	1.0
Saturday matinee	684.0	1.1
Saturday evening	917.1	1.1
Sunday matinee	482.6	*

Note: * There were no Sunday performances in 1970.

Source:

a. TKTS records – Sample taken from July 1973 to April 1974, first week of each of ten months.

b. 1970 Broadway sample – New York Cultural Council Report, *Study of the New York Theatre*, Part II, January 1972, p. 27 (Sample of five productions, October 19–31, 1970).

four the number unsold for Friday and Saturday performances (last column of the table). Comparatively, TKTS sells slightly more tickets on Friday evenings than it does on Tuesday, Wednesday, and Thursday evenings; in other words, it does little to reduce the relative number of unsold tickets in the earlier part of the week.

This suggests that an unvarying 50 percent price reduction for all tickets is not what one would expect to emerge in a completely free market, which might very well call for smaller price reductions for very popular shows and performance times and, very likely, a greater reduction for those whose demand is comparatively small.

On the other hand, the simplicity of the straight 50 percent discount that is currently offered has virtues both from the point of view of administrative cost and comprehensibility of publicity. Perhaps it may be desirable to experiment with some simple variations in discounts, for instance a 40 percent discount on matinees and Friday and Saturday evenings, and a 55 or 60 percent discount on other evenings. Special unannounced bargains might be offered on certain shows if the producer requests such a service. To provide useful information and draw reasonable inferences about still other alternatives in pricing and discount policy, such an experiment requires careful planning to separate out the influence of the price change from other fortuitous influences.

Notes

1. At a central box office the potential purchaser sees the complete selection available, so if there are no tickets for the performance of his first choice, he can select an alternative.
2. The results of this study are described in a report by Theatre Development Fund, 'Survey of Times Square Theatre Centre' (mimeographed), New York, September 1973. Many of the findings are reproduced in this report for comparison with this more recent study.
3. This compares with a total gross of the Broadway theatre for 1973–74 of some $46 million. (Figure supplied by the League of New York Theatres and Producers.)
4. Following *Variety's* usage, a 'sellout' was defined as equalling the estimated capacity gross for that week.
5. The last row of the table, the upper and lower decile, calls for a word of explanation. These are measures of the representativeness of the average figures given in the second row of the table indicating whether the situation is very close to or varies widely from that indicated by the average. Thus, the lower decile tells us how low availability is likely to go after freakish cases have been removed by eliminating the bottom 10 percent of the figures. For example, we see that on the average on Tuesday nights, 47 percent of the shows running have had tickets at TKTS and that 'normally' TKTS offered no less than 23.5 percent of the Broadway shows running. Similarly, the upper decile figure represents an upper limit to the 'normal' range of availability. The 1st figure in the second column of Table III tells us that no more than 66.7 percent of the Broadway shows running offered Tuesday evening tickets through TKTS.
6. See New York City Cultural Council, *Study of the New York Theatre, Basic Report*, New York, 1972, pp. 26–28. The number of performances with over 100 unsold tickets (out of a sample of 18 for each performance time) was Tuesday, Wednesday, and Thursday evening, 18 each; Wednesday matinee, 14; Friday evening, 15; Saturday matinee, 11; Saturday evening, 10. That is, on Saturday evenings, at 10 of the 18 performances examined, more than 100 seats were empty.
7. In this table we used medians rather than averages. For example, *median* education is that educational level such that no more than 50 percent of the sample falls below it and no more than 50 percent above it. Thus, the median education level for the February sample was 'completion of college', which means that less than 50 percent of these persons had gone on to graduate school, but less than 50 percent of the sample had failed to complete college. Statisticians often prefer medians to averages because the former are unaffected by exceptionally high or low values that can pull an average up or down substantially. It was not possible for us to calculate an average

educational attainment figure as our data were not expressed in numerical terms (years of education completed).

8. See W. J. Baumol and W. G. Bowen, *Performing Arts: The Economic Dilemma*, New York, 1966, especially pp. 458–9.
9. One imperfection of the comparisons is this section results from the inclusion of some off-Broadway and Lincoln Center patrons in the TKTS figures. However, the bulk of the users of TKTS bought tickets for Broadway productions, as shown in Figure 1.
10. We would like to emphasize that this is a minimal estimate of the audience new to Broadway, since quite a few respondents replied to these questions with a dash rather than writing a zero. For this purpose, those ambiguous replies were rejected, leaving an absolutely certain 9 percent as our conservative estimate of the proportion of new attendees. This figure represents new attendees to any form of New York theatre, and is therefore naturally weighted heavily toward out-of-town visitors. The group represents less than a quarter of the *new users* of the TKTS booth, many of whom *had* previously attended Broadway and off-Broadway performances. To assure ourselves that this figure did not significantly affect the over-all estimate of TKTS contribution to total box office, we recalculated it on the extremely conservative assumption that absolutely none of the out-of-town users of the booth (even those from Connecticut or New Jersey) would become repeat visitors of the theatre. This extreme assumption naturally affected the result somewhat, but left the overall results entirely within the range that is given later in the text.
11. Compare columns F or G with column C in Table VII.
12. This is done in columns D and E of Table VII, which split the pre-TKTS in two ways. The relevant averages of all shows are: 7 TKTS Shows–column D .90, column E .87; 4 Non-TKTS Shows, column D .97, column E .96.
13. This assumes a steady 10 percent loss in sales every five weeks so that in the first five week period after July 1 $1 in sales would have declined to 81¢ and in the next five week period to 74¢. The average of 81¢ and 74¢ is 77¢, the figure given in the text. If a steady *absolute* loss had been extrapolated instead, the results would have been even more of a net contribution by TKTS.
14. Survey of Times Square Theatre Centre, *op. cit.*, Table VI, p. 9.
15. This indicates why our calculations in this and the following sections are based on the May 1974 figures. These represent the box office after nearly a year of operation when it can be assumed to have achieved an approximation to a longer-run pattern of operations.
16. Appendix B–5 and B–6 give the percentage of patrons who have attended off-Broadway and Lincoln Center performances in the past year. The average number of attendances for all patrons was 5.46 for August 1973, 9.05 for February 1974, and 7.7 for May 1974, probably reflecting the influx of summer visitors.
17. This is simply a weighted average of the numbers given in the 'May' bars in Figure 9, with the last figure assumed to be centered at 26 times per year.
18. For this calculation we used the following formula: Let P_0 be the proportion of new box office users, P_1 the proportion who have been using it one month, etc. Let X be the average attendance rate of persons after they become TKTS patrons. With 2.9 being the pre-TKTS attendance rate of this group, and 5.5 the average rate for the group, we must have:

$$P_0\,(12/12)\,(2.9) + P_1\,[(11/12)(2.9) + 1/12\,X] + P_2\,[(10/12)\,(2.9) + 2/12\,X] + \ldots\ldots + P_{11}\,[(1/12)(2.9) + 11/12\,X] = 5.4$$

This states that newcomers' past year's attendance was entirely at the rate 2.9, that one-month users of the box office spent 11 months at a rate 2.9 and one month at the rate X, etc. The experience of the entire group must then average out to the overall attendance rate of 5.4. The solution of the preceding equation is:

$$X = 11.9.$$

19. This is a straightforward weighted average of ticket prices reported in *The New York Times*, with the prices weighted by the attendance patterns reported in Figure 11 and by reports on midweek vs. end of week attendance patterns of TKTS users.
20. The $4.50 average figure proceeds on the very conservative assumption that no TKTS user ever buys a full-price ticket once he makes his first discount ticket purchase.
21. Note again that the two estimates were derived using completely independent data sources. The first calculation was based on figures on grosses for eleven theatres taken from *Variety*, while the second was obtained from the box office survey. We had no idea in advance what either calculation would show or how the results would compare with one another. As usual, there was a

tense moment as the second result was about to emerge from the calculation process. We also carried out still a third estimate based on other figures from our interviews. These led to a range of values for the net contribution of TKTS ranging between $1.1 million and $1.7 million, also perfectly consistent with the other two estimates.

22. This section is based on interviews and a meeting with a number of treasurers with widely varying opinions.
23. A central box office which would sell tickets to all productions at full price and at a convenient location has been suggested frequently for at least half a century. For several years an approximation to a central ticket booth was operated at Shubert Alley, apparently with mixed results, though some productions seem to have benefitted from it. In any event it seems to have had little publicity and to have served only a limited number of theatres. It seems never to have been possible to get all the theatre owners and producers to participate even in a full-price central box office.

Appendix A: Survey methodology and questionnaires

In the February and May surveys, ticket buying for all nine weekly performances was surveyed, although we found it more convenient to spread the work over a two-week period. One questionnaire was distributed while patrons were waiting to get to the ticket window, and a much shorter one was administered to those who had made purchases. Copies of both questionnaires are reproduced (A–1 and A–2).

The surveys were conducted at various hours of the day from 11:30 a.m. – half an hour before the box office opens – until 5:00 p.m. It was considered futile to try to get people to answer rather lengthy questionnaires after that hour, as after-work purchasers are usually in a rush to buy tickets and have dinner before curtain time. The staggered time meant that we had respondents who waited up to an hour in line and others who just stepped up to the box office and made their purchase (see A–3 for a schedule of the survey times).

Circumstances varied widely depending on the day of week and hour of survey. It was not possible to get a large number of responses on Monday as most of the theatres are dark and very few tickets are sold. Tuesday is also very slow, and we made up the number at other performances that are more popular. We felt this did not seriously bias the results, as general attendance is also much lower on those days.

Before the box office opened, there was always (except Monday) a long queue, and on days when we arrived before 3:00 p.m. our daily quota was reached soon after ticket sales began. When we arrived about 4:00 p.m., however, there was usually a rather short waiting line, and it took at least twice as long to get the required responses.

Pencils and questionnaires were handed out on clipboards to the sample selected. As people tended to stand in groups and socialize rather than wait in an orderly line, we did the best we could to select an unbiased sample. When there were many persons waiting for the booth to open, we tried to choose every fifth person. When the line was shorter, we took every third person. On Mondays and Tuesdays, and sometimes Sunday afternoons, when customers were scarce, we took anyone who came to the window, though always making sure that the respondents were not acquainted. If anyone refused to fill out the questionnaire, we gave it to the person immediately behind.

A word should be said here about the general conditions. The weather was never extremely cold nor extremely hot, but was often quite windy and on two days it rained heavily. The people in the queue would often ask on whose behalf the survey was being conducted, and almost invariably agreed to cooperate when they learned it was for the TKTS booth, usually with some enthusiastic comments. As the queue is not protected from the weather except when it is actually a few steps away from the ticket windows, some questionnaires were filled out in pouring rainstorms and were barely legible. While a fair number of responses had to be rejected for various reasons, the majority were filled in carefully, and we did not lose a single clipboard or pencil.

Table A–1 TKTS Entry Questionnaire

To improve the quality of TKTS service, we would greatly appreciate it if you would fill out this questionnaire. Please check the appropriate response or fill in the blanks.

Date__________ Time__________

1. __Male
   __Female

2. __Married
   __Unmarried

3. Age
   __Under 20
   __20–24
   __25–34
   __35–44
   __45–59
   __60 or over

4. Number of children__

5. Education
   __Currently a student
   __Finished high school
   __Some college
   __Finished college
   __Graduate or professional school

6. Family income. What income category do you fall into?
   __Under $7,000
   __$7,000–14,999
   __$15,000–24,999
   __$25,000 or over

7. Occupation____________________________

8. Where do you live?
   __Manhattan
   __Other boroughs
   __Long Island
   __Rest of NY State
   __New Jersey
   __Other states
   __Other countries

9. How did you hear about TKTS?
   __Newspaper
   __Radio: station name____
   __Television channel no.____
   __Subway billboard
   __Bus poster
   __Railway poster
   __Friend or relative
   __Teacher
   __Noticed booth
   __Other__________
   ____

10. When did you first use the Times Square Ticket booth? __months ago

11. How many performances have you attended on Broadway during the past year?__

12. How many performances have you attended off-Broadway during the past year?__

13. Have you ever attended an off-off-Broadway production?
    __Yes
    __No

14. If yes, how many in the past year?__

15. How many performances (all types) have you attended at Lincoln Center during the past year?__

16. What seat location have you customarily bought during the past year?
    __Orchestra
    __Mezzanine
    __Balcony
    __No preference

17. Where did you purchase your last three sets of tickets? (check if applicable)
    __Box office
    __Ticketron
    __Mail order
    __Student discount
    __Dept. store
    __Ticket broker
    __Two-fer
    __Other

18. Do you order your tickets in advance?
    __Usually
    __Occasionally
    __Rarely

19. If you wanted to purchase tickets for an off-off-Broadway production at less than box office prices, how would you go about it?
    ____
    ____

20. When did you make the decision to attend the theatre today?
    __Today
    __Yesterday
    __Within the last week
    __Within the last two weeks
    __More than two weeks ago

21. If you are unable to get tickets to the play you want, will you:
    __Substitute a different show
    __Get tickets elsewhere. Please specify:
    ____
    __Not go at all

22. Are you on the TDF mailing list?
    __Yes
    __No

If you have any comments or suggestions to make concerning the TKTS operation, please feel free to use the space below or over. Thank you.

Table A–2 TKTS Exit Questionnaire

The TKTS booth is experimental. To improve the services, we would like to know who our customers are and how they feel about it. All information is confidential. Please check the appropriate response or fill in the blank.

1. What is the name of the show for which you just bought tickets?

   ____

2. Which of the following choices was this:
   __The show you had in mind when you first set out for the Times Square Theatre Centre box office
   __First alternative choice
   __Second alternative choice
   __Third alternative choice

3. How many tickets did you buy?__

4. What did you pay for each ticket (including service charge)?___

5. What location in the theatre did you purchase tickets for?
   __Orchestra
   __Mezzanine
   __Balcony
   __Not applicable

6. If this was *not* your first choice of location, which did you first ask for?
   __Orchestra
   __Mezzanine
   __Balcony
   __Other

7. How long did you stand in line to purchase your tickets? __minutes

Table A–3 Schedule of Surveys – February and May 1974

Performance	Date	Number of Usable Responses: Entry Questionnaires	Number of Usable Responses: Exit Questionnaires	Time
Sunday matinee	February 24	18	14	2:20 pm
Saturday evening	March 2	24	20	3:30 pm
Saturday matinee	March 2	22	20	12 noon
Friday evening	February 22	21	20	3:00 pm
Thursday evening	February 21	19	20	4:00 pm
Wednesday evening	February 20	31	25	3:00 pm
Wednesday matinee	February 20	26	24	11:30 am
Tuesday evening	February 26	4	11	4:30 pm
Monday evening	February 25	10	4	2:45 pm
Total		175	158	
Sunday matinee	May 12	22	19	11:40 am
Saturday evening	May 4	29	30	3:00 pm
Saturday matinee	May 4	30	30	12 noon
Friday evening	May 3	29	19	2:30 pm
Thursday evening	May 2	19	19	3:45 pm
Wednesday evening	May 11	20	21	3:00 pm
Wednesday matinee	May 1	30	31	11:30 am
Tuesday evening	May 14	8	30	3:00 pm
Monday evening	May 13	13	7	3:00 pm
Total		200	206	

Appendix B: Information on TKTS users

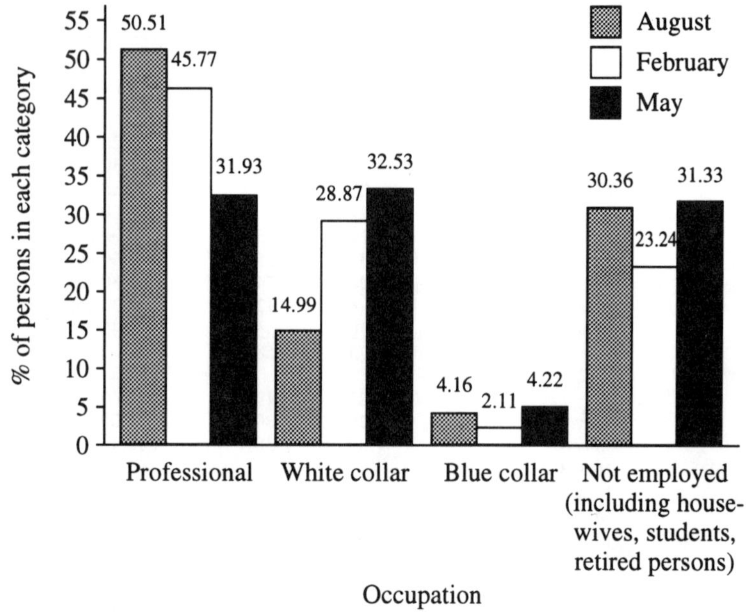

Source: TKTS surveys. Figure 3 of this report uses average of these three surveys.

Figure B–1 Occupations of TKTS Users – Three Surveys: August 1973, February and May 1974

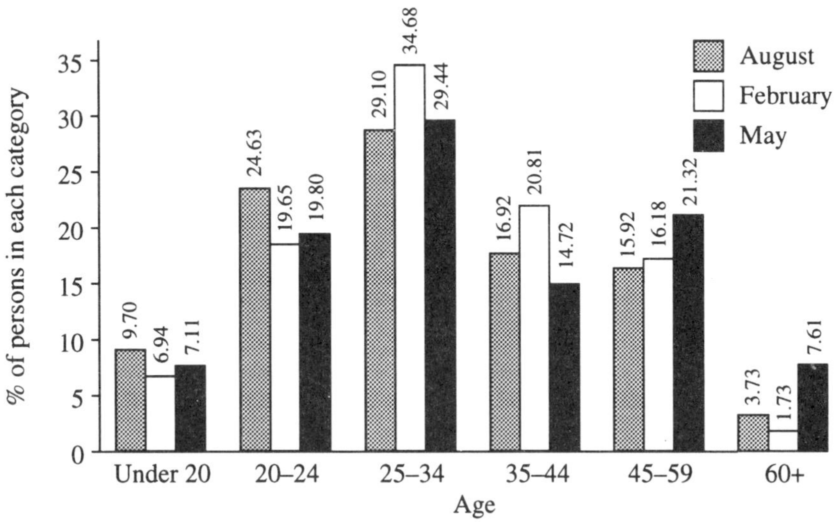

Source: TKTS surveys. Figure 4 in this report uses average of these three surveys.

Figure B–2 Age Composition of TKTS Users – Three Surveys: August 1973, February and May 1974

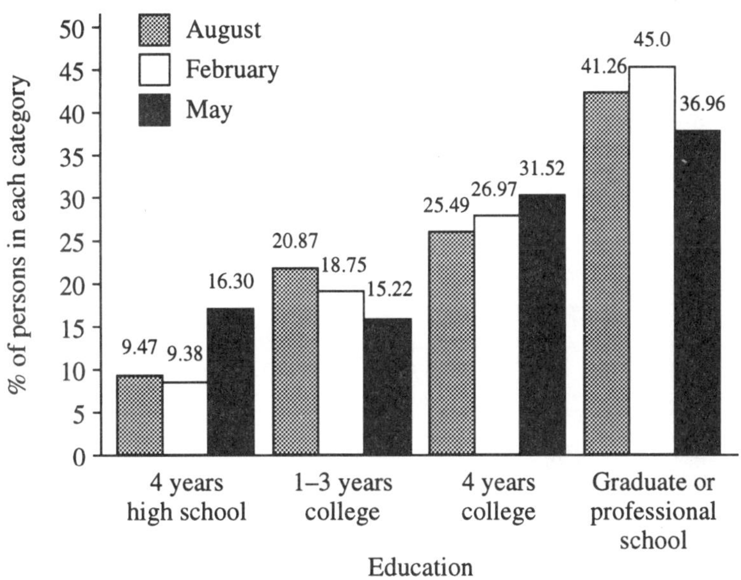

Source: TKTS surveys. Figure 5 of this report uses average of these three surveys.

Figure B–3 Education of TKTS Patrons – Three Surveys: August 1973, February and May 1974

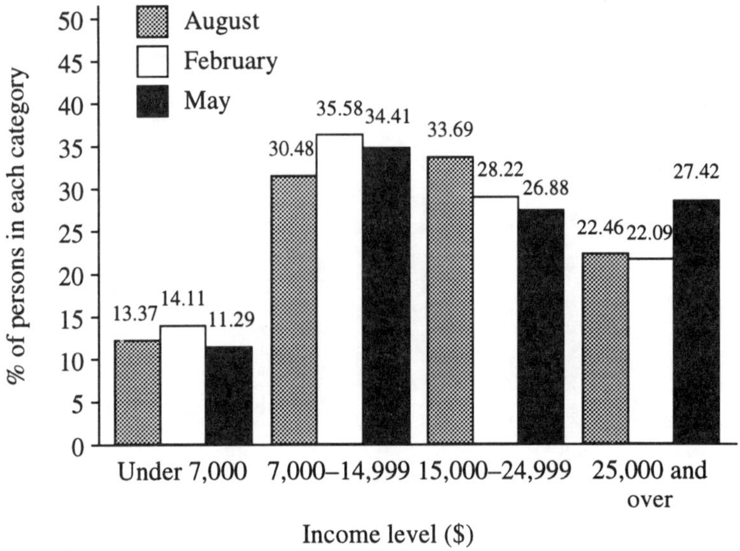

Source: TKTS surveys.

Figure B–4 Income of TKTS Users – Three Surveys: August 1973, February and May 1974

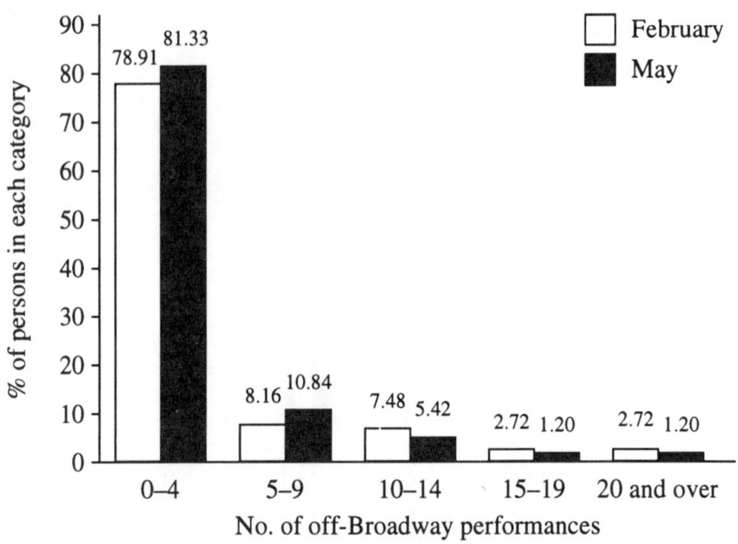

Source: TKTS surveys, February and May 1974.

Figure B–5 TKTS Users Who have Attended Off-Broadway Performances within the Past Year

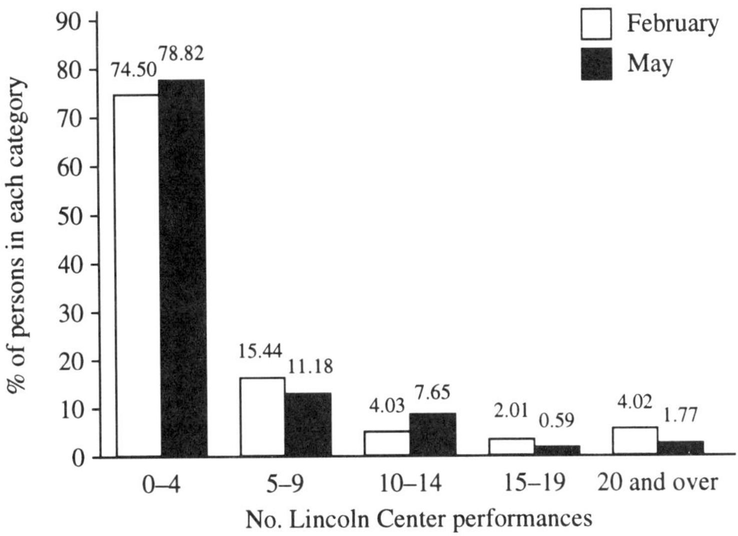

Source: TKTS surveys, February and May 1974.

Figure B–6 TKTS Users Who have Attended Lincoln Center Performances within the Past Year

[24]

The impact of the Broadway theatre on the economy of New York City

with Hilda Baumol

Introduction

The availability of live theatre in New York and other major urban centers across the country has always been recognized as a unique and powerful attraction, but no reliable estimate of the economic contribution of theatre existed. In the usual course of affairs it is impossible to separate theatre-connected expenditures from figures for the total economy. However, an unusual situation presented itself in the fall of 1975, when nine Broadway musical theatres were closed for twentyfive days as a result of a strike by Local 802 of the American Federation of Musicians, reducing total attendance and theatre revenues by some 70 percent. This strike presented the opportunity for a near-controlled experiment indicating the economic impact of the Broadway theatre on the earnings of closely related business activities.

Realizing that such an opportunity might not occur again, and recognizing the importance of understanding theatre's role in the on-going economy of the nation's cities, Professor William Baumol of MATHEMATICA, Inc., Princeton, New Jersey, conducted the first systematic investigation of the indirect economic contribution of the Broadway theatre: the expenditures of audience members related to their theatre attendance. Actual theatre expenditures were also considered to achieve a total picture of the industry's economic impact.

As a result of this work evidence now exists which demonstrates that live theatre makes a substantial financial contribution both to the economy of its immediate community and the economy of the nation. Furthermore, it specifically shows that the commercial theatre in New York City stimulates income and employment amounting to more than a quarter of a billion dollars annually.

Although this report is focused on New York City, the methods used to gather and interpret the information can be applied to other communities, and are applicable to any theatre, whether or not it is profit structured.

The League of New York Theatres and Producers, Inc. is a professional trade association of Broadway theatre owners and producers, founded in 1930.

Part I: Theatre and the economy

1. The main statistical results

The commercial theatre's annual gross revenue from ticket sales amounted to some $57 million in the 1974–1975 season. The study found that, in addition, theatregoers spent nearly an equal amount on transportation, dining, and hotels as a result of their attendance. These outlays stimulated further expenditures totalling $168 million in the metropolitan area, and an additional $110 million across the country – or a national total of about $275 million.

The theatre industry directly contributes $43 million to the economy of New York City. This figure represents expenditures by producers, theatre owners and ticket brokers for performers' salaries, sets, rents, etc. In addition, it was learned that theatregoers annually spend approximately $45 million on restaurants, $10.3 million on taxis, and $4.3 million for parking. Bus tours bring in 600,000 people per year to attend the theatre, and organized theatre tours bring in a minimum of 20,000 visitors every year who often stay the better part of a week. These visitors are estimated to spend another $2.5 million on hotels, shopping, etc. Direct tax payments to New York City are at least $5.7 million. These figures, adjusted for the stimulation they provide to expenditures by the recipients of these amounts (the multiplier effect – see below), yield the figures reported here.

Much of the information was provided directly by the pertinent industries – theatre tour operators, ticket brokers, producers, theatre owners, etc. Our estimates of the theatregoers' contribution to the income of restaurants, taxis and parking lots are based on an investigation and analysis of the reduction in flow of revenues to these activities during the strike which lasted from September 18 to October 13, 1975.

The evidence indicates that during the strike weeks ticket sales and attendance dropped to 30 percent of their normal level for a season and the revenues of taxi owners and operators fell some $117,000 per week. During this period, parking lot operators are shown to have lost about $50,000 per week. However, the largest loss, aside from the theatre itself, is probably that experienced by the restaurants which suffered a decline in revenues of the order of $510,000 per week.

We have deliberately calculated the figures so that all estimates are conservative. In addition, every effort was made to include only expenditures that were demonstrably theatre related; e.g., expenses of theatre tour participants were allowed only on days that they actually attended the theatre rather than visiting a nightclub, etc. Many expenditures, outlays on shopping, nightclubs, sightseeing tours, public transportation and accommodations by theatregoers who made their own arrangements (two-thirds of the total theatre audience), were omitted entirely because there was no way of estimating their magnitude. Very possibly these add up to a considerable amount, but its determination would require a massive survey of theatre audiences.

Thus the figures presented here represent an extreme lower bound of Broadway's contribution to the economy of New York City.

Because it was beyond the scope of this study, no value was assigned to the 'road' activity throughout the country which emanates directly from Broadway, and generates direct returns almost as high as Broadway itself.

2. Analysis of the results

One conclusion follows: the Broadway theatre makes a significant contribution to employment and income, both to the metropolitan area where performances occur and to the national economy. Moreover, some 35 percent of this quarter billion dollar contribution finds its way into portions of the economy lying beyond the metropolitan area, perhaps very far from it.

It also follows that many local businesses have a great deal at stake in the economic health of the theatre, and suggests that where the theatre's future is affected by the quality of the neighborhood or by legislation inhibiting its activities, self-interest calls for a common front between the theatre industry and related businesses.

A case in point is provided by this study, the validity of which was highly dependent on the cooperation of business firms in these related activities, for only they were in a position to supply the requisite information.

When the study was announced it was greeted with universal approbation and promises of support, yet it soon became clear that, despite a stringent system guaranteeing anonymity and confidentiality, it was necessary to overcome fears that proprietary information would somehow became public. Only with great effort by a variety of persons, some of them very well known, was it possible to persuade more than a handful of firms to provide the information that was so clearly in their common interest.

In interpreting the figures in this report, it should be recognized that they are conservative in several important respects beyond those already noted. Aside from the fact that they only deal with the economic effects, deliberately abstracting from the contributions to culture in general and to the quality of life which theatre provides, they also omit one of its economic benefits – its consequences in the choice of geographical location of other activities, which is likely to be more significant in the long run than in the short. For there is evidence that a variety of economic activities are attracted by the availability of cultural resources – firms that are highly dependent upon scientific and technical personnel have found that they run into recruiting difficulties if they try to carry on their work in a cultural wasteland. It is a common experience of professional societies that attendance at their conventions increases markedly when these meetings take place in cities offering a variety of cultural events. All of this implies a very real but largely unquantifiable increment in regional incomes – one which is as much attributable to the presence of the theatre as are the expenditures on restaurants, hotels and taxi cabs investigated here.

3. *The multiplier effects*

A description of the research methods of this study is left almost entirely to Part II, which specifies the details of the evidence and the means by which it was acquired. There is one exception – an explanation of the so-called 'multiplier calculation' which, while it is commonplace to economists, is likely to seem a piece of sleight-of-hand to the non-specialist. Despite its unfamiliarity this part of the calculation is of the utmost importance, both because of its contribution to the final magnitudes of the component of GNP and regional incomes that are attributed to the theatre, and because this element in the calculation permits one to distinguish between the theatre's contribution to the metropolitan area and to the nation's economy.

The point in the multiplier analysis is this: if the theatre were suddenly to disappear from the city, the losses to restaurants, hotels, taxis, etc., would only be those suffered at first remove. Those who derive income from these enterprises would consequently have to tighten their belts and, in their turn, people who cater to them would suffer losses in demand for their products, and so on down the line. If a waiter lost his job, his wife would have less to spend at her grocery store in the Bronx; that grocer in turn would have to put off the purchase of a new pair of shoes or the repair of his television set, etc. This chain of losses is referred to as the multiplier process.

The multiplier process is a standard piece of economic analysis and a detailed explanation is offered in every basic textbook. It is used explicitly or implicitly in every calculation of the effects of government policies upon GNP, inflation and employment within the US Government. It is used routinely by the President's Council of Economic Advisors to calculate its forecasts on the state of the economy and in the design of recommendations for federal policy relating to inflation and employment.

It would be impractical to calculate the value of the multiplier by direct observation of how particular moneys are spent and re-spent. Roughly speaking, it is determined as follows: from statistics about aggregate consumer income and aggregate consumer spending, one determines what proportion any *increase* in income to an average consumer would add to that person's total spending. (This figure is called the 'marginal propensity to consume' or MPC.) For example, with an MPC of 80 percent a theatre patron leaving a $1 restaurant tip will (on the average) induce the waiter to spend an additional 80 cents at the grocery store. The (average) grocer will thereby be induced to spend an additional 80 percent of this amount, i.e., 64 cents, on other items, and so on. Thus the original dollar tip set off a chain of expenditures, 80 cents and 64 cents, etc., and their sum permits us to calculate the multiplier.

Two multiplier figures are pertinent to this study – the intra-city multiplier, and the multiplier for the US economy, as a good part of the chain of expenditures generated by theatre-related outlays 'leak' outside the economy of the city into that of the country as a whole.[1]

There are *direct* economic contributions to the economy outside the city as well. Airline fares paid by theatre tours, babysitting fees, bus rental, gasoline purchases, payment of tolls, etc., are all additions to GNP.

The best estimates of the national multiplier are of the order of magnitude of 2.5, while those for New York City alone are in the vicinity of 1.6. Therefore to obtain an estimate of the full effect of the cessation of theatrical activity in New York City upon the economy outside the city, the numbers obtained in the calculations described up to this point must be multiplied by a factor of 0.9 (the excess of the national multiplier over the New York City multiplier). To obtain the effect upon the economy of the City of New York alone, the figures must be multiplied by 1.6.

Perhaps most important is the inference that can be drawn from this calculation about the contribution of the Broadway theatre to the economy *outside the city*. For it is not the city alone which loses from a contraction of theatrical activity. In fact *for every dollar spent by theatregoers on the Broadway theatre and its ancillary activities, the multiplier effect injects 90 cents outside the city.*

4. Concluding comment

Many statements have been made about the value of theatre and its role in the economic structure. The evidence we give here provides a quantitative evaluation of that contribution, and demonstrates that benefits flow well beyond the immediate neighborhood in which performances take place.

Whatever one's aesthetic predilections or interest in the nation's cultural activities might be, one can be sure that live theatre makes its contribution to the health and vitality of the economy of the country.

Part II: Income and employment contribution of New York's legitimate theatre: research methods and results

1. Nature of the strike and its effects on attendance

To determine the effects of the strike on attendance, the following facts had to be taken into account:

- Nine of the 14 theatres in operation before September 15, 1975 closed during the strike. Only musical productions on Broadway were affected.
- The five dramatic plays which continued running represented more than one-third of the total plays, yet they constituted less than one-third of the total tickets sold.
- Pre-sold tickets for musicals were returned, and some of the patrons purchased tickets to dramatic plays instead.
- The conjunction of inflation and recession that characterized 1975 had its own effects on business, and had to be untangled from the strike.
- The strike was sudden and relatively brief, providing insufficient time for some people to change their plans.
- Some theatre party agents who supply tickets to groups reported few outright cancellations. Instead they had to re-schedule for later dates, incurring doubled overhead charges leading to some loss. Ticketron, forced to cancel 17,000 tickets, estimates that they lost $38,000 in costs for bookkeeping, clerical, overhead and commission (at $2 to $2.35 per check). They experienced no noticeable substitution among their clients.

The evidence is that attendance at the five productions running during the strike rose surprisingly little, and the total attendance fell dramatically. Figure 1 shows the weekly grosses of all 14 theatres for the three weeks preceding the strike, the strike period itself, and the four weeks succeeding it.

The weekly gross fell from a pre-strike average of $1,085,000 to $229,500 during the strike. In the weeks immediately following the average rose to $1,047,500.[2]

Figure 2 charts the attendance patterns during the same period, separating non-musical productions from the musicals closed by the strike. This chart indicates that while there was some increase in attendance at non-musical productions, it was quite small. The weekly total rose on average from about 27,500 to 31,000, or approximately 3 percent of the normal Broadway audience while total attendance fell nearly 70 percent, or some 70,000 persons per week.

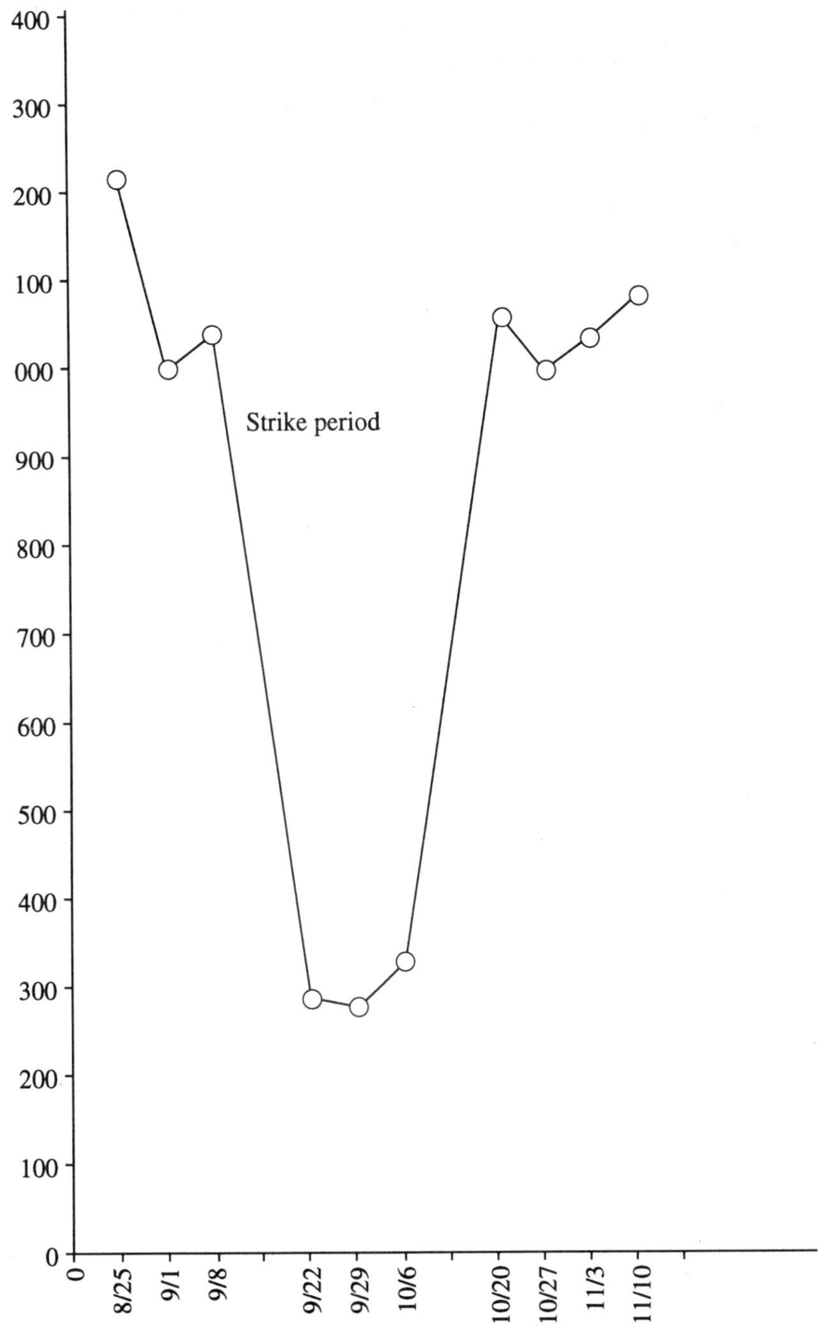

Figure 1 *Combined Total Weekly Grosses, All Theatres (August 28 to November 10, 1975) (in thousands of dollars)*

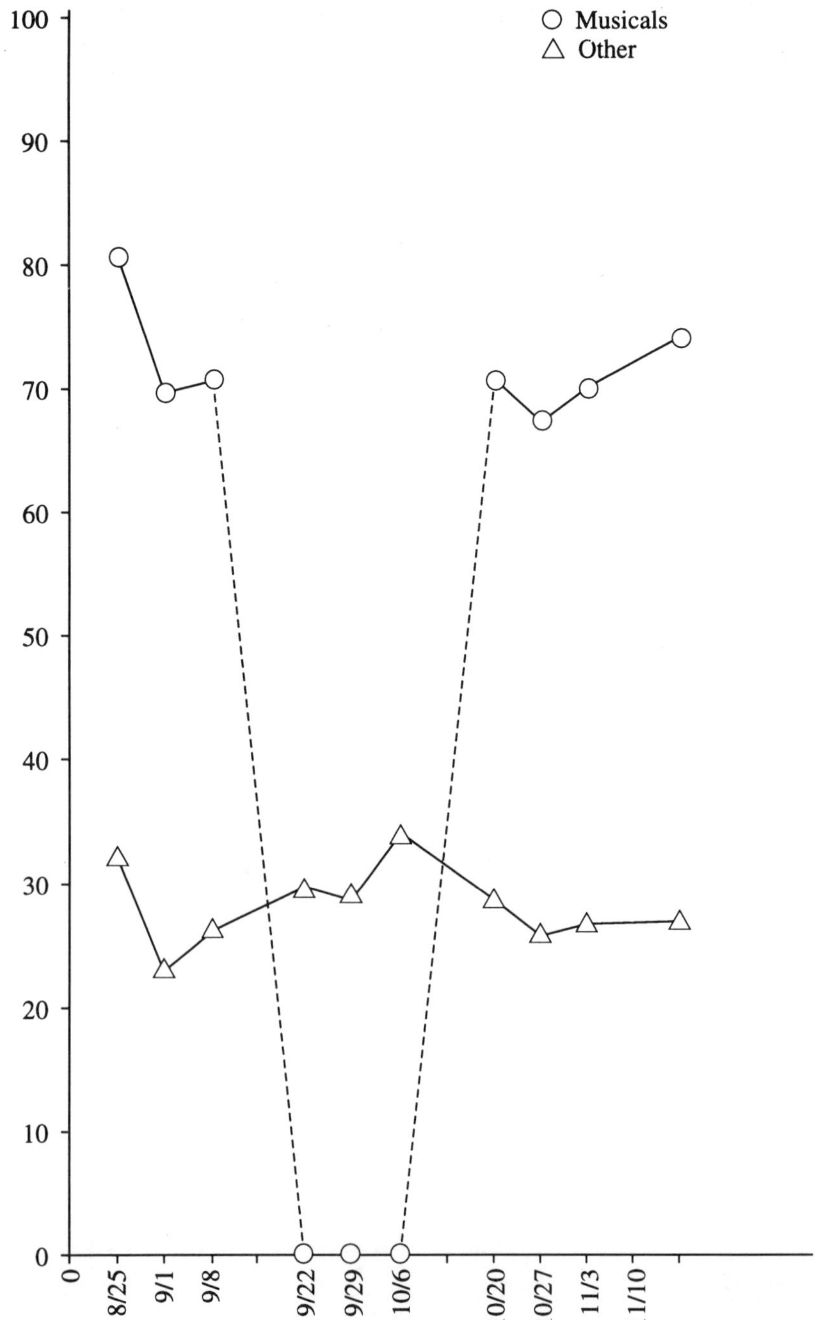

Figure 2 *Pattern of Weekly Attendance, All Theatres (August 28 to November 10, 1975) (in thousands of dollars)*

None of the productions failed to re-open. A few dramatic productions opened during the strike, but except for two (*Trelawny of the Wells* at the Vivian Beaumont Theatre and *Ah, Wilderness* at the Circle-in-the-Square), they closed before the strike was over. A few productions scheduled to open during the strike were delayed for varying lengths of time.

2. Research procedures

The objective of this study was to examine the effects of the entire operation of theatre upon the economy as a whole. The three businesses most likely to have been affected by the theatre strike – restaurants, taxis and parking lots – were asked for data on volume of sales for the period before, during and after the strike, and calculations were made of the losses to these industries attributable to theatre attendance. From this information we determined, within reasonable bounds, the amount of business we could normally attribute to theatre attendees. Theatre tour arrangers, bus tour operators, etc., were approached for information on the magnitude of their bookings.

Figures were gathered on the number of persons annually taking *bona fide* theatre tours and the length of their stay. Their ancillary expenses were estimated using a recent study conducted by the New York Convention and Visitors Bureau which surveyed visitor expenditures for hotels, meals, local transportation, shopping, etc.

These figures for restaurants, taxis, parking lots, and tours have been re-adjusted to put them into comparable terms, added together and adjusted once more for the fact that some one-third of the theatre was still in operation during the strike. We then translated them into an annual equivalent, after seasonal adjustment to take account of the fact that August, September and October usually bring in grosses to the theatres lower than the average for the entire year.

We were fortunate in being able to compare these new calculations against an earlier survey of theatre audiences which provided information about theatre-related expenditures.[3]

This earlier study questioned theatregoers directly on ancillary expenditures of theatregoers: their outlays on food, transportation, babysitters, etc. Since one of the most striking conclusions drawn from the evidence in that report is the extreme stability in the composition and behavior pattern of audiences, one can reasonably infer that the proportions among these various expenditures will not have changed substantially, and the survey results would remain valid subject only to some correction for changes in the price level.

As these data and those in the present study were collected from different sources and under different circumstances, they permit totally independent estimates of the theatre's contribution to the remainder of the economy.

Five different questionnaires were designed and mailed to restaurants and hotel dining rooms, parking lots and garages, convention organizers, theatre owners and producers. Telephone and in-person interviews were conducted with individual businessmen as well as representatives of the Metropolitan Taxicab Board of Trade, New York State Restaurant Association, Restaurant League of New York, Hotel Association of New York City, the League of New York Theatres and Producers,

Select Theatres, Inc., the New York Convention and Visitors Bureau, licensed ticket brokers, theatre party agents, tour operators, an advertising agency, MTA officials, the bridge and tunnel authorities and others.

3. Transportation and food expenditures

a. Taxicab industry Estimated annual theatre-connected receipts: $10,300,000. Figures for the fall-off in business for taxicabs proved somewhat elusive. Two sets of figures were received – one from the Metropolitan Taxicab Board of Trade (representing 54 fleet owners), and the other from the Taxi Drivers Union (independent owners). One figure seemed too high, the other too low. Consequently, an average of the two estimates was taken, giving a figure compatible with other known data such as the number of theatre patrons, percentage parking in lots, and percentage arriving by pre-arranged bus tours.

Our estimate is that 2,750 taxicabs, both fleet and independently owned, are on the night shift in midtown Manhattan. During the strike each lost an average of 2.25 trips per night, for a total loss of 6,200 trips per night or 43,300 per week. As the average metered fare is $2.35, and average tip is $.35 (agreed to by all sources), this means that the weekly losses amounted to $102,000 in fares and $15,000 in tips, or a total loss of $117,000 per week.

This figure implies that some 60 percent of the theatre audience makes the round trip by taxicab, if we assume that two persons make up the average fare. According to our sources the day-long average is 1.4 persons per fare, although the evening figures might be somewhat higher. It must also be considered that taxicabs are used not only by the audience, but by musicians, performers, etc., in this highly labor-intensive industry where the ratio between attendees and the number of persons concerned with a production is unusually high.

Adjusting for normal (non-strike) attendance and the annual seasonal variations, it can be conservatively estimated that $10,300,000 is the annual theatre-connected expenditure on taxicabs in New York City.

b. Parking revenues Estimated annual theatre-connected receipts: $4,300,000. With data on indoor garages from the Metropolitan Garage Board of Trade and a direct census of outdoor parking lots between 42nd and 54th Streets West of Madison Avenue, we estimated that in January, 1976, there were 5,400 indoor spaces at 30 locations and 4,300 outdoor spaces at 40 locations (totaling 9,700 parking spaces at 70 locations in the general area of the theatre district).

While the number of responses to our questionnaire was small (figures were received corresponding to 10 percent of the parking spaces contacted), a check of the results against informed estimates and some precise data obtained from interviews convinced us that our computations describe the real situation with reasonable accuracy.

From firm figures received from six parking facilities, including two on the periphery of the theatre district, it was found that during the strike the total income for these six lots dropped from $24,900 to $17,700, a loss of approximately $7,000. Extrapolating this to the total number of parking spaces in the area, we estimate that the weekly loss amounted to some $50,000 which when adjusted for seasonal variation and normal audience size, gave a total of more than $80,000 weekly. There is also a 6 percent New York City parking tax.

c. Restaurant revenues Estimated annual theatre-connected receipts: $45,000,000. Questionnaires were sent to 132 restaurants between 42nd and 59th Streets, from Park to Ninth Avenues, in every price range. Only 10 percent replied. Because their comments indicated that they range from very inexpensive to fairly high-priced and some denied heavy dependence on theatregoers (one responded that receipts increased during the strike period), we feel this relatively small number of responses can be used to extrapolate to the total number of establishments.

The average restaurant charged $6.47 for lunch and $10.22 for dinner, and normally took in under $35,000 weekly for food and bar receipts.

During the strike they lost an average of $3,700 per establishment. Subtracting the 8 percent tax and adding a 15 percent tip, the total per restaurant loss is $3,900. Extrapolating to 132 restaurants, the normal theatre audience would spend $735,000 for an average week of theatre-related business. Adjusting this figure for the theatre season results in annual theatre-related restaurant receipts of $45,000,000. In addition, $3,600,000 is received in taxes.

4. Expenditures by ticket sales outlets

a. Group sales Estimated annual payroll of group sales agents: $200,000. Estimated annual payroll of ticket brokers: $1,250,000. Individuals who buy their tickets independently still account for more than half of all tickets sold at the theatre box office, either directly or by mail. Our rough estimate is that $8.8 million of the total $57 million in ticket sales in the 1975 season were made by licensed theatre party agents and group sales outlets representing the producers. Upwards of $8 million worth were sold by licensed ticket brokers, $3.4 million were accounted for by the Theatre Development Fund through its production funding programs and mainly through the Times Square Ticket Centers, and about $5 million in sales was effected through Ticketron. These add up to $25 million worth of tickets. The remaining grosses adding up to some $32 million were obtained from tickets sold at the box office.

It was not possible to differentiate sharply between individuals attending the theatre on their own and those traveling with organized groups, because small group operators often patronize the box office rather than recognized group sales outlets. Small and large lots are purchased in the most convenient manner by travel agencies throughout the country, bus owners (many owning only two or three buses) who supply the tickets with the rental of their vehicles for transportation to the theatre, tour organizers, large organizations planning benefits, social groups, teachers arranging theatre trips, and large bus companies who do theatre business in addition to their other travel services, often in conjunction with a professional tour organizer. Some tour organizers or bus operators order large blocks of tickets before the opening of a promising show so they can supply their customers with popular attractions, and some supply their customers only what is available to the general public.

5. *Expenditures on organized theatre tours*

a. One-day bus tours Estimated annual theatre-connected receipts: $1,800,000. A large number of privately chartered buses bring groups to most performances on Broadway from locations within a 300 mile radius of New York City. (Ticket sales records indicate that they come from as far away as Rhode Island and Baltimore.) In addition to school bus tours, three or four large private bus companies rent out over 2,000 buses per year (each carrying over 50 people) to various tour arrangers and travel agencies in the immediate metropolitan area. Throughout the study we kept turning up additional large and small tour operators and travel agencies operating within a few hundred miles of New York City who put together their own local, one-day theatre package using small local bus services, and who serve clubs and organizations throughout the area.

It is difficult to estimate the number of people attending the theatre on organized bus tours, particularly as the tickets are purchased from a variety of sources. Nevertheless, on the basis of the information we acquired from many sources we estimate that licensed theatre party agents and group sales outlets account for the sale of $8.8 million worth of tickets per year. About half this number goes to theatre clubs paying an average ticket price of $12 and other sources not necessarily using bus transportation. It is a plausible conjecture that some $4.5 million worth of tickets are used for one-day bus tours. The average ticket price has been computed with the help of actual sales records to be $7.40 (weighted by the percentage attending musicals as against the less expensive straight plays). Therefore, approximately 600,000 individuals per year travel to the theatre on one-day bus tours. This is a low estimate, since it does not take into account those whose tickets are purchased directly from the theatre or sources other than those who deal only in group sales. The average price is comparatively low as a great many of these tickets are for unpopular nights of the week, matinees, and the least expensive locations.

Buses to matinees typically arrive in New York several hours before curtain to allow time for a meal or shopping, while those arriving in the evening may or may not allow time for anything other than the performance. From actual sales figures we have determined that under 20 percent come from New York City, almost 30 percent from New York State, over 40 percent from New Jersey and Connecticut, and about 11 percent from more distant states.

From interview data we have ascertained that between 15 and 20 percent of these patrons pre-arrange a meal or a visit to a nightclub or hotel restaurant in the area. The meal prices reported to us range from about $6.50 for lunch to $9.50 for dinner, but as they have probably been included in our restaurant figures they are not counted here again.

Assuming that the average bus carries 50 passengers, it follows that 12,000 buses arrive in the theatre district annually. Considering a 40 week season, this amounts to 300 buses per week, 37.5 per performance, or less than two buses per theatre per performance. Some are school buses and probably rent for less than the $150 which is used for our average rental figure, but this is offset by the fact that it would be a very low figure for the outer perimeter of our 300-mile radius. Thus, $1.8 million is spent for bus rentals over the year. Only some $200,000 of this goes to New York City and $540,000 to New York State.

b. Airline tours involving hotel stays Estimated annual theatre-connected expenditure: $3,900,000. Several package tours provide air travel, theatre tickets and hotel accommodations. In some cases the tour is specifically designed for theatre attendance and routinely includes tickets, and in others theatre attendance is one of the options along with visits to a nightclub, or other entertainment. In order to separate theatre attendees taking such tours from other participants, our calculations are based on ticket sales to the tour operators.

During 1975, theatre-tour airline trips were taken by more than 20,000 people who attended the theatre 50,000 times and purchased $770,000 in theatre tickets. On the average, those who attended the theatre rather than selecting trips to nightclubs, sightseeing, etc., as their options, stayed in hotels 59,200 nights.

To estimate the ancillary expenditure of tour participants we employed a 1973 study of vacation visitor expenditures conducted by the Convention and Visitors Bureau which we adjusted for increase in the price level.

Simply multiplying the number of nights spent by these patrons by the 1975 average visitor expenditure figure, we get $3,900,000 spent last year *in addition to ticket outlays*. In our final tabulations we have subtracted restaurant and transpor-

Table 1 Per Diem Expenses of Visitors to New York City Staying in Hotels

Category	Dollar amount 1973	Dollar amount 1975
Hotel rooms	$18.00	$21.00
Hotel restaurant Other restaurants Beverages	$16.00	$19.00
Retail stores	$8.55	$10.00
Local transportation	$2.75	$4.00
Movies Sightseeing, night-clubs Sports events	$5.70	$6.50
Miscellaneous	$3.50	$4.00
Total	$54.50	$64.50

Note:
The 1973 figures are taken from a survey by the New York Convention and Visitors Bureau. They have been adjusted to 1975 levels using figures from the US Department of Labor, Bureau of Labor Statistics, Consumer Price Index, Historical Tabulations for the New York Area. The all-items increase for New York from November, 1973, was 18.7%, but some of the categories such as 'food away from home', 'local transportation', 'reading and recreation', and 'private transportation' are computed separately by the Bureau, and we have used those figures when suitable. All figures rounded.

tation outlays as having been included in those categories. The details of the estimated expenditures of such visitors are provided in Table 1.

We must emphasize again that the figures in Table 1 almost certainly understate the expenditures of theatre patrons by a large amount. The Convention Bureau gives figures for *all* visitors, and it is generally believed that theatre attendees are more affluent than the general population and probably more affluent than typical convention attendees.

Again, the $3,900,000 figure is very conservative. We have considered only patrons of organized theatre tours on days when they actually attended the theatre rather than choosing some other form of diversion offered to them. Not included is the visitor arriving by methods other than an organized tour who combines theatre going with business or social visits. We have also ignored the conventioneer who comes a day or two early with spouse for that purpose, although hotel managers assure us that is sometimes the case.

Two experienced hotel managers representing different priced hotels say that, while their weekday business consists predominantly of business people, their hotels fill up on weekends with couples who come to New York especially to attend the theatre, eat at some special restaurant, and do a good deal of shopping. Some hotels offer special theatre weekends – perhaps two nights in the hotel, one ticket to a musical and one straight play. The clients often drive from Long Island or New Jersey and have not been included in the preceding total because it is not possible to estimate their numbers. Their tickets were probably purchased from ticket brokers or by mail order at the box office, so they cannot be separated from other independent attendees.

Most airline tours do not include transfer to and from airports. Bus transportation is $8 to and from the East Side Terminal, and another $2 each way should be added for cab fare, making this $12 per individual or an additional $250,000.

Assuming conservatively that the average air fare for such a (round) trip is $150, it would follow that organized theatre tours contribute over $3 million in airline fares annually.

6. *Convention visitors*

There are more than three million convention visitors to New York City per year staying an average of 4.5 days and spending, according to a 1973 survey performed by the New York Convention and Visitors Bureau, an average of $69.58 per day (1973 prices).

Because of conflicting reports on theatre attendance by convention visitors, we wrote to 38 convention organizers who had meetings of 2,000 people or more during a three-month period. Nine replies were received, a 24 percent response, including one reply from the American Bankers Association, which is reputedly highest in theatre attendance. Unfortunately, the bankers arrived during the strike period, so that most of the 5,500 seats they had reserved for nine different shows on four nights had to be returned, but their intentions are clear.

The attendance of these nine conventions totalled about 50,500 out-of-town visitors. Theatre parties were planned by two of them, accounting for 5,800 attendances. In other words, at least 11 percent of the participants visited the theatre.

There is no way of estimating the number of individuals who may have purchased tickets on their own, although two of the organizers estimated the figures to be 5 percent and 10 percent of the total. Four of the nine replies emphasized that these were working meetings and there was no free time in the evenings, so their delegates would not be able to attend the theatre.

Because of the exceptional nature of the American Bankers Association, there is no basis for assuming that 11 percent of the 3,000,000 conventioneers who come to New York every year are attracted by the theatre.

7. Digression: ticket outlets

It is interesting to note that almost half of the tickets for tours involving hotel stays are supplied by licensed ticket brokers who charge the legal rate of $1.50 per ticket for the service. The broker serves a clientele which demands the best locations and dates and who are willing to pay for the service. A conservative estimate is that brokers handled over $8,000,000 in business during the 1974–75 season, or slightly less than 15 percent of total ticket sales. They offer such services as charge accounts, telephone orders, ticket booths located in the lobbies of major hotels, and cancellation of orders if necessary. Their clientele is composed of business people who often do a good deal of entertaining (probably one-third to one-half of their customers), habitual theatre attendees willing to pay an additional amount for the services offered, visitors to the city who phone ahead or purchase tickets in hotel lobbies (20 percent to 30 percent of their business) and commercial establishments. Unlike other ticket distributors they do not receive a commission for sales, covering their expenses with the $1.50[4] surcharge that they are permitted. They do, however, require the most popular dates and excellent locations – tickets which the box office itself would find it easiest to dispose of. There are about 30 agencies employing about 150 people with an annual payroll of about $1,250,000.

Over 15 percent of all tickets sold are distributed by theatre party agents who get a commission from the box office and sell blocks of tickets at box office prices. They distribute a great many tickets for less popular times during the week, and do a merchandising job with clubs, schools and tour wholesalers. There are only eight or nine such agents.

The Theatre Development Fund, through its various incentive programs and through the Times Square Ticket Centre, accounted for $3,400,000 worth of tickets in 1974–75, or almost 6 percent of the total. Expenses are paid through a small surcharge upon ticket sales and the purpose of the program is to encourage production and to clear the market of unsold tickets. According to an audience survey the present authors carried out in 1974[5] they serve a younger, less affluent audience than the usual Broadway attendees. About half the patrons are from New York City and Long Island and almost half from other states and abroad.

The other full price ticket outlet is Ticketron, with 60 percent of its outlets in New York City. It charges the customer $.75, gets a commission from the box office to cover expenses, and was responsible for over $5 million in ticket sales during 1975.

Almost two-thirds of Broadway's tickets are still sold at individual theatre box offices, either at the theatres or by mail order, and very little is known about the constitution of their clientele.

8. Expenditures of the theatre itself

Aside from the outlays of theatre audiences on items other than the theatre tickets themselves,[6] the economy of the city benefits from the expenditures of the theatre industry on wages, scenery and costumes, advertising, etc. Its nationwide activities include tryouts and sending of 'road' companies of popular shows to tour throughout the nation.

A survey of individual theatre owners permitted us to arrive at an estimate of their total operating expenses (Table 2). Similarly, we have made estimates of outlays by producers (Tables 3 and 4), based on data provided by a sample of producers. The tables indicate the magnitude of the samples from which the estimates were calculated.

9. Aggregate contribution of the theatre

We are now in a position to put together the information we have gathered from all of the above sources. We carry out this aggregation process in three steps: calculation of annual equivalent of those ancillary expenditures determined during the strike period – outlays on restaurants, taxis, and parking lots, outlays of persons

Table 2 Expenditures – 1974–75 Season, Operations of Broadway Theatres in New York City

	(1) Average week per theatre	(2)[1] Estimated total annual expenditures, all theatres
Expenditures		
Total payroll	7,000	7,707,000
Payroll taxes	400	440,000
Pensions and welfare	750	826,000
Advertising	900	991,000
Commissions	200	220,000
Utilities	675	743,000
Cleaning and maint.	870	958,000
Tickets (printing)	100	110,000
Permits and licenses	30	33,000
Real estate taxes	1,500	1,651,000
Miscellaneous NYC taxes	10	11,000
Total	12,435	13,690,000

Notes:
1. The first column calculates the average expenditure of each theatre on each item per week. In the second column we have multiplied each item by 1,101, the number of playing weeks in the 1974–75 season (*Variety*).

Source: Survey of Broadway theatre owners. Based on a 54% response.

Table 3 Producers' Operating Costs – Broadway Theatres, 1974–75 Season

	(1) Average week per production	(2)[1] Estimated annual expenditure – all productions
Total payroll	9,000	9,909,000
Payroll taxes[2]	1,000	1,101,000
Pension and welfare	450	495,000
Rentals	3,500	3,854,000
Royalties	3,000	3,303,000
Advertising and production	5,800	6,386,000
Other	600	660,000
Total	$23,350	$25,708,000

Notes:
1. The first column calculates the average expenditures of each production on each item per week. In the second column we have multiplied each item by 1,101, the number of playing weeks in the 1974–75 season (*Variety*).
2. This category contains items such as disability insurance, unemployment insurance, payroll expenses, etc.

Source: Survey of producers. Based on 14% response.

participating in tours, and expenditures of the theatres themselves and ticket selling outlets.

We have estimated that during the strike the average weekly reduction in expenditure on restaurants, taxis, parking lots, amounted to $677,000. Three adjustments are required to translate this figure into an estimate of the annual contribution of the theatre to these activities: (i) adjustment to reflect the fact that our data are estimated on the basis of only a *partial* blackout of theatrical activities; (ii) multiplication by 52 to transform the total from a weekly to an annual figure; and (iii) seasonal adjustment to transform them from figures applicable to the August–October period studied to an average week during the year.

The first two adjustments are obvious and require no explanation. Since, during the period of the strike, total attendance of the theatre and weekly grosses each fell by about 70 percent, we can assume that its total contribution to restaurants, taxis, etc., is 30 percent higher than their revenues during the strike. Finally, the seasonal adjustment was carried out by the following method:

(1) We calculated the average weekly gross of the three preceding no-strike years, giving us $952,000.
(2) We calculated the average weekly gross in the same three years for the nine weeks in September–November that the study considered for 1975–76. This came to $806,000.

Table 4 Pre-Opening Expenditures (in dollars) – All Broadway Productions in 1974–75 Season

	(1) Avg. expenditures per production	(2)[1] Estimated annual pre-opening expenditure (all productions)
Scenery and props	30,000	1,770,000
Costumes	4,000	236,000
Rental and purchase of equipment	3,000	177,000
Fees (directors, designers, etc.)	15,000	885,000
Rehearsal salaries	16,500	973,500
Payroll taxes[2]	1,800	106,200
Pensions and welfare	1,500	88,500
Advertising and publicity	16,000	944,000
Other	5,000	295,000
Total	92,800	5,475,200

Notes:
1. The first column calculates average expenditure of each production on each item. In the second column we have multiplied each item by 59, the number of productions in the 1974–75 season (*Variety*).
2. This category contains items such as disability insurance, unemployment insurance, payroll expenses, etc.

Source: Survey of producers. Based on 12% response.

(3) We divided the figure from Step 1 by the figure from Step 2, giving us 1.18, showing how much higher the average grosses are in a typical week than the weeks we studied.
(4) We then adjusted our figures by multiplying them by 1.18 to bring them up to typical weeks, thus ironing out the seasonal influence.

After these adjustments have been completed, we are able to conclude that the theatre's annual contribution to the business of restaurants, taxis, parking lots and traceable miscellaneous activities was $62,000,000.

To the preceding figure, we must now add the $43,000,000 annual outlay of the theatre itself, and the amount expended by ticket merchandising services.

Combining these three figures we obtain a grand total figure of $105 million representing the traceable and direct contributions of the theatre to the economy of the city (see Table 5). As already indicated, however, this only represents the first round in the multiplier process, since every such outlay in turn stimulates a chain of expenditures of these receipts. Using the multiplier estimate of 1.6 for New York City, it follows that we must evaluate the theatre's total contribution to the economy of the city at $168 million per year (see Table 6). Moreover, this is obviously only a

Table 5 Expenditures Related to Broadway Theatre (in dollars) – 1974–75 Season

	(1) Loss per week due to strike	(2) Average weekly theatre-related expenditure – total theatre audience (Col. (1) × 100/70)	(3) Annual theatre-related expenditure	(4) Annual NYC taxes
Taxicabs (including 15% tip)	117,000	167,000	10,300,000[1]	
Parking lots	50,000	70,000	4,300,000[1]	250,000[2]
Restaurants (including 15% tip)	510,000	735,000	45,000,000[1]	3,600,000[3]
Bus tours rentals			200,000 (NYC)	
			540,000 (NYS)[4]	
			1,000,000 (Other)[4]	
Air tours (subsistence @41.50 daily)[5]			2,100,000	185,000[6]
Transfers to and from airport			250,000	
Air fares			3,000,000[1]	
Ticket brokers' payroll			1,250,000	
Group sales agents' payroll			200,000	
Theatre operation			11,600,000	1,700,000
Producers' operating expense			24,600,000	
Producers' pre-opening expense			5,370,000	
Totals[7]	677,000	972,000	105,000,000	5,700,000

Notes:
1. Adjusted for seasonal fluctuations in theatre attendance.
2. Six percent parking tax.
3. New York City sales tax.
4. These are expenditures entirely outside of New York City totalling $4,500,000. They are not included in the totals, but added to the total in Table 6 from which the national multiplier effect is calculated.
5. Food and transportation are subtracted from Table 1 in the text giving average expenditures of visitors to the City.
6. Sales tax and hotel room tax.
7. All figures have been rounded, and consequently the items in the columns do not necessarily add up to the indicated totals.

lower bound, since it excludes a wide variety of expenditures from bridge and tunnel tolls, hotel occupancy of theatregoers not on organized tours, etc., which we have no way of tracing. It also does not include at least \$5.7 million in local taxes generated by the theatre.

Finally, we can form a lower bound estimate of the contributions of the Broadway theatre to the *nation's* economy outside of the city. We can now include outlays on air fares and bus rentals outside the city of \$4,500,000, making a grand total of \$110 million.[7] This total is now multiplied by the national multiplier of 2.5, giving \$275 million, and from this one finally subtracts the estimated total contribution to the economy of New York City, yielding a net figure of about \$110 million as the theatre's contribution outside the city. This again is a conservative estimate of the contribution of Broadway theatre to economic activity of the American economy as a whole and does not include the considerable national touring activity which emanates directly from Broadway. (Tables 5 and 6.)

Table 6 Multiplier calculation (millions of \$s)

	Minimum
Direct contribution to New York metropolitan area	105
Total contribution of theatre to New York metropolitan area	168
Direct contribution of theatre to US economy (total plus expenditures outside of New York City)	110
Total contribution of theatre to US economy	275

10. An alternative estimate

As indicated earlier, our figures can be checked roughly by an independent estimate based upon an earlier survey of theatre audiences which determined, for a substantial sample of audiences in New York City,[8] expenditures on tickets and ancillary outlays on transportation, restaurants, etc. This study indicated that for every dollar spent on admissions approximately 90 cents was laid out on these other items by the average audience member.

Since that study was conducted, all prices have, of course, risen. Assuming that on average the prices in question have risen in roughly the same proportion and that expenditure habits of audiences have not changed drastically,[9] we obtain the following estimates:

1.	Gross ticket sales, 1974–75	\$57 million
2.	Ancillary expenditures	\$52 million
3.	Total direct expenditures by audiences	\$108 million

4. Combined local expenditure stimulus, including multiplier effect — $173 million

5. Combined national expenditure stimulus, including multiplier effect — $270 million

6. Stimulus outside New York metropolitan area — $100 million

It is quite apparent that the data, simply updated from our 11 year old figures with the use of the US Department of Labor annual cost-of-living indexes, come exceedingly close to the data that are laboriously and painstakingly gathered for this study. Thus, the two methods of estimation each help to confirm the accuracy of the other.

In concluding, we note once more that this study, for the first time, provides some indication of the way the theatre contributes to the community in which it is located and the considerable economic activity that it engenders. The figures are not as complete as we would have liked them because of incomplete or inaccessible records, limited response rates, and the necessity for limiting the study to a small geographic area with arbitrarily chosen boundaries. We have always chosen to underestimate rather than exaggerate the figures, and to omit some items rather than relying on unsupported guesses. Yet they certainly do show, beyond reasonable doubt, that the contribution of the theatre extends well beyond its own activities.

Appendix

I. A suggested calculation based on local survey data

If the kind of information supplied by this report is useful for the Broadway theatre, it can be used to similar effect in the many other localities which support theatre in one way or another. While other localities do not have the data revealed by a 25-day gap in theatrical activity, it should be possible to get similar information either by analogy or by administering a simple audience questionnaire. On the basis of our experience with the Broadway study, we are appending a suggested questionnaire along with some suggestions for survey procedures.

A theatre (or any other performing group which carries out such a survey of its audience) can then proceed as follows:

Step 1: Calculate the total annual expenditures by the theatre in question (both production and running costs).

Step 2: Calculate the average expenditure on restaurants, shopping, transportation, etc., for an *average* person in the sample. (That is, calculate total ancillary expenditures for all respondents together, and divide this figure by the number of (usable) responses received.) Here exclude all expenditures which the respondent indicates he would have made anyhow, even if he had not attended the theatre.

Step 3: Multiply the figure in Step 2 by the number of persons who attended the theatre in question during the preceding year (season) to obtain total ancillary expenditures by its audience.

Step 4: Add together the figures in Step 1 and Step 3 to obtain the total direct annual economic contribution of the theatre.

Step 5: Divide the population of the metropolitan area in which the theatre in question is located by 8.8 million[1] (the population of the New York metropolitan area) and multiply the result by 1.6 to obtain an estimate of the local multiplier for the region in question which is to be used instead of the 1.6 in our calculation.

Step 6: Multiply the figure from Step 4 (the direct economic contribution of the theatre) by the figure obtained in Step 5 (the regional multiplier) to obtain an estimate of the contribution of the theatre to the region in question.

Step 7: Multiply the figure obtained in Step 4 (the direct economic contribution of the theatre) by 2.5 (the pertinent national multiplier) to obtain the total economic contribution of the theatre and its audience to the economy of the United States.

II. An alternative calculation method requiring no survey

If it is decided by the theatre that a survey of its audience of the sort described here is impractical, it is still possible to carry out a rough calculation of the contribution of the theatre in question.

While the study of the economic contribution of the theatre has been carried out in terms of New York City, its results can be applied *directly* as an approximation, both to theatres in other cities and to other forms of artistic activity. There is fairly overwhelming evidence documenting the highly homogeneous character of the audience for various forms of live performance in the United States and elsewhere.[2] This fact, which has been documented in a number of independent surveys, permits the application of the results of the present study to the theatres or the orchestras and opera in another part of the country. A simple calculation can be taken, with a reasonable degree of confidence, to constitute a good approximation to the pertinent fact. It must be remembered, however, that local conditions may influence the types of expenditures, particularly on restaurants and car versus taxi transportation.

In the absence of specific data, a rough calculation can be carried out as follows:

Step 1: Calculate the annual gross revenues from sales of tickets to performances by the groups in question.

Step 2: Multiply the gross ticket revenue calculated in Step 1 by 1.6 to obtain an estimated lower bound for ancillary expenditures on items such as restaurant meals, taxis and hotels, by the patron of the theatre (or other type of live performance) that is in question.

Step 3: Add up the gross ticket revenues and ancillary expenditures, as calculated in the two preceding steps, to calculate the direct economic contribution of the audience.

Step 4: Divide the population of the metropolitan area in which the theatre in question is located by 8.8 million (the population of the New York metropolitan area) and multiply the result by 1.6 to obtain the local multiplier for the region in question, which is to be used instead of the 1.6 in our calculation.

Step 5: Multiply the figure from Step 3 (the direct economic contribution of the audience) by the figure in Step 4 (the regional multiplier) to obtain an estimate of the total contribution to the economy of the region.

Step 6: Multiply the figure obtained in Step 3 (the direct contribution of the audience) by 2.5 (the pertinent national multiplier) to estimate the total contribution of the activities in question to the economy of the US.

III. A suggested questionnaire

The questionnaire that can be used for self-administered surveys is divided into two parts which can be employed separately or together. Part I deals with expenditures, and Part II is essentially a reprint of part of the Twentieth Century Fund questionnaire which elicited over 24,000 responses from audiences of theatre, opera, concerts and dance performances from 1963 to 1964.[3]

Ideally, the survey should be carried out more than once (say, a weekday evening, a matinee and Saturday night). It should not be distributed to every member of the audience to minimize the distortion caused by soliciting responses from members of the same family. The best procedure is to stuff the questionnaire into *every other* program[4] (making sure that they are given to the usher in this sequence), and to distribute them as usual. Alternatively, someone can be delegated to stand beside the ticket taker and hand the questionnaire to every other person entering the door. An announcement that the survey is being taken will usually improve the response rate, and receptacles should be provided at the exits for their collection.

The Twentieth Century Fund study had various rates of response depending on the kind of performance. They ranged from as low as 25 percent of questionnaires distributed to the audience at Broadway productions to 60 percent at regional theatres.

In analyzing the responses, you may want to tabulate separately those whose chief purpose in the day's activities was theatre attendance and those who just happened to attend.

QUESTIONNAIRE

From the time you set off from home, was the trip to the theatre:

	Yes	No	
1.	☐	☐	Your sole purpose for making the trip?
2.	☐	☐	Would you have made the trip if you were *not* attending the theatre?

3. How far do you live from the theatre (no. of miles one way)? ______

4. How many people are in your party? ______

Please answer the following questions regardless of whether you made your own arrangements for attending the theatre or if you purchased your ticket through a group. In the latter case, list only expenditures you made yourself that were not included in the price of the theatre package.

For yourself alone, how much did you spend on each of these items? If you did not use them, leave blank.

5. Parking (divide total by number of people in car)? ______

6. Tolls (divide total by number of people in car)? ______

7. Public transportation? ______

8. Taxis (divide total by number of people in party)? ______

9. Restaurant (divide total by number of people in party)? ______

10. Baby sitter (divide total by number of people in family attending)? ______

11. Hotel (if your attendance at the theatre is the reason you are spending the night in (name of city)) __________________? __________

12. Night club or bar (please estimate on basis of past experience if you intend to visit)? ______

13. Shopping? ______

14. Other, please specify? ____

QUESTIONNAIRE (continued)

If you purchased your ticket through an organization or tour organizer, please answer the following.

15. Through which organization did you purchase your ticket? ______________

16. How much did the total package cost? ______

Did it include:

	Yes	No	
17.	☐	☐	Bus transportation?
	☐	☐	Other transportation, please specify? ________________
18.	☐	☐	Lunch?
19.	☐	☐	Dinner?
20.	☐	☐	Hotel accommodation (if your attendance at the theatre is the reason you are spending the night in (name of city)) __________________?
21.	☐	☐	Bar or night club
22.	☐	☐	Other, please specify? ________________________

23. Did you have free time to spend in ____________? How long? ________

We would also like some information about you personally.

24. Male ☐
    Female ☐

25. Married ☐
    Not married ☐

26. No. children ☐

27. Your age

Under 20	☐	20–24	☐	25–34	☐
35–44	☐	45–59	☐	60 or over	☐

QUESTIONNAIRE (continued)

28. What is your occupation? ____________________________________

29. If you are not the head of your household, what is his or her occupation?

____

30. How much formal education have you completed?

Grade school	☐	1–3 years of high school	☐
4 years of high school	☐	1–3 years of college	☐
4 years of college	☐	Graduate or post-college professional school	☐

31. In which group did your total family income (before taxes) for last year fall?

Under $3,000	☐	$3,000–$4,999	☐	$5,000–$6,999	☐
$7,000–$9,999	☐	$10,000–$14,999	☐	$15,000–$24,999	☐
$25,000–$49,999	☐	$50,000 or over	☐		

32. How did you hear about today's performance (check as many as applicable)?

☐ Mailing list announcement

☐ Newspaper advertising

☐ Newspaper story (including reviews)

☐ Radio or television

☐ Billboard advertising

☐ Word-of-mouth

☐ Other (please specify)

33. Yes No

☐ ☐ Are you a subscriber?

Notes:

1. If because of the firing of the waiter the grocer was forced to cut down his consumption of clothing made in the South or of shoes made in New England, obviously these multiplier effects would be felt well outside the city. And, sooner or later, there always are such effects.

   We must emphasize that the pertinence of the national multiplier rests on an assumption not required for the New York City calculation. If the theatre were to close operation it is quite clear that much of the resulting fall in associated expenditure would be lost to the city because it would instead be spent mostly on items imported from outside the city. On the other hand, it will represent a corresponding net loss to the country as a whole if these funds are either withdrawn from expenditure altogether (put into savings) or used to purchase goods from outside the country. Such an heroic assumption is implicit in the claim made on behalf of *any* economic activity that because it generated $X in sales it contributes a corresponding amount to the nation's economy. Thus, our calculation for the contribution of the theatre to the nation's economy rests on as firm a basis as claims that have been made for such industries as shipping and automobile production.
2. In our calculations we deliberately omitted two weeks, one at the beginning and one at the end of the strike, during part of which all theatres were in operation. Thus, all 'non-strike weeks' are to be interpreted as weeks during which all shows were running throughout, and 'strike weeks' refer to weeks when theatres housing musicals were completely dark.
3. Baumol, William J. and William G. Brown, *Performing Arts: The Economic Dilemma*, The MIT Press, Cambridge, Massachusetts and London, England. See Chapter IV and the associated appendix materials.
4. This figure was raised to $2.00 in 1976.
5. Theatre Development Fund, *Last Minute Discounts on Unsold Tickets: A Study of TKTS*, 1974, p. 13.
6. It would involve double counting to include both the gross ticket receipts of the theatres *and* the expenditures of the theatres in our estimate of the contribution of the theatre to the remainder of the economy. The obvious candidate for elimination is the gross ticket income of the theatre, which is not itself a contribution to others.
7. Before, we did not include air fares because they do not contribute directly to the economy of the city in any substantial amounts.
8. Baumol and Bowen, *op. cit.*
9. This too, is a very conservative estimate. If we had just taken the ancillary expenditures from the earlier study and corrected them by the change in the relevant prices over the interviewing period, we would have obtained as our estimate of ancillary outlays a figure exceeding $72 million, rather than the $52 million figure used in the following calculation.

Appendix

1. Department of Commerce, New York City, by telephone.
2. Baumol and Bowen, *op. cit.*
3. Baumol and Bowen, *op. cit.*
4. The reason they are not put into *every* program is to avoid duplication of answers by members of the same family.

PART VI

HISTORICAL STUDIES OF THE ARTS

[25]

THE

QUARTERLY JOURNAL OF ECONOMICS

Vol. LXXXV | August 1971 | No. 3

ECONOMICS OF ATHENIAN DRAMA: ITS RELEVANCE FOR THE ARTS IN A SMALL CITY TODAY *

WILLIAM J. BAUMOL

Perhaps our cities have grown too large for efficiency in the supply of services and amenities to their inhabitants. At least this is a hypothesis one encounters fairly frequently in the literature of urban economics. In discussing this view some writers have suggested that even the arts do not need a large metropolis in order to survive. While today activity in the theater is centered in the biggest cities, in New York, in London, and in Paris, it has been suggested that the drama can, under appropriate circumstances, prosper in smaller communities. The case of ancient Athens has more than once been cited as an example.[1] Greek cities were certainly small towns by current standards, and yet the vitality of its drama and

* I must express my gratitude to the Ford Foundation, whose support of our urban project helped in the completion of this study. I must also thank for their help F. R. B. Godolphin of the Princeton Department of Classics, Lawrence Stone and Henry N. Drewry of the Department of History, as well as K. J. Arrow, my colleague Daniel S. Hamermesh, and my research assistant, Mrs. Sibyl Silverman. My very deepest gratitude must go to my friend and colleague Hourmouzis Georgiadis, for his enormous help in my attempts to arrive at a reasonable translation of the ancient currency.

1. Thus, e.g.: "Finally, still another argument frequently given [for policy to attract the middle classes to the central city rather than the suburbs] is based on increasing returns rather than externalities. It is argued that cultural amenities require for support a large interested public, and this can only come from the middle classes. The necessary size is perhaps not so obvious; Athens in its classical period had a population little bigger than San Jose, and presumably a much lower per capita income, even allowing for tribute payments." (Kenneth J. Arrow, "Criteria, Institutions and Function in Urban Development Decisions," in A. H. Pascal, ed., *Contributions to the Analysis of Urban Problems*; Santa Monica: RAND Corporation P–3868, Aug. 1968, pp. 49–50.)

its other arts is obvious enough. Does this not suggest that cultural activities can flourish without being surrounded by eight million neighbors? I will offer evidence that the circumstances of the Athenian theater were in fact very different from anything we can expect to find in our society and that the lesson of the Greek experience is of very limited significance for the arts today.

The real issue is the replicability of the Greek arrangements. Are the Athenian methods for the financing of the drama readily transferable to our society? By what means did the Greeks attract their audiences and would their methods work for us?

In this note I undertake to describe the relevant facts so far as they are known. Many readers will no doubt find them as surprising as I did. I must add that this foray into a field in which I have no qualifications involves even more than the obvious degree of presumption. One of the standard references tells us in its opening sentence that it undertakes "to treat of a subject concerning hardly a detail of which can any statement be made without the possibility of dispute. . . ."[2] To this we must add the near impossibility of providing a sensible interpretation of the prices and cost figures reported at various points in the discussion.

The economic difficulties of our own theater can usefully be subdivided into two (interrelated) categories: the limited audience, and the high and rising cost of live performance. It will be convenient to divide my discussion of the economics of the Greek drama accordingly.

I. The Greek Audience

The level of attendance at performances of the Greek drama is incredible by current standards. Though the size of the audience at any period is not in fact known, the Theater of Dionysus in Athens (actually built about 340 BC — after the golden age of Greek drama had passed) is estimated to have held some 15,000 to 20,000 spectators.[3] It is even possible that there were additional persons standing on the hillsides above the theater. Audience figures as high as 30,000 have been mentioned but seem implausible.[4] The population of all of Attica at the height of the Periclean Age may have included

2. Roy C. Flickinger, *The Greek Theater and Its Drama* (Chicago: University of Chicago Press, 1918), p. 1.
3. Albert A. Trever, *History of Ancient Civilization,* Vol. I (New York: Harcourt, Brace and World, 1936), p. 266.
4. Sir Arthur Pickard-Cambridge, *The Dramatic Festivals of Athens* (Oxford: Clarendon Press, 1953), p. 268.

40,000 adult male citizens, perhaps some 120,000 free women and children, and perhaps more than 100,000 slaves (though only figures for the free adult males seem to have a dependable basis).[5] It may be guessed that the city of Athens itself contained some 70 percent of those numbers during the period we are discussing.

The enormous size of the Theater of Dionysus becomes clear when we recognize that today no Broadway theater seats more than 2,000 persons. The total audience of all Broadway theaters together on a particularly good evening is on the order of 25,000 persons (with a total of some 33,000 seats available), which as a proportion of New York's eight million population is surely miniscule, comparatively.

A number of elements help to account for the apparently vast Athenian audience. First, it should be recognized that performances were not available throughout the year. One could not simply decide to attend a play next Saturday. In the city itself plays were given only on two occasions — during two festivals. The main performances occurred during the great festival of Dionysus (Bacchus), held annually, early in the spring (roughly, in March). In Athens proper there seems to have been only one other dramatic festival, the Lenaia (held in about January), during which plays were given fairly regularly.[6] Thus, in terms of audience-days per year, Athenian attendance at the theater was not all that large, say two or three days per adult male citizen, since there were about five performance-days per year, with an audience of, say, 20,000 each.[7] In New York City some six or seven million theater tickets are sold annually, so that even relative to its population it does not suffer so much by the comparison.

The number and types of performance at the main festival, the Great Dionysia, varied somewhat with the passage of time, but certainly an enormous number of plays was squeezed into a very few days. During the time of Pericles the festival normally ran for some seven days, four of which were devoted to drama. On the first of

5. See Trever, *op. cit.*, pp. 292–93 and compare H. Mitchell, *The Economics of Ancient Greece* (New York: Macmillan, 1940), pp. 19–20.
6. Pickard-Cambridge, *op. cit.*, p. 38.
7. Perhaps frequency of attendance was even higher. We have no way of knowing since we do not know either the population of the city itself or the number of persons who watched the performances from the hillsides above the theater. As we will see presently, it is plausible that social pressures made it difficult for any free adult male to absent himself from any of the (approximately) five days of performance per year. The number of days on which drama was presented was, incidentally, not the same every year. During wartime one day of performance was, at least sometimes, eliminated from the main festival of Dionysus.

these, five comedies were presented in succession; and on each of the next three succeeding days, three tragedies and one satyr play (a combination, rather scatological in content, of the contemporary tragic drama and an earlier dramatic form — the dithyramb).[8] The performances began at sunrise and lasted through the day. Later, during the Peloponnesian War, the day of comedies was canceled and instead the other three days of dramatic performance were lengthened by the addition of one comedy each evening.[9]

These three- or four-day marathons of drama must have required stamina of the audience, many of them sitting on backless stone (earlier, wooden) benches. Performances began promptly at sunrise and continued on until dusk. Aristophanes must have struck a sympathetic chord when in *The Birds* he listed as one of the advantages of flying the possibility of escaping "from the long-winded tirades of tragedy" to get home for dinner and back in time for the comic performances.

Thus, while the population of the city did not have dramatic performances available to it during most of the year, when the dramatic season did come it seems to have provided a surfeit. How then did the theater manage to keep its audience?

The answer, it would appear, lay in the religious character of the performance. The drama was able to draw so many spectators in fourth-century Athens for the same reason that permitted Bach to draw an audience for his music some 22 centuries later. Going to church simply was the right thing to do, and Bach's performance of his own music was just part of the ritual.

The sacred character of the performance in Athens even affected the Greek attitude toward the actor. Ancient Greece may well have been the only society before very recent times in which the actor was regarded with favor. ". . . the actors were active participants in a religious service and during the festival performances their persons were quasi-sacrosanct. As such, they were entitled to and received the highest respect. . . ."

It was considered essential that everyone attend the dramatic

8. The satyr play may have been introduced about 500 BC as a device to appease the more conservative members of the audience. It represented a return to the Dionysiac subjects from which the tragedy had largely departed. Performers in the satyr play wore goat ears, horns, tails, and hoofs, presumably "in imitation of Dionysus' attendant sprites." In the earlier dithyramb these performers "were sometimes called *tragoi*, which is the Greek word for 'goats.'" Still later, as the form of the play developed, "it came to be called *tragoidia* ('goat-song')" (Flickinger, *op. cit.*, p. 3).

9. Margarete Bieber, *The History of the Greek and Roman Theater* (Princeton: Princeton University Press, 1961), p. 97.

festivals. "Business was abandoned; the law-courts were closed; . . . even prisoners were released from jail, to enable them to share in the common festivities." [1] Boys and slaves were admitted if their tickets were paid for by their parents or owners. Pickard-Cambridge believes (though this has been questioned) that even women and girls were permitted to attend.[2] (!)

It was, indeed, considered so important that everyone attend the festival that the state provided a special fund that paid the daily admission fee (two obols [3] per day at the time of Demosthenes) for

1. Haigh, quoted by Flickinger, p. 120.

2. This is surprising because of the "oriental-like seclusion" of women in the Greek households and because the content of the comedies was decidedly scatological. In the older comedies a large phallic symbol was carried on a pole as part of the ritual procession, and the actor wore a large artificial phallus which subsequently was replaced by a "less indecent" variant. Flickinger remarks (p. 121) that a respectable woman would have invited divorce by being present at real scenes of the character of those they may have been permitted to witness in the Old Comedy and the satyric drama.

3. I may as well attempt at this point to do what I can to translate the currency. The basic coinage ran as follows: 6 obols = 1 drachma, 1 minna = 100 drachmae, 60 minae = 1 talent. Records for the building of a temple about two decades after Pericles indicate that the regular wage for all workers was 1 drachma per day. and jurors were paid 3 obols per day (Trever, p. 296). Thus, admission fees for one day's performances came to a third of a day's normal wages and were by no means nominal. As we will see later, standards of living in ancient Greece were very low even at the height of the Greek civilization. As a very crude standard of comparison, I will take a day's wage to have been worth $3 in current dollars. (This is slightly more than one quarter of what is now considered to constitute the poverty line for a family of four by the Department of Health, Education and Welfare.) Then, the daily admission price to the festival would have been about $1. Clearly, such a translation into dollars is largely fantasy, but it will serve as a convenient mnemonic device. In any event, since it has been suggested (Trever, p. 269) that 1 drachma sufficed to cover all the daily expenses of a family of four, the proposed convention, 1 drachma = $3, may not be excessive in terms of dollars of 1970 purchasing power.

After writing an earlier draft of this footnote, I came across Colin Clark's much more careful attempt to reconstruct the purchasing power of ancient currencies. Using dollars of 1925–34 purchasing power as his standard, Clark assigns the following values for the drachma at the dates indicated: 480 BC, $4; 400 BC, $2; 300 BC, $1.20. Since the price level in the United States has risen two to three times from 1925–34 until 1970, my conversion rate seems to be moderately consistent with his for the age of Pericles (about 460–430), though my rate gives somewhat fewer 1970 dollars to the drachma than his. (See Colin Clark, *The Conditions of Economic Progress*, London: Macmillan, 1951, p. 551.)

Professor Georgiadis has helped me to conduct some further checks of the suggested conversion rate. We have some figures for wheat prices in Periclean Athens indicating that 50 liters of wheat cost some 3 drachmas. Making a rough attempt to calculate a retail price equivalent for today gives us something less than $2 per drachma. On the other hand, utilizing a weighted average for the urban and rural work force for modern Greece, we arrive at an average daily wage that translates into a bit less than $4. If, as Clark suggests, the output per man-year in ancient Greece was higher than it is today, the drachma, one day's wage, should perhaps be valued somewhat higher. In any event, the choice within the range that seems plausible does not affect the discussion materially since I am concerned primarily with the *ratio* of the ticket price to the daily wage, the ratio between the subsidy to the festivals and the total budget of the state, etc. My attempt to find a reasonable conversion rate

anyone who felt he could not afford it. There are even hints that potential members of the audience were bribed more substantially for attending.[4] Thus, state subsidy for the drama seems to have begun rather early.

II. Financing the Greek Festival

We turn next to the costs of the festival and the means by which they were met. The revenues were clearly not inconsiderable. Assume that the audience was in fact 15,000 per day and that each attendee paid his 2 obols admission. Over the course of the festival if admissions were collected for six days (including the two days in which no plays were performed) this would yield a gross of 5 talents or, at our arbitrary conversion rate of $6 per drachma, about $90,000.

The expenses of the festival are not entirely clear. The personnel involved in the dramatic portion included the author of the play, the chorus, which for the tragedy at different times consisted of twelve to fifteen persons, and the actors, who at the time we are considering, according to Flickinger,[5] generally numbered no more than four persons.[6] Of course, expenses were reduced substantially by the very small number of actors, and for that reason it is still considerably cheaper to produce a Greek drama than, say, a typical Elizabethan play.[7] Nevertheless, because of the sheer number of presentations, despite the small number of actors in each play, the combined size of the casts involved in the festival was enormous. "The number of participants was also astonishing. The dithyrambs alone needed 500 choreutai, with at least ten flute players. In each comedy there were about five actors and 24 choreutai with their flute players and sometimes citharists. In each tragedy, of which nine were presented, there were three actors, fifteen chorus members, and probably at last two musicians. In each of the three satyr

is intended only to convey a rough sense of order of magnitude, indicating that the drachma was worth neither 5 cents nor $50.

4. Pickard-Cambridge, pp. 270–73, and Mitchell, p. 364.

5. Flickinger, pp. 182–83.

6. This often required the actors to play several parts. Sometimes, moreover, a single part seems to have been divided among several actors. Thus, Flickinger suggests that the important role of Theseus in Sophocles' *Oedipus at Colonus* was "played in turn by each of the three actors!" (p. 181).

7. Moreover, the cast had grown only gradually to this size. In the earlier choral performances there was a chorus leader (coryphaeus), usually the poet himself, who answered questions posed by the chorus. Gradually he was given a more distinctive role and replaced by an actor. Aeschylus apparently introduced the second actor, and Sophocles the third (in about 470 BC) (Flickinger, pp. 166–67). It was only with Sophocles, whose voice seems to have been weak, that the poet ceased taking the leading roles.

dramas there were three actors, and chorus members with their flute player. There must have been 700–800 choreutai, 30–50 actors and 20–40 musicians. If we add the mute characters, choregi, chorus teachers, magistrates, judges and stage hands, the number of active participants must have been not much less than one thousand."[8] Today even grand opera rarely involves much over 300 performers. However, the figures refer to the entire festival, including some seventeen plays. If we subtract the 500 performers in the dithyrambs, this leaves us with some thirty performers per play. In any event, when plays went on the road after the Athenian festival, the companies were kept very small.

We do not seem to know how much the actors were paid. We do know that in the middle of the third century they were organized into a guild, called the "Dionysiac Artists," apparently a powerful organization. The guild members formed themselves into companies. A record for the years 272–69 BC of twenty-two companies, all members of the Athenian guild, lists exactly three actors' names for each company. The actors were normally paid by the state. They also took part in contests and may have been able to supplement their incomes with prizes.

Prizes, substantial in magnitude, were also offered to the playwrights. We do not know their amounts in the Athenian festivals. However, we do know that toward the close of the fourth century prizes of 10, 8, and 6 minae were presented to the dithyrambic victors at the festival of Piraeus, with one such prize to each contestant who had been selected to participate.[9] Recalling that a mina was equivalent to 100 drachmae, and that a drachma could cover a day's expenses for a family of four, we see that the poet could probably live comfortably for over a year on his prize money. (At our fictitious rates of exchange the first prize of 10 minae comes to $3,000.)

The finances of the festival involved, primarily, three different groups: the lessees of the theater, the government itself, and a very interesting institution, the choregus. The first of these was the only source of funds not amounting to pure subsidy. ". . . although the dramatic festivals were under the direct control of the state, the financial management was relegated to lessees, who agreed to keep the theater in repair and to pay a stipulated sum into the public treasury in return for the privilege of collecting an admission fee. During the fourth century BC the lessees of the Piraeus theater paid

8. Bieber, p. 53.
9. Flickinger, p. 269.

thirty-three minae [about $10,000 on our concocted exchange rate] annually. This system explains why the authorities, when they wished to enable even the poorest citizens to attend the dramatic exhibitions, did not simply throw open the doors to all. . . ." [1]

The state seems to have contributed the wages of the actors, their costuming, the honoraria of the poets, and the prizes, as well as the admissions subsidies that we have already noted.[2] These must have constituted some of the more substantial outlays on the festivals.

However, a very heavy burden also fell on the choregi. The highest state official involved in the festival had as one of his first duties the appointment of a number of choregi from among the wealthier citizens. These persons, in effect, were "volunteered" to bear a substantial portion of the expenses of the Dionysia. They paid for the training of the chorus, for their costumes, the wages of the singers and their trainer, perhaps also for the flute player, and were responsible for any special scenery that was needed. There is a speech listing the expenses of one choregus who may have been on the generous side. It lists 30 minae ($9,000) for choregia in tragedy in 410 and 50 minae ($15,000) for a dithyrambic chorus of men in 409. In another year his expenses for a comedy came to 16 minae (about $5,000 at our artificial exchange rate). In a country in which wealth was scare, these were very heavy sums.[3]

The choregi were selected from among the wealthy Athenian citizens in rotation. A citizen appointed to take on the position of choregus could ask to be excused on the ground that he had already assumed other public burdens, or he could suggest that it be taken on by someone else better able to do so. Under the law the person who was challenged in this way either had to assume the position of choregus *or had to trade estates with the challenger.*[4] However, citizens would characteristically take on the task more often and would spend more generously than they were required to.[5] This was fortunate from the point of view of the playwrights, the success

1. *Ibid.*, pp. 269–70.
2. Pickard-Cambridge, p. 91.
3. *Ibid.*, pp. 88–89.
4. Flickinger, p. 270.
5. The choregi had a very considerable incentive to contribute to the theater. Sponsors financed the plays of specific playwrights, and when the prizes were awarded, naturally, a great deal of the honor went not only to the author but also to the financial backer. When inscriptions of the festival prizes were prepared, the name of the financial sponsor was at least sometimes inscribed above that of the author of the winning play. For example, the name of Pericles is written above that of Aeschylus, who won the prize for the play *The Persians* in 472 BC. Moreover, financial supporters would sometimes back plays with a particular political slant coinciding with their own interests.

of whose production might be damaged severely by the niggardliness of a choregus.

In sum, the dramatic festivals were made possible by a two-part system of subsidy, involving generous grants by the state and lavish contributions by private citizens that were, in part, voluntary but whose philanthropy was enforced by law and custom.

III. The Magnitude of the Financial Burden

The fragmentary state of our financial information clearly makes it very difficult to draw any conclusions about the real strain that drama imposed on the Greek economy. Before turning to what little information we have on the public finances of the Athenian state, we may first consider some relevant general principles.

Live performance is, of course, very close to being a pure service activity. Because of the *comparative* difficulty in instituting labor-saving innovation in the services,[6] they rise cumulatively in relative cost as an economy's productivity and real income grows. We all know how rapidly the relative price of a haircut rises as we go from an underdeveloped country to a country of moderate wealth to a highly prosperous area. We have also seen the cost of household services rising with the growing prosperity of our economy. Our theater has suffered from just this problem. Cost per performance has risen cumulatively at a rate significantly exceeding the general price level (and the rate of increase in ticket prices, for that matter). For wages in the theater have gone up steadily along with the level of real incomes in our economy, while productivity of the actor in live performance has remained essentially unchanged — it takes as many man-hours today to produce a play of Sheridan's as it did in the eighteenth century. With man-hour productivity in the economy as a whole growing as much as 4 percent per year, the continued rise in the cost of theatrical performance becomes easier to understand.[7]

6. Cf. Victor R. Fuchs, *The Service Economy* (New York: National Bureau of Economic Research, 1968), pp. 50 *ff*. I emphasize the word "comparative" to avoid being misunderstood to be saying that productivity increases in the services are impossible.

7. In the United States one manifestation of this phenomenon has been the increasing length of runs of plays in the commercial theaters. One simply cannot afford to produce plays unless the period of time over which they can be expected to run increases along with the production cost. It is noteworthy, therefore, that in ancient Athens a play was normally performed only once, though a successful drama might be repeated in the provinces. Only after 386 BC, after the great age of playwriting was over, was provision made for revival of earlier dramas as part of the Athenian festivals (Pickard-Cambridge, p. 100).

Thus, the surprising poverty of the ancient Greeks suggests that the opportunity cost of services must have been much lower than it is today. That is, the relative cost, in terms of material consumption goods, of an hour of theatrical performance must have been miniscule compared to what it is currently.[8]

Some idea of the standard of living of the Athenian in the age of Pericles is offered by the nature of his food and shelter. The ordinary houses were built side by side with a common wall between them. Burglars found it easier to break through the walls than to pick the locks. The bedrooms were "mere cells." "The average Athenian was satisfied with the most meager fare — barley or wheat cake or porridge with a much diluted sour wine and relish (opsonion) of salt fish or onions to make it go down. The monotony might be relieved by goat's cheese, honey, green vegetables, and an occasional egg or bit of mutton, but meat was usually reserved for festival days."[9] Perhaps this passage, as one reader has commented, describes consumption patterns that were more Spartan than Athenian, but it is, nevertheless, suggestive.

Even the relatively affluent Athenians were not terribly wealthy. In figures on the distribution of wealth in fourth-century Athens only seventeen persons are reported to have possessed over 5 talents ($90,000 on our contrived standard). All of this suggests that industry and productivity were indeed at a stage at which the cost of performance was relatively low.[1]

Despite this, and despite the substantial contributions of the choregi, the public festivals made very great inroads on the public purse. The budget for the purpose has been estimated by Mitchell[2] at no less than 40 talents per year (about 3/4 million dollars on our conversion scale) out of a total annual budget on the order of 700 talents (about $12 million).[3] That is, the festival expenses came

8. Clark (p. 552) uses the data provided by the Edict of Diocletian (301 AD) to investigate relative costs of various types of goods and services in the ancient world. He concludes that "the purchasing power of the denarius was highest . . . over personal services . . ." (i.e., these were relatively cheap), as our discussion suggests.

9. Trever, p. 295. See also Mitchell, pp. 132 *ff*.

1. Yet, Clark estimates (p. 461) that ". . . the average production per man-year of the whole working community was still probably in the neighborhood of [$500 of 1925–34 purchasing power]. This is a good deal higher than that of present-day Greece or of most southern or eastern European countries."

2. Mitchell, p. 371.

3. In a letter, Professor Arrow comments rather persuasively that the subsidy figure seems very high. If half the total budget for the festivals were devoted to the roughly seventeen plays offered during the Great Dionysia, the reported figure comes to some $20,000 per performance. In a period of low real wages the figure is hard to believe.

Mitchell does, however, cite another writer who "reduces the estimate [of

to well over 5 percent of the annual costs of the entire government, including the "military and naval forces." It is hard to imagine a contemporary government that is prepared to budget that high a proportion of its revenues for the arts. In New York City, for example, it would call for an annual subvention to the arts of some $250 million — more than twice the 1964–65 budget for all non-profit organizations of fully professional performance in the United States combined!

IV. Concluding Comment: Relevance for Contemporary Urban Planning

This superficial survey of the economics of the Athenian theater offers us little reason to expect that in our modern economy a small community can serve as a center for the performing arts. Certainly the circumstances of the arts in Athens were vastly different from those in our society, and there is nothing to lead us to expect that we can replicate them. There seems little prospect of government subsidy on the vast relative scale provided by the Athenian state. It is hard to imagine our wealthier citizens agreeing to be appointed as involuntary philanthropists — and then vying in the generosity of their patronage.

Perhaps most important, we have no substitute for the religious associations of the Greek drama, which helped to make possible the large public subsidies and private subventions, and which brought huge audiences into the theater. Today, with no religious fervor to pack the houses and with television competing for the audiences, a community in which 5 percent of the population is drawn to a live dramatic performance is unusual indeed. The enormous proportion of the Athenian population that attended the theater is surely unattainable for today's cities.

Even if all this could somehow be duplicated, the rising relative costs of live performance mean that the opportunity cost of this support would have grown enormously since the time of Pericles. It would no doubt cost much more today in terms of goods and services foregone, i.e., relative to the general price level, to finance a given level of dramatic activity, and we can expect these costs to continue to grow cumulatively.

the festival's budget] to 40,000 drs. [$180,000], a very small sum" (p. 371, fn. 2). Actually even this amount is not all that small — it is nearly 1½ percent of the total expenditure of the Athenian state. Clark (p. 466) reports the revenue of the Athenian treasury at 6 million drachmae ($18 million) in 433 BC and states that "in 422 BC, a war year, this revenue was doubled." He adds that "the former figure represents 17 percent of the national income."

The sad fact is that, short of a revolution in attendance patterns, the minimum size of city needed to support a theater or a symphony orchestra seems very likely to grow even larger than it is today as rising real costs of performance make it necessary to look ever more widely for sources of support.

PRINCETON UNIVERSITY AND NEW YORK UNIVERSITY

ON THE ECONOMICS OF THE THEATER IN RENAISSANCE LONDON*

Mary I. Oates and William J. Baumol

Princeton University and New York University, USA

Summary

The theater of Elizabeth and James (1576–1642) was entirely commercial, receiving virtually no subsidy from patrons. Though not always profitable, some theatrical entrepreneurs made fortunes and many actors lived comfortably. The profitability of runs of two weeks (today some 35 weeks are required) helps explain the many plays produced. The high attendance rate was necessary for prosperity of the theater in a city under 200 000. It was also probably helped by the Tudor inflation which apparently reduced real wages to their lowest level from the late Middle Ages to the present. Today, with real wages many times higher and attendance rates lower, such small cities cannot provide prosperous unsubsidized theater.

Introduction

The outburst of dramatic activity that included the work of Marlowe, Shakespeare, Jonson, and scores of others was relatively brief. It lasted somewhat less than seventy years, that is, from the second half of the reign of Elizabeth until, after a period of decline, Cromwell's associates finally closed it down in 1642. It was, for the most part, a vigorous and successful activity. The immediate issue we explore in this paper is how, in a community so small as London at the end of the sixteenth century, the commercial theater was able to thrive as it did. Our ultimate objective, however, is to throw light on two broader issues.

First, we hope to offer evidence on the influence of city size on the vitality of the performing arts, and on the doubts expressed by Professor Arrow (1968), among others, about the assumption that there are a great many significant activities that can be provided only by the large metropolis. The second of the

* We would like to thank the National Science Foundation whose grant assisted materially in this study. And we are deeply grateful to Professor G. E. Bentley for his careful reading of our manuscript and for his many useful suggestions that helped us to avoid a number of serious errors. We must also thank Kenneth Arrow, A. Walton Litz, Wallace Oates, C. Patrick O'Donnell Jr., Joseph Parvin, and Lawrence Stone, each of whom was extremely helpful to us at various stages of our work.

broad issues considered is the relationship between the level of real wages and the supply of services. It has been argued elsewhere (Baumol & Bowen, 1966) that rising real wages generally put personal services at a cost and, hence, a price disadvantage, because in these activities it is relatively difficult to introduce labor-saving innovations that offset increasing wage costs. One tends to think of the Elizabethan period as one of great prosperity and relatively high real wages. However, we will see that, although incomes were apparently rising for some classes, there is evidence suggesting that real wages toward the end of the sixteenth century were in fact extraordinarily low. It will be suggested that the *low level of real wages may have contributed substantially to the prosperity of the drama,* thus leading to the conclusion that general economic prosperity, with the increase in real wages that normally accompanies it, may actually depress some of those activities which are usually taken to contribute to "the quality of life".

1. Nature of the Data

Much of the information we have about the workings of the theater in Shakespeare's London rests on inference, some of it quite tenuous. The surviving plays occasionally refer to the workings of the theater: for example, after Hamlet's theatrical venture—his attempt to catch the conscience of a king—he asks Horatio whether his efforts have earned him a "fellowship in a cry of players", and Horatio replies, "Half a share". From such allusions, as well as from legal documents, scholars have deduced that the leading actors in a theatrical company held stock in the company, shared in its profits, and were called "sharers" or "fellows": the half a share to which Horatio refers represented, Professor Bentley tells us in a letter (October, 1970), the size of the player's original investment. Since information about the earnings of these entrepreneurs, who sometimes doubled as actors, is more difficult to come by, it is fortunate that a diary has survived kept by Philip Henslowe, financier of the Admiral's Men, the leading rivals of Shakespeare's company. This diary records such information as the dimensions of a theater that Henslowe ordered built, and, for each performance over most of a three year period, his own share of the daily receipts (half the gallery seats sold). However, we do not know enough about the number of persons admitted at each of the various prices to permit us to translate with any degree of accuracy Henslowe's share to figures for attendance and gross revenue. If we add to that complexity the suspicion that prices doubled on opening nights[1] and may have been higher for holiday occasions, the inaccuracies are, of course, compounded. The traveler, Samuel Kiechel, furnishes us with the only surviving record of

[1] Samuel Kiechel, a German traveler, said flatly in 1585 that the price for a new play was double that for a repeat performance (quoted by Rye, p. 88). See also Jonson, Induction to *Bartholomew Fair*.

gross receipts as such. Kiechel either noticed, or was told, in 1585, that The Theater was grossing £10–£12 per day for a new play (Rye, p. 88), and while the figure may have been a mere guess, it does accord fairly well with both the inferential data upon which we are otherwise dependent, and with the usual payment (£10) for a performance at court.[1]

Legal records can also be valuable. On the important issue of total audience size for all theaters on a given day, for example, the most dependable source is a sworn statement that was not challenged by the plaintiff's adversaries.[2] It names what is likely, therefore, to be a lower bound, 3 000. For the capacities of individual theaters we are in worse case: in contrast with the surviving evidence on the Greek drama, no Elizabethan or Jacobean theater buildings remain, so that we are dependent on documents such as Henslowe's specifications for the dimensions of a house. Using such figures Alfred Harbage has actually experimented to determine the possible number of standees and the seats one could have crowded into the available areas (1941, pp. 19–23). This is, essentially, the basis of current estimates of the number of places offered in each price range, the size of a capacity audience, and total revenue that it would have yielded.

For data on wages and prices in the economy generally we use the figures furnished by E. H. Phelps Brown and Shiela Hopkins that report wages of building laborers and building craftsmen in Southern England, which may not have been quite the same as wages paid to workmen in London. The few references to earnings in London that we have come across are a bit higher, but are generally consistent with the figures that we use.[3]

---

[1] For a slightly later period, the office book kept by Sir Henry Herbert, James' and Charles' Master of the Revels for the period 1622–1641 is useful, since Herbert agreed on one occasion to accept the profits from two "benefit" performances per year for the period 1628–32, the most profitable of which, played at Blackfriars, yielded £17 10*s.*, and the least, at the Globe, £1 5*s.* After the "daily expenses" of the company, averaged and estimated by them at £2 5*s.*, were deducted, Herbert netted an average of £8 19*s.* 4*d.*, the average gross being thus £11 4*s.* 4*d.* (Bentley, 1941–68, I, p. 24). This figure, slightly higher than the £10 mentioned in the text reflects the higher profits of the 1630's, during which Prof. Bentley has players' bills as high as £20 for a single performance at Hampton Court or Richmond: because they had to go farther afield, they note, the additional bounty was justified since, as one accountant's item reads: "[We] lost our day at our house" (quoted in Bentley Letter).

[2] In 1612 the Waterman's Company, who represented the bargemen on the Thames, presented a legal brief which complained that the fashionable new theaters on the North Bank were attracting some 3 000 spectators a day, the grievance being that this clientele had formerly employed the watermen to convey them across the Thames for performances at the large public theaters on Bankside or for bear-baiting at the Paris Garden. John Taylor, who presented the plaintiffs' case, was himself a playwright, and so probably had a fairly accurate idea of total daily audience-size at the North-Bank theaters; at all events, as noted, the defendants did not contest his claim (Harbage, 1941, pp. 36–37).

[3] The figures on prices and wages were originally gathered by Thorold Rogers and William Beveridge. More recently E. H. Phelps Brown and Sheila Hopkins used these data to construct, with considerable care and all the appropriate reservations, indices of wages and prices of a "composite unit of consumables running from 1260 to 1954". The price figures are based, however, on institutional records which may or may not represent retail prices, and unfortunately, such historical records can be affected by "kick-backs" and other distorting influences. The price index is based on a calculation of "an aggregate price year

2. Interpretation of Elizabethan Prices

It will be helpful to have some sort of crude translation of Elizabethan money into current terms. Such a translation is unavoidably suspect since it must be based on imperfect data, and because patterns of consumption, working hours and conditions have changed over the four intervening centuries. Nevertheless, we offer our calculations for what they may be worth, since we feel that the only thing worse than an attempt to interpret the sixteenth and seventeenth century currency in modern terms would be failure to do so.

Even if we had all the information we would like, the translation from Elizabethan pounds to 1970 dollars would still not be unique because of the very large difference in the behavior of prices of different items over the centuries. The calculated relative purchasing power of the two currencies will therefore vary materially with the type of item whose purchase is used as the standard of comparison. For our purposes two such standards seem particularly pertinent: labor time and a market basket of commodities. With the aid of the former one can hope to evaluate, say, an Elizabethan ticket price in terms of today's incomes. It will indicate the current dollar ticket price which would require as many hours of work for its purchase as the one penny admission paid by the Elizabethan attendee. The second standard, the market basket of consumer's goods, indicates the relative amounts of consumption given up in exchange for a ticket then and now. In both these calculations we rely primarily on the Phelps Brown-Hopkins figures.

The labor time translation is the more direct of the two, though here there is also an ambiguity. One can translate in terms of daily or in terms of hourly wages, but since the length of the working day has changed substantially over the centuries, from perhaps 8–12 hours in 1600 to some 7 or 8 hours today, the results will not be the same. The daily wage comparison may give us a better feeling for the relative total incomes available in the two periods, while the translation in terms of hourly wages indicates the relative purchasing power of a given amount of labor time, then and now. For the period 1580–1629, we are given a daily wage of 1 shilling for a building craftsman and 8 pence for a laborer. In the United States in 1968 union wages in construction in five major cities averaged $5.75/hour for a journeyman and $4.50 for helpers and laborers (U.S. Department of Labor, Table 11). Assuming that they work a seven hour day, this gives us a daily wage of approximately $40 and $31.50 for the respec-

---

by year for a composite commodity, made up always of the same amounts of some of the main heads of consumption ... bread-stuffs, meat, cloth, and so on". The specific items included in each category are varied to reflect the available evidence on changes in consumption patterns. Unfortunately, the calculation excludes a number of important cost components, notably, rents and the prices utilized are described as "more wholesale than retail". Recent evidence (Kerridge, pp. 208–226) suggests that rents in Tudor and early Stuart England did not lag behind other prices, though this view has not been accepted by all economic historians. If Kerridge's views are valid, the inclusion of rent data in the Phelps Brown–Hopkins index would, if anything, have strengthened our conclusions.

Table 1. *1970 Dollar equivalent in terms of Elizabethan currency*

	Purchasing power $	Wages $	
		Daily	Hourly
1 penny	0.17	3.30	4.60
1 shilling	2.00	40.00	56.00
1 pound	40.00	800.00	1 120.00

tive categories. Either of these two pairs of figures then indicates that a daily wage of a shilling in 1600 can be translated into a daily wage of some $40 today, i.e., that one Elizabethan pound is worth about $800 in its ability to purchase days of labor. Since in 1970 the workday was not only more remunerative but also shorter, the translation of Elizabethan currency on the basis of hourly wages gives us still higher figures. Using a ten and a seven hour day as very rough estimates for the building industries in the two periods, the hourly wage equivalents are about 1.4 times as high as the daily figures.

The translation in terms of a market basket of goods uses the Phelps Brown–Hopkins price index. The average value of that index for the 50 year period 1576–1625 is 456. By 1950 the index had reached 3155. Using the U.K. "Price Index Number" (Department of Employment and Productivity, p. 115) to bring this figure up to date we find that between 1950 and 1969 the Price Index number went from 100 to 205. Guessing that it had risen to 215 by 1970 we obtain an extrapolation of the Phelps Brown–Hopkins series that gives us an index number of about 6 800 for 1970. This means that the market basket of consumables rose in cost by about 15 times over the period 1600–1970. To translate this into dollars requires only one more step. We have an estimate for the cost of a "median weekly family food basket" which indicates that a pound in the U.K. can purchase as much as $2.60 here.[1] Multiplying by this factor we conclude that a pound in 1600 could buy as much as £15 or about $40 today.

If we believe the calculation, the real daily wages of an American worker today are 20 times as high as those of an Elizabethan,[2] whose daily wage in

[1] See Bush. An extrapolation of some earlier United Nations figures gives a rate of exchange of about $2.90 to the pound. This obviously does not affect our calculations substantially.

[2] And the real hourly wage is about 28 times as high! The figures at first glance may seem implausible, but a simple calculation suggests that it is quite credible. Data furnished in the *Economic Report of the President* (1965, p. 227) indicate that since World War I productivity per man hour in the United States has risen rather steadily at an average rate of 2.5 percent per year and somewhat more rapidly since World War II. Assume that in 1800 productivity in the U.S. was still exactly the same as that in Elizabethan London but that, with the advent of the Industrial Revolution, it rose at an average rate of 2 percent between 1800 and 1910, then increasing 2.5 percent per annum thereafter. This suffices to produce the estimated increase in real wages.

What little information we have about working-class living conditions suggests that they were indeed minimal. "For Dekker ... workmen were 'Stinkards': herrings and onions, alas, were among the few foods they could afford to buy; bread was an expensive luxury" (Harbage, 1941, p. 56).

terms of 1970 dollars is seen to be only $2! As we will see later, he did not normally live on his wages alone, but the calculation is nevertheless rather disturbing.

Table 1 may serve as a handy summary of our results.

3. The Public and Private Theaters[1]

The Elizabethan and Jacobean Theaters fell into two types, very different in character and in mode of operation: the public and the private playhouses. Their difference will play a significant role in the subsequent discussion. The public theater was a mass entertainment enterprise. It offered some 200 performances per year, although it was often forced to suspend its operations during Lent and during the plague-ridden summer months. The audience capacity of a single theater has been estimated at 3 000,[2] which is more than twice that of the typical Broadway house, and more than a third larger than the largest of the Broadway theaters. Prices of admission began at one penny,[3] which in terms of other consumables foregone amounts to less than twenty cents, but as a proportion of a worker's daily wage is equivalent to more than three dollars. The best seats seem to have cost threepence, and a very few, "The Lords", 6 or even 12 (Harbage, 1941, p. 26).

---

[1] A fine introductory discussion of the structure of the Elizabethan theater is found in Bentley, 1961, Chapters 4 and 5. Most of our discussion of the private and the public theaters is based on Harbage, 1952.

[2] "There are only two known contemporary estimates of the capacity of Elizabethan public theaters, one made by a touring Dutchman named Johannes De Witt, who visited the Swan Theater in 1596, and the other by the Spanish Ambassador, who reported to his government about the size of the crowds at the Globe Theater at several performances of a smash hit play in the summer of 1625. Both men name the same capacity figure, 3 000" (Bentley, 1961, p. 130). See also note 3, above, which refers, of course, to total theatrical attendance on a given day.

[3] Since the period of great theatrical activity lasted over half a century of general inflation, most prices, including those of tickets, must have changed over the course of the period. Most of our data are based on Henslowe's figures for the decade of the 1590's, just before the middle of the period. The 1590's must not, however, be taken as a "representative" decade. It included a very serious outbreak of the Plague, several years of crop failure and some extraordinarily sharp price rises. We have evidence indicating that, while before 1600 the minimum price of admission was one penny, by 1625 this had doubled. Thus Harbage quotes Platter (another German traveler) to this effect:

"... Whoever cares to stand below pays one English penny, but if he wishes to sit he enters by another door, and pays another penny, while if he desires to sit in the most comfortable seats which are cushioned, where he not only sees everything well, but can also be seen, then he pays yet another English penny at another door (1599)."

The later figures we get from Bentley, who quotes an allusion from a play performed about 1625. Thrift, "a citizen", is speaking:

> And I will hasten to the money box,
> And take my shilling out again,
> I'll go to th' Bull, or Fortune, and there see
> A play for two pense, with a Jig to boot.

(*The Careless Shepherdess*, quoted in Bentley, 1941–68, VI, p. 111.) Thrift is attending a play in a "private" house. The "two pense" seems to refer to standing room at one of the two public theaters mentioned.

The private theaters, which began as boys' companies with exclusively juvenile casts drawn from the great choir schools, only assumed a degree of commercial importance in about 1600. No adult company that we know of played in a private house until 1608, when Shakespeare's company, the King's Men, purchased Blackfriars, formerly used by the boys of the Queen's Chapel (who served as a company of child performers). At first the profits from both seem to have been about equal. By 1634, however, the balance had swung in favor of the Blackfriars, although the company continued to play both there and at its public, i.e., open air, theater for the remainder of its existence. Even as early as 1612 Edward Kirkham, who was both a theatrical investor and Revels Office official, said that "they took in £ 1 000 in a winter more at the Blackfriars than they had formerly taken at the Globe" (Bentley, 1948, p. 47).

Figure 1 provides an overview of the level of dramatic activity in London over the entire period, and indicates the number of public and private houses in operation. The numbers are only approximate, several unimportant and short lived theaters having been omitted; in a few cases the date of construction is unknown, and some of the buildings were later converted into prize fighting arenas. Nevertheless, the graph is a reasonably good representation of the course of events in the London theater, and it shows strikingly how the private theaters which, as just noted, only began to operate on fully professional basis some years after 1600, constituted at least 25 percent of the theater's operating units after 1615, and eventually reached 50 percent of the total. Note also that the number of private theaters actually in operation at a given time does not reflect very accurately the demand for their services. In contrast to managers of the public theaters, which lay across the Thames, the North Bank entrepreneurs were continually threatened with eviction by their Puritan-minded neighbors in the City. These worthies frequently entered successful complaints in the courts, insisting that the houses were a neighborhood nuisance, not to mention a moral threat. In the second decade of the seventeenth century, for example, knowledgeable theatrical investors sank vast sums into the building of a private theater ("Rosseter's Blackfriars", or Puddle Wharf) to replace Whitefriars, the lease on which expired in 1613. Although work began to convert the house at Puddle Wharf into a theater, and plays were actually performed there ca. 1613–1616, the legal authorities finally insisted on its demolition. Such failure, however, did not deter the backers of the Phoenix in Drury Lane, which was used as a playhouse from 1616–1642. The very vehemence of the watchdogs of public morals points to a greater demand for these theaters than the existing ones could meet.

Jonson, Beaumont and Fletcher were among those who wrote at least partly for the private theaters. Performances at these theaters were, at least during the first half of our period, given only once or at most twice a week, and their season was short, probably fewer than 30 weeks a year. The buildings which, unlike the public theaters, were entirely enclosed, were also very small. Estimates run to a seating capacity of perhaps 400, though some of them were later rebuilt to hold an audience of somewhat more than 600 persons.

Admission prices started at six pence (Harbage, 1952, pp. 43–44) and went up to a shilling or even one and six. Most seats sold at a shilling and occupants of sixpenny seats were sneered at as "groundlings".[1] Since in terms of today's daily wages this is a price scale whose cheapest tickets sold at some $20.00, it is clear that the private theater was *not* the theater of the common man.

4. The Theater as Commercial Private Enterprise

The fact that each theatrical company had its noble patron may suggest that the drama was subsidized. In fact, this simply was not so. Neither governmental nor private philanthropy was ordinarily provided to the theater: "The role of the patron cost little or nothing ... What a company could normally expect from its lord was a document declaring that its members were his servants and should be respected accordingly, occasional intercession on their behalf, if they got into trouble, a payment when they performed before him (such as they would receive in similar circumstances from any other lord), and, occasionally, a 'badge' or livery—an allowance of cloth so that they might wear the colors of his house" (Harbage, 1952). Bentley adds that royal companies received payment for livery every other year (1941–1968, I, 53). Typically, for a performance at court or at the home of one of the barons, the company received £10, which is very slightly more than what in the earlier period of the Elizabethan theater seems to have been the normal gross from a performance at its own theater—some 8 or 9 pounds. The role of the patron was primarily the protection of the actors from harassment as "Roges, Vacaboundes and Sturdy Beggers",[2] and no benefits other than prestige and suits of clothing for the coronation seem to have accrued to Shakespeare's company when, from "the Lord Chamberlain's Men", they were transformed into "the King's Men" after James' accession.

That the ordinary, commercial drama was far from being subsidized is indicated by the sizeable fees a company had to pay to the Master of the Revels, a sort of censorship arm of the Lord Chamberlain himself. The fees the Master might collect varied: Henslowe records what appear to be regular monthly

[1] Jonson (1632) refers to "the *Faeces*, or grounds, of your people, that sit in the oblique caves and wedges of your house, your sinfull sixe-penny Mechanicks ..." (*Introduction to the Magnetick Lady*, Vol. V, p. 504).

[2] "all Fencers Bearewardes Comon Players in Enterludes & Minstrels, not belonging to any Baron of this Realme or Towardes any other honorable Personage of greater Degree ... whiche ... shall wander ... shalbee taken adjudged and deemed Roges Vacaboundes and Sturdy Beggers, intended of this present Act" *Act* 16 *Elizabeth*, c. 5, p. 5 (1572), quoted by Simpson, Vol. II, p. 240.

£3 payments, perhaps simply for the license to use his theater as a playhouse, while Herbert seems to have applied a sliding scale for the censorship of the plays themselves, depending on whether the scripts were old or new, or whether they contained "dangerous matter" (Bentley, 1941–1968, III, 265). One of the few cases of outright royal grants to a commercial company occurred during James' reign when he granted the King's Men several subsidies to keep them together during plague seasons (Thaler, pp. 86–87, and Cunningham, pp. 82–96). But the King's Men by this time were clearly the premiere London company; others were not so fortunate, and were forced either to take to the road, where they seldom made expenses, or to disband completely. Aside from these rather rare instances of royal patronage, the picture is, as Baldwin says, that of the acting company as a "monopoly under license or patent" (Baldwin, p. 286), a privilege for which the Revels Office might collect as much as £100 per year from a successful company.

Theatrical enterprise then was, essentially, an unsubsidized commercial venture. Certainly, most if not all of the theatrical entrepreneurs were in the business for money and there is little reason to believe that they were reluctant to sacrifice "artistry" where that was dictated by financial considerations. Alleyn, who was Henslowe's partner and one of the age's great tragic actors was also an accomplished bear-baiter, and the two built the Hope in 1614 with the intention of using it for baiting at least two days in six (Briley, p. 106).[1] As another example, we note that new plays were simply placed on order by Henslowe as business needs dictated. He kept a stable of authors and often utilized several playwrights to produce one piece, somewhat in the spirit of Hollywood's procedure at the height of its prosperity. Professor Bentley (letter cited above) reports on the basis of a review of all English plays known to have been written between 1590 and 1640 that well under half of the total were works of collaboration, but the number was nevertheless substantial. With the market requiring a company to produce as many as 40 new plays in a year there was little time to waste on playwriting. Marchette Chute reports: "Thomas Dekker, for instance, worked for four years for Henslowe at a rate of nearly a script a

[1] As Murray Bromberg has observed, Henslowe's methods were matched if not equalled by more "respectable" entrepreneurs. "There are repeated suggestions that [Christopher] Beeston [another actor-manager] was more shrewd than honest in his business dealings with the actors ... A Beeston's Diary would probably offer many parallels to Henslowe's Diary ... (II, 364)". The impressment of children for the boys' companies; the beating in 1606 of Thomas Woodford, backer of a rival juvenile company by an Edward Pierce, who was probably Master of Paul's Boys, over what may have been a business dispute (Hillebrand, p. 213); and, on the positive side, the comfortable retirements of Shakespeare, Burbage, and other members of the King's Men, several of whom had even bought "gentility" in the form of coats of arms, suggest parallels between these "aesthetic" entrepreneurs and the eager money-makers of the City. Briley documents Alleyn's bear-baiting activity by a quotation from Alleyn's diary: "Baighted before ye king a my men washt my shep & pd 2*d* a skore ... 0.1.0." 11 June 1622. The Henslowe-Alleyn partnership considered baiting profitable enough to use the Hope two days out of seven for baiting, the stage "being made to take up and downe when they please". (Quoted from a manuscript continuation of Stow's *Annales* (1631) by Sir Edmund Chambers, *ES* (1923), II, 374–5, and by Briley, p. 106.)

month, and Michael Drayton ... produced seventeen scripts for Henslowe in a single year."[1]

With such devotion to their business interests it is not surprising that some of those involved in theatrical activities made out very well. We know of a number of cases of financial success. Certainly, the Henslowe–Alleyn partnership prospered. They are reported to have provided for the foundation of the College of God's Gift in Dulwich an endowment of £10 000, for those days an enormous sum, comparable in terms of workers' daily earnings with some $8 million today. John Heminges, Shakespeare's fellow-housekeeper was said to be of "Greate Lyveinge wealth and power", and Richard Burbage is reported to have died with holdings worth £300 annually (Harbage, 1952, p. 24).

Nevertheless, these success stories are about as unrepresentative as those we encounter in the theater today. We know that Henslowe was perpetually bailing his lackeys out of debt, and that much of his power resulted from their financial dependence on him. Few of the theatrical companies survived very long. Only Shakespeare's company managed to go on for 50 years, and no more than three or four others were able to continue for 20 years (Bentley, 1961, p. 88). Despite (or perhaps because of) their high prices, the early private theaters were constantly in financial straits (Harbage, 1952, p. 45).

In sum, the Renaissance theater in London was very much a private enterprise, dedicated to the pursuit of profit and not subsidized either by government or private philanthropy. It was a risky business in which some did manage to make their fortunes. The natural question, then, is how, in a city so small as London in 1600, it was possible for the theater to survive at all, and how it was able to support so many new productions. Since the answer may lie in the frequency of attendance of the average Londoner and in the relative cost of a production we will, therefore, next examine these in turn.

London one immediately runs into a problem: just what does one mean by "London" in 1600?—only the area within the political boundaries of "the City" or also suburbs, such as Westminster, from which one could reach the theaters on foot? In fact, many of the demographers' estimates do not specify which entity they have in mind. We are, therefore, not quite sure what to make of Roger Mols' figures (p. 47) that report London's population to have been over 100 000 but under 200 000 toward 1600. Similarly, we cannot readily interpret

5. Size of the Elizabethan Audience

There simply are no good records on audiences and populations three or four centuries ago. In examining the specialists' guesses about the population of

[1] (Chute, p. 56). Baldwin (pp. 28–29), however, cites several instances of individual playwrights who worked under bond to particular companies to provide about two or three new plays a year. Shakespeare's output was almost exactly two plays per year which may have represented an informal agreement with his company.

Trevelyan's estimate (p. 142) that "... when Elizabeth died [the population of London] may already have touched 200 000." Harbage, though no specialist in demography, has, however, undertaken a painstaking calculation, based on bills of mortality and other related evidence, on the population of areas within fairly easy walking distance of the theaters. He arrives (1941, p. 38) at a figure of 160 000 for 1605. Since this figure is consistent with the other estimates we have been able to find, we may take it to be correct in order of magnitude.

For the audience figures we must also turn to Harbage. He calculates his figure from the number of theaters in operation, which we do know with some degree of certitude, from the average capacity of the theaters, which, as we have said, is a very crude guess at best, from Henslowe's figures for gallery receipts,[1] and from estimates of the number of places available at each ticket price, which Harbage calculates from the known dimensions of the theaters. As already mentioned, the only surviving contemporary estimates mention "3 000" as the capacity of two *different* public theaters (see note 8). The same figure as a rough estimate of "ordinary" *total* attendance at all the theaters in operation in 1612 may possibly include the Bear Garden (see note 3).

The estimated size of the daily average audience of all theaters in London taken together varies by date. In 1595 it is put at 2 500. By 1601 it may have grown to 3 000. For 1605 there is an estimate of 3 500 and for 1613 a figure of 3 000–4 000 (Harbage, 1941, pp. 36–38). Harbage multiplies these figures by six to obtain a weekly attendance figure.[2] From this calculation Harbage deduces that weekly attendance, in 1605, the period when he believes attendance relative to the population was at its peak was about 21 000 persons. Since the relevant population was apparently 160 000 this means that at this time about 13 percent of the population attended the theater every week.

To indicate whether this figure is particularly large we offer two comparisons. First, we consider attendance at the New York theater which seems to have reached its peak in about 1928, just before the advent of the talking picture. We have an estimate of weekly attendance in February of 1928–29 of 286 thousand persons (Moore, p. 149). At this time (interpolating between the 1920

---

[1] Among many other entries, Henslowe's diary records his share of the gallery receipts at the Rose Theater from 1594 through 1597. It indicates that this figure on holidays (about 50 shillings) and at opening performances (55 shillings) tended to be much higher than it was on an "ordinary day" (28 shillings) (see Harbage, 1941, Appendix B) [the figures are averages for the two "more normal" seasons, 1595–1596]. It is surprising that there was so little fall in receipts from the galleries during the winter season considering that even the twopenny seats, while protected from snow, were probably not heated. November and December receipts were low (about 22 shillings) compared with the overall average of some 27 shillings. February revenues, however, perhaps owing to pre-Lenten celebration, averaged a healthy 32 shillings. The high receipts at opening performances are undoubtedly, in part, a consequence of the higher prices charged on those occasions.

[2] The estimate may be somewhat low because it is based on the assumption that the ban on Sunday performances was, in fact, enforced. There is evidence that Sunday performances and even performances during Lent were winked at, at least under James (Henslowe, pp. xxvii).

and the 1930 census data) the population of New York City proper was slightly more than 6.5 million, and, to use a somewhat broader geographic unit, the total population of incorporated places within 20 miles of New York City Hall was slightly over 9.5 million (Laidlaw, p. 43). Thus, the weekly attendance figure is roughly 4.5 percent of the New York City population and about 3 percent of that of the metropolitan area, well below the 13 percent figure for Elizabethan London, but not so far below it as one might have suspected.

A second comparison is provided by Harbage himself who considers

> "... the oft-used analogy of theater attendance in Shakespeare's day and movie attendance in our own", and concludes that "eighty-five million Americans are said to go to the movies every week [1941] ... about 65 percent of our population, or 10 persons in 15. In light of this modern devotion to drama the Elizabethan Londoner begins to appear almost apathetic."[1]

Thus, theatrical attendance during the period we are considering was high[2] but not astonishingly high. The data also lead us to question the notion that (in contrast with all evidence on today's audience) the Elizabethan theater attracted as many persons from the lower income groups as is generally supposed. Performances took place in the daytime, during working hours, and this suggests that the activity was not designed primarily to attract an audience of laboring poor.[3] But there is a stronger reason for suspicion. The decline in the number of public theaters and the rapid rise in the demand for performances at "private" houses so soon after the innovation had been introduced (Figure 1) suggests that the market for theater was to be found primarily among the upper classes. The commercial instincts of the Jacobean entrepreneurs would hardly have led them toward private theaters with their small seating capacity and their very high ticket prices if the masses were a primary source of demand.

Perhaps the "Theater of a Nation" was mainly an Elizabethan phenomenon: it does appear that shortly after James' accession in 1603, by approximately 1610, the lower income groups were beginning to go back to prize fighting, bear-baiting, visits to madhouses, and public executions for their entertainment. It is also likely that Puritan scruples were beginning to take their toll. There was growing Puritan sentiment among the well-off urban middle classes that was shared to a much smaller degree by the country gentry and aristocracy, and, although those sharing this sentiment frowned on public spectacles of almost any sort, they were particularly hard on the "common stage". Whatever the

---

[1] Harbage, 1941, p. 42. Harbage does go on, however, to point out various reasons, convenience of location being one, why the analogy between motion pictures and Elizabethan drama is of limited validity.

[2] A reader has suggested that the size of the audience during the period in question may be conditioned in part by the fact that so many "Londoners" were transients. This, plus the fact that the range of services, like the range of commodities, was narrow, would no doubt have contributed to the demand for theatrical entertainment.

[3] But see Harbage 1941, p. 67 for an account of the way in which members of this class might have been less "regimented by time clocks" than they are now.

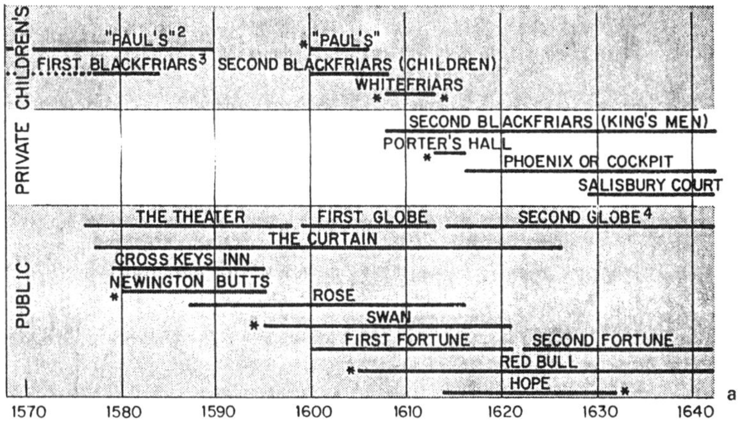

Fig. 1a. Life spans of London theaters 1575–1642.[1]
(* indicates approximate date)

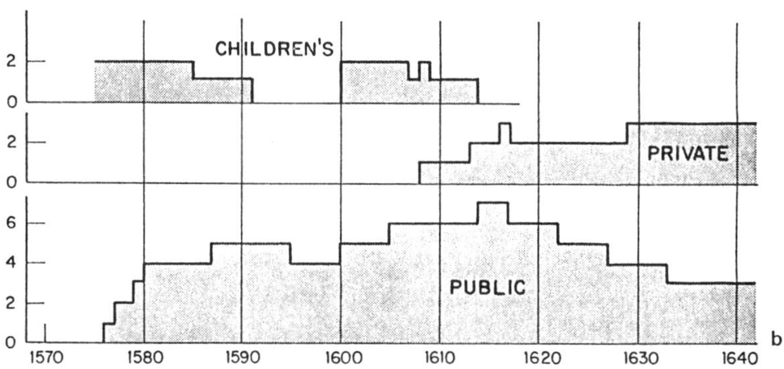

Fig. 1b. Number of theaters in use 1575–1642. Sources: Hillebrand; Chambers (1923) vol. II; Bentley (1941–68) vol. VI.

[1] Excludes the following theaters because of very problematic dates: The Bell Inn; The Bel Savage Inn; The Boar's Head; The Bull Inn; The Red Lion; Le Fevre's Riding Academy.

[2] Since no actual building has been identified, references to "Paul's" Theater rest upon accounts of activities undertaken by this boys' company, and the assumption that they must have had a fairly permanent playing place. See Hillebrand, p. 114. Children, including those of Paul's, continued to play sporadically in various "adult" houses until about 1616, when Hillebrand places their virtual disappearance from the London stage, p. 274.

[3] Both children's companies, the Boys of Paul's and the Children of The Chapel Royal (later the Children of the Queen's Revels, finally Children of the Revels) had begun public performances before 1575. The Chapel Children did not actually occupy the First Blackfriars until 1577, but must have used another playing place (denoted by a broken line) previously.

[4] Assumes the theaters did comply with the Parliamentary closing order of 1642. For surreptitious performances following the order, see Bentley (1941–1968), VI, p. 173.

reason, by 1620 the theater's business interests were turning toward a smaller, more affluent audience.

6. Prices, Wages, and the Prosperity of the Theater

Live performance is a labor-intensive activity. Today some 30 percent of the budget of a Broadway play is devoted to the wages of the actors and musicians, and, when one includes payment to the author, to stagehands, carpenters, and the like, the figure is probably over 50 percent (Moore, p. 64). In the Elizabethan theater, as indicated in the appendix, the proportions do not seem to have been much different. In such an activity financial viability must then depend strongly on the level of real wages. When costs of labor are low the theater can more easily afford to take risks in its choice of plays, since even a rather short run can then show a profit. A relatively large number of companies can survive in a given market, and tickets can be offered at prices that are low in comparison with the cost of less labor-intensive goods and services.

The energy and expansionism of Elizabethan England are likely to foster the impression that it was a period of general prosperity in which most classes benefited. As we will see, the picture is considerably more mixed. At this point we are interested primarily in the real incomes of wage earners and the rural residents without secure land tenure, the copyholders and the tenants at will, from among whom one might expect the theater to have obtained its personnel. Here, the Phelps Brown–Hopkins indices can help us again. We have reproduced from the Phelps Brown–Hopkins articles graphs indicating the movement of prices, and of wages in comparison with prices, for the remarkably long period 1264–1954 (Figures 2 and 3). The authors themselves point out the dangers in such long-term comparisons, yet the broad general movements are probably not badly misrepresented.

The Tudor inflation is a phenomenon which excited a great deal of contemporary comment. By today's standards, the rate of price increase was very mild. The Phelps Brown–Hopkins figures indicate that during the 50 years 1576–1625, which encompass the period of greatest theatrical vitality, consumer prices rose only about 1.1 percent per annum.[1] Nevertheless, it is easy to see why Englishmen of the period were impressed by the rate of price increase. Figure 2, the graph of the Phelps Brown–Hopkins index of the price of consumables, shows that by the time Shakespeare began to write prices had been rising fairly steadily for about three quarters of a century. In the 1590's, with a series

[1] Any initial and terminal dates must be arbitrary to some extent. However, the results of our calculations are unlikely to be affected substantially by the choice of these dates since, as Figure 2 indicates, the inflation began much earlier and ended considerably later. For the entire period of the Tudor inflation, say 1510–1600, even though the price level increased eight-fold, the average annual price rise, as calculated by logarithmic least squares regression, using the Phelps–Brown Hopkins figures, was only 1.3 percent. Such is the power of compounding over long periods. Even during the catastrophic decade 1590–1600 the rate of increase was only 3.5 percent, pretty mild stuff by current standards.

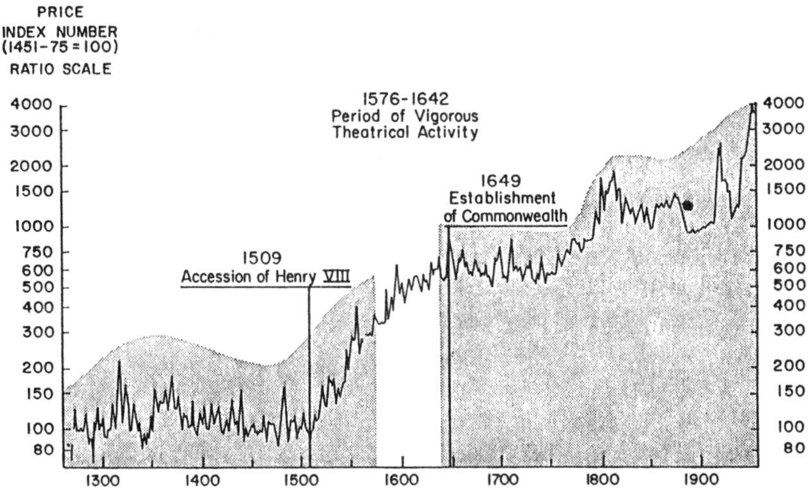

Fig. 2. Price of a composite unit of consumables in southern England 1264–1954. Reprinted by permission of *Economica.*

of bad harvests, prices really rose very sharply, the index going from a low of 356 in 1593 to a peak of 579 in 1598. Thereafter the index again drops, but by the 1630's it twice reaches the vicinity of 700.

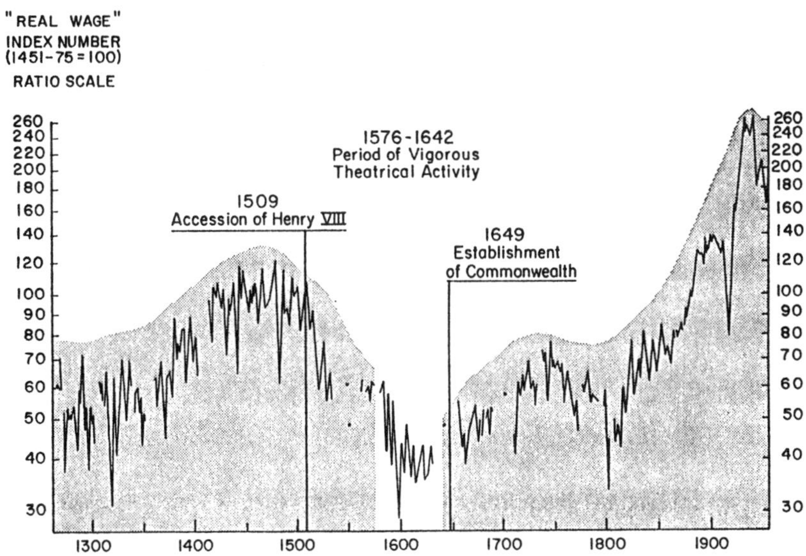

Fig. 3. Changes in the equivalent of the wage rate of a building craftsman expressed in a composite physical unit of consumables in southern England 1264–1954. Reprinted by permission of *Economica.*

Wages, on the other hand changed rather slowly over this period. The daily wage of a craftsman toward the beginning of our period is reported to have been 10 to 12 pence, rising to a range of 12 to 16 pence about half a century later. The common laborer's wage followed the same pattern, increasing from 8 pence to 10 to 12 pence in this interval. Thus wages may be taken to have gone up by 30 to 40 percent during a half century when the price index increased some 80 percent.

The Phelps Brown–Hopkins calculations confirm that there was a fall in real wages. The drop in purchasing power of wages was particularly severe during the great price upsurge of the 1590's, as Figure 3 shows. Using a base period of 1451–1475, coinciding roughly with the Wars of the Roses, after 1594 the index of purchasing power rises above 45 only once before 1629 (after which there is a long gap in the series). And in 1597, the year in which the *Merchant of Venice* may first have been performed, the index falls to its all-time low, 29, presumably representing a level of purchasing power more than two thirds lower than that during the late Middle Ages!

These figures must, as one historian has suggested, be treated with a great deal of scepticism:

> "It seems hardly possible that such a drop can have taken place without far greater outcry than we have record of. To accept the figures at their face-value would mean that urban workers were dying of starvation in thousands at the end of the 16th century and in the early Stuart period. Some factors have surely been left out of account: ... the building labourer may ... have received a supplement to his wages in the form of meals and accomodation on the job, and such payments in kind would cushion him against inflation. More important still, the urban labourer of the 16th century was not as fully urbanised as his 20th century successor, and would often have a plot of land or at least a garden on which he could cultivate his own food ...
>
> "But with this said it remains true that the urban worker did suffer a substantial fall in his standard of living ... Tudor workers lacked trade unions and political representatives to plead their case effectively, and the legislation of 1563 was designed to hold wages down rather than force them up. Cheap labor may have aided the prosperity of industrial employers in Elizabeth's reign. It meant real hunger and hardship for a substantial number of the working population." (Ramsey, pp. 137–38.)

Because it is so labor-intensive an activity the theater may have benefited even more than many of the "industrial employers" from the low real wages of the period. By giving opportunities to a sufficient number of new playwrights, it may have made it easier to find and encourage the ones whom we consider to have been great, as well as a host of others, to try their hands at the task.

We have evidence suggesting how the economics of the theater was affected by the wage levels. A change in real wages affects significantly the length of time a play must run before it can recoup the initial investment in rehearsal time, costumes and so forth. Today, it is estimated that a play generally has to run over 30 weeks in order to break even, at an average of 70 percent of capacity. For the period just before the onset of the Great Depression the estimated figures range from 5 1/2 to 8 weeks, and a calculation for 1913 for a comparable production sets the breakeven run at 4 weeks (all assuming attendance at 60 percent of capacity). (Bernheim, p. 206 and Poggi, p. 74.)

Harbage (1941, pp. 51–52) offers us some illustrations taken from Henslowe's *Diary* that permit a rough comparison: "*Julian the Apostate* with three performances was a failure; *Philipo and Hippolito* with twelve, an average success; and *Wise Man of West Chester* with thirty-two, a great hit." In other words, *a run of two weeks seems to have given a comfortable margin to the company.* Clearly, the figures are not perfectly comparable with the more recent data. The Elizabethan public theater had, easily, twice the audience capacity of our own. Moreover, several elements of production cost that are important today were less significant in Shakespeare's time. On the other hand, in terms of purchasing power, the admission prices to the Elizabethan public theaters were a fraction of today's. Yet it does seem fairly clear that a new play then represented a much smaller financial commitment than it does today. The profitability of a short run must be ascribed not so much to the magnitude of demand for the theater, but to low real wages, perhaps one twentieth of their current level in the United States.

Low real wages also permitted inexpensive ticket prices. The penny admission to the public theater was very cheap in terms of commodity purchasing power, even if it did amount to about a tenth of a day's wages. No doubt it helped to widen the audience. However, the growing importance of the private theaters, with their admission prices that are high by virtually any standards suggests that low ticket prices did not play an important role in the prosperity of the theater of James and Charles.

Burenstam Linder has drawn our attention to a more subtle connection between real wages and the demand for the arts. He points out that rising real wages increase the economic value of time. Hence, they raise the *relative* real cost of activities like theatrical attendance whose consumption time is high relative to their price. Low real wages will *always* produce a substitution effect that favors this type of activity.[1] Thus, the low real earnings of this period—

[1] *Proof:* let x_1 represent the individual's level of consumption of the service in which we are interested, i.e., theater; let r be his number of hours of labor-time and x_2 be the quantity he consumes of the Hicksian "all other goods". Since any consumption process takes time, the consumer will maximize the utility function

$$u(x_1, x_2, r)$$

subject to two constraints

$$p_1x_1 + p_2x_2 = m + wr \quad \text{(his budget constraint)}$$

perhaps (as already noted several times) one twentieth of their level today—may also in this way have contributed to the demand for the services of the theater, especially during the last two decades of the sixteenth century, when the new public theaters seem to have attracted at least some of the lower classes of wage earners.

There are other observations that may cause one to suspect that there is an association between the level of real wages and the viability of the drama. The theater of ancient Athens also flourished in a society in which real incomes were very low by our standards (see, e.g. Mitchell, p. 132 ff.). Greek theater, however, was very highly subsidized (Pickard–Cambridge, pp. 270–73), so that it is impossible to infer from the limited financial data available on the subject whether low wages really contributed a great deal to the success of the Greek drama. However, there is a more suggestive case. If we look again at Fig. 3, we see that there is one earlier period of unusually low real wages in English history. This occurs in the 1320's, and certainly wages do not seem to have been very high in the immediately preceding or the immediately succeeding decades. Now, it may largely be coincidence that this was the period of the Corpus Christi plays that represent the first known English instance of popular, secular drama, written in the vernacular (Chambers, 1903, I, pp. 108–109). These dramas were produced at the expense of the guild itself, which is to say, at the expense of the masters who supported it. The guild owned costumes, props, and pageant wagons, and provided acting personnel from among its own members. Since journeymen were probably paid their normal wages during rehearsals, and apprentices worked for food and lodging, the master absorbed whatever opportunity costs were incurred. Although the guilds did provide what amounted to subsidized drama, real wage rates in the half century before first

---

and

$t_1x_1 + t_2x_2 + r = t$ (his time constraint)

where p_1, p_2 and w are the respective prices of x_1, x_2 and r; t_1, t_2 and unity are their utilization times (with none of the coefficients necessarily constant); and m is non-wage income. Since time can be converted into income via changes in the value of r, the two constraints really amount to only one effective constraint. Eliminating r and collecting terms, they may be rewritten as

$$(p_1 + wt_1)x_1 + (p_2 + wt_2)x_2 = wt + m \qquad (1)$$

which is a budget constraint of the normal Hicksian form, with Becker's "time prices", $p_i + wt_i$, substituted for the ordinary commodity prices, p_i.

Now a rise in real wage, w, will lower the relative time price of x_1 if and only if

$$\frac{d(p_1 + wt_1)/(p_2 + wt_2)}{dw} = \frac{t_1(p_2 + wt_2) - t_2(p_1 + wt_1)}{(p_2 + wt_2)^2} = \frac{t_1p_2 - t_2p_1}{(p_2 + wt_2)^2} < 0$$

i.e., if and only if $(t_1/p_1) < (t_2/p_2)$. The result now follows directly by the usual derivation of the Slutsky theorem. For there will be a substitution in favor of x_1 only if its relative (time) price falls when w increases, and this will be true, as we have just seen if t_1/p_1, the consumption time-price ratio, is relatively low for this commodity: this is not how we would normally characterize theatrical attendance.

the Black Death and then the Hundred Years War decimated the working population were so low, that the subsidies were not onerous.[1]

In sum, while we cannot conclude with any certainty that low real wages did play a critical role in helping to make the Elizabethan theater viable, all the evidence seems to suggest that it did not hurt then, or in earlier periods of flourishing dramatic activity.

7. Conclusions

One is never entitled to generalize from a single historical case, and the gaps in our information about the drama in Renaissance London make such an attempt all the more foolhardy. Nevertheless, from our information we can draw several negative conclusions which we believe to be still significant today.

First, the Elizabethan case offers little basis for the hope that professional live theater will be able to prosper in small communities in the foreseeable future without some sort of subsidy. At the beginning of the seventeenth century, several circumstances conspired to make it possible for the theater to finance itself. Real wages seem to have been unusually low—a considerable financial advantage to a labor-intensive activity such as the theater. Several economic classes, particularly the gentry, were attracted to London where they sought entertainment (see Fisher) and, apparently, the wealth of this class was rising,[2] making it easier for its members to purchase the more expensive tickets which even in the public theaters must have been important for the prosperity of the company. One may surmise that the large number of transients who visited London on business, for education at the Inns of the Court, or simply for a change from rural life, as well as the unusual interest in the arts and the hunger for entertainment that characterized the Renaissance also contributed to the size of the audience. Even then theater had to compete with cock fighting, boxing and other popular entertainments but these did not have the convenience and perhaps not the attraction of today's mass media. Low real wages may also have helped to attract audiences by permitting admission fees low in comparison with other prices and by generating a substitution effect favoring time-intensive activities such as theater attendance. These conditions (aside, perhaps, from the prosperity of the middle classes) are unlikely to be replicated

[1] It is generally thought that popular or folk, i.e., amateur, drama did survive the period of high real wages of the 15th century, and lasted down to Shakespeare's time (*vid.* the "craft" drama in *Midsummer Night's Dream*), but documentation is scanty.

[2] R. H. Tawney and Lawrence Stone are the leading proponents of the view that the real wealth of the gentry increased significantly during the Tudor period. This conclusion has, however, been disputed, particularly by Hugh Trevor-Roper. The importance of the higher priced tickets for the company reflected more than the obvious fact that these tickets are more lucrative than inexpensive ones. We have seen that in the smaller private theaters of the early seventeenth century *all* tickets were comparatively expensive. Without a wealthy clientele it would have been impossible for these theaters to operate using the financial arrangements they did.

in our economy. Certainly, with today's real wages differing by an order of magnitude from those of 1600, the financing of theatrical activity can be expected to remain correspondingly more difficult (compare, for example, the 30 with the 2 week breakeven runs for the two periods). From the fact that, despite all these favorable circumstances, the Elizabethan theater was a highly risky business, one can infer how much more difficult it would be for a self-financed professional theater to survive in a small community today.[1]

A second conslusion that can be drawn from our study is that economic prosperity does not automatically bring with it all the things that are usually taken to contribute to the "quality of life", and if it is accompanied by rising real incomes for all economic classes, it may be a positive detriment to such activities. Whether or not it was largely a coincidence, we have seen that several of the most celebrated periods in the history of the theater were also periods of low real wages, and we can also find periods of prosperity of a more general character, in which dramatic activity is not considered outstanding. The Roman theater, for example, is generally considered artistically inferior to the Greek, despite Rome's greater wealth, and, as we have seen, the unusually high real wages of the fifteenth century seem to have coincided with a long hiatus in theatrical activity that was either professional in organization or characterized by a willingness to experiment. It follows that one cannot simply assume that growth in GNP will bring with it a prosperous and innovative drama.

APPENDIX

Costs and Returns in the Theater of Elizabeth and James

Theatrical budgets from the first half of the eighteenth century have come down to us, but the data from the period studied in this paper are very fragmentary. This appendix summarizes our attempts to put together something resembling a budget from the available figures, from inference, and from a generous dose of guesswork.

Since many of our cost and revenue figures are calculated per-day or per-week of performance, it is first necessary to estimate the number of days and weeks that a successful company played in a typical year. We have already seen that for adult companies there were about six performances per week. We have data for the Swan Theater indicating that in 1610–11 it offered 208 performances; in 1611–12, 248; in 1612–13, 252; in 1613–14, 146; and in 1614–15, 46 (Baldwin, p. 334). The approximate average of these figures (leaving out the last, since in the autumn of 1615 the

[1] "(In 1968–69) the twenty-six regional theaters comprising the League of Resident Theaters had a combined operating deficit (before allowing for gifts or grants) in excess of $6 million. Grants and gifts covered all but $1.6 million. However, these uncovered deficits, added to previous years' deficits, left the regional theaters with accumulated deficits of just over $5 million, and these deficits have occurred despite the fact that actors, technicians, and other staff members in these theaters subsist on extremely meager earnings. Salaries for full-time employees of $50, $60, and $75 a week are common; the average salary for all full-time employees in these theaters, including managing and artistic directors and top actors was less than $150 a week [in 1968–69]. And for most of these employees, their work is only seasonal." (Fitchandler, p. 44.)

resident company moved to a new theater), 200 seems a reasonable estimate of the number of performances per year; the Swan figures also suggest how widely the number must have varied.

The cost of the Elizabethan theater seems to have included two major components: the cost of the building itself, and the earnings of its personnel. There was virtually no scenery and the cost of the costumes, though sometimes very high,[1] was held down by the fact that new costumes were not provided for every new production. It is true that some elaborate dramatic effects were employed – the First Globe burned down when sparks from a simulated cannonade set fire to the roof. But aside from such catastrophes, we may surmise that the cost of such effects did not amount to a great deal.

Initially, the theaters were constructed by investors in real estate who leased them to the companies at high rentals. Later, the more prosperous acting companies purchased or constructed their own theatrical houses. We have firm data about the costs of various theaters (Harbage, 1951, p. 23). The pathbreaking 1576 Theater cost £666 to construct – about $30 000 in terms of commodity purchasing power and over $500 000 in terms of modern daily wages. The Rose was built in 1587 at a cost of £816. We are not sure of the cost of the First Globe (1599) but it is estimated to have been comparatively low, £400–600. The First Fortune cost £520 to construct in 1600. By the time the Second Globe (1614) and the Second Fortune (1622) were built, costs had risen substantially, to £1 400 and £1 000 respectively, presumably at least in part as a result of the inflation.

There is evidence that rates of interest in our period ranged somewhere between 8 and 10 percent[2] as one might expect in an inflationary era. This means that if the theater buildings had been very durable and their use had been expected to continue indefinitely they should have rented for a little more than 10 percent of their building cost. In fact, rental charges were much higher than that. The 1576 Theater rented at £100, so that over £30 per year may be taken to represent amortization of the original £666 cost. We are told that the rent on the Rose amounted to the enormous sum of £346, as compared to the (roughly) £80 interest cost on the original capital. Rental on the First Globe is reported to have been an incredible £420–560 per annum, almost returning its original cost every year! It is easy to see why the theater was rebuilt almost immediately after its destruction by fire fourteen years after it was built.[3]

Before turning to the payments to the actors, we must consider the compensation of the playwrights, which on their own showing at least, was less than munificent.[4]

---

[1] Marchette Chute (p. 55) comments, "Stage costumes were expensive and accounted for a large part of the company's expenses. The taffeta for a single gown cost as much as the salary of a hired actor for fifteen weeks, and even a robe "for to go invisible" represented a considerable investment".

[2] See Kerridge, pp. 213–14. Figures as low as 6 percent are also mentioned.

[3] It is also easy to understand why some companies decided to construct their own theaters under these circumstances. The figures cited represent an annual rate of return on investment in the theaters averaging over forty percent! It is a bit harder to explain why, with such returns, competitive theaters were not constructed in order to drive down the rents. One conjecture is that it required a license which would not be granted for the construction of more theaters than the available acting companies were able to use (some companies did use two theaters—performing sometimes at one, sometimes at the other). The number of companies licensed to perform was indeed strictly limited. Financial difficulties were capable of reducing rents. When local residents prevented Burbage from using the Second Blackfriars as a theater for an adult company after he had purchased and reconstructed it for a total of £900 in 1596, he rented it out for 8 years for only £40 per annum.

[4] Prof. Bentley takes issue with the playwrights' complaints, pointing out that Chettle and Dekker earned more in a year than a curate or a schoolmaster (Bentley, 1971, Chap. V).

Ben Jonson complained to Drummond in 1619 that "of all his playes he never gained 2 hundreth pounds" and he may be fairly accurate, especially if he meant to exclude his numerous court masques (Jonson, 1925, 1, 148). By 1619 the canon of plays either entirely or mostly attributable to Jonson seems to have extended to about 14, although the figure may well have been higher. £10 was probably the top price for a new play, and Henslowe records a payment of 20 shillings to Chettle for a revision (Henslowe, 1961, p. 175). The playwrights (or teams of writers who manufactured many Elizabethan plays) appear to have been paid some £6–£10 per play. In Chapter V of his forthcoming book, however, Prof. Bentley points out that emoluments to playwrights seem to have been rising more rapidly than the general price level: he cites, as one example, the correspondence that appears in W. W. Greg. (ed.) *Henslowe Papers,* Articles 70, 71, 72, 84. This exchange between Robert Daborne and Henslowe (1613–1614) suggests that the playwright was earning approximately £20 per play (Bentley, 1971). As was noted in the text, an average success" might have been performed about twelve times, but a great many plays were performed only four or five times and some only once. This suggests that, with 200 performances per year, there may have been as many as 15 new productions per year. Consequently £120 per annum seems a fair estimate of the sum devoted to playwrights' compensation.

We come next to earnings in the company itself. There are estimates of the earnings of the actor-sharers. In Shakespeare's company these are said to have amounted to about £25–35 (Baldwin, p. 162), which is only about $1 000 to $1 300 per year in terms of 1970 purchasing power. Even the estimate of £55 per year (based on 1635 figures) given by Thaler does not come out much higher. It is noteworthy that these are figures for what was surely the most successful of the acting companies. However, if a leading actor were also a "housekeeper," i.e., part-owner of the building itself, he might expect additional income from the rental of the playhouse. It seems possible, too, that if he were a playwright as well (Shakespeare and a few others were involved in all three roles), he would realize the normal £6–£10 payment for his literary labors. Altogether, though low by today's standards, these compensation levels were reasonably good in comparison with contemporary wage rates. Assuming that the company performed 200 times per year on the average, a £25–35 annual payment per actor-sharer meant an earnings rate of 2 1/2 to 3 1/2 shillings per day, compared with 14 to 16 pence per day for a master craftsman in London. Taken as a whole, the actor-sharers in a single company seem to have earned in a year somewhere between £225 (the Rose in 1592–3) and £300 (average for the Globe in 1599–1608).

Data on wage costs of hirelings (the paid professional actors, musicians, etc. who were not sharers) record that in Henslowe's companies, which cannot have been atypical, they were paid from 5 to 10 shillings per week, and 6 shillings weekly appears to have been a typical wage.[1] The Henslowe diary does tell of an actor hired apparently for 10 shillings every week he played in London in 1597, on a two year arrangement. The contract was negotiated and signed by Henslowe's son-in-law, Edward Alleyn.[2] As for the number of hirelings ordinarily employed at one time by

---

[1] Thaler, p. 85. Gosson states that in 1579 the wages of a hireling were 6 shillings per week, which is probably accurate, since even though Gosson is hostile to the theater, the figures were a matter of public knowledge.

[2] The diary reports:
Md y^{t} this 8th of december 1597 my father philyp
hinchlow hiered as A Covenauant servant willyam kendall for
ij years after The statute of winchester w^{t} ij single penc

a single company, Ringler (p. 113) quotes the observant German traveler, Platter, as having reported "seeing on 21 September 1599, in the thatched playhouse across the Thames [the Globe], a performance of *Julius Caesar 'mitt ohngefehr 15 personen ... Agieren'*." Ringler goes on to observe that "since a member of the audience would not ordinarily be able to identify the individual actors who doubled in the various parts (49 in our only text), someone must have told Platter that the Chamberlain's company numbered 'about fifteen' in September, 1599." Ringler's detailed analysis of the text shows that "*Julius Caesar* can easily be produced by a company of sixteen actors, and cannot be produced with less than sixteen" (Ringler, p. 121). Since we know that at the time of the building of the Globe there were six actor-sharers, the number of hireling actors cannot have been more than ten and was probably closer to 7 or 8, since a few boy-apprentices were employed as well. It is well to remember of course that, as Bentley points out (1961, p. 90), the "hired men" often included "musicians, stage managers, wardrobe keepers and prompters, as well as minor actors", so that even Platter's statement is ambiguous for our purposes. It seems reasonable to surmise that including these other persons the total number of hirelings may have been as high as 15. This gives us an annual expenditure estimate for their wages of some £200 (15 hirelings × 33 weeks at, say, 8*s*./week).

The members of the last group in the company, the boy actors, were treated as apprentices. While they received no money, their keep was provided by the company at a cost which plausibly may be taken to have been somewhat less than £100 per year.

Having gone over the major cost categories we undertake next a rough estimate of receipts. With earnings perhaps slightly above £8 per performance and about 200 performances per year per company, we end up with a total revenue figure of some £1 600, that is, about sixty thousand dollars per year in terms of modern purchasing power.

Subtracting from this sum about £400 for rental of the theater, £300 per year as the compensation of the actor-sharers, £120 per year as payment of playwrights, and £200 per year for hirelings, and, say, £80 for the maintenance of the boy actors and payment to the roughly 20 gatherers (admissions collectors), this leaves over some £500 for miscellaneous expenses of which perhaps £50 or more went as tax payments to the Master of the Revels. The reader should notice that over 40 percent of the total cost is devoted to labor if we include the income of the actor-sharer and the payment to the playwright. This is very similar to the corresponding figure for today's theater,[1] despite the fact that today's productions are much more elaborate and require heavy outlays for stagehands, electricians, etc.

A to geue hym for his sayd servis everi
week of his playng in london xs & in ye
Cuntrie v^{s} for the wch he covenaunteth for ye space
of those ij years To be redy att all Tymes to play in ye howse
of the sayd philyp & in no other during the sayd Terme

wittnes my self the writer
ofThis EAlleyn

(Henslowe, pp. 268–269)

The "two single pence" mentioned in this passage may be by way of "earnest money", a small amount customarily paid upon the signing of an agreement, as a means of signaling good faith.

[1] Indeed, the structure of Elizabethan theatrical costs as estimated and that of the more recent commercial theater is remarkably similar, as the following table shows.

Bibliography

Arrow, K.: Criteria, institutions, and function in urban development decisions. In A. H. Pascal (ed.), *Contributions to the analysis of urban problems*. Santa Monica, 1968.

Baldwin, T. W.: *The organization and personnel of the Shakespearean company*. Princeton, 1927.

Baumol, W. J. & Bowen, W. G.: *Performing arts: The economic dilemma*. New York, 1966.

Bentley, G. E.: Shakespeare and the Blackfriars Theater. *Shakespeare Survey no. 1*, pp. 38–50, 1948.

Bentley, G. E.: *Shakespeare, A biographical handbook*. New Haven, 1961.

Bentley, G. E.: *The Jacobean and Caroline stage*. (7 Vols.) Oxford, 1941–1968.

Bentley, G. E.: Letter to W. Baumol, Oct. 24, 1970.

Bentley, G. E.: *The profession of the dramatist in Shakespeare's time*. Princeton, 1971.

Bernheim, A. L.: *The business of the theater*. New York, 1932.

Briley, J.: Of stake and stage. *Shakespeare Survey*, No. 8, pp. 106–108, 1955.

Bromberg, M.: The reputation of Philip Henslowe. *Shakespeare Quarterly I*, 135–145, 1950.

Bush, K.: A comparison of retail prices in the United States, the USSR and Western Europe in April 1969. *Radio Liberty Research Paper*, no. 33, New York, 1969.

Carus-Wilson, E. M.: *Essays in Economic History*. (3 Vols.) Vol. II. London, 1962.

Chambers, E. K.: *The Elizabethan stage*. (4 Vols.) Vol. I. Oxford, 1923.

Chambers, E. K.: *The Medieval stage*. (2 Vols.) Vol. II. Oxford, 1903.

Chute, M.: *Ben Jonson of Westminster*. New York, 1953.

Department of Employment and Productivity, *Statistics on Incomes, Prices, Employment and Production*, June, 1969, No. 29, London, 1969.

Economic Report of the President, Washington, January 1965.

Fitchandler, Th.: Regional theater: filling the vacuum. *Cultural Affairs*, pp. 43–44, 1970.

Fisher, F. J.: The development of London as a centre of conspicuous consumption in the sixteenth and seventeenth centuries. *Transactions of the Royal Historical Society*, p. 30, 1948. Reprinted in Carus-Wilson, 197–207.

Gosson, S.: *School of Abuse*. London, 1579.

Harbage, A.: *Shakespeare's audience*. New York, 1941.

Harbage, A.: *Shakespeare and the rival traditions*. New York, 1952.

Henslowe, Ph.: *Henslowe's diary* (ed. R. A. Foakes and R. T. Rickert. Cambridge, 1961.

Hillebrand, H. Newcomb: *The child actors: A chapter in Elizabethan stage history*. Urbana, 1926.

Jonson, Ben: Conversations with Drummond. In *Works* (ed. C. H. Herford &

Table 2.

	Estimated % of total budget ca. 1600	% of itemized costs, Broadway Theater, 1960–1
Theatrical Rental	25	28
Playwright's Fees	7.5	8
Artists & Managerial	30–35	34

Broadway figures are taken from Moore, p. 155. Unfortunately, despite Moore's careful work, he was unable to obtain information about some 15 % of the relevant costs, which may or may not include salaries, playwright's royalties, etc. This may distort our percentage figures slightly, for example, perhaps reducing the rent figure from 28 to 23 percent of the total. More recent unpublished data for Broadway indicate that the theater rental figure has in fact risen and that the shares of the performers and the playwright have fallen.

Percy Simpson). (11 Vols) Vol. I. Oxford, 1925.

Jonson, Ben: Induction to Bartholomew Fair. In *Works* (ed. C. H. Hereford & Percy Simpson). Vol. VI. Oxford, 1925.

Kerridge, E.: The movement of rent, 1540–1640. In Carus-Wilson, 208–226.

Laidlaw, W. (ed.): *Population of the City of New York,, 1890–1930*. New York, 1932.

Linder, S. B.: *The harried leisure class*. New York, 1970.

Mitchell, E. H.: *The Economics of Ancient Greece*. New York, 1940.

Mols, R.: *Introduction á la démographie historique des villes d'Europe* du XIVe au XVIIIe siècle, tome troisième. Louvain, 1955.

Moore, Th. G.: *The economics of the American theater*. Durham, 1968.

Poggi, J.: *Theater in America*. Ithaca, 1968.

Phelps Brown, E. H. & Hopkins, S. V.: Seven centuries of building wages. *Economica*, N.S. 22, 195–206, Aug. 1955, Reprinted in Carus-Wilson, 168–178.

Phelps Brown, E. H. & Hopkins, S. V.: Seven centuries of the prices of consumables. *Economica*, N.S. 23, 296–314, Nov. 1956. Reprinted in Carus-Wilson, 179–196.

Pickard-Cambridge, A.: *The dramatic festivals of Athens*. Oxford, 1953.

Ramsey, P.: *Tudor economic problems*. London, 1963.

Ringler, W. A., Jr: The number of actors in Shakespeare's early plays. In Bentley (ed.) *The seventeenth century stage*. Chicago, 1968.

Rye, W. B.: *England as seen by foreigners, in the days of Elizabeth and James I*. London, 1865.

Simpson, P.: Actors and acting. In *Shakespeare's England: An account of life and manners of his age*. (2 Vols.) London, 1916–17.

Stone, L.: The anatomy of the Elizabethan aristocracy. *Economic History Review 18*, 1–38, 1948.

Tawney, R. H.: Harrington's interpretation of his age. Raleigh Lecture, *Proceedings of the British Academy 18*, 1–38, 1948.

Thaler, A.: Shakespeare's income. *Studies in Philology*, 82–96, 1918.

Trevelyan, G. M.: *English social history*. London, 1944.

Trevor-Roper, H. R.: The Gentry, 1540–1640. *Economic History Review*, Supplement 1, 1953.

US Department of Labor, Bureau of Labor Statistics, *Union Wages and Hours: Building Trades*, Bulletin No. 1621, Washington.

Journal of Cultural Economics **18:** 171–198, 1994.

On The Economics of Musical Composition in Mozart's Vienna

WILLIAM J. BAUMOL and HILDA BAUMOL
CV Starr Center for Applied Economics, New York University, U.S.A.

Abstract. The article provides historical evidence suggesting that a substantial element in the explanation of the profusion of talented composers in the 18th century Habsburg empire was the fragmentation of the state into many near-independent states, each with its own court seeking entertainment and prestige through new musical offerings. The resulting profusion of jobs attracted people into the profession and provided hearings for their work. The article also examines the data on Mozart's finances and using a rough translation of 18th century Austrian currency into current dollars supports recent revisionist findings that, with the exception of several years, he was relatively well off.

Key words: Employment opportunities for composers, patronage versus market income, Mozart's earnings, Mozart's expenses

> "Perhaps in this neglected spot is laid/Some heart once pregnant with celestial fire,/Hands, that the rod of empire might have sway'd,/Or wak'd to extasy the living lyre."
>
> Thomas Gray, *Elegy Written in a Country Church Yard*

> "'Aren't the myriad of princely [German] courts,' asked Leibnitz in 1679, 'a glorious means to allow so many people to distinguish themselves who would otherwise remain lying in the dust?'"
>
> (Vierhaus, 1988, p. 39).

> "Believe me, my sole purpose is to make as much money as possible; for after good health it is the best thing to have."
>
> Mozart to his father, Vienna, April 4, 1781
> (Anderson, 1938, Vol. 3, p. 1072)

The primary object of this paper is to help to explain the extraordinary confluence of composers whose activities centered in Vienna around Mozart's time. These included Gluck, Haydn, Dittersdorf, Salieri, Beethoven and, of course, Wolfgang Amadeus Mozart. We will suggest some possible reasons for this phenomenon and the underlying economic causes which had a profound effect on music and musicians, entailing some descriptive materials on the economic and political climate characterizing Mozart's period of residence in Vienna – the decade 1781–1791. Finally, we have been unable to resist some discussion of several recent revisionist targets, in particular the denial by a number of scholars of the widely held vision of a Mozart beset by grinding poverty.

Our central purpose, however, is an attempt to help account for the period's extraordinary abundance of musical talent. Why at the end of the eighteenth century? Why in the Holy Roman Empire and the associated lands (the Germanic states, Bohemia, Hungary and Italy)?

Obviously, economic and political conditions cannot create talent, but they certainly can either inhibit it or provide opportunities for its exercise. Our main hypothesis is intended to narrow the pertinent geography – to help account for the striking level of composing activity emanating from Germany and Italy. This hypothesis suggests that the political division of the Holy Roman Empire and the Habsburg possessions into numerous petty states worked to produce the circumstances (notably substantial demand and a profusion of jobs) that help to explain the profusion of musical productivity. It is our secondary hypothesis that in the Empire, as in England and France, the rising prosperity of the eighteenth century – the first stirrings of the industrial revolution and associated developments such as the rise in the wealth and position of the small body of the bourgeoisie as consumers of culture – contributed to the demand that underlay the creation of a free market in musical composition. Through this development, demand helped to elicit supply.

While much private support continued, the composer was beginning to emerge from a state of servitude to take control of his own professional life. By the second half of the eighteenth century demand for the work of the composer derived from the two sources: continued patronage of royalty and nobility, and the emerging free market. The resulting availability of employment opportunities served to attract into the profession many who would otherwise have sought to earn a living elsewhere. Among this profusion of composers many, predictably, proved to have no outstanding talent. But among the group there were the few who, as the poet put it, might otherwise have been "born to blush unseen and waste their sweetness on the desert air."

1. The Period and Its Circumstances

1.1. The Extraordinary Decade

The last ten years of Mozart's life, the period when he lived in Vienna, is arguably one of the most dramatic in history. It encompassed the end of the American Revolution, the adoption of the Constitution of the United States, the widely accepted date of the beginnings of the industrial revolution in England (including the development of Watt's improved steam engine), and the first years of the French Revolution. Its intellectual life was shaped by such luminaries as Rousseau, Voltaire, Franklin, Hume, Samuel Johnson, Adam Smith, Goethe and Schiller.

Germany (as a result of its fragmentation, as we will suggest) had a comparative advantage in the supply of two products: composers and royalty. It contributed a striking number of European monarchs of great ability, domineering personalities with at least nominal allegiance to the ideas of the Enlightenment: Gustav III of

Sweden,[1] Catherine the Great of Russia, Frederick the Great of Prussia and, by no means least, Joseph II of Austria, Mozart's emperor. But that was by no means all. George III of England derived from Hanover, as everyone knows, and while Louis XVI[2] was obviously not (primarily) Teutonic, the queen of France, Marie Antoinette, was the younger sister of Emperor Joseph II.

Despite their great inherited power, their efforts to hold together a liberalized modification of the old order were to be undermined by the French Revolution and other disturbing circumstances. The enlightened rulers sought to preserve their vestiges of absolute power by using the bourgeoisie as a counterpoise to the aristocracy, whose influence they sought to curtail. The bourgeoisie, somewhat expanded and enriched by the first stirrings of the Industrial Revolution, though still very small in numbers by modern standards (see below), used this opportunity to acquire for themselves benefits suited to the wealth they were accumulating.

1.2. Prosperity of the Habsburg Territories

Economic historians suggest that in the 18th century considerable portions of the Habsburg territories, and the Austrian lands in particular, which included Vienna, were highly prosperous at the end of the 18th century, at least in relative terms. Their per-capita incomes were probably well ahead of those of Brandenburg (Prussia), and very likely higher than that of France. Only England and the low countries may have been in a superior position. Prosperity brought great wealth to well-placed members of the nobility and the small group constituting the upper bourgeoisie of Vienna and the nearby territories, among them Hungary and Bohemia (including Prague). They spent liberally, running their courts and mansions in a lavish style which included the services of many composers and performers. At the same time, because real wages, and those of musicians in particular, were relatively low, a given real expenditure could purchase much more than today in the way of musician service. This is a matter to which we will return presently.

1.3. Joseph II – The Holy Roman Emperor

Mozart's Emperor, Joseph II, was perhaps the most enlightened of the "enlightened despots" of the era (see e.g., Padover, 1934). Like Frederick the Great, he was a dedicated amateur performer of chamber music, but, unlike the latter, Joseph admired German culture and sought to promote it, for example, through his efforts to encourage German opera at the expense of the fashionable opera of Italy.

Joseph's remarkable measures of liberalism included an attempt to introduce universal and compulsory education, virtual abolition of censorship, steps toward the ending of serfdom, (near) abolition of the death penalty and elimination of the most oppressive restrictions upon Protestants and Jews. Had the Emperor not had a fatal attraction to military activity (probably stimulated by admiration and envy of Frederick the Great), for which he apparently had little talent, he might have been

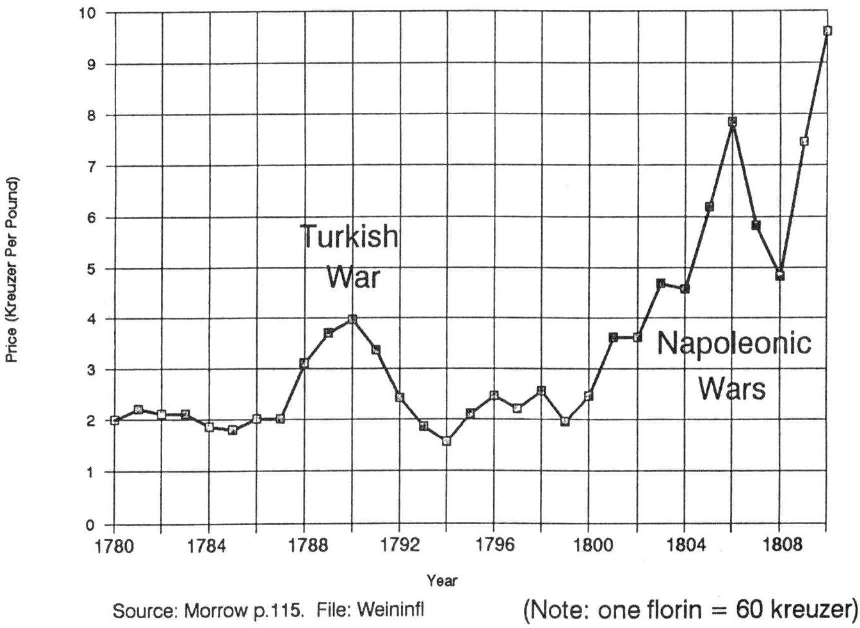

Fig. 1. Vienna: bread prices, 1780–1810.

remembered universally as a prime contributor to the spread of the rule of law and modern standards of freedom and public welfare. Unfortunately, the Turkish War, his Vietnam, proved fatal to him, to his achievements and to his reputation. The war was, incidentally, probably in part responsible for Mozart's financial difficulties during his two very troubled years, 1789–1790 (the years when Mozart repeatedly sought to borrow money), his income having been made precarious when the Emperor and part of the music-supporting nobility left Vienna (at least some for the front). Concurrently, a sharp but short-lived inflation, which may have doubled prices (see Figure 1), is likely to have cut severely into the purchasing power of Mozart's income.[3]

Despite his enlightenment Joseph retained a degree of despotism. He felt it appropriate to intervene in a variety of activities in ways that hardly contributed to his popularity. Though he intended to abolish the death penalty, when a nobleman was found to have killed an old woman for her wealth, Joseph condemned the murderer to an execution medieval in its cruelty. He prohibited ballet during opera performances (though he was persuaded, apparently by Da Ponte, to make an exception for *The Marriage of Figaro*). He forbade the wearing of corsets for reasons of health, and for the same reason promulgated the highly-unpopular restrictions on burial practices which, apparently, form the basis for the legend that

Mozart was given a "pauper's burial," a subject we will go into in slightly more detail later.

Characteristically prudent in his expenditures, Joseph seems to have had a strong desire to keep Mozart in Vienna, but to do so at the lowest possible expense. So while he rewarded Mozart with commissions and a stipend, they seem not to have been overly generous.

1.4. Emergence of the Market for Musical Services

Mozart's Vienna decade is noteworthy as a period of transition in the economics of music and, in particular, of composition. It was part of the changeover from the universal system of private patronage to the beginnings of a market mechanism under which the product of the composer and the performer became a commodity that could be bought and sold, the prices ranging from niggardly to spectacularly generous, depending on what the composer or performer could command in the market place. Mozart was among the first in Vienna to turn his talents as composer and virtuoso pianist into a commodity. He usually composed on commission or to advance his career, and he seldom composed without a commercial incentive.[4]

Haydn was perhaps the most telling example of the transition. When he was freed from Esterhazy patronage upon the death of his sponsor, his income leaped from the modest level at which it had been held for many years to the spectacular earnings he received in England (sweetened by the honors conferred upon him by the ancient universities). By our calculations, the British market mechanism made him the equivalent of a 1990 millionaire in the United States (for details on our methods of currency translation see the appendices to this paper). When Mozart died in 1791 arrangements were being made for him to follow Haydn to London, where he might well have had the opportunity to add considerably to his earnings.[5]

Some profound changes helped to make such musical entrepreneurship feasible at this time. One was the gradual replacement of the old *Kapelle* arrangement by hired, professional musicians, a replacement which had begun approximately with the Seven Years War (1756–1763). Under the old system the musical demands of a noble household were supplied by a cadre of household servants led by a *Kapellmeister*, who was little more than a servant himself. Working, probably, for a royal or noble patron or a prince of the church, he was responsible for all musical activities – composing, performing, overseeing musicians, giving musical instruction, and so on. His compositions were not his own property but belonged to his master, and he had to seek permission to accept outside commissions or even to resign from the service of the master. Sometimes he had additional assignments, as when even as famous a *Kapellmeister* as Karl Ditters von Dittersdorf is believed to have had to wait on tables every other night (Moore, 1987, p. 66).

The reasons for the decline of this system may have been rooted in fashion as well as economics. Early in the eighteenth century the most aristocratic patrons of music had established *Kapellen* in their own households, in which servant-musicians were organized to provide all musical needs including the most elaborate productions.[6]

The *Kapelle* system was largely replaced in the latter part of the eighteenth century when it became fashionable to maintain only smaller *Harmonien* to be augmented by hired musicians. Concurrently there emerged dilettante concerts in which amateurs (often members of the highest aristocracy) performed in private salons along with professional musicians hired for the occasion, sometimes of the caliber of Mozart himself.

The imperial court had abandoned its reliance on the *Kapelle* under Maria Theresa and limited its support of music mainly to opera. Moore comments: "... it seems that a particular source of prestige when adopted by a given social class quickly lost its prestige among the next higher social class. By the middle of the eighteenth century, the Imperial court could outshine the private musical performances of aristocratic households only in the area of full-scale opera productions; therefore, the Imperial court virtually abandoned those forms of music that no longer represented its special status. Were the four music-loving emperors who preceded Maria Theresa born music-lovers, or were they conditioned to love music by the fact that they reigned during a period when the Imperial court could command musical resources far superior to those of the aristocracy in general?" (Moore, 1987, p. 100).

While the long process of the decay of royal theaters and the disbanding of large private musical establishments proceeded, those composers and musicians who were partially or entirely displaced declared themselves for hire. They earned their livings in new ways. Public concerts featuring their own works and charging admission began to be organized either by the composer for his own benefit or by one of the new public concert societies. Musicians also gave lessons, had their own works published for sale to the public and accepted commissions and part-time employment.

Publication also began to expand, though so slowly that significant proceeds seem to have largely benefited Mozart's estate rather than himself. The popularity of the new "galant" style of composition, as opposed to the difficult contrapuntal style, increased the feasibility of amateur musical performance. This led to a great demand for published compositions of varying levels of difficulty. The emergence of the music-publishing industry facilitated wide dissemination of the composer's product. The composer, of course, profited from the sale of his work, for which he was often compensated by fixed payment by the publisher. The new publication arrangement also served to advertise the composer's work at home and abroad.

This was the situation when Mozart, having figuratively thumbed his nose at Salzburg's Prince Archbishop and been physically booted out in return, went to Vienna where he found the opportunities for support through patronage only modestly rewarding[7] and augmented his earnings by private enterprise with noteworthy financial success, as we shall see. By the time of Beethoven, reliance on the market was far greater, and while he still benefited from private patronage, severe inflation had cut deeply into its value.

1.5. Introduction of the Pianoforte

The eighteenth century brought with it a spate of inventions – the "wave of gadgets" that underlay the industrial revolution. Musical instruments also benefited from this trend. Mozart, one of the earliest virtuoso pianists, had the advantage of improvements that were being made in keyboard instruments. Before the emergence of the pianoforte in the second half of the century, the organ, the clavichord and the harpsichord were the only keyboard instruments available. "The clavichord was simple and cheap to construct, and it allowed the player an intimate control over the intensity and quality of its sound. Sensitive gradations of tone, even a vibrato – the *bebung* – could be achieved. But the clavichord was quiet [it could hardly be heard from a few yards away], and therefore a private instrument. The harpsichord, by contrast, was sufficiently loud and brilliant for hall, theater and church, but could not produce subtle gradations of volume ..." (Ehrlich, 1990, p. 11).

Closson (1947, p. 85) reports, "From the moment that Mozart in 1777 discovered the pianos of Stein, he definitely gave up the harpsichord. Haydn did the same ... so did Beethoven." Kellett and Naylor (1889, p. 131) concur: "... Mozart, the first world-virtuoso, the idol of the concert hall, thinking only of sound-effects in the great halls, never hesitated for a moment between clavicymbal and piano." The piano helped to expand the market for the composer's efforts in at least two ways. First, it facilitated concert performance and made it possible to perform before larger audiences. Second, as pianos entered an increasing number of private homes, the demand for (new) music (see below) also rose. Thus, the evolution of the technology of musical instruments was yet another influence that expanded the free market available to composers and increased the demand for their services in the second half of the eighteenth century.

1.6. Other Influences: Cost, Musical Style, Pursuit of Prestige and Lack of Interest in "Ancient Music"

Low wages, as we shall see, stimulated the production of plays and the demand for playwrights' services in renaissance London. In 18th century Germany the demand for musicians' services, generated by the profusion of courts and princes, was also reinforced by low wages, although it is impossible to estimate the value of the perquisites that accompanied them. No doubt they varied for each individual case. At the lowest rung, a musician such as Haydn's brother, tenor Johann Evangelist, might receive (aside from his servants' compensation in kind) starvation wages of 60 florins per annum – roughly equivalent to a wage of $4000 today, and half the pay of the most lowly school teacher (Braunbehrens, 1986, 1990, pp. 127, 129. For more on the currency and its purchasing power, see the Appendix to this paper).

It is, of course, dangerous to take such figures literally, since so large a proportion of the earnings of musicians and others were paid in kind – food, lodging, etc. Moreover, many musicians were paid far better. But still, if the producer were economical, musical services could be provided at far lower relative cost than today. For example, we know that in 1791 on the occasion of the coronation of Leopold II, Joseph's successor, the impresario Domenico Guardasoni undertook to produce *La Clemenza di Tito* for less than 7000 florins. This was less than 20 times the *monetary* salary of a high school teacher in Vienna at the time. Included in this sum were composer's fees, costumes, scenery, performers' salaries and candles (no minor outlay) (Robbins Landon, 1988, pp. 88–89 and 116–117). The example is not meant to deny that extravagant production could be very expensive, sometimes ruinously so to a minor ruler. (On this, see, e.g., Yorke-Long, 1954, pp. 7, 60–61, 71). However, it does mean that the activity *could* be carried out at astonishingly low cost when compared (in real terms) to the outlays required today.

Not only the possibility of economical presentation of musical performance stimulated demand for the composers' work. The advent of the *galant* style of musical writing, with its expressiveness and avoidance of contrapuntal complexities, made attendance at operas and concerts more popular, and also facilitated amateur performance and the demand by amateurs for new compositions.

Musical activities were also sought out as a matter of honor and prestige. "Music, especially instrumental music, then, was a highly honorific indoor sport in Vienna: any Viennese understood that it was something the best people cultivated in a big way ... If music was eminently socially correct ... it would not fail to be impressive to the bevies of newly rich and newly noble. They could think to better themselves cheaply by aping their betters, so they too assiduously cultivated their musical talents and interests" (Loesser, 1954, p. 119).

Moore quotes the letters of a Count Franz Anton von Sporck who, while professing himself a music lover, was induced to engage an opera company, "... after I learned that princess Schwarzenberg was to take a cure only a mile from here on her husband's estate ... I hoped that the illustrious princess would remain in the vicinity for the entire summer" (Moore, 1987, pp. 95–6), quoting from Freeman (1987, p. 52).

Added to the stimulation of the demand for music and musical *composition* both by genuine appreciation and the pursuit of prestige was the fact that audiences generally were prepared to listen only to *new* music, usually to works written no more than a decade earlier.[8]

It is true that societies of "ancient music" had been formed in London and Vienna in an effort to save the works of composers like Handel and Bach from oblivion, but these "ancient" works were only some 30 years old – closer in time to Mozart's Vienna than, say, George Gershwin is to ours. Moreover, these were esoteric activities of interest only to highly dedicated amateurs and professional musicians. It consequently required the constant efforts of living composers to supply enough *new* works to keep the market supplied.[9]

1.7. Mozart's Vienna – A Few Remarks

During Mozart's decade in Vienna, the city was probably the largest and the wealthiest in the German lands. Still, its population of nearly a quarter of a million was only about half of that of Paris and less than one-fourth of London's. Vienna, then, had somewhat fewer inhabitants than Baton Rouge or Rochester or Tampa have today. As the location of the main court of the Holy Roman Emperor the city attracted both nobility and ambitious members of the rising bourgeoisie, and that, in turn, meant business opportunities for composers, tradesmen and others who served the wealthy, as well as for others who provided goods and services to the latter in the multiplier chain of expenditure.

Vienna lagged behind other capitals in forming societies organized for the purpose of presenting public concerts, and also lacked an adequate concert hall. Instead, the Viennese depended on the two imperial theaters. The leading one was the Burgtheater, probably accommodating between 1600 and 1700 people (the Haymarket in London is reputed to have accommodated 4000), and the other, smaller, one was the Karntnerthortheater. "Both were under the jurisdiction, at least theoretically, of the Emperor. Their connection with concert history derives from the fact that religious practice dictated that no staged drama, spoken or sung, be presented during the Advent and Lent" (Morrow, p. 42). The practice arose of providing musical performances during those periods as a substitute for the usual presentations of drama, and, thus, in Vienna, musical performance was presented at these premises six weeks of the year, and musicians had to make do with much smaller makeshift rooms and parks for the rest of the year.

For whatever reasons, by the end of the century musical salons were the basis of musical life in Vienna. This included the significant dilettante movement in which amateurs from various social strata, including the very highest, gave musical performances and often hired professionals (Mozart among them) to participate. There was much music-making in the home at all economic levels and at gala occasions, and professional musicians were hired by those who could afford them to provide after-dinner music and other services.

The sizes of the special groups from which consumers of musical services were largely drawn have been estimated. Moore (1989, p. 34) cites Pezzl's estimate that the aristocracy constituted 1 percent of the population of Vienna, while the middle class came to 2.5 percent of the total. This means that the middle class of that time could hardly offer anything resembling a mass market for music, but it might possibly have added substantially to the audience provided by the even-smaller aristocratic portion of the population.

Toward the end of the eighteenth century, when the 25-year old Mozart settled in Vienna, that city could hardly claim to be the unchallenged musical capital of Europe. Paris and London provided a greater number of lucrative musical opportunities, higher fees and were more attractive to a number of composers like Handel, Gluck and Haydn. Vienna had neither a public concert hall nor a Friends of Music Society, but it held the advantage of proximity to the sources of supply of musical talent which at the time flowed predominantly from Italy and from the great number of German and Habsburg non-German centers (notably Hungary and Bohemia). Among the most noteworthy were places such as Berlin (where Frederick the Great employed C.P.E. Bach), Salzburg, Munich, Leipzig, Stuttgart, Prague and Mannheim, among others. Nevertheless, Vienna, as the seat of Empire, was surely the focus of musical life in the German lands, so that it is not difficult to account for the fact that most of the great composers of this part of the world eventually made their way to that city.

2. The Basic Hypothesis

2.1. The Role of German Disunity

We turn next to the main subject of our study – influences that led to the extraordinary profusion of composing talent in the Habsburg empire during Mozart's period and neighboring decades. One can, of course, never determine all of *the* causes of such a phenomenon, even if such a listing were conceivable. However, it is our basic contention that the fragmentation of the Holy Roman Empire and the attendant circumstances go a considerable way toward explaining the incentives for composition in Vienna at the end of the eighteenth century.

In a sense we are suggesting that the opportunities for Gluck, Haydn, Mozart and Beethoven have their origin in Canossa in 1077 when Henry IV's submission to Pope Gregory served to perpetuate the dismemberment of Germany, and in the submission in Venice, precisely one century later, of Frederick Barbarossa to Pope Alexander, which confirmed this fate. In the eighteenth century the Holy Roman Empire included something like 1,800 more-or-less independent German states (to be contrasted with the less than 200 states on the entire planet recognized by the United Nations in 1990). It is certainly true that effective power resided in, perhaps, a half-dozen to a dozen major secular and ecclesiastical dominions, but the fact is that Germany and Italy, unlike France and the United Kingdom, were subdivided into a multitude of petty states, each with its own provincial capital, and each with its own small court in which boredom was a principal concern of the ruler, and where musical activity frequently served as the main antidote. "Each [of the many states of the Holy Roman Empire] was headed by an absolute sovereign princelet, who ... strutted about, affectionately coddling his ornamental army, his hunting apparatus, and his little orchestra .... Of the kings and dukes, the greater and richer ones maintained their own opera establishments. These were very expensive, fancy luxuries, requiring incredibly luxurious stage machinery .... Princelets who could not afford their own operas contented themselves with keeping little chamber orchestras" (Loesser, 1954, pp. 4–7).

Here, of course, some principalities were more equal than others. Mannheim was a major focus of musical activity with its own "style" and magnificent orchestra. Wittenberg and Dresden were great musical centers, and Berlin was not far behind.[10]

Vienna and Prague were the main centers in the Habsburg possessions. Germany, Bohemia and Hungary were flooded with composers and musicians, many, undoubtedly, very minor talents and long deservedly forgotten, but their sheer number was surely astonishing.

As was already noted, old music was almost never played, and programs consisted of newly composed music, often by the court composer. This made for an abundance of employment opportunities for a host of composers and musicians spanning the full range of ability. It is well known that many of the court musicians were treated as servants, but also, in many cases, in order to qualify for employment as a servant the candidate was expected to display some musical skills. It also seems obvious that the necessity to practice these skills, often in the company of extremely accomplished musicians, served to hone them to a higher level. It is even reported (though it may strain credulity) that in Bohemia, "Every schoolmaster was expected to compose, rehearse, and perform at least one mass each year" (Braunbehrens, 1990, 1986, p. 295).

It is our conclusion that this profusion of outlets for the work of the composer served in a manner analogous to the bush leagues in baseball today, attracting and bringing to light the prospective superstars, along with a horde of less-talented aspirants, into musical composition rather than the other, often vastly different, occupations of their ancestors. The courts that valued music the most and were willing to spend the most money picked off the best.

We can hardly claim that anything approximating proof is provided by the evidence offered here for the hypothesis that the availability of a very large number of composers' posts brought forward many practitioners of the art, among them some geniuses who might otherwise never have written any music. Yet we believe that this line of reasoning, coupled with that of the next subsections, is sufficiently persuasive to convince dispassionate observers that it constitutes a substantial part of the story.

2.2. Economic Circumstances and the Availability of Artistic Opportunity

In an era in which sons often followed the occupations of their fathers (as did Bach and his own numerous sons), what else can have led these great German composers to seek a career other than the ones traditionally followed by their forefathers? In the absence of an enormous demand for the services of composers, one might never have suspected that the son of a forester (Gluck), the son of a wheelwright and distinguished town official (Haydn) and the grandson of a bookbinder and a government official (Mozart) were potential giants of musical composition (Robbins Landon, 1989, p. 11) See also the pertinent entries in the Grove Dictionary).[11]

The implication is that while suitable economic circumstances are, in themselves, hardly sufficient to elicit an abundance of musical genius, they may constitute a necessary condition for this result. As we have said before, economics can hardly be the entire story, but neither can its role be denied altogether. And surely it is plausible that many of those entering the labor market would turn to careers for which they thought themselves suitable in fields where there existed opportunities.

We have already seen evidence suggesting strongly that the political fragmentation of Germany (and Italy) provided opportunities for musicians which France and England did not offer. Despite the considerable musical activity in Paris and London, much of the talent seems to have been imported. Opportunities for native musicians must have been very limited because France and the United Kingdom had no secondary cities with a thriving musical life. Lyons and Rouen were not Mannheim, and York or Bath were not Berlin. One is led to surmise that the incentive for young job seekers to turn to music were far more modest than in Germany.

The role of economics in such matters is eloquently expressed in another context by that noted defender of historical materialism, G.V. Plekhanov. He observes, "In order that a man who possesses a particular kind of talent may, by means of it, greatly influence the course of events ... the existing social order must not bar the road to the person possessing the talent which is needed and useful precisely at the given time .... Napoleon would have died as the barely known General or Colonel Bonaparte had the old order in France existed another seventy-five years. In 1789 ... Augereau was a fencing master; Lannes was a dyer; Gouvion Saint-Cyr was an actor; Jourdan was a peddler; Bessières was a barber; Brune was a compositor; Joubert and Junot were law students; Kléber was an architect .... Had the old order continued until our day it would never have occurred to any of us that in France at the end of the 18th century, certain actors, compositors, barbers, dyers, lawyers, peddlers and fencing masters had been potential military geniuses" (Plekhanov, 1878, 1969, pp. 169–70).

2.3. Analog: The Economics of Theater in Renaissance London[12]

The case can, perhaps, be made more plausible by an analogy. The reason for the profusion of memorable composers in Germany towards the end of the 18th century clearly has its counterpart in the large number of great playwrights in London during the reigns of the first Elizabeth and James. Marlowe, Jonson and Shakespeare are only the most notable of these figures. Once again, economics surely cannot have created their genius, but it can be argued with some degree of plausibility that it gave them their opportunity.

The Phelps Brown-Hopkins indices[13] extending back to the 13th century, indicate that the plague and its decimation of the labor force raised real wages to levels unduplicated until the end of the 19th century. But with the accession of Henry VIII there began the great Tudor inflation which lasted nearly one and a half centuries, and which eroded the purchasing power of wages, bringing them, by the decade of Shakespeare's greatest productivity, to the lowest level in the entire seven centuries covered by the statistics. Undoubtedly, wages of theater builders, costume makers and actors followed a similar pattern.

The consequence for the economics of play production was dramatic. Today it takes well over a year for a non-musical play to recoup the expenses of its production, and before World War I it required a run of less than two months to break even. However, at the time the Globe Theater was in operation if a play ran for two weeks it was a great and profitable success. Low wages made a labor-intensive activity like theatrical production relatively cheap, and the result was that the demand for new plays was enormous. Producers had to maintain a stable of playwrights. They even resorted to the services of playwriting committees which were sometimes ordered to grind out new plays in a matter of days if the previous production proved to be disappointing commercially. With so much opportunity it is easily imagined that persons in search of employment would turn to the dramatist's occupation, and that out of the large number of entrants into the craft a small number who might otherwise never have been suspected of possession of the talent would turn out to be extremely capable, in some cases even able to write for the ages.

As has been argued, a different but equally powerful set of influences stimulated the market for composers' services in the Holy Roman Empire in the second half of the eighteenth century and, arguably, led many of those in search of gainful employment to turn to this activity. We may surmise that the bulk of those who did so might well have gone into forestry, farming or bookbinding. But, surely, it was among those many that society turned up those few whose works were to endure. Thus, it is our conclusion that a crucial influence helping to explain the profusion of great composers in Vienna at the time was a combination of circumstances, perhaps the most important of which was the fragmented state of the Empire that added greatly to the number of job opportunities for composers – an ideal situation for Mozart and others to pioneer abandonment of the old retainer system and become a musical entrepreneur.

3. On Revisionist Views of Mozart's Circumstances

This completes the discussion of our central topic. But we cannot end without offering some comments on the recent revisionist literature on Mozart's life and economic circumstances. Though it represents a digression for us, we think we have something pertinent to say about some of the romantic legends that have grown up about Mozart. Most of these have been dispelled by biographers like Braunbehrens (1986, 1990) and Robbins Landon (1988, 1989), and on those we will, consequently, be very brief.

3.1. MISCELLANEOUS LEGENDS

We have already alluded to the circumstances which inspired the tale of Mozart's "pauper's burial." Joseph II, as an enlightened ruler, decreed that for reasons of sanitation, economy and rationality, burial masses would be celebrated in Viennese churches, and the bodies then transported in (reusable) wooden boxes to mass graves outside the city limits in special carts. Not many people chose to argue with the Emperor, and it became the custom to conclude the burial service at the Church rather than to follow the funeral cart on its long trip to the mass burial ground. Only members of the highest nobility managed to avoid this sort of "pauper's burial," and so it is true that Mozart, along with the wealthy bourgeoisie, did not escape it. Incidentally, it was customary to dig the bones out of the mass graves after a number of years, depositing them in the ossuaries that tourists still visit in Vienna, so that the cemetery grounds could be used again.

The evidence also leads one to spring to the defense of Constanze against the accusation that she was a silly, uncaring woman. It is true that Mozart's father disapproved of the marriage and that her family may have been opportunists, but the deep affection displayed in Mozart's letters to her (none of her letters to him is preserved), the intelligence and care with which she oversaw posthumous publication of his works (with unwillingness to accept lucrative offers that threatened shoddy publication) and her contributions to the material for Nissen's biography of Mozart all make the traditional depiction of her extremely questionable.

Only those whose total knowledge of Mozart's life is limited to attendance at the play or movie, *Amadeus*, can believe that Salieri poisoned Mozart. Actually, when the deed was alleged to have been committed Joseph II had died, and his successor, in a great economy sweep, had fired Salieri and abolished his post, to which Mozart may conceivably once have aspired.

It is difficult to picture Mozart as an unmannered lout when we know the company he kept, which included some of the most distinguished people in Vienna. He was a Mason, a suspect liberal organization at that time. Like other artists and writers, he selected his librettos to promote the liberal ideas that found fruition in the French Revolution, testing the limits of censorship in the process. It is hard to believe that it was merely fortuitous that his librettists and sources included Da Ponte and Beaumarchais, who were often in trouble with the authorities. Incidentally, the profusion of common themes in his librettos written by different librettists, surely indicates that he must have taken a substantial role in their writing. An example is the recurrence of the revolutionary theme of the exploitation of servants by masters and the superior intelligence, leadership and/or morality of the servants (Blonde in the *Abduction*, Suzanna and Figaro in the *Marriage*, Despina in *Cosi*, and even, to some degree, Leporello and Zerlina in *Don Giovanni*). Another illustration is the repeated appearance of the theme of forgiveness. The point is that these operas, all written with different librettists, are rare in their literary sophistication, something that can be accounted for only by an influence they shared in common. They all clearly show the hand of a talented and powerful intellect, one with clear ideas about human nature, justice, marriage[14] and the appropriate role of humor.

We are also inclined to concur with Julia Moore's educated guess about his character, "I would describe him rather as high-spirited, energetic, hard-working, fun-loving, absolutely assured of his talent and impatient with the lesser talents of most fellow musicians, and usually buoyant in the face of adversity" (1991 p. 22).

3.2. MOZART'S SUPPOSED POVERTY

As we will show next, Mozart earned a good deal of money during his decade in Vienna. For some years now, it has become increasingly clear that, whether or not it placed him in the most affluent portion of the middle class – a subject still disputed – Mozart's income put him well above the poverty level (see Braunbehrens, Robbins Landon and the data provided by Moore (1989, p. 21). However, the magnitude of his earnings seems not to have been evaluated defensibly in terms of today's dollars, so that their size was not readily apparent to the reader. We will attempt to provide such a translation.

It is true that there were periods when Mozart was in financial difficulties. In part, as we will see, this was attributable to his high standard of living. In addition, the two years (about 1789 to 1790) in which he seems to have been seriously strapped coincided with an expensive illness of Constanze's and a period probably characterized by high inflation and reduced demand for musical services by the court and that part of the nobility who were occupied with the Turkish War. Clearly, the inflation considerably (if temporarily) reduced the purchasing power of Mozart's earnings (see Figure 1, which shows the price of bread, as reported by Morrow (1984) for the period 1780 to 1810, including all of Mozart's time of residence in Vienna).[15]

Steptoe, in his review of the evidence (1984), also notes that in the years when Mozart appears to have been in financial trouble he suffered a sharp drop in the number of his concert appearances, which may well be, to some degree, attributable to the dispersion of the court and the fall in demand resulting from the war. There may also have been a general drop in Mozart's popularity caused, perhaps, by overexposure on the Viennese concert stage, as Steptoe proposes. Certainly Mozart undertook several onerous trips between 1785 and 1791, possibly to duplicate his Viennese success in other cities. Unfortunately, they seem to have been only mildly remunerative if at all.

It is noteworthy that by 1791, Mozart's last year, Constanze was apparently no longer taking the cure, the Turkish war was over, prices appear to have returned to their pre-war level and the documented part of Mozart's income was higher than its 1783–91 average. Offers were arriving from England and Russia and honorary pensions were being gathered to attract him to Amsterdam and Hungary

(Braunbehrens, p. 141). Had he but lived, his financial troubles might possibly soon have vanished[16] (perhaps only to rise again during the terrible inflation of the Napoleonic wars, as happened to Haydn and Beethoven).

3.3. MOZART'S FINANCIAL STATE: TRANSLATING 1780S AUSTRIAN CURRENCY INTO CURRENT DOLLARS

Before going into more detail on Mozart's income and expenditures we must try to arrive at an understanding of what those figures mean in terms comprehensible to us today. There is no really accurate way to translate the currency of another land in another era into money here and now. The most obvious reason is that people have changed their requirements and patterns of consumption. They now buy very different combinations of things whose relative prices vary greatly.

Specialists have designed methods that do the job in a rough and ready manner. Part 1 of the Appendix to this article describes two such methods which yield two different numbers, each with a legitimate and significant interpretation.

The first simply corrects for the change over time in the price level, which has risen considerably since 1786 (the mid-point of Mozart's residence in Vienna), so that it takes many more dollars or pounds today to buy a given bundle of goods than it would have in 1786. Moreover, the contents of a representative market basket have changed, and some effort must be made to take this into account. Our appendix calculation indicates that the 2,500 florin estimate of Mozart's average income in his Viennese period, which we believe to be quite conservative, would have enabled him to purchase a bundle of goods whose 1990 equivalent would cost somewhere near $25,000 today (see part 2 of the Appendix). That is hardly great wealth, though it is not abject poverty either. But it neglects the fact that in those days Europe was far poorer than it is today, and so the purchasing power of almost everyone was far lower than that of his or her 20th century counterpart.

To deal with this fact, the second method of calculation undertakes a comparison of the *hierarchy* of earnings in Mozart's time and the present. Even the 1700 florins, which was the average of Mozart's documented earnings alone, came to more than five times the 300 florin money income that was the top of the scale for a high school teacher at that time. If we assume that the average teacher received as much again in kind (such payments were common practice then), and that Mozart received absolutely no such nonmonetary remuneration,[17] the *known and documented portion* of Mozart's income alone would have come to more than 2.8 times (1,700 = (2.8) × (600), approximately) that of the teacher. Thus, if Mozart were to be in the same income position relative to a New York City high school teacher today (whose top salary is $50,000), he would have to earn more than 2.8 times that amount, or nearly $150,000 per annum! This comparison cannot be taken to be more than a suggestive guess, but it illustrates that our second translation of Mozart's income into todays dollars is based on a comparison of Mozart's income with earnings of others in Vienna at the time. It also suggests that Mozart's earnings put him well into the bracket of the middle class of his Vienna, when, according to Pezzl's guidebook, the 1786 budget of a typical middle class bachelor (actually, a rather impecunious middle-class bachelor) amounted to some 550 florins, that is, well under 25 percent of our (we think conservative) guess about Mozart's average income (see below). There is an abundance of other evidence that supports this general conclusion, though the numbers just suggested should not be accepted as more than gross approximations. Yet it is important to note that there has just emerged, through the capable scholarship of Dr. Moore a re-revisionist position that holds that the recent studies that have concluded that Mozart's income was substantial, constitute an exaggeration, if not worse.

It is reasonable to surmise that Mozart, like so many businessmen today, experienced cash flow problems. No doubt he was pressed for payment for expenditures connected with his musical activities, and we know that at least some of his receipts came in very slowly. He had probably borrowed a substantial amount while establishing himself in Vienna and for various other purposes, though it is interesting that he did not leave a particularly large burden of debt on his death – less than 2000 gulden (Braunbehrens, p. 424). By his final year, however, his finances appear to have been under somewhat better control,[18] and he had reason to expect in the next year to follow Haydn to London, where the latter had been able to earn far more than Mozart earned in Vienna, even in his most prosperous periods.[19]

3.4. More on Mozart's Income

Over a century ago, Jahn (1856–9) provided the then currently known evidence on Mozart's recorded earnings during his decade in Vienna (for a careful review of what is known and what is not known about Mozart's income, see Steptoe). Jahn's figures on Mozart's income, are all (more or less) documented and, apparently, were not disputed until very recently. After Braunbehrens took them over as the basis for his calculations, Moore examined the figures more critically, and took issue with such things as the inclusion of Mozart's borrowings as income, and the inclusion as 1791 income of a 2000 florin figure that Mozart mentions as an expected receipt in a letter seeking to borrow money, a receipt for which absolutely no confirming evidence appears to exist. Because of Moore's careful scholarship our calculations are based on her figures rather than Braunbehrens'.[20]

These figures must be interpreted with considerable caution because they represent only the documented portion of Mozart's actual income. In addition, these figures represent only gross income, with no deductions for professional expenses (see below). Many sources of income, including publication fees, payments for lessons, private concerts, payments for the composition of some of his operas and so on, have been omitted because we do not know the precise amounts he received for them. However, for many of the omitted items we do know the customary fees and the amounts Mozart had received for other similar activities. For example, we know that for *Figaro* he was paid 100 ducats or 425 florins (equivalent, roughly to a wage of $30,000 in 1989).[21] Yet, because we do not know his fee for the *Abduction*, this fee is here very conservatively treated as though it was zero.

The jagged curve in Figure 2 reports, year by year, just the *documented* and, hence, known income received by Mozart. Its considerable volatility is probably attributable to the haphazard nature of the information that survives as much as to changes in the market for his services. Even if we consider only this known part of his income, we find that it averaged some 1,700 florins per year (the wage equivalent of about 120,000 1990 dollars), and surpassed 2,000 florins (or 140,000 in 1990 dollars) in three of the nine years depicted in the graph.

Braunbehrens calculates that if we add to these figures reasonable evaluations of his undocumented income, his average earnings during his Vienna years are conservatively estimated at 3,000–4,000 florins per annum.[22]

We adopt a far more conservative guess, for purposes of comparison. We assume (without evidence) that no more than two thirds of his total income is included explicitly in the documentation provided by the surviving papers, and therefore comes to some 2,500 florins.

The purchasing power of our estimate of Mozart's average income – the 2500 florins – is estimated by the crude methods available for the purpose to be about that of $25,000 today, but measured in terms of the ratio of 1786 Viennese wages to today's wages in the U.S., it amounted to approximately[23] $175,000 relative to the average U.S. wage in 1989 (for the evidence, see the appendices).

It should be emphasized, however, that these figures can, at best, be accepted as reasonable estimates of Mozart's *gross* income, because they do not deduct unavoidable professional expenses, whose magnitude has proved very difficult to estimate (see the discussion of his expenses, below.)

Mozart had five principal sources of income: patronage, performance, music lessons, publication, and commissions. His income from patronage in Vienna was limited – principally the sinecure stipend, 800 florins per year, granted by the Emperor in 1787. The grant came late in Mozart's life, and the amount, though hardly negligible, was far smaller than others, such as Gluck, had received.

A large part of Mozart's income was probably earned as virtuoso pianist. He played often at the all-important "... private salons ... where most of the music making took place," and where "Mozart ... maintained a dizzying schedule of private appearances at his zenith in the mid 1980's" (Morrow, pp. 37–8). Payment was at the discretion of the host and probably varied greatly. He composed 26 pianoforte concertos for performance at his own concerts which are considered to be among his greatest works. He organized subscription series of three or four concerts or more, at least sometimes aided by, perhaps, the first private impresarios, Philipp Jacques Martin and Ignaz Schuppanzigh. Such concerts were held in the inadequate private facilities that existed in Vienna. Mozart claimed to have 174 subscribers for one such projected series, and his series of six concerts in the Mehlgrube attracted 150 subscribers (Morrow, pp. 56–7). They may have been extremely lucrative.

How much did he earn at public concerts? Again Morrow's careful scholarship comes to our aid: "Generalizing ... is impossible ... . If the circumstances were right, one performance could bring in 1,000–1,500 gulden [florins] or more (two to three times the court orchestra concert master's annual salary). Even a half-empty hall at Jahn's (the concert hall of the Court Caterer in the Himmelpfortgasse (Gate of Heaven Road)) would have brought in 400 gulden and left *ca.* 250 gulden after expenses. The situation in Vienna offered musicians a good chance to make money, if they had the business sense and the talent to take advantage of it" (Morrow, p. 146).

We have more evidence on how much Mozart could earn at his peak as concert performer. His father, in a letter to his daughter on February 16, 1785, wrote of "... his first subscription concert, where there was a vast concourse of people of rank. Each person pays one souverain d'or ($13\frac{1}{2}$ gulden) or 3 ducats [$900 in today's wage equivalent] for the 6 Lenten concerts ... for the use of the room he pays only *one half a souverain d'or*" (quoted in Robbins Landon, 1989, p. 125).

It was the opinion of Jahn that Mozart did not earn much from publication of his works: "... the music trade of the day was small and insignificant; indeed, the first impulse was given to it by the publication of an edition of all Mozart's works soon after his death. During his life ... compositions were more often copied than printed; and the composer was obliged to keep careful watch lest copies should be distributed which were ... never paid for." He points out that such caution was not in Mozart's nature, but adds, "He was careful only of his concertos ... not allowing any one to play them who chose" (Jahn, 1891, 1970, p. 293). Certainly his letters reflect this view.

Mozart insisted on the high price for lessons of 6 ducats (some $1800 in 1989 wage equivalent) for 12 lessons to be given every day. The work was limited to the winter season and was a highly undependable source of income. Some teachers, e.g., Clementi, charged more than Mozart for lessons, but Mozart's fee was far above the norm (Steptoe, p. 197). It is possible that he resorted to private teaching when he was in great need of money. It may have been his principal source of income before the premiere of *The Abduction* in 1782, his first great popular success.

For composition Mozart also received fees toward the high end of the scale of customary fees, e.g., normally 100 ducats per opera. He probably sometimes received more, but not as much as Paisiello at his most popular.

3.5. On Mozart's Expenditures

As Mozart, so to speak, ran his own business, it is interesting to learn his professional expenses. One component may have been the necessity of adequate premises. Robbins Landon writes: "In Vienna, at that time [1784], Mozart's name was on every tongue ... . It was a heady success, also financially, and the Mozarts urgently required a new and much larger apartment, where they could accommodate the constant presence of copyists, pupils and the complicated organization needed to deal with academy concerts, subscription invitations, and so on ... The move was to be made ... to splendid, very expensive, and spacious quarters, for which the rent was 460 gulden [florins] p.a. [per annum] (compared with the 150 gulden for his previous flat)" (Robbins Landon, 1989, pp. 119–120). That is, he was now paying a rent equivalent to $30,000, measured in 1989 U.S. wages. It should be said that rents in Vienna were very high, and this was less than rents paid by many of Mozart's friends – highly compensated actors, opera singers, members of the nobility and the wealthy bourgeoisie. Keeping up with them must have been a strain on the Mozart budget.

Pianos were also costly. Mozart reports that Stein's price for his higher-quality pianos was no "... less than three hundred gulden ... [over $20,000 in wage equivalent]" (letter of October 17, 1777, as quoted in King, 1955, p. 243). This was the same as his father's base annual income. Mozart also undoubtedly increased the outlay on his pianoforte further by having it fitted with a complicated pedal board "... built like the pianoforte, with similar hammers, dampers, etc., but the keys are much enlarged and so disposed that they can be played with the feet" (King, p. 245, quoting an 1806 description).

As we have seen, there is no reason to suggest that Mozart was economical in most of his outlays. Jahn refers to his "thoughtless liberality." His love of costly clothing was probably carried to extremes. On April 16, 1785, Leopold writes to his daughter that Madame Lange and Wolfgang had intended going with him to Munich, but nothing was likely to come of it, "although each of them have now had six pairs of shoes made, which are all standing there now."

Bär (1978) carefully reviews much more such evidence, both on Mozart's outlays and on expenditure patterns in Vienna at the time. He concludes that the family must have been spending approximately at the rate of 2000 florins per year. However, he does not include medical expenses (including Constanze's six pregnancies), maintenance of a horse, attendance at the theater (of which Mozart was extremely fond), books and musical scores, among other things.

The itemization of Mozart's estate, which there is good reason to believe was deliberately undervalued (in accord with current custom), also suggests that his expenditures were rather generous. His estate contained many suits of expensive clothing, many porcelain figures and boxes, a billiard table, and four couches with matching upholstered chairs that normally appeared only in the estates of the very rich.[24]

He was certainly a liberal spender in some ways, but it does not follow that such outlays were excessive in light of his income level, and certainly not compared to those of his friends and acquaintances. On Mozart's death he left debts of less than 2,000 gulden, not a huge amount for one who had been so liberal a spender. Perhaps he paid off some of his debts when the money rolled in again in 1791. It may be illuminating to end with Steptoe's summation: "The financial difficulties Mozart encountered later in his life were almost inevitable for an artist reliant on irregular sources, who was in ill-health and somewhat unpopular at the same time. It is not necessary to infer that Mozart and Constanze were profligate or (as is often claimed without evidence) that Mozart gambled his income away in order to account for their predicament. She in particular has received an excessive degree of blame. Her supposed thriftlessness and caprice are hard to reconcile with her financial shrewdness as a widow" (p. 200).

4. Concluding Comment

It would appear that it was not Vienna, but its hinterlands, to which one should assign the bulk of the credit for the emergence of so great a number of great composers. Vienna usually attracted them from other parts of Germany after the first stages of their career paths had been completed. Probably no one explanation can account for the extraordinary profusion of Germanic composition that spanned the end of one century and the beginning of another, but it is difficult to believe that the political fragmentation of the country and the associated proliferation of job opportunities for musicians had little or no role in attracting into the profession many persons who otherwise might have gone elsewhere, and in helping to ferret out those among the recruits who displayed unusual ability.

5. Appendix – Method of Conversion: 1786 Pounds to 1989 Dollars, With Some Notes on Mozart's Income, 1781–1791[25]

A.1. Translation of 1786 Currency into 1989 Terms

The task of interpreting Mozart's eighteenth century income into today's terms cannot be carried out unambiguously, given the vast differences in consumption patterns and living standards. Two different conversions of 1786 pounds to 1989 dollars will be used here to present a fuller picture.

The first of these is a comparison of the *purchasing power* of a unit of currency today with that of the eighteenth century, using the Phelps Brown-Hopkins index for a market basket of consumables for the years 1786 through 1950 in southern England. This is then extended to 1989 using the United Kingdom GDP deflator as reported by the U.S. Bureau of Labor Statistics. Finally, the resulting 1989 *British pound* figure (taking 1786 = 100) is converted to dollars using the BLS purchasing-power-parity (PPP) exchange rate between pounds and dollars, as calculated by the BLS. The figure obtained in this way is an estimate of the number of 1989 U.S. dollars required to purchase a market basket of consumer goods that is roughly equivalent to a market basket that could have bought for one pound in southern England in 1786. This figure will be used to calculate the 1989 *purchasing power* of Mozart's income.

Also offered is a second pound-dollar conversion which estimates an *earnings equivalent* comparison. This takes into account both the change in the purchasing power of money and, in addition, the rise in average standards of living. It gives us the ratio of the number of dollars earned by a "typical" worker in 1989 to the comparable earnings figure for 1786. It does so by adding to the information used in the calculations of the preceding paragraph an estimate of the rise in real wages in England over the two hundred and four years in question. To estimate that rise in real wages we start, once again, with the Phelps Brown-Hopkins data, this time using their index of real building wages, and then bring their figures up to date with the aid of BLS data for the UK. Since real wages are estimated, on this calculation, to have risen by a factor of 7.2 over the period,[26] the figure in the preceding paragraph is simply multiplied by this factor. The result is almost certainly an underestimate, since use of the PPP exchange-rate figure ignores the fact that US 1989 real wages were substantially higher than the British, and so have risen even more in relation to 1786 British wages. This second approach to 1989 dollar translation of a 1786 pound is to be interpreted as the number of dollars an American must earn in 1989 to be in the same relative position, vis-a-vis an "average worker," that the earner of one pound sterling would have been in England in 1786. This figure will be used to determine in 1989 terms where Mozart's income placed him in the hierarchy of earnings in Vienna in about 1786.

The pertinent data are given in Table I.

Thus, we conclude that the number of 1989 pounds equivalent to one 1786 pound equals

in purchasing power: $(3.76) \times (14.3) = 53.9$
in relative wage: $(53.9) \times (3.1) \times (2.3) = 388$.

We then obtain via a pound-dollar translation: 1989 dollar equivalent of a 1786 pound (at PPP 1989 exchange rate 0.6161 pounds per dollar) equals

in purchasing power: 53.9/0.6161 = \$87.50;
in relative wage: 388/0.6161 = \$630.

To sum up the results of the two approaches, one British pound in 1786 could purchase a bundle of goods equivalent to one worth about \$87.50 today; and to be in the same place in the earnings hierarchy as the earner of one pound in 1786, one must earn (approximately) \$630 today.

To evaluate today's dollar equivalent of Austrian money in Mozart's time we took 9 Viennese florins (gulden) to have been equivalent to one pound during that period.

According to the authoritative information supplied by Professor John J. McCusker (Department of History, University of Maryland), to whom we are deeply grateful, this is consistent with the reports in the Viennese financial press of the day, and is approximately the figure given by Ruelle (1798, p. 425). Robbins Landon uses 10 florins to the pound, while Braunbehrens uses 8, so the figure selected here falls precisely between the two.

TABLE I. Data for calculation of 1989 dollar equivalent of 1786 pound

	Price of market basket		Real wage	
	Phelps Brown-Hopkins Index	BLS Index	Phelps Brown-Hopkins Index	BLS Index
1786	839.0	NA	58.0	NA
1950	3155.0	18.3	180.0	53.3
Ratio (1950/1786)	4.76		3.1	
1989	NA	262.4	NA	123.9
Ratio (1989/1950)		14.3		2.3

TABLE II. Translation of 1786 Austrian currency into 1989 dollars

	1 florin =	1 ducat =
In Purchasing Power	$10 (approx)	$45 (approx)
In Wage Equivalent	$70 (approx)	$300 (approx)

This meant that the ducat, worth about 4.5 florins, was equivalent to half of a British pound. This readily gives us the 1989 dollar translations of one florin and one ducat, respectively, that is shown in Table II.

A.2. Mozart's Income in 1989 Terms

Mozart's average annual documented income during his years 1783–91 in Vienna has been calculated from Moore's data (1989, p. 21) to have been a bit more than 1711 florins.

Our reason for omission of the years 1791–92 has already been described.

Guessing that no more than 2/3 of his total income is listed in surviving documents, we have estimated his total income to have averaged 2500 florins. This can be translated into 1989 dollars, very approximately, with the aid of the figures in Table II, yielding:

1989 purchasing power, Mozart's estimated average annual income: $25,000;

1989 real wage equivalent of that income: $175,000.

If the guess at Mozart's average annual income is considered too shaky, one can perform a similar calculation upon the average of Mozart's known income figures as reported by Moore. As we have seen, for the years 1783–91 this is somewhat in excess of 1700 florins. Performing the same calculations as before, this figure translates into a 1989 purchasing power of $17,000, and a real wage equivalent of

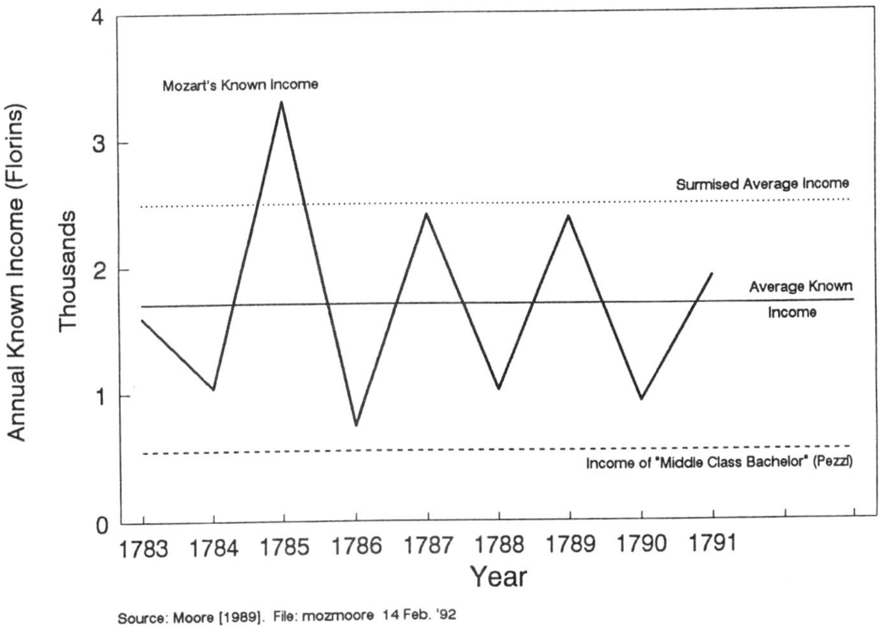

Fig. 2. Mozart's *known* income, 1783–1791 (Moore's calculations, omitting undocumented income).

about $120,000. This clear underestimate of Mozart's income does not amount to vast wealth, but it is surely far from grinding poverty.

Figure 2 shows Mozart's *known* income, year by year, during his last nine years in Vienna. The data are the numbers provided by Moore (1989, p. 21) and generally constitute a downward revision of the data first documented by Otto Jahn in his 1856–59 biography of Mozart. Also included in the graph for purposes of comparison, are three horizontal lines. The lowest shows Pezzl's estimate of the annual income required by a (lower) middle class bachelor. The middle line is the average of the known income figures reported by Moore for the years in question. The top line depicts our guess about the magnitude of Mozart's average income, documented and undocumented.

Notes

* The authors are, respectively, professor of economics at Princeton and New York Universities, and president of Consultants in Industry Economics, Inc. We are deeply grateful for comments and suggestions to Edward T. Cone, Timothy Guinnane, Richard Kapp, Arno Mayer, John J. McCusker and Maynard Solomon. We are particularly indebted to Dr. Julia Moore, who saved us from some embarrassing mistakes on matters musical or historical – fields in which our standing is strictly that of amateurs (both in the original and current senses of the word). Of

course, none of these can be held responsible for our conclusions, and Dr. Moore in particular takes a different view from ourselves on Mozart's finances. None of the work reported here is based on direct archival study and it undertakes only to explore the implications of the published materials. This paper was originally prepared for the Woodrow Wilson International Center for Scholars, which has published an abbreviated version and with whose kind permission this article is published. We are also very much indebted to New York University's C.V. Starr Center for Applied Economics for facilitating our work on this paper.

1. The assassination victim of *Un Ballo in Maschera.*
2. Of course, royal marriage patterns made it difficult to say of any monarch that he had no significant amount of German blood. Among the ancestors of Louis XVI there was, for example, Anne of Austria, wife of Louis XIII and mother of the Sun King, she whose association with the Duke of Buckingham is the focus of *The Three Musketeers.*
3. Figure 1 is based only on the price of bread, *faute de mieux,* as a crude indicator of inflation. Moore's excellent index of food and rent prices (probably as accurate as the surviving data permit), which she used in her analysis of Beethoven's income, does not begin until 1790. The use of bread prices is particularly dangerous because some governments in Europe at that time placed controls on the price of bread to forestall disorder and revolution. This suggests that the rise in bread prices during the Turkish War probably provides an *underestimate* of the general rate of the war inflation, with the government permitting a doubling in bread prices only when it could no longer hold them back. This suggestive use of bread price is the only way that figure is used in the current paper, its purpose being to apply Moore's cogent argument about Beethoven to Mozart – that one cannot understand his real income without taking into account the role of inflation..
4. His letters affirm this repeatedly, as in the quotation at the beginning of this article. However, such statements may well exaggerate Mozart's dedication to money making, perhaps having been intended to reassure his father and to stem the flow of stern fatherly advice. Professor Edward T. Cone reminds us that Mozart wrote pieces for his own family: four-hand sonatas that he played with his sister, violin sonatas that he played with his wife and pieces he wrote for his pupils. Thus, as is to be expected, his objective was not quite undeviatingly pecuniary.
5. Still, this oft repeated report may be viewed with some skepticism, given the lack of attention to Mozart's music in London at this period. According to McVeigh Haydn had tried repeatedly but unsuccessfully to convince the English of Mozart's greatness (McVeigh, 1993, p. 127).
6. Below, we report the evaluation by Moore who concludes that aristocratic and bourgeois demand for musical composition and performance was as much, and perhaps more, a matter of ostentation and the pursuit of status and prestige, as it was of appreciation of the arts.
7. However, in 1787, he was appointed to the post of Imperial Chamber Musician, largely a sinecure, at a fairly generous stipend of 800 florins per annum.
8. The expected impermanence of musical works is underscored by the fact that they were often written with particular performers in mind. There are many examples in Mozart's writings, and he was known to criticize performances because they were not given by the performer for whom the composer intended them. He describes his attendance at a Holzhauer opera in Mannheim thus: The *prima donna*, Madame Wending, "... is always indisposed and, what is more, the opera was not written for her, but for a certain Danzi, who is at present in England; consequently it is not suited to her voice, but is too high for her" (Mozart to his father, November, 14–16, 1777; Anderson, 1938, Vol. 2, pp. 549–50).
9. By Mozart's Viennese period "ancient musick" had begun to acquire some status in London with Paris and Berlin lagging behind. "In the year 1700 [in London] it would have seemed more than mildly ludicrous to put on regular public concerts offering only music more than twenty or so years old ... . Yet in 1776 a group of noblemen founded just such a musical society, the proudly backward-looking Concert of Ancient Music ... . In 1784 its august directors put on a grand festival in honour of George Frederick Handel, then twenty-five years in his grave, that brought 525 musicians and over four and a half thousand listeners to Westminster Abbey and seized the attention of newspapers from Boston to Berlin. Ancient music now rivalled the modern; old works had acquired a certain chic ... . [Yet, up until then in England] Works were composed, used, and discarded ... *La musique ancienne* did not become rooted in French musical

life as ancient music did in British concerts [and in Vienna the movement was represented by Swieten's] private readings." (Weber, 1992, pp. 1–4).

10. On all this see, e.g., York-Long (1954).
11. None of this is meant to suggest that any of these composers suffered from a deprived childhood (Gluck's forester father seems, for example, to have been prosperous), but only that their occupations were radically different from those of their forebears.
12. This section is based on material provided in Baumol and Oates (1972).
13. The Phelps Brown-Hopkins indices of real wages and prices are a carefully constructed and widely used set of statistics based on the records of building wages and prices recorded in manors in southern England and in the ancient universities.
14. "People of noble birth must never marry from inclination or love, but only from interest and all kinds of secondary considerations. Again, it would not at all suit a grandee to love his wife after she had done her duty and brought into the world a bouncing son and heir. But we poor humble people can not only choose a wife whom we love and who loves us, but we may, can and do take such a one, because we are neither noble, nor highly born, nor aristocratic, nor rich ... ." (Mozart to his father, February 7, 1778; Anderson 1938, Vol. 2, pp. 690–91).
15. The figures are in kreuzer per pound of bread; a florin was equivalent to 60 kreuzer. By our calculation, bread sold at a wage equivalent of about two 1989 dollars per pound. That is, an average income earner in Mozart's Vienna worked about the same time to earn a pound of bread as it requires an average American worker to earn two dollars today. The data in the graph are taken from Morrow in her extremely illuminating dissertation. On the dangers of use of the controlled price of bread as an index of the general price level see note 3, above.

    Incidentally, because it ends in 1810, the graph only begins to show how much more serious was the inflation with which Beethoven had to deal. It was only after 1810 that Austrian prices really exploded (perhaps more than 30-fold between 1795 and 1817), and the bankrupt Austrian government debased its currency on a five-to-one ratio in 1812 (see Moore's (1987) very careful analysis). Naturally, this severely eroded the 4000 florin annual stipend that had been granted to him in 1899 by the Archduke and two princes. Like many others at the time, Beethoven resorted to the courts and sued the creditors of the bankrupt Prince Lobkowitz and the estate of the dead Prince Kinsky. In 1815 he was awarded partial adjustment for the debasement of the currency by the government (but no adjustment for the severe inflationary erosion, see Moore, e.g., pp. 3, 126–27). All of this evidence supports Moore's contention that Beethoven's financial problems were very real and severe. It certainly suggests that there is as little basis for the widespread skepticism on Beethoven's financial complaints as there is for the equally common view that Mozart was chronically impoverished.
16. Mozart was well aware of the bitter irony in the fact that this all came too late. During his final illness, according to his first biographer (Georg Nikolaus Nissen, Constanze's second husband), Mozart wrote, "... now ... when I could compose freely and independently whatever my heart dictates! I must leave my family ... in that moment when I would be in a better condition to care for them ... ." (Robbins Landon, 1988, p. 153, who cites Nissen, 1828).
17. As a matter of fact Mozart *did* receive some nonmonetary income which at least in earlier years was likely to have been substantial. Thus, Moore (1989 p. 22 note 10) cites Angermüller's report that "The Mozart family returned from their European concert tour of 1763–6 with nine gold watches, 12 gold snuff boxes, countless gold rings with precious stones, earrings, necklaces, miscellaneous gold objects and *galanterie* clothing worth perhaps 12,000 fl[orins]."
18. However, a document has turned up indicating that only a month before his death, Mozart was sued by Count Lischinowsky, later a patron of Beethoven, for the considerable sum of 1435 florins and 32 kreuzer. The claims of either side in this case, or its outcome (if it ever did reach a hearing) are unknown, since all other documents related to the case have disappeared. On this see Brauneis (1991).
19. The known income of Mozart's last year, 1925 florins, is well above the average. However, he was still plagued by debt and he may have lost a costly lawsuit, so that while the future seems to have looked promising, as already noted, his financial difficulties undoubtedly were not quite over.

20. Still, it should be noted that for the years 1783–1791 Moore's figures total only 11 percent less than Braunbehrens' – his average annual figure for the known portion of Mozart's income during those years is 1928 florins, while hers is 1711. We use her figures for only the years 1783–91, ignoring 1791–92, the first two years of Mozart's residence in Vienna. We think the available information is so poor that the known portion of his income for those years must be a ludicrous underestimate of his actual income. For example, no payments are recorded for *Idomeneo* (1781) or *the Abduction* (1782), so nothing is included in Moore's figures for those years.
21. Since standards of living in the eighteenth century were far lower than now, this amount provided far less in terms of purchasing power – probably something in excess of $4000 today.
22. Kraemer proposes a figure well above 10,000 florins for Mozart's annual income, but that far exceeds every carefully calculated estimate, and from the evidence it seems highly implausible. Steptoe's estimate is that the average figure was slightly *less* than 3000 florins (1984, p. 198). However, this number excludes earnings from private performances, which were probably not negligible. In any event, since just the documented portion of his income averages nearly 2000 florins, it is implausible that the total was far below 3000 florins.
23. That is, the ratio (1700 florins/ estimated Viennese wage in 1786) is approximately equal to ($175,000/ average U.S. wage in 1989). The factor (seven) by which we multiply the estimate of Mozart's purchasing power (25,000 in 1989 dollars) to arrive at the wage equivalent is demonstrably and deliberately exceedingly conservative. It assumes that the average real income of an American in 1989 is seven times as high as that of an inhabitant of Vienna two centuries earlier. Yet, careful calculations by economic historians indicate that 1989 average U.S. real income was some eight times as great as it was in 1870, for which some considerable evidence, including surviving family budgets, is available. In sum, we are proceeding on the absurdly conservative assumption that the average standard of living in eighteenth century Vienna was higher than that in the U.S. in 1870. Clearly, exaggeration of the estimate of average income in 1789 Vienna serves to *reduce* the calculated figure for Mozart's relative income – that is, to arrive at a more defensible figure a multiplier considerably higher than seven should undoubtedly have been used to bring it up to its modern U.S. wage equivalent.
24. Beethoven's estate included only one couch. But that is not all we can learn from a comparison of the two estates. According to Moore (pp. 452–454), Mozart's clothing and furniture were valued, respectively, at 55 and 229 florin of 1781, while the corresponding figures for Beethoven were only 37 and 57 florins of 1827. But this vastly underestimates the true difference because it ignores the probably more than twentyfold inflation in prices that occurred between 1791 and 1827. When corrected for this, in 1827 florins we must estimate the value of the clothing in Mozart's estate at over 1100 florins and his furniture at more than 4500 florins of 1827, that is, more than 80 times as great a value as Beethoven's.
25. We are extremely grateful to Timothy Guinnane and John J. McCusker for their very valuable help in the preparation of this Appendix.
26. Real annual wages have almost certainly risen far more slowly than output per worker, since the number of hours worked per year has probably fallen some 40 percent in just the past hundred years.

References

Anderson, Emily (trans.) (1938) *The Letters of Mozart and His Family*. Macmillan, London.

Bär, Carl (1978) "Er war ... -kein guter Wirth' Eine Studie über Mozarts Verhältnis zum Geld." *Acta Mozartiana* 25: 30–53.

Baumol, W.J. and Oates, Mary I. (1972) "On the Economics of the Theater in Renaissance London." *Swedish Journal of Economics* 74: 136–160.

Braunbehrens, Volkmar (1990) *Mozart in Vienna*. Grove Weidenfeld, New York (German edition, 1986). Reprinted in the United States, Harper Perennial, 1991.

Brauneis, Von Walther (1991) "'... wegen schuldigen 1435 f 32 xr' Neuer Archivfund zur Finanzmisere Mozarts im November 1791." *Mitteilungen der Internationalen Stiftung Mozarteum*, 158–163.

Closson, Ernest (1947) *History of the Piano*. Paul Elek, London.
Ehrlich, Cyril (1990) *The Piano: A History*. Clarendon Press, Oxford.
Freeman, Daniel (1987) *The Opera Theater of Count Franz Anton von Sporck in Prague 1724–35*. Ph.D. Dissertation, University of Illinois.
Good, David P. (1984) *The Economic Rise of the Habsburg Empire, 1750–1914*, University of California Press, Berkeley.
Jahn, Otto (1891) *Life of Mozart (1856–59)*. English translation, Novello, Ewer and Co., London. Reprinted Cooper Square Publishers, New York, 1970.
Kellett, E.E. and Naylor, E.W. (1889) *A History of the Pianoforte and Pianoforte Players* (Tr. and Rev. from the German of Oscar Bie, "Das Klavier"). E.P. Dutton, New York.
King, A. Hyatt (1955) *Mozart in Retrospect*, Oxford University Press, London.
Kraemer, Uwe (1976) "Wer hat Mozart verhungern lassen?" *Musica* 30: 203–211.
Loesser, Arthur (1954) *Men, Women and Pianos*. Simon and Schuster, New York.
McVeigh, Simon (1993) *Concert Life in London From Mozart to Haydn*. Cambridge University Press, Cambridge.
Moore, Julia V. (1987) *Beethoven and Musical Economics*. Ph.D. dissertation, University of Illinois at Urbana-Champaign.
Moore, Julia V. (1989) "Mozart in the Market Place." *Journal of the Royal Musical Association* 114: 18–42.
Moore, Julia V. (1991) "Review Essay: Mozart Mythologized or Modernized?" *Journal of Musicological Research*: 1–27.
Morrow, Mary Sue (1984) *Concert Life in Vienna 1780–1810*. Ph.D. dissertation, University of Indiana.
Nissen, Georg Nikolaus (1972) *Anhang zu W.A. Mozarts Biographie*, Hrsg. von Constanze Maria Weber von Nissen, New York. Hildesheim, Olms (first edition, Breitkopf and Hartel, Leipzig, 1828).
Padover, S.K. (1934) *The Revolutionary Emperor*. R.O. Ballou, New York.
Phelps Brown, E.H. and Hopkins, S.V. (1955) "Seven Centuries of Building Wages." *Economica* N.S. 22: 195–206.
Phelps Brown, E.H and Hopkins, S.V. (1956) "Seven Centuries of the Prices of Consumables." *Economica* N.S.23: 296–314.
Plekhanov, G.V. (1969) "The Role of the Individual in History." (first published in 1898) in *Fundamental Problems of Marxism*. International Publishers, New York.
Robbins Landon, H.C. (1988) *Mozart's Last Year, 1791*. Thames and Hudson, London.
Robbins Landon, H.C. (1989) *Mozart: The Golden Years, 1781–1791*. Thames and Hudson, London.
Ruelle, J.R. (1798) *Opérations des Changes des Principales Places de l'Europe Lyons*, 3rd. ed.

ECONOMIC ISSUES IN THE ARTS[†]

Unnatural Value: or Art Investment as Floating Crap Game

By WILLIAM J. BAUMOL*

I shall suggest on the basis of a priori considerations and several centuries of price data that in the market for the visual arts, particularly the works of noted creators who are no longer living, there may exist no equilibrium level, so that the prices of such art objects may be strictly *un*natural in the classical sense. Their prices can float more or less aimlessly and their unpredictable oscillations are apt to be the exacerbated by the activities of those who treat such art objects as "investments," and who, according to the data, earn a real rate of return very close to zero on the average. If the art marketing process really is inherently rudderless, the imperfection of the available information on prices and transactions does not matter in the sense that better information about the behavior of the market really would not help anyone to make decisions more effectively.

I. Supply Response: The Pricing Anchor for Manufactures

The art market contrasts sharply with those for manufactured products, such as steel bolts or ball bearings, in terms of determinancy of equilibrium price level. There the key to equilibration is responsiveness of supply. If, for example, a manufactured product's current market price happens to be well above its equilibrium level, as the text books tell us, capital will flow into the production of the overpriced commodity, its output will be increased and its price driven downward. Thus the equilibrium price comes equipped with a powerful magnet capable of attracting actual market prices to it.

It is this mechanism that imparts value to pertinent information, for data on costs, on the nature of demand, and on the cost of capital are of value primarily because they help the observer to evaluate the equilibrium price, which is of practical interest *only* if there exist reliable forces pulling the actual prices in its direction.

II. The Unanchored Prices of Noted Works of Art

We may well suspect, in contrast with the manufacturing case, that the equilibration process will be considerably weakened in a market where elasticity of supply is absolutely zero, as it is in the market for the noted works of noted but deceased artists (an occasional intrusion of forgeries aside).[1] One may even surmise that, as in stock prices, the market values of such works of art will exhibit random behavior.

Indeed, there are several distinctions between the workings of the securities and arts markets, all of which suggest that an equilibration mechanism is likely to be more feeble in the latter.

First, the inventory of a particular stock is made up of a large number of homogeneous securities, all perfect substitutes for one

[†]*Discussants*: William S. Hendon, *Journal of Cultural Economics*; Harold Horowitz, National Endowment for the Arts; Virginia Lee Owen, Illinois State University.

*Princeton University, 108 Dickinson Hall, Princeton, NJ 08542, and New York University. I should like to express my deep gratitude to the C.V. Starr Center for Applied Economics for its generous support of the research underlying this paper. I am heavily indebted to Michael Goldberg for his analysis of the price data, and to Michael Montias for his very valuable comments, though some differences in views remain between us.

[1] I deal here with noted works by noted artists because the markets for the products of what are considered minor schools work very differently. As Montias has pointed out, a sudden rise in the popularity of such a group can elicit a flow of their works from attics and basements, thereby rapidly expanding their available supply.

another. Widely known paintings and sculptures are unique, and even two works on the same theme by a given artist are imperfect substitutes.

Second, a given stock is held by many individuals who are potentially independent traders on the near perfectly competitive stock market. The owner of a Cranach or a Caravaggio holds what may be interpreted as a monopoly on that work of art.

Third, transactions in a given stock take place frequently, indeed, almost continuously. The resale of a given art object may not even occur once in a century.

Fourth, the price at which a stock is exchanged is, generally, public information. The price at which an art work is acquired is frequently known only to the parties immediately involved. While, as I will argue, the availability of such information is not so helpful as is sometimes believed, it surely is unlikely to impede equilibration.

Finally, in the case of a stock we know, at least in principle, what its "true" (equilibrium) price should be—it is the stock's pro rata share of the discounted present value of the company's expected stream of future earnings. But, for a work of art, who would dare to claim to know the true equilibrium price? Distorting Oscar Wilde to my purposes, even those critics who claim to know the value of everything may know the true price of nothing.

In these circumstances it seems implausible that art markets possess anything like long-run equilibrium prices, let alone that there exist reliable forces that drive market prices toward them.

III. On the Economic Value of Art Market Information

Those economists who helped to achieve it are proud of their role in the unbundling of the services of stock brokers, in good part because, as a result, the securities purchaser is no longer required to pay for research which most economists consider to be useless to the investor. If stock prices do indeed approximate random walks, as the evidence strongly indicates, then there is little that information can do to improve estimates of future prices, the key forecast for the purchaser of stocks.

But, if art prices are no more orderly than the prices of stocks, and perhaps even considerably less so, how can data on past activity in the art market conceivably serve as a portent for the future? If stock market research is worthless for the stock market investor; if the stock purchaser can select as well by throwing darts at the financial pages as by following the advice of professional analysts (see, for example, Burton Malkiel, 1973), how much better off can the investor in art hope to emerge with the aid of similar data on art sales with all their warts and blemishes, or even with the help of someone who conducts some sort of "analysis" of those data, perhaps on the lines of the fundamental or technical approaches fashionable among stock market analysts?

IV. Some Data and their Rate of Return Implications

While data on the art market are woefully incomplete and even those that are available are not easy to come by, there exists a remarkable source which permits analysis going beyond anything I have encountered in the literature. In one book of a three-volume set, Gerald Reitlinger (1961) provides an extensive compendium of the sales of art works by "...the best known painters of the world,"[2] extending over more than five centuries. A price is given for each reported sale, which seems to include every transaction involving the work of a painter on Reitlinger's list for which price data are known to be recorded. As the author describes it, "unless otherwise stated, the items refer to London sales. Until 1920 or thereabouts this means with few exceptions sales at Christie's" (p. 242).

[2] It is a noteworthy comment on the haphazard fluctuation of tastes that in the same passage in which Reitlinger ponders on the curiously long period during which Vermeer was ignored, he justifies his inclusion of Turner by the fact that he was a "...Monarch...in the salesroom of [his] day and a very curious chapter in the history of taste, which is so often the history of bad taste" (p. 241).

The art market simply does not provide the continuous data or even the continuous transactions that would be required for a systematic analysis of sophisticated issues such as a random walk hypothesis. However, analysis of simpler issues remains possible. Specifically, I will turn now to examination of the rate of return on investment in art.

Of the thousands of sales recorded between pages 241 and 506 of Reitlinger's book, there are a substantial number of cases in which a given work of art was resold two times and more during a 300-year period. We compiled a complete list of such multiple sales and their prices, and sought to determine what range of rates of return the investor could have hoped for during this period.

Specifically, the following procedure was employed: from the complete list of multiple sales we eliminated all cases in which an interval of less than 20 years intervened between the sales. Approximately 25 listings involved some inconsistencies and were eliminated. In another 25 or so, there were no firm price figures but only word of mouth financial information, and they too were eliminated.

This left us with a total of 640 transactions extending from 1652 to 1961. The reported prices were then deflated by a price index to transform them into pounds of constant purchasing power. For the years 1652 to 1952, the E. H. Phelps-Brown and Sheila Hopkins (1956) index of the prices of consumables was employed. For the period 1955–61, deflation was carried out using the International Monetary Fund Consumer Price Index (1979). The two indices, of course, do not match perfectly but permit a workable deflation procedure.

Finally, from these deflated figures, rate of return figures were calculated for each painting for the period between adjacent transactions. These were calculated from the standard continuous compounding formula $y_t = y_0 e^{r(t-t_0)}$. From these a set of measures of central tendency, that is, the mean, median, standard deviation, etc. were determined and a histogram of the observations was prepared. Let us, then, see what these showed.

V. Results

As a standard of reference it should be noted that, apart from the time of the Napoleonic wars and a few other episodes that were relatively brief, the rate of inflation during the period that encompasses our data was extraordinarily low by current standards. Indeed, by and large the nineteenth century can be characterized as a period of deflation. Over the 300-year span containing our cases, the Phelps-Brown and Hopkins price index rose at an average rate less than 0.7 percent per year. At the same time, according to Sidney Homer (1977), the rate of interest on the safest securities of the British government ranged from a high of some 6 percent near 1800 during the Napoleonic wars, to a low of about 2.25 percent during the Victorian "great depression" of the 1890's in Britain. These include the famous "consols" which have no redemption date and which, literature recounts, were the mainstay of Victorian widows or surviving spinster daughters from financially comfortable families. Probably about 3.25 percent was a representative nominal rate of return for the period, providing a real return of, perhaps, 2.5 percent.

Now it should be recognized that ownership of a painting is a risky affair, aside from whatever financial uncertainty may be involved. A painting can be stolen or destroyed in a fire. English collectors after the restoration were spared the risk caused by wars and revolution (though the affair of the '45 glamorized by "Bonnie Prince Charlie" may have seemed rather a near thing at the time). Yet, London had undergone its great fire in 1666 which left, perhaps, one-fifth of the walled city intact, and organized firefighting techniques only arose well into the nineteenth century. The implication is that whatever the apparent rate of return the ownership of a painting yields, a substantial risk premium must be deducted from the figure to get at the true underlying rate of return.

In addition, the sales commissions charged by the sales agent should of course be subtracted from an art work's resale price in

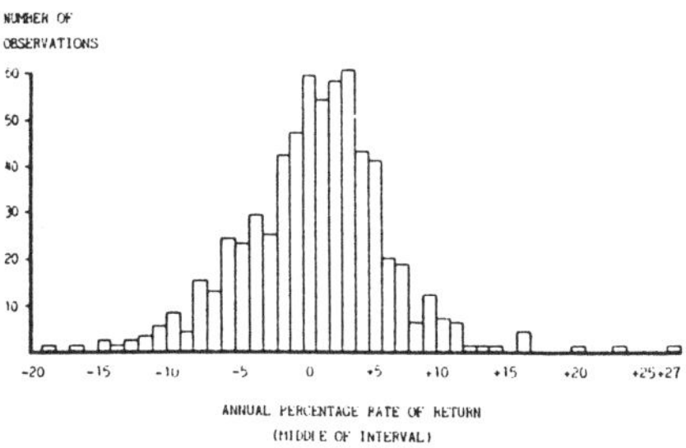

FIGURE 1

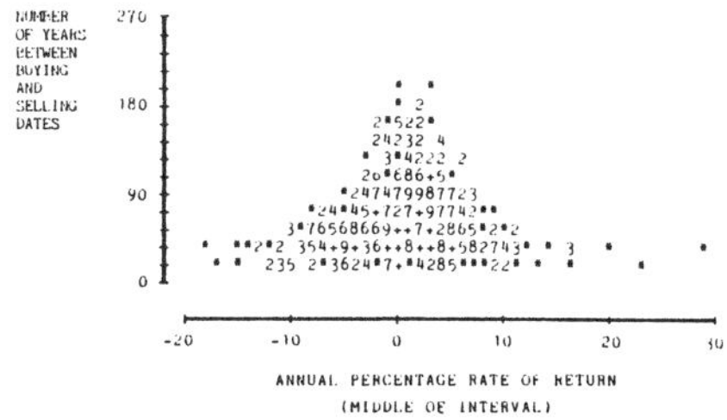

FIGURE 2

Note: Each point is plotted with an asterisk. When more than one point falls on the same plotting position, a count of the number of points falling there is given. When more than nine points fall on the same plotting position, the + symbol is given.

order to evaluate the true rate of return to the investor. Having no data on such selling fees in earlier centuries, we made no attempt to carry out the required subtraction. As a result of the omission of this adjustment as well as that of the risk premium, our calculated rates of return are undoubtedly overevaluations.

With these observations in mind, what do our data show? To come to the central point they show that, on the average, the purchase and subsequent resale of a painting (making no allowance) for sales commissions, maintenance costs, etc.) brought an annual compounded rate of return of 0.55 percent in real terms. The median was somewhat higher: 0.85 percent. These returns are obviously far from princely. In comparison with government securities they imposed an opportunity loss upon the holder of the painting of close to two percentage points per year. That is, the rate of return on a median painting was about one-third as high as that on a government security, and the average return was only about one-sixth of the latter.

Not only were rates of return on painting as investment remarkably low, they were also remarkably dispersed, meaning that this form of investment was quite risky. Figure 1 is a histogram showing the frequency distribution of the rates of return on resales of paintings. We see that there are cases with compounded rates of return as high as 27 percent per year and others as low as −19 percent per year. In more than 40 percent of the cases returns were negative, and about 60 percent of the cases incurred an opportunity loss in the sense that they returned less than the real yield of government securities.

It may be noted that Figure 1 bears a remarkable resemblance to a normal probability distribution. This conjecture derived support from a Kolmogorov-Smirnov test of the divergence of our observed distribution from a normal distribution. Our calculation showed that the hypothesis that the two distributions are the same could not be rejected at the 0.05 percent confidence level. To that degree we can indeed conclude that art prices do behave randomly.

Figure 2 shows another attribute of our observations. The vertical axis represents length of time that elapsed between the purchase and sale of an art work, while the horizontal axis shows annual rate of return. The graph indicates that large gains or losses are experienced only by persons who hold works for a *relatively* brief period (say, less than fifty years) while as the holding period increases beyond that the range of earnings narrows and approaches very close to zero. This is, of course, what one should expect in a random process whose mean is approximately zero.

VI. More on the Possibility of Profiting Through Knowledge

It is tempting, after looking at the preceding results and the Reitlinger data, to conclude that investment in art is indeed perilous, but that it is dangerous primarily for the amateur who does not know what he is doing. According to this view, people who understand art, who can foresee what works will emerge triumphant from the test of time, can surely do better. Particularly the professionals who have devoted their lives to art can expect to outperform the amateur who ventures into purchasing with the temerity derived from ignorance.

Dispassionate judgement of such contentions can only give rise to skepticism. First of all, the notion that professionals are better than amateurs as prophets of price in anchorless markets is certainly belied by the well-documented performance of stock market analysts.

Beyond the caution with which the analogy with the stock market should imbue us, the evidence of the history of art connoisseurship provides strong warnings of its own. It tells us that the main lesson imparted by the test of time is the fickleness of taste whose meanderings defy prediction. Vermeer, as we know, virtually disappeared from sight for several centuries, only to be resurrected as a producer of works of the most priceless variety. El Greco is another modern rediscovery. Turner, who for a while was a leader of the British art world, is said later to have become an embarrassment to the Tate gallery because of the large collection of his works stored in their cellars; though they are now among the most valued items in the museum's collection. The pre-Raphaelites are "in" once more. Reitlinger's list of painters contains many unrecognizable names such as Wouverman, Berchem, and Van Ostade, who once were anxiously sought after but who were all but forgotten when Reitlinger wrote. Apparently some of them have again become more fashionable. Who knows if that will happen to others and, if so, when that will occur?

It is true, of course, that the profitable investments in our sample were made by those who purchased Vermeers, Turners, and pre-Raphaelites when they were not à la mode, and the heavy losers were the early buyers of Berchem, Van Ostade, and their ilk. But that is only to say that a winner is a winner and a loser is a loser. It is, perhaps, a helpful observation to the art historian, whose very legitimate metier is an exercise in hindsight. It is, however, no help to those who would foresee the future in making art purchases for investment. Only those critics who have succeeded as instruments for the redirection of general tastes seem really to have been in a position to profit from their judgement.

VII. Concluding Comment

I have argued here that if prediction as applied to stock prices is a losing game, it is certainly unlikely to be a winner in the market for works of art. Of course, none of this implies that people should desist from the ownership of art works. It may well represent a very rational choice for those who derive a high rate of return in the form of aesthetic pleasure. They should not, however, let themselves be lured into the purchase of art by the illusion that they can beat the game financially and select with any degree of reliability the combination of purchase dates and art works that will produce a rate of return exceeding the opportunity cost of their investment.

REFERENCES

Homer, Sidney, *A History of Interest Rates*, 2nd ed., New Brunswick: Rutgers University Press, 1977.

Malkiel, Burton G., *A Random Walk Down Wall Street*, New York: W. W. Norton, 1973.

Phelps-Brown, E. H. and Hopkins, Sheila, "Seven Centuries of the Prices of Consumables," *Economica*, November 1956, *23*, 296–314.

Reitlinger, Gerald, *The Economics of Taste: The Rise and Fall of the Picture Market, 1760–1960*,. New York: Holt, Reinhart and Winston, 1961.

International Monetary Fund, *1949–1978 International Statistics Yearbook*, Washington, D.C., 1979.

PART VII

THE COST DISEASE SPREADS: LIBRARIES, HEALTH AND EDUCATION

[29]

Library Costs in 678 Four-Year Colleges and Universities, 1967 and 1968

In the previous chapter, the trends in various library variables were examined and their relationships to size of collection and growth rate were presented. The data used in chapter 1 were those collected annually by the Association of Research Libraries. This chapter examines the same variables at a given point in time in order to identify the factors which determine library costs and to estimate the magnitude of their effects. More specifically, in this chapter, we examine the factors which appear to explain variations in library costs for a large number of institutions (678 four-year colleges and universities) in a recent year.[1]

This approach complements the time trend analysis in a number of ways. First, by concentrating on a single year, we practically remove the inflationary factor, permitting us to deal thoroughly with the other variables affecting library costs. Second, since this part of the study included a very large number of institutions, it was possible to incorporate additional factors into the analysis and to perform more extensive statistical tests.

The primary purpose of this chapter is analytical. Here we are in a position to evaluate the determinants of the variables

1. The data for this chapter are those gathered by the National Center for Educational Statistics of the U.S. Office of Education for *Library Statistics of Colleges and Universities: Data for Individual Institutions, Fall 1967* and *Fall 1968* (Washington, D.C.: Government Printing Office, 1969). These data are discussed more fully in chapter 4.

whose behavior over time was observed in the previous chapter. This analysis, determining the influence of variables such as size of collection, size of staff, etc., is essential if a study of costs is to be helpful in budget planning and for decision making.

The study yielded a large number of findings. Before turning to a full discussion of the procedures and the results, it may be worthwhile to present here a brief general summary of the more important findings.

1. Statistical models which incorporate library holdings, acquisitions, and staff explain almost entirely the differences in library operating costs among a large number of institutions.

2. Private institutions appear to have more freedom to adapt their budgetary structure to changing circumstances than do public institutions. This freedom manifests itself in several ways. The library budgets of private institutions typically reflect more closely the institutions' expenditures (per student) on nonlibrary educational programs; the budgets are also more consistently related to the size of the library's holdings. Private institutions also permit greater increases in staff with growth in enrollment.

3. Libraries, in both private and public institutions, do not adjust their inputs, i.e., staff and acquisitions, to small or moderate changes in enrollment; only moves from one enrollment class to another are associated with discernible and systematic changes in library operations. The enrollment-related effects we observed were, in any event, surprisingly small in magnitude.

4. Medium-sized and large public institutions appear to be less adequately staffed than private institutions falling in comparable enrollment categories; these differences were primarily attributable to the larger holdings of the private schools and their higher levels of educational expenditures per student. Staff costs, however, were typically lower in private institutions, especially in the smallest (1,000-2,499

students) colleges and universities. This difference is apparently the result of lower compensation levels in these schools.

5. As expected, acquisitions were found to be correlated with size of holdings, with public institutions generally responding more strongly to a rise in holdings. Acquisitions in private institutions also increase with the level of educational expenditures per student. No such relationship was observed for public institutions.

6. Acquisition costs per volume were lower for institutions in the very smallest enrollment group (1,000-2,500 students), but hardly varied among the larger-enrollment categories. In private institutions, cost per volume rises, on the average, with size of holdings; such a relationship was not displayed in public institutions. Surprisingly, the percentage of science books (physical science, biomedicine, and technology) in the holdings did not appear to affect per volume acquisition costs.

7. The classification of schools as universities or colleges has little, if any, effect on library costs when one is able to account for differences in enrollment, size of holdings, acquisitions, and staff.

The Sample and the Methodological Approach

The analysis encompassed 678 four-year colleges and universities with enrollments exceeding 1,000; the sample constituted almost 80 percent of all institutions falling in this category. The distribution of the institutions by enrollment and status (private or public, college or university) is reported in table 2.1. The institutions not considered—all two-year colleges and all other institutions with enrollments less than 1,000—differ in important respects from the other groups, and we therefore felt that it would be best to exclude them.

The two largest components of library costs are acquisition of library materials and staff salaries and wages. In 1967-68, for example, these two costs constituted about 90 percent of the half billion dollars spent by all college libraries in the U.S. This fact suggests that an investigation which concerns itself primarily with acquisitions and library staffing will explain a preponderant portion of library operating costs.

In the course of the study, we considered and experimented with many factors suggested to us by members of the Council on Library Resources. Not surprisingly, variations in library costs turned out to be largely explainable by relating them to enrollment, type of control of institution (public or private), size of book collection, and level of expenditures per student. As we report below, these factors accounted in most instances for a very large portion of the variation in costs among institutions.

Table 2.1

Distribution of Institutions in Sample

ENROLLMENT CLASS	PRIVATE		PUBLIC	
	College	*University*	*College*	*University*
1,000-2,499	282	–	66	–
2,500-4,999	59	8	73	–
5,000-9,999	14	22	69	14
10,000-19,999 ...	–	16	11	23
20,000+	–	8	–	13

Because the values of the variables under study are often affected by a number of influences, one cannot rely on simple correlation of variables when seeking to isolate their effects. For example, since staff will generally increase with both enrollment and collection size, one cannot determine the separate effect of either, unless both are considered simultaneously. Multivariate regression analysis is the statistical approach designed to solve this problem, and we employed it throughout the analysis. Because this technique must be understood if our results are to be of maximum use, we turn now to a discussion of regression analysis and will illustrate how the results are to be interpreted and employed.

Use of Regression in the Analysis of Library Operations

Multivariate regression analysis presupposes a causal relationship between a number of explanatory (independent) variables and one dependent variable. For example, if library staff is *assumed* to be determined both by the level of holdings and by enrollment, regression analysis can be used to determine the quantitative effect of each of these variables. The least squares technique is used to estimate these effects. As explained in chapter 1, the least squares method provides estimated values (coefficients) which are best predictors in the sense that they minimize the sum of the squared deviations of the actual from the predicted observations. Tables 2.2 and 2.3 present typical results for private and public colleges with enrollments over 1,000, respectively. The results of the calculations for libraries in other types of institutions are offered in tables A.5–A.12 of the appendix.

These tables are, at first, likely to seem complex to readers unfamiliar with regression techniques, and consequently rather careful explanations seem appropriate. As an illustration, consider the third column of table 2.2. In the corresponding equation,[2] we set out to explain variations in the number of volumes added among institutions in the sample by relating acquisitions to several control (or independent) variables: number of volumes held, expenditures per student, and size of enrollment. The upper coefficient across from the first explanatory variable, 0.0278 (first row, third column) indicates that one unit change in volumes held was, on the average, associated with a 0.0278-unit change in the level of additions. Since both variables were measured in units of 10,000 volumes, we may expect a difference of 10,000 volumes in holdings to result in an incremental acquisition of 278 volumes. We must emphasize that this figure is an incremental and not an average measure; that is, it indicates the

2. The complete equation has the following mathematical form: Volumes added = $a_0 + a_1$ (volumes held) + a_2 (expenditures) + u; where a_0, a_1, and a_2 are coefficients whose values are to be estimated (the numbers in our tables), and u is an error term.

effect on the dependent variable (acquisitions) of a given change in the value of the explanatory variable (volumes held). Indeed, the average ratio of additions to holdings in this group was far larger, in excess of 5 percent. But there is really little point in examining *average* relationships of this kind since they do not provide us with the independent effect of the particular variable, which is, of course, the magnitude required for planning. In other words, average ratios represent the combined effect of several factors while the regression coefficient provides an estimate of the independent effect of a single variable. This coefficient cannot, by itself, explain acquisition levels of colleges which differ in other respects besides level of holdings (for example, in enrollment and educational expenses per student) unless their *separate* effects are explicitly taken into account.

Since the coefficient is only an estimate of whatever the true relationship may be, one must obtain some notion of its statistical reliability before it can be used for prediction. A standard statistical measure, the *t*-ratio, is used for this purpose. The *t*-ratio for each coefficient is the number reported immediately below it in the table. The higher this figure, the more confident we can be that even under repeated sampling, the value of the coefficients would not differ much. Although proper evaluation of the *t*-ratio is possible only after examining the appropriate probability distribution, any *t*-ratio larger than 1.7 in the present study can be taken to indicate a normally acceptable degree of reliability. The coefficient is then said to be statistically significant. In the present case, the value of the *t*-ratio exceeds 36; therefore, the coefficient clearly is statistically significant.

The next coefficient in the same equation (second row, third column in table 2.2) is the estimate of the effect of a unit ($1,000) change in educational expenditures *per student* on acquisition levels. It suggests that a difference of $1,000 in educational expenditures per student will result in a difference of 1,249 in new acquisitions, assuming of course that collection size and enrollment are not changed. Once again,

Table 2.2

Regression Results for Private Colleges with Enrollments over 1,000

EXPLANATORY VARIABLE	DEPENDENT VARIABLE				
	Number of Professional Librarians	*Total Library Staff*	*Volumes Added, 1967-68 (x 10,000)*	*Cost of Volumes Added (x $100,000)*	*Total Library Operating Costs (x $100,000)*
Volumes held, 1966-67 (x 10,000)	0.3478	1.3929	0.0278	0.004	0.0531
t-ratio	35.8022	20.7189	36.5042	0.3194	21.1494
Expenditures per student (x $1,000)	1.4881	6.3905	0.1249	–	–
t-ratio	7.6933	4.7746	8.2247	–	–
Volumes added, 1967-68 (x 10,000)	–	–	–	0.7153	1.0184
t-ratio	–	–	–	19.4872	14.5315
College enrollment 2.500-4.999 (x 1,000)	2.2598	12.9504	0.3152	0.2058	0.2047
t-ratio	2.2807	1.8889	4.0530	3.2824	1.8695
College enrollment 5.000-9.999 (x 1,000)	8.6859	27.2886	1.0170	0.2645	0.0234
t-ratio	6.5645	2.9805	9.7931	2.8969	0.1455
College enrollment 10.000-19.999 (x 1,000)	14.0553	66.0509	2.7906	0.2978	1.1335
t-ratio	6.9020	4.6874	17.4600	1.8121	3.9515
College enrollment 20+ (x 1,000)	23.4637	175.4912	2.9594	0.4512	0.3280
t-ratio	6.7577	7.3045	10.8598	1.9416	0.8063
Number of professional librarians	–	–	–	–	0.0568
t-ratio	–	–	–	–	10.2256
Constant term	0.7082	–1.7981	0.2056	–0.0506	–0.3718
t-ratio	1.3758	–0.5048	5.0878	–1.6438	–6.8929
$\bar{R}^2$	0.9004	0.7742	0.9238	0.9229	0.9831

See note on facing page.

the *t*-ratio (8.2247) suggests that the coefficient is statistically significant.

The next group of variables, usually referred to as "dummy variables," is intended to represent the average effect of a given enrollment category on acquisition levels. This effect is calculated by classifying all institutions into one of four enrollment classes and determining simultaneously the effect of membership in each particular group on acquisitions. An alternate approach to the evaluation of the effect of enrollment is to calculate a separate statistical relationship for each enrollment category and then compare the coefficients in the different equations. In our analysis, both approaches have been employed.

When the actual enrollment figures for the institutions were introduced, they did not show a significant relationship to library activities *within* an individual size category. This result indicates that acquisitions, staffing, and total operating costs are not responsive to small changes in enrollment. Only

---

Note: Data used for the regression analysis were those gathered by the U.S. Office of Education for *Library Statistics, Fall 1967* and *Fall 1968.* With the exception of the volumes held figures, all data were for 1967-68. The variable definitions which follow are taken from *Library Statistics, Fall 1968*, pp. 169, 172.

Volume
: A volume is a physical unit of any printed, typewritten, handwritten, mimeographed, or processed work contained in one binding or portfolio, which has been classified, cataloged, or otherwise prepared for use. Included are bound periodical volumes and all nonperiodical government documents.

Expenditures per student
: Total educational and general expenses less total operating expenditures for library, divided by total enrollment.

Professional librarians
: Staff doing work that requires training and skill in the theoretical or scientific aspects of library work, as distinct from its mechanical and clerical aspects.

Total library staff
: All staff serving libraries in regular positions (that is, full-time or part-time positions functioning at least during the fall term).

Cost of volumes added
: Expenditures for books and other library materials.

Total library operating costs
: Consist of total salaries before deductions; salary equivalence of contributed-service staff; wages paid to students and other hourly assistants; expenditures for books and materials, for binding and rebinding; and all other operating expenditures.

Table 2.3

Regression Results for Public Colleges with Enrollments over 1,000

EXPLANATORY VARIABLE	DEPENDENT VARIABLE				
	Number of Professional Librarians	*Total Library Staff*	*Volumes Added, 1967-68 (× 10,000)*	*Cost of Volumes Added (× $100,000)*	*Total Library Operating Costs (× $100,000)*
Volumes held, 1966-67 (× 10,000)	0.5465	1.6919	0.0449	0.0015	0.0200
t-ratio	22.6188	17.7744	12.6788	0.5384	3.0521
Expenditures per student (× $1,000)	0.5446	4.8960	−0.0202	–	–
t-ratio	1.3547	3.0913	−0.3424	–	–
Volumes added, 1967-68 (× 10,000)	–	–	–	0.6587	0.9826
t-ratio	–	–	–	16.8044	14.8332
College enrollment 2.500-4.999 (× 1,000)	3.2971	8.3700	0.4133	0.2048	0.1939
t-ratio	2.0289	1.3073	1.7351	1.3490	0.7755
College enrollment 5.000-9.999 (×1,000)	5.3873	10.0149	0.9020	0.1981	0.1479
t-ratio	3.3428	1.5773	3.8183	1.2901	0.5819
College enrollment 10.000-19.999 (× 1,000)	6.0033	5.4640	2.2789	0.5446	0.6838
t-ratio	2.5779	0.5956	6.6766	2.3249	1.7781
College enrollment 20+ (× 1,000)	32.8283	88.8756	3.3586	1.4354	3.3754
t-ratio	9.3777	6.4443	6.5457	4.1074	5.9034
Number of professional librarians	–	–	–	–	0.0947
t-ratio	–	–	–	–	9.7886
Constant term	0.2309	−2.9410	0.5468	0.0311	0.0271
t-ratio	0.1775	−0.5738	2.8673	0.2776	0.1477
$\bar{R}^2$	0.8447	0.7638	0.6974	0.8258	0.9384

Note: Definitions of variables can be found in the note to table 2.2 on page 23.

major enrollment shifts from one category to another showed significant effects.

Within the framework of the model which we employed, the enrollment effect for a given size category is the difference between the value of the dependent variable (in our example, the level of acquisitions) for this category and that for the smallest enrollment category. For instance, the coefficient reported for private colleges with 2,500-4,999 students shows that institutions falling into this enrollment category acquired, on the average, 3,152 more volumes than institutions in the smallest (1,000-2,499 students) category. Similarly, institutions in the next group (enrollments of 5,000-9,999) acquired about 10,000 more volumes each than those in the smallest category and, by implication, about 7,000 more than those in the 2,500-4,999 enrollment group. Institutions in the 10,000-19,999 category acquired an amount larger than those in the preceding group by about 18,000, and 27,906 more than those in the smallest group. All these coefficients showed t-ratios substantially over 2 and can be considered statistically significant.

The enrollment class effect, as one factor in a multivariate equation, does not take into account the effect of changes in other variables which may typically accompany large enrollment changes. Thus, while in reality an institution's shift from one enrollment class to the next is probably associated with a larger collection size, the effect of the latter on acquisitions must be added on when the total change in acquisitions is calculated from our equations.

All reported equations also include a value referred to as the constant. This value may be considered the level of the dependent variable which will continue no matter what the values of the independent variables, at least within some relevant range. For example, if in order to maintain its quality, a library must continue to acquire x volumes per year no matter what happens to enrollment at the institution, the magnitude of x should be indicated by the constant term.

Statistically, this value must be taken into account in estimating the *magnitude* of the dependent variable (i.e., total acquisitions equal x plus acquisitions resulting from increased enrollment). However, the x value is irrelevant in studying responses–i.e., *changes*–in the dependent variable precisely because it is a constant.

The last term in each column is the $\bar{R}^2$. As discussed more fully earlier, this term measures the percentage variation in the statistic under study accounted for by the variation in the independent variables when these are assumed to exert the influence specified by the estimated coefficients of the equation. Thus, in the equation of the third column of table 2.2, we see that as much as 92 percent of the variation in the level of acquisitions is explained by the variables used in this particular equation.

The regression coefficients have many important uses. At a minimum, they offer estimates of the quantitative interrelationships affecting the economics of university libraries and provide estimates of the net effects of a number of variables that influence library operations.

These effects can be viewed as comparative norms by individual institutions seeking to determine whether they lag behind similar institutions. Of course, one must caution against viewing the results as the standards for adequate library services; they merely reflect prevailing practices.

The regression coefficients can also help the librarian in planning his operation and budgeting. For example, if he has information indicating that his institution plans a 25 percent increase in enrollment, the relevant coefficients will help him in planning the appropriate budgetary response. We return to the subject of enrollment-related effects in the last section of this chapter.

Library Staff

The role of the college library staff in providing adequate services is well known, if not always fully appreciated. It includes instructional and research activities, planning to

Table 2.4

Mean Number of Professional Librarians and Other Library Staff

ENROLLMENT CLASS	PRIVATE INSTITUTIONS		PUBLIC INSTITUTIONS	
	Professional Librarians	*Total Staff Other than Professional Librarians*	*Professional Librarians*	*Total Staff Other than Professional Librarians*
1,000-4,999	5.2	6.7	7.3	8.6
5,000-9,999	24.9	44.6	15.9	22.1
10,000+	60.6	127.1	56.8	97.8

Source: U.S. Office of Education, *Library Statistics of Colleges and Universities: Analytic Report, Fall 1968* (Washington, D.C.: Government Printing Office, 1970), table 15.

meet academic needs for library services, coordination with faculty, planning and management of acquisitions, development of cooperative programs with other institutions, processing of publications, and general management responsibilities. It is therefore not surprising that the quality of library services is strongly related to the size and composition of the staff. From a budgetary point of view, staff constitutes the largest expense category, and hence clearly deserves careful attention in a study of this nature.

The Office of Education distinguishes among three categories of library personnel: professional librarians, other professional staff, and nonprofessional staff.[3] However, our discussions with members of the Council on Library Resources suggested that not all universities adhere to the Office of Education definitions in classifying personnel; this fact must be borne in mind when the statistical results are interpreted.

A look at average size of staff, by type and size of institution (table 2.4), reveals that for institutions with over 5,000

3. "*Professional librarians* are defined as staff doing work that requires training and skill in the theoretical or scientific aspects of library work as distinct from its mechanical and clerical aspects. *Other professional staff* are personnel who, though not professional librarians, are in positions normally requiring at least a bachelor's degree. *Nonprofessional staff* are persons who perform receiving, shipping, storing, and secretarial duties, and similar personnel, exclusive of maintenance staff and students or other assistants serving on an hourly basis" (U.S. Office of Education, *Library Statistics, Fall 1967*, p. 4).

students, private schools employ more professional librarians and other staff than do public institutions. Thus, while some sixteen professional librarians were employed on the average in a public institution with 5,000-9,999 students, for the corresponding private institutions, the figure was nearly twenty-five. In the very large and very small institutions, the mean values for the number of professional librarians do not differ much between public and private institutions. But useful inferences cannot be drawn from such a gross comparison of public and private universities. One must take into account other factors that are likely to influence staff size.

After experimenting with various variables, we found that one can obtain a fairly good statistical explanation of the differences in size of staff by taking into account size of collection, educational expenditures per student, type of institution, and enrollment class. Indeed, these factors explain 90 percent and 84 percent of the variation in number of professional librarians in private and public institutions respectively. (See tables 2.2 and 2.3.) Table 2.4 presents the difference in staff size between private and public institutions after removing statistically the influence of differences in the size of holdings and expenditures per student.

Size of Collection and Size of Staff. The regression results suggest that in both public and private institutions, professional librarians and all other staff vary significantly with the size of collection, though not at the same rate. More specifically, for institutions within the same enrollment class and with equal educational expenditures per student, more professional librarians are added as size of collection is increased (tables 2.2 and 2.3). In both types of institution, however, the indicated additions are surprisingly low in absolute value: if the collection is increased by 100,000 volumes, the number of librarians increases in public institutions by 5.5, in private institutions by 3.5.

The impact of collection size on staff *other than librarians* is about the same for private and public institutions: a 10-member staff increase for an addition of 100,000 volumes. We should note, however, that the effect of collection size in public institutions, unlike that in private institutions, was not uniformly significant or stable in value when estimated for the separate enrollment categories. Only at the 10,000- to 20,000-student range do we find public and private institutions exhibiting almost identical values.

Role of Educational Expenditures per Student. The level of educational outlays per student was found to influence library staff size, but not in all enrollment categories. No significant effect was established for the 10,000-19,999 enrollment category for either public or private institutions, nor for the 1,000-2,499 category in public institutions; that is, in these cases the statistical evidence is not sufficiently strong to permit us to be confident of its conclusions. With this caveat in mind, one may suggest, nonetheless, that on the average, a given increase in educational outlays per student in private schools would be associated with an increase in the number of librarians three times as large as that shown for public institutions. These data seem to suggest that in public institutions a relatively low priority is assigned to library activities as additional funds are made available for educational expenditures. We will see later that a similar relationship seems to characterize public institutions' acquisition policy.

Effects of Enrollment Size. Size of library staff was also strongly associated with the enrollment class in which an institution fell, though it was not responsive to minor differences *within* enrollment categories.[4] The magnitude of

4. In evaluating the significance of the enrollment-related effects, we must consider the possibility that they merely reflect an associated increase in the percentage of universities as one moves to successively larger enrollment sizes. However, the evidence leads us to discount the role of this effect. Separating colleges from universities did not suggest the presence of a consistent or significant difference in size of library staff in three instances (private 5,000-9,999, public 5,000-9,999, and public 10,000-20,000). Only in one group, private 2,500-4,999, did colleges employ a significantly smaller number of professional librarians than universities with the same holdings and educational outlays per student. (An institution was classified as a university if it gives considerable emphasis to graduate instruction, awards advanced degrees as well as baccalaureates in a variety of liberal arts fields, and has at least two professional schools that are not exclusively technological in nature.) See the effect of classification as a college in equation 3 of table A.13.

these enrollment effects, when collection size and educational outlays per student are held constant by statistical means, is summarized in table 2.5. We see that in most cases, with an increase in enrollment, the library staff in private institutions increases by a larger number than that in public institutions. When considering staff members other than librarians, the patterns of response of public institutions are far less regular. This fact seems to suggest that public institutions may not be as free as private institutions to reapportion their total budgets in response to variations in user needs.

Table 2.5

Size of Library Staff in Institutions with 2,500 or More Students Relative to Staff Size in Institutions with Enrollments of 1,000-2,499

ENROLLMENT CLASS	PRIVATE INSTITUTIONS		PUBLIC INSTITUTIONS	
	Difference in Number of Professional Librarians	*Difference in Number of Other Staff*	*Difference in Number of Professional Librarians*	*Difference in Number of Other Staff*
2,500-4,999	2.25	10.70	3.30	**
5,000-9,999	8.68	18.60	5.39	**
10,000-19,999 . . .	14.05	52.00	6.00	**
20,000+	23.46	152.03	32.83	55.00

Note: Data, which are based on regression results in tables 2.2 and 2.4, assume collection size and educational expenditures per student are held constant.

**Estimates were not statistically significant.

The figures in table 2.5 suggest that the effect of enrollment on library staff size is astonishingly small; in public institutions, professional librarians are added at a rate of less than one for 1,000 additional students, except in the few largest institutions (20,000+ students). For example, in the 10,000-19,999 enrollment category (average size, 15,000), there are only six more professional staff members than in the 1,000-2,499 enrollment group. The additions are only slightly higher in private institutions.

Acquisition of Library Materials

College libraries have been adding to their holdings at a substantial rate; in 1967-68 alone, college libraries in the U.S. added 25 million volumes, or about 8.25 percent of their entire collection. While acquisition policy is in part dependent upon the rate at which new publications appear, there are obviously great differences in acquisition policies among institutions. To determine which variables can account for these variations, we experimented with several formulations but finally settled on the relationship represented by the third column in tables 2.2 and 2.3. Basically, the equation described in this column enables us to identify the separate effects of collection size, educational expenditures per student, enrollment, and type of institution (public or private).

Effect of Size of Collection. Turning to specific findings, we first note the relationship between the level of acquisitions and collection size. A difference of 10,000 volumes was associated with a difference of 278 acquisitions for private institutions, when other factors are taken into account. For public institutions, a 10,000-volume difference in holdings produces a substantially larger effect on acquisitions—a 449-volume increase.

Educational Expenditures per Student. The degree of budgetary restrictiveness of the institution is undoubtedly also important in explaining the level of acquisitions. One naturally expects schools able to provide relatively generous support to their instructional programs also to acquire a larger number of volumes for their libraries. To evaluate this influence, we incorporated educational expenditures per student (excluding library costs) into the analysis. Generally, the results show that this variable does have a consistent, if moderate, effect on the level of acquisitions. A difference of $100 in educational outlays per student in private institutions is associated with 125 acquisitions, other factors assumed constant. This influence is not as pronounced in public institutions, appearing significant only in institutions with enrollments from 5,000 to 10,000. In private institutions, on the other hand, outlays per student were a statistically significant factor in most enrollment categories. This result suggests the hypothesis, which seems not entirely implausible, that there is a smaller degree of freedom for public institutions in determining how best to allocate their total budgets.

Enrollment and Acquisitions. The last influence on the volume of acquisitions to be considered is enrollment. Perhaps surprisingly, we found no relationship between enrollment and acquisition levels *within* any of the four enrollment categories, suggesting that acquisition policies are not affected by small differences in enrollment. However, when one considers differences in acquisition levels across enrollment categories, the picture changes. More specifically, for any given level of library holdings and educational expenditures per student, the higher the enrollment class, the larger the acquisition level. Enrollment effects on acquisitions hardly differ between private and public institutions.

There are probably several reasons why enrollment affects acquisitions. Larger schools are likely to have a greater number of educational programs requiring continuing additions to their holdings. Also, the percentage of universities in the sample increases as we move up to larger enrollment categories, and since universities place heavier emphasis on research, their acquisitions may be larger. The role of this variable was evaluated by incorporating an additional control variable, designation of each institution as a college or university. The results of this analysis were mixed, suggesting that this factor has at best a limited role in explaining the effect of large enrollment changes on acquisitions.

Cost of Acquisitions

If all colleges purchased the same mix of books, paid the same prices, and had the same ratio of donated-to-purchased materials, cost per volume would differ little from one institution to another. Obviously, these three conditions do not hold, and one does in fact observe a considerable degree of variation in per-unit acquisition costs.

An increase of 10,000 volumes added was found to produce an incremental expenditure of about $70,000, yielding a cost per volume of $7 (the figure is slightly lower for public institutions). This cost increases with size (enrollment class) of institution. Thus, private institutions in the 2,500-19,999 enrollment groups will incur an additional cost of $2-$3 per volume over the smallest institutions. In public institutions the effect of college size on acquisition costs is less consistent.

We may note here what appears to be an important difference between private and public institutions. For the former we found that, *within* individual enrollment classes, acquisition costs increased with the size of holdings. This trend may be caused by a change in the kind of volumes ordered as total holdings rise. It is reasonable to assume that after the most elementary needs are met, libraries would order a greater percentage of more expensive items–research materials, periodicals, and the like. But such a relationship could not be established for public institutions with the exception of the 10,000-19,999 enrollment class. Although we cannot be certain of the significance of this finding, it may suggest that more expensive materials are generally not selected by small and medium public institutions when they expand the size of their collection. This phenomenon may be caused either by budgetary restrictions or by a lesser emphasis on the research role of the library. Specifically, only in the very large public institutions–those with 10,000-19,999 students–do we find acquisition costs to be affected by collection size in a manner similar to private institutions.

Library Operating Costs

In the previous two sections, we examined libraries' staffing and acquisition levels. Although these functions account for the bulk of library operating costs (almost 90 percent), other cost items are also of interest and their analysis can certainly be useful for budgetary purposes. We therefore turn to the analysis of total library operating costs, an aggregate which reflects all expenditure items.

The model we employed utilizes collection size, level of acquisition, staff, enrollment, and type of institution. A brief explanation why collection size is introduced here is in order. Its inclusion was designed to capture operating costs other than salaries, wages, and cost of acquisitions. Among these are binding, equipment, other operating expenditures, and interlibrary loans. These cost items can be expected to vary with size of collection.

The results we obtained, which will be described presently, suggest that the chosen explanatory factors explain virtually the entire variation of operating costs among institutions (98 percent of the variation of private, and 94 percent of that of public institutions). Therefore, the estimates which the analysis yielded can be viewed with a considerable degree of confidence.

Size of Collection. The regression results show that the effect of collection size on operating costs was higher and statistically more significant in private than in public institutions. A difference in collection of 10,000 volumes at private institutions produces on average an additional library expense of about $5,000 annually. In public institutions, on the other hand, the association with collection size is weaker, and the indicated budgetary support rises are considerably lower–only about $2,000 for an increase of 10,000 volumes in collection size. This difference suggests that in public institutions, budgetary support for those functions related to collection size is less consistent and of lower magnitude.

Acquisitions. The effect of acquisitions on total library operating costs is very similar; on the average, in both private and public institutions, roughly a $10 increase per year is required for each addition to the number of volumes acquired (per year). This estimate exceeds the figure for direct acquisition costs obtained earlier by a substantial amount, reaffirming the well-known observation that the full cost of a newly acquired volume far exceeds its purchase price since a new acquisition requires cataloging and other types of processing.

Staff Size. Some of our more aggregate models indicated that public and private institutions differ in the influence of staff size on total operating costs, with public institutions showing a substantially higher cost figure for additional librarians. Closer examination of the data suggests that this result may not hold for every enrollment category, but may well reflect the disproportionately large number of very small private institutions in the total. In the small private schools, low salaries and a large portion of donated services apparently combine to yield astonishingly low cost estimates for library employees.

When we examine the second size class (2,500-4,999 students), we find that the cost effect of librarians is the same in both private and public institutions. In the remaining enrollment categories (5,000+), public institutions show slightly higher staff-related costs.

Enrollment. The relationship between enrollment and total operating costs may appear somewhat surprising. Enrollment and operating costs *within* individual enrollment categories show little correlation, in line with earlier findings that staffing and acquisitions were not significantly correlated with enrollment. Although the correlation improves markedly when all enrollment classes are pooled, the regression results show that the independent effect of enrollment on costs (i.e., any effect apart from the association of enrollment with collection and staff size) is small and not very significant. Very roughly, it is on the order of $10 for each additional student.

The low association between enrollment and total costs does not, upon reflection, appear surprising. For it is only through the expansion of library inputs (staff, collection, etc.) that costs are incurred, and these cost factors are accounted for separately in the model.

Applications of the Findings to Budget Preparation

The results described so far go beyond the provision of a clearer understanding of the economics of library operations; they can be of direct help in budget preparation and for long-term planning. In this section, we indicate in specific terms how such planning might proceed.

Obviously, no single approach to budget making is likely to meet the particular needs and circumstances of each and every institution. Our discussion will therefore point out a range of procedures, from the very simple to the relatively more complex.

Some institutions may prefer to rely entirely on a time series analysis such as that presented in chapter 1. This is clearly the simplest tool and at the same time fairly reliable, at least in the statistical sense. Consulting tables 1.3 and 1.4, the reader will immediately note that the annual compound rate of increase in the total library budget falls within a very narrow range, between 9.8 and 11.7 percent, depending upon the size and growth category of the institution.

The total operating budget can be broken up into its two most important components: expenditures on staff and on acquisitions. The growth rates of these series are found in rows 12 and 14 of tables 1.3 and 1.4, and can be used with a reasonable degree of confidence. Since the student is one of the primary recipients of library services,[5] when requesting additional funds, some institutions may find it useful to break out explicitly a component that is required merely to compensate for the growth of the student body and a com-

5. Of course, we do not mean to suggest that the number of students is the most significant influence on library costs. The range and type of research programs, the number of faculty, and the distribution of their fields are undoubtedly more influential, but we simply did not have the data to estimate these influences statistically.

ponent attributable to all other factors (improved services, inflation, etc.). In the most simplistic variant of this approach, a school which expects its enrollment to increase by, say, 5 percent per annum would grant the library an increase of 5 percent, *plus* the expected rate of increase in cost per student as reported in row 11 in tables 1.3 and 1.4, as a proxy for the other important components of future requirements.

A more complex, yet somewhat more analytic approach to budget making would utilize both our cross-sectional results, reported in this chapter, and the time series trends discussed in the previous chapter.

As a concrete illustration, let us start with the projection of professional manpower requirements. The first step in such a procedure is to calculate the expected levels of library holdings and expenditures per student in the year for which the requirement is to be estimated. Next, one turns to the statistical table pertaining to the group in which the school in question falls (among tables A.5–A.12). Each of the expected values (holdings and expenditures per student) will then be multiplied by its associated coefficient from column 1. The sum of these products plus the constant, also reported in column 1, will yield the required level of professional librarians if 1968 service norms are not to deteriorate. To this figure, one must add the somewhat less precise enrollment effects on the number of librarians. To obtain these, the librarian can turn to the data reported in table 2.5.

To make this discussion more specific, let us use some numbers (selected for arithmetic simplicity rather than realism). Suppose our illustrative librarian works at a private college with 2,500-4,999 students. This librarian would then utilize table A.6, which applies to his category of institution. Suppose that in 1971-72 he finds that his library holds 200,000 volumes and that educational expenditures per student at his college are $2,000. Using table 1.4, he will see that in small libraries, the number of volumes held can be expected to grow by 5.4 percent while expenditures per student grow at about 6.1 percent. Hence, for 1972-73, he can project the following figures:

Volumes held	210,800
Expenditures per student	\$2,122

Now, the table A.6 equation for number of librarians can be written as:

$$\text{Number of librarians} = -0.6153 + 0.3258 \times \text{volumes held} + 3.9027 \times \text{expenditures per student}$$

with -0.6153 as the constant term. Rounding the coefficients in the equation (for purposes of illustrative simplicity) and inserting the projections just obtained,[6] we have:

$$\text{Number of librarians} = -0.6 + 0.3\,(21.08) + 4.0\,(2.122) \cong 14.$$

This equation gives the librarian his initial projection for the number of professional librarians, indicating as a norm what can be expected to hold for institutions in circumstances similar to those at his.

A major concern of many libraries is the preparation and projection of their overall operating budgets. This task can be accomplished with the aid of equation 5 (i.e., the entries in the fifth column) in the appropriate table from among A.5 to A.12.

The application of this model requires estimates of the level of holdings, acquisitions, and the number of librarians in the year for which the projection is to be made. The sum of these, each multiplied by its associated coefficient in equation 5, plus the constant of the equation, provides an estimate of the required operating budget of the library.

Again, an illustrative calculation may be helpful. Let us assume that a public institution with an enrollment between

6. Note that table A.6 measures number of volumes held in units of 10,000, so that our projected number of volumes becomes 21.08. Similarly, educational expenditures per student are expressed in units of \$1,000.

10,000 and 20,000 is preparing its annual budget. Assume that in the forecast year, the collection is expected to hold 1,500,000 volumes; acquisitions are projected at 100,000; and a staff of 50 professional librarians will be employed. (These projections can be obtained in various ways, the simplest being an extrapolation based on tables 1.3 and 1.4.)

The equation for this operating budget (from table A.12) can be written as:

$$\text{Operating budget} = 0.5571 + 0.0139 \times \text{volumes held} + 0.8139 \times \text{volumes added} + 0.1317 \times \text{professional librarians}$$

where 0.5571 is the constant term. Rounding the coefficients for illustrative simplicity and substituting the projections into the equation in units of 10,000 volumes, we obtain:

$$\text{Operating budget} = 0.56 + 0.014\,(150) + 0.814\,(10) + 0.132\,(50) = 17.4.$$

Since costs are expressed in units of $100,000, the projected budget is $1,740,000.

Two points are noteworthy. A projection of the operating budget can also be carried out with the use of a more aggregate model, whose central equation is estimated for all public institutions (table 2.3). In the illustration just carried out, this calculation calls for a slightly higher budget, totaling $1,839,000. Thus, in each case, there are at least two equations on which a projection can be based: the one based on data for all enrollment sizes simultaneously (table 2.2 or 2.3) and the one fitted to the individual enrollment class data (from tables A.5 to A.12). The precise conditions under which the use of one or the other equation is preferable is a matter of judgment. There is a case for the employment of the equation which has the higher $\bar{R}^2$ if these figures differ markedly for the two equations, but this is not a cast-iron precept.

We might also reiterate here that in the last illustration, the projection provides for an allowance based on collection size

($210,000 in our example) apart from allowances for staff and acquisitions. The only adjustment that remains is one for inflationary effects. Inflation primarily affects the prices of acquisitions and levels of staff salaries. As demonstrated in table 1.4 by the differences between growth rates for book expenditures and volumes added, and between growth rates for salaries and total staff, the price of acquisitions grew at a rate of 4.8 percent per annum (compounded) and staff salaries at 4.4 percent. The expected inflationary impact will be a weighted average of these figures (4.5 percent in our example), the weights being proportional to the share of the budget going to each activity in the most recent period.

The budget can now be converted from our 1968 base to the desired year, say 1973. A price increase of 4.5 percent compounded over five years adds up to a 24.6 percent increase, and the budget is $1,740,000 X 1.246 = $2,168,040.

The type of calculation described in the preceding sections is not meant to deny that at each individual institution there will be additional factors which must be considered in budget preparation. Nor does our calculation pretend to serve as some sort of indicator of optimality. A budget based on the computations described would reflect practices at other institutions comparable to that of the library in question. Our findings do not preclude the possibility that prevailing practices can be improved upon to reduce the costs of a given volume of activity or to improve the service made possible by a given outlay.

However, there is an important reason why budget preparation must take cognizance of prevailing standards in other libraries, as the calculations of this chapter have done. Every college and university must keep up with the standards offered by others if it is to obtain students and faculty members of comparable quality. This element has been critical in the budgeting of faculty salaries and their improvement over the past decade and can certainly play an important role in effective financial planning for libraries.

Table A.5

Regression Results for Private Colleges with Enrollments of 1,000-2,499

EXPLANATORY VARIABLE	DEPENDENT VARIABLE				
	Number of Professional Librarians	*Total Library Staff*	*Volumes Added, 1967-68 (× 10,000)*	*Cost of Volumes Added (× $100,000)*	*Total Library Operating Costs (× $100,000)*
Volumes held, 1966-67 (× 10,000)	0.3716	1.4454	0.0229	0.0125	0.0464
t-ratio	8.0949	9.8580	8.7212	7.3166	12.6317
Expenditures per student (× $1,000) .	0.1061	0.3344	0.0350	–	–
t-ratio	0.4026	0.3973	2.3195	–	–
Volumes added, 1967-68 (× 10,000)	–	–	–	0.4946	0.9050
t-ratio	–	–	–	13.3206	12.5955
Number of professional librarians . . .	–	–	–	–	0.0139
t-ratio	–	–	–	–	3.3561
Constant term	2.6595	7.2665	0.3970	–0.0209	0.0512
t-ratio	4.7219	4.0393	12.3206	–0.8798	1.0669
$\bar{R}^2$	0.2288	0.3053	0.3023	0.6369	0.7554

Note: Definitions of variables can be found in the note to table 2.2 on page 23.

Table A.6

Regression Results for Private Colleges with Enrollments of 2,500-4,999

EXPLANATORY VARIABLE	DEPENDENT VARIABLE				
	Number of Professional Librarians	*Total Library Staff*	*Volumes Added, 1967-68 (x 10,000)*	*Cost of Volumes Added (x $100,000)*	*Total Library Operating Costs (x $100,000)*
Volumes held, 1966-67 (x 10,000)	0.3258	1.5009	0.0248	0.0186	0.0609
t-ratio	6.5193	5.3382	5.4915	4.9441	6.8161
Expenditures per student (x $1,000)	3.9027	11.5751	0.2257	–	–
t-ratio	4.8525	2.5582	3.1003	–	–
Volumes added, 1967-68 (x 10,000)	–	–	–	0.7962	0.7477
t-ratio	–	–	–	8.9655	3.9546
Number of professional librarians . . .	–	–	–	–	0.0782
t-ratio	–	–	–	–	4.9859
Constant term	–0.6153	0.6744	0.4084	–0.2707	–0.2258
t-ratio	–0.6031	0.1175	4.4232	–3.5070	–1.5198
$\bar{R}^2$	0.8627	0.7524	0.7821	0.9191	0.9554

Note: Definitions of variables can be found in the note to table 2.2 on page 23.

Table A.7

Regression Results for Private Colleges with Enrollments of 5,000-9,999

EXPLANATORY VARIABLE	DEPENDENT VARIABLE				
	Number of Professional Librarians	*Total Library Staff*	*Volumes Added, 1967-68 (× 10,000)*	*Cost of Volumes Added (× \$100,000)*	*Total Library Operating Costs (× \$100,000)*
Volumes held, 1966-67 (× 10,000)	0.3378	1.1471	0.0363	0.0191	0.0505
t-ratio	5.7098	4.3983	9.8556	4.6885	4.3127
Expenditures per student (× \$1,000)	2.0734	7.6514	0.1292	–	–
t-ratio	3.9235	3.2842	3.9231	–	–
Volumes added, 1967-68 (× 10,000)	–	–	–	0.4087	0.6849
t-ratio	–	–	–	4.9254	2.4972
Number of professional librarians . . .	–	–	–	–	0.0732
t-ratio	–	–	–	–	4.2793
Constant term	8.1691	32.5164	0.8431	0.2611	0.2187
t-ratio	2.7201	2.4559	4.5029	1.9961	0.5849
$\bar{R}^2$	0.7274	0.6253	0.8527	0.9243	0.9368

Note: Definitions of variables can be found in the note to table 2.2 on page 23.

Table A.8

Regression Results for Private Colleges with Enrollments of 10,000-20,000

	DEPENDENT VARIABLE				
EXPLANATORY VARIABLE	*Number of Professional Librarians*	*Total Library Staff*	*Volumes Added, 1967-68 (x 10,000)*	*Cost of Volumes Added (x $100,000)*	*Total Library Operating Costs (x $100,000)*
Volumes held, 1966-67 (x 10,000)	0.5059	3.1531	0.0430	0.0132	0.0493
t-ratio	6.8471	3.9149	4.8789	1.6853	2.6507
Expenditures per student (x $1,000)	−1.2052	−17.2125	−0.0545	–	–
t-ratio	−0.8096	−1.0607	−0.3070	–	–
Volumes added, 1967-68 (x 10,000)	–	–	–	0.4830	0.8175
t-ratio	–	–	–	2.7339	2.4375
Number of professional librarians . . .	–	–	–	–	0.1093
t-ratio	–	–	–	–	2.7932
Constant term	9.5538	−19.5912	2.1800	0.4120	−0.5432
t-ratio	1.7301	−0.3255	3.3120	0.7215	−0.5411
$\bar{R}^2$	0.8894	0.6559	0.8159	0.8844	0.9755

Note: Definitions of variables can be found in the note to table 2.2 on page 23.

Table A.9

Regression Results for Public Colleges with Enrollments of 1,000-2,499

EXPLANATORY VARIABLE	DEPENDENT VARIABLE				
	Number of Professional Librarians	*Total Library Staff*	*Volumes Added, 1967-68 (× 10,000)*	*Cost of Volumes Added (× $100,000)*	*Total Library Operating Costs (× $100,000)*
Volumes held, 1966-67 (× 10,000)	0.1945	−0.2708	0.0269	−0.0124	0.0293
t-ratio	1.6223	−0.3442	1.4669	−1.1543	1.7021
Expenditures per student (× $1,000)	0.1860	0.6131	0.0337	–	–
t-ratio	0.9199	0.4619	1.0899	–	–
Volumes added, 1967-68 (× 10,000)	–	–	–	0.3954	0.6027
t-ratio	–	–	–	5.4439	4.9540
Number of professional librarians	–	–	–	–	0.0932
t-ratio	–	–	–	–	5.0011
Constant term	3.0015	15.7266	0.5868	0.3335	0.2807
t-ratio	3.4292	2.7374	4.3868	3.7741	1.9592
$\overline{R}^2$	0.0292	−0.0269	0.0276	0.2984	0.5751

Note: Definitions of variables can be found in the note to table 2.2 on page 23.

Table A.10

Regression Results for Public Colleges with Enrollments of 2,500-4,999

EXPLANATORY VARIABLE	DEPENDENT VARIABLE				
	Number of Professional Librarians	*Total Library Staff*	*Volumes Added, 1967-68 (× 10,000)*	*Cost of Volumes Added (× $100,000)*	*Total Library Operating Costs (× $100,000)*
Volumes held, 1966-67 (× 10,000)	0.4148	2.2671	0.0990	−0.0102	0.0260
t-ratio	3.0659	3.0610	4.8310	−0.8057	1.1667
Expenditures per student (× $1,000)	1.0555	1.3984	−0.0323	–	–
t-ratio	2.0156	0.4878	−0.4072	–	–
Volumes added, 1967-68 (× 10,000)	–	–	–	0.8350	1.2566
t-ratio	–	–	–	12.0912	9.4737
Number of professional librarians	–	–	–	–	0.0704
t-ratio	–	–	–	–	3.6003
Constant term	4.3316	3.4556	0.3896	0.1126	0.0122
t-ratio	2.9036	0.4231	1.7234	0.8442	0.0516
$\overline{R}^2$	0.2166	0.1311	0.2508	0.7201	0.7843

Note: Definitions of variables can be found in the note to table 2.2 on page 23.

Table A.11

Regression Results for Public Colleges with Enrollments of 5,000-9,999

EXPLANATORY VARIABLE	DEPENDENT VARIABLE				
	Number of Professional Librarians	*Total Library Staff*	*Volumes Added, 1967-68 (x 10,000)*	*Cost of Volumes Added (x $100,000)*	*Total Library Operating Costs (x $100,000)*
Volumes held, 1966-67 (x 10,000)	0.1382	–0.0432	0.0412	–0.0137	–0.0068
t-ratio	1.1774	–0.0950	3.1891	–1.3613	–0.3872
Expenditures per student (x $1,000)	5.0462	37.1404	0.4557	–	–
t-ratio	2.4277	4.6165	1.9915	–	–
Volumes added, 1967-68 (x 10,000)	–	–	–	0.7751	1.0654
t-ratio	–	–	–	8.7785	6.1204
Number of professional librarians	–	–	–	–	0.1125
t-ratio	–	–	–	–	5.9410
Constant term	8.4672	3.5601	0.9568	0.2651	0.2129
t-ratio	3.2468	0.3527	3.3331	1.1430	0.5089
$\bar{R}^2$	0.1312	0.2482	0.2485	0.5109	0.6694

Note: Definitions of variables can be found in the note to table 2.2 on page 23.

Table A.12

Regression Results for Public Colleges with Enrollments of 10,000-20,000

EXPLANATORY VARIABLE	DEPENDENT VARIABLE				
	Number of Professional Librarians	*Total Library Staff*	*Volumes Added, 1967-68 (× 10,000)*	*Cost of Volumes Added (× $100,000)*	*Total Library Operating Costs (× $100,000)*
Volumes held, 1966-67 (× 10,000)	0.5017	1.2095	0.0530	0.0185	0.0139
t-ratio	6.1896	5.2880	3.9557	2.5034	0.8003
Expenditures per student (× $1,000)	−3.0781	−0.2633	−0.3359	–	–
t-ratio	−0.9451	−0.0286	−0.6235	–	–
Volumes added, 1967-68 (× 10,000)	–	–	–	0.4927	0.8139
t-ratio	–	–	–	4.8356	4.3756
Number of professional librarians	–	–	–	–	0.1317
t-ratio	–	–	–	–	4.3132
Constant term	14.7724	37.9067	2.9018	0.5114	0.5571
t-ratio	3.1951	2.9052	3.7945	1.1058	0.6520
$\bar{R}^2$	0.6312	0.6025	0.3971	0.7008	0.8420

Note: Definitions of variables can be found in the note to table 2.2 on page 23.

Table A.13

Regression Results for Private Colleges with Enrollments of 2,500-4,999 with Effect of Classification as College Added

EXPLANATORY VARIABLE	DEPENDENT VARIABLE				
	Number of Professional Librarians	*Total Library Staff*	*Volumes Added, 1967-68 (× 10,000)*	*Cost of Volumes Added (× $100,000)*	*Total Library Operating Costs (× $100,000)*
Volumes held, 1966-67 (× 10,000)	0.3416	1.5347	0.0258	0.0192	0.0637
t-ratio	7.1272	5.4191	5.7403	5.4497	6.8409
Expenditures per student (× $1,000)	2.8771	9.3799	0.1658	–	–
t-ratio	3.3788	1.8643	2.0791	–	–
Volumes added, 1967-68 (× 10,000)	–	–	–	0.7051	0.7147
t-ratio	–	–	–	7.9546	3.7351
Number of professional librarians . . .	–	–	–	–	0.0711
t-ratio	–	–	–	–	4.1714
Effect of classification as college[a] . .	–6.9845	–14.9500	–0.4080	–0.5047	–0.3898
t-ratio	–2.7548	–0.9979	–1.7186	–3.0618	–1.0677
Constant term	6.9417	16.8499	0.8498	0.2747	0.1895
t-ratio	2.3853	0.9799	3.1190	1.4283	0.4552
$\bar{R}^2$	0.8755	0.7524	0.7886	0.9285	0.9555

Note: Definitions of variables can be found in the note to table 2.2 on page 23.

[a]Institutions were classified as universities if they (1) give considerable emphasis to graduate instruction, (2) award advanced degrees as well as baccalaureates in a variety of liberal arts fields, and (3) have at least two professional schools that are not exclusively technological. All other four-year institutions of higher education were classified as colleges.

Cost Trends and Longer-Range Plans

The literature of library technology has made much of the prospects of an electronic revolution. Extravagant claims and overly sanguine predictions have undoubtedly reduced the credibility of much that has been said about such innovations. Certainly, there is reason to believe that for the immediate future changes in library technology will continue to be gradual. To date, the majority of successful data processing applications in libraries have involved mechanization of nonprofessional tasks such as circulation control and typing of bibliographic aids. At the same time, there are trends in process which may in the next two decades change the range of innovation that is economically feasible.[1] These are: (1) the achievement of a standard format for bibliographic records in machine-readable form and the associated production at the Library of Congress and elsewhere of a sizable data base of such records; (2) a continuing sharp decrease in the cost of certain components of electronic data processing systems; (3) continuing increases in the capacity and reliability of electronic communications channels with concomitant decreases in the unit costs of the channels; and (4) the creation of evolving modular, computer-based library systems, which take advantage of the three other changes just

1. We are particularly grateful to Carl M. Spaulding of the Council on Library Resources for his invaluable contributions to the preparation of this chapter.

mentioned. In these systems the electronic computers involved are not a substitute for the intellectual work of professional library personnel. Instead, they facilitate that work and multiply its effect through a great reduction of needless duplication. In addition, they accomplish enormous amounts of nonintellectual work in the form of computer printing of catalog cards, spine labels, order forms, and the like. But because of the growing complexity of the demands upon the librarian and the increase in the quantity of materials to be handled, no decline in the demand for the services of the skilled professional is imminent. In addition, there is every reason to expect that new (and, it is hoped, better) services to library patrons will require large numbers of librarians educated in new library functions, including the application of electronic information-handling systems. In short, library technology is apparently entering a period of important change, but the change will evolve over a period of quite a few years and while unit costs of some functions may gradually begin to level off or even decrease, overall costs of libraries will be appreciably higher than at present.

The cost-trend information gathered in this report suggests that in a few decades some profound modification in the manner in which libraries are run may virtually be inevitable. If this is so (and this chapter will discuss the basis for that assertion), libraries must begin planning for the changeover in a systematic manner, rather than leave the shape of the new arrangement to haphazard developments.

Planning in this area must be undertaken early because of the long lags inherent in the decision process and the very long-term commitment implicit in these decisions. For example, a library building is usually constructed with the expectation that it will serve its users for many decades. A building designed to be compatible only with methods of operation prevalent at the time of its construction may lock the institution into obsolete activity patterns which will constitute an intolerable drain upon its budget. Add to this problem the time lag inherent in the very process of design, and the plea for early planning of future library operations becomes more than a routine reaffirmation of belief in foresight, research, and motherhood!

Relevance of the Cost Trends

Obviously, economic forces are only one factor among the set of elements that determines the course of developments in library organization. Yet under some circumstances, their role becomes crucial. If the cost of some activity or mode of operation is prohibitive, this fact alone can obviously be decisive. In the process we are now discussing, cost may play this role twice–initially, by limiting severely the libraries' use of electronic equipment, and later, perhaps, by forcing them to embrace it.

Decision making in this area must then take into account future as well as present costs; i.e., it must give heavy weight to the relevant cost trends. Some of these trends have already been reported here. We will presently examine more closely those that are critical for our discussion and also bring out some figures on cost trends in other areas relevant to our topic.

Forecasting on the basis of past trends can often be hazardous. The fact that a statistical series has moved in a particular direction in the past gives us little reason to trust that it will continue on this same course indefinitely. We know too many cases in which very protracted cycles or simply sharp breaks in behavior have led to total departure from linear trends that had been followed for substantial periods. However, as will be shown later, in the case we will be discussing, we have strong analytical reasons for confidence in the belief that the observed trends are likely to continue unchanged at least in direction, if not in absolute magnitude. In other words, in projecting the cost figures which are the basis for our discussion, we are not simply engaging in mechanical extrapolation; we do have a solid analytical basis for our forecast.

In the next section we will examine some of the statistical evidence on comparative cost trends. Then we will digress briefly to review the analytic explanation for these trends, showing the grounds for our belief in their reliability as portents of the future. Finally, we will examine in some detail the nature of their longer-run implications for library operations.

Some Postwar Trends in Library and Computer Costs

For reasons that will emerge presently, libraries and computers may be considered two opposite polar cases among information channels from the point of view of past and prospective cost behavior. In this section, some data are provided to illustrate the nature of these differences in cost behavior.

As we have already noted, the cost *per unit* of library services has been rising rapidly and steadily *relative to the average cost of commodities* in the United States as a whole while the real cost (cost corrected for changes in purchasing power) of electronic computers has been behaving in precisely the opposite fashion. In brief, library costs have been *rising* sharply while the costs of electronic computers have been *falling.*

Before some illustrative statistics are presented, the interpretation of rising library cost figures merits a bit of discussion. Two obvious–and frequently encountered–explanations of the rising costs of library services are inflation in the general economy and increases in the size of the population served, notably in the size of the student body at colleges and universities. The results summarized here show that neither is a tenable explanation for the bulk of the cost increases. Since the trends are apparent in terms of unit costs (cost per volume held or cost per student), the rises cannot be explained simply as a matter of a larger volume of activity. Of course, if costs per student increase and simultaneously the number of students grows, we can expect a still larger rise in the total budget; but something besides the expansion of the student population underlies the observed trends.

General inflation is not the sole influence underlying the rises, nor can inflation *plus* rising activity levels account for the observed facts. During the postwar period, the price level in the United States was relatively stable until the acceleration of military activities in Vietnam. Our data show that library costs *per unit* have risen at a compound rate far greater than that of the general price level. Obviously, in a period in which the wholesale price index was increasing at an annual rate of less than 1 percent while library costs *per student* increased at more than 5 percent a year compounded, the growth in student body and the rise in price level still leave unexplained an annual rise of more than 4 percent.[2]

We turn now to the data. Figure 3.1 shows how college and university library costs per unit have risen relative to the wholesale price index. In the graph, for comparability, the curves have been put on an index basis (1951 = 100). They show dramatically how much more rapid has been the increase in per unit library costs than that in general price level.

Table 3.1 indicates explicitly these relative growth rates from 1951 to 1969. We see for example that, calculated on a per volume basis, the cost per student of operation of university libraries went up at an annual rate of slightly over 6 percent while during the same period, the wholesale price index was increasing at a rate of less than 1 percent per

2. We do not intend to imply that rising prices have been no problem for libraries. On the contrary, as table 3.1 indicates, prices of books and periodicals, a principal expenditure of libraries, have themselves risen at a rate far exceeding that of the general price level. The point is that in *both* of these activity sectors, there are special economic relationships at work (other than the general economic pressures besetting the economy) which account for their atypical price behavior.

Figure 3.1

Unit Costs in Fifty-eight University Research Libraries in Comparison with Wholesale Price Index, 1951-69

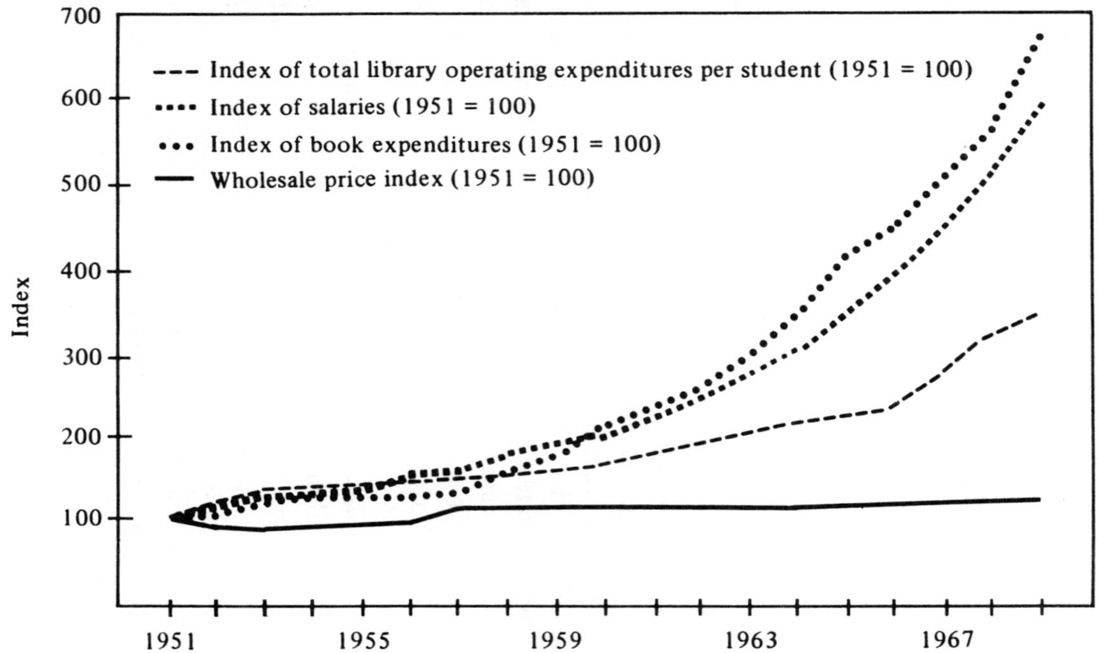

Source: Table 2.2.

annum. The table does, indeed, confirm that costs per unit of library services have tended to rise far more rapidly than the price level.

Table 3.1

Growth Rates in per Unit Operating Costs and Prices for Fifty-eight University Research Libraries, Fiscal 1951-69

	Growth Rate per Volume Owned	*Growth Rate per Student Enrolled*	*Growth Rate in Selected Price Indices*
Total expenditures	6.3	6.1	—
Staff salaries	5.5	5.3	—
Growth rate in wholesale price index (1951-69)	—	—	0.9
Growth rate in price of library acquisitions (1958-68)	—	—	6.5

Sources: For library expenditures and staff salaries, Association of Research Libraries (see table 1.3); for growth of wholesale price index, figure 3.2; for growth of library acquisitions, chapter 1.

Note: The growth rates have been calculated by logarithmic least squares regression.

Let us contrast this cost behavior with the cost pattern for electronic computer systems. Improvement in the cost-performance ratio for certain principal computer components in the past twenty years has been rather phenomenal. Figure 3.2 illustrates, in a most dramatic way, the decrease in the cost of performing a set of operations, each occurring with a relative frequency corresponding to average commercial use.[3] (In this diagram, a logarithmic scale has been employed to compress the data and reduce the slope of the graph in order

3. The costs of commercial rather than scientific calculations are reported because of their similarity to library operations in the use of storage, comparison, etc. Nevertheless, one must be careful *not* to interpret the reported trends in computation costs to represent the costs of automation in libraries, where the nature of the appropriate equipment may have to be far more specialized and where manual operations will unavoidably continue to play an important role.

Figure 3.2

Comparison of Cost of Computation with Wholesale Price Index

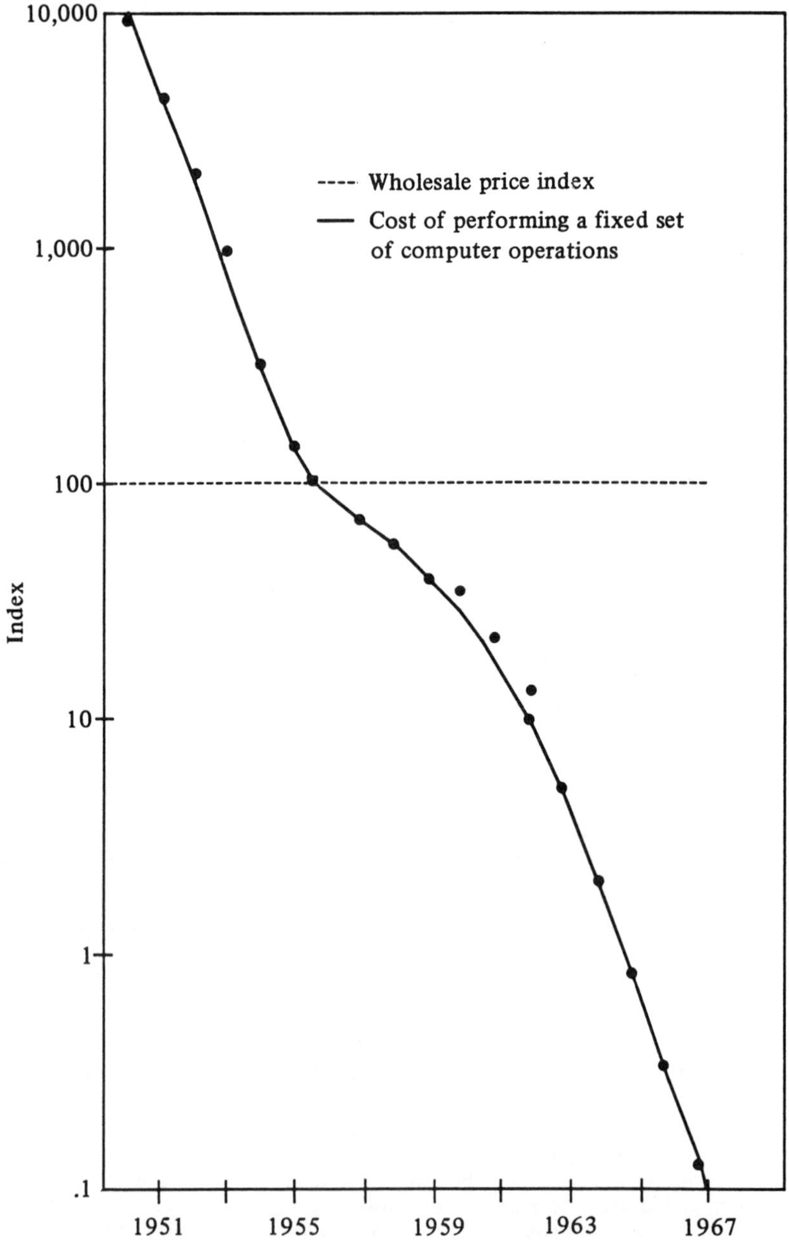

See notes on facing page.

to fit it into a standard page.)[4] The cost decrease follows a step-like pattern with the rate of decrease about 55 percent a year (except between 1955 and 1960 when the decrease was about 20 percent).[5]

The cost of on-line storage (computer memory) is perhaps of slightly more direct interest for a comparison with library systems. The reduction in computer storage costs has not been as impressive as the increase in computer performance, but it has nevertheless been quite spectacular. For example, in the 1960s, the speed of ferrite core memories improved by a factor of 4 while the cost per unit decreased by a factor of 7.[6]

Central processing units (CPUs) for computers are expected to experience cost decreases of from 80 to 90 percent by 1980 with large processors showing the greatest percentage reduction. Random-access mass storage devices (e.g., disk files) are likely to exhibit even greater cost decreases during the eighties, reaching a cost per basic unit of storage equal to

4. A logarithmic scale is one in which equal intervals represent constant *percentage* increases rather than constant *absolute* increases. For example, if on the vertical scale the first inch above the axis represents an increase in cost from $100 to $200, the second inch will go from $200 to $400, and the third from $400 to $800. That is, the intervals proceed in the geometric sequence 1, 2, 4, 8, 16, etc., rather than the usual arithmetic sequence, 1, 2, 3, etc.

5. The years 1955 to 1966 are reported to have been periods of saturation in the use of old models, and in the years after 1960, there was a sharp increase in the marketing of larger computers.

6. R. J. Petschauer, "Trends in Memory Element and Subsystem Design in the 1970's," *Computer* 3, no. 6 (November-December 1970): 13.

Sources: Data from 1950 to 1962, Kenneth E. Knight, "Change in Computer Performance," *Datamation* 12, no. 9 (September 1966): 40-42+. Data from 1963 to 1966, Kenneth E. Knight, "Evolving Computer Performance, 1963-1967," *Datamation* 14, no. 1 (January 1968): 31-35.

Note: Each point represents the cost of performing the same "mix" of operations using the computers available during the time period under consideration. The operations used in this mix were grouped into five categories:

1. Fixed add (and subtract) and compare instructions performed
2. Floating add (and subtract) instructions required
3. Multiply instructions
4. Divide instructions
5. Other manipulations and logic instructions

The relative frequencies with which the five operations were used correspond to a typical pattern of commercial use. The year 1956 has been taken as the base year.

no more than 1 percent of today's cost.[7] Generally, this savings will be reflected in the availability of devices with much larger capacities for the current price rather than a 99 percent price reduction for today's devices.

Concurrently, telecommunications technology will continue for some time to provide ever higher capacity methods as well as facilities for transmitting and switching data streams from computer to computer and between user terminals and computers. For the past 130 years, communications technology has advanced with remarkable consistency in that it has, over each successive period of approximately 17 years, provided a new or improved technique having a per channel capacity ten times that of its predecessor. It is entirely possible that this remarkably consistent performance will be improved on in the next two decades.[8]

These items, central processing units, random-access storage, core memory, and telecommunications facilities, are all important elements in library automation systems. Central processing units are the unifying and controlling components of any computer hardware configuration, and the size and speed of the associated core memories directly affect the efficiency of software. Large capacity, low unit-cost random-access storage is vital for the enormous bibliographic data bases which are fundamental for computerization of library functions. Finally, network development and other resource- and facility-sharing operations among libraries cannot be truly efficient until electronic communications channels become highly reliable, relatively low in cost, automatically switched, and capable of carrying very large volumes of digital traffic.

The difference between the rate of change in the general price level and the rates of change of library and computer

7. Frederic G. Withington, "The Next (and Last?) Generation," *Datamation* 18, no. 5 (May 1972): 71-74.

8. James Martin, *Future Developments in Telecommunication* (Englewood Cliffs, N.J.: Prentice-Hall, 1971), p. 341 ff.

costs are small numbers when stated as annual percentages but are not minor matters when compounded for a period of a few years. For example, with a 7 percent rate of increase a variable doubles in a single decade and expands by a factor of 8 in only thirty years (the time interval since the beginning of the second World War).

Specifically, a service now provided by conventional library methods at substantially less than it would cost if provided by means of a computer-based system could become cheaper to do by computer in a few years. At the same time, these overall trends do *not* indicate that a continuing increase in the cost of library operations and a continuing decrease in the cost of computer technology will *necessarily* cause any particular library operation to become less expensive through automation. The susceptibility of the specific function to replacement of human effort by machinery and the way in which the total library operation is organized must be considered. Some human capabilities are very difficult—perhaps impossible—to duplicate or supersede by electronic and mechanical hardware.

More important than the evolving capability of electronic machinery to carry out (or assist with) the tasks presently making up library operations is the potential for using new technological developments and management methods in order to: (1) provide new or improved services to library patrons, (2) enhance greatly the management of resources, and (3) restructure the way libraries and related organizations function individually and collectively. For example, multi-library sharing of infrequently used resources might be facilitated by a computer-based system for more effective determination of the location and availability of those resources. The same system could be used to help select titles appropriate for shared collections and to determine the cost of library resources, services, and facilities required to support curriculum changes being considered in conjunction with resource sharing. In sum, the computer properly applied is but an element, albeit an important one, in a gradual prospective reorganization of the operation of libraries and other information transfer agencies. Consequently, costs in the computer era will be more a function of those new systems whose development is feasible financially than of the costs of computerization of the functions of existing systems. In any event, the overriding constraint will be the funds available.

A Model of Service and Nonservice Cost Trends

Let us now attempt to account for the behavior of the data just reported.[9] Again, it is convenient to think in terms of two polar cases because they simplify the discussion and do not undermine the validity of the analysis. However, in actuality the economy is composed largely of activities that fall in between the two extremes and share some of the characteristics of each in varying degrees.

We consider two economic activities. In one activity, the quality of the end product is directly dependent on the amount of labor expended per unit of production; as a consequence, it is difficult for technological progress to effect any significant decreases in the quantity of labor input. In the other activity, however, cumulative savings in the labor input occur steadily.

Examples of both types of activity can be easily provided. Among relatively inflexible labor-content activities, one can list education, medicine, live artistic performances, legal services, fire protection, and certain library services. Examples of industries that have benefited over the years from labor-saving innovations are even more numerous: telecommunications, electric power, automotive production, and electronics, to name a few. The examples show that the distinction is a very real one. Moreover, while from time to time, breakthroughs have increased productivity in some activities of the

9. This section is intended as a brief summary of the analysis of Part III, "On the Economics of Library Operations" in Douglas M. Knight and E. Shepley Nourse, *Libraries at Large: Tradition, Innovation, and the National Interest* (New York: R. R. Bowker Co., 1969).

first category, these advances have rarely been followed by a steady stream of labor-saving innovations as has typically been the case in manufacturing. This result has not been a matter of accident. The difference is inherent in the nature of the two types of products and the technology of their supply. The first category consists largely of services requiring personal attention, in which the quality of the end product depends primarily on the amount of human effort devoted to it. Such products are not easily standardized or automated. In many cases, the quantity of labor involved per unit of output is virtually fixed by the nature of the product; e.g., a performance of a trio scored for one-half hour clearly requires a one and a half man-hour performance.

Now, the evidence indicates that wages in the labor-inflexible industries have often lagged behind those in the rest of the economy, but have generally caught up over longer periods. For example, while right after the war school teachers' wages had fallen behind those in industry, the gap has now been closed. Economic pressures simply do not permit growing divergences in real wages in different economic activities, for, if growing disparities were to persist, labor would move into the increasingly better paid occupations, and the resulting shortages would force wages up in the activities where they had lagged. A good deal of evidence shows that things do work out this way in practice.

The implication of the analysis for the cost behavior of the service and manufacturing sectors is straightforward. With costs of labor rising at comparable rates, but labor requirements falling cumulatively and steadily in the one sector while remaining fairly constant in the other, a differential in cost behavior becomes inevitable. Costs of the service sector must rise steadily and cumulatively relative to those in the remainder of the economy at a percentage rate directly related to the differential in their productivity.

If wages in the economy rise at a rate of 5 percent per year, and productivity in manufacturing increases by 4 percent per annum while productivity in the services remains almost unchanged, costs of manufactured goods will go up at an annual rate of 1 percent, but those of services will rise at 5 percent. The difference in the technologies of the two sectors forces this differential upon them, and, with occasional exceptions, we can expect such a differential to persist year after year.

The empirical evidence supports this conclusion. In one personal service after another, costs per unit of output have risen over 4 percent more rapidly over the postwar period than the rate of increase in price level. The *relative* costs *per unit* of these services have doubled every fourteen years and quadrupled over less than three decades. Understandably these sectors have faced budgetary difficulties that have grown more critical with the passage of time.

As we have already noted, conventional library operation is a fairly inflexible labor-content activity; its success requires personal services and depends heavily on the amount of human thought and attention devoted to it. The preceding analysis can thus help explain a significant portion of the rising demands upon library budgets.

Other Sources of Rising Library Costs

Like any analytic model, the preceding analysis constitutes something of an oversimplification of the facts. Library cost increases over the postwar period obviously reflect to some extent the general expansion in the nation's institutions of higher education, including the proliferation of new programs. Yet the fact that, calculated on a *per student* basis, library expenditures increased at some 6 percent per year suggests that there is more to the matter than the expansion of higher education.

The volume of world book production also has been increasing very rapidly, implying that a library must acquire more books per year simply to obtain the same percentage of new publications for its collections. Added to this increase in production is the rising price of books and journals. As indicated in table 3.1, their price on the average has increased at just about the same annual rate as library expenditures per enrolled student—at something in excess of 6 percent per year.

Each of these elements must be assigned some role in any adequate explanation of the rising costs of library operations. Yet over the long run, a critical place must be assigned to the technological component stressed in the preceding section. Unlike the service character of library operations, many of the influences that have just been listed may well be transitory. Thus, for example, the expansion in educational programs as well as in the size of student bodies is undoubtedly decelerating.

Moreover, some of these cost-increasing influences themselves are engendered by the cost problem imposed by service technology, this difficulty thereby affecting the libraries indirectly as well as directly. For example, the scope for productivity increases in the publications industry has apparently proven very limited, and our analysis therefore also helps to explain the rise in costs of books and periodicals, which has contributed so much to the growth in library expenses.

Finally, we should observe that other service industries have exhibited cost patterns very similar to those characterizing the libraries. For example, between 1949 and 1969, the cost per pupil-day of elementary education in the United States rose some 6.5 percent per year. At public and private universities, over the two decades, instructional costs per student rose at average rates of 5.0 and 7.5 percent per year, respectively. Between 1946 and 1965, hospital expenses per patient-day, after elimination of the effects of the increase in personnel per patient, grew at an annual rate of 6.2 percent.[10] The similarity in all these figures certainly lends credence to the notion that some common element is at work.

10. These figures, some of them updated and revised, are based on D. A. Bradford, R. A. Malt, and W. E. Oates, "The Rising Cost of Local Public Services: Some Evidence and Reflections," *National Tax Journal* 22, no. 2 (June 1969): 185-202.

Implications of the Analysis

The simple model of service and manufacturing cost trends presented earlier in this chapter should be of interest for a number of reasons. The analysis shows that the rising costs of library operations emanate from what may be described as the technological structure of library operations. The most frequently cited villains—inefficiency and mismanagement—need have nothing to do with the problem, and general inflation explains only a limited part of it. Similar cost trends have been documented for various activities in other inflexible labor-content portions of the economy. The largest single activity of American municipalities in terms of size of budgetary requirements is education, and we have just seen that educational costs per pupil rise at just about the same rate as those of library services. The same is true of various other public services. For nonprofit institutions such as hospitals, private universities, and orchestras, costs have been rising about as rapidly. Among business enterprises in the services sector, one finds automotive insurance, restaurants, and law firms, and here again the trend is similar. The diversity of areas whose cost trends are consistent with the predictions of the model is important as is the fact that the differences in cost trends between service and nonservice activities continue through all sorts of economic circumstances—periods of inflation and recession. These trends indicate, in accord with the analysis, that this cost increase for services is not a fortuitous phenomenon whose effects can be expected to be transitory nor one ascribable to peculiar circumstances within one or a few activities.

Another important implication of our analysis is that the source of the rising relative costs of library operations—its *comparatively* slow rate of labor-saving innovation—means that society can, if it chooses, meet these rising costs. The rapid growth of productivity in other sectors in the economy that drives up the costs of service activities automatically increases the wealth of the community. The notion that a community can afford less in the way of services because the productivity of its manufacturing is increasing is a patent absurdity. While services will undoubtedly continue to grow more expensive, the analysis shows that the community will well be able to afford to pay these rising costs, and that failure to do so may simply represent a misguided reallocation of social priorities rather than an unavoidable economy measure.

Finally, the analysis suggests that certain components of electronic data processing systems do not suffer from the technological cost problems that now beset libraries. Electronics has benefited more than most industries from increased productivity through innovation. Few areas have proven to provide such fertile ground for technological change. The implications of our model are perfectly consistent with the cost behavior of these two activities as indicated earlier by our statistics.

The model leads us to conclude that the observed cost patterns are neither fortuitous nor temporary. The same technological differences that have accounted for the divergent cost trends for data processing systems and conventional library operations in the past are likely to be with us in the years to come. This stability is precisely why cost forecasting in this area is a reasonable undertaking and why one can have some degree of confidence in its results. For the analysis offers us an explanation of the behavior of relative costs that indicates why the future can be expected to bring with it a continuation of the trends observed in the past for the two types of activities, trends whose differences are substantial and significant.

Longer-Run Implications for Library Operations

There are no doubt many reasons why the use of electronic systems in libraries has proceeded far less rapidly than some of its more sanguine advocates had predicted. In part, the electronic systems seem to have proven less flexible and less useful (at least in their present state of design) than had been claimed. In addition, library operations are more complex than computer adherents had realized. Undoubtedly also, as in any profession, there is some degree of natural conservatism and resistance to innovation.

Yet, a major impediment to a change in library operations turned out to be the cost of the electronic equipment itself and of its operation. The investment in purchase or rental of the equipment is enormous, and rapid obsolescence does not make matters easier. Moreover, sophisticated equipment requires the use of highly skilled personnel for maintenance, operation, programming, and so on, and such personnel are never cheap. As a result, the use of electronic equipment for the performance of library functions has been, for the most part, financially prohibitive.

However, the long-run trends—if they continue to behave as in the recent past—are likely to change the cost relationship dramatically and may conceivably do so more quickly than is generally expected. With recent rates of change in their costs continuing, only a decade would be required to eliminate a ten-fold operational cost differential between service activity and a purely electronic substitute (assuming a purely electronic substitute exists or can be developed). By the time two decades had passed, the cost of the labor-intensive conventional process would have risen to twenty times that of its electronic substitute!

Such an extrapolation undoubtedly exaggerates matters. It is quite possible that the burst of innovation that has accompanied the inauguration of computer technology may not continue very long. In any event, the electronic processing cost calculations as they have been derived here are not directly applicable to libraries. The requirements of library computerization are quite unique, and the necessary technology is still far from being settled. It would be foolish to take data derived from the application of general-purpose computers for other uses and simply attempt to use them unmodified and unanalyzed as a predictor of future library costs.

Yet the figures are suggestive. They indicate that within the foreseeable future, electronization of a significant portion of library operations may perhaps become feasible financially, and in some cases may become unavoidable. For, with a time path of costs such as the libraries have experienced, not much time is required before the use of some conventional methods is priced out of consideration. Obviously, the date at which this circumstance occurs will vary by library and by the operation in question. Some critical parts of the workings of the library will probably never lend themselves to electronic assistance to any significant extent. The point of this discussion is not to argue that the computer can, or will, or should do everything, but merely to indicate that in those aspects of library operation for which the computer is potentially useful, the cost trends will ultimately render its use feasible financially.

Computerization and electronic operation are not the only alternatives to conventional library operations. For example, proposals for increased sharing of resources among libraries may prove a promising means to decelerate the expansion in the size of individual collections. Microfilm, microfiche, and other types of miniaturization may help reduce growing storage costs, as will be emphasized in the next section. Both these alternatives can be expected to depend upon, and be imbedded in, electronic technology and each other. At present, resource sharing is commonly inefficient and has a high per unit cost. It appears highly likely that message communication, record keeping, and document transmission for resource sharing will, in the coming years, be more and more efficiently carried out with the aid of advanced telecommunications under computer direction. An increasing amount of resource sharing may also be effected by computer-controlled retrieval, inexpensive duplication, and rapid delivery of microforms. A more advanced system would transmit images of the computer-retrieved microforms by telefacsimile.

Emphasis must be given to the fact that while hardware and software for these systems are technically feasible even now, their utilization in practice on any substantial scale would almost certainly take a decade or more and would require hard-won progress in nontechnological areas. For example, legislative and judicial action would have to be taken on copyright matters, user-acceptance of microforms would need to be improved, and new methods of remunerating publishers would have to be worked out.

The authors of this volume lay no claim to expertise in the technology of library operation, and there is nothing further from our objective than specific recommendations about the type of innovation that will prove most amenable to use by libraries. Rather, our intention is merely to point out the implications of current cost trends and our analytic results, which indicate that these trends can be expected to persist over the foreseeable future. The economist is in no position to judge in any detail how the shape of library operations will change with the passage of time. He can, however, assert with some degree of confidence that some fairly radical changes may become inevitable within a matter of decades.

Other Relevant Trends

In chapter 1 we examined growth rates of various library indices and came across several that were rather high. One growth rate particularly pertinent for this discussion is the figure for volumes held, which over the two decades investigated grew at a cumulative rate of more than 4 percent per annum. At that rate, the average size of a library collection doubles in less than eighteen years and quadruples in less than thirty-five years.

The storage problems that this prospect entails are clear enough. But the volumes held statistics may well understate the problem by a considerable margin. For the evidence indicates that the expansion of libraries is in fact accelerating, and at a remarkable rate. The number of volumes *added* has been increasing far more rapidly than the number of volumes held. The former has been growing cumulatively at an average annual rate exceeding 7 percent. Within four decades, if this trend continues, the number of volumes added annually will be sixteen times as large as it is today. The processing and storage problems may prove overwhelming for a very substantial proportion of college and university libraries.

Well before that time one may expect the search for alternative forms of storage and retrieval to become a matter of the highest priority. Already it has begun to emerge as a critical issue, and various new forms of microfilm are now available. However, most of these forms have serious drawbacks, such as the requirement for special equipment which the reader must utilize at a location away from his normal working and reading area, or high cost when produced in small numbers of copies. Here again, it has been suggested that electronic means can be found to help matters, but specific and detailed remedial methods have, at least as yet, not been designed.

Requisites of Planning

In these circumstances, an institution with a large conventional library plant that does not lend itself to conversion may be at an enormous disadvantage. To protect their interests, institutions should begin as soon as possible to examine the implications of library cost trends for their own operations and to lay out procedures for an orderly transition that keeps down dislocations and costs.

Most of the work of library planning, of course, requires skills and knowledge which the economist normally does not possess. Such planning calls for intimate acquaintance with both the details of library operations and the capabilities—current and prospective—of the pertinent types of electronic equipment.

Yet, three observations are perhaps useful for us to offer:

1. Continuing surveillance of the cost trends of library operations, with particular attention to significant changes in any of these trends, is desirable.

2. In designing additions to library plants, serious consideration should be given to the incorporation into the design of elements of *flexibility* which permit easier conversion from conventional to electronic models of operation. However, flexibility is itself *not* a free commodity, and a balance between cost and flexibility must be sought for each library. A building readily convertible from one type of operation to another will be more expensive than one much more specialized. Moreover, large-scale conversion to electronic modes of operation or a fundamental redefinition of the functions of libraries is impractical for the immediate future. But since the costs of conventional operations are likely to continue to rise so dramatically, built-in flexibility, despite its cost, may prove to be the most rational approach to the matter. In any event, this possibility should be investigated carefully with some study of the nature of the specific design modifications required, the likely range of their costs, and their relative suitability for libraries that differ in size and in other characteristics.

3. Because ultimate responsibility for the proper design and performance of new library systems lies with the professional library staff, the movement of schools of library science into study areas dealing with library management, computer technology, systems analysis, and the economics of library operations is highly desirable. While not turning librarians into experts in these areas, such programs do enable them to work with the specialists, thereby facilitating the rapid and optimal employment of the newer management methods.

Concluding Comment

The analysis of cost trends just described shows that the observed behavior of costs of library operations and of related activities cannot be considered a chance occurrence. The trends arise at least in considerable part out of the nature of the technology involved and hence they can be expected, with a considerable degree of confidence, to continue for the foreseeable future.

These cost changes are likely to have a revolutionary impact on the nature of library operations, and the general outlines of these changes can be anticipated. Increased sophistication in technology and recourse to automated equipment may be unavoidable within a matter of decades. So profound a change can be extremely disturbing to the orderly functioning of libraries unless steps are taken early to plan for the transition and to assure that its advent occurs in an organized manner.

[30]

Electronics, the Cost Disease, and the Operation of Libraries

William J. Baumol
Princeton University, Princeton, NJ 08544 and
New York University, New York, NY 10003

Sue Anne Batey Blackman
Princeton University, Princeton, NJ 08544

This article analyzes the prospects for costs of computerized operation of libraries relative to costs of more conventional operation. Conventional library operation is labor intensive and not readily amenable to cumulative increases in labor productivity. This helps to explain the rapid and cumulative rise in cost per volume and/or student served relative to the rise in the economy's price level during the earlier postwar period. Because the price of computer hardware has been falling at a spectacular rate, it has been expected that computerized operation of libraries would become increasingly inexpensive relative to conventional procedures. Yet the evidence indicates that such a differential has not materialized. It is shown why the costs of computerized operation should in fact not be expected to fall along with the price of computer hardware. The reason is that the very decline in computer hardware prices has increased the share of software and other labor-intensive activities in the total budget of computer operation. The implications of this relationship for library operations are analyzed.

The age of electronics may bring with it profound changes in the operation of libraries. Some of these changes may be adopted because they will expand the capacities of the individual institution and permit improvements in library services. But other changes may be forced upon libraries by financial pressures—by cost relationships which leave the librarian no alternative. It is the second of these sources of change that will concern us here.

In this article we examine trends in the costs of conventional library operation and trends in the costs of the electronic devices which may pervade the libraries of the future. We also describe some alternative scenarios for the use of computerized facilities by libraries. Then we present some evidence on the rate of adoption of electronic techniques which has so far occurred and, finally, offer some analytic material which seeks to account for the observed developments in this area.

We began our investigation with a hypothesis that seemed to follow indisputably from the underlying technological relationship between libraries and electronics. For reasons which will be reviewed in the next section, library costs have until recently been rising at a compounded rate significantly greater than the rate of inflation in the rest of the economy, and the underlying problem can be expected with some confidence to continue in the future. At the same time, costs associated with computers have exhibited a persistent downward trend of astonishing magnitude. The conclusion that appeared to follow inescapably from these observations is that even if electronic library operation is now more expensive than traditional methods, the latter must soon catch up and, indeed, ultimately cost substantially more than computerized methods. When that happens librarians will find themselves with little choice: Traditional methods of library operation will have to give way to the computer.

This "technocratic" view of the future is a radical departure from today's libraries. It envisions at least partial replacement of the written page by the television screen. And that television screen is to be located not at a central library, but at the reader's premises. Rather than handling a technical journal physically, the reader can command the library's central computer to transmit a particular article (or a particular page of an article) via his own television screen. Or he can first ask the computer for a bibliography relating to a particular topic, and can then summon up items from that bibliography at his convenience.

When a particular item is likely to be needed repeatedly or annotation is required, hard copy can be made from a page of the television screen with the aid of an attached photocopying unit which produces a copy automatically charged to the user's account. For such mate-

Received January 27, 1982; accepted September 7, 1982

rial no local library need be involved. A central memory bank, perhaps operated by the Library of Congress, will be able to serve the needs of all scholars and the delays engendered by interlibrary loans will become a thing of the past.

With these developments the publication of technical journals and reference books is likely to vanish, for materials such as statistical tables will be more accessible, more easily kept up to date, and less difficult to store in electronic rather than printed form.* This is not to say that all book publication will cease. Those works whose subject matter requires the aesthetic qualities of the printed book will undoubtedly survive the electronic revolution, but little else will continue to be the same.

This, then, is the technocratic vision of the library of tomorrow. Curiously, there is a sense in which none of it can be classed as science fiction. The requisite hardware has all been invented, and prototypes are already available.† Given the desire and the requisite funds, it *can* all be realized.

On this view of things, it is only temporarily prohibitive costs or conservatism that impede the widespread adoption of electronic techniques, and librarians who will apparently have little choice in terms of overall mode of operation are best advised to plan how to adapt themselves to the inevitable electronic future.

This, as already indicated, was the hypothesis with which our study began. As we will see, however, neither the facts nor the underlying relationships turned out to support the hypothesis. What emerges is much less categorical in its implications and suggests that the choice of techniques of library operations is not nearly as open-and-shut as the initial hypothesis indicated. For, paradoxically, the astonishing rate of decline in computer costs can be expected in the future to *limit* the rate of decrease of the overall cost of electronic library operation.

1. The Cost Disease of Library Operation

Libraries are among a set of activities in our economy which are especially vulnerable to a debilitating "cost disease" which causes their costs to rise far more rapidly than costs in the rest of the economy. The source of this cost disease is in the technology that characterizes the affected activities. It is important to understand the relationships involved in order to recognize the persistence of the phenomenon and the likelihood of its continuation in the future. Baumol and Marcus [2] explained the cost disease in the following words:

> Consider two economic activities: in one activity, the quality of the end product is directly dependent on the amount of labor expended per unit of production; as a consequence, it is difficult for technological progress to effect any significant decreases in the quantity of labor input. In the other activity, however, cumulative savings in the labor input occur steadily.
>
> Examples of both types of activity can be easily provided. Among relatively inflexible labor-content activities, one can list education, medicine, live artistic performances, legal services, fire protection, and certain library services. Examples of industries that have benefitted over the years from labor-saving innovations are even more numerous: telecommunications, electric power, automotive production, and electronics, to name a few. The examples show that the distinction is a very real one. Moreover, while from time to time, breakthroughs have increased productivity in some activities of the first category, these advances have rarely been followed by a steady stream of labor-saving innovations as has typically been the case in manufacturing. This result has not been a matter of accident. The difference is inherent in the nature of the two types of products and the technology of their supply. The first category consists largely of services requiring personal attention, in which the quality of the end product depends primarily on the amount of human effort devoted to it. Such products are not easily standardized or automated. In many cases, the quantity of labor involved per unit of output is virtually fixed by the nature of the product; e.g., a performance of a trio scored for one-half hour clearly requires a one and a half man-hour performance.
>
> Now, the evidence indicates that wages in the labor-inflexible industries have often lagged behind those in the rest of the economy, but have generally caught up over longer periods. For example, while right after the war school teachers' wages had fallen behind those in industry, [by the end of the 1960s] the gap [had] been closed. Economic pressures simply do not permit growing divergences in real wages in different economic activities, for, if growing disparities were to persist, labor would move into the increasingly better paid occupations, and the resulting shortages would force wages up in the activities where they had lagged. A good deal of evidence shows that things do work out this way in practice.
>
> The implication of the analysis for the cost behavior of the service and manufacturing sectors is straightforward. With costs of labor rising at comparable rates, but labor requirements falling cumulatively and steadily in the one sector while remaining fairly constant in the other, a differential in cost behavior

*The transition to this brave new world will undoubtedly bring with it a number of curious problems. What will replace the refereeing process that precedes publication in a technical journal and serves as a rough attestation of quality? What, indeed, can be taken to constitute "publication" and serve as evidence of the merit of an author seeking academic tenure?

†Indeed, at least one library, that of Clarkson College, is reported already to be well on its way to achieving such a mode of operation. See ref. [1, p. C1] and ref. [44].

becomes inevitable. Costs of the service sector must rise steadily and cumulatively relative to those in the remainder of the economy at a percentage rate directly related to the differential in their productivity.

If wages in the economy rise at a rate of 5 percent per year, and productivity in manufacturing increases by 4 percent per annum while productivity in the services remains almost unchanged, costs of manufactured goods will go up at an annual rate of 1 percent, but those of services will rise at 5 percent. The difference in the technologies of the two sectors forces this differential upon them, and, with occasional exceptions, we can expected such a differential to persist year after year.

The empirical evidence supports this conclusion. In one personal service after another, costs per unit of output have risen over 4 percent more rapidly over [much of] the postwar period than the rate of increase in price level. The *relative* costs *per unit* of these services have doubled every fourteen years and quadrupled over less than three decades. Understandably these sectors have faced budgetary difficulties that have grown more critical with the passage of time.

[To apply this discussion to our central topic we must recognize that] conventional library operation is a fairly inflexible labor-content activity; its success requires personal services and depends heavily on the amount of human thought and attention devoted to it. The preceding analysis [may] thus help [to] explain a significant portion of the [pressures] upon library budgets. (pp. 52-54)*

To see how well library cost data compare with this cost disease analysis, we will divide the postwar era into two subperiods: the period before 1970 in which inflation was, by and large, extremely moderate and library funding was relatively abundant, and the subsequent period in which all of that changed.

2. Library Costs in the Fifties and Sixties

Much of the postwar period before the 1970s was a time of relative prosperity for the libraries. Of course, they have never enjoyed an overabundance of funds. Still, before the baby boom began to subside and before the Vietnam War and OPEC had produced their inflationary consequences, colleges and universities found themselves in easier financial circumstances than anyone could remember, and their libraries were among the beneficiaries. Libraries unconnected with educational institutions also enjoyed reduced economic pressures at that time.

The statistics confirm that, measured both in terms of cost per student and cost per volume held, library costs over the period rose at rates significantly exceeding the rise in the general price level, that is, far faster than the economy's overall rate of inflation.* For a sample of 58 university libraries, between 1951 and 1969 expenditure per volume held grew at 6.3% per year, while expenditure per student served grew at an annual rate of 6.1% [2, p. 47]. In contrast (although this now seems hard to believe), the wholesale price index (used as a measure of the overall inflation rate) grew only 0.9% per year. Put in a different way, measured in dollars of constant purchasing power, library cost per volume held and per student grew at compounded rates of about 5.4 and 5.2% per year, respectively. These are very substantial rates and imply that, if continued, real cost per volume held or per student must double in less than 14 years!

One may well suspect, however, that this enormous rate of increase is not entirely attributable to the cost disease. The relative prosperity of the libraries during the fifties and sixties may well have encouraged costly improvements in standards of library operation. Real incomes, college-age population, and university enrollments were all rising during this period; with relatively stable book and journal prices and increasing budgets rapid growth in library collections and staff was possible, and stable prices also permitted construction of new facilities [4, p. 7]. In 1951 only 14 research libraries in the U.S. and Canada had collections exceeding 1 million volumes; by 1973-1974 there were 76 with more than 1 million volumes, 25 with more than 2 million volumes, and 14 with more than 3 million volumes [5]. Library cost increases may also have been exacerbated by other special problems of the period, such as the rapidity of the surge in number of students and the explosion in technical publications. It is therefore of some importance to determine what happened to real costs during the decade of the 1970s, and we will turn to that shortly. First, however, we will examine the trends in computer costs in order to see what they suggest about the financial prospects of electronic operation of the libraries.

3. Trends in Computer Costs

The rise in the real cost of conventional library operations in the 1950s and 1960s seems very substantial. Yet it

*For a contrary view, see White [3]. White measures productivity in public libraries directly in terms of circulation relative to labor time and an index of other inputs. White concludes that from 1951 to 1963 library productivity rose about as fast as it did in the economy as a whole, although it then began to fall, perhaps because of overgenerosity of budgets.

*It is necessary to calculate some sort of cost *per unit* of library operation (however one may choose to define that concept). The period under discussion was one in which both number of students served and number of volumes held was increasing rapidly. Should it have proven that the total budget of a library, while expanding, was doing so at a rate significantly slower than the growth rate of the student body or the number of volumes stocked, then one would have to conclude that in substance costs were actually declining. As crude indices of unit costs, cost per student and cost per volume held were, consequently, calculated.

involves a rate of change that is extremely moderate in comparison with the costs of computer hardware. The rate of decline of hardware prices per unit of computing capacity is simply sensational. While there are no cost figures which are both representative and precise, because the components in question are so heterogeneous, the following excerpts are suggestive of the magnitudes involved.*

> The increase in computational power and memory for a fixed price has been approximately exponential over time. Cost-effectiveness doubles every two years—this means, for example, that the cost effectiveness of computing has increased by a factor of more than a million since World War II. It seems likely that this doubling will continue through the 1980's. One crucial factor has been the astonishing increase in the number of active elements on a single silicon chip. (Lipson [6], p. 23)

> The cost/performance of electronics is improving at a rate variously estimated at from 20-25 percent per year. (Triebwasser [7], p. 176-177)

> The most significant...future development involving [data] communications modes will be the drop in the dollar cost of transferring a bit of information from here to there. The carrier component of this cost has been calculated as declining by about 15 percent per year since about 1960, and is forecast to continue at that rate into the 80s. (Ferreira and Nilles [8], p. 51)

Kubitz [9], who provides a detailed description of trends in the electronics industries, estimates that computer performance per unit cost has been increasing at 25 to 30% per year (p. 135). Burns [10] offers the following breakdown of the rate of cost change for various components over the next decade: People (labor) up 6% per year, communications down 11% per year, computer logic down 25% per year, and computer memory down 40% per year.

This is just a small part of the cost evidence available. We can easily provide other quotations offering similar and sometimes identical estimates. But what all these observers seem to suggest is that the cost of the computer components relevant for library operations is likely to continue to decline about 25% per year even without adjustment for inflation, which means that the real decline will probably be considerably higher.

*It is noteworthy that most of these calculations apparently make no correction for the effects of inflation. This means that if adjusted to reflect constant purchasing power the decrease in computer costs would have been even more remarkable; for example, if in a year when inflation proceeds at an annual rate of 10%, the cost of an electronic component declines, say, 18% (unadjusted for inflation), in constant dollars the (*real*) rate of decline will be closer to 28%!

Our empirical observations so far would seem to imply that the widespread conversion of libraries to electronic techniques should be fast upon us. During the 1950s and 1960s library costs rose at a rate exceeding 5% per year in constant dollars, while computer costs have plummeted at a rate of 25% per year, even without adjusting for inflation. Simple extrapolation of these cost trends would at first glance imply that in fairly short order a thoroughgoing electronic overhaul of library operations will be transformed from a luxury into a financial necessity.* But we will see next that things have not worked out quite as might have been expected.

4. The Cost Disease and Library Costs in the 1970s

Earlier, we deliberately broke off our story at the end of the 1960s, since the advent of the next decade clearly would bring with it a new era in library financing. The seventies were, as we know, not a particularly fortunate time for the libraries, which were faced by sudden and sharp decreases in funding.

Before examining the actual consequences of the new stringency, it is important to note how the cost disease generally behaves in periods of inflation. During inflationary periods the cost disease has, characteristically, departed from its usual pattern. Historically, whenever the economy's price level has been steady or declining, the costs of the services have generally risen relative to the price level in the rest of the economy. That is, the constant dollar cost of services has always risen in such circumstances. However, during inflationary periods, at least as far as nonprofit institutions like universities, orchestras, and libraries are concerned, matters have been quite different. Per unit expenditures, rather than outpacing the rate of inflation, have tended to lag behind it, so that in terms of dollars of constant purchasing power the unit costs of these services have actually fallen.†

The explanation, presumably, is that inflation has eroded these nonprofit organizations' sources of funding. As a result, they have been forced to adopt cutbacks in service, reduce the real compensation of their staffs, and even skimp on quality. It is in these ways that the activities subject to the cost disease have been able to reduce their costs (measured in constant dollars) during inflations.

*It is helpful to see what these figures mean if extrapolated into the future. If we adopt the exaggerated premise that unit costs of an unspecified electronic library operation are ten times as high as manual costs, simple arithmetic confirms that if the cost of conventional operations continues to rise at 5% per year while that of electronics falls 25% per year, then within eight years the disparity in costs virtually will have been wiped out. By the ninth year electronic operation will have become the less expensive alternative.

†Data for the orchestras bring this out most clearly because there exist data on orchestral costs going back to the first half of the 19th century. Financial figures for the New York Philharmonic since 1842 show that costs rose more quickly than the general price level except for the periods of inflation associated with the Civil War and World Wars I and

In light of all this, it should come as little surprise that library costs did not manage to keep up with inflation during the 1970s. Figure 1 shows total expenditures between 1951 and 1980 for a median member library of the Association of Research Libraries. The curve marked current dollars, which is uncorrected for inflation, shows a fairly steady rise from $350,869 in 1951 to $4,783,864 in 1979-1980. But when the figures are translated into dollars of constant purchasing power matters change substantially. While *total* outlays still rise until 1969-1970, after that they level off or even decline slightly. But this pattern holds only for total cost. When measured per student served and per volume held, unit costs in constant dollars actually fell. Figure 2 shows per student costs of U.S. academic libraries. In constant 1972 dollars, funds per student increased steadily from $75 per student in 1967 to $94 in 1972. But since then they have declined almost every year until in 1981 the figure had dropped to $69 per student. Finally, Figure 3 shows the trends in library expenditures per volume held. It tells the same story—a more or less steady rise in real cost per volume from 1951 to 1970, with the cost figure more than doubling over that interval. But between 1970 and 1980, cost per volume held, in constant dollars, fell almost without let-up, declining about 40% over the ten year period.

The conclusion to be drawn from these cost trends is that for the libraries the cost disease has been suspended during the recent period of inflation. Since many economists feel that inflation is here to stay for a while and the financial stringency besetting the libraries also seems likely to continue, this may suggest that the cost incentives for the adoption of electronic library operations may have been blunted, if not eliminated entirely. But such a conclusion is premature. There are at least two reasons why such a revised view may not be justified.

First, the suspension of the cost disease occurs, apparently, not because inflation in some way increases the technological efficiency of conventional library operations, but because the financial stringency which accompanies the inflation imposes painful and much-regretted economies upon the libraries. In such circumstances, if it turns out that electronic operation is less expensive, then the motivation for its adoption should surely be enhanced and certainly not reduced. The suspension of the cost disease during inflation is no reprieve from pressures for the libraries to economize. The second reason for this conclusion is related to the sheer magnitude of the decrease in computer hardware costs. Even if the cost disease for conventional library operation is halted, if hardware costs are dropping at 25% per year, then the date at which the cost superiority of electronic library operation occurs would seem merely to be postponed for a few years.*

There can be no doubt, then, that computers and electronics generally will play a role in the libraries of the future. But the transformation of the libraries into futuristic automated institutions has not occurred at the pace that might have been expected back in the sixties. In the next section, we will look at what libraries have actually done to computerize their operations.

5. How Libraries Have Automated

Certainly few, if any, major libraries are still run as they were in the 1950s, essentially as handicraft enterprises. The trauma of the transformation to computerized record keeping, circulation procedures, and the like has achieved the status of a "shared experience." But, by and large, the changes have been fairly conservative in character. The bulk of the library computerization process that has occurred so far has not radically transformed library services, but has enabled libraries to do basically what they always did, albeit more efficiently and less labor-intensively than before. Cataloguing procedures, circulation techniques, and record keeping, rather than the form of the reading matter and the place and manner of its delivery, are the items that have been primarily affected.

Automated systems are still mainly the preserve of large libraries with big holdings and enormous clerical tasks, or very innovative, technical-oriented libraries, but more and more libraries are installing computerized systems.† Automated circulation is a particularly active

II (Baumol and Bowen [11, p. 190]). More recent figures indicate that the behavior of orchestral costs during the 1970s has not been identical with that in earlier inflationary periods. Data provided by the American Symphony Orchestra League (ASOL) indicate that between 1973-1974 and 1979-1980, inclusive, in constant dollars cost per attendee actually rose some 2.6% per year, though cost per performance declined at an annual rate of 1.6%.

The apparent inconsistency of the behavior of cost per attendee and cost per performance is explainable largely by special conditions and new practices in the orchestras. In recent years 52 week annual contracts with musicians have become common, and this has led to a proliferation of small scale chamber concerts each involving only a small number of an orchestra's musicians and aimed at smaller audiences.

The rise in cost per attendee is attributable to the surprisingly felicitous experience of the arts during the 1970s in terms of financial support both from private and public sources. The evidence indicates that giving to the arts in the U.S. (and a number of other countries) rose far faster than the price level during this period. For example, for the orchestras during the period 1973-1974 to 1979-1980, financial support rose more than 5% per year, compounded, *measured in constant dollars*.

*Our earlier hypothetical extrapolation (see Section 3, second footnote) enables us to illustrate the point. It will be recalled that we started from the assumption that electronic operation is initially ten times as costly as conventional operation. We calculated that with the cost disease raising conventional library costs as it did before the onset of inflation, in only nine years the costs of electronic operation will have become lower than conventional costs. But even if the cost disease is suspended completely, the same sort of calculation shows that the catchup period is extended only to 11 years.

†Apparently, a rule of thumb for adopting automated circulation systems is that libraries with fewer than 200,000 transactions per year can easily handle their workload manually; for larger libraries it is more efficient and economical to automate.

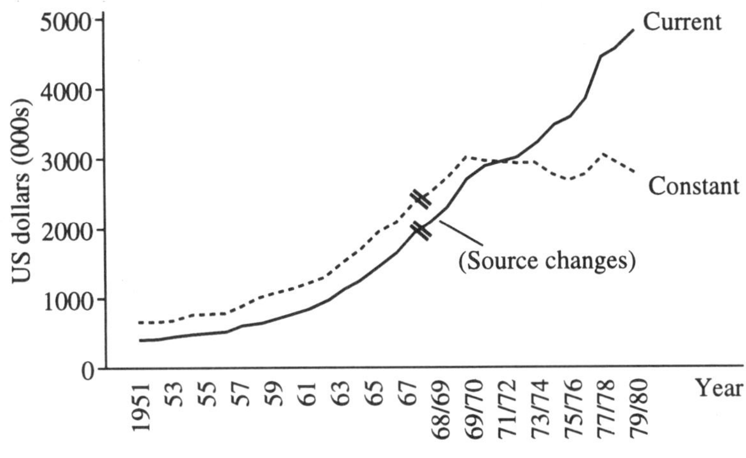

FIG. 1. Total library operating expenditures, median ARL university library, 1951-1980, in current and constant dollars (source: see Appendix A).

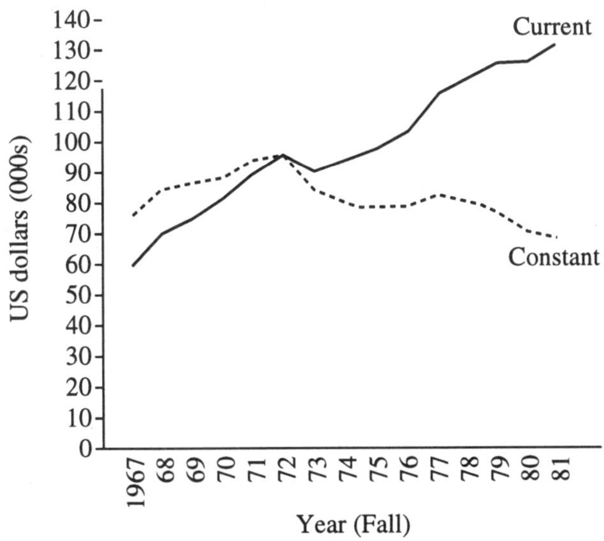

FIG. 2. Total operating expenditures per student served, U.S. college and university libraries, 1967-1981, in current and constant dollars (source: see Appendix B).

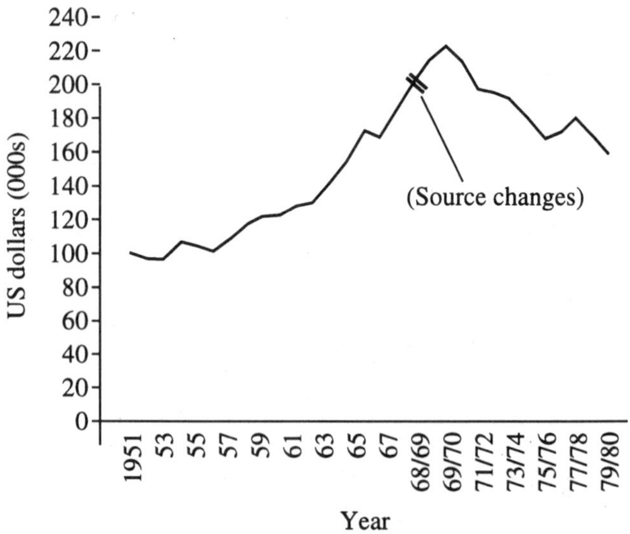

FIG. 3. Total expenditures per volume held, median university library, 1951–1980, in constant dollars (source: see Appendix A).

area. The development of low cost minicomputers, microprocessors, and "light pens" able to read and transmit data from bar-coded labels has spurred the adoption of these systems. The typical online inventory circulation system provides instant access to a database of library holdings and can provide patron receipts, bibliographies, print out a variety of statistical and managerial reports, trap delinquent borrowers, compute fines, and determine book and patron status. Minimum costs today for such systems are high, but the development of microcomputers is predicted by some observers to reduce costs dramatically, and system sharing and increased vendor competition have helped make these systems accessible to smaller libraries.

Another significant development in library automation in the last ten years has been the emergence of online bibliographic utilities—organizations that maintain large online bibliographic databases and provide customer libraries with various cataloguing-related services and products. The groundbreaking and still dominant online utility is OCLC, Inc. (formerly Ohio College Library Center). Under the aegis of OCLC, more than 2000 libraries interact daily with more than five and a half million records. There are now a number of utilities besides OCLC, including RLIN (owned and managed by the Research Libraries Group), geared to large academic research libraries, UTLAS (University of Toronto Library Automation Systems), serving Canadian libraries, and WLN (Washington Library Network), a Pacific Northwest regional utility.

Other developments in library automation include computerized ordering and receipt of materials, payment systems, search techniques, and theft detection. Some particularly innovative libraries around the country are trying out video techniques, one of the newer areas of library automation. Video disks have tremendous potential for low cost storage and retrieval of information, and may some day replace microfilm and microfiche. The optical disk may represent the most significant electronic breakthrough for libraries (Kubitz [9]).

In investigating how and why libraries have automated their operations, we found that the motivation was often *not* financial but service-oriented and designed to obtain better control over the library collection. According to Bahr [12] only a few libraries can justify automation of circulation on the basis of cost alone. Apparently, some libraries have saved money by automating (see, for example, Druschel [13], Berger and Cerutti [14], and Saffady [15]), some have spent more (see, for example, Mosley [16]), and some have spent about the same for an automated system as for a manual system (see Frohmberg and Moffett [17]). A Mitre study of 193 public libraries reported that one third of the libraries had found automated circulation to be less expensive than a manual system, one third found it more expensive, and one third found the cost to be the same (Simpson [18]). In 1979 the Association of Research Libraries reported that:

> In general, while the promises and potentials of automation are high, it seems that automation has not had as much impact upon library procedures and performance as was predicted in the 1960's. Only a few librarians report having truly integrated multi-functional systems and there is little evidence that automation has resulted in large-scale redefinition of library tasks. However, academic libraries have benefitted from the use of automated systems. Some of these have been economic but the most important have been performance-based. (*ARL Statistics* [19], p. 114)

Thus, the switch to automated libraries so far has not brought with it enormous cost savings and some observers are quick to point out the problems. Mick [20] contends that:

> ...computer hardware and software vendors offer the seductive temptations of reduced labor costs and increased production through automation, but although system performance may improve, overall costs rarely go down. (p. 37)

Price [21] is also skeptical:

> In the halcyon days of the early 1960s there was a plethora of promises about the marvelous things computers could do for libraries—and everybody else, for that matter. Unfortunately, performance seldom, if ever, lived up to the promises. Tickets for the automation bandwagon command a high price, and all too many found themselves saddled with ill-conceived and poorly planned automation, which, contrary to the promises, increased costs, degraded performance, and generally caused problems. (p. 84)

Veaner [22], too, claims automation has failed to achieve the cost advantages that were promised:

> With automation we have still failed to realize significant staff savings (especially in cataloging)...as computers and systems become more sophisticated, they require an ever increasing staff of highly sophisticated and expensive software people for maintenance and development. The rise of this personnel component of the computer far offsets any personnel savings in actual library operations... For every decline in [computer] hardware costs, there appears to be a correspondingly greater increase in the cost of staff required to support that hardware... (p. 6)

6. Electronic Library Operation: The Paradox of Increasing Costs

Clearly, electronic library operation has not marched rapidly toward overwhelming cost superiority. This has been so despite the continued decline in the cost of electronic components at a rate of perhaps 25% per year. As we will see, the explanation for this curious behavior sheds quite a different light on our general subject.

Paradoxically, the extraordinary rate of technological progress in the field of electronics, and the probability that this rate of progress will continue, implies that the remarkable decline in computation costs is likely to "self-destruct," conceivably leaving this activity vulnerable to the cost disease. How is this possible? The answer lies in the labor component of electronic operations.

Computer hardware (the mechanical, magnetic, and electronic designs, structures, and devices of a computer) is only one component of an automated system. Also required is the human labor devoted to operation, creation of software (the programs and data), and the performance of other tasks, including those peculiar to the operation of a library. In the early days of automation, computer hardware was the relatively expensive component and dominated the entire cost structure. But as hardware costs have fallen dramatically, they have assumed less and less significance in the total, and software (i.e., labor) costs are becoming more important.

Dramatic evidence of this phenomenon is available. For example, Kubitz [9] reports "the major factor in the decreasing cost of computing is the falling cost of the electronics. To use a computer, however, it must be programmed. The cost of software...has been increasing. In 1973 software represented 5 percent of the microprocessor system cost; in 1978 this increased to 80 percent..." (p. 143). Schindler [23] also writes, "Having risen from 50 percent of total system development cost in 1975 to 80 percent this year, software is expected to exceed 90 percent by 1980" (p. 88). There is some dispute about the prospects for the software-hardware cost ratio, as we will see in a moment. But we may note first that if those figures are roughly correct, they have profound implications for the likely course of computer costs. Accepting the ratio of cost shares as 90% software to 10% hardware for the sake of argument, assume that in a year real labor costs rise 5%, while real hardware costs fall 25%. Then, a computer operation which costs \$100 (\$10 in hardware and \$90 in software) in 1981, will rise to \$102 (\$10 − 25% plus \$90 + 5%) in 1982 (in constant dollars). That is, while the same spectacular rate of cost decrease may continue to apply to the hardware, that very process will have reduced the *share* of total cost to which these savings apply to a very small proportion of the whole. As a result, the component of the cost which is subject to the cost disease will take over, and computation cost, instead of continuing to fall, will actually begin to rise, even in constant dollars. We call such an activity *asymptotically stagnant* because it is characterized by initially spectacular cost

APPENDIX A. Total Operating Expenditures, Median ARL Library, 1951-1980, in Current and Constant Dollars; and Total Operating Expenditures Per Volume Held.

Year	Total expenditures, median university library, curent dollars[a] (1)	GNP implicit price deflator (1972 = 100)[b] (2)	Total expenditures in constant dollars; [(1) ÷ (2)] (3)	Volumes held, median university library[a] (4)	Expenditures per volume held, in constant dollars [(3) ÷ (4)] (5)
1951	$ 350,869	57.27	$ 612,657	615,963	$0.99
1952	354,322	58.00	610,900	642,154	0.95
1953	370,446	58.88	629,154	664,496	0.95
1954	434,652	59.69	728,182	691,752	1.05
1955	458,160	60.98	751,328	732,268	1.03
1956	476,543	62.90	757,620	758,568	1.00
1957	563,249	65.02	866,270	804,577	1.08
1958	633,511	66.06	958,993	824,545	1.16
1959	698,148	67.52	1,033,986	862,921	1.20
1960	767,104	68.67	1,117,087	917,256	1.22
1961	849,988	69.28	1,226,887	965,131	1.27
1962	931,653	70.55	1,320,557	1,031,781	1.28
1963	1,072,618	71.59	1,498,279	1,080,902	1.39
1964	1,214,947	72.71	1,670,948	1,091,396	1.53
1965	1,455,411	74.32	1,958,303	1,146,552	1.71
1966	1,582,758	76.76	2,061,956	1,219,432	1.69
1967	1,871,480	79.02	2,368,362	1,277,422	1.85
1968/1969	2,293,112	84.64[c]	2,709,253	1,268,159	2.14
1969/1970	2,698,072	89.04	3,030,179	1,370,902	2.21
1970/1971	2,776,105	93.69	2,963,075	1,390,167	2.13
1971/1972	2,855,735	98.01	2,913,717	1,486,412	1.96
1972/1973	3,026,243	102.96	2,939,241	1,522,964	1.93
1973/1974	3,243,492	111.16	2,917,858	1,553,192	1.88
1974/1975	3,366,697	121.83	2,763,438	1,549,589	1.78
1975/1976	3,490,754	130.56	2,673,678	1,592,582	1.68
1976/1977	3,863,299	137.58	2,808,038	1,656,275	1.70
1977/1978	4,467,578	146.67	3,046,006	1,707,493	1.78
1978/1979	4,605,041	157.41	2,925,507	1,741,760	1.68
1979/1980	4,783,864	170.06	2,813,044	1,792,048	1.57

[a]Sources, 1951-1967: see ref. [26]; 1968/1969-1979/1980: see ref. [19].
[b]Sources, 1951-1973: see ref. [27]; 1974-1980: see ref. [28].
[c]In column (2) starting with 1968/1969, the implicit price deflator is calculated by averaging one year and the next to accomodate data change to academic year figures, e.g., 1968/1969 is calculated by averaging the GNP implicit price deflators for 1968 and 1969.

decreases, which automatically extinguish themselves because the component of cost which manifests the rising efficiency to which the savings are attributable necessarily soon accounts for only a small part of the total cost. The more spectacular its initial cost performance, the sooner that felicitous state must come to an end.

Now the future is yet to determine whether the field of electronics itself is really an asymptotically stagnant activity. Computers are now being designed to take over a considerable portion of the task of software creation, with the job becoming progressively easier and less time consuming. There are those who suggest (see, for example, Schindler [23] and Spencer [24]) that such changes may even be able to reverse the trend in the share of software costs. Not all observers agree with this assessment (see, for example, Heines [25] and Kubitz [9]), but if it does transpire that software costs can be reduced and held to anything like their initial share of the total, the cost per unit of computation may be able to resume its downward march.

Casual observation suggests, however, that no such remission can be expected for electronic library operation. This is so because even in the most sophisticated of automated libraries there are associated labor-intensive activities which do not seem susceptible to any considerable retrenchment. Some conventional books and other physically printed or written items will continue to be held in the electronic library, and these must be handled along more or less conventional lines. Librarians will have to be available to make decisions and to disseminate information too unstandardized for computers to handle. Tasks as mundane as repair and building maintenance do not seem about to be eliminated. Automation may reduce these residual labor costs somewhat, but it seems inconceivable that there will not be a substantial residue of labor-intensive activities which strongly resists a steady rate of cost reduction, and this means that eventually this component of library cost must increase to a significant proportion of the whole. With that, the electronic library, like the conventional library, becomes fully vulnerable to the symptoms of the cost disease.

Acknowledgment

The authors are extremely grateful to the Division of Information Science and Technology of the National Science Foundation whose Grant No. IST 79 15235 made possible the writing of this paper.

APPENDIX B. U.S. College and University Libraries, Total Operating Expenditures per Student Served, 1967-1981 (Current and Constant Dollars).

Year	(1) Current dollars[a]	(2) GNP Deflator (1972 = 100)[b]	(3) Constant dollars[c]
Fall 1967	$ 59.29	79.02	$75.03
Fall 1968	69.86	82.57	84.60
Fall 1969	74.95	86.72	86.42
Fall 1970	81.25	91.36	88.93
Fall 1971	89.88	96.02	93.60
Fall 1972	94.76	100.00	94.76
Fall 1973	89.38	105.92	84.38
Fall 1974	93.24	116.41	80.09
Fall 1975	97.50	127.25	76.62
Fall 1976	102.60	133.88	76.63
Fall 1977	115.92	141.29	82.04
Fall 1978	121.05	152.05	79.61
Fall 1979	125.32	162.77	76.99
Fall 1980	125.46 (estimate)	177.36	70.73
Fall 1981	131.85 (estimate)	191.17 (2nd Quarter)	68.97

[a]Sources for 1967-1976 total operating expenditures per student and number of students served, 1977 and 1978, see ref. [29]. Sources for 1977-1981 total operating expenditures, see ref. [30]. Sources for number of students served, 1979-1981, see ref. [31].

[b]Sources for 1951-1981, se refs. [27] and [28].

[c](1) ÷ (2).

References

1. Kleiman, D. "Futuristic library does away with books." *The New York Times*, October 21, 1980; C6 and C1.
2. Baumol, W. J.; Marcus, M. *Economics of Academic Libraries*. Washington, DC: American Council on Education; 1973.
3. White, L. J. "Is productivity stagnant in public libraries? Some evidence for public libraries." New York University Graduate School of Public Administration, 1978, unpublished.
4. Drake, M. A. "Academic research libraries: A study of growth." Purdue University, West Lafayette, IN; 1977.
5. De Gennaro, R. "Austerity, technology, and resource sharing: Research libraries face the future." *Library Journal*. 100(10): 917-923; 1975.
6. Lipson, J. I. "Technology and science education: The next 10 years." *Computer*. 13(7):23-28; 1980.
7. Triebwasser, S. "Impact of semiconductor microelectronics." *Computer Technology: Status, Limits, Alternatives*. New York: Institute of Electrical and Electronics Engineers, Inc.; 1978: 176-177.
8. Ferreira, J.; Nilles, J. M. "Five year planning for data communications." *Datamation*. 22(10):51-57; 1976.
9. Kubitz, W. J. "Computer technology, A forecast for the future." In F. Wilfrid Lancaster, Ed., *Proceedings of the 1979 Clinic on Library Applications of Data Processing. The Role of the Library in an Electronic Society*. Urbana-Champaign, IL: University of Illinois Graduate School of Library Science; 1980; 135-161.
10. Burns, C. "The evolution of office information systems." *Datamation*. 23(4):60-64; 1977.
11. Baumol, W. J.; Bowen, W. G. *Performing Arts: The Economic Dilemma*. New York: Twentieth Century Fund; 1966.
12. Bahr, A. H. *Automated Library Circulation Systems, 1979-80*, 2nd ed. White Plains, NY: Knowledge Industry Publications; 1979.
13. Druschel, J. "Costs analysis of an automated and manual cataloging and book processing system." *Journal of Library Automation*. 14(1):24-49; 1981.
14. Berger, P. W.; Cerutti, E. "The management of online reference search services in federal libraries." *Science and Technology Libraries*. 1(1):81-107; 1980.
15. Saffady, W. "The economics of online bibliographic searching: costs and cost justifications." *Library Technology Reports*. 15: 567-653; 1979.
16. Mosley, I. J. "Cost effectiveness analysis of the automation of a circulation system." *Journal of Library Automation*. 10(3):240-254; 1977.
17. Frohmberg, K. A.; Moffett, W. A. "Research on the impact of a computerized circulation system on the performance of a large college library, Part 1: The main library." National Science Foundation Grant 78-10821, Oberlin College, Oberlin, OH; April 1981.
18. Simpson, G.; et al. *Automated Circulation Systems in Public Libraries*. McLean, VA: The Mitre Corporation; 1978.
19. *ARL Statistics*. Washington, DC: Association of Research Libraries, various years.
20. Mick, C. K. "Cost analysis of information systems and services." *Annual Review of Information Science and Technology*. 14:37-64; 1979.
21. Price, D. S. "Cost analysis and reporting as a basis for decisions." In J. L. Divilbiss, Ed., *Proceedings of the 1976 Clinic on Library Applications of Data Processing: The Economics of Library Automation*. Champaign, IL: University of Illinois; 1977.
22. Veaner, A. B. "What hath technology wrought?" In F. W. Lancaster, Ed., *Problems and Failures in Library Automation: Proceedings of the 1978 Clinic on Library Applications of Data Processing*. Urbana-Champaign, IL: University of Illinois Graduate School of Library Science; 1979.
23. Schindler, M. "Computers, big and small, still spreading as software grows." *Electronic Design*. 27(1):88; 1979.
24. Spencer, Jr., R. F. "VLSI and minicomputers." *Computer Technology: Status, Limits, Alternatives*. New York: Institute of Electrical and Electronics Engineers, Inc.; 1978: 13-25.
25. Heines, J. M. "Courseware development and the NSF." *Computer*. 13(7):31-34; 1980.
26. Dunn, O. C.; Seibert, W. F.; Scheuneman, J. A. *The Past and Likely Future of 58 Research Libraries, 1951-1980: A Statistical Study of Growth and Change*. West Lafayette, IN: Purdue University, University Libraries and Audio Visual Center; 1965 and 1968.
27. U.S. Dept. of Commerce, Bureau of Economic Analysis. *The National Income and Products Accounts of the United States, 1929-1974*, statistical tables, a supplement to *Survey of Current Business*.
28. U.S. Dept. of Commerce, Bureau of Economic Analysis. *Survey of Current Business*, various years.
29. Samore, T. "College and university library statistics: Analysis of NCES survey." *The Bowker Annual of Library & Book Trade Information*, 23rd ed. New York: R. R. Bowker; 1978: 243-248, *The Bowker Annual of Library & Book Trade Information*, 23rd ed. New York: R. R. Bowker; 1978: 236; *The Bowker Annual of Library & Book Trade Information*, 25th ed. New York: R. R. Bowker; 1980: 372.
30. Samore, T. Personal correspondence, October 29, 1981.
31. Edles, N. Personal communication, November 4, 1981.
32. *American Libraries*. "Understanding the utilities." 11(5):262-264; 1980.
33. Atkinson, H. "Personnel savings through computerized library systems." *Library Trends*. 23:587-594; 1975.
34. Abelson, P. H.; Hammond, A. L. "The electronics revolution." *Science*. 195(4283):1087-1091; 1977.
35. Caswell, H. L.; et al. "Basic technology." *Computer*. 11(9): 10-19; 1978.
36. Council on Library Resources, Inc. *24th Annual Report*. Washington, DC; 1980.
37. Christian, R. *The Electronic Library: Bibliographic Data Bases, 1978-79*. White Plains, NY: Knowledge Industry Publications; 1978.

38. Cohen J.; Leeson, K. W. "Sources and uses of funds of academic libraries." *Library Trends*. 28(1):25–46; 1979.
39. De Gennaro, R. "Escalating journal prices, time to fight back." *American Libraries*. 8(2):69–74; 1977.
40. Dowlin, K. E. "The electronic, eclectic library." *Library Journal*. 2265-2270; November 1, 1980.
41. Dunn, O. C.; Tolliver, D. L.; Drake, M. A. *The Past and Likely Future of 58 Research Libraries, 1951–1980: A Statistical Study of Growth and Change*. West Lafayette, IN: Purdue University, University Libraries and Audio Visual Center; 1973.
42. De Gennaro, R. "Research libraries enter the information age." *Library Journal*. 104(20):2405–2410; 1979.
43. Drake, M. A.; Olsen, H. A. "The economics of library innovation." *Library Trends*. 28(1):89–106; 1979.
44. Ferrell, T. "Libraries face up to the new technological imperatives." *The New York Times*. June 29, 1980; 20E.
45. Fiske, E. B. "Traditional library use threatened." *The New York Times*. August 12, 1980; C1 and C4.
46. Gorman, M. "Network!" *American Libraries*. 11(1):48; 1980.
47. Holton, W. C. "The large-scale integration of microelectronic circuits." *Scientific American*. 237(3):111; 1977.
48. King, D. W.; et al. "Statistical indicators of scientific and technical communication updated to 1975." *The Information Age in Perspective: Proceedings of the ASIS Annual Meeting*. 15: 177-179; 1978.
49. Kennedy, R. A. "Bell Laboratories library network." April 15, 1980. (Based on a chapter in *Industrial Information Systems*, Jackson, E. B.; Jackson, R. L. Stroudsburg, PA: Dowden, Hutchinson, and Ross; 1978.)
50. Lancaster, F. W.; Drasgow, L. S.; Marks, E. B. "The role of the library in an electronic society." In F. W. Lancaster, Ed., *Proceedings of the 1979 Clinic on Library Applications of Data Processing*. Urbana-Champaign, IL: University of Illinois Graduate School of Library Science; 1980.
51. Lancaster, F. W. "Whither libraries? or, wither libraries." *College and Research Libraries*. 39(5):345–357; 1978.
52. Lancaster, F. W. "The dissemination of scientific and technical information: Toward a paperless society." University of Illinois Graduate School of Library Science *Occasional Papers*. 127; April 1977.
53. Markuson, B. E. "Granting amnesty and other fascinating aspects of automated circulation." *American Libraries*. 9(4):205–211; 1978.
54. McCarn, D. "Trends in information." *Information Utilities*. American Society for Information Science, 1974.
55. Mayo, J. S. "The Role of microelectronics in communication." *Scientific American*. 237(3):192 and 208; 1977.
56. Noyce, R. N. "Microelectronics." *Scientific American*. 237(3): 63–69; 1977.
57. Nelson, B. R. "Implementation of on-line circulation at New York University." *Journal of Library Automation*. 12(3):219–232; 1979.
58. Oldham, W. G. "The fabrication of microelectronic circuits." *Scientific American*. 237(3):111; 1977.
59. Pobst Reed, M. J.; Vrooman, H. T. "Library automation." *Annual Review of Information Science and Technology*. 14; 1979.
60. Roistacher, R. C. "The virtual journal: Reaching the reader." In F. W. Lancaster, Ed., *Proceedings of the 1979 Clinic on Library Applications of Data Processing*. Urbana-Champaign, IL: University of Illinois Graduate School of Library Science; 1980.
61. Terman, L. M. "The role of microelectronics in data processing." *Scientific American*. 237(3):163; 1977.
62. Yencharis, L. "Technology survey predicts big jump for computer hardware and software." *Electronic Design*. 27:40 and 51; 1979.
63. *Advanced Technology/Libraries*. 10(4):2; 1981.

[31]

A growing economy can pay its bills

The expanding army of homeless, the increasing filth of our streets, tightening educational and police protection budgets, and the snowballing real price of medical care, higher education, performing arts, legal services and insurance are all inescapable realities of life. Every industrial country suffers from these symptoms to some degree, but, as in other fields, they are still a few years behind us.

What has gone wrong and what, if anything, can be done? While no single cause can account for these complex problems, one influence explains a good deal, and suggests the way out.

Productivity stagnation in the service industries has led to persistent rises in their costs. The laggard services include, most notably, health care, education, legal services, welfare programs for the poor, postal service, police protection, sanitation, repair services, the performing arts and restaurants. Their common element is the handicraft character of their production, requiring larger labor inputs that are resistant to curtailment.

Hard to standardize

There are at least two reasons why rapid and persistent productivity growth has eluded these stagnant services. First, some of them are inherently hard to standardize. Before one can cure a patient or repair a broken piece of machinery, it is necessary to determine, case by case, just what is wrong, and the treatment must then be tailored to the individual case.

A second reason why it has been difficult to reduce the labor content of these services is that in many of them quality is, or is believed to be, inescapably correlated with the amount of labor expended on them. Teachers who cut down the time they spend on their classes or who increase class size, doctors who speed up the examination of patients, or a police force that spends less time on the beat, are all held to be shortchanging those whom they serve.

To see how all this affects costs and prices imagine an economy with two sectors: one in which productivity is rising steadily, and another in which productivity is constant. The first sector produces automobiles; the second, performances of Mozart quartets. If each year the average auto worker's wage goes up by 4%, but his output increases by exactly the same percentage, labour cost per unit of output remains absolutely unchanged. This can continue indefinitely, with auto workers earning more each year, and no rise in prices needed to maintain profits.

But with productivity per work-hour in quartet-playing constant, any increase in the musicians' wage rates, however modest, must cause a corresponding increase in costs. If performer incomes rise every year by only 2%, the labor cost of each performance must also increase by 2%.

The upshot is that these stagnant services suffer from a terrifyingly rapid and frighteningly persistent rise in costs. For instance, the annual rate of increase in the price of a visit to a general medical practitioner between 1947 and 1986 was nearly 5.5%, compared to an average annual increase of 4.2% in the Consumer Price Index. While this difference may not seem very large, over those 39 years it has resulted in an increase in the price of a physician visit of approximately 750% in absolute terms, or 150% in relation to the general price level. This disturbing price pattern is often attributed to physician greed, but over much of the post-World War II period the inflation-adjusted earnings of doctors in the US have remained virtually constant.

Cost per pupil-day of elementary schooling has also risen steadily and cumulatively at a rate markedly outstripping that of inflation, and there are similar trends in the prices of automobile insurance and automotive maintenance and repair. For the entire period 1947–1989 the CPI grew at a compound rate of a bit more than 4%. The price increase averaged nearly 5% for auto maintenance and repair, and about 6.5% for auto insurance.

It has been suggested that other countries exercise firmer control over their medical costs, take better care of their indigent citizens and continue to offer better public services. Yet there are few industrialized countries in which complaints of 'public squalor' are not heard. Adjusting for inflation, the cost of education per student in five other major industrial democracies – Britain, Canada, France, Germany and Japan – has risen quite consistently faster than the general price level. In Canada, France and Japan, it rose even faster than in the US.

We also have some health-care cost figures, for whatever they may be worth. In 1990 the Organization for Economic Cooperation and Development provided a new 'total medical consumption index', which is calculated for the years 1965 through 1987 for 19 countries, including the major industrial democracies. In all of them, the nominal health-care price index rose rapidly. After correction for inflation, in 13 of the 19 countries, health care prices rose more rapidly than prices in general. The US cost *level* was higher than that in all the other countries, but the US *rate of increase* was exceeded by that of Austria, Australia, Canada, the Netherlands, Norway and Switzerland.

Happily, the very structure of the problem offers society the solution. Contrary to appearances, we can afford ever more ample medical care, ever more plentiful education, ever more adequate support of the indigent, and all this along with a growing abundance of private comforts and luxuries. It is an illusion that we cannot do so, and the main step needed to deal effectively with the fiscal problem underlying the growing public squalor is to overcome that illusion.

Even in the stagnant services, there is a small but positive growth of productivity. It may take just as much labor time today to perform a Mozart quartet as when it was composed. However, a group of Viennese musicians performing in Frankfurt can get there in a few hours. When Mozart made the trip in 1790, it took six days.

More important, however, productivity growth in the rest of the economy means we can afford more of everything. In an economy in which productivity is growing in almost every sector and declining in none, consumers can have more of every good and service. To achieve this, a limited quantity of the inputs used to produce goods whose productivity is growing need merely be transferred to the production of stagnant services.

Productivity growth will still permit the progressive outputs to expand, despite the small cut in their inputs, while the influx of inputs to the stagnant services will make them grow also. To achieve greater abundance of everything, society must change the *proportion* of its income that it devotes to the different products but not the *total amount* of labor or products it gives up in exchange. It is a fiscal illusion that underlies the view that consumers as a group cannot afford to pay the rising costs of education, health care and other such services.

Look what happens if the real prices of education and health care were to continue growing at their current rates (respectively, 2.9% and 2.2% per year), for the next 50 years, if overall US productivity rises at its historic rate of 2% and if real educational and health care outputs retain their current shares of total gross domestic product. Medical outlays, instead of constituting less than 12% of the total as they did in 1989, would rise to more than 35% in 2039. And the share of expenditure on education will have risen from less than 7% of the total at the beginning of the period to more than 29% at the end.

In other words, if relative price trends and output proportions continue as they are now, by the time four decades of the next century have passed, education and health care alone will absorb well over half of GDP! But even so, rising productivity means that consumers will be able to nearly *triple* their consumption of each and every other good and service, including manufactured necessities and luxuries of every variety.

Budgetary reorientation

A little thought will confirm that this can continue indefinitely. Obviously this sanguine conclusion is simplistic. The path to actual practice is beset by difficulties. Not the least of these is the hard educational task of getting the public to recognize the difference between reality and illusion in the behavior of costs. Without this, effective budgetary reorientation will be politically impossible.

Financing the required shift in expenditures is of course a daunting task. For example, if the real outlays on municipal services such as police protection, libraries and welfare will have to treble and more before the middle of the 21st century, then either taxes will have to rise correspondingly, or the tasks must be shifted to the private sector, while freeing it from any regulatory interference that prevents the business firms from making a profit despite rising costs. It is surely urgent to begin to think about these problems.

Public Choice 77: 17–28, 1993.

Health care, education and the cost disease: A looming crisis for public choice*

WILLIAM J. BAUMOL
C.V. Starr Center for Applied Economics, New York University, 269 Mercer Street, New York, NY 10003

An economic specter haunts the democratic governments of the world's most prosperous economies. The rising cost of health care and education casts a shadow over virtually every election, while increasing costs of other services play a part in the growth of the homeless population and the deteriorating sanitation of city streets. It will be shown here that both an explanation and a solution *in principle* are available. However, while the solution is, in one sense, simple and straightforward, in another it poses a problem of frightening magnitude for public choice. If the citizens of these countries are willing to do what is necessary for the supply of educational, health care and other related services to keep up with the expansion in overall economic output made possible by rising productivity, then, if my analysis is correct, a difficult choice will be required: either ever more of gross national product will have to be channeled through the public sector, with all the problems we know that to entail; or, alternatively, these services will have to be transferred to private enterprise, in fields where private business firms can hope to succeed only if granted an (improbably) immunity from the temptation of unwise governmental interference. This, is indeed, Scylla and Charybdis in spades.

1. The problem of the personal services: Some empirical evidence

A quarter-century has passed since William G. Bowen and I (1966) drew attention to the phenomenon of continuing and compounded rises in the real costs of a special class of economic activities that includes the live performing arts, automotive repair, health care, education, postal services, automotive and accident insurance and care of the indigent. The statistical data for the postwar period, including the decades since we wrote, have confirmed the presence and persistence of these trends. Figure 1, showing real cost of education per student (based on data from UNESCO and the U.S. Department of Education for the

* I am extremely grateful to the Alfred P. Sloan Foundation, the Price Institute for Entrepreneurial Studies and the C.V. Starr Center for their generous support of this work, and to Ms. S.A.B. Blackman for her invaluable help in the research.

18

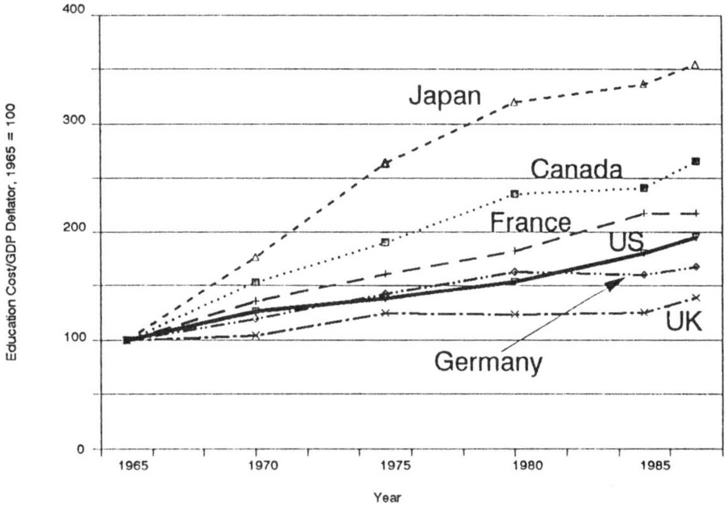

Figure 1. Education: Real cost per student (Education cost/GDP deflator), 1965 to 1987. Source: UNESCO, various years.

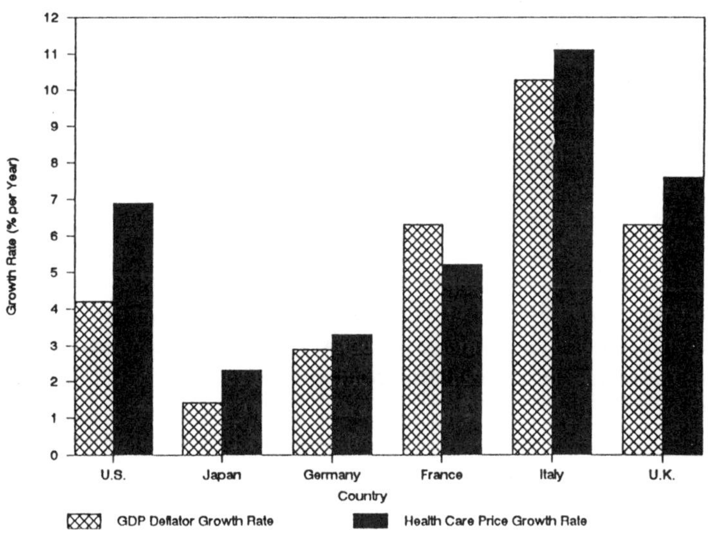

Figure 2. Growth rates: Health care price index and GDP deflator, 1980 to 1990. Source: OECD (1990).

period 1965 to 1987), confirms that these expenditures have indeed grown everywhere over the bulk of the period since World War II. Similarly, Figure 2, comparing (for six countries for the decade 1970–1980) the growth rate of

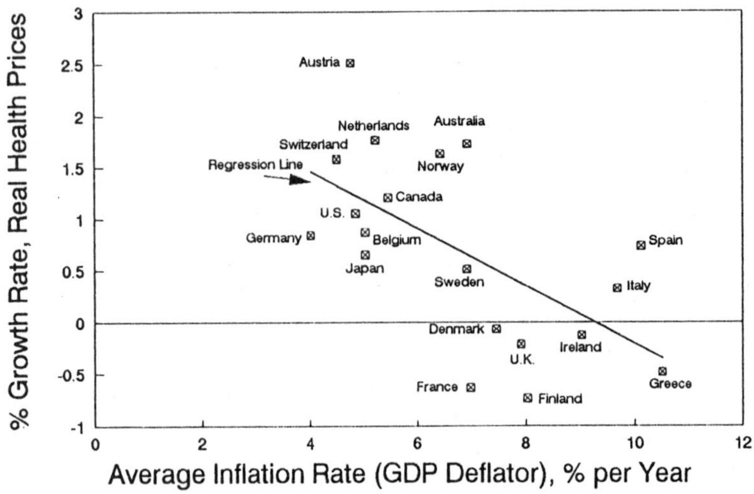

Figure 3. Real health prices versus inflation: Growth rates, 1960 to 1987.
Source: OECD (1990).

the health care cost index with that of the GDP deflator, also confirms that real health care expenditures have grown over the decade in five of the countries – that is, health care prices have grown faster than the GDP deflator (France being the exception).[1] These figures confirm that the problem of rising health care costs is not overcome either by private or public sector operation. Indeed, (Figure 3) over the period 1960–1987, six of the 19 countries in the available sample had real growth rates of medical costs higher than those in the U.S., even though those countries all offer public health care systems.

Finally, Figure 4 shows for the U.S. for the period 1947–1989 the relative prices of automobile repair and auto insurance, compared to the Consumer Price Index, confirming that these private sector activities have had persistent real price trends similar to those just reported for education and health care. In other words, all of them suffer from what we call the "cost disease of the personal services."

2. Explaining the cost disease: Low productivity growth in the personal services

Of course, no single influence can account for any such complex phenomenon. For example, litigation and rent seeking probably play a considerable role in affecting the magnitude of medical costs.[2] However, there is reason to believe that relatively low productivity growth in the personal services is a substantial contributory influence: the services that have been infected by the cost disease are precisely those in which the human touch is crucial, and are thus resistant to labor productivity growth.[3]

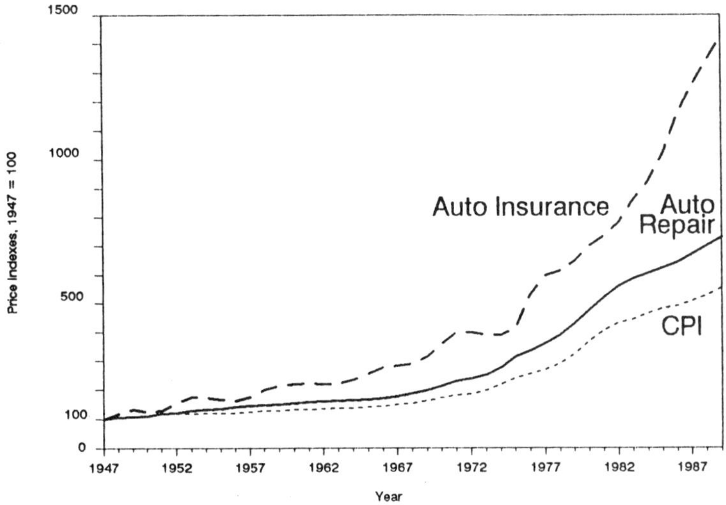

Figure 4. U.S. price indices, 1947 to 1989: Auto insurance, auto repair and consumer price index. Source: U.S. Department Commerce, Bureau of Labor Statistics, various years.

We would expect that the productivity of some economic activities would grow more slowly than others, but what *is* surprising is that those services whose productivity grows slowly today are the same ones whose productivity grew slowly as far back as there are data available. These stagnant services are the very items that have already been listed here.

There are at least two reasons why rapid and persistent productivity growth has eluded the stagnant services. First, some of them entail production processes that are inconsistent with standardization. Before one can undertake to cure a patient or to repair a broken piece of machinery it is necessary to determine, case by case, just what is wrong, and then the treatment must be tailored to the individual case. The manufacture of thousands of identical automobiles can be carried out on an assembly line and much of the work done by industrial robots, but the repair of a car just hauled to a garage from the site of an accident cannot be entrusted to automated processes. A second reason why it has been difficult to reduce the labor content of these services is the fact that in many of them quality is, or is at least believed to be, inescapably correlated with the amount of human labor devoted to their production. Teachers who cut down the time they spend on their classes or who increase class size, doctors who speed up the examination of their patients, or a police force that spends less time on the beat are all held to be shortchanging those whom they serve. This, then, is why the stagnant services have consistently proved unamenable to productivity growth.[4]

The relation to cost behavior should be clear. If, in the telecommunications industry, nominal wages rise at a compounded annual rate of 4 percent, but productivity goes up at an even higher rate of 5 percent, then cost per unit of output in this industry will actually fall. But if, in education, the pupil-teacher ratio remains constant, so that crude productivity growth per teacher-hour is zero, then a 3 percent rise in nominal teacher salaries (or *any* growth at all in those salaries, for that matter) will lead to a commensurate rise in cost per pupil. Since the overall price level in the economy is made up of an average of these two types of product, and since market forces in the long run push nominal wages up everywhere (even in the zero-productivity-growth services), then it follows that the cost of education will rise, not only more quickly than that of telecommunications, but more rapidly that the general price level.

3. Toward viable policy: Can we afford the stagnant services?

The pervasive fiscal difficulties that threaten the quality of life in the industrialized countries have many roots. However, the evidence indicates that a considerable share of the problem is attributable to the cost disease. If inflation proceeds at a rate of, say, four percent per year, but the cost of education per pupil and other municipal services rises at a rate of six percent, then a tax base that expands only a little faster than the rate of inflation is sure to lead to growing financial problems for the city. And medical costs and insurance premiums that considerably outstrip the rate of inflation year after year would appear to put such vital services beyond the reach of all but the wealthiest families. If the cause of this predicament is, indeed, the nature of the technology of the supply of these services, and the course of the development of such technology does not lend itself to easy modification, then the implication would seem grim indeed – the conclusion would appear to be one that befits the natural pessimism of a practitioner of the dismal science.

Yet, I will argue next that, far from there being no exit, the very structure of the problem is such as to offer society all the resources requisite for its solution. Contrary to appearances, we *can* afford ever more ample medical care, ever more abundant education, ever more adequate support of the indigent, and all this along with a growing profusion of private comforts and luxuries. It is only an *illusion* that we cannot do so, and the main step needed to deal effectively with our fiscal problems is to overcome that illusion. This conclusion may strike the reader as implausible in light of all that has been said. Yet, if our future overall productivity record bears any resemblance to that of the decades past, then this conclusion is inescapable. There are two fundamental reasons that will be described in turn:

22

3.1. The small, but positive, growth rate of productivity in the stagnant services

In *A Connecticut Yankee in King Arthur's Court*, Mark Twain devotes an entire chapter to Sir Boss's unsuccessful attempt to explain the concept of real wages to his primitive hosts. Sir Boss argues with some passion that the monetary magnitudes of wages are irrelevant; that, regardless of their value as expressed in terms of money, wages are really higher only if it takes fewer hours of labor to earn the wages needed to purchase a given set of goods. Yet, as will be shown now, precisely that is true of the stagnant services. Their money prices are indeed rising ever higher, and their exchange rate against manufactured goods is constantly increasing, just as has been shown. But in terms of the number of labor hours it takes to acquire them over the longer run, their cost is decreasing steadily, albeit relatively slowly. So, the claim that we cannot afford them is simply a manifestation of money illusion.

In fact, even the most technologically stagnant of services is undergoing productivity growth – slowly, and not very steadily, but some growth nevertheless. Our cost disease analysis does not claim otherwise; its workings merely require productivity in the stagnant services to grow substantially more *slowly* than that of the economy overall. To illustrate the point, let me return to my favorite example. If a hypothetical Mozart string quartet had been scored for a half-hour performance, then its performance in 1990 required two persons-hours of labor, just as it did in 1790, when it might have been written. Thus, here, there appears to be absolutely no scope for the slightest increase in labor productivity.[5] Yet that is only an illusion. To see why, assume that the 1990 performance was by a Viennese group of musicians, and that the piece was played in Frankfurt am Main. A trip from their Austrian home base to the German auditorium surely would normally have taken the performers no more than several hours in 1990. But when Mozart made the trip in 1790 it required *six days* of travelling in extreme discomfort (and, at that, Mozart wrote that he was surprised at the speed of the journey, (Letter of 28 September, 1790). Certainly, technical progress *has* reduced the number of hours of labor required to provide a unit of the output in question, thus raising the labor productivity of every itinerant performer, even in live performance (and we know that performers are virtually all itinerant).

This example clearly suggests that there is no personal service whose productivity is untouched by technical progress to some degree. The consequent rise in labor productivity means, by definition, that it requires ever less labor time to produce a unit of such a service. And every resulting reduction in labor-time expended in producing the service means that those purchasing the service must expend that much less labor-time to acquire the wherewithal needed to purchase it. That is the sense in which even education and medical care have really grown steadily cheaper (albeit at a snail's pace, compared to other outputs), even as they appear to become steadily more unaffordable. Productivity growth in the stagnant services means that their real costs are steadily, if slowly, declining despite the dramatic inflation in their money prices. However, this, at best, can only make a minor contribution toward solution of the politico-budgetary problems that stem from the cost disease. More powerful aid must come from a second source:

3.2. Productivity growth in the economy means we can afford more of everything

There is a good deal more to the sanguine side of the cost disease story. Even if it were true that productivity in the stagnant services was not increasing one iota, their rising prices could still not put them beyond the reach of the community; on the contrary, it would remain true that society could afford ever more of them, just as it has in fact been getting ever more of the health care and education that seem to grow steadily toward becoming too expensive to afford.

As was pointed out some time ago by David Bradford (1969), in an economy in which productivity is growing in almost every sector and declining in none, consumers can have more of *every* good and service. To achieve this goal, some limited quantity of the inputs used to produce goods whose productivity is growing (the "progressive" outputs) must be transferred into the production of the stagnant services. Then productivity growth will still permit expansion of the progressive output quantities (despite the small subtraction from their inputs), while the outputs of the stagnant services will grow because more input is being devoted to their production. To achieve such a goal – greater abundance of everything – society must change the *proportions* of its income that it devotes to the different products. It is a fiscal illusion that underlies the view that consumers as a group cannot afford to pay the rising costs of education, health care, and other such services.

But over the longer run, the size of the required transfer of income is startling. We can suggest the magnitudes that may possibly be involved by using current U.S. data on price trends and expenditures on health care and education to illustrate the point. It should be emphasized that the figures that follow make no pretence of being forecasts – they are intended as no more than suggestive extrapolations. We will now see what would be entailed if: 1) the *real* prices of education and health care were to continue to grow at their current rates for 50 years; 2) overall U.S. productivity were to rise for that period at its historic rate of (approximately) two percent; and, 3) real educational and health care outputs were to maintain an unchanged share of GNP – that is, the economy were to produce more education, health care and everything else, in their current relative proportions.

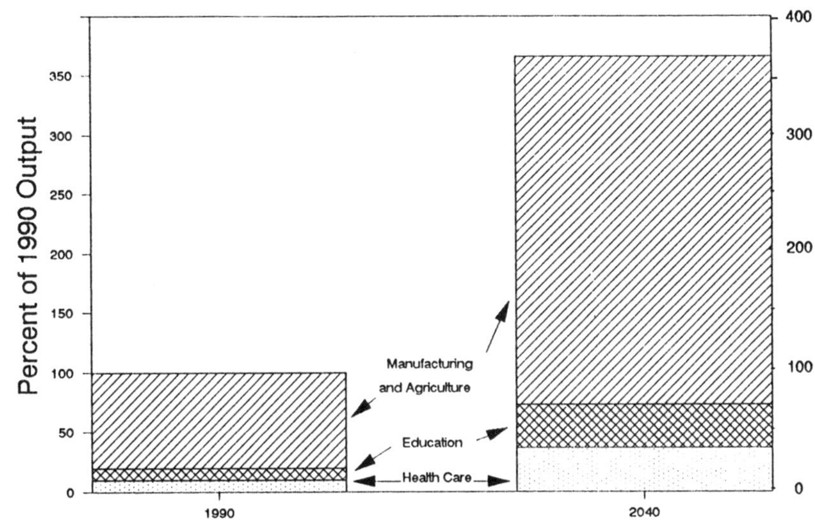

Figure 5. Hypothetical changes in total outputs, over 50 years, assuming historic sectoral productivity growth rates.
Source: Calculated by author with data from OECD (1990), U.S. Department of Education (1990) and U.S. Department of Commerce, Bureau of the Census, various years.

In both Figures 5 and 6 the left-hand bar shows the actual shares of gross national product constituted by health care, education, and the remainder in the year 1990. It shows that these two services then constituted less than 20 percent of the total. In Figure 5 the right-hand bar reports what will happen to GNP in 50 years if the number of hours of labor performed in the U.S. remains constant but productivity in the economy grows at its historic average rate and each industry's output level is adjusted to retain the same *share* of GNP. It shows that over those fifty years the output of *every* good and service, including education and health care, can increase to more than 3.5 times their 1990 magnitudes. This growth is indicated by the relative heights of the corresponding segments of the two bars in Figure 5 – that for 1990 and the one for the year 2040. That is, we see that the right-hand bar (for the year 2040), *and every one of its segments*, is more than 3.5 times as tall as in the left-hand bar (1990).

Figure 6, however, is the crucial one for our analysis, for it shows the modification of *real expenditures* required to achieve the result of Figure 5, in effect, measuring spending on each product by the relative number of hours of labor needed to earn enough to purchase it. Our assumption that the total hours of labor does not change means that total spending on GNP, measured in terms of labor hours used, must also be constant. Thus, the 1990 bar and the 2040 bar, representing total (labor-hour) expenditure on GNP in the two years, must be exactly equal in height. However, expenditure *proportions* will have

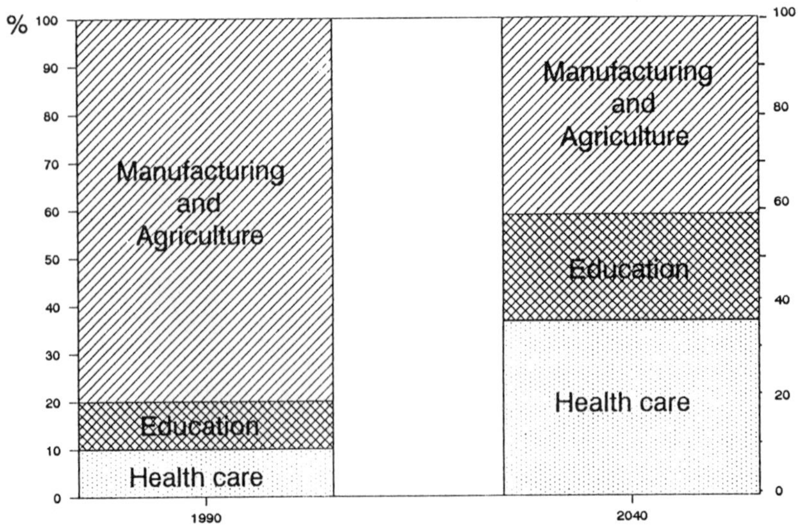

Figure 6. Hypothetical changes in total spending, over 50 years, assuming historic sectoral productivity growth rates.
Sources: Calculated by author with data from OECD (1990), U.S. Department of Education (1990), and U.S. Department of Commerce, Bureau of the Census, various years.

changed drastically. Medical care outlays, instead of constituting 11 percent of the total, as they did in 1987, must rise to more than 35 percent of GNP in 2039. And the share of expenditure devoted to education will have risen from under 10 percent of GNP in 1990 to more than 20 percent fifty years later. In other words, if current relative price trends and output proportions continue as they are now, by the time four decades of the next century have passed, education and health care alone will absorb well over half of GNP! *But that will not prevent consumers from nearly trebling their consumptions of each and every good and service,* including manufactured necessities and luxuries of every variety. And a little thought will confirm that this can continue indefinitely.

4. The problem of communication

Yet, this sanguine conclusion is more than a bit simplistic. The path from theory to practice is beset by daunting difficulties. Not the least of these is the difficult educational task of getting the public to recognize the difference between the reality and the illusion in the behavior of costs. It will not be easy to convince the intelligent layperson that, even though the prices of personal services appear to be rising at a rate that is out of control, in fact the costs of those services (in terms of their labor-time equivalent) are really gradually declining, because of small increases in their labor productivity. One can hardly blame such persons for their reluctance to be taken in by what appears to be pure academic sleight of hand, or mere theoretical gobbledygook. The difficulty of convincing those who are not trained to think about these matters analytically that an item really becomes cheaper when its price doubles if, at the same time, wages rise by a factor of 2.1 is, after all, the main moral that Mark Twain seems to want the reader to draw from Sir Boss's vain attempt to make the matter clear. Yet the task of explanation to the public should not be beyond the most skilled of journalists and others who specialize in the art of effective communication. And an indispensable task it is, for without it effective budgetary reorientation along the lines described will undoubtedly be politically impossible in a democratic society.

5. The fundamental problem for public choice

There is a second problem that besets effective treatment of the cost disease – one that is arguably much more serious than the first. The cost disease analysis implies that our governments, perhaps particularly those of our towns and cities, face a daunting task in the future, in acquiring the revenues necessary to prevent municipal services from collapsing even more completely than they have already. A large portion of the budgets of town and city governments consists of education, health care, and other services likely to exhibit similar price behavior: police protection, libraries, welfare, and so on. This means that we can expect that the *real* outlays on these services may have to treble and more (!) before the middle of the 21st century, if these service outputs are not to fall behind the outputs of the economy's remaining activities.

But this is not the fundamental difficulty. Rather, the threat lies in the prospect that more than half of the value of the economy's total output will have to be devoted to services whose funding derives predominantly from the public sector. The consequences of so enormous an increase of the share of GNP that will have to flow through government channels rather than the private sector of the economy are hardly an attractive prospect. With the resounding failure of the centrally directed economies so recently before us, it is disturbing, to say the least, to recognize that we are beset by apparently inexorable forces driving the free-market economies toward governmental funding and control of the purse strings, if not outright governmental provision of the outputs in question.

The obvious answer, *à la mode*, is privatization – putting more and more of these activities into the hands of private enterprise. One can be confident that such a move will elicit determined opposition, which already has shown itself, for example, whenever any measure is proposed that is perceived as even a minor threat to the public schools. Moreover, whatever ultimate position one may take on these matters, a dispassionate evaluation will surely recognize that many of the objections raised against privatization of some of these traditionally public activities are not entirely without merit.

No matter how one feels about those arguments it should also be recognized that, for activities beset by the cost disease, privatization poses a very special problem, and one that will not be easy to overcome. The very fact that the stagnant, personal services are likely to be beset by persistent, cumulative and compounded rises in their costs is certain to make their suppliers the subject of suspicion and hostility. They are sure to be accused of greed, incompetence and worse. Insurance companies, as suppliers of bundles of stagnant services (medical, legal, automotive repair, etc.), provide a foretaste of what is to be expected. These companies have become the target of one politician after another who seeks an easy way to curry public favor. But in every case the politician's remedy has turned out to be some form of price control, which, in an industry whose costs are driven by technological imperatives to rapid rise, can only result in deterioration in the quality of the service and, ultimately, withdrawal altogether of a service that is presumably valuable to society. Thus, the danger is that privatized services subject to the cost disease will find themselves harassed and undermined by public hostility and the resulting governmental intervention. The prospect is that public pressure will be the enemy of the public interest as in so many cases where price control has been invoked as the magic formula for cost reduction.

Here is a problem for public choice that is likely to prove critical for our quality of life. An unfortunate choice in this arena does indeed threaten to bring us an economy, in the words of the poet, "where wealth accumulates and men decay." But the nature of the right choice is by no means clear.

Notes

1. It should be noted that during the period 1970–1980, a period of very rapid inflation, the health care index rose more slowly than the GDP deflator in four of the six countries. Historically, this has always been the exception (see Baumol and Bowen, 1966). In periods of rapid inflation expenditure on such services has typically been unable to keep abreast of the price level, and so real cost per unit of output of these services has tended to fall. Indeed, in this set of six countries, the two for which real health care cost rose during the 1970s were those with the *lowest* inflation rates. Moreover, in the entire sample of 19 countries for which we have been able to obtain health care cost data for the period 1960–1987, real cost increased in 13, with only those whose inflation rate was high falling behind (Figure 3).
2. However, while these probably help to account for the relatively high *level* of health care costs in the U.S., it does not seem plausible that they play much of a role in the *rate of growth* of those costs, which is the focus of this paper. For to play such a role, rent seeking presumably would have to be characterized by a secularly rising trend, and to do so in all of the many coun-

28

tries in which health care costs are rising faster or nearly as rapidly as ours. The fact that the compounded rise in real costs extends over so many countries with such differences in health care systems, and that it has persisted for so long a period seems to me to strengthen the case for an important role for a mechanism such as the cost disease.

3. For this purpose, productivity measurement must deliberately avoid any attempt for correction for improvement in quality, and must, rather, focus on crude indices such as number of patients per physician-hour, because cost to the patient per physician-visit depends directly on the average annual physician salary divided by sheer number of patients seen by the doctor per year, and is affected only indirectly by quality of service rendered.
4. Of course, technological change in health care has hardly been negligible. However, study of the evidence indicates that it has been predominantly quality improving rather than labor saving in character.
5. Or even for any increase in total factor productivity, for that matter; the latter appears frozen by the fact that the same number of instruments, the capital equipment, was required at the two dates.

References

Baumol, W.J. and Bowen, W.G. (1966). *Performing arts: The economic dilemma*. New York: Twentieth Century Fund.

Bradford, D.F. (1969). Balance on unbalanced growth. *Zeitschrift für Nationalökonomie* 29: 291–304.

Organization for Economic Cooperation and Development (OECD) (1990). *Health care systems in transition: The search for efficiency*. Paris.

United Nations Educational, Scientific and Cultural Organization (UNESCO). *Statistical yearbook*. Paris. Various issues.

U.S. Department of Commerce, Bureau of the Census. *Statistical Abstract of the United States*. Washington, DC: U.S. Government Printing Office. Various years.

U.S. Department of Commerce, Bureau of Labor Statistics. *CPI Detailed Report*. Various issues.

U.S. Department of Education (1990). *Digest of education statistics*. Washington, DC: National Center for Education Statistics.

Name index